DICTIONARY OF CONCEPTS IN ARCHAEOLOGY

Recent Titles in
Reference Sources for the Social Sciences and Humanities

Research Guide for Psychology
Raymond G. McInnis

Dictionary of Concepts in Human Geography
Robert P. Larkin and Gary L. Peters

Dictionary of Concepts in History
Harry Ritter

A Research Guide to the Health Sciences: Medical, Nutritional, and Environmental
Kathleen J. Haselbauer

Dictionary of Concepts in Physical Geography
Thomas P. Huber, Robert P. Larkin, and Gary L. Peters

Dictionary of Concepts in the Philosophy of Science
Paul T. Durbin

Dictionary of Concepts in General Psychology
John A. Popplestone and Marion White McPherson

Research Guide for Studies in Infancy and Childhood
Enid E. Haag

Dictionary of Concepts in Recreation and Leisure Studies
Stephen L. J. Smith

Dictionary of Concepts in Physical Anthropology
Joan C. Stevenson

Dictionary of Concepts in Cultural Anthropology
Robert H. Winthrop

Dictionary of Concepts in Literary Criticism and Theory
Wendell V. Harris

DICTIONARY OF CONCEPTS IN ARCHAEOLOGY

Molly Raymond Mignon

Reference Sources for the Social Sciences and Humanities, Number 13
Raymond G. McInnis, Series Editor

Greenwood Press
Westport, Connecticut • London

Library of Congress Cataloging-in-Publication Data

Mignon, Molly Raymond.
    Dictionary of concepts in archaeology / Molly Raymond Mignon.
       p.   cm.—(Reference sources for the social sciences and
humanities, ISSN 0730–3335 ; no. 13)
    Includes index.
    ISBN 0–313–24659–9 (alk. paper)
    1. Archaeology—Dictionaries. I. Title. II. Series.
CC70.M45   1993
930.1′03—dc20   92–43151

British Library Cataloguing in Publication Data is available.

Library of Congress Catalog Card Number: 92–43151
ISBN: 0–313–24659–9
ISSN: 0730–3335

First published in 1993

Greenwood Press, 88 Post Road West, Westport, CT 06881
An imprint of Greenwood Publishing Group, Inc.

Printed in the United States of America

The paper used in this book complies with the
Permanent Paper Standard issued by the National
Information Standards Organization (Z39.48–1984).

10 9 8 7 6 5 4 3 2 1

Contents

Series Foreword   vii

Preface   ix

List of Concepts   xi

The Dictionary   1

Name Index   357

Subject Index   361

Series Foreword

In all disciplines, scholars seek to understand and explain the subject matter in their area of specialization. The object of their activity is to produce a body of knowledge about specific fields of inquiry. As they achieve an understanding of their subject, scholars publish the results of their interpretations (that is, their research findings) in the form of explanations.

Explanation, then, can be said to organize and communicate understanding. When reduced to agreed-upon theoretical principles, the explanations that emerge from this process of organizing understanding are called concepts.

Concepts serve many functions. They help us identify topics we think about, help classify these topics into related sets, relate them to specific times and places, and provide us with definitions. Without concepts, someone has said, "man could hardly be said to think."

Like knowledge itself, the meanings of concepts are fluid. From the moment an authority introduces a concept into a discipline's vocabulary, where it is given a specific meaning, that concept has the potential to acquire a variety of meanings. As new understandings develop in the discipline, inevitably the meanings of concepts are revised.

Although this pattern in the formation of the meaning of concepts is widely recognized, few dictionaries—certainly none in a consistent manner—trace the path a concept takes as it becomes embedded in a research topic's literature.

Dictionaries in this series uniformly present brief, substantive discussions of the etymological development and contemporary use of the significant concepts in a discipline or subdiscipline. Another feature that distinguishes these dictionaries from others in the field is their emphasis upon bibliographic information.

Volumes contain about 100 entries. Consistently, entries comprise four parts. In the first part, brief statements give the current meaning of a concept. Next, discursive paragraphs trace a concept's historical origins and connotative development. In part three, sources mentioned in part two are cited, and where appropriate, additional notes briefly highlight other aspects of individual references. Finally, in part four, sources of additional information (that is, extensive reviews, encyclopedia articles, and so forth) are indicated.

Thus, with these volumes, whatever the level of their need, students can explore the range of meanings of a discipline's concepts.

For some, it is the most fundamental need. What is the current meaning of Concept X? Of Concept Y? For others with more intensive needs, entries are departure points for more detailed investigation.

These concept dictionaries, then, fill a long-standing need. They make more accessible the extensive, often scattered literature necessary to knowing a discipline. To have helped in their development and production is very rewarding.

Raymond G. McInnis

Preface

The conceptual content of the field of archaeology is broad and often subtle, and a comprehensive coverage of its entirety is far beyond the scope of a single volume. The terms and concepts selected for inclusion here are, it is hoped, those most in need of definition and explanation for persons outside the field. This book is addressed to them, as well as to students of archaeology. In cases where the terminology has not become standardized, alternative terms have been included. In every instance, the use of jargon terms has been avoided in favor of standard English words. It is hoped that these discussions will make the content of the archaeological literature more accessible to laypersons, as well as provide some guidance into the vast literature for those both inside and outside the field of archaeology.

The literature of archaeology and its subdisciplines is of awesome size, and is increasing exponentially. Since comprehensive coverage was not possible here, criteria for inclusion had to be selected. In most instances, publications referred to in the text and discussed in the accompanying bibliographic essays are either basic, original sources of vital importance in the development of the concept under discussion; intermediary sources, such as review articles, providing access to a sizable portion of the literature related to the concept; or recent publications representative of current directions in relevant research.

Many people have contributed to this volume in some degree, and it is not possible to mention them all by name. Some have made outstanding contributions. These include Priscilla Machia, who assisted immeasurably in the library research, as well as in checking the bibliographic citations in the text; series editor Ray McInnis, whose continued patience and support throughout the project are deeply appreciated; and especially my husband, Edmond Mignon, without whose unfailing encouragement, feedback, and forbearance throughout the long years of writing and research this volume could never have reached completion, and whose comments and corrections to the manuscript have been invaluable.

Finally, I would like to thank my former students, and all the archaeology enthusiasts who have traveled with me to Mesoamerican archaeological sites since 1986, for their many penetrating and stimulating questions that have guided my thoughts in writing this book, questions frequently posed in circumstances of tropical heat, mud, vermin, and innumerable discomforts about which they never complained. It is to them that this book is dedicated.

List of Concepts

Adaptation

Analogy

Anthropological Archaeology

Antiquarianism

Archaeoastronomy

Archaeological Record

Archaeology

Archaeometry

Artifact

Assemblage

Bioarchaeology

Biocultural Studies

Carrying Capacity

Catchment Analysis

Central Place Theory

Ceramic Analysis

Chiefdom

Chronometric Dating

Cognitive Archaeology

Context

Cultural Complexity

Cultural Ecology

Cultural Materialism

Cultural Resource Management (CRM)

Culture

Culture Area

Culture History

Curation

Decipherment

Diffusion

Ethnoarchaeology

Evolution

Exchange

Field Archaeology

Food Production

Geoarchaeology

Household Archaeology

Hunter-Gatherer Archaeology

Inference

Interaction Sphere

Lithics

Middle-Range Research

Migration
Mortuary Analysis
"New" Archaeology
New World Archaeology
Old World Archaeology
Paleoanthropology
Paleodemography
Prehistory
Pseudoarchaeology
Quantification
Relative Dating
Sampling
Seasonality
Sedentariness
Seriation

Settlement Pattern
Site
Social Organization
Spatial Analysis
Specialization
State
Stratigraphy
Style
Subsistence
Survey
System Theory
Taphonomy
Three-Age System
Typology
Uniformitarianism
Zooarchaeology

*DICTIONARY OF
CONCEPTS IN
ARCHAEOLOGY*

A

ADAPTATION. 1. In evolutionary theory, the process of genetic change exhibited by living organisms through time, as a result of selection for traits promoting their survival in particular environmental situations. 2. In archaeology, the effects discernible in the ARCHAEOLOGICAL RECORD of behavioral processes and cultural features (or traits) that promoted human survival in a given environment during a particular period of time in the past. 3. An overall human ecological pattern or lifeway based on a specific type of SUBSISTENCE or economic strategy, such as a *hunting-gathering adaptation*, a *maritime adaptation*, or a *village agricultural adaptation*, each of which implies a range of predictable regularities in the demographic, residential, and technological characteristics of communities pursuing such a strategy. (See also EVOLUTION; SUBSISTENCE.)

The idea of adaptation as a state of being fitted or suited to some specific set of environmental conditions has been present in Western intellectual history since at least the early seventeenth century. Since the late eighteenth century, the term has been used to refer to the process of biological or behavioral modification to fit a new or changing set of conditions (Alland and McCay 1973:144).

A state of adaptedness, or fitness, may be defined as possession of biological or behavioral characteristics that optimize the individual's chances of reproducing, thereby ensuring the survival of his/her own genetic material in future generations of the species. According to evolutionary theory, fitness is achieved through genetic change resulting from the mechanism of natural selection (Alland 1975; see also EVOLUTION).

The concept of adaptation was an important one in nineteenth-century Darwinian theory, in which it specifically denoted changes in response to alterations in environmental conditions (Darwin 1958 [1859]). The term and concept were introduced into ARCHAEOLOGY by way of nineteenth-century social anthropology, and adaptation was considered an intrinsic part of the evolution of human society by the social evolutionist Herbert Spencer (Spencer 1876–1896).

It has been proposed that CULTURE is humankind's unique extrasomatic means of adaptation (White 1959; Binford 1968), and that culture itself is an entity subject to the same selective pressures and evolutionary processes as biological organisms (Dunnell 1980). Human populations are therefore subject to natural selection of two kinds, biological and cultural. This proposition has been challenged in recent years, and the idea of cultural evolution has itself been called into question by sociobiologists, who regard human behavior as a strictly biological phenomenon and therefore subject to natural selection (Irons 1979), as well as by some archaeologists and anthropologists (Wenke 1981; Rindos 1984, 1985, 1986, 1989). The concept of culture as the key mechanism of human adaptation is, however, firmly established in ARCHAEOLOGY, and has served as a guiding principle in the work of Julian Steward, Marshall Sahlins, and Elman Service (Steward 1956; Sahlins and Service 1960; Service 1975), as well as of such later archaeologists as Kent Flannery (1972).

In the 1960s and 1970s, Lewis Binford, David Clarke, and other "new" archaeologists emphasized the processual, systemic nature of culture as mankind's principal strategy of adaptation, an idea traceable to Leslie White's earlier definition of the adaptive function of culture. White's theory, however, conceives of culture as a separate entity evolving through cultural selection, a process he regards as distinct from the biological evolutionary process (White 1959).

An important point related to adaptation and other aspects of EVOLUTION is the level at which the selection process operates, that is, whether the primary unit selected is the individual, the social group, or the entire population. Alland and McCay (1973) devised an evolutionary model of human cultural adaptation based on the biological model, in which selection operates at the population level. Adaptive behaviors, whether learned or genetically influenced, are "shaped by the environment in the same way as a somatic trait. . . . The adaptive [cultural] behavior of a single individual can be transmitted to others independently of genes" (Alland and McCay 1973:172). Others, such as William Durham, who proposes that human evolution is a dualistic phenomenon, with both biological and cultural selective processes operating in a complementary relationship to one another, have suggested that selection operates at more than one level, affecting the reproductive fitness of both individuals and groups (Durham 1976, 1979, 1990).

Patrick Kirch has outlined a theoretical basis for investigating human behavior as adaptation using archaeological data, employing a model of relationships between environment, adaptive strategy, and demographic factors that he believes will predict human behavioral responses to specific environmental pressures (Kirch 1980). More recently, however, Michael O'Brien and Thomas Holland, in a critical review of the present status of adaptation as an explanatory concept in archaeology, state:

Anthropology in general, and archaeology in particular, are not even close to having a developed set of methods for the study of human adaptation . . . not only are the methods lacking but . . . a critical lack of understanding exists . . . of what adaptation and its closely allied concept of adaptedness (fitness) are and are not. This misunderstanding not only cripples attempts to identify and understand specific human adaptations but also calls into question our understanding of principles that have received extraordinary treatment by evolutionary biologists and philosophers of biology, who themselves diverge sharply on the concepts of adaptation and adaptedness. (O'Brien and Holland 1992:36–37)

As this statement demonstrates, the specific applicability of the concept of adaptation in archaeological research, like that of evolution, remains a subject of controversy. Robert Dunnell has repeatedly noted that the concepts of evolutionary theory may hold considerable potential for theoretical applications in archaeology (Dunnell 1980, 1989); but to date only a few rigorous attempts have been made by archaeologists to develop a general evolutionary theory based on Darwinian principles (see, e.g., Rindos 1984; Leonard and Jones 1987).

A major problem in the archaeological study of adaptation is that the archaeological record does not provide all the data required for documenting prehistoric adaptation. Although the material record may preserve evidence of *realized* adaptations, it may provide little or no data on those potentially adaptive but unsuccessful innovations that occurred in the past, at least at our present level of ability to interpret the evidence (O'Brien and Holland 1992). Clearly, new methodologies need to be developed for assessing archaeological evidence of adaptedness in PREHISTORY.

REFERENCES

Alland, Alexander, Jr. 1975. Adaptation. Annual Review of Anthropology 4:59–73.
Alland, Alexander, Jr., and Bonnie McCay. 1973. The concept of adaptation in biological and cultural evolution. In Handbook of social and cultural anthropology, J. Honigmann, ed. Rand McNally, Chicago, pp. 142–178.
Binford, Lewis R. 1968. Post-Pleistocene adaptations. In New perspectives in archaeology, S. R. Binford and L. R. Binford, eds. Aldine, Chicago, pp. 313–341.
Darwin, Charles. 1958. On the origin of species by means of natural selection, or the preservation of favoured races in the struggle for life; with an introduction by Sir Julian Huxley. New American Library, New York. (Reprint edition of a work first published in 1859)
Dunnell, Robert C. 1980. Evolutionary theory and archaeology. Advances in Archaeological Method and Theory 3:35–99.
———. 1989. Aspects of the application of evolutionary theory in archaeology. In Archaeological thought in America, C. C. Lamberg-Karlovsky, ed. Cambridge University Press, pp. 35–49.
Durham, W. H. 1976. The adaptive significance of cultural behavior. Human Ecology 4(2):89–121.
———. 1979. Toward a coevolutionary theory of human biology and culture. In Evo-

lutionary biology and human social behavior, N. A. Chagnon and William Irons, eds. Duxbury Press, Boston, pp. 39–59.

———. 1990. Advances in evolutionary culture theory. Annual Review of Anthropology 19:187–210.

Flannery, Kent V. 1972. The cultural evolution of civilizations. Annual Review of Ecology and Systematics 3:399–426.

Hardesty, D. L. 1986. Rethinking cultural adaptation. Professional Geographer 38(1):11–18.

Irons, William. 1979. Natural selection, adaptation and human social behavior. In Evolutionary biology and human social behavior, N. A. Chagnon and William Irons, eds. Duxbury Press, Boston, pp. 4–39.

Kirch, Patrick V. 1980. The archaeological study of adaptation: theoretical and methodological issues. Advances in Archaeological Method and Theory 3:101–156.

Leonard, R. D., and G. T. Jones. 1987. Elements of an inclusive evolutionary model for archaeology. Journal of Anthropological Archaeology 6:199–219.

O'Brien, Michael J., and Thomas D. Holland. 1992. The role of adaptation in archaeological explanation. American Antiquity 57(1):36–59.

Rindos, David. 1984. The origins of agriculture: an evolutionary perspective. Academic Press, New York.

———. 1985 Darwinian selection, symbolic variation, and the evolution of culture. Current Anthropology 26:65–88.

———. 1986. The evolution of the capacity for culture: sociobiology, structuralism, and cultural selection. Current Anthropology 17:315–332.

———. 1989. Undirected variation and the Darwinian explanation of cultural change. Archaeological Method and Theory 1:1–45.

Sahlins, Marshall, and Elman R. Service, eds. 1960. Evolution and culture. University of Michigan Press, Ann Arbor.

Service, Elman R. 1975. Origins of the state and civilization: the process of cultural evolution. W. W. Norton, New York.

Spencer, Herbert. 1876–1896. The principles of sociology. 3 vols. Appleton, New York.

Steward, Julian H. 1956. Cultural evolution. Scientific American 194(5):69–80.

Wenke, Robert J. 1981. Explaining the evolution of cultural complexity: a review. Advances in Archaeological Method and Theory 4:79–127.

White, Leslie A. 1959. The evolution of culture. McGraw-Hill, New York.

SOURCES OF ADDITIONAL INFORMATION

For further background material, consult the overviews of adaptation from biological and cultural anthropological perspectives, respectively, in each of two articles titled "Adaptation," in Joan Stevenson, *A Dictionary of Concepts in Physical Anthropology* (Westport, Conn., Greenwood Press, 1991), pp. 11–18; and in Robert Winthrop, *A Dictionary of Concepts in Cultural Anthropology* (Westport, Conn., Greenwood Press, 1991), pp. 6–10, both of which include substantial bibliographies. An unusual treatment of adaptation may be found in Alexander Alland, Jr., "Adaptation," *Annual Review of Anthropology* 4 (1975):59–73. Alland considers the relationship between mind, behavior, and ecological adaptation, and attempts to reconcile the ecological and structuralist approaches to human adaptation in a position he calls "structural ecology." The collection of papers edited by Elliott Sober, *Conceptual Issues in Evolutionary Biology: An Anthology* (Cambridge, Mass., MIT Press, 1984), includes reprints of two important papers on adaptation. The first, by Robert Brandon, "Adaptation and evolutionary theory" (pp. 58–82), presents a definition of adaptedness as a biological property. The second, "Adaptation," by Richard C. Lewontin (pp. 235–251), considers the concept in its historical context and discusses its relationship to natural selection and the ideological uses that have been made of it.

A treatment of adaptation as an explanatory concept in archaeology is Michael J. O'Brien and Thomas D. Holland, "The role of adaptation in archaeological explanation," *American Antiquity* 57(1) (1992):36–59, which includes the most up-to-date literature review available. To update this entry, consult current issues of *American Antiquity* and *Journal of Anthropological Archaeology* for articles and book reviews on the changing role of the adaptation concept in archaeological research.

ANALOGY. In archaeology, the use of a form of reasoning based on observed similarities between ARTIFACTS, or patterns of spatial dispersement of artifacts and features, among human groups now living, and material remains and patterns discernible in the prehistoric ARCHAEOLOGICAL RECORD. Such similarities are used in interpreting archaeological remains by making INFERENCES about tool functions and various kinds of past behavior, extrapolating to the past from behavior directly observable in the present.

Analogical reasoning from ethnographic data has long been a standard archaeological interpretative technique. In North America, it has been employed since the late nineteenth century, constituting the basic method of the "direct historical approach" first used by Cyrus Thomas, and later by Alfred Kidder (Thomas 1894; Kidder 1936). However, it was not until the late 1950s and early 1960s that this process was adopted as an explicitly conscious method by experimental archaeologists and ethnoarchaeologists (Kleindienst and Watson 1956; Thompson 1958; Ascher 1961; Binford 1967, 1978).

In the 1960s and 1970s, some of the so-called "new" archaeologists sought to establish relationships between elements of pottery design and patterns of postmarital residence in the prehistoric ancestors of living human groups (Deetz 1960, 1965, 1968; Longacre 1964, 1966, 1968; Hill 1966, 1968). Observations of the modern descendants revealed that postmarital residence was usually matrilocal, and pottery was manufactured by the women; these factors were assumed to hold for the prehistoric past. Spatial analyses of archaeological remains showed that parts of SITES where pottery had been manufactured were located near the residences of matrilineages, and distinctive pottery STYLES were found to develop in these sectors, with decorative and stylistic motifs that may have been associated with specific matrilineal descent groups. Although they have been faulted on various grounds, these studies have become classic examples of the productive use of analogy in archaeological research.

Archaeological analogies may be based on historical links known to exist between present and past populations, or they may be based only on general comparative principles. Analogy is the basis of a large part of archaeological interpretation using inference to reconstruct past behavior from material or documentary evidence, or a combination of the two. It is a basic principle underlying the methods of ETHNOARCHAEOLOGY. Like all methods of MIDDLE-RANGE RESEARCH, reasoning by analogy is based on the assumption of UNIFOR-MITARIANISM, the idea that processes observable in the present are similar to those operating in the past.

The current procedure for using ethnographic analogy in American archaeology usually consists of selecting cases from the ethnographic or historical literature that appear to be applicable to the investigation of a particular problem or a specific locality, and testing these against archaeological data for goodness of fit. Results must be quantifiable, and may be further tested by ethnoarchaeological studies, in which the practices of contemporary groups are observed for discard patterns or other data supporting the analogy (e.g., Hayden and Cannon 1984).

According to the "direct historical approach" developed in American archaeology early in the twentieth century (see NEW WORLD ARCHAEOLOGY), which applied ethnographic analogy in the interpretation of prehistoric Indian remains, the most valid analogies between living and past populations are those in which some known genetic or historical connection exists between past and present groups, and the assumption of cultural continuity is therefore a reasonable one. Analogies between living and past populations are thought to become weaker and more subject to error the further they are extended into the past, and the use of this technique is widely regarded as appropriate only for seeking comparative data for prehistoric groups who have clearly established modern descendants, now living or historically known.

The "general comparative approach," in which appropriate analogues for an archaeological population may be sought anywhere in time and space, has been rejected by many archaeologists, since it is impossible to establish with certainty which analogues may be appropriate (Ascher 1961; Gould and Watson 1982). Extrapolation from modern hunter-gatherers, for example, to early hominid groups would be inappropriate, on psychological as well as cultural grounds, since too little is known of how these early populations differed biologically from contemporary humans. But although most archaeologists would probably agree that direct historical analogies are stronger than general comparative ones, this is difficult to justify logically, and both types of analogy may in fact generate equally testable hypotheses (Gould and Watson 1982:359).

The use of analogy has been widely criticized as a method that encourages misleading and inaccurate interpretations of the past. Its defenders argue that since the mental processes and overt behavior that resulted in the formation of the prehistoric material record cannot be reconstructed, analogy is essential to interpreting the archaeological traces of these processes.

Ethnoarchaeologist Richard Gould has contended that the assumption of uniformitarianism may not be applicable to cultural behavior generally, and suggests it may be more enlightening to look for evidence of dissonance between present behavior and the ARCHAEOLOGICAL RECORD, and to seek anomalies rather than analogies between present and past behavior (Gould 1980; Gould and Watson 1982:367). Exactly how this would differ in practice from analogical reasoning is not made clear. As Alison Wylie has noted, in her critique of the published dialogue between Patty Jo Watson and Richard Gould on the use of analogy (Gould and Watson 1982), the approach Gould favors is basically that of reasoning by analogy, and although he uses different terminology, the procedure is essentially similar, only disguised by "rhetorical sleight of hand" (Wylie 1982:385).

Despite criticisms and arguments over its validity (see, e.g., Wylie 1985), there is currently an overall awareness among archaeologists that analogy, properly used, is an essential tool for testing archaeological hypotheses with ethnographic data, one that can shed considerable light on elements of past cognitive systems as well as on questions relating to technology and subsistence. Current research practices clearly indicate that analogy will continue to be an indispensable technique for interpreting the past until it is replaced by more satisfactory methods that do not yet exist.

REFERENCES

Ascher, Robert. 1961. Analogy in archaeological interpretation. Southwestern Journal of Anthropology 17:317–325.

Binford, Lewis R. 1967. Smudge pits and hide smoking: the use of analogy in archaeological reasoning. American Antiquity 32(1):1–12.

———. 1978. Nunamiut ethnoarchaeology. Academic Press, New York.

Deetz, James. 1960. An archaeological approach to kinship change in eighteenth century Arikara culture. Ph.D. dissertation, Harvard University.

———. 1965. The dynamics of stylistic change in Arikara ceramic. University of Illinois Series in Anthropology No. 4. University of Illinois Press, Urbana.

———. 1968. The inference of residence and descent rules from archaeological data. In New perspectives in archaeology, S. R. Binford and L. R. Binford, eds. Aldine, Chicago, pp. 41–49.

Gould, Richard A. 1980. Living archaeology. Cambridge University Press.

Gould, Richard A., and Patty Jo Watson. 1982. A dialogue on the meaning and use of analogy in ethnoarchaeological reasoning. Journal of Anthropological Archaeology 1:355–381.

Hayden, Brian, and Aubrey Cannon. 1984. The structure of material systems: ethnoarchaeology in the Maya highlands. SAA Papers No. 3. Society for American Archaeology, Washington, D.C.

Hill, James N. 1966. A prehistoric community in eastern Arizona. Southwestern Journal of Anthropology 22(1):9–30.

———. 1968. Broken K Pueblo: patterns of form and function. In New perspectives in archaeology, S. R. Binford and L. R. Binford, eds. Aldine, Chicago, pp. 103–143.

Kidder, Alfred V. 1936. Speculations on New World prehistory. In Essays in anthropology, Robert H. Lowie, ed. University of California Press, Berkeley, pp. 143–152.

Kleindienst, Maxine R., and Patty Jo Watson. 1956. "Action archeology": the archeological inventory of a living community. Anthropology Tomorrow 5:75–78.

Longacre, William A. 1964. Archaeology as anthropology: a case study. Science 144(3625):1454–1455.

———. 1966. Changing pattern of social integration: a prehistoric example from the American Southwest. American Anthropologist 68(1):94–102.

———. 1968. Some aspects of prehistoric society in east-central Arizona. In New perspectives in archaeology, S. R. Binford and L. R. Binford, eds. Aldine, Chicago, pp. 89–102.

Thomas, Cyrus. 1894. Report of the mound explorations of the Bureau of Ethnology. Smithsonian Institution, Bureau of Ethnology, Twelfth Annual Report, 1890–1891. Washington, D.C.

Thompson, Raymond H. 1958. Modern Yucatecan pottery making. Society for American Archaeology Memoir 96. Washington, D.C.

Wylie, Alison. 1982. An analogy by any other name is just as analogical: a commentary on the Gould-Watson dialogue. Journal of Anthropological Archaeology 1:382–401.

———. 1985. The reaction against analogy. Advances in Archaeological Method and Theory 8:63–111.

SOURCES OF ADDITIONAL INFORMATION

For material on the logical aspects of analogical reasoning, see A. I. Uemov, "The basic forms and rules of inference by analogy," in *Problems in the Logic of Scientific Knowledge*, P. V. Tavener, ed. (Dordrecht, Netherlands, Reidel, 1970) and Merrilee Salmon, "Analogy and functional ascription," in *Philosophy and Archaeology* (New York, Academic Press, 1982), pp. 57–83, a philosophical work primarily concerned with archaeological applications.

For further discussion of the archaeological uses of analogy, see Jane H. Kelley and Marsha P. Hanen, *Archaeology and the Methodology of Science* (Albuquerque, University of New Mexico Press, 1988); the 1982 Richard Gould-Patty Jo Watson dialogue in *Journal of Anthropological Archaeology* (see References); and the two papers by Alison Wylie (1982, 1985), also in References above.

An unusual application of analogy by Nicholas David, one of the first to use analogy in ethnoarchaeological studies, is in Nicholas David, Judy Sterner, and Kodzo Gavua, "Why pots are decorated," *Current Anthropology* 29(3)(1988):365–389, which includes commentary and a substantial bibliography of recent literature. For more recent material, consult most recent issues of *Current Anthropology*, *American Antiquity*, and *Journal of Anthropological Archaeology*, as well as the standard annual reviews.

ANTHROPOLOGICAL ARCHAEOLOGY. The current synthetic approach to archaeological research adopted by most North American archaeologists, combining the principles of evolutionary theory, scientific method, a systemic view of cultural and environmental factors, and an emphasis on variability in the analysis and interpretation of archaeological data. See also "NEW" ARCHAEOLOGY.

In North America, the disciplines of archaeology and anthropology evolved together, drawing upon each other's methods, and have usually been combined in academic departments. This was a striking contrast with the development of European archaeology, which has traditionally been much more strongly aligned with ANTIQUARIANISM and with a humanistic and historical, rather than scientific, approach to material culture and its interpretation. American archaeology has always been more anthropologically oriented, and it is therefore more than coincidence that anthropological archaeology remains primarily an American phenomenon.

Anthropological archaeologists are concerned with defining archaeology's subject matter and appropriate goals, as well as with the development of theory and method for attaining these goals (Gibbon 1984). An important aspect of this approach is the emphasis placed on the dynamic behavioral dimension of the human past, in which material ARTIFACTS are viewed within the CONTEXT of the human actions that led to their production and use.

An explicitly self-conscious anthropological approach to archaeological research was a product of the "NEW" ARCHAEOLOGY of the 1960s and 1970s. Lewis Binford first outlined the principles of this approach in a series of landmark papers defining the goals and methods of a scientific archaeology that rejected arguments based solely on authority in favor of a pragmatic, problem-oriented type of research design aimed at deriving general principles from specific observations. Such an inductive procedure would, Binford believed, allow archaeologists to identify and characterize the past human behavior that left its traces in the existing material record (Binford 1962, 1964, 1965; Binford and Binford 1968).

Binford's impetus stimulated widespread interest in the use of an explicitly scientific approach to archaeological problems, which resulted in a plethora of theoretical and methodological publications (Watson, Leblanc, and Redman 1971, 1984; Schiffer 1975, 1976); as well as works devoted to the philosophical foundations and implications of the new orientation (Chang 1967; Schiffer 1981; Salmon 1982; Kelley and Hanen 1988). A comparable phenomenon occurred in British archaeology at about the same time, stimulated by the work of David Clarke (Clarke 1968). These and other contributions resulted in more explicitly defined research problems, and in the widespread application of statistical methods and computer simulation modeling in archaeology (Willey and Shimkin 1973; Cowgill 1986). The use of these techniques, together with the accompanying shift in philosophical orientation, led to the synthesis now called anthropological archaeology, which currently constitutes the mainstream of archaeological thinking in North America (Trigger 1989). Its characteristics have been succinctly summarized by Richard Diehl and Janet Berlo:

> . . . the post-1960 generation of . . . [archaeologists] . . . practice the once New but now Orthodox Archaeology. Their approach . . . utilizes theoretical models derived from cultural anthropology and other social and natural sciences, attempts to investigate all socioeconomic levels of ancient societies rather than just elites, and emphasizes scientific rigor in the entire research process. (Diehl and Berlo 1989:4–5)

The only serious challenge to this prevailing synthesis is the position of European postprocessualists, which is in many respects a direct outgrowth of the humanistic, historically oriented roots of European archaeology (see OLD WORLD ARCHAEOLOGY; PREHISTORY). The mentalist position of the latter is in marked contrast with prevailing American materialism, and has stimulated considerable debate (see, e.g., Leone 1982; Price 1982), and has divided archaeologists into two opposing camps in a dispute that shows no signs of imminent resolution (see ARCHAEOLOGY).

REFERENCES

Binford, Lewis R. 1962. Archaeology as anthropology. American Antiquity 28(2):217–225.
———. 1964. A consideration of archaeological research design. American Antiquity 29(4):425–441.
———. 1965. Archaeological systematics and the study of culture process. American Antiquity 31(2):203–210.
Binford, Sally R., and Lewis R. Binford, eds. 1968. New perspectives in archaeology. Aldine, Chicago.
Chang, K. C. 1967. Rethinking archaeology. Random House, New York.
Clarke, David L. 1968. Analytical archaeology. Methuen, London.
Cowgill, George L. 1986. Archaeological applications of mathematical and formal methods. In American archaeology past and future, D. J. Meltzer, D. D. Fowler, and J. A. Sabloff, eds. Society for American Archaeology/Smithsonian Press, Washington, D.C., pp. 369–394.
Diehl, Richard A., and Janet Catherine Berlo. 1989. Introduction. In Mesoamerica after the decline of Teotihuacan, AD 700–900, Richard A. Diehl and Janet Catherine Berlo, eds. Dumbarton Oaks Research Library, Washington, D.C., pp. 1–8.
Gibbon, Guy. 1984. Anthropological archaeology. Columbia University Press, New York.
Kelley, Jane H., and Marsha P. Hanen. 1988. Archaeology and the methodology of science. University of New Mexico Press, Albuquerque.
Leone, Mark. 1982. Some opinions about recovering mind. American Antiquity 47(4):742–760.
Price, Barbara J. 1982. Cultural materialism: a theoretical review. American Antiquity 47(4):709–741.
Salmon, Merrilee H. 1982. Philosophy and archaeology. Academic Press, New York.
Schiffer, Michael B. 1975. Archaeology as a behavioral science. American Anthropologist 77:836–848.
———. 1976. Behavioral archaeology. Academic Press, New York.
———. 1981. Some issues in the philosophy of science and archaeology. American Antiquity 46:899–908.
Trigger, Bruce. 1989. A history of archaeological thought. Cambridge University Press.
Watson, Patty Jo, Stephen A. Leblanc, and Charles L. Redman. 1971. Explanation in archaeology: an explicitly scientific approach. Columbia University Press, New York.
———. 1984. Archaeological explanation. Columbia University Press, New York.
Willey, Gordon R., and Dimitri B. Shimkin. 1973. The Maya collapse: a summary view.

In The classic Maya collapse, T. Patrick Culbert, ed. University of New Mexico Press, Albuquerque, pp. 457–501.

SOURCES OF ADDITIONAL INFORMATION

Two views of anthropological archaeology by archaeologists outside the mainstream of the "new" archaeology are presented in A. M. Snodgrass, "The new archaeology and the classical archaeologist," *American Journal of Archaeology* 89(1)(1985):31–37, which suggests classical archaeology could benefit from the adoption of some of "new" archaeology's methods; and K. Paddayya, *The New Archaeology and Aftermath, a View from Outside the Anglo-American World* (Pune, India, Ravish Publishers, 1990). Retrospective evaluations of the "new" anthropological archaeology are now beginning to appear, including Charles L. Redman's "Distinguished Lecture in Archaeology, In defense of the seventies: the adolescence of new archaeology," *American Anthropologist* 93 (2)(1991):295–307; and R. A. Watson, "What the new archaeology accomplished," *Current Anthropology* 32(3)(1991):275–291. For latest developments in this field, see current issues of *Journal of Anthropological Archaeology, American Antiquity, American Anthropologist,* and *Current Anthropology.*

ANTIQUARIANISM. 1. A movement that arose in early Renaissance Europe, rooted in interest in the recently rediscovered classical world and its civilizations, and associated with historical and humanistic studies. Although primarily motivated by the desire to acquire relics of the past, some early antiquarians were genuinely interested in the origins of these curios, and their antiquarian interests significantly contributed to the development of archaeology. 2. Currently, interest in collecting ARTIFACTS of the past as curios or works of art, rather than for their scientific value as sources of information about ancient cultures.

Antiquarianism has often been considered a consequence of natural human curiosity, aroused by the presence of prehistoric artifacts or ruins. Questions about the makers of such objects, their origins, and their motivations have prompted antiquarian studies and collecting in many parts of the world, including ancient China, where remnants of early civilization are numerous (Daniel 1975:13, 1985; Chang 1986).

The classical Greeks were the first Western people known to have pursued antiquarian interests, stimulated by their widespread contacts with other CULTURES (Wace 1949). The Greek historian Herodotus described the material culture of such peoples as the Scythians and Macedonians, as well as their customs, in considerable detail. This early interest in past lifeways became dormant after the decline of the Roman Empire, and remained largely so until the Renaissance, although interest in the past was kept alive on a small scale by a few popes and priests during the Middle Ages (Sanford 1944; Laming-Emperaire 1964; Trigger 1989).

With the beginning of the Renaissance, the revival of classical learning stimulated humanistic interest in the past, and also created a new interest in the Roman ruins and monuments of prehistoric peoples scattered over the European continent. The stone tools of early European inhabitants were also objects of curiosity. Variously called by such folk terms as thunderstones, fairy arrows, and elfshot, the nature of these artifacts would not be recognized by scholars until the early nineteenth century, after the antiquity of humanity had been established by geological and paleontological evidence, and the resulting intellectual changes produced by this new knowledge (Grayson 1983).

Antiquarianism began to flourish in Europe in the sixteenth century, a time when discovery and exploration of hitherto unknown cultures served as a further stimulus to interest in and study of exotic peoples and their artifacts and customs (Walters 1934; Fagan 1975; Hodgen 1964; Piggott 1976, 1978; Sklenar 1983). Some members of the British aristocracy undertook systematic efforts to amass antiquities from ancient Greece, resulting in collections that eventually formed the core of many museums (Daniel 1975). However, since these early collectors, like their modern counterparts, had no contextual information about the artifacts they amassed, virtually nothing could be learned from them about the peoples who had fashioned them, and not even relative methods of dating them had been developed. The situation was well described in a statement by Rasmus Nyerup, a nineteenth-century Danish collector who established a small museum at the University of Copenhagen:

> Everything which has come down to us from heathendom is wrapped in a thick fog. . . . We know that it is older than Christendom, but whether by a couple of years or a couple of centuries, or even by more than a millennium, we can do no more than guess. (Nyreup 1806, *Oversyn over foedrelandets mindesmaerker fra oldtiden*; quoted in Daniel 1975:38)

Such ignorance and lack of temporal context were echoed by many of Nyerup's antiquarian contemporaries, who searched the writings of the classical authors for informational clues they might use to interpret these relics of the past.

A first step toward developing a relative chronology for organizing collections of artifacts was the contribution of another Danish scholar, Christian Thomsen, whose THREE-AGE SYSTEM was designed to arrange the collections of the Danish National Museum according to their material of manufacture (Thomsen 1836). Thomsen's Stone, Bronze, and Iron ages became the first roughly developmental chronologic scheme in archaeology; it was subsequently popularized by his student J. J. A. Worsaae, and adopted as a classificatory system for museum collections in many parts of Europe. Thomsen and Worsaae also developed descriptive and functional categories for classifying artifacts based on the taxonomic principles of Linnaeus (Linnaeus 1735).

The early antiquarians began to organize into societies composed of members who shared similar interests in collecting and in the past (Clark 1961; Lynch and Lynch 1968; Marsden 1974, 1984; Levine 1986). In 1572 a society for the preservation of national antiquities was formed in England, and applied to Queen Elizabeth I for a charter; after her death, James I opposed it and the society was abolished. This organization, like its successor, the Society of Antiquaries, held meetings at which the members read papers summarizing their research. The papers were published in 1720 by Thomas Hearne as *A Collection of Curious Discoveries by Eminent Antiquaries* (Daniel 1975:18). Similar societies were founded in several European countries during the seventeenth century, including the Accademia dei Lincei in Rome; the Accademia del Cimento in Florence; the Académie des Sciences in Paris; the Royal Society of London; and, in 1718, the Society of Antiquaries of London (Daniel 1975:23; Evans 1956). These societies fostered interest in natural history as well as in antiquarianism, and the research of their members contributed to the foundation of several modern scientific disciplines, including archaeology.

In the twentieth century, antiquarianism still persists among collectors of artifacts, from pothunters who remove arrowheads and pottery from Indian sites in the United States, to the customers of professional traffickers in artifacts obtained by the systematic looting of ruins in many parts of the world, whose activities persist despite legislation designed to put an end to them (Coggins 1969, 1970; Adams 1971; Beals 1971; Clewlow, Hallinan, and Ambro 1971; Meyer 1973; Sheets 1973; Fagan 1975; UNESCO 1983; Bassett 1986; Graham 1986; Nevaer 1988; Messenger 1989). Although pothunting and the vandalism associated with it are illegal in the United States and most other nations of the world, it is a practice with a long history that does not seem likely to disappear. Legislation designed to protect sites from looters has been extremely difficult to enforce. A majority of prehistoric sites have been seriously vandalized, and the cultural data they could have provided to archaeologists have been irretrievably destroyed. In some areas, such as the Department of Petén in Guatemala, looting has affected virtually 100 percent of sites in the region (Meyer 1973). A movement to return artifacts to the nations from which they have been stolen, supported by many museums, is now developing (Greenfield 1989).

The long-standing willingness of antiquarian collectors, and even of unscrupulous archaeologists, to buy artifacts from local pothunters has contributed to the continuation of looting and has impeded effective enforcement of existing laws. Evidential requirements for convicting looters may also inhibit enforcement (Bassett 1986); but the principal problem remains the existence and attitude of the private collector, rooted in the antiquarian tradition, which regards the artifact as desirable merchandise and a thing of primarily aesthetic value, rather than as an important piece of cultural information that, once removed from its CONTEXT, loses most of its archaeological value. It is an ironic fact of history that the heritage of antiquarianism, which contributed so much to the growth of archaeology in its early years, is now contributing to the systematic destruction of many of the world's surviving archaeological SITES.

REFERENCES

Adams, Robert McC. 1971. Illicit international traffic in antiquities. American Antiquity 36(1):ii–iii.
Bassett, Carol Ann. 1986. The culture thieves. Science 86 (July/August):22–29.
Beals, Ralph L. 1971. Traffic in antiquities. American Antiquity 36:374–375.

Chang, Kwang-chih. 1986. The archaeology of ancient China. 4th ed. Yale University Press, New Haven.

Clark, L. K. 1961. Pioneers of prehistory in England. Sheed and Ward, London.

Clewlow, C. William, Jr., P. I. Hallinan, and R. D. Ambro. 1971. A crisis in archaeology. American Antiquity 36:472–473.

Coggins, Clemency. 1969. Illicit traffic of pre-Columbian antiquities. Art Journal 29:94–114.

———. 1970. The Maya scandal: how thieves strip sites of past cultures. Smithsonian 8:1–7.

Daniel, Glyn. 1975. A hundred and fifty years of archaeology. Harvard University Press, Cambridge, Mass.

———. 1985. A divine antiquarian? Antiquity 59(225):55.

Evans, Joan. 1956. History of the Society of Antiquaries. The Society of Antiquaries, London.

Fagan, Brian M. 1975. The rape of the Nile. Scribner's, New York.

Fox, L., ed. 1956. English historical scholarship in the sixteenth and seventeenth centuries. Oxford University Press, London.

Graham, Ian. 1986. Looters rob graves and history. National Geographic 169(4):452–461.

Grayson, Donald K. 1983. The establishment of human antiquity. Academic Press, New York.

Greenfield, Jeanette. 1989. The return of cultural treasures. Cambridge University Press, New York.

Hodgen, M. T. 1964. Early anthropology in the sixteenth and seventeenth centuries. University of Pennsylvania Press, Philadelphia.

Laming-Emperaire, A. 1964. Origenes de l'archéologie préhistorique en France dès superstitions mediévales à la découverte de l'homme fossile. Picard, Paris.

Levine, P. 1986. The amateur and the professional: antiquarians, historians and archaeologists in Victorian England, 1838–1886. Cambridge University Press.

Linnaeus, C. 1735. Systema naturae, sive Regna tria naturae systematice proposita per classes, ordines, genera et species. T. Haak, Leiden.

Lynch, B. D., and T. F. Lynch. 1968. The beginnings of a scientific approach to prehistoric archaeology in 17th and 18th century Britain. Southwestern Journal of Anthropology 24:33–65.

Marsden, B. M. 1974. The early barrow-diggers. Noyes Press, Park Ridge, Ill.

———. 1984. Pioneers of prehistory: leaders and landmarks in English archaeology (1500–1900). Hesketh, Ormskirk, U.K.

Messenger, Phyllis Mauch, ed. 1989. The ethics of collecting cultural property: whose culture? whose property? University of New Mexico Press, Albuquerque.

Meyer, Karl E. 1973. The plundered past. Athenaeum, New York.

Nevaer, Louis E. V. 1988. The black market traffic in pre-Columbian artifacts. Part 1: The supply. Mesoamerica 1(3) (Winter): 27–29.

Piggott, Stuart. 1976. Ruins in a landscape: essays in antiquarianism. Edinburgh University Press.

———. 1978. Antiquity depicted: aspects of archaeological illustration. Thames and Hudson, London.

Sanford, E. M. 1944. The study of ancient history in the Middle Ages. Journal of the History of Ideas 5:21–43.

Sheets, Payson D. 1973. The pillage of prehistory. American Antiquity 38(3):317–320.

Sklenar, K. 1983. Archaeology in central Europe: the first 500 years. Leicester University Press.

Thomsen, Christian Juergen. 1836. Ledetraad til nordisk oldkyndighed. National Museum, Copenhagen. (Translated into English, 1848)

Trigger, Bruce. 1989. A history of archaeological thought. Cambridge University Press.

UNESCO. 1983. Conventions and recommendations of UNESCO concerning the protection of the cultural heritage. UNESCO, Paris.

Wace, A. J. B. 1949. The Greeks and Romans as archaeologists. Société Royale d'Archéologie d'Alexandrie, Bulletin 38:21–35.

Walters, H. B. 1934. The English antiquaries of the sixteenth, seventeenth and eighteenth centuries. Walters, London.

SOURCES OF ADDITIONAL INFORMATION

For additional information on the antiquarian background of archaeology, see Joan Evans's *History of the Society of Antiquaries* (London, The Society, 1956); the book by P. Levine (cited in References, above); and other historical works cited above. More recent treatments of the subject include W. Chapman, "The organizational context in the history of archaeology," *Antiquaries Journal* 69(1989):23–42; P. B. Wood, "The natural history of man in the Scottish Enlightenment," *History of Science* 28 (1990):89–123; and Alice B. Kehoe's work on the heritage of the antiquarian Daniel Wilson, "The invention of prehistory," *Current Anthropology* 32(1991):467–476. To update this information, see latest issues of *American Journal of Archaeology*, *Antiquity*, and *Antiquaries Journal*.

For ongoing coverage of the problem of site looting, see the regular feature in *Journal of Field Archaeology* titled "The antiquities market," and consult latest issues of *Archaeology*, which also has regular coverage of this subject.

ARCHAEOASTRONOMY. The interdisciplinary study of ancient astronomical systems, using both written records and archaeological evidence; specifically, the investigation of existing archaeological evidence for such systems in the prehistoric past. Also called *astroarchaeology*.

Archaeoastronomy has been defined as an interdisciplinary science that attempts to probe the astronomical knowledge of early peoples (Hicks 1976:372) and as a subdiscipline combining astronomy, engineering, and archaeology that arose out of interest in apparent uses of astronomical techniques in ancient construction (Baity 1973:389). As a distinct category of study, it has existed since the early 1960s.

Evidence of prehistoric astronomy may consist of building orientations suggesting intentional astronomical alignments; prehistoric structures that appear to have been designed as observatories or calendric devices, such as the "henge" structures and other megalithic monuments in Europe and the so-called medicine wheels of North America; and prehistoric artworks that may record astronomical events in the past or illustrate the use of astronomical sighting devices (Miller 1955; Digby 1974).

Anthony Aveni, who was a major contributor to the development of archaeoastronomy, distinguishes three approaches to the study of ancient astronomical systems. The first is *astroarchaeology*, which he equates with the field methodology of archaeoastronomy. Second is the study of the history of astronomy, a branch of the history of science relying on written records, which emphasizes astronomical systems of Old World cultures. The third approach is ethnoastronomy, a branch of cultural anthropology utilizing material from ethnographic field studies and ethnohistorical records to investigate the origins of astronomical systems (Aveni 1981:1–2).

Although archaeoastronomy as an interdisciplinary study has existed only since the early 1960s, it had some antecedents. In the 1890s, British astronomer J. Norman Lockyer published a work that may be considered the first archaeoastronomical inquiry, in which he suggested ancient Egyptian temples and pyramids were laid out to correspond with rising and setting positions of the sun and other celestial bodies at particular times of the year, such as the solstices (Lockyer 1894). Unfortunately, his supporting data were used as a basis for wild speculations about Egyptian religion and society; Lockyer's methodological contribution to the development of archaeoastronomy was thereby demeaned, and his work was largely rejected by archaeologists.

Little further activity occurred in archaeoastronomical studies until the 1960s, when Gerald Hawkins published his ideas on the astronomical nature of Stonehenge (Hawkins 1963, 1964, 1965), interpreting the famous monument as a structure designed for predicting lunar eclipses. Hawkins, like many later archaeoastronomers, was trained in astronomy but had little knowledge of archaeology or PREHISTORY. His ideas, like Lockyer's before him, were largely ignored by archaeologists until engineer Alexander Thom's studies of over 300 megalithic rings in the British Isles convinced at least some archaeologists that such ancient structures may indeed constitute astronomical records of prehistoric CULTURES (Thom 1955, 1961, 1966, 1967). While Lockyer and Hawkins made the pioneering efforts, it was Thom's work that attained some respectability for archaeoastronomy as a legitimate field of scholarly inquiry (Aveni 1981:7).

The initial focus in archaeoastronomy was on Old World megalithic structures, particularly in Britain, as represented in the work of Thom and Hawkins, although some astronomical investigations were carried out in Europe, Asia, and even Africa (Thom 1972; Thom et al. 1975, 1988; Stencel, Gifford, and Moron 1976; Lynch and Robbins 1978). In the New World, the earliest studies of archaeological evidence for pre-Columbian astronomical knowledge were directed toward Mesoamerica, where, in addition to astronomically aligned structures and others earlier identified as observatories, a body of written astronomical records survived. The Classic Maya, whose hieroglyphic inscriptions contain numerous references to celestial events, also produced astronomical tables, such as those in the Dresden Codex, recording eclipses and predicting their occurrence in the future (Spinden 1928; Teeple 1930; Aveni 1972, 1975, 1977, 1979a, 1979b, 1980; Aveni and Linsley 1972; Thompson 1974; Aveni, ed. 1975; Aveni and

Gibbs 1976; Lounsbury 1978; Aveni, Hartung, and Kelley 1982; Aveni and Urton 1982). Evidence of astronomical alignments, as well as of observatories, has been found in both Central and South America (Dow 1967; Rowe 1979; Dearborn et al. 1987; Zuidema 1988).

While the study of prehistoric Mesoamerican astronomy began in the early decades of the twentieth century, archaeoastronomical investigations of prehistoric North America did not begin until somewhat later. In addition to the "medicine wheels" of Canada and the northern United States, which have been interpreted as astronomical/calendric structures with functions similar to those of megalithic monuments in Europe, many other indications of early astronomical knowledge are present. Among these are the prehistoric effigy mounds of the American Midwest; the remnants of a wooden "henge" at the prehistoric Mississippian city of Cahokia in Illinois; evidence of astronomical building alignments at several complex sites in the southwestern United States; and representations in rock art of datable astronomical events that occurred before European contact (Brandt and Williamson 1975). All of these have been interpreted as evidence of early American astronomical knowledge (Kehoe 1954, 1974; Miller 1955; Wedel 1967, 1977; Wittry 1969; Brandt, Williamson et al. 1973; Britt 1973; Cowan 1973; Eddy 1974, 1977, 1978; Brandt and Williamson 1975; Mayer 1975; Williamson et al. 1973, 1977; Hicks 1976; Reyman 1976; McCluskey 1977; Brandt 1979; Frazier 1979; Evans and Hillman 1981).

Archaeoastronomical studies have revealed that ancient buildings were sometimes not only aligned to the rising or setting positions of celestial bodies at particular times, or in a manner that recorded or predicted such astronomical events as solstices or equinoxes, but also were sometimes designed to dramatize these events by producing special visual effects, or hierophanies, when they occurred. A notable example in Mesoamerica is the "descending serpent" pattern visible on the principal temple at Chichén Itzá, Yucatán, produced by the reflected light of the setting sun at the equinoxes. In the Maya culture that produced this building, as in most early civilizations, astronomy was practiced not as a science but as an adjunct to religion, ritual, and even politics. Hierophanies such as this would have served as valuable propaganda devices for priests and rulers, providing public evidence of their knowledge and power.

Astronomical observations are essential for keeping track of time and the seasons. This is necessary among agricultural peoples for such practical reasons as determining optimum dates for planting; but at least as often, astronomy has served ritual specialists for determining the proper times for performing the ceremonies associated with planting, to ensure sufficient rainfall and good crops. Such rituals may have been held on days of astronomical events, such as the solstices and equinoxes, and buildings designed to mark these events were often temples where the associated ceremonies were performed. Religion was usually inseparable from astronomy prior to the beginning of Western science and, like the rituals themselves, astronomical knowledge was motivated by practical considerations, as a means of enlisting the aid of both natural and supernatural forces in promoting human welfare. It also frequently served as a method for predicting future events. Resulting knowledge was valued not for its own sake but for what it might contribute to human survival and well-being.

Today the concepts of archaeoastronomy are part of mainstream archaeological study, and archaeologists are alert to possible astronomical alignments in early structures, as well as to evidence of instruments used for astronomical observation, which have sometimes been identified from depictions in prehistoric art (Digby 1974; Aveni 1980). Alignments to points of rising and setting of the sun, moon, planets, and constellations on important dates have been found to be fairly common, especially in the Americas, and are now routinely looked for during archaeological field investigations.

REFERENCES

Aveni, Anthony F. 1972. Astronomical tables intended for use in astroarchaeological studies. American Antiquity 37:531–540.
————. 1975. Possible astronomical orientations in ancient Mesoamerica. In Archaeoastronomy in precolumbian America, A. F. Aveni, ed. University of Texas Press, Austin, pp. 163–190.
————. 1977. Concepts of positional astronomy employed in ancient Mesoamerican architecture. In Native American astronomy, A. F. Aveni, ed. University of Texas Press, Austin, pp. 3–19.
————. 1979a. Old and New World naked-eye astronomy. In Astronomy of the ancients, Kenneth Brecher and Michael Feirtag, eds. MIT Press, Cambridge, Mass., pp. 61–89.
————. 1979b. Venus and the Maya. American Scientist 67:274–285.
————. 1980. Skywatchers of ancient Mexico. University of Texas Press, Austin.
————. 1981. Archaeoastronomy. Advances in Archaeological Method and Theory 4:1–77.
————, ed. 1975. Archaeoastronomy in pre-Columbian America. University of Texas Press, Austin.
Aveni, Anthony F., and S. Gibbs. 1976. On the orientation of pre-Columbian buildings in central Mexico. American Antiquity 41:510–517.
Aveni, Anthony F., Horst Hartung, and J. Charles Kelley. 1982. Alta Vista (Chalchihuites), astronomical implications of a Mesoamerican ceremonial outpost at the Tropic of Cancer. American Antiquity 47(2):316–335.
Aveni, Anthony F., and R. Linsley. 1972. Mound J., Monte Alban: possible astronomical orientation. American Antiquity 37:528–531.
Aveni, Anthony F., and Gary Urton, eds. 1982. Ethnoastronomy and archaeoastronomy in the American tropics. Annals of the New York Academy of Sciences 385.
Baity, Elisabeth C. 1973. Archaeoastronomy and ethnoastronomy so far. Current Anthropology 14:389–449.
Brandt, John C. 1979. Pictographs and petroglyphs of the Southwest Indians. In Astronomy of the ancients, Kenneth Brecher and Michael Feirtag, eds. MIT Press, Cambridge, Mass., pp. 25–38.
Brandt, John C., and Ray A. Williamson. 1975. Rock art representations of the A.D. 1054 supernova: a progress report. In Native American astronomy, A. F. Aveni, ed. University of Texas Press, Austin, pp. 171–177.

Brandt, John C., Ray A. Williamson, et al. 1975. Possible rock art records of the Crab Nebula Supernova in the western United States. In Archaeoastronomy in pre-Columbian America, A. F. Aveni, ed. University of Texas Press, Austin, pp. 45–58.

Britt, Claude, Jr. 1975. Early Navajo astronomical pictographs in Canyon de Chelly, northeastern Arizona, U.S.A. In Archaeoastronomy in pre-Columbian America, A. F. Aveni, ed. University of Texas Press, Austin, pp. 89–107.

Cowan, Thaddeus M. 1975. Effigy mounds and stellar representation: a comparison of Old World and New World alignment schemes. In Archaeoastronomy in pre-Columbian America, A. F. Aveni, ed. University of Texas Press, Austin, pp. 218–235.

Dearborn, David S. P., Katharina J. Schrieber, and Raymond E. White. 1987. Intimachay: a December solstice observatory at Machu Picchu, Peru. American Antiquity 52(2):346–352.

Digby, A. 1974. Crossed trapezes: a pre-Columbian astronomical instrument. In Mesoamerican archaeology: new approaches, Norman Hammond, ed. University of Texas Press, Austin, pp. 271–283.

Dow, J. 1967. Astronomical orientations at Teotihuacán, a case study in astroarchaeology. American Antiquity 32:326–334.

Eddy, J. A. 1974. Astronomical alignment of the Big Horn medicine wheel. Science 184:1035–1043.

———. 1977. Medicine wheels and plains Indian astronomy. In Native American astronomy, A. F. Aveni, ed. University of Texas Press, Austin, pp. 59–87.

———. 1978. Archaeoastronomy of North America: cliffs, mounds, and medicine wheels. In In search of ancient astronomies, E. C. Krupp, ed. Doubleday, New York, pp. 133–163.

Evans, J., and H. Hillman. 1981. Documentation of some lunar and solar events at Casa Grande. In Archaeoastronomy in the Americas, R. Williamson, ed. Ballena Press, Santa Barbara, Calif.

Frazier, K. 1979. The Anasazi sun dagger. Science '80 1:56–67.

Hawkins, Gerald S. 1963. Stonehenge decoded. Nature 200:306–308.

———. 1964. Stonehenge: a neolithic computer. Nature 202:1258–1261.

———. 1965. Stonehenge decoded. Delta-Dell, New York.

Hicks, Robert D. III. 1976. Astronomy in the ancient Americas. Sky and Telescope 51:372–377.

Kehoe, Thomas F. 1954. Stone "medicine wheels" in southern Alberta and the adjacent portion of Montana. Journal of the Washington Academy of Sciences 44:133–137.

———. 1974. Stone "medicine wheel" monuments in the northern plains of North America. Atti de XL Congreso Internazionale degli Americanisti, Rome, pp. 183–189.

Lockyer, J. N. 1894. The dawn of astronomy. Cassel, London. Reprinted by MIT Press, Cambridge, Mass., 1964.

Lounsbury, Floyd. 1978. Maya numeration, computation and calendric astronomy. In Dictionary of scientific biography, C. C. Gillispie, ed. Scribner's, New York, vol. 15, suppl. 1, pp. 759–818.

Lynch, B., and L. Robbins. 1978. Namoratunga: the first archaeoastronomical evidence in Sub-Saharan Africa. Science 200:766–768.

McCluskey, S. 1977. The astronomy of the Hopi Indians. Journal for the History of Astronomy 8:174–195.

Mayer, Dorothy. 1975. Star patterns in Great Basin petroglyphs. In Archaeoastronomy in pre-Columbian America, A. F. Aveni, ed. University of Texas Press, Austin, pp. 109–130.

Miller, W. C. 1955. Two possible astronomical pictographs found in northern Arizona. Plateau 27(4):7–13.

Reyman, Jonathan E. 1976. Astronomy, architecture, and adaptation at Pueblo Bonito. Science 193:957–962.

Rowe, J. 1979. Archaeoastronomy in Mesoamerica and Peru. Latin American Research Review 14:227–233.

Spinden, Herbert J. 1928. Ancient Mayan astronomy. Scientific American 138:8–12.

Stencel, R., F. Gifford, and E. Moron. 1976. Astronomy and cosmology at Angkor Wat. Science 193:281–287.

Teeple, J. E. 1930. Maya astronomy. CIW Contributions to American Archaeology No. 403. Carnegie Institution of Washington, Washington, D.C., pp. 29–115.

Thom, A. 1955. A statistical examination of the megalithic sites in Britain. Journal of the Royal Statistical Society A118:275–295.

———. 1961. The geometry of megalithic man. Mathematical Gazette 45:83–93.

———. 1966. Megaliths and mathematics. Antiquity 40:121–128.

———. 1967. Megalithic sites in Britain. Oxford University Press (Clarendon), New York and London.

———. 1972. The Carnac alignments. Journal for the History of Astronomy 3:11–26.

Thom, A., A. S. Thom, and A. S. Thom. 1975. Stonehenge as a possible lunar observatory. Journal for the History of Astronomy 6:19–30.

Thom, A. S., J. M. D. Ker, and T. R. Burrows. 1988. The Bush barrow gold lozenge: is it a solar and lunar calendar for Stonehenge? Antiquity 62:492–502.

Thompson, J. Eric S. 1974. Maya astronomy. Philosophical Transactions of the Royal Society of London A276:83–98.

Wedel, Waldo R. 1967. The council circles of central Kansas: were they solstice registers? American Antiquity 32:54–63.

———. 1977. Native astronomy and the Plains Caddoans. In Native American astronomy, A. F. Aveni, ed. University of Texas Press, Austin, pp. 131–145.

Williamson, Ray A., et al. 1975. The astronomical record in Chaco Canyon, New Mexico. In Archaeoastronomy in pre-Columbian America, A. F. Aveni, ed. University of Texas Press, Austin, pp. 33–34.

———. 1977. Anasazi solar observatories. In Native American Astronomy, A. F. Aveni, ed. University of Texas Press, Austin, pp. 203–217.

Wittry, W. L. 1964. An American woodhenge. Cranbrook Institute of Science News Letter 33(4):102–107.

———. 1969. The American woodhenge. In Explorations in Cahokia archaeology, Melvin L. Fowler, ed. Illinois Archaeological Survey Bulletin 7:43–48.

Zuidema, R. Tom. 1988. The pillars of Cuzco: which two dates of sunset did they define? In Proceedings, 46th International Congress of Americanists, Amsterdam, Netherlands 1988: New directions in American archaeoastronomy, A. F. Aveni, ed. BAR International Series 454. Oxford, pp. 143–169.

SOURCES OF ADDITIONAL INFORMATION

Information on archaeoastronomy outside the western hemisphere may be found in D. C. Heggie, *Archaeoastronomy in the Old World* (Cambridge, Cambridge University Press, 1982); and J. Barnatt, "Megalithic astronomy, a new archaeological and statistical study of 300 western Scottish sites," *Journal of Archaeological Science* 12(4):243–245.

Materials on New World astronomy are more abundant, and include Anthony Aveni, "Tropical archaeoastronomy," *Science* 213(4504) (1983):161–171; *Archaeoastronomy in the New World, Proceedings of the 1981 International Conference on American Primitive Astronomy, Oxford* (Cambridge, Cambridge University Press, 1982); D. S. Dearborn and R. E. White, "Archaeoastronomy at Machu Picchu," *Annals of the New York Academy of Sciences* 385 (1982):249–259; C. S. Kidwell, "Native knowledge in the Americas," *Osiris* 1(1985):209–228; and J. McKim Malville and Claudia Putnam, *Prehistoric Astronomy in the Southwest* (Boulder, Colo., Johnson, 1989), which discusses the astronomy of the prehistoric Anasazi of Chaco Canyon and the "Four Corners" area.

R. Collea and Anthony F. Aveni, *A Selected Bibliography on Native American Astronomy* (Hamilton, N.Y., Colgate University, 1978), is now seriously out of date. To update this publication and monitor current and future literature in the field, forthcoming issues of the following journals should be scanned: *Journal of Archaeological Science*; *Archaeoastronomy*, a supplement of the *Journal of Astronomy* (published at Churchill College, Cambridge, since 1977); and *Archaeoastronomy Bulletin* (College Park, Center for Archaeoastronomy, University of Maryland). Future annual issues of *Archaeological Method and Theory* and *Annual Review of Anthropology* should also be consulted for reviews.

ARCHAEOLOGICAL RECORD. The totality of material remains of human activity in the past that survives in the present, whether in a region, a SITE, or the world as a whole, consisting of ARTIFACTS, features, sites, settlements, and all other material consequences of past human behavior.

Although the archaeological record is one of the most basic of all archaeological concepts, and one long used by archaeologists in many parts of the world, it has remained undefined and largely unexamined, and its precise meaning has rarely been discussed.

Linda Patrik, in a review (Patrik 1985), has noted that in current archaeological studies there exist two distinct views of the nature of the archaeological record, reflecting the orientations of the two major schools of archaeological theory and interpretation, the materialist/processualist and the structuralist/idealist, the latter also encompassing some elements of historical particularism that are frequently lumped together under the rubric of "postprocessual archaeology" (Leone 1982; Price 1982; Hodder 1986; see also ARCHAEOLOGY).

According to the materialists, the archaeological record may be conceived of as a static remnant of dynamic behavior in the past, a purely physical phenomenon analogous to the fossil record of paleontology (Binford 1983b; Sabloff, Binford, and McAnany 1987). In the idealist/structuralist view, now held by a number of European archaeologists, the record is viewed as a kind of historical text for the prehistoric past, in which artifacts function as material symbols encoding the meanings originally attached to them by those who manufactured and used them (Hodder 1982, 1986).

Lewis Binford, a principal author of the "new" archaeology of the 1960s and 1970s, has been one of the most vocal of the materialists on the subject of the archaeological record. According to Binford, the record encompasses not only the material remains of past activity but also the taphonomic processes affecting these remains up to the time of their discovery.

> The archaeological record is . . . above all a static phenomenon. It is what remains in static form of dynamics which occurred in the past as well as dynamics occurring up until present observations are made. . . . The only statements we can make directly from the archaeological record are some form of descriptive statics. (Binford 1983a:23)

Binford also emphasizes the contemporaneous nature of the archaeological record as well as its physical character.

> The archaeological record is here with us in the present. . . . It is out there under the ground, quite likely to be hit by someone building a new road. . . . The archaeological record is not made up of symbols, words or concepts, but of material things and arrangements of matter. (Binford 1983b:19)

The alternative model, in which the record is conceived as an encoded text made up of material symbols, is exemplified in the writings of the British archaeologist Ian Hodder. In Hodder's view, artifacts in archaeological deposits are not merely material objects distributed in a manner reflecting past behavior but also meaningful iconic symbols that can be "read" to reveal their meaning to those who created them.

> There is little one can do by focussing only on the object as physical object . . . most statements about the past involve making assumptions about . . . meanings—whether one is talking of prestige exchange, the economy or the population size. . . . (Hodder 1986:171)
>
> Material culture often appears to be a simpler but more ambiguous language . . . in comparison to speech. . . . But a material culture "word" such as a photograph or sculpture . . . is not an arbitrary representation of that which is signified . . . material culture signs are iconic . . . archaeologists have to develop their own theory and method for reading their own particular data. (Hodder 1986:177)

Although the textual model implied in the above quotation has been likened to historical models, it also has strong ties to the field of linguistics, which is concerned with the analysis and interpretation of symbols and their meanings. The archaeological record may, according to the textual or linguistic model, be viewed as meaningful in itself. As Alison Wylie has put it, it "is meaningful in the sense that systems of meaning are instrumental in its formation" (Wylie 1982:41).

Materialist archaeologists find the archaeological record a useful concept, but some would suggest that new methodologies are required in order to give it meaning. The need for "bridging" or middle-range theory that would link the statics of the record with past dynamics is often mentioned, and such theory is usually seen as being derived from actualistic or historical studies (Sabloff, Binford, and McAnany 1987). So far, however, such studies have not generated the requisite body of theory; and inferences continue to be made from an archaeological record that remains an implicit, "commonsense" concept that is used by archaeologists every day, but almost never examined or discussed.

REFERENCES

Binford, Lewis R. 1975. Sampling, judgment and the archaeological record. In Sampling in archaeology, James W. Mueller, ed. University of Arizona Press, Tucson. Reprinted in Working at archaeology, Academic Press, New York, 1983, pp. 251–257.

————. 1982. Meaning, inference and the material record. In Ranking, resources and exchange, C. Renfrew and S. Shennan, eds. Cambridge University Press. Reprinted in Working at Archaeology, Academic Press, New York, 1983, pp. 57–62.

————. 1983a. Working at archaeology. Academic Press, New York.

————. 1983b. Translating the archaeological record. In In pursuit of the past: decoding the archaeological record. Thames and Hudson, New York, pp. 19–30.

Hodder, Ian. 1986. Reading the past. Cambridge University Press.

————, ed. 1982. Symbolic and structural archaeology. Cambridge University Press.

Leone, Mark. 1982. Some opinions about recovering mind. American Antiquity 47(4):742–760.

Patrik, Linda E. 1985. Is there an archaeological record? Advances in Archaeological Method and Theory 8:27–62.

Price, Barbara J. 1982. Cultural materialism: a theoretical review. American Antiquity 47(4):709–741.

Sabloff, Jeremy A., Lewis R. Binford, and Patricia A. McAnany. 1987. Understanding the archaeological record. Antiquity 61:203–209.

Schiffer, Michael B., and William L. Rathje. 1973. Efficient exploitation of the archaeological record: penetrating problems. In Research and theory in current archaeology, Charles Redman, ed. Wiley-Interscience, New York, pp. 169–179.

Tilley, Christopher, ed. 1990. Reading material culture: structuralism, hermeneutics and post-structuralism. Basil Blackwell, Oxford, U.K. and Cambridge, Mass.

Wylie, Alison. 1982. Epistemological issues raised by a structuralist archaeology. In Symbolic and structural archaeology, Ian Hodder, ed. Cambridge University Press, pp. 39–46.

SOURCES OF ADDITIONAL INFORMATION

The best introductory, general discussions of the concept of the archaeological record are in Patrik (1985) and in Sabloff, Binford, and McAnany (1987) (see References for full citations). The latter paper includes several definitions of the archaeological record as well as discussion of the problems of assigning meaning to it and the need for middle-range theory.

For information on current postprocessual interpretations of the archaeological record, see T. C. Patterson, "History and the postprocessual archaeologies," *Man* 24(1989):555–566; Tilley (1990; see References above); and P. J. Watson and Michael Fotiadis, "The razor's edge: symbolic-structural archaeology and the expansion of archaeological inference," *American Anthropologist* 92(1990):613–629. Other publications include Linda S. Cordell, Steadman Upham, and S. L. Brock, "Obscuring cultural patterns in the archaeological record, a discussion from southwestern archaeology," *American Antiquity* 52(3)(1987):565–577; and S. A. Chomko and B. M. Gilbert, "Bone refuse and insect remains, their potential for temporal resolution of the archaeological record," *American Antiquity* 56(4) (1991):680–686. A review article that includes over 100 bibliographic references is M. J. Shott, "Diversity, organization, and behavior in the material record: ethnographic and archaeological examples," *Current Anthropology* 30(3)(1989):283–315.

To update the information above, the journals *American Antiquity*, *Current Anthropology*, *American Anthropologist*, and *Journal of Anthropological Archaeology* should be monitored regularly, as well as latest volumes of *Archaeological Method and Theory* and *Annual Review of Anthropology*.

ARCHAEOLOGY. The discipline concerned with the study of the human past and the reconstruction of past lifeways, through the systematic recovery, analysis, and interpretation of the material remains of past human CULTURES. See also ANTIQUARIANISM; CHRONOMETRIC DATING; FIELD ARCHAEOLOGY; NEW WORLD ARCHAEOLOGY; OLD WORLD ARCHAEOLOGY; PALEOANTHROPOLOGY; PREHISTORY; RELATIVE DATING.

> The history of archaeology is . . . in the first instance a history of *ideas*, of theory, of ways of looking at the past. Next it is a history of developing research methods, employing those ideas and investigating those questions. And only thirdly is it a history of actual discoveries. (Renfrew and Bahn 1991:17)

Archaeology has rarely been considered as a pluralistic discipline. While specialized areas such as classical, Americanist, and historical archaeology have been traditionally recognized, only since the mid-1980s have some archaeologists noted and discussed the existence of "alternative" archaeologies, each representing different viewpoints on the past that may or may not include the basic underlying assumptions of the Western intellectual tradition from which contemporary mainstream archaeology has drawn its concepts, methods, and biases (Glock 1985; Hodder 1982, 1986; Tilley 1990). While recognizing that "archaeology" is therefore not a monolithic entity, the following discussion is centered upon the origin and development of contemporary mainstream archaeology, or what Albert Glock has called "the archaeology reported in *American Antiquity* and meetings of the Society for American Archaeology" (Glock 1985:464).

The roots of modern archaeology are a tangled web reaching far down into the past. The discipline's historical development from the matrix of natural history and ANTIQUARIANISM spawned by the European Renaissance is well known (Walters 1934; Clark 1961; Daniel 1950, 1976, 1978; Lynch and Lynch 1968; Piggott 1976; Grayson 1983; Sklenar 1983; Marsden 1984; Levine 1986;

Daniel and Renfrew 1988; Christenson 1989; Trigger 1989; see also ANTIQUAR-
IANISM; PREHISTORY; OLD WORLD ARCHAEOLOGY). However, its earliest origins
may well lie much further back, in the antiquarian interests and intellectual
curiosity of rulers and collectors in the earliest Old World civilizations.

While very little is known of such things, there is a small amount of tantalizing
evidence. We know that King Ashurbanipal of Assyria collected a large library,
whose catalog has survived to be published in the twentieth century; we know
that Nabonidus, the last king of the Chaldean dynasty of Babylonia, in the sixth
century B.C. excavated a temple floor down to a 3,200-year-old foundation, and
that his daughter had a collection of local antiquities. King Sesostris III of the
Egyptian Twelfth Dynasty had two sarcophagi of Third Dynasty royalty removed
from their tombs and buried in his own pyramid enclosure; and there is further
evidence of the antiquarian interests of ancient Egyptians who tunneled into old
monuments in order to copy their decorations on later buildings (Dodson 1988).
We also know that a fifth-century Thracian princess was buried with her collection
of Neolithic stone axes. Suetonius tells us that Caesar Augustus collected dinosaur
bones and those of other extinct species, as well as ancient weapons, and had
the glass sarcophagus of Alexander the Great exhumed and opened so he could
study the features of the ruler's mummy (Daniel 1985:55). The few records that
have come down to us of these activities clearly demonstrate that antiquarianism was not an invention of the European Renaissance, and that the human
desire to recover material remains of the ancient past is itself a very ancient
phenomenon.

The Intellectual Matrix

The modern discipline of archaeology had its immediate antecedents in the
uniformitarian reaction to biblical catastrophism and the first intimations of EVO-
LUTION to be recognized in the paleontological record. From this evidence of a
long development—and of occasional extinctions—of animal species, it was
perhaps only a small leap to the idea of human antiquity and human descent
from earlier species. But this was not so simple to accomplish in an era of
religious doctrine which held that every living thing occupied its own unique,
permanent place in a great chain of being established by God at the moment of
creation, to which nothing could be added and from which nothing could be
removed. At the beginning of the Enlightenment, no species could be created
or destroyed; and man was still the living exemplar of God's image.

It is perhaps not possible for scholars at the end of the twentieth century fully
to grasp the intellectual situation in which archaeology's immediate predecessor,
natural science, made its debut. The human past was considered to be brief,
beginning in 4004 B.C., according to Bishop James Ussher, and human history
was believed to be entirely recorded in the Old and New Testaments. The
awareness of the antiquity of the human species, and of a prehistoric period in
the human career of immeasurable length, would come only after several cen-

turies of scholarly research and debate among natural historians, antiquarians, and academicians (Grayson 1983; see also OLD WORLD ARCHAEOLOGY; PREHISTORY). It was only after this awareness of humanity's early past had been established that archaeology was able to begin its long search for the material remains of that past.

The Development of Method

In developing its methodology, archaeology has borrowed heavily from many other disciplines. In its earliest stages the field was closely aligned with geology, especially paleontology, from which the highly important principles of STRATIGRAPHY and superposition were derived, along with some basic field methods. Excavation as the primary field method may be said to have been established with the work of John Frere at Hoxne (Frere 1800), and of Boucher de Perthes on the Somme at Abbeville (Boucher de Perthes 1859), although numerous unrecorded efforts doubtless preceded these. Mapping and SURVEY techniques were derived in the late nineteenth century from military engineering methods, and incorporated into archaeology by General Augustus Lane-Fox Pitt-Rivers, who utilized his training in military survey methods in excavations on his estates in England in the latter part of the nineteenth century (Renfrew and Bahn 1991).

Long before the "NEW" ARCHAEOLOGY, archaeologists employed ethnographic ANALOGY and inferential reasoning in reconstructing past lifeways, using the patterns observed among exotic non-Western peoples discovered on the voyages of exploration from the end of the fifteenth century on, whose lifeways formed the basis of speculation by anthropologists of the nineteenth century (e.g., Lubbock 1865). Anthropology has continued to be a fertile source of concepts for archaeology, although it did not contribute specifically to the development of method until the second half of the twentieth century, with the beginning of ETHNOARCHAEOLOGY, in which anthropological and archaeological field methods have been combined, together with those of ethnohistory.

In the twentieth century, archaeology has borrowed from locational geography (CENTRAL PLACE THEORY, the principles of SPATIAL ANALYSIS), from the biological sciences and medicine (in BIOCULTURAL STUDIES and PALEOANTHROPOLOGY, plus the analytic techniques of palynology and paleoethnobotany), and increasingly from the physical sciences and their associated technologies. The latter have given us radiocarbon dating and dendrochronology (invented by an astronomer), as well as a variety of other CHRONOMETRIC DATING methods, and many chemical and physical techniques for analyzing archaeological materials, from human bone to ceramic wares. Statistical and other quantitative methods have been adopted from mathematics, and since the 1960s the use of computers and the principles of information theory have been routinely incorporated into archaeological analysis. Methods of remote sensing and a wide range of archaeometric techniques have contributed to SITE location and field investigations, as well as to the analysis of archaeological materials. At present, there is scarcely an academic discipline or technical field whose expertise has not been incorporated in some measure into the body of archaeological methods now in use.

Interpretation, Analysis, and the Search for Theory

The wealth of borrowed methods now in use by archaeologists has not resulted in comparable riches in the realm of theory. Archaeology has not lacked for theoretical efforts during its two-hundred-year history, and the history of the field in the second half of the twentieth century has been, more than anything else, the history of the quest for a general theory of archaeology; yet the field has remained atheoretic. While the reasons for this paradox may be as elusive as the long-sought body of theory itself, some of the barriers to the development of archaeological theory may be identified, and traced to peculiarities inherent in the field itself.

In the earlier years of the twentieth century, up to the 1940s, the development of chronology had served in some measure as a substitute for a body of theory. During this time it was widely believed that the ARCHAEOLOGICAL RECORD was too incomplete to supply the evidence needed to fill in more than the most general outlines of prehistoric cultures and their lifeways, and arranging material remains in a roughly developmental sequence was viewed by some as a sufficient disciplinary goal.

The need for reform in archaeology's methods and objectives became increasingly apparent in the 1940s and 1950s, as reflected in critical statements such as that of Walter Taylor (Taylor 1948). The revolution of the 1960s was, of course, to change archaeology's goals, as well as its methods, setting as its aim no less than the recovery of the behavioral processes of the past that had left their traces in the material record. A further, and at least equally important, goal in the early years of the "new" archaeology was the development of a truly scientific general theory, a body of lawlike generalizing statements that would direct all future archaeological research, generating hypotheses that could be empirically tested and undergo continuous revision and refinement in the light of the new knowledge that would be gained. At the same time, the assumptions on which methods had been based in the past were critically examined, and research designs were now required to make investigators' assumptions, as well as their procedures and goals, explicit. Some "new" archaeologists, such as Lewis Binford, set out to do no less for archaeology than what Darwin had done for biology a century earlier, by discovering and articulating a general theory that would stand the test of time and permit archaeologists to explain the past in terms of causal relationships. Application of a rigorously scientific approach to research was believed to be the avenue that would lead to such a body of general theory that would form the basis for archaeological explanation (Binford 1968; Watson, LeBlanc, and Redman 1971).

Today, in the early 1990s, archaeologists are still keenly aware of the absence of general theory; and while the methods and methodological goals of the "new" archaeology constitute the mainstream core of archaeological practice, there is little expectation or optimism that such theory will be created in the near future. Current efforts have usually been directed toward adapting theory derived from other disciplines, in particular Darwinian evolutionary theory, to archaeology (e.g., Rindos 1984; Leonard and Jones 1987), in accordance with the long-standing archaeological practice of borrowing from other fields.

One problem area in theory development is the nature and characteristics of archaeology's subject matter. Archaeologists must deal with an unknown universe. Sampling from the archaeological record is SAMPLING from a universe or population (in the statistical sense) for which there are no known parameters. The size, location, distribution, and other characteristics of the world's material record of the past, considered as a whole, cannot be described, nor is there any way to determine what portion of it has been recovered. Given this situation, the possibility of deriving general laws that can be meaningfully tested with existing data is greatly diminished, since the degree to which the sampled data are representative of the record as a whole cannot be determined.

Another problem may lie in reliance on the methods of science that, like many of the concepts employed in archaeology, have been borrowed from other fields and put to uses for which they were never intended. Archaeology is not an exact or "hard" science, and perhaps can never be entirely a science at all, although it has taken on many of the characteristics of a scientific discipline since the 1960s (experimentation, formulation of testable hypotheses, quantifiable results) and has found these to produce useful data. But the productivity of scientific method in other fields has created expectations that may be unrealistic for archaeology. Perhaps the possibilities of positivism, both as a method and as a paradigm for theory-building in archaeology, have been exhausted, and what is needed is a different approach, a new worldview or "paradigm," and a new methodology built upon it. This is the position now adopted by some of the "postprocessualists," who have abandoned the traditional materialist approach to archaeological interpretation altogether, in favor of various mentalist orientations whose conclusions cannot be objectively verified (see Tilley 1990).

Archaeology has borrowed many of its theoretical concepts, like its methods, from other disciplines, and adapted them to its own specific needs and problems. From anthropology came first the idea of cultural EVOLUTION, followed by the synchronic reactions against nineteenth-century evolutionism, including diffusionism with its CULTURE AREA concept, and functionalism. The culture historical approach, which prevailed during much of the early twentieth-century preoccupation with chronology, was eventually abandoned as lacking in explanatory potential when the "new" archaeologists established explanation as one of their primary goals.

Like all theoretical positions, each of these has exercised considerable influence on the kinds of questions archaeologists have addressed to their data at various times. But the causal links here are two-directional: archaeological research questions are greatly influenced by the nature of the available data, linking theoretical concerns and the archaeological record in a feedback relationship that affects both in ways that have not always been explicitly examined. It is therefore appropriate to consider some of the kinds of questions posed by archaeologists over the years, in relation to the ways in which these have affected theoretical concerns and concepts.

Colin Renfrew and Paul Bahn, whose archaeology text is organized around a set of basic questions archaeologists now frequently pursue in their research (Renfrew and Bahn 1991), focus on those concerned with technology, SUBSISTENCE, and environmental factors. Unlike many such introductory treatments of archaeology, however, these authors are also concerned with the biological, cognitive, and social aspects of prehistoric peoples, as are most contemporary archaeologists, and with the ways in which these different aspects of human existence are interconnected. Archaeologists now demand a great deal from their data, and have devised ingenious means of expanding their applications, which have in turn expanded their research goals. Such goals are, however, as clearly linked to contemporary concerns as was true in the past.

While sixteenth-century Europeans had as many questions about the inhabitants of the recently discovered New World as archaeologists still have today, these were directly generated by the prevailing worldview of the time, which determined the kinds of questions that were considered important enough to pursue. Among these were Who were the American natives, and where did they come from? Were they, like the Europeans, the descendants of Israel, and if so, how had they fallen into such an ignorant and degraded state? Did they even have souls?

These questions, which may have little relevance for our time, illustrate how the prevailing paradigm determines what matters may be considered worthy of pursuing at any particular time. Equally apparent is how our present concerns condition the questions archaeologists now investigate. Our interests are very evident in the preoccupation with matters of environment, population dynamics, productivity, resource exhaustion, and related concerns in contemporary archaeological studies. We may also pose such specifically pragmatic questions as What relevance has archaeology to our present condition? Can it help us to avoid the errors of the past? To whom does the heritage of that past belong? Such questions as these, which clearly reflect modern biases, would have been as meaningless to archaeologists in 1900 as the sixteenth-century concern with the souls of the New World Indians is to archaeologists today. While the goal of scientific objectivity continues to be an ideal, our research goals are still very much a product of contemporary worldview and present practical concerns.

Archaeology Now

Today archaeology appears to be in a stage of "normal science" (Kuhn 1970), with the innovative methods introduced by the "new" archaeologists solidly incorporated into the mainstream of current research. While deriving of general laws is rarely discussed, middle-range studies continue (Grayson 1986; see also MIDDLE-RANGE RESEARCH; ETHNOARCHAEOLOGY). These studies have perhaps contributed more to archaeological interpretation than any other single innovative approach since the 1960s, and have resulted in some valuable, although usually case-specific, explanatory efforts. Little progress has been made, however, toward a formal body of middle-range theory, a set of propositions that would elucidate and make possible the prediction of the specific "dynamic processes" of the past that generate observed patterns in the material record.

The overall effect of the "new" archaeology has been a rigorous and careful stocktaking, a reexamination of archaeology's methods, assumptions, goals, and epistemological foundations. The results of this effort are very apparent in the quality of field data now being produced, if not always in the efforts that have been made to explain these data in generalizing terms.

Present-day archaeology is fragmented into many subdisciplines practiced by a new breed of archaeological technologists that did not exist in the 1960s: palynologists, taphonomists, geoarchaeologists, archaeometrists, and a plethora of other specialists now populate the archaeological landscape. The discipline has become fragmented along other lines as well. While in 1960 the great majority of North American archaeologists were scholars with doctorates, who divided their time between university teaching and field research, today the majority are either self-employed contractors or government employees, who may or may not hold a doctorate and whose time is spent in conducting rescue operations in areas where cultural resources are threatened with immediate destruction by development projects. Research, if attempted at all in these conditions, must be subject to the limitations on time, funding, and data collection opportunities imposed by the constraints of the individual field project. Reporting and publication of the results of any such research are often in the form of limited-distribution documents that are inaccessible to most other archaeologists.

Major field research efforts are increasingly few in number, and are typically directed by the few remaining academic archaeologists. These are usually large-scale operations, often conducted outside the United States as cooperative efforts with foreign government agencies, funded largely by private and foreign sources, and carried out by an international array of field personnel (see, e.g., Sharer and Ashmore 1979:120–143). Publication of results of these projects is often delayed, and may require several decades to complete.

Archaeology as a whole is further divided into two major and opposing theoretical camps. The "processualists," who include most North American archaeologists, represent the traditional mainstream of materialist interpretation and the methods of the "new" archaeology. "Postprocessualists" comprise a whole range of theoretic persuasions, from various forms of structuralism derived from the theories of Claude Lévi-Strauss (Lévi-Strauss 1963) to the linguistic-textual school of interpretation, structural Marxists, and proponents of the new hermeneutics, their one unifying thread being the rejection of materialism in favor of one mentalist approach or another (Hodder 1982, 1986; Leone 1982; Tilley 1984, 1990; Kosso 1991; Johnson and Olsen 1992). This group includes the British archaeologist Ian Hodder and his students, as well as a number of other British and European archaeologists, and a few Americans. The interpretative emphasis favored by many of this group is based on the concept of ARTIFACTS as material symbols comprising an archaeological record that can be "read" as a "text" of the past in which material symbols constitute the meaningful elements. Artifacts are viewed as dynamic symbols of the events of the past, encoding the information with which their creators endowed them; their meanings can be decoded by archaeologists through their "readings" of the material record. In this approach, archaeological interpretation becomes entirely a mental exercise, and each "reading" an individual effort to reconstruct and revive the dynamic aspects of mental life in the past. The problem of how the validity of any such interpretation can be verified has not been adequately addressed in terms acceptable to archaeological materialists.

These two schools of thought represent basically different epistemologies and philosophical approaches to archaeological research and data, and their reconciliation or synthesis seems unlikely in the foreseeable future.

REFERENCES

Binford, Lewis R. 1968. Archaeological perspectives. In New perspectives in archaeology, S. R. and L. R. Binford, eds. Aldine, Chicago, pp. 5–32.

Boucher de Perthes, J. 1859. Sur les silex taillés des bancs diluviens de la Somme. Comptes Rendus Hebdomadaires de l'Académie des Sciences 49:581.

Christenson, Andrew L., ed. 1989. Tracing archaeology's past: the historiography of archaeology. Southern Illinois University Press, Carbondale and Edwardsville.

Clark, L. K. 1961. Pioneers of prehistory in England. Sheed and Ward, London.

Daniel, Glyn. 1950. A hundred years of archaeology. Duckworth, London.

———. 1976. A hundred and fifty years of archaeology. Harvard University Press, Cambridge, Mass.

———. 1985. A divine antiquarian? Antiquity 59:55.

———, ed. 1978. Towards a history of archaeology. Thames and Hudson, London.

Daniel, Glyn, and Colin Renfrew. 1988. The idea of prehistory. 2nd ed. Edinburgh University Press.

Dodson, Aidan. 1988. Egypt's first antiquarians? Antiquity 62:513–517.

Frere, John. 1800. Account of the flint weapons discovered at Hoxne in Suffolk. Archaeologia 13:204–205.

Glock, A. E. 1985. Tradition and change in two archaeologies. American Antiquity 50(2):464–477.

Grayson, Donald K. 1983. The establishment of human antiquity. Academic Press, New York.

———. 1986. Eoliths, archaeological ambiguity, and the generation of "middle-range" research. In American archaeology past and future, D. J. Meltzer, D. D. Fowler, and J. A. Sabloff, eds. Society for American Archaeology, Washington, D.C., pp. 77–133.

Hodder, Ian. 1982. Theoretical archaeology: a reactionary view. In Symbolic and structural archaeology, I. Hodder, ed. Cambridge University Press, pp. 1–16.

———. 1984. Survey 2. Ideology and power—the archaeological debate. Environment and Planning D—Society & Space 2(3):347–353.

————. 1986. Reading the past: current approaches to interpretation in archaeology. Cambridge University Press.

Johnson, Harald, and Bjornar Olsen. 1992. Hermeneutics and archaeology: on the philosophy of contextual archaeology. American Antiquity 57(3):419–436.

Kosso, Peter. 1991. Method in archaeology: middle-range theory as hermeneutics. American Antiquity 56(4):621–627.

Kuhn, T. S. 1970. The structure of scientific revolutions. 2nd ed. University of Chicago Press.

Leonard, R. D., and G. T. Jones. 1987. Elements of an inclusive evolutionary model for archaeology. Journal of Anthropological Archaeology 6(3):199–219.

Leone, Mark. 1982. Some opinions about recovering mind. American Antiquity 47(4):742–760.

Lévi-Strauss, Claude. 1963. Structural anthropology, C. Jacobson and B. Schoepf, trans. Basic Books, New York. (Originally published in 1958)

Levine, P. 1986. The amateur and the professional: antiquarians, historians and archaeologists in Victorian England, 1838–1886. Cambridge University Press.

Lubbock, J., Lord Avebury. 1865. Pre-historic times, as illustrated by ancient remains, and the manners and customs of modern savages. Williams and Norgate, London.

Lynch, B. D., and T. F. Lynch. 1968. The beginnings of a scientific approach to prehistoric archaeology in 17th and 18th century Britain. Southwestern Journal of Anthropology 24:33–65.

Marsden, B. M. 1984. Pioneers of prehistory: leaders and landmarks in English archaeology (1500–1900). Hesketh, Ormskirk, U.K.

Piggott, Stuart. 1976. Ruins in a landscape: essays in antiquarianism. Edinburgh University Press.

Renfrew, Colin, and Paul Bahn. 1991. Archaeology; theories, methods and practice. Thames and Hudson, New York.

Rindos, D. 1984. The origins of agriculture: an evolutionary perspective. Academic Press, New York.

Sharer, Robert J., and Wendy Ashmore. 1979. A case study in research design: the Quirigua project. In Fundamentals of Archaeology, by R. J. Sharer and W. Ashmore. Benjamin Cummings, Menlo Park, Calif., pp. 120–143.

Sklenar, K. 1983. Archaeology in central Europe: the first 500 years. Leicester University Press, Leicester, U.K.

Taylor, Walter W. 1948. A study of archaeology. American Anthropological Association Memoirs No. 69. Washington, D.C.

Tilley, Christopher. 1984. Ideology and the legitimation of power in the Middle Neolithic of southern Sweden. In Ideology, power and prehistory, D. Miller and C. Tilley, eds. Cambridge University Press.

————. 1990. Reading material culture: structuralism, hermeneutics and post-structuralism. Basil Blackwell, Oxford and Cambridge, Mass.

Trigger, Bruce G. 1989. A history of archaeological thought. Cambridge University Press.

Walters, H. B. 1934. The English antiquaries of the sixteenth, seventeenth and eighteenth centuries. Walter, London.

Watson, Patty Jo, Steven A. LeBlanc, and Charles L. Redman. 1971. Explanation in archaeology: an explicitly scientific approach. Columbia University Press, New York.

————. 1984. Archaeological explanation: the scientific method in archeology. Columbia University Press, New York.

SOURCES OF ADDITIONAL INFORMATION

For comprehensive overviews of the historical development of archaeology, see Bruce Trigger, *A History of Archaeological Thought* (Cambridge, Cambridge University Press, 1989); the earlier books by Glyn Daniel (Daniel 1950, 1976, 1978); and Daniel and Renfrew (1988), all cited in the References. Philosophical statements of the foundations of the "new" archaeology are in Watson, LeBlanc, and Redman 1971 (cited above); Patty Jo Watson, Steve LeBlanc, and Charles Redman, *Archaeological Explanation: The Scientific Method in Archaeology* (New York, Columbia University Press, 1984); and Merrilee H. Salmon, *Philosophy and Archaeology* (New York, Academic Press, 1982).

For expositions of the positions of some of the postprocessualists, see Leone 1982; Hodder 1982; Tilley 1984 and 1990; and the articles on hermeneutics by Kosso (1991) and Johnson and Olsen 1992 (see References above for complete citations). For brief reviews of a number of contemporary theoretical positions see Ian Hodder, *Reading the Past* (Cambridge, Cambridge University Press, 1986). Discussions of some of these issues are included in Frederick Baker and Julian Thomas, eds., *Writing the Past in the Present* (Lampeter, U.K., Saint David's University, 1990); and in Valerie Pinsky and Alison Wylie, eds., *Critical Traditions in Contemporary Archaeology* (Cambridge, Cambridge University Press, 1989).

Full discussions of the "new" archaeology and its long-term effects on the discipline are in Guy Gibbon, *Anthropological Archaeology* (New York, Columbia University Press, 1984); Jane Kelley and Marsha Hanen, *Archaeology and the Methodology of Science* (Albuquerque, University of New Mexico Press, 1988); and Richard A. Watson, "What the new archaeology has accomplished," *Current Anthropology* 32(3)(1991):275–291.

For an example of the effects of bias on theoretical research, see Marvin Harris's classic Marxist work, *Cultural Materialism: The Struggle for a Science of Culture* (New York, Random House, 1979).

Further discussion of postprocessualism may be found in Patty Jo Watson and M. Fotiadis, "The razor's edge: symbolic-structuralist archaeology and the expansion of archaeological inference," *American Anthropologist* 92(3)(1990):613–629, which includes an extensive bibliography. A critique of both the "new" archaeology and postprocessualist archaeology is in Richard A. Gould, *Recovering the Past* (Albuquerque, University of New Mexico Press, 1990), in which the author discusses a number of major issues in contemporary archaeology. For a discussion of the possibilities of developing a Darwinian evolutionary theory for archaeology, see Leonard and Jones 1987 (for complete citation, see References above).

For descriptions of archaeological methods adopted from the sciences, see Don Brothwell and Eric Higgs, eds., *Science in Archaeology: A Survey of Progress and Research*, rev. and enl. ed. (New York, Praeger, 1970). The material in this volume may be updated in part by M. J. Aitken, *Science-based Dating in Archaeology* (London, Longman, 1990); see also relevant articles in this volume, including ARCHAEOMETRY, BIOARCHAEOLOGY, and CHRONOMETRIC DATING.

To update the material in the publications cited above, consult latest issues of *American Antiquity, Current Anthropology, Journal of Anthropological Archaeology,* and annual volumes of *Archaeological Method and Theory* and *Annual Review of Anthropology*.

ARCHAEOMETRY. A broadly inclusive term used to refer to the diversity of quantitative methods involving technology and instrumentation developed in the physical, chemical, and engineering sciences over the past several decades that are now routinely used in the analysis and characterization of archaeological materials. Archaeometric studies encompass procedures employed in archaeological dating and chronology; investigations of ARTIFACTS using physicochemical techniques; paleobiological studies of prehistoric diet and nutrition by chemical analysis of human and animal remains; and the location of archaeological SITES and buried remains by remote sensing. See also BIOCULTURAL STUDIES; CHRONOMETRIC DATING; QUANTIFICATION.

The application of methods and techniques from the physical and biological sciences to archaeological problems, in particular to problems requiring precise metric data and chemical testing of artifacts, ecofacts, or human remains, developed as a result of the interdisciplinary approach to archaeological research that began in the 1950s. The word *archaeometry* was originally coined by Sir Christopher Hawkes, who used it as the title for the publication, *Archaeometry, Bulletin of the Research Laboratory for Archeology and Art* at Oxford University, which began publication in 1958. Its more general usage and application resulted from the widespread distribution of this journal (Taylor and Payen 1979:241).

Archaeometric studies may be divided into four broad subdivisions: (a) archaeological chronology or "archaeochronometrics" (CHRONOMETRIC DATING); (b) archaeological analytics (physical, chemical, and engineering analyses of artifact materials); (c) paleo-environmental and paleoecological reconstructive studies; and (d) archaeological remote sensing applications, such as the use of underground magnetometry to locate buried structures and large features, and the use of airborne radar to discover such features and constructions as irrigation works and agricultural terracing and raised field systems, canals, and concentrations of human settlement on ancient landscapes (Taylor and Payen 1979:241).

One of the earliest archaeometric applications was the use of radioactive carbon samples for dating organic materials from archaeological contexts (Arnold and Libby 1949; Aitken 1990), which provided archaeologists with one of the first reliable methods of CHRONOMETRIC DATING. Since that time, the variety of archaeometric techniques available has greatly increased. Such techniques now include methods for identifying early cultigens from pottery residues (Hill and Evans 1988), and for studying a variety of technical processes in the past, including pyrotechnology, methods of medical treatment, and early mining and metalworking (Craddock and Gale 1988), to mention only a few.

Until quite recently, archaeometric studies were usually focused on questions concerned with establishing the age or provenience of artifacts such as pottery, glass, and lithic tools, or information on prehistoric diet and SUBSISTENCE obtained from chemical analyses of bone and other organic materials (Schoeninger 1979; Chisholm, Nelson and Schwarz 1982, 1983; Price 1989). In 1979, Taylor and Payen described their primary role in archaeology in these terms:

... The current emphasis [is] on archaeometry's role of providing an interface between the archaeologist and the collaborating physical or natural scientist. Perhaps its most valuable contribution has been in the matching of archaeological problem and perspective with the physical scientist's priorities, capabilities, and interests. (Taylor and Payen 1979:241)

Traditionally, archaeometric studies have concentrated on techniques and methods of analysis, and have reported purely quantitative results rather than producing generalizing conclusions (see, e.g., the papers in Brothwell and Higgs 1970). This situation is now beginning to change, and there is a growing emphasis on using archaeometric data to address broader research questions and explanatory issues, as well as for testing hypotheses.

Current archaeometric studies encompass applications of procedures for tracing raw materials used in manufacturing artifacts to their sources by neutron activation (Slater and Willett 1988); methods for detecting buried archaeological deposits that employ geophysical instrumentation and other geophysical techniques (Walker 1988); and a variety of computer applications. Uses of statistical techniques in SERIATION of artifacts (Orton 1980) and the development of artifact typologies have been implemented by computer technology, which has also enabled archaeologists to assemble data banks for storing archaeometric data, to compile computerized excavation archives, to store SURVEY data, and to utilize computer analysis for interpreting aerial photographs and other remote-sensing data acquired from surveys. Papers presented at an international conference on the application of scientific techniques in ARCHAEOLOGY (Slater and Tate 1988) span the broad range of current archaeometric studies, demonstrating the great variety of techniques now available for analyzing archaeological data, as well as the variety of research problems that can be addressed using these methods.

Archaeometry has ceased to be merely a collection of technical procedures, and has begun to acquire importance as an area of research contributing to the development and testing of archaeological hypotheses. Increasingly, it is becoming a part of theory-conscious research designed to answer conceptual questions, in addition to its continuing importance for descriptive studies. It appears quite likely that in the future, when a majority of archaeologists have acquired sufficient technical training and skill to master their use, archaeometric techniques will become the standard methods of archaeological analysis, superseding traditional methods based on intuition and sense data (Dunnell 1991).

REFERENCES

Aitken, M. J. 1990. Science-based dating in archaeology. Longman, London.
Arnold, J. R., and W. F. Libby. 1949. Age determinations by radiocarbon content. Science 110:678–680.
Brothwell, Don and Eric Higgs, eds. 1970. Science in archaeology: a survey of progress and research. Rev. and enl. ed. Praeger, New York.
Chisholm, Brian S., D. Erle Nelson, and H. P. Schwarz. 1982. Stable isotope ratios as

a measure of marine versus terrestrial protein in ancient diets. Science 216:1131–1132.

——. 1983. Marine and terrestrial protein in prehistoric diets on the British Columbia coast. Current Anthropology 24(3):396–398.

Craddock, P. T., and D. Gale. 1988. Evidence for early mining and extractive metallurgy in the British Isles: problems and potentials. In Science and archaeology, Glasgow 1987, E. A. Slater and J. O. Tate, eds. BAR International Series 196. Oxford, vol. 1, pp. 167–191.

Dunnell, Robert C. 1991. Discussion and comments [verbal] on using archaeometry: the role of physical sciences in archaeology, a symposium held at the 56th annual meeting of the Society for American Archaeology, New Orleans, April 1991, Christopher Pierce, organizer.

Hill, H. E., and J. Evans. 1988. Vegeculture in Solomon Islands prehistory from pottery residues. In Science and archaeology, Glasgow 1987, E. A. Slater and J. O. Tate, eds. BAR International Series 196. Oxford, vol. 2, pp. 449–458.

Orton, Clive. 1980. Mathematics in archaeology. Collins, London.

Price, T. Douglas, ed. 1989. The chemistry of prehistoric human bone. Cambridge University Press.

Schoeninger, Margaret J. 1979. Diet and status at Chalcatzingo: some empirical and technical aspects of strontium analysis. American Journal of Physical Anthropology 51:295–309.

Slater, Elizabeth A., and James O. Tate, eds. 1988. Science and archaeology, Glasgow 1987: proceedings of a conference on the application of scientific techniques to archaeology. . . . 2 vols. BAR International Series 196. Oxford, vols. 1 and 2.

Slater, E. A., and F. Willett. 1988. Neutron activation analysis of clay cores from Nigerian castings. In Science and archaeology, Glasgow 1987, E. A. Slater and J. O. Tate, eds. BAR International Series 196. Oxford, vol. 1, pp. 247–257.

Taylor, R. E., and Louis A. Payen. 1979. The role of archaeometry in American archaeology: approaches to the evaluation of the antiquity of Homo sapiens in California. Advances in Archaeological Method and Theory 2:239–283.

Walker, R. 1988. Geophysical instrumentation for archaeological prospection. (Abstract). In Science and archaeology, Glasgow 1987, E. A. Slater and J. O. Tate, eds. BAR International Series 196. Oxford, vol. 2, p. 485.

SOURCES OF ADDITIONAL INFORMATION

For background material on archaeometry, see Ulrich Leute, *Archaeometry: An Introduction to Physical Methods in Archaeology and the History of Art* (New York, Weinham, 1987); and the review by Taylor and Payen in *Advances in Archaeological Method and Theory* (see References above for complete citation). The variety of archaeometric applications may be sampled in the papers published in Elizabeth A. Slater and James O. Tate, eds., *Science and Archaeology, Glasgow 1987: Proceedings of a Conference on the Application of Scientific Techniques to Archaeology* (Oxford, British Archaeological Reports, 1988), BAR British Series 196, vols. 1 and 2; and Yannis Maniatis, *Archaeometry: Proceedings of the 25th International Symposium* (Amsterdam, Elsevier, 1989).

The most comprehensive review of physical and chemical methods is Brothwell and Higgs (1970; see References for citation), but this is now quite out of date, and needs to be updated by the papers in Slater and Tate (1988) and Maniatis (1989) (see References for both).

For continuing update of developments in archaeometry, see the regular feature "Archaeometric clearinghouse" in *Journal of Field Archaeology*, and future issues of the journals *Archaeometry* and *Archaeomaterials*.

ARTIFACT. Any material item manufactured by humans, or utilized and modified by humans.

Artifacts are portable objects such as tools, pottery, baskets, clothing, and personal ornaments, and permanently fixed features on the human landscape, including buildings, fences, hearths, and trash dumps. Natural objects, or *ecofacts*, such as shells, animal bones, seeds, or tree branches that have been used by humans as tools, for food, or for decorative purposes, may also be considered artifacts, if there is clear evidence in the ARCHAEOLOGICAL RECORD of such utilization. Any object that exhibits clear signs of human modification or utilization may be considered an artifact, "whether a scatter of broken bones, a ruined house, a gold mask, or a vast temple plaza" (Fagan 1988:92). Artifacts comprise all material items and traces of human cultural behavior (Spaulding 1960), and are distinguished from ecofacts by virtue of possessing distinctive attributes resulting from human activity (Dunnell 1971:130). Such objects constitute the primary material data of ARCHAEOLOGY, and are studied in terms of their forms and temporal contexts in efforts to reconstruct human events and lifeways of the past.

Archaeologists may distinguish between several broad categories of artifact, such as features, structures, portable artifacts, and ecofacts (Sharer and Ashmore 1979:70–72; Fagan 1988:92); all, however, share the common attribute of reflecting past behavior in the overall patterned nature of their characteristics, which is a key feature used to distinguish them from natural objects (Fagan 1988:101). Artifacts may be defined and categorized in terms of either their functions or their physical attributes (see TYPOLOGY).

Prior to the eighteenth century, prehistoric stone tools discovered in Europe were customarily considered to be objects of natural or supernatural origin. References to "thunderstones" and "elf-arrows," attributed respectively to lightning and to supernatural beings, are some of the earliest recorded discoveries of Paleolithic hand axes (Lynch and Lynch 1968; Daniel 1975; Trigger 1989). In the 1650s, William Dugdale was among the first to interpret stone tools as the manufactured products of early inhabitants of England who had not yet developed metallurgy (Dugdale 1656). The earliest known artifact to be collected by an antiquarian is the Conyors hand ax, a Lower Paleolithic implement found in 1690 and still in the collection of the British Museum (Jessup 1961:4; Lynch and Lynch 1968:37). Robert Plot and others noted similarities between the early European stone axes and some of the tools found in America by explorers and colonists (Plot 1677, 1686; Evans 1872; Lynch and Lynch 1968:46). The German Johann Esper correctly identified as early as human implements the tools found with bones of extinct mammals in a cave near Bamberg, and published an account of this in the 1770s (Daniel 1975:25), before the antiquity of the human species had become established in European intellectual circles (Grayson 1983).

The industrial revolution, which stimulated mining and excavation for building materials, led to many discoveries of early stone artifacts. In 1800, an English antiquarian, John Frere, illustrated hand axes he had recovered from a brick pit near Hoxne in a paper of considerable sophistication for that time, in which he described not only the artifacts but also their stratigraphic associations (Frere 1800).

A continuing problem in the interpretation of the earliest stone artifacts, especially those associated with prehuman hominids, is that of distinguishing the marks of purposeful activity from the modifications produced by the action of natural processes. This difficulty prompted a number of experimental studies early in the twentieth century, in which stones were subjected to various machine-produced processes designed to approximate the action of natural agencies, and the results compared with problematical artifacts, in attempts to distinguish differences that would allow the unequivocal identification of the results of human agency and thereby distinguish artifacts from "geofacts," as they have sometimes been called (Dalton 1905; Kendall 1905; Warren 1905; Schwartz and Beavor 1909). The results were not as conclusive as could have been desired, and this problem has persisted up to the present time, producing a sizable body of literature, as well as a considerable amount of further experimental research, without reaching a completely satisfactory resolution (Moir 1914; Barnes 1939; Haynes 1973; Payen 1982; Budinger 1983, 1984; Grayson 1983). As Brian Fagan has noted, however, the detection of patterning is a crucial factor in solving this problem (Fagan 1988); but identifying such patterning according to a set of objective, quantifiable criteria remains almost as elusive a goal for stone artifact analysis as for identifying the effects of human agency on bone (Bonnichsen and Sorg 1989). Recent research in LITHICS has generated some new theoretical approaches to this problem (see Dibble and Rolland 1990; Rolland and Dibble 1990) that may eventually lead to the development of reliable criteria for separating the work of humans from the actions of nature.

REFERENCES

Barnes, A. S. 1939. The differences between natural and human flaking in prehistoric flint implements. American Anthropologist 41(1):99–112.

Bonnichsen, R., and M. H. Sorg, eds. 1989. Bone modification: proceedings of the First International Conference on Bone Modification, Carson City, Nevada, August 1984. University of Maine, Center for Studies of Early Man, Orono.

Budinger, F. E., Jr. 1983. Evidence for Pleistocene man in America: the Calico early man site. California Geology 36:75–82.

———. 1984. Calico debitage. Friends of Calico Newsletter 6(4):5–7.

Dalton, O. M. 1905. Machine-made eoliths. Man 5:123.

Daniel, Glyn E. 1975. One hundred and fifty years of archaeology. Harvard University Press, Cambridge, Mass.

Dibble, Harold L., and N. Rolland. 1990. Beyond the Bordes-Binford debate: a new synthesis of factors underlying assemblage variability in the Middle Paleolithic of western Europe. In New perspectives on human adaptation and behavior in the Middle Paleolithic, H. Dibble and P. Mellars, eds. University of Pennsylvania Press, Philadelphia.

Dugdale, William. 1656. The antiquities of Warwickshire. Warren, London.

Dunnell, Robert C. 1971. Systematics in prehistory. Free Press, New York.

Evans, J. 1872. The ancient stone implements, weapons, and ornaments of Great Britain. Appleton, New York.

Fagan, Brian M. 1988. In the beginning: an introduction to archaeology. 6th ed. Scott, Foresman, Glenview, Ill.

Frere, John. 1800. Account of flint weapons discovered at Hoxne in Suffolk. Archaeologia 13:204–205.

Grayson, Donald K. 1983. The establishment of human antiquity. Academic Press, New York.

Haynes, C. Vance. 1973. The Calico site: artifacts or geofacts? Science 181:305–311.

Jessup, Ronald, ed. 1961. Curiosities of British archaeology. Butterworth, London.

Kendall, G. O. 1905. Eoliths and pseudo-eoliths. Man 5:163–165.

Lynch, Barbara D., and Thomas F. Lynch. 1968. The beginnings of a scientific approach to prehistoric archaeology in 17th and 18th century Britain. Southwestern Journal of Anthropology 24:33–65.

Moir, J. R. 1914. A defence of the "humanity" of the Pre-river Valley implements of the Ipswich district. Proceedings of the Prehistoric Society of East Anglia 1(4):368–374.

Payen, L. A. 1982. Artifacts or geofacts at Calico: application of the Barnes test. In Peopling of the New World, J. E. Ericson, R. E. Taylor, and R. Berger, eds. Ballena Press Anthropological Papers 23. Menlo Park, Calif., pp. 193–201.

Plot, Robert. 1677. The natural history of Oxfordshire. Oxford.

———. 1686. The natural history of Staffordshire. Oxford.

Rolland, Nicolas, and Harold L. Dibble. 1990. A new synthesis of Middle Paleolithic variability. American Antiquity 55(3):480–499.

Schwartz, A. S., and H. R. Beavor. 1909. The dawn of human invention: an experimental and comparative study of eoliths. Memoirs and Proceedings of the Manchester Literary and Philosophical Society 53(3):1–34.

Sharer, Robert J., and Wendy Ashmore. 1979. Fundamentals of archaeology. Benjamin/ Cummings Publishing Company, Inc., Menlo Park, Calif.

Spaulding, Albert D. 1960. Statistical description and comparison of artifact assemblages. In The application of quantitative methods in archeology, R. F. Heizer and S. F. Cook, eds. Quadrangle Books, Chicago, pp. 60–90.

Trigger, Bruce. 1989. A history of archaeological thought. Cambridge University Press.

Warren, S. H. 1905. On the origin of "eolithic" flints by natural causes, especially by the foundering of drifts. Journal of the Royal Anthropological Institute of Great Britain and Ireland 35:337–364.

SOURCES OF ADDITIONAL INFORMATION

For further discussion of artifacts, see articles in this volume titled ARCHAEOLOGICAL RECORD; CULTURE; LITHICS; and TYPOLOGY. Artifacts as data are discussed in L. Biek, "Artifacts," in *Science in Archaeology*, Don Brothwell and Eric S. Higgs, eds. 2nd ed. (New York, Praeger, 1970), pp. 567–570. Considerations of artifacts from a structuralist-textual interpretative viewpoint may be found in D. Miller, "Artifacts as products of human categorisation processes," in *Symbolic and Structural Archaeology*, I. Hodder, ed. (Cambridge, Cambridge University Press, 1982), pp. 17–25; and Ian Hodder, *Reading the Past* (Cambridge, Cambridge University Press, 1986). For future publications, consult the journals *American Antiquity* and *Journal of Anthropological Archaeology*.

ASSEMBLAGE. 1. A collection of ARTIFACTS and utilized ecofacts thought to represent the total range of activities shared by a past community. 2. A varied collection of a specific category or class of archaeological materials, or one derived from a particular geographical locale or cultural tradition, such as a faunal assemblage of animal bones; a surface assemblage of stone tools collected from the ground surface of a site; or a Paleo-Indian assemblage of implements all datable to the earliest cultural period in New World prehistory. See also ARTIFACT; CULTURE; LITHICS.

An assemblage has been variously defined as "a collection of artifacts . . . thought to represent the products of a single society over a short period of time" (Spaulding 1960:62); "associations of tools . . . thought to be contemporary" (Fagan 1988:137); a "gross grouping of all subassemblages assumed to represent the sum of human activities carried out within an ancient community" (Sharer and Ashmore 1979: 560); and "the totality of the *lithic* artifacts recovered from a single archaeological unit, [which] forms the basis for the description and definition of a site" (Cahan, Keeley, and Van Noten 1979:661; emphasis added). The maximum group of all assemblages from all contemporaneous sites in the same area composes an *archaeological culture* (Sharer and Ashmore 1979:559; see also CULTURE).

The common element present in such definitions as those above is the idea that an assemblage consists of the totality of artifacts from a single archaeological unit, and therefore provides an adequate sample for describing and characterizing the nature of a SITE or other unit by providing an inventory of the tools typically made and used by its past occupants to serve their needs. However, the ARTIFACTS composing any assemblage inevitably reflect the operation of many variables, including the cultural and personal preferences of the people who made them, the activities they performed, the length of time the SITE was occupied, and especially accidents of preservation or nonpreservation, postdepositional disturbance processes, and many other factors (Cahan, Keeley, and Van Noten 1979; see also SITE; TAPHONOMY).

The comprehensiveness of an assemblage distinguishes it from a *subassemblage* or *toolkit*, which is a group of tools or other artifacts consistently used together in performing a particular economic, SUBSISTENCE, or artistic activity, such as butchering, stonecutting, or woodcarving, and which is usually confined to a particular location or activity area within a SITE where the remains of the activity are deposited.

The concept of the assemblage as a collection of artifacts that display patterning or groups of regularly associated traits, occurring in different sites from the same

CULTURE and showing repeated regularities, appears in some of the earliest archaeological literature, and underlies the related concept of archaeological cultures or "industries" as larger units representing types or species of culture easily identified from their material remains, which display recurring characteristics or traits. Culture historians of the early twentieth century viewed assemblages produced by groups inhabiting different sites but sharing the same culture as distinct categories similar to biological species, which remained formally the same regardless of their locational CONTEXT (Childe 1925, 1956; Sackett 1981). This view, which led to difficulties in accounting for observed variability between assemblages from different sites belonging to the same culture, persisted into the 1950s, when it began to be challenged by the use of statistical methods for identifying and characterizing assemblages (Spaulding 1960; Cannon 1983; Fagan 1988:308).

The traditional view of CULTURE HISTORY prior to this time had been that a specific cultural tradition created only one type of lithic industry, and this would be unvaryingly repeated at all sites belonging to that culture. American archaeologists have often adopted a different position, one allowing for the influence of different local environmental characteristics on assemblages produced and used by groups sharing the same culture. The late French archaeologist François Bordes took a very different view, attributing interassemblage variability observed in tool collections from the Mousterian culture of the Middle Paleolithic, associated with Neanderthal populations, to ethnic differences between the groups who produced them (Bordes 1953, 1961, 1969; Bordes and Sonneville-Bordes 1970). The American archaeologist Lewis Binford has interpreted this variation as evidence that different kinds of activities were performed by the Mousterians in different spatial areas, and has supported his conclusions with ethnoarchaeological data. His findings would suggest that the so-called variant assemblages Bordes regarded as evidence of the presence of different ethnic groups are in fact subassemblages, or toolkits, associated with particular kinds of processes, and do not represent the entire range of activities performed by Middle Paleolithic peoples of the Mousterian culture (Binford and Binford 1966, 1969; Binford 1973, 1983).

The concept of an assemblage as representing the totality of activities engaged in by an entire community may be misleading, since it implies a completeness of material remains that occurs very rarely in archaeological sites. Under even the best of preservation conditions, only a fragment of a community's total productive activity will leave its traces in the ARCHAEOLOGICAL RECORD. The stone tools that are most likely to survive represent only a portion of this activity; artifacts made from organic materials, such as wooden and bone tools and utensils, fabrics, and basketry, will usually not be preserved. An assemblage is therefore better conceived as a collection of *surviving remains* of a past community that represents the activities of that community to a limited and highly variable degree, or as an uncontrolled sample of an unknown population of artifacts whose representativeness of total community output cannot be statistically determined or measured. As a key to the lifeways of the past, assemblages require very careful interpretation, taking into account factors of preservation, context, and the totality of what is known of the cultures that produced them. In the interpretative process, assemblage data may be supplemented by well-supported inferences based on appropriate ethnohistorical or ethnoarchaeological data, when available.

REFERENCES

Binford, Lewis R. 1973. Interassemblage variability—the Mousterian and the "functional" argument. In The explanation of culture change, C. Renfrew, ed. Duckworth, London, 227–254.

————. 1983. In pursuit of the past. Thames and Hudson, New York.

Binford, Lewis R., and Sally R. Binford. 1966. A preliminary analysis of functional variability in the Mousterian of Levallois facies. American Anthropologist 68(2), pt. 2:238–295.

————. 1969. Stone tools and human behavior. Scientific American 220(4):70–84.

Bordes, François. 1953. Essai de classification des industries "mousteriennes." Bulletin de la Société Préhistorique Française 50(7–8):457–466.

————. 1961. Mousterian cultures in France. Science 134(3482): 803–810.

————. 1969. Reflections on typology and techniques in the Paleolithic. Arctic Anthropology 6(1):1–29.

Bordes, François, and Denise de Sonneville-Bordes. 1970. The significance of variability in Paleolithic assemblages. World Archaeology 2(1):61–73.

Cahan, D., L. H. Keeley, and F. L. Van Noten. 1979. Stone tools, toolkits, and human behavior in prehistory. Current Anthropology 20(4):661–683.

Cannon, Aubrey. 1983. The quantification of artifactual assemblages: some implications for behavioral inferences. American Antiquity 48(4):785–792.

Childe, V. Gordon. 1925. The dawn of European civilization. Routledge and Kegan Paul, London.

————. 1956. Piecing together the past. Routledge and Kegan Paul, London.

Fagan, Brian M. 1988. In the beginning: an introduction to archaeology. 6th ed. Scott, Foresman, Glenview, Ill.

Sackett, James. 1981. From de Mortillet to Bordes: a century of French Upper Paleolithic research. In Towards a history of archaeology, Glyn Daniel, ed. Thames and Hudson, London, pp. 85–99.

Sharer, Robert J., and Wendy Ashmore. 1979. Fundamentals of archaeology. Benjamin Cummings, Menlo Park, Calif.

Spaulding, A. C. 1960. Statistical description and comparison of artifact assemblages. In The application of quantitative methods in archaeology, R. F. Heizer and S. F. Cook, eds. University of Chicago Press, pp. 60–90.

SOURCES OF ADDITIONAL INFORMATION

For discussions of assemblage formation processes, see A. Ammerman and M. Feldman, "On the making of an assemblage of stone tools," *American Antiquity* 39(1974):610–616; M. G. Stevenson, "The formation of artifact assemblages at workshop/habitation sites: models from Peace Point in northern Alberta," *American Antiquity*

50(1)(1985):63–81; and M. J. Shott, "On tool class use lives and the formation of archaeological assemblages," *American Antiquity* 54(1)(1989):9–30.

For a view of intersite variability in the Mousterian outside western Europe, see F. C. Munday, "Intersite variability in the Mousterian of the central Negev," in *Prehistory and Palaeoenvironments in the Central Negev, Israel, vol. 1*, S. Marks, ed. (Dallas, Southern Methodist University Press, 1976), pp. 113–140.

An overview of the increasing importance of surface assemblages in archaeological interpretation, together with a bibliography of the literature up to the early 1980s, is in the review by Dennis E. Lewarch and Michael J. O'Brien, "The expanding role of surface assemblages in archaeological research," *Advances in Archaeological Method and Theory* 4(1981):297–342.

Recent emphases on assemblage structure, diversity, quantification, and modeling are reflected in B. J. Mills, "Integrating functional analyses of vessels and sherds through models of ceramic assemblage formation," *World Archaeology* 21(2)(1989):133–147; K. D. Schick, "Modeling the formation of early stone-age artifact concentrations", *Journal of Human Evolution* 16(7–8)(1987):789–807; J. C. Chatters, "Hunter-gatherer adaptations and assemblage structure," *Journal of Anthropological Archaeology* 6(4)(1987):336–375; and M. J. Shott, "Diversity, organization, and behavior in the material record, ethnographic and archaeological examples," *Current Anthropology* 30(3)(1989):283–315. A volume of papers devoted entirely to the measurement of assemblage diversity is R. Leonard and G. Jones, eds., *Quantifying Diversity in Archaeology* (Cambridge, Cambridge University Press, 1989).

For future developments in the study of assemblage formation and variability, see forthcoming issues of *American Antiquity, Journal of Anthropological Archaeology, Journal of Archaeological Science*, and *Current Anthropology*.

B
_____

BIOARCHAEOLOGY. The study of preserved remains of once-living orga-nisms recovered from archaeological deposits, for information they may reveal on prehistoric human ecology, SUBSISTENCE, health, or cultural behavior. Bioar-chaeological investigations are usually conducted by interdisciplinary research teams, and may include paleoecological and paleoenvironmental research aimed at reconstructing the physical environment of the past, as well as investigation of human interaction with that environment. See also BIOCULTURAL STUDIES; PALEOANTHROPOLOGY; SUBSISTENCE; ZOOARCHAEOLOGY.

Bioarchaeology encompasses a number of specialized subfields of ARCHAE-OLOGY, including *palynology*, the study of prehistoric pollen profiles; *paleo-botany* (also called paleoethnobotany and archaeobotany; Miksicek 1987:211); the study of preserved plant remains from archaeological contexts; and faunal analysis, or ZOOARCHAEOLOGY. A related specialized area of bioarchaeological investigation, BIOCULTURAL STUDIES, combines the analysis of human physical remains with ecological and cultural data, frequently to study nutrition, disease, or genetic factors in the past, and is often carried on by a physical anthropologist working with an archaeologist.

Bioarchaeology was a product of the period of interdisciplinary archaeological research that began in the 1940s and 1950s with the work of Robert Braidwood at early village sites in Iraq, and Grahame Clark's environmentally-oriented excavations at the Mesolithic site of Star Carr in northern England (Braidwood 1974; Braidwood and Howe 1960; Clark 1952, 1954, 1972). The cultural eco-logical research of Julian Steward and his students was an important stimulus to paleoenvironmental research in North America. Since the time of these earliest investigations, studies of plant and animal remains from archaeological sites have become a routine part of a majority of archaeological field projects, and personnel trained in palynology, paleoethnobotany, and faunal analysis are now part of most archaeological research teams.

The primary subject matter of bioarchaeology is composed of *ecofacts*, the unaltered, preserved organic remains of plants and animals utilized by past human populations. If these materials have been altered by humans, they are considered ARTIFACTS, and are subject to cultural analysis. Bioarchaeologists, however, deal primarily with unaltered ecofacts. Plant materials studied may include phytoliths (Rovner 1971, 1983; Piperno 1984, 1985a, 1985b; Bozarth 1987), pollen (Behre 1968; Bryant and Holloway 1983), diatoms, spores, carbonized seeds, wood and charcoal, or any other plant parts preserved in archaeological deposits that may have been of economic importance to a prehistoric population (Adams 1980; Bottema 1984). Animal remains collected and analyzed may include bone, shell, insect chitons, and fish otoliths (see ZOOARCHAEOLOGY). Bioarchaeologists also examine food remains preserved in human fossil feces (coprolites) for information on prehistoric diet and nutrition (Callen 1967; Marquardt 1974). Those specializing in the related field of biocultural studies may examine human remains from burials for data on diet and nutrition in the past, and utilize resulting data in the study of health and disease patterns, demographic factors, and genetic relationships among members of an archaeological population. The study of paleobotany has been an area of considerable research activity in recent years, and has generated a substantial literature (Helbaek 1970; Yarnell 1970; Renfrew 1973; Ford 1979; Meyen 1987; Hastorf and Popper 1989; Pearsall 1989).

Since many of the materials of interest to the bioarchaeologist are of very small size, special field techniques such as fine screening, wet screening and flotation are often necessary for their recovery (Jarman et al. 1972; Keeley 1978; Doebley 1981; Minnis 1981; see also FIELD ARCHAEOLOGY). Laboratory techniques for their analysis frequently require the use of high-powered microscopes, including the scanning electron microscope (Keepax 1975).

In addition to problems involved in recovering their primary data in the field, bioarchaeologists must deal with the ongoing problems of small sample sizes. Since organic materials, especially those of small size, are frequently preserved only in very small quantities, it is often difficult or inadvisable to generalize from the sparse data that may be available, and doing so will require the use of specialized statistical methods (see also QUANTIFICATION; ZOOARCHAEOLOGY). For this reason, the interpretation of food remains may require the use of models based on ethnographic or ethnoarchaeological data (Greenhouse, Gasser, and Gish 1981; Jones 1984).

Bioarchaeological data are important for reconstructing past environments inhabited by prehistoric populations. Studies of floral remains can provide information on vegetation patterns that existed at various times in the past, indicating the plant foods available to humans. Pollen diagrams indicate which plant species were most numerous at different times, and are useful indicators of the presence of human agriculturists, since episodes of cultivation will be reflected in dramatic increases in the proportion of *Graminae* pollen, representing concentrations of the grains that were usually cultivated as staple crops. Carbonized seeds recovered from sites give further indications of species gathered or cultivated for food. Studies of human coprolites, and of stomach contents of human bodies preserved by dry mummification or in anaerobic wet deposits, can yield similar data, and may sometimes even tell the archaeologist how foods were cooked in the past (Glob 1971). Such studies may be supplemented by the work of lithic specialists, since microexamination of stone tools will sometimes reveal wear patterns indicating the kinds of plants the tools were used to process, and occasionally residues of plant or animal fibers or blood will be found on tools. Such painstaking analysis produces data of great value in reconstructing prehistoric SUBSISTENCE strategies and technology.

Today bioarchaeological studies are central to virtually all major field projects, and new techniques for the analysis of biological remains continue to be developed, enabling archaeologists to pose new questions about past lifeways that can be answered by using the data now available through bioarchaeological research.

REFERENCES

Adams, K. R. 1980. Pollen, parched seeds and prehistory: a pilot investigation of prehistoric plant remains from Salmon Ruin, a Chacoan pueblo in northwestern New Mexico. Contributions in Anthropology 9. Eastern New Mexico University, Portales.

Behre, K. E. 1968. The interpretation of anthropogenic indicators in pollen diagrams. Pollen et Spores 23:225–245.

Bottema, S. 1984. The composition of modern charred seed assemblages. In Plants and ancient man, W. van Zeist and W. A. Casparie, eds. A. A. Balkema, Boston, pp. 207–212.

Bozarth, Steven R. 1987. Diagnostic opal phytoliths from rinds of selected *Cucurbita* species. American Antiquity 52(3):607–615.

Braidwood, Robert J. 1974. The Iraq Jarmo project. In Archaeological researches in retrospect, Gordon R. Willey, ed. Winthrop, Cambridge, Mass., pp. 61–83.

Braidwood, Robert J., and B. Howe. 1960. Investigations in Iraqi Kurdistan. Studies in Ancient Oriental Civilization No. 31. Oriental Institute, University of Chicago.

Bryant, Vaughn M., Jr., and Richard G. Holloway. 1983. The role of palynology in archaeology. Advances in Archaeological Method and Theory 6:191–224.

Callen, E. O. 1967. Analysis of Tehuacán coprolites. In The prehistory of the Tehuacán Valley. Vol. 1: Environment and subsistence, D. S. Byers, ed. University of Texas Press, Austin, pp. 261–269.

Clark, Grahame (J. G. D.). 1952. Prehistoric Europe: the economic basis. Methuen, London.

———. 1954. Excavations at Star Carr, an Early Mesolithic site at Seamer, near Scarborough, Yorkshire [with chapters by D. Walker, H. Goodwin and F. C. Fraser, and J. E. King]. Cambridge University Press.

———. 1972. Star Carr: a case study in bioarchaeology. McCaleb Module in Anthropology, No. 10. Addison-Wesley, Chicago.

Doebley, J. F. 1981. Plant remains recovered by flotation from trash at Salmon Ruin, New Mexico. The Kiva 46(3):169–187.

Ford, Richard I. 1979. Paleoethnobotany in American archaeology. Advances in Archaeological Method and Theory 2:285–336.

Glob, P. V. 1971. The bog people: Iron Age man preserved. Ballantine Books, New York.

Greenhouse, R., R. E. Gasser, and J. W. Gish. 1981. Cholla bud roasting pits: an ethnoarchaeological example. The Kiva 46:227–242.

Hastorf, Christine A., and Virginia S. Popper, eds. 1989. Current paleoethnobotany: analytical methods and cultural interpretations of archaeological plant remains. University of Chicago Press.

Helbaek, Hans. 1970. Palaeo-ethnobotany. In Science in archaeology, 2nd ed., Don Brothwell and Eric Higgs, eds. Praeger, New York, pp. 206–214.

Jarman, H. N., A. J. Legge, and J. A. Charles. 1972. Retrieval of plant remains from archaeological sites by froth flotation. In Papers in economic prehistory, E. S. Higgs, ed. Cambridge University Press, pp. 39–48.

Jones, G. 1984. Interpretation of archaeological plant remains: ethnographic models from Greece. In Plants and ancient man, W. van Zeist and W. A. Casparie, eds. A. A. Balkema, Boston, pp. 43–69.

Keeley, H. C. M. 1978. The cost effectiveness of certain methods of recovering macroscopic organic remains from archaeological deposits. Journal of Archaeological Science 5:179–184.

Keepax, C. 1975. Scanning electron microscopy of wood replaced by iron corrosion products. Journal of Archaeological Science 2:145–150.

Marquardt, W. H. 1974. A statistical analysis of constituents in human paleofeces specimens from Mammoth Cave. In Archaeology of the Mammoth Cave area, P. J. Watson, ed. Academic Press, New York, pp. 193–202.

Meyen (also Meien), Sergei V. 1987. Fundamentals of palaeobotany. Chapman and Hall, London and New York.

Miksicek, Charles H. 1987. Formation processes of the archaeobotanical record. Advances in Archaeological Method and Theory 10:211–247.

Minnis, P. E. 1981. Seeds in archaeological sites: sources and some interpretive problems. American Antiquity 46:143–152.

Pearsall, Deborah M. 1989. Paleoethnobotany: a handbook of procedures. Academic Press, San Diego.

Piperno, Dolores. 1984. A comparison and differentiation of phytoliths from maize and wild grasses: use of morphological criteria. American Antiquity 49(2):361–383.

———. 1985a. Phytolithic analysis of geological sediments from Panama. Antiquity 59:13–19.

———. 1985b. Preceramic maize in central Panama: phytolith and pollen evidence. American Anthropologist 87(4):871–878.

Renfrew, J. M. 1973. Paleoethnobotany: the prehistoric food plants of the Near East and Europe. Methuen, London.

Rovner, I. 1971. Potential of opal phytoliths for use in paleogeological reconstruction. Quaternary Research 1:343–359.

———. 1983. Plant opal phytolith analysis: major advances in archaeobotanical research. Advances in Archaeological Method and Theory 6:225–266.

Yarnell, Richard A. 1970. Palaeo-ethnobotany in America. In Science in Archaeology, 2nd ed., Don Brothwell and Eric Higgs, eds. Praeger, New York, pp. 215–228.

SOURCES OF ADDITIONAL INFORMATION

For further background on bioarchaeology see the series of classic papers by R. W. Dennell, "The interpretation of plant remains: Bulgaria," in *Papers in Economic Prehistory*, E. S. Higgs, ed. (Cambridge: Cambridge University Press, 1972), pp. 149–160; "The economic importance of plant remains represented in archaeological sites," *Journal of Archaeological Science* 3(1976):229–247; and "Archaeobotany and early farming in Europe," *Archaeology* 31(1978):8–13. Additional material may be found in H. K. Kenward, "The value of insect remains as evidence of ecological conditions on archaeological sites," in *Research Problems in Zooarchaeology*, D. Brothwell, K. D. Thomas, and J. Clutton-Brock, eds., Institute of Archaeology Occasional Papers No. 3(1978):25–28; K. R. Adams and R. E. Gasser, "Plant microfossils from archaeological sites: research questions and sampling techniques and approaches," *The Kiva* 45(4)(1980):293–300, which outlines sampling techniques and field methods for recovering and preserving botanical remains from archaeological sites; and W. Van Zeist and W. A. Casparie, eds., *Plants and Ancient Man* (Boston, A. A. Balkema, 1984). For material on methods of faunal analysis, see ZOOARCHAEOLOGY.

To update this material, consult future issues of the *Journal of Archaeological Science*, *Paleobiology*, *Quaternary Research*, and *American Anthropologist*.

BIOCULTURAL STUDIES. A specialized interdisciplinary area of studies combining theoretical approaches and methods derived from ARCHAEOLOGY, physical anthropology, and the biological and physical sciences, to investigate interactions between the physical and cultural environments and human health, growth, and survival in the past.

Biocultural studies are concerned with documenting the mutual relationship between cultural practices and health, diet, morbidity, and demographic factors in the past. Its subject matter includes paleonutritional studies, some types of paleodemographic investigations, paleoepidemiological studies, and paleopathological examination of prehistoric human skeletal remains (Crosby 1972; Perzigian 1977; Cockburn and Cockburn 1980; Larsen 1981; Martin and Bumsted 1981; Huss-Ashmore, Goodman, and Armelagos 1982; Merbs 1983; Klepinger 1984; Buikstra and Konigsberg 1985; Buikstra and Mielke 1985; Eaton and Konner 1985; Merbs and Miller 1985; Clark et al. 1987; Baker and Armelagos 1988). The field is somewhat diffuse, and includes researchers whose primary professional training has been in archaeology, physical anthropology, ARCHAEOMETRY, and the medical and physical sciences. Terminology is not completely standardized, nor is there a formal body of either theory or method for the field as a whole. Investigators employ methods derived from anthropology, archaeology, and the laboratory sciences; interpretations and reporting have usually followed prevailing practice in the "new" anthropological archaeology.

Biocultural studies encompass archaeological investigations of prehistoric human skeletal remains and food remains for information on prehistoric diets, SUBSISTENCE practices, health and disease, and the effects of interaction among all these factors on human behavior in the past. Those engaged in such studies also consider the impact of different lifeways on the human skeleton, as recorded in both nonpathological and pathological changes in joints, bone form and function, tooth wear and decay, and evidence of fractures, lesions, or other bone trauma. Biocultural studies include chemical analyses of isotopes and trace elements in human bone for evidence of diet (Gilbert 1977; Lambert, Szpunar, and Buikstra 1979; Schoeninger 1979; Price and Kavanagh 1982; Chisholm, Nelson, and Schwarz 1983; Sillen and Smith 1984; Bumsted 1985; Farnsworth et al. 1985; Lynott et al. 1986; Sealy and Sillen 1988); paleopathological studies of skeletal remains for markers of disease and nutritional deficiencies (Morse 1969; Saul 1973; Clarke 1978; Buikstra 1981; Huss-Ashmore 1981; Cook et al. 1983; Manchester 1983; Molnar and Molnar 1985; Andersen and Manchester 1988; Baker and Armelagos 1988; Manchester and Roberts 1989); and studies of faunal and botanical remains as evidence of prehistoric human diets, using the techniques of BIOARCHAEOLOGY and ZOOARCHAEOLOGY (Holden 1991).

Examination of human burial populations for traits and skeletal markers suggesting genetic relationships among individuals that may reveal aspects of SOCIAL ORGANIZATION in the past, such as kinship systems and marriage rules, is another area of investigation (Lane and Sublett 1972; Wilkinson and Norelli 1981; see also ARCHAEOMETRY). Skeletal studies can also sometimes yield information about prehistoric subsistence strategies (Sealy and Van der Merwe 1986; Larsen 1987); mortality and morbidity rates (Clarke 1980; Storey 1985); and the effects on health of the transition from hunting and gathering to FOOD PRODUCTION (Cohen and Armelagos 1984).

Although some isolated early studies relate pathologies observed in skeletal remains to past diet and lifeways (e.g., Mummery 1870; Hrdlicka 1909; Hooton 1930), biocultural studies as a distinctive interdisciplinary area evolved as part of the expanded investigative methods of the ''NEW'' ARCHAEOLOGY during the 1960s. The use of improved archaeological field techniques made possible the recovery of data that had previously been lost or destroyed. Human skeletal remains that could be examined for clues to the health and nutritional status of individuals were recovered in far greater numbers, as well as floral and faunal materials that could be analyzed for information on prehistoric diets. These materials provided a data base for the study of diet, nutrition, and pathology in the past that could be related to subsistence, SOCIAL ORGANIZATION, and other cultural factors, affording opportunities to develop far more detailed information on the interaction of culture and human biological factors in the past than had previously been possible.

Some of the earliest paleonutritional studies were the result of extensive collections of faunal remains made by investigators such as Elizabeth Wing, whose work in Mesoamerica revealed status-related differences in patterns of meat consumption in the past, as well as temporal changes in the animal species of greatest dietary importance (Wing 1974, 1978, 1981; Wing and Hammond 1975; Wing and Steadman 1980). By the 1970s, chemical and trace element studies of human bone brought further refinements in knowledge of prehistoric diets, including such data as relative proportions of animal and plant foods consumed (Gilbert 1977; Lambert, Szpunar, and Buikstra 1979; Chisholm, Nelson, and Schwarz 1983; Sealy and Sillen 1988). In 1979, the first major theoretical and methodological work on paleonutrition was published (Wing and Brown 1979).

Paleopathological studies of human skeletal remains were also a product of the 1960s. The first major collection of papers reporting research on prehistoric disease and pathology appeared in the late 1960s (Brothwell and Sandison 1967), and was followed by numerous studies based on field data, as well as some attempts at synthesis (Morse 1969; Saul 1972, 1973; Buikstra and Cook 1981; Mignon 1982; Manchester 1983; Cohen and Armelagos 1984; Cohen 1989). Skeletal studies relating paleopathology and PALEODEMOGRAPHY to paleonutrition also began to appear (Buikstra 1981; Corruccini 1983; Buikstra and Mielke 1985), as well as others that derived social and cultural information from investigations of burial populations (Haviland 1967; Lane and Sublett 1972; Nickens 1976; Wilkinson and Norelli 1981; Sillen and Smith 1984). Bone studies also became a valuable source of information on prehistoric subsistence patterns (Lynott et al. 1986; Sealy and Van der Merwe 1986).

The extensive use of human skeletal material from archaeological SITES as the primary data of biocultural studies became an area of considerable controversy in the United States during the 1980s. Many Native American groups have protested the excavation and laboratory study of the bones of those they regard as their ancestors, and have demanded that such remains not continue to be excavated, and that those now in laboratory collections be returned to the appropriate persons for reburial. This matter has generated heated discussions at meetings of professional societies, and has led to careful examination of the legal and ethical issues involved. Legal considerations in the collection and study of human remains were discussed as early as 1979 by Wing and Brown in their volume on paleonutritional studies, and then-existing laws at local, state, federal, and international levels were reviewed (Wing and Brown 1979:175–178).

The reburial issue has significantly affected the availability of skeletal material for study by paleonutritionists and paleopathologists since the mid-1980s, because human remains are now being returned to Native American groups in large numbers, and some archaeologists will no longer excavate human burials. These factors have made the future of biocultural studies extremely uncertain.

REFERENCES

Andersen, Johannes G., and Keith Manchester. 1988. Dorsal tarsal exostoses in leprosy: a palaeopathological and radiological study. Journal of Archaeological Science 15:51–56.

Baker, Brenda J., and George J. Armelagos. 1988. The origin and antiquity of syphilis: paleopathological diagnosis and interpretation. Current Anthropology 29(5):703–738.

Brothwell, Don R., and A. T. Sandison. 1967. Diseases in antiquity. C. Thomas, Springfield, Ill.

Buikstra, Jane E., ed. 1981. Prehistoric tuberculosis in the Americas. Archaeological Program Scientific Papers 5. Northwestern University, Evanston, Ill.

Buikstra, Jane E., and Della C. Cook. 1981. Paleopathology: an American account. Annual Review of Anthropology 9:433–470.

Buikstra, Jane E., and L. Konigsberg. 1985. Paleodemography: critiques and controversies. American Anthropologist 87:316–333.

Buikstra, Jane E., and J. H. Mielke. 1985. Demography, diet, and health. In The analysis of prehistoric diets, R. I. Gilbert, Jr., and J. H. Mielke, eds. Academic Press, Orlando, Fla., pp. 362–422.

Bumsted, M. Pamela. 1985. Past human behavior from bone chemical analysis—respects and prospects. Journal of Human Evolution 14:539–551.

Chisholm, Brian S., D. Erle Nelson, and Henry P. Schwarz. 1983. Marine and terrestrial protein in prehistoric diets on the British Columbia coast. Current Anthropology 24:396–398.

Clark, George A., Marc A. Kelley, J. M. Grange, and M. Cassandra Hill. 1987. The evolution of mycobacterial disease in human populations: a re-evaluation. Current Anthropology 28(1):45–62.

Clarke, S. K. 1978. Markers of metabolic insult: the association of radiopaque transverse lines, enamel hypoplasias, and enamel histopathologies in a prehistoric human skeletal sample. Doctoral dissertation, Department of Anthropology, University of Colorado, Boulder.

———. 1980. Early childhood morbidity trends in prehistoric populations. Human Biology 52:79–85.

Cockburn, A., and E. Cockburn, eds. 1980. Mummies, disease, and ancient cultures. Cambridge University Press.

Cohen, Mark N. 1989. Paleopathology and the interpretation of economic change in prehistory. In Archaeological thought in America, C. C. Lamberg-Karlovsky, ed. Cambridge University Press, pp. 117–132.

Cohen, Mark N., and G. J. Armelagos, eds. 1984. Paleopathology at the origins of agriculture. Academic Press, Orlando, Fla.

Cook, Della C., Jane E. Buikstra, C. J. DeRousseau, and Don C. Johanson. 1983. Vertebral pathology in the Afar australopithecines. American Journal of Physical Anthropology 60:83–101.

Corruccini, Robert S. 1983. Pathologies relative to subsistence and settlement at Casas Grandes. American Antiquity 48:609–610.

Crosby, A. W., Jr. 1972. The Columbian exchange: biological and cultural consequences of 1492. Greenwood Press, Westport, Conn.

Eaton, S., and Melvin Konner. 1985. Paleolithic nutrition. New England Journal of Medicine 312:283–289.

Farnsworth, Paul, James E. Brady, Michael J. DeNiro, and Richard S. MacNeish. 1985. A re-evaluation of the isotopic and archaeological reconstruction of diet in the Tehuacán Valley. American Antiquity 50(1):102–116.

Gilbert, Robert I., Jr. 1977. Applications of trace element research to problems in archeology. In Biocultural adaptation in prehistoric America, R. I. Blakely, ed. University of Georgia Press, Athens, pp. 85–100.

Gilbert, Robert I., Jr., and James H. Mielke, eds. 1985. The analysis of prehistoric diets. Academic Press, New York.

Haviland, William A. 1967. Stature at Tikal, Guatemala: implications for ancient Maya demography and social organization. American Antiquity 32:316–325.

Holden, Timothy G. 1991. Evidence of prehistoric diet from northern Chile: coprolites, gut contents and flotation samples from the Tulan Quebrada. World Archaeology 22(3):320–331.

Hooton, Ernest Albert. 1930. The Indians of Pecos Pueblo: a study of their skeletal remains. Yale University Press, New Haven.

Hrdlicka, Ales. 1909. Report on an additional collection of skeletal remains from Arkansas and Louisiana. Journal of the Academy of Natural Science (Philadelphia) 14:173–249.

Huss-Ashmore, Rebecca. 1981. Bone growth and remodeling as a measure of nutritional stress. In Biocultural adaptation: comprehensive approaches to skeletal analysis, D. I. Martin and M. P. Bumsted, eds. Department of Anthropology Research Reports 20. University of Massachusetts, Amherst, p. 95.

Huss-Ashmore, Rebecca, Alan H. Goodman, and George J. Armelagos. 1982. Nutritional inference from paleopathology. Advances in Archaeological Method and Theory 5:395–474.

Klepinger, Linda L. 1984. Nutritional assessment from bone. Annual Review of Anthropology 13:75–96.

Lambert, J. B., C. B. Szpunar, and J. E. Buikstra. 1979. Chemical analysis of excavated human bone from Middle and Late Woodland sites. Archaeometry 21:115–129.

Lane, Rebecca A., and Audrey J. Sublett. 1972. Osteology of social organization: residence pattern. American Antiquity 37(2):186–201.

Larsen, Clark Spencer. 1981. Skeletal and dental adaptations to the shift to agriculture on the Georgia coast. Current Anthropology 22:422–423.

―――. 1987. Bioarchaeological interpretations of subsistence economy and behavior from human skeletal remains. Advances in Archaeological Method and Theory 10:339–445.

Lynott, Mark J., Thomas W. Boutton, James E. Price, and Dwight E. Nelson. 1986. Stable carbon isotopic evidence for maize agriculture in southeast Missouri and northeast Arkansas. American Antiquity 51(1):51–65.

Manchester, Keith. 1983. The archaeology of disease. University of Bradford, Bradford, U.K.

Manchester, Keith, and Charlotte Roberts. 1989. The paleopathology of leprosy in Britain: a review. World Archaeology 21(2):265–272.

Martin, D. L., and M. P. Bumsted, eds. 1981. Biocultural adaptation: comprehensive approaches to skeletal analysis. Department of Anthropology Research Reports 20. University of Massachusetts, Amherst.

Merbs, C. F. 1983. Patterns of activity-induced pathology in a Canadian Inuit population. National Museum of Man Mercury Series, Archaeological Survey of Canada Paper 119. Ottawa.

Merbs, C. F., and R. J. Miller, eds. 1985. Health and disease in the prehistoric Southwest. Anthropological Research Papers 34. Arizona State University, Tempe.

Mignon, Molly R. 1982. Health, nutrition and pathology of the pre-Columbian Maya Indians. M.A. thesis, Department of Anthropology, Western Washington University, Bellingham.

Molnar, S., and I. Molnar. 1985. The incidence of enamel hypoplasias among the Krapina Neanderthals. American Anthropologist 87(3):536–549.

Morse, Dan. 1969. Ancient disease in the Midwest. Illinois State Museum Reports of Investigations No. 15. Springfield.

Mummery, J. R. 1870. On the relations which dental caries, as discovered among the ancient inhabitants of Britain and amongst existing aboriginal races, may be supposed to hold to their food and social conditions. Transactions of the Odontological Society of Great Britain 2:7–24, 27–80.

Nickens, P. R. 1976. Stature reduction as an adaptation to food production in Mesoamerica. Journal of Archaeological Science 3:31–41.

Perzigian, Anthony J. 1977. Teeth as tools for prehistoric studies. In Biocultural adaptation in prehistoric America, R. L. Blakeley, ed. University of Georgia Press, Athens, pp. 101–114.

Powell, M. L. 1986. Late prehistoric community health in the central deep South: biological and social dimensions of the Mississippian chiefdom at Moundville, Alabama. In Skeletal analysis in southeastern archaeology, J. E. Levy, ed. North Carolina Archaeological Council Publication No. 24. Raleigh, N.C., pp. 127–149.

Price, T. Douglas, and Maureen Kavanagh. 1982. Bone composition and the reconstruction of diet: examples from the midwestern United States. Midcontinental Journal of Archaeology 7:61–79.

Saul, Frank. 1972. The human skeletal remains of Altar de Sacrificios: an osteobiographic analysis. Papers of the Peabody Museum of Archaeology and Ethnology 63, no. 2. Harvard University, Cambridge, Mass.

———. 1973. Disease in the Maya area: the pre-Columbian evidence. In The Classic Maya collapse, T. Patrick Culbert, ed. University of New Mexico Press, Albuquerque.

Schoeninger, Margaret. 1979. Diet and status at Chalcatzingo: some empirical and technical aspects of strontium analysis. American Journal of Physical Anthropology 51:295–310.

Sealy, Judith C., and Andrew Sillen. 1988. Sr and Sr/Ca in marine and terrestrial foodwebs in the southwestern Cape, South Africa. Journal of Archaeological Science 15:425–438.

Sealy, Judith C., and Nikolaas J. Van der Merwe. 1986. Isotope assessment and the seasonal-mobility hypothesis in the southwestern Cape of South Africa. Current Anthropology 27(2):135–150.

Sillen, Andrew, and P. Smith. 1984. Weaning patterns are reflected in strontium-calcium ratios of juvenile skeletons. Journal of Archaeological Science 11(3):237–246.

Storey, Rebecca. 1985. An estimate of mortality in a pre-Columbian urban population. American Anthropologist 87(3):519–535.

Wilkinson, Richard G., and Richard J. Norelli. 1981. A biocultural analysis of social organization at Monte Alban. American Antiquity 46(4):743–758.

Wing, Elizabeth S. 1974. Vertebrate faunal remains. In Excavation of an early shell midden on Isla Cancún. Tulane University, Mesoamerican Research Institute Publication 31, no. 6. New Orleans, pp. 186–188.

———. 1978. Use of dogs for food: an adaptation to the coastal environment. In Prehistoric coastal adaptations, Barbara L. Stark and Barbara Voorhies, eds. Academic Press, New York.

————. 1981. A comparison of Olmec and Maya foodways. In The Olmec and their neighbors, essays in memory of Matthew W. Stirling. Dumbarton Oaks Research Library, Washington, D.C.

Wing, Elizabeth S., and A. B. Brown. 1979. Paleonutrition: method and theory in prehistoric foodways. Academic Press, New York.

Wing, Elizabeth S., and Norman Hammond. 1975. Animal remains from Lubaantun . . . with additional references by Norman Hammond. In Lubaantun, a Classic Maya realm, by Norman Hammond. Peabody Museum of Archaeology and Ethnology Monographs No. 20. Harvard University, Cambridge, Mass., pp. 379–383.

Wing, Elizabeth S., and David Steadman. 1980. Vertebrate faunal remains from Dzibilchaltun; appendix to Excavations at Dzibilchaltun, Yucatan, Mexico, by E. Willys Andrews IV and E. Wyllys Andrews V. Middle American Research Institute Publication 48. Tulane University, New Orleans.

SOURCES OF ADDITIONAL INFORMATION

Further background on paleonutritional studies may be found in Wing and Brown 1979; for paleopathology, see the papers in Brothwell and Sandison 1967; Cockburn and Cockburn 1980; and the review by Buikstra and Cook (1981). (See References above for complete citations to all these publications.) A review on the exchange of trace elements between bone and soil, affecting the results of chemical analysis of archaeological bone, is Ann M. Whitmer, Ann F. Ramenofsky, Jacob Thomas, Louis J. Thibodeaux, Stephen D. Field, and Bob J. Miller, "Stability or instability: the role of diffusion in trace element studies," *Archaeological Method and Theory* 1(1989):205–273, which includes more than 100 bibliographic references.

These materials and those listed in the References above should be updated by consulting current and forthcoming issues of *Journal of Archaeological Science, American Journal of Physical Anthropology*, and *Current Anthropology*, as well as *Annual Review of Anthropology* and *Archaeological Method and Theory*.

For material on the reburial issue, see Lawrence Rosen, "The excavation of American Indian burial sites: a problem of law and professional responsibility," *American Anthropologist* 82(1980):5–27; Anthony L. Klesert and Michael J. Andres, "The treatment of human remains on Navajo lands," *American Antiquity* 53(2)(1988):310–320; "The question of reburial: archeologists debate the handling of prehistoric human skeletal remains" [editorial, in "Issues in archeology" feature], *Early Man Magazine* (Autumn 1981):25; Jane E. Buikstra, "A specialist in ancient cemetery studies looks at the reburial issue," *Early Man Magazine* (Autumn 1981):26–27; D. H. Ubelaker and L. G. Grant, "Human skeletal remains, preservation or reburial?" *Yearbook of Physical Anthropology* 32(1989):249–287; and L. Goldstein and K. Kintigh, "Ethics and the reburial controversy," *American Antiquity* 55(3)(1990):585–591.

C

CARRYING CAPACITY. 1. The maximum population that can be supported indefinitely within a given environment, using a specific level of extractive technology, without producing irreversible damage to the environment; "the critical population size before land degradation begins" (Brush 1975:800). 2. A measure of the relationship between a human population and its environment, or of some specific aspect of that relationship, such as "the productive capacity of the environment divided by the per capita [economic] requirements of a human population" (Dewar 1984:602). 3. The "man-land balance . . . maintained by native populations practicing simple food producing methods such as shifting cultivation" (Brush 1975:799). See also PALEODEMOGRAPHY; SUBSISTENCE.

The concept of carrying capacity originated in wildlife biology, where it appears to have been first used by D. L. Errington and F. N. Hammerstrom in their studies of quail populations in Iowa and Wisconsin in the 1930s, in which they observed that each of the 20 areas they investigated supported a characteristic number of birds (Hassan 1981:164). However, the conceptual basis for the idea has been present in Western culture since Thomas Malthus's famous 1826 essay on population, in which he pointed out the limiting effect of SUBSISTENCE practices on human population, and the potential of technology for altering this relationship (Brush 1975:799; Hassan 1981:161).

Anthropologists and ecologically oriented archaeologists concerned with relationships between environment, human population size, and economic/SUBSISTENCE patterns (e.g., Dumond 1965, 1972, 1975, 1976a, 1976b; Zubrow 1971, 1975; Casteel 1972; Brush 1975; Hayden 1975) have found carrying capacity to be a useful concept for the study of prehistoric human populations. This is especially true of those who regard population size as a "limiting factor," in accordance with Esther Boserup's theory of population growth and its relationship to subsistence practices (Boserup 1965).

Among human populations, carrying capacity is a function of technology, as well as of environmental factors (Alland and McCay 1973). Technology is one method of changing the carrying capacity through increasing productivity by using technological means. Such changes may be only temporarily effective, however, if environmental destruction results from the intensification methods utilized.

Many problems have arisen in the quantitative application of the carrying capacity concept, due to the difficulty of assessing values of such key variables as environmental productivity potential or the amount of food obtainable from a particular environment using a given technology (Hayden 1975:11–14). The usefulness of being able to calculate such values has stimulated a search for improved quantitative measures of population and environmental variables (Glassow 1978:45).

A number of formulas have been suggested for calculating carrying capacity, and have been applied by anthropologists and archaeologists such as Robert Carneiro (1960) and Roy Rappaport (1968), in order to predict how a given human ecosystem will respond at particular points in time to continued population growth and resulting resource pressure (see discussion in Brush 1975:800–802).

Carrying capacity played an important role in the growth of the ecological paradigm in ARCHAEOLOGY (Vayda and Rappaport 1968; Vayda and McCay 1975; Vayda 1976), and remains a very important concept in the archaeological study of SUBSISTENCE and economic patterns, particularly among those interested in testing Boserup's population pressure hypothesis with respect to the beginning and intensification of FOOD PRODUCTION (Boserup 1965). Its advantages include providing a deductive method for studying man/land relationships that lends itself to quantitative treatment and testing, allowing comparisons to be made between human populations and communities of other biological species. In addition, it permits the formulation and testing of hypotheses regarding human population control in the past, and how such practices may have been related to environmental factors among prehistoric peoples (Hayden 1972; Brush 1975; Dumond 1975; Dewar 1984, 1985; Keegan, Johnson, and Earle 1985).

REFERENCES

Alland, Alexander, Jr., and Bonnie McCay. 1973. The concept of adaptation in biological and cultural evolution. In Handbook of social and cultural anthropology, John J. Honigmann, ed. Rand McNally, Chicago, pp. 143–178.

Boserup, Esther. 1965. The conditions of agricultural growth. Aldine, Chicago.

Brush, S. B. 1975. The concept of carrying capacity for systems of shifting cultivation. American Anthropologist 77:799–811.

Carneiro, Robert. 1960. Slash-and-burn agriculture: a closer look at its implications for settlement patterns. In Men and cultures, Anthony F. C. Wallace, ed. University of Pennsylvania Press, Philadelphia, pp. 229–234.

Casteel, R. W. 1972. Two static models for hunter-gatherers: a first approximation. World Archaeology 3:19–40.

Dewar, Robert E. 1984. Environmental productivity, population regulation and carrying capacity. American Anthropologist 86(3):601–614.

———. 1985. The pitfalls of supply-side ecology: a reply to Keegan, Johnson and Earle. American Anthropologist 87(3):663–664.

Dumond, Don E. 1965. Population growth and cultural change. Southwestern Journal of Anthropology 21:302–324.

———. 1972. Population growth and political centralization. In Population growth: anthropological implications, B. Spooner, ed. MIT Press, Cambridge, Mass., pp. 286–310.

———. 1975. The limitation of human population: a natural history. Science 187:713–721.

———. 1976a. Response to Zubrow. American Anthropologist 78:896.

———. 1976b. Review of Prehistoric carrying capacity: a model, by Ezra B. W. Zubrow. American Anthropologist 78:710–711.

Glassow, Michael A. 1978. The concept of carrying capacity in the study of culture process. Advances in Archaeological Method and Theory 1:32–48.

Hassan, Fekri A. 1981. Carrying capacity and population pressure. In Demographic archaeology. Academic Press, New York, pp. 161–175.

Hayden, Brian. 1972. Population control among hunter-gatherers. World Archaeology 4:205–221.

———. 1975. The carrying capacity dilemma. In Population studies in archaeology and physical anthropology, A. C. Swedlund, ed. SAA Memoir No. 30, issued as American Antiquity 40(2, pt.2):11–21.

Keegan, William, Allen Johnson, and Timothy Earle. 1985. Carrying capacity and population regulation: a comment on Dewar. American Anthropologist 87(3):659–663.

Rappaport, Roy A. 1968. Pigs for the ancestors. Yale University Press, New Haven.

Vayda, Andrew P. 1976. On the "new ecology" paradigm. American Anthropologist 73:645–646.

Vayda, Andrew P., and Bonnie J. McCay. 1975. New directions in ecology and ecological anthropology. Annual Review of Anthropology 4:293–306.

Vayda, Andrew P., and Roy A. Rappaport. 1968. Ecology, cultural and noncultural. In Introduction to cultural anthropology: essays in the scope and methods of the science of man, James A. Clifton, ed. Houghton Mifflin, Boston, pp. 477–497.

Zubrow, Ezra. 1971. Carrying capacity and dynamic equilibrium in the prehistoric Southwest. American Antiquity 36:127–138.

———. 1975. Prehistoric carrying capacity: a model. Benjamin Cummings, Menlo Park, Calif.

SOURCES OF ADDITIONAL INFORMATION

Fekri Hassan, "Carrying Capacity and Population Pressure," in his *Demographic Archaeology* (New York, Academic Press, 1981), pp. 161–175, discusses the concept of carrying capacity in relation to Esther Boserup's "population pressure" theory of agricultural development; for a critique of this concept, see G. L. Cowgill, "Population pressure as a non-explanation," in *Population Studies in Archaeology and Biological Anthropology*, A. C. Swedlund, ed. (SAA Memoir 30), issued as *American Antiquity* 49(2, pt.2):127–131. Donald Hardesty, *Ecological Anthropology* (New York, Wiley 1977), pp. 195–211, is also devoted to a discussion of carrying capacity, and includes a summary of quantitative methods for its estimation (pp. 199–203). S. B. Brush (1975; see References for full citation) discusses the background, advantages, and principal formulas; Michael Glassow (see References) summarizes carrying capacity and the population pressure model, and provides a bibliography (which now requires updating). For a critical evaluation of the carrying capacity concept, see John Street, "An evaluation of the concept of carrying capacity," *The Professional Geographer* 21(1969):104–107.

A study using data from early ethnohistoric documents to test a carrying capacity model developed by William Sanders and his associates for the Basin of Mexico in the early sixteenth century is Barbara Williams, "Contact period rural overpopulation in the Basin of Mexico: carrying capacity models tested with documentary data," *American Antiquity* 54(4)(1989):715–732; results indicate that carrying capacity had been exceeded by the time of contact in rural areas of this region.

Future issues of *American Anthropologist*, *American Antiquity*, and *Annual Review of Anthropology* should be consulted to update the information in the resources listed above.

CATCHMENT ANALYSIS. The term *catchment* is borrowed from geography, where it denotes a watershed or drainage basin. In archaeology, *catchment* refers to the geographic area from which a SITE's former inhabitants drew the natural resources needed to support their community. Catchment analysis is a technique used in the SPATIAL ANALYSIS of archaeological sites, usually as part of SETTLEMENT PATTERN research specifically directed toward reconstructing the prehistoric economy or SUBSISTENCE pattern of a local population.

A catchment area is a behavioral as well as a territorial unit (Jarman 1972), consisting of the geographic zone from which the material content of a site was derived. It is usually defined as being roughly circular in shape, given a flat or relatively uniform environment, but will depart from this circular pattern where relief is pronounced (Jarman, Vita-Finzi, and Higgs 1972:63; Roper 1979:124). Catchment analysis attempts to define a site catchment area in order to reconstruct patterns of resource procurement and their role in the local economy of a prehistoric community.

Catchment analysis, the technique of reconstructing the resource area utilized by a past population, assumes that humans act rationally in choosing locations for their activities, and make such decisions in accordance with the law of least effort. Sites can therefore be expected to lie close to those essential resources most frequently and intensively exploited. Resources located at greater distance, and consequently requiring greater expenditures of human energy for their procurement, will therefore be of relatively less importance in the economy. As one moves away from a site, the intensity of resource exploitation will tend to decrease with distance, eventually reaching a point beyond which such exploitation is no longer practical or profitable.

Catchment analysis as a specifically archaeological method dates to the late 1960s. The term was first used by Claudio Vita-Finzi (1969), who, with Eric Higgs, is usually credited with developing both the technique and its conceptual rationale. In developing the concepts of catchment analysis, Vita-Finzi and Higgs drew on the work of Michael Chisholm (1968), who, in turn, made use of principles introduced by Johann von Thünen in an economic model developed early in the nineteenth century (Von Thünen 1875; Vita-Finzi and Higgs 1970; Clarke 1977; Sallade and Braun 1982), and later elaborated by the geographer Walter Christaller in his central place model of settlement location (Christaller 1966). The relationships between site location and site function, and their connection to environmental factors, can be traced back to Julian Steward's studies in the Great Basin during the 1930s (Steward 1938).

Catchment analysts may plot site resource areas as a series of concentric circles of increasing size, each having the site as its center, and each representing the area from which a particular resource or category of resources was procured. The arbitrary circular pattern will need to be modified to allow for geophysical features of the land, such as bodies of water, variations in elevation, and other factors that may affect vegetation patterns, game habitats, and other resources, as well as the ease of procurement, resulting in catchment areas of different shapes. This technique is most frequently employed in analysis from a distance, using data from maps rather than data collected in the field by the analyst. Some analysts have constructed Thiessen polygons around sites to define catchment areas (see, e.g., Cassels 1972).

Analysts whose studies are based on field research more often use a temporal unit to define catchment areas. For hunting-and-gathering populations with seasonally variable residence patterns, for example, the primary resource zone may be defined as encompassing the area within a one-hour walk, or less, from the community (Vita-Finzi and Higgs 1970; Jarman, Vita-Finzi, and Higgs 1972:62–63; Roper 1979:123).

Some of the unverified assumptions of site catchment analysis may restrict the validity of its results. Among these are (a) that adjacent sites were occupied contemporaneously; (b) that catchment areas of adjacent sites do not overlap; and (c) that the catchment area was the only resource zone utilized, and no essential resources were procured through trade with groups exploiting other catchment areas with different resources.

Attempts to circumvent these difficulties have included the approach used by Kent V. Flannery in his catchment studies of sites in Mesoamerica (Flannery 1976a). Instead of using either spatially or temporally based analytical techniques, he began with empirical data, the material remains found in the site itself, and then traced these to their nearest environmental sources. The frequencies of particular classes of remains in the site, as well as the nearest distances from which they could have been procured, were then taken as indicators of the catchment area. Flannery and his associates used statistical techniques to analyze their results (Flannery 1976b; Rossman 1976; Zarky 1976). Unfortunately, environmental and taphonomic factors contributed to poor preservation of organic remains in Mesoamerican sites, reducing the likelihood that Flannery's samples are representative of the resources utilized by early Mesoamericans.

Another problem with using catchment models to reconstruct past economic patterns is the assumption that modern resource distributions are similar to those in past times when an archaeological site was occupied. Changes in climate and environments, and their effects on biological and other resources, may present an immeasurable distorting factor that is not always taken into consideration.

Despite these problems, and the contention that catchment analysis has frequently been misapplied (e.g., Sallade and Braun 1982), the technique has several advantages. It may enable the archaeologist to compare site locations and to identify contemporaneous sites that were economically complementary, such as locations of summer and winter residences and resource procurement activity sites used seasonally by the same population group. It also provides a method for checking on the economic conclusions derived from excavation; and it may in addition provide data for classifying a prehistoric economy as "mobile" or "sedentary" in its settlement and economic patterns, or as displaying some combination of these two (Jarman, Vita-Finzi, and Higgs 1972:65–66; see also SEASONALITY; SEDENTARINESS; SETTLEMENT PATTERN; SUBSISTENCE).

REFERENCES

Cassels, R. 1972. Locational analysis of prehistoric settlement in New Zealand. Mankind 8:212–222.

Chisholm, Michael. 1968. Rural settlement and land use, an essay in location. Hutchinson University Library, London.

Christaller, Walter. 1966. Central places in southern Germany, Carlisle W. Baskin, trans. Prentice-Hall, Englewood Cliffs, N.J.

Clarke, David L. 1977. Spatial information in archaeology. In Spatial archaeology, David L. Clarke, ed. Academic Press, London, pp. 1–32.

Flannery, Kent V. 1976a. Empirical determination of site catchments in Oaxaca and Tehuacán. In The early Mesoamerican village, K. V. Flannery, ed. Academic Press, New York, pp. 103–177.

————. 1976b. The village and its catchment area: introduction. In The early Mesoamerican village, pp. 91–95.

Jarman, M. R. 1972. A territorial model for archaeology: a behavioral and geographic approach. In Models in archaeology, David L. Clarke, ed. Methuen, London, pp. 705–733.

Jarman, M. R., C. Vita-Finzi, and E. S. Higgs. 1972. Site catchment analysis in archaeology. In Man, settlement and urbanism, P. J. Ucko, R. Tringham, and G. W. Dimbleby, eds. Duckworth, London, pp. 61–66.

Roper, Donna C. 1979. The method and theory of site catchment analysis: a review. Advances in Archaeological Method and Theory 2:119–140.

Rossman, D. L. 1976. A site catchment analysis of San Lorenzo, Veracruz. In The early Mesoamerican village, K. V. Flannery, ed. Academic Press, New York, pp. 95–103.

Sallade, Jane K., and David P. Braun. 1982. Spatial organization of peasant agricultural subsistence territories: distance factors and crop location. In Ethnography by archaeologists, Elisabeth Tooker, ed. American Ethnological Society, Washington, D.C., pp. 19–41.

Steward, Julian H. 1938. Basin-plateau aboriginal socio-political groups. Bureau of American Ethnology Bulletin No. 120. Washington, D.C.

Vita-Finzi, C. 1969. Early man and environment. In Trends in geography—an introductory survey, U. Cooke and J. H. Johnson, eds. Pergamon, Oxford, pp. 102–108.

Vita-Finzi, C., and E. S. Higgs. 1970. Prehistoric economy in the Mount Carmel area of Palestine: site catchment analysis. Proceedings of the Prehistoric Society 36:1–37.

Von Thünen, J. H. 1826. Der isolierte staat in beziehung auf landwirtschaft und nationalökonomie. F. Perthes, Hamburg.

Zarky, A. 1976. Statistical analysis of site catchments at Ocos, Guatemala. In The early Mesoamerican village, K. V. Flannery, ed. Academic Press, New York, pp. 117–128.

SOURCES OF ADDITIONAL INFORMATION

For further background on catchment analysis, see the review article by Donna Roper (cited in References, above). The ongoing usefulness of the technique is discussed in D. A. Sturdy and D. D. Webley, "Paleolithic geography, or Where are the deer?" *World Archaeology* 19(3)(1988):262–280.

Some further applications of catchment analysis in archaeology are described in J. E. Ericson and R. Goldstein, "Work space: a new approach to the analysis of energy-expenditure within site catchments," *Anthropology UCLA* 10(1–2)(1980):21–30; J. A. Tiffany and L. R. Abbott, "Site catchment analysis, applications to Iowa archaeology," *Journal of Field Archaeology* 9(3)(1982):313–322; G. N. Bailey and I. Davidson, "Site exploitation territories and topography, two case studies from Paleolithic Spain," *Journal of Archaeological Science* 10(21)(1983):87–115, which includes a bibliography of over 130 references; K. G. Hirth, "Catchment analysis and Formative settlement in the Valley of Mexico," *American Anthropologist* 86(1)(1984):136–143; V. P. Steponaitis, "Catchments, nonproducers, and tribute flow in the Valley of Mexico: some further remarks," *American Anthropologist* 86(1)(1984):143–148; L. G. Straus, "Late Würm adaptive systems in Cantabrian Spain, the case of eastern Asturias," *Journal of Anthropological Archaeology* 5(1986):330–368; James L. Boone III, "Defining and measuring midden catchment," *American Antiquity* 52(2)(1987):336–345; and D. A. Davison and C. M. Green, "An analysis of site catchment areas for chambered cairns on the island of Arran," *Journal of Archaeological Science* 16(4)(1989):419–426.

For current studies and reviews, consult future issues of *American Anthropologist*, *American Antiquity*, *Journal of Field Archaeology*, *Journal of Archaeological Science*, and *Annual Review of Anthropology*.

CENTRAL PLACE THEORY. A theory, borrowed by archaeologists from locational geography, which predicts that human settlements will be located at roughly equal intervals across a landscape, placed according to patterns of resource availability and routes of trade and communication, and will be distributed in a hierarchical pattern centered around service centers called central places.

Central place theory was developed by the German geographer Walter Christaller, whose classic work *Die zentralen Orte in Suddeutschland* was published in 1933. Christaller was convinced that the distribution of human communities resulted from economic as well as geographical factors, and set out to discover an underlying principle governing the number, locations, and sizes of towns within a region. He concluded that centralization was the organizing principle determining settlement location, and he called the economic service centers of geographic regions *central places* (Christaller 1966). Each central place serves a "complementary region" for different kinds of goods and services.

Christaller identified a hierarchical pattern of relationships among central places, based on their economic importance rather than population or physical size; his principle of centrality "refers less to the merely spatial central location than to the central *function*" (Christaller 1966:19; emphasis added). All central places of similar function will tend to be roughly equal in size, and higher-order central places will comprise all the functions of smaller (lower-order) central places within the same region, resulting in a hierarchically nested system of central places of differing functional sizes that, with their associated hexagonally shaped complementary regions, form an intricate lattice pattern on the landscape (Johnson 1972:769).

An economic model based on somewhat similar concepts, embodying the principle of least effort and concentric activity zones, had been developed by the German economist Johann von Thünen in the nineteenth century (Von Thünen 1875). This model was a significant influence on Christaller's work, although, unlike the central place model, von Thünen's considered sites as isolated units without economic ties to other communities (Clarke 1977:21–22). The von Thünen model was later adapted for archaeological applications by Claudio Vita-Finzi and Eric Higgs to provide the basis for CATCHMENT ANALYSIS (Chisholm 1968; Vita-Finzi and Higgs 1970).

It should be noted that centrality is an effort-minimizing principle, and the shape of the area served by a central place involves effort minimization (Hodder and Orton 1976:56). If the landscape is assumed to be a flat, featureless plain (as in von Thünen's model), the shape of the complementary region will be circular. In a later modification of Christaller's model, Peter Haggett showed that the hexagon is a more efficient shape than the circle, since it allows for the closest and densest packing together of complementary regions around their central places, and minimizes movement and boundary length (Haggett 1965:49). There have, however, been relatively few studies conducted to determine whether hexagonally shaped service areas exist in reality (Hodder and Orton 1976:56), although Haggett found some evidence for them in Brazil (Haggett 1965:50–51). Other investigators have discovered complementary regions with different geometric shapes, including the rhomboid (Johnson 1972).

The classic central place model of hierarchically nested communities and complementary regions, each serving a particular set of economic functions, may be graphically represented as a network of contiguous hexagons, each having a higher-order central place at its center and lower-order centers surrounding it at approximately equal distances. Christaller tested this model in southern Germany, where he was able to verify a seven-level hierarchy of communities ranging from small hamlets to regional capitals. The number of hierarchical levels identifiable is taken as an indicator of the relative degree of social and economic complexity represented in the region.

Areas served by central place service centers are commonly represented on maps by Thiessen polygons, produced by drawing perpendiculars at the midpoints between towns. The area enclosed within each resulting hexagon will be the area most efficiently served by the market center, assuming access is uniform, a principle testable archaeologically by using ARTIFACT distributions over the landscape. Deviations from the predicted pattern are to be expected, for as Christaller himself noted, the model does not include all possible variables that may affect community locations and intercommunity economic relationships (Johnson 1972:770).

Christaller's model was further modified by August Lösch (1954), who suggested that settlements of similar size need not necessarily serve the same function, and that large (i.e., higher-order) central places need not contain all the functions of smaller ones (Haggett 1965; Marcus 1976). A prior modification was introduced by John Harrison Kolb and Edmund de S. Brunner (1946), who suggested that the size of the area using a particular category of goods provided by a central place will vary with the size of the central service center. Furthermore, the broader range of services available in a higher-order center will attract people from greater distances, reducing the areas served by lower-order centers in even the primary and secondary services they provide, which are usually duplicated in the higher-order center (Brush 1953:392; Hodder and Orton 1976:63). This modification is a better reflection of reality than Christaller's original model.

Another modification usually employed by archaeologists using central place models is to discard the notion inherited from von Thünen of a service center surrounded by a flat, featureless plain, and changing the shapes of service areas from circular to hexagonal or other forms to reflect and accommodate physical features of real landscapes, as well as the modified intercommunity patterns these will produce.

The utility of central place theory in archaeology has been tested using data from sites in ancient Iraq (Johnson 1972), medieval England (Brush and Bracey 1955), West Africa (B. W. Hodder 1963), Roman Britain (I. Hodder 1972), and the American state of Wisconsin (Brush 1953). It has occasionally been adopted as an analytic technique by archaeologists engaged in the study of SETTLEMENT PATTERNS at the regional scale, and to explain observed locations of past communities and apparent hierarchical relationships among them. The success of such attempts has been limited, however, by the common problems of small sample size and of establishing site contemporaneity. It is extremely difficult, and often impossible, to identify all the prehistoric communities within a region, or to establish how representative any available sample of SITES may be of settlement distribution at any point in the past. The use of ethnohistoric documentary evidence, when available, may alleviate this problem to some extent.

An interesting application of central place theory to settlement data in the Maya lowlands of Mesoamerica was made by archaeologist Joyce Marcus (Marcus 1976), who attempted to establish a central place hierarchy of Maya cities of the Classic period in this region, based on the use of "emblem glyphs" (Berlin 1958). Using hieroglyphic evidence, Marcus attempted to demonstrate temporal changes in the hierarchical relationships between cities that appeared to be reflected in changing patterns of the use of emblem glyphs (unique identifying signs, each associated with a particular city) over time. The value of her analysis was unfortunately reduced by the incomplete nature of settlement data for the Maya lowlands, where exploration has been limited and an unknown number of sites remain undiscovered, as well as by the impossibility of verifying the exact significance of emblem glyph usage, and the very scanty data available on ancient Maya sociopolitical organization.

Gregory Johnson (1972) devised a test of central place theory and its archaeological applicability, using settlement data collected by Robert McC. Adams (1965) for the Early Dynastic I period (ca. 2800 B.C.) on the Diyala Plains of Iraq. His results indicated that, with some modifications, the marketing and transport principles developed by Christaller appear to be good predictors of site location patterns in this complex society.

A major difficulty in the archaeological application of central place theory is the virtual impossibility of ascertaining whether all the archaeologically identified communities in a region were occupied at the same time, and should therefore be included in the sample, and which belonged to earlier or later occupations. Without this information, central place analyses can have little validity. Other limitations are rooted in the limits of the theory itself, which may have greater applicability to economic relationships among complex urban centers of modern industrial civilization than to the prehistoric past. Geographers have noted that even contemporary reality does not necessarily reflect the principle of centralization defined by Christaller, and modifications in the classic model are usually required to correct for variables the model does not include. Its greatest usefulness appears to be in geography, since the assumptions and requirements of the central place model can rarely, if ever, be entirely satisfied using archaeological data.

REFERENCES

Adams, R. McC. 1965. Land behind Baghdad: a history of settlement on the Diyala Plains. University of Chicago Press.
Berlin, Heinrich. 1958. El glifo "emblema" en las inscripciones mayas. Journal de la Société des Americanistes [Paris] n.s. 47:11–119.
Brush, J. E. 1953. The hierarchy of central places in southwestern Wisconsin. Geographical Review 43:380–402.
Brush, J. E., and H. E. Bracey. 1955. Rural service centres in southwestern Wisconsin and southern England. Geographic Review 45:559–569.
Chisholm, Michael. 1968. Rural settlement and land use, an essay in location. Hutchinson University Library, London.

Christaller, Walter. 1966. Central places in southern Germany, Carlisle W. Baskin, trans. Prentice-Hall, Englewood Cliffs, N.J.

Clarke, David L. 1977. Spatial information in archaeology. In Spatial archaeology, David L. Clarke, ed. Academic Press, London, pp. 1–32.

Haggett, Peter. 1965. Locational analysis in human geography. St. Martin's Press, New York.

Hodder, B. W. 1963. Markets in Yorubaland. Ph.D. thesis, University of London.

Hodder, Ian. 1972. Locational models and the study of Romano-British settlement. In Models in archaeology, D. L. Clarke, ed. Methuen, London, pp. 887–909.

Hodder, Ian, and Clive Orton. 1976. Spatial analysis in archaeology. Cambridge University Press.

Johnson, Gregory A. 1972. A test of the utility of central place theory in archaeology. In Man, settlement and urbanism, P. J. Ucko, R. Thingham, and G. Dimbleby, eds. Duckworth, London, pp. 769–785.

Kolb, J. H., and E. de S. Brunner. 1946. A study of rural society. Houghton Mifflin, Boston.

Lösch, August. 1954. The economics of location. Yale University Press, New Haven.

Marcus, Joyce. 1976. Emblem and state in the Classic Maya lowlands. Dumbarton Oaks Research Library, Washington, D.C.

Vita-Finzi, C., and Eric S. Higgs. 1970. Prehistoric economy in the Mt. Carmel area of Palestine. Proceedings of the Prehistoric Society 36:1–37.

Von Thünen, J. H. 1826. Der isolierte staat in beziehung auf landwirtschaft und nationalökonomie. F. Perthes, Hamburg.

SOURCES OF ADDITIONAL INFORMATION

Most introductory archaeology texts include an explanation of the basic principles of central place theory and its application in archaeology. See, for instance, Robert Sharer and Wendy Ashmore, *Fundamentals of Archaeology* (Menlo Park, Calif., Benjamin Cummings, 1979), pp. 429-432; David Hurst Thomas, *Archaeology* (New York, Holt, Rinehart and Winston, 1979), pp. 306–308; and Brian Fagan, *In the Beginning*, 6th ed. (Glenview, Ill., Scott, Foresman, 1988), pp. 456–460. Other sources of background information include discussions by Robert Larkin and Gary L. Peters in their *Dictionary of Concepts in Human Geography* (Westport, Conn., Greenwood Press, 1983), pp. 39–42; David Clarke (1977); Walter Christaller (1966); August Losch (1954); and Hodder and Orton 1976, chapter 4 (see References above for complete citations). Most of these publications also have material illustrating the typical "hexagonal lattice" patterns.

Some more recent publications discussing or applying central place theory in archaeology include S. T. Evans, "Spatial analysis of Basin of Mexico settlement: problems with the use of the central place model," *American Antiquity* 45(4)(1980):866–875; H. P. Pollard, "Central places and cities, a consideration of the protohistoric Tarascan state," *American Antiquity* 45(4)(1980):677–696; and M. E. Smith, "The Aztec marketing system and settlement pattern in the Valley of Mexico, central place analysis," *American Antiquity* 44(1)(1979):110–125.

The bibliographies included in the above-mentioned background resources, especially those in Hodder and Orton (1976) and Clarke (1977), are still useful, although they need to be updated. Current issues of journals such as *American Antiquity*, *Geography*, and *Geographical Journal* should be consulted for more recent literature, as well as pertinent annual reviews for current applications of the concepts of central place theory in archaeology.

CERAMIC ANALYSIS. The study of ceramic remains as a category of AR-TIFACT, by archaeologists who may specialize in this kind of investigation, as a means of acquiring various kinds of information about prehistoric societies.

Ceramic remains analyzed by archaeologists include a variety of artifact types: figurines, clay musical instruments, beads, and other decorative items, as well as the pottery vessels and their broken shards that constitute the ceramic analyst's primary subject matter.

Pottery is a very significant category of material to archaeologists, one that can be used to obtain information about past technology, art and design conventions, changing cultural traditions, trade patterns, costume, customs, and even SOCIAL ORGANIZATION (Gifford 1960; Deetz 1965; Millett 1979; Longacre 1981; Steponaitis 1983; Shapiro 1984; Kolb 1988, 1989). Pottery shards are second only to stone tools as the most abundant and durable artifacts archaeologists find. In addition to their usefulness as temporal and stylistic markers for developing chronologies and cultural sequences, potsherds can be a significant indicator of the overall technological level achieved by a society.

Potterymaking was once thought to have been an invention linked to the beginning of FOOD PRODUCTION, when sturdy, airtight vessels would have become a necessity for long-term grain storage. It has now become apparent that ceramic manufacture appears in the earliest permanent settlements, whether or not these were supported by cultivation or by specialized hunting and collecting activities. The presence of pottery is therefore a better indicator of technological achievement, and of social patterns characteristic of life in permanent communities, than of any particular economic or SUBSISTENCE pattern.

Ceramic analysis as a means of acquiring data for understanding the past developed in the 1930s among archaeologists working in the southeastern and southwestern United States. The goals of these early analysts were centered on constructing cultural chronologies utilizing ceramic ASSEMBLAGES to identify temporal phases and culture areas. For this reason, the techniques they employed were primarily descriptive and classificatory. The type/variety method of ceramic analysis, largely the work of James A. Ford, employs a hierarchical classification system based on descriptive attributes, and has remained the principal approach to stylistic pottery analysis among archaeologists (Gifford 1960, 1976; Smith, Willey, and Gifford 1960; Willey and Sabloff 1980).

With the advent of interdisciplinary research and the "NEW" ARCHAEOLOGY of the 1960s and 1970s, ceramic analysis began to acquire new objectives. Some of these involved the use of techniques from the physical sciences for examining the physicochemical characteristics of ceramic wares to trace the origins of the clays used as raw materials, as well as to determine the technological knowledge of past potters. Ceramic remains also began to take on new functions in problem-oriented research designs, as exemplified in the work of archaeologists such as James Deetz (1965), and especially of William Longacre (Longacre 1981) and James N. Hill (Hill 1968, 1985), who used distribution patterns of ceramics in archaeological SITES to reconstruct some aspects of social organization in past communities, with the aid of analogies based on ethnographic data (see also ETHNOARCHAEOLOGY).

More recently, attempts have been made to develop ceramic theory, a variety of middle-range theory, to connect static ceramic remains with the dynamic behavior that generated them. Dean Arnold has noted that the classificatory analytic paradigm, whose influence is apparent in the work of most ceramic analysts, is basically atomistic, relying on arbitrary units of analysis that are difficult to relate to behavioral reality. Arnold proposes a broader theoretical approach, incorporating principles of system theory and cultural ecology, as potentially more productive for ceramic analysis (Arnold 1985).

Ceramics may be described or classified in terms of their artistic or decorative attributes; their form and function; methods used in their manufacture; or the physical and chemical properties of the raw materials used to produce them. The four major approaches to ceramic studies in current use by archaeologists may be categorized according to which of these aspects is adopted as the primary basis of analysis.

Stylistic analysis has traditionally been the approach favored by the majority of archaeologists. This method is grounded in the assumption that stylistic regularities are culturally determined, embodying modes or consistencies representing the aesthetic preferences of the potter's cultural group. The definition of pottery types based on stylistic attributes has many pitfalls, since the attributes used for classification tend to be subjectively derived, making comparisons of assemblages difficult or impossible unless a standardized system of nomenclature or definitional criteria is adopted. Two general theories of pottery STYLE, one viewing stylistic variation as reflecting social interaction and the other approaching stylistic factors as a form of information exchange, are now recognized by those involved in stylistic analysis of archaeological ceramics (Sackett 1977; Hill 1985; see also STYLE).

The widespread use of *type-variety analysis*, the principal method of stylistic analysis now practiced by archaeologists, represents an attempt to achieve standardization of concepts and categories. This method employs a hierarchical classification scheme based on minimal attributes derived from sense data, both visual and tactile, sometimes supplemented by formal and technological attributes, to define pottery types and varieties that are used as units of classification (see TYPOLOGY). Beginning with the minimal attributes derived from direct observation, the analyst groups pottery remnants into the varieties and types defined in the late 1950s by Philip Phillips (1985), Joe Ben Wheat, James C. Gifford, and William W. Wasley (1958), and Robert Smith, Gordon Willey, and James Gifford (1960), and proceeds from this point to the next highest level of classification, that of the ceramic group, and from there to the ceramic complex or system, and the ceramic sphere (Gifford 1960, 1976; Sharer and Ashmore 1979:312). Each of these classificatory levels represents a broader spatial distribution of pottery displaying the characteristics that define the type, which is presumed to reflect the distribution of a particular cultural pattern associated with and shared by the populations producing and using this pottery type. The method therefore assumes that its criteria and levels of classification reflect social and behavioral reality, an assumption that has yet to be conclusively demonstrated. Although its basic assumptions may be questioned, the type-variety method of analysis has the advantages of allowing intersite comparisons of ceramic artifacts based on standardized classificatory categories, and of promoting the recognition of temporal and spatial patterning and variation in the distribution of ceramic complexes.

Formal/functional analysis is a less popular method, although its principles are often combined with stylistic criteria by archaeologists using a stylistic method. In this approach, types are defined according to formal attributes based on clusters of basic vessel shapes, or consistent shapes of physical vessel components, such as base or lip (Holly 1986; Smith 1988; Hagstrom and Hildebrand 1990). Classes derived from formal attributes are usually broad categories that may also reflect vessel function (bowl, cup, plate, vase), since form and function are closely linked. When not immediately apparent, vessel function is often inferred from the vessel's archaeological CONTEXT and associations, which are also utilized to distinguish utilitarian wares, typically found in domestic contexts, from ceremonial pottery, which is usually much more elaborate and occurs most often in burials or ritual contexts.

Functional analysis also includes examination of ceramic vessels for residues that reflect their use, such as incense, food, or seeds (see also BIOCULTURAL STUDIES). In the absence of residues, the analyst must sometimes rely upon contextual data and ethnographic ANALOGY to determine vessel function.

Technological analysis is aimed at reconstruction of the manufacturing operations involved in pottery production, from acquisition of the raw material through firing, and includes determination of the basic technique—modeling, coiling, or throwing on a potter's wheel—used in vessel manufacture. Decoration (incising, carving, punctation, painting), slip or glaze application, and drying are among the other complex operations of interest. Microscopic examination of the pottery fabric and chemical analysis of glazes and pigments may be among the techniques employed. Thermal analysis allows the analyst to determine firing temperatures used, an important indicator of technological level (Shepard 1956:145–146; Matson 1970; Rice 1987).

The technological analyst of ceramic wares will usually need to supplement the examination of vessels with observations of pottery manufacturing processes in use today, in order to reconstruct those used in the past to produce any particular vessel or group of vessels. In this way, parts of the process that may leave no traces in the ARCHAEOLOGICAL RECORD may be inferred by using analogical reasoning and ethnoarchaeological methods (Kramer 1985).

Source analysis, or sourcing of raw material (clays, temper and other inclusions) used in pottery manufacture, is done to identify the locations from which nonlocal clays were obtained, a kind of information useful in the study of prehistoric trade. X-ray diffraction, optical emission spectrometry, and other techniques adopted from the physical sciences are typically used by the source analyst to identify clays, making it possible to distinguish vessels made from local materials from those of exotic origin. Neutron activation analysis is now frequently employed to identify sources of nonlocal clays, enabling archaeologists to trace patterns of prehistoric trade both in pottery vessels and in the raw materials used in their manufacture. Clays, like finished vessels, were often transported from their source locations over long distances, sometimes to specialized sites of pottery manufacture. The identification of such ceramic "workshop" sites can be an important indicator of developing craft SPECIALIZATION in a prehistoric society, usually a marker of increasing social complexity and CULTURAL COMPLEXITY. Temper and other inclusions in the pottery fabric were also sometimes of exotic origin, and tracing fragments of, for example, marine shell used as temper for vessels found at inland locations, provides a means of reconstructing patterns of past interaction over long distances.

Other kinds of information archaeologists may infer from the analysis of ceramic remains include the artistic and aesthetic canons or conventions represented in ceramic forms and decorative designs, as well as symbolic information that may be encoded in such decorative elements. Data on daily life in the past can be recovered from scenes, costumes, or ceremonies sometimes depicted in the painted representations on pots. Prudence Rice has noted that technological analysis of ceramics yields data that can be used to formulate and test hypotheses concerning "socioeconomic activities, such as organization of ceramic production, distribution and trade" (Rice 1984:xvii).

Ceramic analysis has become an indispensable methodological tool for archaeologists, and is now beginning to be conceptualized in attempts to incorporate its underlying assumptions into theoretical principles (Arnold 1985; Hill 1985), a pattern of concept development from method that has many counterparts in the history of archaeology.

REFERENCES

Arnold, Dean E. 1985. Ceramic theory and cultural process. Cambridge University Press.
Bronitsky, Gordon. 1986. The use of materials science techniques in the study of pottery construction and use. Advances in Archaeological Method and Theory 8:209–276.
———, ed. Pottery technology: ideas and approaches. Westview Press, Boulder, Colo.
Bronitsky, Gordon, and Robert Hamer. 1986. Experiments in ceramic technology: the effects of various tempering materials on impact and thermal-shock resistance. American Antiquity 51(1):89–101.
Deetz, James. 1965. The dynamics of stylistic change in Arikara ceramics. University of Illinois Press, Urbana.

Gifford, James C. 1960. The type-variety method of ceramic classification as an indicator of cultural phenomena. American Antiquity 25:341–347.

———. 1976. Prehistoric pottery analysis and the ceramics of Barton Ramie in the Belize Valley. Peabody Museum of Archaeology and Ethnology, Memoirs No. 18. Harvard University, Cambridge, Mass.

Hagstrom, Melissa B., and John A. Hildebrand. 1990. The two-curvature method for reconstructing ceramic morphology. American Antiquity 55(2):388–403.

Hill, James N. 1968. Broken K Pueblo: patterns of form and function. In New perspectives in archaeology, S. R. Binford and L. R. Binford, eds. Aldine, Chicago, pp. 103–142.

———. 1985. Style: a conceptual evolutionary framework. In Decoding prehistoric ceramics, Ben A. Nelson, ed. Southern Illinois University Press, Carbondale and Edwardsville, pp. 362–385.

Holly, David J. 1986. The identification of vessel function: a case study from northwest Georgia. American Antiquity 51(2):267–295.

Kolb, Charles C., ed. 1988. Ceramic ecology revisited, 1987: the technology and socioeconomics of pottery, pt. 2. BAR International Series 436, Oxford.

———. 1989. Ceramic ecology, 1988: current research on ceramic materials. BAR International Series 513, Oxford.

Kramer, Carole. 1985. Ceramic ethnoarchaeology. Annual Review of Anthropology 14:77–102.

Longacre, William. 1981. Kalinga pottery: an ethnoarchaeological study. In Pattern of the past, studies in honour of David Clarke, I. Hodder, G. Isaac, and N. Hammond, eds. Cambridge University Press, pp. 49–66.

Matson, Frederick R. 1970. Some aspects of ceramic technology. In Science in archaeology, Don Brothwell and Eric Higgs, eds. Praeger, New York, pp. 592–602. (Revised and enlarged edition)

Millett, M., ed. 1979. Pottery and the archaeologist. Institute of Archaeology Occasional Publication No. 4. University of London.

Mommsen, H., A. Kreuser, and J. Weber. 1988. A method for grouping pottery by chemical composition. Archaeometry 30(1):47–57.

Phillips, Philip. 1958. Application of the Wheat-Gifford-Wasley taxonomy to Eastern ceramics. American Antiquity 24(2):117–125.

Rice, Prudence M. 1987. Pottery analysis: a sourcebook. University of Chicago Press.

———, ed. 1984. Pots and potters: current approaches in ceramic archaeology. Institute of Archaeology Monograph 24. University of California at Los Angeles, Los Angeles.

Sackett, James R. 1977. The meaning of style in archaeology: a general model. American Antiquity 42(3):369–380.

Shapiro, Gary. 1984. Ceramic vessels, site permanence, and group size: a Mississippian example. American Antiquity 49(4):696–712.

Sharer, Robert J., and Wendy Ashmore. 1979. Fundamentals of archaeology. Benjamin Cummings, Menlo Park, Calif.

Shepard, Anna O. 1956. Ceramics for the archaeologist. Carnegie Institution of Washington, Washington, D.C.

———. 1965. Ceramics for the archaeologist [with foreword on ceramic studies 1954–1964]. Carnegie Institution of Washington Publication 609. Washington, D.C.

Smith, Marion F., Jr. 1988. Function from whole vessel shape: a method and an application to Anasazi Black Mesa, Arizona. American Anthropologist 90(4):912–923.

Smith, Robert E., Gordon R. Willey, and James C. Gifford. 1960. The type-variety concept as a basis for the analysis of Maya pottery. American Antiquity 25(3):330–339.

Steponaitis, Vincas P. 1983. Ceramics, chronology and community patterns. Academic Press, New York.

Wheat, Joe Ben, J. C. Gifford, and William W. Wasley. 1958. Ceramic variety, type cluster, and ceramic system in southwestern pottery analysis. American Antiquity 24(1):34–47.

Willey, Gordon R., and Jeremy A. Sabloff. 1980. A history of American archaeology. 2nd ed. W. H. Freeman, San Francisco.

SOURCES OF ADDITIONAL INFORMATION

Most introductory books on archaeology contain general information on ceramic analysis, although the relative emphasis placed on the various approaches varies greatly from one work to another. Robert Sharer and Wendy Ashmore, in *Fundamentals of Archaeology*, chapter 9 (see References above for complete citation), discuss several analytic approaches, and give the most complete treatment of stylistic analysis, including the type/variety method. Martha Joukowsky, in her introductory book *A Complete Manual of Field Archaeology* (Prentice-Hall, Englewood Cliffs, N.J., 1980), has an informative chapter on ceramic analysis for beginners, oriented toward basic information including category recognition, forms, terminology, and such practical matters as recordkeeping in the field.

The standard and most comprehensive reference source on archaeological pottery analysis has long been Anna O. Shepard's *Ceramics for the Archaeologist* (Washington, D.C., Carnegie Institution of Washington, 1956, 1965). Prudence Rice's synthetic work (1987; see References) may eventually supersede Shepard as the standard source, at least for pottery technology, although Shepard will continue to be useful for stylistic analysis.

There is a wealth of literature on specific approaches to ceramic analysis. For technological analysis, the 1986 review article by Gordon Bronitsky in *Advances in Archaeological Method and Theory* (see References) is very useful, both in its content and for the bibliographical references provided; a somewhat earlier article by Ronald L. Bishop, Robert L. Rands, and George R. Holley, "Ceramic compositional analysis in archaeological perspective," *Advances in Archaeological Method and Theory* 5(1982):275–330, gives similar coverage to compositional analysis and sourcing. The collection of papers edited by Gordon Bronitsky (1989; see References) presents information on various aspects of ceramic technology and its social and economic contexts.

A collection of papers edited by Ben A. Nelson, *Decoding Prehistoric Ceramics* (Carbondale and Edwardsville, Southern Illinois University, 1985), contains 14 very informative papers by specialists on a variety of topics in ceramic analysis, including the relationship between stylistic variation and social organization; form, function, and context; the organization of ceramic production in Mesoamerica; and the uses of ethnoarchaeology in ceramic studies.

For updating the material in these publications, the reader should consult current and future issues of *Archaeometry*, *Journal of Archaeological Science*, *World Archaeology*, *American Anthropologist*, and *American Antiquity*, as well as annual volumes of *Archaeological Method and Theory* and *Annual Review of Anthropology*.

CHIEFDOM. A type of political organization in which the leadership structure is headed by a hereditary chief, who is invested with authority and power over a social group extending beyond the local community level. See also CULTURAL COMPLEXITY; SOCIAL ORGANIZATION; STATE.

In cultural evolutionary terms, the chiefdom is believed to represent a developmental stage intervening between the local community and the STATE as the highest level of sociopolitical organization present in a society. According to Robert Carneiro, a chiefdom is the first form of SOCIAL ORGANIZATION transcending local autonomy.

> ... with chiefdoms, multicommunity political units emerged for the first time. . . .
> The transcending of local sovereignty and the aggregation of previously autonomous
> villages into chiefdoms was a critical step in political development. . . . It crossed a
> threshold, and once crossed, unlimited further advances in the same direction became
> possible. (Carneiro 1981:37–38)

In this statement, as well as in his definition of a chiefdom as ''an autonomous political unit comprising a number of villages or communities under the permanent control of a paramount chief'' (Carneiro 1981:45), Carneiro stressed the concept of *permanent, centralized political control* as the essential defining characteristic of the chiefdom, an interpretation representing its current meaning in archaeology.

The chiefdom form of organization is associated with relatively large and complex societies with well-defined hierarchies of social ranking and well-developed external trading networks. Ranks normally include full-time specialized occupational groups.

The chiefdom lacks the self-perpetuating bureaucratic structure of the state, as well as the state's legitimate enforcing power based on a formal body of law. The chief may have the power to enforce social controls, that is, police powers, but these will be based upon custom rather than being legitimized by law. In a chiefdom there may be no formalized rule other than inheritance for perpetuating governmental authority on the death of a chief. The office and authority of a ruling chief are usually conceived as being independent of the person who holds the position of paramount chief at any time, and there will be some traditional mechanism, usually based on kinship principles, for succession to the chiefly office. Kin groups, such as clans, hold a prominent place in the social structure of a chiefdom, and entire clans may occupy permanent ranks relative to one another (Kirchoff 1955; Fried 1957; Sahlins 1963). In addition to the position of paramount chief, a chiefdom society may include a variety of lesser chiefs, whose authority is restricted to certain well-defined functions, such as waging war.

The earliest usage of the term *chiefdom* in its current meaning was by Kalervo Oberg (Oberg 1955), who placed it in an intermediate position in his typology of sociopolitical units (Carneiro 1981:40). The concept and political form had previously been discussed by Julian Steward, in his introduction to volume 4 of the *Handbook of South American Indians*, on the circum-Caribbean tribes (Steward 1948). He identified several important attributes of the chiefdom, including supralocal organization into units above the village level; relatively large and dense populations; planned communities with storage facilities; and a ranked society in which wealth was concentrated in the chiefly class, where it was frequently acquired or enhanced by a system of tribute. Steward focused on the elevated social status of the chief as a key feature, while Oberg, like Carneiro, defined chiefdoms in terms of political control.

> . . . the distinguishing feature . . . is that the chiefs have judicial powers to settle disputes and to punish offenders even by death and . . . to requisition men and supplies for war. . . . (Oberg 1955; quoted in Carneiro 1981:41)

Elman Service proposed the chiefdom as an evolutionary stage in the development of human sociopolitical organization, defining chiefdoms as "redistributional societies with a permanent central agency of coordination" (Service 1962:145), a definition emphasizing one particular economic characteristic (redistribution) as the chiefdom's distinguishing feature, which has not been supported by cross-cultural ethnographic evidence.

Ever since its initial popularization by Service (1962, 1975), the chiefdom has been used by cultural evolutionists as a category or type of society representing a developmental stage on the way to statehood. Those who favor schemes of continuous social change, and therefore object to the assignment of discrete categories to particular levels or stages of social evolution, have criticized the concept as being either too specific or too vague. Others have avoided the use of the term altogether (e.g., Sahlins 1958) or have suggested alternative terms, such as *middle-range society*, for what is essentially the chiefdom form of political organization (Feinman and Neitzel 1984; Upham 1987).

Since the 1960s, the chiefdom concept has evolved from one defined in primarily economic terms to one defined along political lines, with a shift in emphasis from economic to administrative characteristics as its defining feature (Earle 1977, 1978, 1987, 1989, 1991; Spencer 1987:369). Earle (1989) and Steponaitis (1978) have discussed the political strategies implicated in creating and maintaining regional polities such as chiefdoms, which frequently rely on warfare, ideological innovation, and the manipulation of wealth and resources for maintaining as well as extending the sphere of a paramount chief's power and control.

Despite the imprecision of the chiefdom concept, it is an improvement on the earlier idea of the tribe, or tribal society, which was more vague and broadly inclusive, and therefore resistant to precise definition (Plog 1989). In its current usage, the term *chiefdom* has acquired sufficient specificity to be readily understood as denoting a particular form of sociopolitical organization, and has become widely employed in the archaeological literature (Helms 1980; Kirch 1984; Hudson et al. 1985; Drennan and Uribe 1987; Widmer 1988). Problems remain, however, in determining and defining what constitutes distinctive archaeological evidence for the presence of a chiefdom level of organization. Minimally, such material evidence will include settlement data indicating the presence of a ranked, multilevel society organized into a hierarchy of communities with one large principal center at its apex; and indications of consistent differences in burial practices reflecting variations in wealth and status that are ascribed, that is, inherited rather than achieved, such as the presence of elaborate grave goods in burials of young children. Another form of evidence is the existence of some type of symbolic communication that may occur in advanced chiefdoms, as well as states, in which iconographic signs or symbols function as indicators of the perpetuation of chiefly power through time, by hereditary or other means, although these may present considerable interpretative problems. Differentiating between developed chiefdoms and states on the basis of material evidence alone can be very difficult, and archaeologists must often rely on models developed from ethnohistoric and ethnographic evidence for making such distinctions.

REFERENCES

Carneiro, Robert L. 1981. The chiefdom: precursor of the state. In The transition to statehood in the New World, Grant D. Jones and R. R. Kautz, eds. Cambridge University Press, pp. 37–79.

Drennan, Robert D., and Carlos A. Uribe, eds. 1987. Chiefdoms in the Americas. University Press of America, Lanham, Md.

Earle, Timothy K. 1977. A reappraisal of redistribution: complex Hawaiian chiefdoms. In Exchange systems in prehistory, T. K. Earle and J. E. Ericson, eds. Academic Press, New York, pp. 213–229.

———. 1978. Economic and social organization of a complex chiefdom: the Halelea District, Kaua'i, Hawaii. Museum of Anthropology Anthropological Papers 63. University of Michigan, Ann Arbor.

———. 1987. Chiefdoms in archaeological and ethnohistorical perspective. Annual Review of Anthropology 16:279–308.

———. 1989. The evolution of chiefdoms. Current Anthropology 30(1):84–88.

———. 1991. Chiefdoms: power, economy, ideology. Cambridge University Press.

Feinman, Gary, and Jill Neitzel. 1984. Too many types: an overview of prestate societies in the Americas. Advances in Archaeological Method and Theory 7:39–102.

Fried, Morton H. 1975. The classification of corporate lineal descent groups. Journal of the Royal Anthropological Institute 87:1–29.

Helms, M. W. 1980. Succession to high office in pre-Columbian, circum-Caribbean chiefdoms. Man 15(4):718–731.

Hudson, Charles, Marvin Smith, David Hally, Richard Polhemus, and Chester DePratter. 1985. Coosa: a chiefdom in the sixteenth-century southeastern United States. American Antiquity 50(4):723–737.

Kirch, Patrick V. 1984. The evolution of the Polynesian chiefdom. Cambridge University Press.

Kirchhoff, Paul. 1955. The principles of clanship in human society. Davidson Anthropological Journal 1:1–10.

Oberg, Kalervo. 1955. Types of social structure among the lowland tribes of South and Central America. American Anthropologist 57:472–487.

Plog, Fred. 1989. Studying complexity. In The sociopolitical structure of pre-historic southwestern societies, Steadman Upham, Kent G. Lightfoot, and Roberta A. Jewett, eds. Westview Press, Boulder, Colo., pp. 103–125.

Sahlins, Marshall D. 1958. Social stratification in Polynesia. University of Washington Press, Seattle.

———. 1963. Poor man, rich man, big man, chief: political types in Melanesia and Polynesia. In Peoples and cultures of the Pacific, A. P. Vayda, ed. Natural History Press, Garden City, N.Y.

Service, Elman R. 1962. Primitive social organization. Random House, New York.

———. 1975. Origins of the state and civilization: the process of cultural evolution. W. W. Norton, New York.

Spencer, Charles S. 1987. Rethinking the chiefdom. In Chiefdoms in the Americas, Robert D. Drennan and Carlos A. Uribe, eds. University Press of America, Lanham, Md., pp. 369–390.

Steponaitis, Vincas P. 1978. Location theory and complex chiefdoms: a Mississippian example. In Mississippian settlement patterns, Bruce D. Smith, ed. Academic Press, New York, pp. 417–453.

Steward, Julian H. 1948. The circum-Caribbean tribes: An introduction. In Handbook of South American Indians. Vol. 4: The circum-Caribbean tribes, Julian H. Steward, ed. Smithsonian Institution, Bureau of American Ethnology Bulletin 143. Washington, D.C., pp. 1–41.

Upham, Steadman. 1987. A theoretical consideration of middle-range societies. In Chiefdoms in the Americas, Robert D. Drennan and Carlos A. Uribe, eds. University Press of America, Lanham, Md., pp. 345–368.

Widmer, Randolph J. 1988. The evolution of the Calusa: a nonagricultural chiefdom on the southwest Florida coast. University of Alabama Press, Tuscaloosa.

SOURCES OF ADDITIONAL INFORMATION

Further background information on the chiefdom concept may be found in Carneiro 1981; the 1987 review by Timothy Earle in *Annual Review of Anthropology*; and the papers by Charles Spencer and Steadman Upham in the 1987 volume edited by Robert Drennan and Carlos Uribe (see References for complete citations). More recent publications include Robert L. Carneiro, ''The evolution of complexity in human societies and its mathematical expression,'' *International Journal of Comparative Sociology* 28 (3–4) (1987):111–128, plus all the articles in *American Behavioral Scientist* 31 (4) (1988), devoted entirely to Carneiro's circumscription theory of the development of the STATE. Regional interaction and trade in chiefdoms are discussed in R. D. Drennan, L. G. Jaramillo, E. Ramos, C. A. Sánchez, M. A. Ramírez, and C. A. Uribe, ''Regional dynamics of chiefdoms in the Valle de la Plata, Colombia,'' *Journal of Field Archaeology* 18(3) (1991):297–317; and R. S. Kipp and E. M. Schortman, ''The political impact of trade in chiefdoms,'' *American Anthropologist* 91(2) (1989):370–385. More recent publications on pre-Columbian chiefdoms in Latin America include W. Creamer and J. Haas, ''Tribe versus chiefdom in lower Central America,'' *American Antiquity* 50(4) (1985):738–754; and C. S. Spencer and E. M. Redmond, ''Prehispanic chiefdoms of the western Venezuelan llanos,'' *World Archaeology* 24(1) (1992):134–157. The journals *American Anthropologist*, *American Antiquity*, *Journal of Field Archaeology*, and *Journal of Anthropological Archaeology* should be consulted for future publications on the chiefdom, as should forthcoming annual review volumes.

CHRONOMETRIC DATING. The dating of archaeological remains in actual calendar years; also called *absolute dating*. ARTIFACTS, ecofacts, or matrix material from archaeological deposits may be chronometrically dated by one or more methods that permit precise estimation of their age within a definable range of error, using a variety of techniques derived from the physical or biological sciences. Absolute dating of archaeological SITES and materials from cultures with written records and calendars is also possible, if such records include decipherable dates that can be correlated with modern calendars. See also ARCHAEOMETRY; RELATIVE DATING.

Establishing the ages of archaeological materials has been a central problem in archaeology since its earliest beginnings. With the appearance of the first RELATIVE DATING methods, such as the THREE-AGE SYSTEM, in the nineteenth century, archaeologists were able to establish cultural sequences and relative chronologies. However, it was not until the early years of the twentieth century that dating of archaeological materials in actual calendar years became possible.

His discovery in the late 1940s of the C14, or radiocarbon, method for dating organic materials in calendar years, using a calculated half-life for the radioactive decay of the carbon 14 isotope in organic materials as a basis for determining their age, earned Willard Libby the Nobel Prize for chemistry in 1960, and was hailed as a universal solution to dating problems in archaeology (Arnold and Libby 1949; Libby, Anderson, and Arnold 1949; Libby 1955, 1965; Willis 1970). This was not quite true, however, and the limitations and calibration problems of radiocarbon dating have proved it was not exactly the panacea it was initially believed to be (Renfrew 1979; Browman 1981; Adovasio, Donahue, and Stuckenrath 1990). Used in conjunction with other methods, however, it has remained the most important and most widely used method of absolute dating for organic materials, and has permitted archaeologists to resolve some long-standing problems in chronology (Clark 1975; Read 1979; Scott, Baxter, and Aitchison 1984; Taylor et al. 1985; Creel and Long 1986; Hester 1987; Kra 1988; Timei and Sixun 1988; Gowlett, Hedges, and Lack 1989; Williams 1989; Shott 1992).

Radiocarbon dating was not the first absolute dating method to be employed by archaeologists. Cross-dating of materials from the Minoan and Greek civilizations with Egyptian hieroglyphic inscriptions had been accomplished by Sir Arthur Evans near the turn of the twentieth century. Dendrochronology, or tree-ring dating, was another chronometric technique developed in the early years of the twentieth century by A. E. Douglass, an astronomer, in the southwestern United States. This method, based on the existence of annual growth rings in trees, which are visible on a cross section of the trunk, has remained extremely important both in its own right and, since the 1970s, as a means of calibration and error correction for radiocarbon dates (Antevs 1938; Clark 1975; Fritts 1976; Fletcher 1978; Renfrew 1979; Baillie 1982; Eckstein, Baillie, and Egger 1984; Stahle, Cook, and White 1985; Stahle and Wolfman 1985). Its principal limitation is its restricted geographic range, which has been considerably expanded in recent years.

Absolute techniques include those contributed by the physical sciences, many of them suited to particular categories of artifacts or materials. Some of these, such as potassium-argon, obsidian hydration, and amino acid racemization, have very broad time ranges, extending from approximately 1,000 years before the present, to dates in excess of 1 million years ago (Aitken 1990:4). Amino acid racemization has greatly extended the datable range of organic materials beyond the limits of the radiocarbon method, although its results tend to be less reliable. Archaeomagnetic methods, based on variability and directionality of the earth's magnetic field, and the periodic variation of declination between true north and magnetic north in the past, have proved useful for some applications, especially for dating archaeological features such as fired clay floors, kilns, and hearths (Aitken 1990). Obsidian hydration layers that form at fracture sites on obsidian tools can also be used to determine their date of manufacture (Taylor 1976; Michels and Tsong 1980). Fission-track dating is another method used by archaeologists to date obsidian, as well as early hominid remains stratigraphically associated with volcanic mineral deposits. This method, like the potassium-argon method, dates high-temperature events in the remote past, and has been used on remains from such early sites as Olduvai Gorge, the "Lucy" site in the Hadar (Ethiopia), and the *Homo erectus* finds at Zhoukoudian, China (Aitken 1988, 1990). Thermoluminescence, a method developed for dating pottery and other forms of baked clay, has a greater range than radiocarbon but less precision (Aitken 1985). Electron spin resonance has proved a useful method for dating flowstone, stalagmites and stalactites in caves associated with cultural or skeletal remains of Paleolithic occupations, and tooth enamel (Aitken 1990).

In addition to radiocarbon dating, some other methods have been developed for dating biological remains. Amino acid racemization of fossil bones and teeth is a method with a greater time range than carbon 14 but less accuracy (see above), and many of the dates produced using this technique have proved to be unreliable (Hare, Hoering, and King 1980; Masters 1986; Bada 1987).

In recent years, the value of ancient writing and calendrics as sources of absolute dates has been underscored by decipherment of the Maya script of Mesoamerica, enabling archaeologists to date in absolute years the inscribed monuments and their associated buildings and artifacts at many sites. Calendric dates from inscriptions have the added importance of allowing archaeologists to check the accuracy of radiocarbon dates and those obtained by other methods.

Despite the variety of methods now available, and the considerable refinements these have undergone in recent years, no chronometric method is completely reliable. This has proven to be especially true of the most popular method, radiocarbon dating, which has produced series of dates that continue to be controversial and even unacceptable, although the grounds for their rejection may in some cases be highly questionable (see, e.g., Meltzer 1989; Lynch 1990; Guidon and Arnaud 1991). Acceptance of radiocarbon dates obtained anywhere in the Americas that suggest a human presence prior to the so-called Clovis occupation of North America has unfortunately become a political issue among many American archaeologists, one that may have little relevance to the accuracy of the dates themselves. Such controversies highlight the fact that, regardless of the accuracy or dependability of chronometric dating methods now available to archaeologists, they are still subject to the often imperfect interpretations of very human archaeologists.

REFERENCES

Adovasio, J. M., J. Donahue, and R. Stuckenrath. 1990. The Meadowcroft rockshelter radiocarbon chronology 1975–1990. American Antiquity 55(2):348–354.

Aitken, Martin J. 1985. Thermoluminescence dating. Academic Press, London and Orlando, Fla.

———. 1988. The Thera eruption: continuing discussion of the dating I. Resume of dating. Archaeometry 30(1):165–182.

———. 1990. Science-based dating in archaeology. Longman, London.

Antevs, E. 1938. Rainfall and tree growth in the Great Basin. Carnegie Institution of Washington Publication 469. Washington, D.C.

Arnold, J. R., and W. F. Libby. 1949. Age determination by radiocarbon content. Science 110:678–680.

Bada, J. L. 1987. Palaeoanthropological applications of amino acid racemization of fossil bones and teeth. Anthropologischer Anzeiger 45:1–8.

Baillie, M. G. L. 1982. Tree-ring dating and archaeology. Croom Helm, London.

———. 1991. Marking in marker dates: towards an archaeology with historical precision. World Archaeology 23(2):233–243.

Browman, D. L. 1981. Isotopic discrimination and correction factors in radiocarbon dating. Advances in Archaeological Method and Theory 4:241–295.

Clark, R. M. 1975. A calibration curve for radiocarbon dates. Antiquity 49:251–266.

Creel, Darrell, and Austin Long. 1986. Radiocarbon dating of corn. American Antiquity 51(4):826–837.

Eckstein, D., M. G. L. Baillie, and H. Egger. 1984. Handbook for archaeologists no. 2: Dendrochronological dating. European Science Foundation, Strasbourg, France.

Fletcher, J. M., ed. 1978. Dendrochronology in Europe. BAR International Series 51. Oxford.

Fritts, H. C. 1976. Tree rings and climate. Academic Press, New York.

Gowlett, J. A. J., R. E. M. Hedges, and I. A. Lack. 1989. Radiocarbon accelerator (AMS) dating of Lindow man. Antiquity 63(238):71–79.

Guidon, N., and B. Arnaud. 1991. The chronology of the New World: two faces of one reality. World Archaeology 23(2):167–178.

Hare, P. E., T. C. Hoering, and K. King, eds. 1980. Biogeochemistry of amino acids. Wiley, New York.

Hester, James J. 1987. The significance of accelerator dating in archaeological method and theory. Journal of Field Archaeology 14(4):445–451.

Kra, Renée. 1988. Updating the past: the establishment of the International Radiocarbon Data Base. American Antiquity 53(1):118–125.

Libby, Willard F. 1955. Radiocarbon dating. University of Chicago Press.

———. 1965. Radiocarbon dating. 2nd ed. University of Chicago Press.

Libby, Willard F., E. C. Anderson, and J. R. Arnold. 1949. Age determination by radiocarbon content: worldwide assay of natural radiocarbons. Science 109:227–228.

Lynch, T. F. 1990. Glacial-age man in South America? A critical review. American Antiquity 55(1):12–36.

Masters, Patricia M. 1986. Amino acid racemization dating—a review. In Dating and age determination of biological materials, M. R. Zimmer and J. L. Angel, eds. Croom Helm, London, pp. 39–58.

Meltzer, David J. 1989. Why don't we know when the first people came to North America? American Antiquity 54(3):471–490.

Michels, Joseph W., and Ignatius S. T. Tsong. 1980. Obsidian hydration dating: a coming of age. Advances in Archaeological Method and Theory 3:405–444.

Renfrew, Colin. 1979. Before civilization: the radiocarbon revolution and prehistoric Europe. Cambridge University Press.

Read, Dwight W. 1979. The effective use of radiocarbon dates in the seriation of archaeological sites. In Radiocarbon dating, R. Berger and H. E. Suess, eds. University of California Press, Los Angeles, pp. 89–94.

Scott, E. M., M. S. Baxter, and T. C. Aitchison. 1984. A comparison of the treatment of errors in radiocarbon dating calibration methods. Journal of Archaeological Science 11:455–466.

Shott, Michael J. 1992. Radiocarbon dating as a probabilistic technique: the Childers site and Late Woodland occupation in the Ohio Valley. American Antiquity 57(2):202–230.

Stahle, David W., Edward R. Cook, and James W. C. White. 1985. Tree-ring dating of bald cypress and the potential for millennia-long chronologies in the Southeast. American Antiquity 50(4):796–802.

Stahle, David W., and Daniel Wolfman. 1985. The potential for archaeological tree-ring dating in eastern North America. Advances in Archaeological Method and Theory 8:279–302.

Taylor, R. E., ed. 1976. Advances in obsidian glass studies. Noyes Press, Park Ridge, N.J.

Taylor, R. E., et al. 1985. Major revisions in the Pleistocene age assignments for North American human skeletons by C-14 accelerator mass spectrometry: none older than 11,000 C-14 years B.P. American Antiquity 50(1):136–140.

Timei Chen and Yuan Sixun. 1988. Uranium-series dating of bones and teeth from Chinese Paleolithic sites. Archaeometry 30(1):59–76. (Uranium series studies of fossil bones and teeth yielded an absolute age sequence for 20+ Chinese Paleolithic sites, the first such chronology in China)

Williams, E. 1989. Dating the introduction of food production into Britain and Ireland. Antiquity 63:510–521.

Willis, E. H. 1970. Radiocarbon dating. In Science in archaeology, Don Brothwell and Eric Higgs, eds. Praeger, New York, pp. 46–57. (Revised and enlarged edition)

SOURCES OF ADDITIONAL INFORMATION

Dating methods applied in constructing New World chronologies have been comprehensively covered in R. E. Taylor and Clement Meighan, *Chronologies in New World Archaeology* (New York, Academic Press, 1978). The opening chapter by R. E. Taylor, "Dating methods in New World archaeology" (pp. 1–28), outlines 12 basic chronometric methods derived from the physical and natural sciences, all but two of which were developed after 1950. All the chapters include bibliographies, now in need of updating. The final chapter, "A summary scan," by Gordon R. Willey (pp. 513–563), is a still-useful overview, summarizing the development of dating techniques and chronological sequences in the 24 cultural areas discussed in 13 of the book's 15 chapters. Also still extremely useful is the "hemispheric projection" of New World chronologies in the volume endpapers (North and Middle American chronologies are charted on the front endpaper, Lower Central and South American chronologies on the back endpaper).

An excellent source for updating the information in Taylor and Meighan is M. J. Aitken, *Science-Based Dating in Archaeology* (London and New York, Longman, 1990), which covers later developments in the methods discussed in Taylor and Meighan's first chapter. Aitken's opening chapter also provides a very brief introduction to the problem of dating archaeological materials, which includes two charts graphically summarizing the age ranges of the principal chronometric dating methods, the types of materials for which each is appropriate, and their relative reliability (pp. 3–4). Succeeding chapters are devoted to detailed description and discussion of all major chronometric techniques now in use. The individual chapter bibliographies provide access to relevant literature published through 1989.

For an extended discussion of the radiocarbon dating method and its calibration by the tree-ring method, as well as some of the ways in which the calibration of radiocarbon dates affected traditional interpretations of Old World prehistory, see Colin Renfrew's *Before Civilization: The Radiocarbon Revolution and Prehistoric Europe* (Cambridge, Cambridge University Press, 1979). To update the information in this volume, see chapters 3 and 4 (pp. 56–75) in Aitken 1990, described above. Additional material on calibration and correction problems may be found in D. L. Browman, "Isotopic discrimination and correction factors in radiocarbon dating," *Advances in Archaeological Method and Theory* 4(1981):241–295, which also includes many bibliographic references.

The first two decades of the voluminous literature on radiocarbon dating has been covered by Dilette Polach, *Radiocarbon Dating Literature: the First 21 Years, 1947–1968: An Annotated Bibliography* (London, Academic Press, 1988). The bibliography in Browman (1981; see above) will update this to 1980; for references to more recent literature, see Taylor 1987 and Bowman 1990, described below.

Publications on the radiocarbon method include R. E. Taylor, "The beginnings of radiocarbon dating in *American Antiquity*: a historical perspective," *American Antiquity* 50(2)(1985):309–325, a retrospective article in the journal's fiftieth anniversary issue, which includes a substantial bibliography; and Taylor's book *Radiocarbon Dating: An Archaeological Perspective* (Orlando, Fla., Academic Press, 1987). Other materials on radiocarbon dating include R. Berger and H. E. Suess, eds., *Radiocarbon Dating* (Los Angeles, University of California Press, 1979); Sheridan Bowman, *Radiocarbon Dating, Interpreting the Past* (London, British Museum Publications, 1990); and Zhiman An, "Radiocarbon dating and the pre-historic archaeology of China," *World Archaeology* 23(2)(1991):193–200. Radiocarbon and other methods for dating organic materials are the subject of M. R. Zimmerman and J. R. Angel, eds., *Dating and Age Determination of Biological Materials* (London, Croom Helm, 1986).

Review articles covering other chronometric methods include Jeffrey S. Dean, "Independent dating in archaeological analysis," *Advances in Archaeological Method and Theory* 1(1978):223–255; Daniel Wolfman, "Geomagnetic dating methods in archaeology," *Advances in Archaeological Method and Theory* 7(1984):363–458; and A. J. Clark,

D. H. Tarling, and M. Noel, "Developments in archaeomagnetic dating in Britain," *Journal of Archaeological Science* 15(1988):645–667. All include bibliographies.

An excellent summary of the development of chronometric dating is Joan Stevenson's "Absolute or chronometric dating," in her *Dictionary of Concepts in Physical Anthropology* (Westport, Conn., Greenwood Press, 1991), pp. 3–11, which includes an abundance of bibliographic information, both in its list of references and the accompanying bibliographic essay.

World Archaeology 23, no. 2 (October 1991) is devoted to various aspects of chronology. Most of its 11 articles discuss both relative and chronometric dating methods, and the usefulness of their combination in constructing archaeological chronologies; all include lists of references.

For further access to recent literature, see the extensive bibliographies in Taylor et al. 1985; Creel and Long 1986; and Meltzer 1989 (see References above for complete citations). Future issues of *Archaeometry, Journal of Archaeological Science*, and *Radiocarbon* should be consulted for information on new developments in chronometric dating techniques.

COGNITIVE ARCHAEOLOGY. The archaeological study from material evidence of symbolic behavior in the past.

Cognitive archaeology attempts to document, from archaeological data, the existence of a distinctively human mentality among prehistoric populations, and to identify temporally, with as much precision as possible, when the first evidence of this appears in the ARCHAEOLOGICAL RECORD. Such evidence consists of symbolic ARTIFACTS, including works of art; ceremonial paraphernalia; decoration applied to functional items such as tools or clothing; public monuments; inscriptions; grave goods (material items placed in graves with the dead); and ceremonial and mortuary architecture, or other indicators of religious belief or special treatment accorded the dead. "Cognitive archaeology [is] the study of past ways of thought from material remains" (Renfrew and Bahn 1991:339; see also MORTUARY ANALYSIS).

Although the art and writing of past peoples have always been subjects of interest to archaeologists, these have until recently been considered the province of the art historian and the epigraphist, respectively, and have not been an integral part of archaeological studies per se. In the 1980s, this began to change, and efforts are now being made to develop explicit procedures for analyzing the material remains of past cognitive systems, and for deciphering the information encoded in symbolic objects (Hodder 1982, 1986; Renfrew 1982; Renfrew and Bahn 1991:339). The use of the phrase "cognitive archaeology" to denote this type of analysis is quite new; the first published discussion of this area of study under this rubric is in Renfrew and Bahn (1991; see also Renfrew 1982). The goals and focus of cognitive archaeology are in a general way similar to those of semiotic studies in anthropology, which have developed in roughly the same time frame (Hawkes 1977).

Different kinds of archaeological data may be utilized in cognitive analysis. Among these are items reflecting systems of measurement or numeration, such as weights used by people of the Indus Valley civilization, or the bar-and-dot notation used by many pre-Columbian peoples of Mesoamerica; plans and layouts of ancient communities and monuments, which often can be reconstructed from contemporary surveys (e.g., Harrison 1989) or from any surviving maps or topographic models. Other items providing clues to past values and mental life include "elite" artifacts buried with persons of high status, revealing the categories of material goods that were most highly valued, which may have symbolized authority or power. Works of art, as well as mortuary customs, may convey information on ways prehistoric peoples conceived of the supernatural and expressed these conceptions in their behavior (Leroi-Gourhan 1964; Grieder 1975; Alland 1977). Other reflections of symbolic behavior occur in the form of astronomical observatories or calendric structures, and alignments of buildings or cities toward positions on the horizon where stars or planets were seen to rise or set on significant dates (see ARCHAEOASTRONOMY), and artifacts that functioned as currency or "primitive valuables" in EXCHANGE systems.

Other categories of material evidence from which the cognitive aspects of prehistoric life may be inferred include artifacts and architecture designed for religious ritual, and symbolic records such as writing systems, emblems, and pictographs or petroglyphs. Symbolic information may also be encoded in devices for counting or tallying, such as the *quipu*, an abacus-like device employed by the pre-Columbian Incas of Peru; the coup sticks and other tallying devices used for recordkeeping by North American Indian groups; and similar objects found in both New World and European Paleolithic contexts (Marshack 1972, 1985, 1989). Calendric markers, which may have been utilized in rituals, occur in many forms, including the "woodhenges" and numerous so-called medicine wheels of North America.

Such symbolic records as these, embodying quantitative concepts and relationships, are more amenable to accurate interpretation and testing than the kind of information encoded in such works of art as the European cave paintings of the Upper Paleolithic (Leroi-Gourhan 1965, 1982; Conkey 1978, 1983). The central problem in interpreting such works of art is not only that of decoding their symbolic information but also that of verifying the accuracy of the interpretation, which is often not possible. The problems of cognitive archaeological studies are similar to those of the cryptographer who undertakes to decipher an unknown code, to which no known key exists; or of the epigraphist attempting to decipher a text in an unknown script for which there is no equivalent text in a known language. Such decipherments do occasionally occur (see DECIPHERMENT), but these are rare events; and verification remains a continuing problem, usually contingent on the independent acquisition of additional information from other material sources.

All symbolic behavior is dependent on abstract thought, which has its basis in the use of language, or articulate speech. Speech is a uniquely human communication system, based on the patterned use of arbitrary vocal signals that, in various combinations, are perceived as representing or symbolizing particular material objects or nonmaterial concepts, and expressing relationships among them. The appearance of language, and of the material culture associated with its use, are therefore believed to mark the biological transition from earlier forms of the genus *Homo* to fully modern *H. sapiens sapiens* (Mellars 1973; Conkey 1978; Harrold 1980; Pfeiffer 1982; White 1982, 1985; Isaac 1983; Orguera 1984; Binford 1989). Although the exact point in the course of EVOLUTION when humans began to speak remains unknown, evidence of the beginnings of symbolic communication and its consequences are visible in the ARCHAEOLOGICAL RECORD, making it possible to estimate when this momentous landmark in the human career occurred (Binford 1989; Bateman et al. 1990). At present, the time of this transition is still a matter of debate that has aroused much discussion and controversy; but there is increasing evidence for the appearance of fully modern humans possessing articulate speech in the late Pleistocene, in at least some geographical locations; or, in terms of traditional cultural chronologies, at about the time when the Middle Paleolithic merged into the Upper Paleolithic, roughly 50,000 years ago (Marshack 1972, 1975; Isaac 1976; Pfeiffer 1982; Orguera 1984; White 1985; Wynn 1985, 1986; Chase and Dibble 1987; Davidson and Noble 1989; Mellars and Stringer 1989; Stringer 1989a, 1989b; Trinkaus 1989; Lindly and Clark 1990).

Symbolic behavior appears to be unique to the human species, and may be presumed to serve an adaptive function, although the exact manner in which it contributes to human survival has not been determined. Symbolic systems exist in all human groups, from the fundamental use of languages to the creation of ideologies, religious belief systems, and works of art. Indeed, all systems of human communication are of a symbolic nature, since they depend on the use of symbols, arbitrary signs that have agreed-upon standardized meanings to those who use them, for transmitting information from one human to another.

An area of current controversy related to the study of cognitive and symbolic systems of the past is the ongoing debate among archaeologists and anthropologists over the intellectual and verbal abilities of *Homo neanderthalensis* versus those of *H. Sapiens sapiens*, with particular respect to the interpretation of Paleolithic cave art, tool manufacture, and archaeological evidence of planning behavior (Isaac 1972, 1981; Stringer 1982; Trinkaus 1983; Binford 1985, 1989; Chase and Dibble 1987; Davidson and Noble 1989; Mellars and Stringer 1989; Whallon 1989; see also PALEOANTHROPOLOGY). According to many present students of the Paleolithic, there is scant evidence that archaic forms of *Homo*, such as Neanderthal man, possessed articulate language or the ability to symbolize, and therefore should be excluded from the species *sapiens*. On the other hand, there is currently no evidence definitively refuting the "human" status of Neanderthal man, despite claims based on skeletal studies and anatomical reconstructions that suggest these protohumans were incapable of speech as we know it (see, e.g., Lieberman 1984). For these reasons, some archaeologists regard it as improper to attribute human CULTURE to Neanderthals, and would place the lifeway of these archaic humans beyond the acceptable range of ethnographic ANALOGY.

Obviously, archaeologists can have no direct access to the religious beliefs, unwritten languages, or other symbolic systems that existed in the past. Inferring the meanings encoded in material objects by their prehistoric manufacturers is therefore a risk-laden activity, one that has traditionally been avoided by materialist archaeologists. According to the materialist view of PREHISTORY, symbolic systems of the past can be inferred only from the archaeological CONTEXT in which certain classes of artifacts predictably occur, in combination with the use of analogies based on observations of recent human behavior, preferably among peoples who are likely descendants of the archaeological population. Such analogies may be rejected as unacceptable for testing archaeological data derived from prehistoric populations of archaic humans such as Neanderthals, whose mentality and behavior may have been different from our own.

The structuralist and postprocessualist schools of contemporary archaeological interpretation, unlike the materialists, take the view that ideology and symbolic systems may have played an active, determinative role in structuring past societies and in producing social change (Hodder 1982, 1986). In this view, artifacts are seen as a dynamic feature of culture, constituting material symbols that not only reveal the mental lives of their producers but also constitute active expressions of that mental life that can be "read" as if they were texts describing its features and characteristics. Such readings, however, remain dependent upon the acceptance of a mentalist point of view, such as that of the structuralists, a view that does not address the problem of objective verification of the "meanings" assigned to artifacts by postprocessualists. Since such verification is of paramount importance to any scientifically oriented archaeologist, this problem illustrates the essence of the fundamental dichotomy between the two major competing theoretical positions in contemporary archaeology, which does not appear to be in imminent likelihood of resolution. Meanwhile, materialist archaeologists continue to pursue their studies of the cognitive characteristics of prehistoric peoples using the set of methods outlined above. (See ARCHAEOLOGY; "NEW" ARCHAEOLOGY.)

REFERENCES

Alland, Alexander, Jr. 1977. The artistic animal: an inquiry into the biological roots of art. Anchor Press/Doubleday, Garden City, N.Y.

Bateman, Richard, Ives Goddard, Richard O'Grady, V. A. Funk, Rich Mooi, W. John Kress, and Peter Cannell. 1990. Speaking of forked tongues: the feasibility of reconciling human phylogeny and the history of language. Current Anthropology 31(1):1–24.

Binford, Lewis R. 1985. Human ancestors: changing views of their behavior. Journal of Anthropological Archaeology 4(4):292–327.

————. 1989. Isolating the transition to cultural adaptations: an organizational approach.

In The emergence of modern humans: biocultural adaptations in the later Pleistocene, Erik Trinkaus, ed. Cambridge University Press, pp. 18–41.

Chase, Philip G., and Harold L. Dibble. 1987. Middle Paleolithic symbolism: a review of current evidence and interpretations. Journal of Anthropological Archaeology 6:263–296.

Conkey, Margaret. 1978. Style and information in cultural evolution: toward a predictive model for the Paleolithic. In Social archaeology: beyond subsistence and dating, C. Redman et al., eds. Academic Press, New York, pp. 61–85.

––––––. 1983. On the origins of Paleolithic art: a review and some critical thought. In The Mousterian legacy, E. Trinkaus, ed. BAR, Oxford.

Davidson, Iain, and William Noble. 1989. The archaeology of perception: traces of depiction and language. Current Anthropology 30(2):125–155.

Grieder, Terence. 1975. The interpretation of ancient symbols. American Anthropologist 77:849–855.

Harrold, F. B. 1980. A comparative analysis of Eurasian Palaeolithic burials. World Archaeology 12:195–211.

Harrison, Peter D. 1989. Spatial geometry and logic in the ancient Maya mind. Part 2: architecture. Proceedings of the 7th Mesa Redonda de Palenque, June 1989. (In press)

Hawkes, Terence. 1977. Structuralism and semiotics. University of California Press, Berkeley.

Hodder, Ian. 1982. Symbols in action. Cambridge University Press.

––––––. 1986. Reading the past. Cambridge University Press.

Isaac, Glyn. 1972. Early phases of human behavior: Models in Lower Paleolithic archaeology. In Models in archaeology, David Clarke, ed. Methuen, London.

––––––. 1976. Stages of cultural elaboration in the Pleistocene: possible archaeological indicators of the development of language capabilities. Annals of the New York Academy of Sciences 280:275–288.

––––––. 1981. Archaeological tests of alternative models of early hominid behavior: excavation and experiments. Philosophical Transactions of the Royal Society of London B292:177–188.

––––––. 1983. Aspects of the evolution of human behaviour: An archaeological perspective. Canadian Journal of Anthropology 3:233–243.

Leroi-Gourhan, A. 1964. Les religions de la préhistoire. Presses Universitaires de France, Paris.

––––––. 1965. Treasures of prehistoric art. Abrams, New York.

––––––. 1982. The dawn of European art. Cambridge University Press.

Lieberman, P. 1984. The biology and evolution of language. Harvard University Press, Cambridge, Mass.

Lindly, J. M., and G. A. Clark. 1990. Symbolism and modern human origins. Current Anthropology 31(3):233–261.

Marshack, Alexander. 1972. Upper Paleolithic notation and symbol. Science 178:817–828.

––––––. 1975. Exploring the mind of Ice Age man. National Geographic 147(1):62–89.

––––––. 1985. A lunar-solar year calendar stick from North America. American Antiquity 50(1):27–51.

––––––. 1989. On wishful thinking and lunar "calendars." Current Anthropology 30(4):491–500.

Mellars, P. 1973. The character of the Middle-Upper Paleolithic transition in southwest France. In The explanation of culture change, C. Renfrew, ed. Duckworth, London, pp. 255–276.

Mellars, P., and C. B. Stringer, eds. 1989. The human revolution. . . . University of Edinburgh Press.

Orguera, L. 1984. Specialization and the Middle/Upper Paleolithic transition. Current Anthropology 25:73–98.

Pfeiffer, J. E. 1982. The creative explosion. Harper & Row, New York.

Renfrew, Colin. 1982. Towards an archaeology of mind. Cambridge University Press.

Renfrew, Colin, and Paul Bahn. 1991. What did they think? cognitive archaeology, art, and religion. In Archaeology: theories, methods, and practice. Thames and Hudson, New York, pp. 339–370.

Stringer, C. B. 1982. Towards a solution to the Neanderthal problem. Journal of Human Evolution 11:431–438.

————. 1989a. The origins of early modern humans: a comparison of the European and non-European evidence. In The human revolution, P. Mellars and C. B. Stringer, eds. University of Edinburgh Press, pp. 232–244.

————. 1989b. Documenting the origin of modern humans. In The emergence of modern humans, Erik Trinkaus, ed. Cambridge University Press, pp. 67–96.

Trinkaus, Erik, ed. 1983. The Mousterian legacy. BAR, Oxford.

————. 1989. The emergence of modern humans, biocultural adaptations in the later Pleistocene. School of American Research/Cambridge University Press.

Whallon, R. 1989. Elements of cultural change in the later Palaeolithic. In The human revolution: behavioural and biological perspectives on the origins of modern humans, vol. 1, P. Mellars and C. B. Stringer, eds. Edinburgh University Press, pp. 433–454.

White, Randall. 1982. Rethinking the Middle/Upper Paleolithic transition. Current Anthropology 23:169–92.

————. 1985. Thoughts on social relationships and language in hominid evolution. Journal of Social and Personal Relationships 2:95–115.

Wynn, Thomas. 1985. Piaget, stone tools, and the evolution of human intelligence. World Archaeology 17(1):32–43.

————. 1986. Archaeological evidence for the evolution of modern human intelligence. In The Pleistocene perspective: precirculated papers of the World Archaeological Congress, Southampton, 1986, M. Day, R. Foley, and Wu Rukang, eds. Allen and Unwin, London.

SOURCES OF ADDITIONAL INFORMATION

At present, published general discussions of materialist cognitive archaeology are relatively few. Those available include the Renfrew address, "Towards an archaeology of mind" (Renfrew 1982); and a chapter in the archaeology text by Colin Renfrew and Paul Bahn, "What did they think? cognitive archaeology, art, and religion," in *Archaeology: Theories, Methods and Practice* (New York, Thames and Hudson, 1991), pp. 339–370. In addition, a portion of chapter 12 in this work (pp. 431–434) discusses "Cognitive-processual archaeology: the new synthesis"; in it Renfrew melds his own cognitive approach with that of the mainstream materialist processualists, and distinguishes it from its antecedents in a number of ways. An interesting somewhat earlier discussion of the cognitive aspects of the past is the final chapter, "The Dawn of Self

Awareness,'' in Grahame Clark's *Aspects of Prehistory* (Berkeley and Los Angeles, University of California Press, 1970), pp. 103–146.

Reports of applied cognitive studies are more common; see, for instance, the reviews in recent issues of *Current Anthropology* cited above, and material in Wynn 1985, 1986; White 1985; the papers in Mellars and Stringer 1989; and Lindly and Clark 1990 (see References for complete bibliographic information). Mark Leone, "Some opinions about recovering mind," *American Antiquity* 47(4)(1982):742–760, discusses some possible applications of cognitive theory in archaeology from several perspectives, including the structuralist and Marxist positions, and concludes that the materialist approach offers the greatest potential for cognitive archaeology.

Cognitive studies of specific topics include Steven J. Mithen, "Looking and learning: Upper Palaeolithic art and information gathering," *World Archaeology* 19(3) (February 1988):297–327, which emphasizes the communication function of the European cave paintings as repositories of environmental information; Thomas N. Huffman, "Cognitive studies of the Iron Age in southern Africa," *World Archaeology* 18(1) (June 1986):84–95, in which the author applies two models based on ethnographic data to infer political organization and cosmology in the African Iron Age; and Peter W. Stahl, "Hallucinatory imagery and the origin of early South American figurine art," *World Archaeology* 18(1) (June 1986):134–150, in which artistic objects are interpreted as representations of shamanic visions induced by intoxication. The latter article includes a very extensive bibliography. A paper treating a similar theme is J. D. Lewis-Williams and T. A. Dowson, "The signs of all times: Entoptic phenomena in Upper Paleolithic art," *Current Anthropology* 29(2) (April 1988):201–245, whose authors use a "neuropsychological" model to interpret geometric signs in cave art, which they first applied to shamanic rock art of the San of South Africa and the Shoshonean Coso. Lewis-Williams and Dowson argue that these signs were representations of mental images perceived in altered states of consciousness. Two other articles concerned with the interpretation of art are John Halvorson, "Art for art's sake in the Paleolithic," *Current Anthropology* 28(1) (February 1987):63–69; and Whitney Davis, "The origins of image making," *Current Anthropology* 27(3) (June 1986):193–215.

World Archaeology 19, no. 2 (October 1987), was devoted to the archaeological study of rock art and its interpretation, with eight papers discussing various aspects of this art form in many parts of the world. A treatment of monumental architecture as symbolic behavior from a fundamentally Marxist point of view is Bruce Trigger, "Monumental architecture: a thermodynamic explanation of symbolic behaviour," *World Archaeology* 22(2) (October 1990):119–132. Trigger argues that control of energy expenditures is a basic expression of sociopolitical power, which is given material form in monumental structures.

A study of pottery decoration as a form of symbolic expression, as well as a way of endowing physical objects with power, is Nicholas David, Judy Sterner, and Kodzo Gavua, "Why pots are decorated," *Current Anthropology* 29(3) (June 1988):365–389, which includes a lengthy bibliography of relevant literature.

A paper on another pertinent topic, the origins of language, is Sue Taylor Parker, "A socio-technological model for the evolution of language," *Current Anthropology* 26(5) (December 1985):617–639. Parker applies a sociobiological model of communication as an adaptive method of social manipulation to the development of language, which she also regards as an adaptive device for this purpose.

All the articles in *Current Anthropology* cited above have extensive bibliographies that include citations contributed by the referees whose commentaries accompany each article, as well as the authors' references, and may serve as useful introductions to the literature of the topics discussed. To update these, future issues of *Current Anthropology*, *World Archaeology*, the pertinent annual reviews, and current issues of other archaeological journals, such as *American Antiquity*, *Antiquity*, and *American Anthropologist* should be consulted for more recent articles.

CONTEXT. 1. The in situ position of an ARTIFACT in three-dimensional space, measured horizontally and vertically from reference points established from a survey SITE map, together with its temporal/cultural position determined from its associations with dated materials located adjacent to it within the same three-dimensional unit of space. Also called *provenance* or *provenience*. 2. The functional nature of an artifact's in situ location in a site, determined from study of the associated artifacts and features. This functional context may be a *ritual* one, if associated materials are ceremonial objects; *domestic*, if associated materials are those used in everyday household activities; *burial*, if it accompanies a human interment; or *manufacturing*, when associated materials suggest its location was a specialized workshop area.

The critical importance of the physical location in which an artifact, ecofact, feature, or group of associated objects is found in relation to the physical matrix (usually soil) in which it lies has been recognized by archaeologists since the beginnings of FIELD ARCHAEOLOGY in the early nineteenth century. Provenance—the three-dimensional location of an artifact or feature in space, its horizontal and vertical position within the surrounding matrix material—is always recorded, normally with reference to the grid system established when the site is surveyed prior to the beginning of excavation (see FIELD ARCHAEOLOGY; SURVEY). These descriptive data, together with similar information on other materials occurring in association within the same matrix and excavation level, will be used by the archaeologist to interpret the find. Context is the information that allows the first step to be made in linking the material remains of a past CULTURE to the behavior that produced them.

Archaeological context has been defined as "the position of an archaeological find in time and space, established by measuring and assessing its associations, matrix, and provenience . . . *includ[ing the] study of what has happened to the find since it was buried in the ground*" (Fagan 1988:575; emphasis added). In other words, the recovery context of an artifact, ecofact, or feature encompasses not only its position in space and its functional associations but also its post-depositional history, the result of both natural and human events that have affected the position and condition in which it is recovered by the archaeologist (see TAPHONOMY).

Context may be primary or secondary. Primary context refers to the position of an object in the original spatial location where it was placed or discarded by those who manufactured and used it. An item that has been redeposited, that is, moved from its original location of deposition as the result of subsequent human or animal activity or natural disturbance processes, is said to occur in secondary context. The original or primary context of an archaeological find is a phenomenon of the past, a consequence of the set of past circumstances in which the item was originally discarded, buried, or otherwise deposited in the ARCHAEOLOGICAL RECORD. The recovery context is the present set of circumstances in which the object is found, which may be significantly different from the original context, due to the operation of intervening processes. Only the recovery context is directly perceived by the archaeologist, who must infer the original context from the available evidence. The recovery context may be either primary or secondary, and is a phenomenon of the present archaeological record, while the original context is a phenomenon of the past (Sullivan 1978).

Context provides all the most significant clues to the original behavior that created a need for this particular object, as well as the behavior involved in its manufacture and use. While the cultural meaning an excavated knife, painted pottery vessel, or image of a deity had for its original owner cannot be fully comprehended by the archaeologist, the information provided by its physical location and surroundings may lead to important and revealing insights into its owner's behavior and motivations. It is for these reasons that the preservation and recording of contextual data are of such crucial importance, since such information inevitably is permanently destroyed by the excavation process. If the excavation is uncontrolled and unrecorded, as looters' excavations always are, the possibility of reconstructing context is permanently lost. Although the artifacts themselves may be preserved, and may eventually find their way into the hands of an archaeologist, their value as sources of information about human behavior in the past is irretrievably lost (Sharer and Ashmore 1979:84).

Most artifacts in private collections are of unknown provenance, as are many in museum collections. The former have usually been illegally removed from their original context by professional thieves, and many of the latter have been acquired from persons who know nothing of their original context, usually through distributors and middlemen connected with the illegal antiquities market (Meyer 1973; Muscarella 1984). The acquisition of such objects by museums is now considered unethical, as well as being illegal, and is avoided, although many were acquired in past years. Such artifacts may be compared to isolated words written in an unknown language that cannot be deciphered because their grammatical context has been lost. The preservation of archaeological context information is therefore at least as important as the preservation of artifacts themselves for purposes of archaeological interpretation, and in some instances more cultural and behavioral information may be acquired from a well-preserved primary context than from a poorly preserved artifact found within it (Sullivan 1978; Wiseman 1984).

Alan Sullivan treats the information from both artifact and context as comprising a set of archaeological "traces" of past behavior. The recovery of such traces in ways that preserve their information intact requires, he believes, a careful methodology of its own (Sullivan 1978:204).

Sharer and Ashmore (1979) distinguish a variety of types of context, both primary and secondary. The most informative type they define as a *primary* (or undisturbed) *use-related context*, which preserves the ancient human behavior pattern the artifact was designed to serve. The survival of this kind of context is due to chance factors that preserve the material object in its original location without the interference of natural processes or human agency. Good examples of such preservation are undisturbed tombs or burials, where the placement of grave goods interred with the dead reflects the society's belief system and its associated rituals, as well as cultural behavior surrounding the death of an individual (see MORTUARY ANALYSIS). Sir Leonard Woolley was able to develop considerable information about mortuary customs and beliefs of the ancient Chaldeans from his careful observation and recording of contextual information preserved in the intact royal tombs of Ur, which he excavated in the 1920s. In only one of the tomb chambers that had been looted was this information lost; surviving materials here had been moved from their original location, placing them in *use-related secondary context*, which preserved their original purpose and function (as grave goods) but not their original physical provenance (Sharer and Ashmore 1979:88–89).

Most often, the recovery context of an artifact reflects not its daily use and behavioral associations but the discard and disposal habits of its producers. This is true for all materials recovered from middens, or trash accumulations, which are probably the most common source of artifacts recovered by archaeologists. Occasionally tools will be discarded or abandoned at the site of their use in such activities as butchering carcasses or manufacturing other tools, but this is less likely to occur than discard of a broken tool in a disposal area or dump. Use-related context is therefore relatively rare, and artifacts are commonly repaired and reused until they become worn out and unrepairable and find their way into a midden pile, where, if undisturbed, the archaeologist will find them in *transposed primary context*.

An additional category of context is *natural secondary context*, resulting from the movement of deeply buried artifacts into higher depositional levels representing later cultural periods, through the action of natural processes such as freezing and thawing, the activities of burrowing rodents, or human activities such as plowing, all of which pose considerable interpretative problems (Sharer and Ashmore 1979:90–92).

Even the best-preserved context will require careful interpretation. Since what survives in the archaeological record is only a fragment of the total material output of any past society, the physical position and associations surrounding these material finds are an invaluable source of information that may often allow the archaeologist to flesh out his or her discoveries and place the artifacts recovered in their original behavioral context.

REFERENCES

Fagan, Brian M. 1988. In the beginning: an introduction to archaeology. 6th ed. Scott, Foresman, Glenview, Ill.

Meyer, Karl E. 1973. The plundered past. Athenaeum, New York.

Muscarella, Oscar White. 1984. On publishing unexcavated artifacts. Journal of Field Archaeology 11(1):61–66.

Sharer, Robert J., and Wendy Ashmore. 1979. The nature of archaeological data. In Fundamentals of archaeology, by Robert J. Sharer and Wendy Ashmore. Benjamin Cummings, Menlo Park, Calif., pp. 69–106.

Sullivan, Alan P. 1978. Inference and evidence in archaeology: a discussion of the conceptual problems. Advances in Archaeological Method and Theory 1:183–222.

Wiseman, James. 1984. Scholarship and provenience in the study of artifacts. Journal of Field Archaeology 11(1):67–77.

SOURCES OF ADDITIONAL INFORMATION

The subject of context has not been frequently discussed in the archaeological literature. The fullest, most informative treatment of all aspects of context and its importance is in Chapter 3, "The nature of Archaeological Data", in Sharer and Ashmore's *Fundamentals of Archaeology* (see References), especially pp. 82–92. There is further useful discussion in the Sullivan review article (see References). Additional material related to the importance of context in exploiting the archaeological record may be found in Michael B. Schiffer, "Archaeological context and systemic context," *American Antiquity* 37(1972):156–165; Michael B. Schiffer and W. I. Rathje, "Efficient exploitation of the archaeological record," in *Research and Theory in Current Archaeology*, Charles L. Redman, ed. (New York, Wiley, 1973), pp. 169–179; and Michael B. Schiffer and J. J. Reid, "A system for designating behaviorally significant proveniences," in *The Cache River Archaeological Project: An Experiment in Contract Archaeology*, M. B. Schiffer and J. H. House, comps. Arkansas Archaeological Survey, Research Series No. 8, Fayetteville.

Practical instructions for determining and describing the context of excavated items may be found in chapter 4, "Excavation procedures," of the field manual by Knud R. Fladmark, *A Guide to Basic Archaeological Field Procedures* (Burnaby, B.C., Department of Archaeology, Simon Fraser University, Publication No. 4, 1978). Similar material is available in most other field manuals.

For more current information on context, issues of *Journal of Field Archaeology* and *American Antiquity*, as well as the annual review *Archaeological Method and Theory*, should be consulted.

CULTURAL COMPLEXITY. A term frequently used in describing societies in which social distinctions, such as ranks, classes, or other types of status differences, exist, in contrast with societies that are egalitarian, or lacking in social inequalities between individuals or groups. (See also CHIEFDOM; SOCIAL ORGANIZATION; STATE.)

The evolutionary principle that social systems, like living organisms, evolve from simpler to more complex forms is implicit in the notion of complexity, which is assumed by evolutionists to increase through time in any situation in the normal course of events. The term has also been used interchangeably with *civilization* to denote a quite specific level of social and political integration, characterized by large populations, urbanism, food-producing economies, multiple hereditary social statuses, and (frequently) written records. The term *complexity* is now sometimes used by archaeologists to refer to almost any type of SOCIAL ORGANIZATION beyond that of the small nomadic band, and references to "complex hunter-gatherers" are now quite common in the archaeological literature (e.g., Price and Brown 1985; Hayden and Gargett 1990). However, the phrase is more accurately restricted to groups in which permanent social inequalities, or ascribed status differences, exist between groups comprising ranks, or classes of elites and commoners, that are perpetuated through time, a type of social inequality quite distinct from the transitory individual differences in power or wealth that may arise from the efforts of particularly charismatic, enterprising, or exploitative persons, but that do not survive their individual lifetimes.

Typologies of social organization, which are frequently organized on evolutionary principles, assume that in the normal course of events, EVOLUTION will be "a movement toward greater organization, greater differentiation of structure, increased specialization of function, higher levels of integration, and greater degrees of energy concentration" (White 1949:367)—in a word, toward *increasing complexity*. The concept of complexity in this sense has been an implicit one in evolutionary theory since its early-nineteenth-century origins (White 1959; Murdock and Provost 1973; Moore 1974; Blau 1977; Sanders and Webster 1978; Steponaitis 1981; Wenke 1981; Braun and Plog 1982; McGuire 1983; Earle 1984; Cohen 1985; Brumfiel and Earle 1987; Kristiansen 1987; Trinkaus 1987; Plog 1989; Braun 1990; Kowalewski 1990), although it has seldom been defined in a manner useful to archaeologists seeking to identify traces of the beginnings of "complexity" in the ARCHAEOLOGICAL RECORD.

The level of social organization denoted by the term *civilization* has traditionally been considered to represent the greatest possible degree of collective human organizational complexity, that which appears as the end point in most sociocultural evolutionary schemes (Steward 1949; Braidwood 1952; Frankfort 1956; Service 1975; Butzer 1976; Wright 1986). But while civilization implies urbanism (by its derivation from the Latin *civitas*), *complexity*, which has become the alternative term now most frequently used by archaeologists in their discussions of cultural typologies or prehistoric cultural change, has no such connotation.

The concept of civilization, since it refers to a type of organization that is qualitatively different from its antecedents, and can be defined in terms of the presence or absence of particular institutions or phenomena, such as urbanism (Adams 1966, 1969), fits easily into evolutionary schemes. *Complexity*, on the other hand, implies a comparative phenomenon that can be conceived of in degrees, or as a series of possible points along a continuum, rather than a discrete category, and therefore does not readily lend itself to use in hierarchical developmental schemes. As a result, problems arise from attempts to treat complexity as a single, unitary variable in characterizing social groups, since it encompasses a whole set of sociocultural traits and variables—although there has been little agreement concerning how many of these must be present to constitute a "complex" society or culture. *Complexity* has unfortunately become a catchall term without precise meaning, used to describe a phenomenon that has not been precisely defined. The concept is therefore not an especially useful one, since it not only is lacking in explanatory value or power but also has resisted satisfactory definition. However, since it continues to be used in the archaeological literature, it is in need of discussion and elucidation.

Robert Wenke, in a review article on the evolution of cultural complexity (Wenke 1981), distinguished between functional and evolutionary explanations of complexity, but never defined the concept itself, although he treated it as a concept of importance in cultural evolutionary theory. Wenke also touched on the problems of documenting complexity from archaeological evidence; and in a later discussion of the origin of complex society in Egypt (Wenke 1989), he noted the lack of "powerful theories of history or archaeology that tell us how ancient complex societies can best be categorized and measured for . . . explaining their origins." He went on to give a conventional definition of "complex society" as "a nonquantitative composite of monumental architecture, inferred mortuary cults, rank and wealth hierarchies, specialized craft production etc.," but admitted that "such trait lists must be considered descriptive, not analytical" (Wenke 1989:130).

The traditional cultural evolutionist view of what constitutes a complex society has most often described such a society in terms of collections of institutions or traits. Some, however, have emphasized control hierarchies, levels of political integration, or the development of particular forms of political structures, such as CHIEFDOMS and primary states (Wright 1986). This is a popular view, and is basically the one adopted by Elman Service (Service 1975), William Sanders and Barbara Price (1968), and other cultural evolutionists who imply that sociocultural development is goal-directed toward increasing complexity, which is usually defined (when definition is attempted) in terms that emphasize greater numbers of statuses or social ranks, control hierarchies, and lists of particular cultural "traits" or behavior patterns that include long-distance trade networks, wealth, intensified agriculture, large populations, hereditary statuses, and sometimes a specific economic pattern, such as redistribution (Service 1962).

Alternative evolutionary models of complexity include the much-cited systemic one developed by Kent Flannery (Flannery 1972), which identified some of the variables and mechanisms leading to sociocultural change toward increasing complexity, but made no attempt at causal explanation of the processes involved.

Other treatments of the subject have attempted to isolate key variables in the growth of complex organizational structures, such as Randall McGuire's "inequality" and "heterogeneity" (McGuire 1983). Fred Plog has tried to evade the linear developmental model and to construct a multidimensional model, based on pairs of dichotomies, such as simple/complex; predictability/unpredictability; stability/resiliency, and the possible forms societies may take when these are combined and permuted according to different patterns (Plog 1989). Some recent discussions addressing the processes leading to complex society have emphasized the role of personal aggrandizement and individual power and wealth accumulation. A notable example is presented by Brian Hayden and Rob Gargett (1990), who attribute the emergence of social inequalities to the activities of "accumulators," ambitious persons who, through conscious competitive effort, seek to acquire control of strategic resources and thereby increase their influence and power. Another approach is that of Robert Paynter (Paynter 1989), who begins his discussion by citing social inequality and stratification as markers of complexity, and asking whether inequality itself constitutes complexity. Paynter notes that

> The concept of complexity concerns the degree of internal differentiation and the intricacy of relations within a system. . . . Complex societies involve many different social entities, whose members affect each other along intricate pathways. Simple societies have relatively similar social entities, whose members interact with one another in similar ways. Inequality exists when socially distinct entities have differential access to strategic resources. . . . (Paynter 1989:369)

Beyond the central problem of adequately defining complexity, its archaeological study has two dimensions or aspects. The first of these is how to explain, in operational terms, why and how socioeconomic inequalities begin to emerge in originally simple, egalitarian societies; and second, to develop valid criteria for identifying the material correlates of this phenomenon in the ARCHAEOLOGICAL RECORD (Peebles and Kus 1977; Smith 1987). Both these problems have been addressed to some extent in the archaeological literature. Some common themes mentioned repeatedly in the literature as diagnostics of complexity are the appearance of differential access to strategic or critical resources by different social groups (Paynter 1989; Hayden and Gargett 1990); the presence of resource abundance, which is often enhanced by new technology or new strategies that increase the efficiency of resource utilization (Hayden and Gargett 1990); and a shift from reciprocity and food sharing among persons of equal status to *new forms and patterns of social interaction.*

It is the latter shift that appears to be the key factor distinguishing the complex society from the simple, egalitarian one. In the complex society, interpersonal relationships are no longer based upon the mutual support of equals to promote their mutual survival, but become based on principles of dominance and submission, on relative differences in economic power and resource control between individuals that formerly did not exist. These social changes appear to constitute the most basic difference between simple and complex societies. Other variables often cited as diagnostics of "complexity"—large populations, long-distance trade, new social-organizational forms or units such as chiefdoms and states, bureaucracies and specialists—are of secondary importance, and can be regarded as among the *effects* of complexity rather than as among its causes or diagnostic characteristics.

For the purposes of ARCHAEOLOGY, then, complexity itself is perhaps best defined as *a particular kind of basic change in the fundamental conventions of social interaction, and the socioeconomic consequences of this change.* The overall effect is to convert an egalitarian society into a stratified society, with primary social divisions based less on kinship affiliations than on differences in access to resources or wealth (economic advantage) and/or power (social advantage), both forms of advantage that do not normally exist in egalitarian society. These new social patterns will have the effect of creating new organizational structures and a new value system in the complex society. The basis for membership in corporate groups is likely to change. Whereas such membership is frequently determined by genetic relatedness in the egalitarian society, in the complex society it is more likely to be determined by one's status relative to some important, powerful key figure (big man, chief, king).

The emphasis in ethical values is likely to shift from sharing with relatives (to insure one's own survival or one's inclusive fitness) as the desired norm, to acquiring status, political power, or wealth as the preferred behavior to insure one's survival. Survival thus becomes more contingent and less certain, and relationships under the new order are less predictable and therefore less stable, creating a social system that is inherently more unstable than that of an egalitarian, kin-based society. Consequently, new roles and statuses are created and multiplied as a hedge against this inherent instability. The result is the creation of bureaucracies, which are usually of a hierarchical nature, in keeping with the predominant new pattern of social structure. Since bureaucracies can, and usually do, acquire a degree of inertia that makes them self-perpetuating, they provide some insurance against sudden disruptions that might lead to system collapse—that is, they function as *system buffers* in developing complex social systems.

These changed patterns of social interaction will be documented in the archaeological record by the appearance of material items symbolizing the new social differences between groups of individuals, such as artifacts used only by elites (rulers, priests, "accumulators," or other bureaucrats; see Hayden and Gargett 1990), whose value is symbolic rather than functional. Such ARTIFACTS serve to signal and emphasize the presence of significant social distance between their possessors and those who do not possess them. Although they may be replicas of utilitarian items, such as knives, axes, or other tools, bowls or other vessels, their symbolic or ornamental nature will usually be made clear by the intrinsic value of the scarce or expensive raw materials from which they are fashioned, and the difficulty of obtaining these from distant sources; the elaborate, ornamental nature of their form or decoration, which implies the skill and artistry

of full-time specialized artisans; or a combination of all these factors, plus the
lack of wear from use, which clearly sets them apart from their utilitarian pro-
totypes. The locational contexts and distribution patterns of such items in archaeological SITES are also important, since these will pinpoint areas of elite
residence and activity, as well as those of persons of lower social status who
did not possess or use such items.

In discussing the archaeology of equality and inequality, Robert Paynter (1989)
deals with some of these points. He further notes that the appearance of complexity creates a host of new social problems. While specific responses to these
problems will vary from one case to another, those which occur with repetitive
frequency include an increase in the division of labor, the creation of more social
boundaries, and the development of a hierarchy of warrior-priest elites to deal
with conflicts resulting from the new social diversity. But in the neoevolutionary
paradigm, complex society should be a problem solver, not a problem creator.
In his critique of the neoevolutionist view of complexity, Paynter quotes Mark
Cohen on this point:

> Complex social organization not only solves logistic problems in coordinating people
> with resources, it also relieves interpersonal tensions generated by relatively inflex-
> ible, close association with large numbers of other people. (Cohen 1985:112; quoted
> in Paynter 1989:374)

In other words, new rules are required to handle more people and greater social
diversity; and the new complex social structures generate and facilitate these
rules. Paynter goes on to criticize the neoevolutionists for attributing stability to
complex systems—he cites numerous examples to show they clearly are *not*
stable, but highly vulnerable to disruption and collapse (Paynter 1989:375; see
also Tainter 1988).

If archaeologists have developed some plausible models for ways in which
cultures may become more complex, there still remains the problem of explaining
why complexity develops in stable, egalitarian societies (see Binford 1983:221;
Hayden and Gargett 1990. Lewis Binford (1983) has approached this question
from a pragmatic, problem-solving point of view.

> . . . I think . . . the most practical principle . . . to adopt . . . is an analog to the prin-
> ciple of inertia. A system will remain stable until acted upon by forces external to
> its organization as a system. When . . . faced with a question such as why complex
> systems come into being, my first reaction is to ask what problem people were
> attempting to solve by a new means. Experimenting with novel ways of doing things
> is surely worthwhile only if some fresh problem has emerged for which no previous
> solution appears satisfactory. (Binford 1983:221)
>   . . . a major shift in social forms, such as those represented by the appearance of
> ranking and stratification, must represent some kind of major break with earlier
> patterns of growth . . . at some point in the trajectory . . . a major structural break
> with earlier forms . . . appears . . . basic units of production and generalized reci-
> procity . . . instead of duplicating themselves, begin to develop conventions for *ex-
> cluding* individuals. (Binford 1983:223–224)

Binford goes on to point out that the first successful competitive individuals (those Hayden and Gargett call "accumulators") are the first to work outside the system since, in order to capitalize on their own productivity, they must become social mavericks; the resulting isolation gives them greater freedom to maneuver in promoting their own interests, unlike the others, who are still playing by the established rules. They therefore become entrepreneurs who develop profitable relations with persons outside the system, and by doing so further enhance their personal advantage (Binford 1983:227). These are the first people to acquire "elite" or exotic goods from distant trading partners. In this scenario, change is initiated by unconventional individuals who are willing to take risks, including the risk of not being supported by their relatives in a crisis, in order to increase their own wealth, power, and influence. And it is their actions, taken on their own behalf (and perhaps secondarily on behalf of their fellows), that eventually cause the entire society to change its form and structure from egalitarianism to ranking, from kin-based social organization to hierarchical political forms of organization, from simplicity to complexity.

REFERENCES

Adams, R. M. 1969. The rise of urban society. Aldine, Chicago.
Adams, R. McC. 1966. The evolution of urban society. Aldine, Chicago.
Binford, Lewis R. 1983. "Paths to complexity." In In pursuit of the past: decoding the archaeological record. Thames and Hudson, New York, pp. 214–232.
Blau, P. 1977. Inequality and heterogeneity: a primitive theory of social structure. Free Press, New York.
Braidwood, Robert J. 1952. The Near East and the foundations for civilization: an essay in appraisal of the general evidence. State System of Higher Education, Eugene, Ore.
Braun, D. P. 1990. Selection and evolution in nonhierarchical organization. In The evolution of political systems: sociopolitics in small-scale sedentary societies, Steadman Upham, ed. Cambridge University Press, pp. 62–86.
Braun, D. P., and S. Plog. 1982. Evolution of "tribal" social networks: theory and prehistoric North American evidence. American Antiquity 47:504–525.
Brumfiel, Elizabeth M., and Timothy K. Earle, eds. 1987. Specialization, exchange and complex societies. Cambridge University Press.
Butzer, Karl W. 1976. Early hydraulic civilization in Egypt. University of Chicago Press.
Cohen, M. N. 1985. Prehistoric hunter-gatherers: the meaning of social complexity. In Prehistoric hunter-gatherers, T. D. Price and J. A. Brown, eds. Academic Press, Orlando, Fla., pp. 99–119.
Earle, Timothy K., ed. 1984. On the evolution of complex societies. Undena, Malibu, Calif.
Flannery, Kent V. 1972. The cultural evolution of civilizations. Annual Review of Ecology and Systematics 3:399–416.
Frankfort, H. 1956. The birth of civilization in the Near East. Indiana University Press, Bloomington.
Hayden, Brian, and Rob Gargett. 1990. Big man, big heart? a Mesoamerican view of the emergence of complex society. Ancient Mesoamerica 1(1):3–20.

Kowalewski, Stephen A. 1990. The evolution of complexity in the Valley of Oaxaca. Annual Review of Anthropology 19:39–58.

Kristiansen, K. 1987. From stone to bronze: the evolution of social complexity in northern Europe, 2300–1200 B.C. In Specialization, exchange and complex societies, E. Brumfiel and T. K. Earle, eds. Cambridge University Press, pp. 30–51.

McGuire, Randall H. 1983. Breaking down cultural complexity: inequality and heterogeneity. Advances in Archaeological Method and Theory 6:91–142.

Moore, Charlotte B., ed. 1974. Reconstructing complex societies: an archaeological colloquium. American School of Oriental Research, Cambridge, Mass.

Murdock, George P., and Caterina Provost. 1973. Measurement of cultural complexity. Ethnology 12:379–392.

Paynter, R. 1989. The archaeology of equality and inequality. Annual Review of Anthropology 18:369–399.

Peebles, C. S., and S. M. Kus. 1977. Some archaeological correlates of ranked society. American Antiquity 42:421–448.

Plog, Fred. 1989. Studying complexity. In The sociopolitical structure of prehistoric southwestern societies, Steadman Upham, Kent G. Lightfoot, and Roberta A. Jewett, eds. Westview Press, Boulder, Colo., pp. 103–125.

Price, T. Douglas, and James A. Brown, eds. 1985. Prehistoric hunter-gatherers: The emergence of cultural complexity. Academic Press, New York.

Sanders, William T., and Barbara Price. 1968. Mesoamerica: the evolution of a civilization. Random House, New York.

Sanders, William T., and D. Webster. 1978. Unilinealism, multilinealism and the evolution of complex societies. In Social archaeology, beyond subsistence and dating, Sanders and Webster et al., eds. Academic Press, New York, pp. 249–302.

Service, Elman R. 1962. Primitive social organization: an evolutionary perspective. Random House, New York.

———. 1975. Origins of the state and civilization: the process of cultural evolution. W. W. Norton, New York.

Smith, M. E. 1987. Household possessions and wealth in agrarian states—implications for archaeology. Journal of Anthropological Archaeology 6(4):297–335.

Steponaitis, Vincas. 1981. Settlement hierarchies and political complexity in nonmarket societies. American Anthropologist 83:320–363.

Steward, Julian. 1949. Cultural causality and law: a trial formulation of the development of early civilizations. American Anthropologist 51(1):1–27.

Tainter, Joseph A. 1988. The collapse of complex societies. Cambridge University Press.

Trinkaus, Kathryn Maurer, ed. 1987. Polities and partitions: human boundaries and the growth of complex societies. Department of Anthropology Anthropological Research Papers No. 37. Arizona State University, Tempe.

Wenke, Robert J. 1981. Explaining the evolution of cultural complexity: a review. Advances in Archaeological Method and Theory 4:79–127.

———. 1989. Egypt—origins of complex societies. Annual Review of Anthropology 18:129–155.

White, Leslie. 1949. Energy and the evolution of culture. In The science of culture, L. White, ed. Farrar, Straus & Giroux, New York, pp. 363–393.

———. 1959. The evolution of culture. McGraw-Hill, New York.

Wright, Henry T. 1986. The evolution of civilizations. In American archaeology past and future, David J. Meltzer, Don D. Fowler, and Jeremy A. Sabloff, eds., pp. 323–365. Smithsonian Institution Press, Washington, D.C.

SOURCES OF ADDITIONAL INFORMATION

The literature on cultural complexity is vast, and comprehensive coverage of it is not attempted here. In addition to the basic sources cited in the text and listed in the References above, Robert Carneiro, "The evolution of complexity in human society and its mathematical expression," *International Journal of Comparative Sociology* 28(3–4) (1987):111–128, revives the idea of quantifying complexity, which was anticipated in the early 1970s by George Murdock (see Murdock and Provost 1973, cited above). *American Behavioral Scientist* 31, no. 4 (1987) is devoted to papers on the evolution of complexity, with particular reference to Carneiro's theory of circumscription as the principal mechanism leading to the formation of the state. These include bibliographies of additional publications relating to cultural complexity, which should be consulted.

The proceedings of the sixteenth annual Chacmool Conference, held at the University of Calgary, *Status, Structure and Stratification: Current Archaeological Reconstructions*, Marc Thompson, Maria Teresa Garcia, and Francois J. Kense, eds. (Calgary, University of Calgary Archaeological Association, 1985), includes several relevant papers. Among these are Linda S. Cordell, "Status differentiation and social complexity in the prehistoric Southwest: a discussion" (pp. 191–195); J. Jefferson Reid, "Measuring social complexity in the American Southwest" (pp. 167–173); and Steadman Upham, "Interpretations of prehistoric complexity in the central and northern Southwest" (pp. 175–180).

Additional literature is listed in the bibliographies in the review articles cited above (e.g., Paynter 1989; Kowalewski 1990), as well as in the articles in the "circumscription" issue of *American Behavioral Scientist* (1988). The journals *American Antiquity* and *American Anthropologist*, and the appropriate annual reviews, should be consulted for forthcoming publications and information on cultural complexity.

CULTURAL ECOLOGY. 1. A theoretical approach to the study of human ecological ADAPTATION, in which culture and its institutions are viewed as adaptations to specific environmental conditions. 2. A method of analyzing human CULTURES, including those known only through the ARCHAEOLOGICAL RECORD, as environmental adaptations, emphasizing the dynamic interaction between cultural factors and the biological and physical environment.

Cultural ecology is concerned with determining the extent to which human societies represent adjustments to particular environmental conditions that require certain modes of behavioral adaptation for survival. Such environmental situations may be seen as playing a causal role in determining particular cultural practices, which are interpreted as human responses to specific environmental constraints or the presence of specific resources.

The focus of cultural ecological studies is principally on those human behaviors "which empirical analysis shows to be most closely involved in the utilization of environment in culturally prescribed ways" (Steward 1959:88). Such behaviors will ordinarily include SUBSISTENCE practices and their requisite technology, a set of cultural features that in cultural ecological theory is considered to constitute the cultural "core."

As a theoretical orientation, cultural ecology differs from environmental determinism in apportioning causality between cultural and environmental factors, rather than assigning exclusive causal force to the environment in seeking to explain cultural phenomena in adaptive terms. In their analyses of human ecosystems, cultural ecologists investigate dynamic relationships between human groups and the environments they occupy and exploit, focusing upon interconnections among various cultural subsystems and their overall contribution to promoting survival. In such investigations, the environment is considered to be an independent variable, while the cultural features, including the level of CULTURAL COMPLEXITY, constitute dependent variables. Relationships between technology and environment are emphasized, as is the material culture associated with extractive or productive activities involved in subsistence. Human SETTLEMENT PATTERNS are also examined as reflections of environmental factors.

Although the roots of cultural ecology have been traced back as far as the fourteenth century (Larkin and Peters 1983:49), the concept as it is currently understood and applied in archaeology is usually attributed to Julian Steward, who first outlined its principles and enunciated a method for cultural ecology studies in the late 1930s (Steward 1955, 1959, 1968; Vayda and Rappaport 1968; Murphy 1977). Steward's interest in the effects of environmental factors on culture was initially stimulated by his contact at Berkeley with the geographer Carl Sauer, which affected his later research in the Great Basin (Orlove 1980:237), research that also exercised an important influence on the development of his cultural ecological approach. In his theoretical exposition of ecology, Steward undertook "to develop the concept of ecology in relation to human beings as an heuristic device for understanding the effect of environment upon culture" (Steward 1959:81).

Steward sought a method of analysis in which culture was considered as a dynamic adaptive process rather than a static collection of traits. Cultural ecology, with its emphasis on the importance of local environments in shaping localized cultural adaptations, was an important reaction against the culture historical orientation fostered by Alfred Kroeber and his students (Vayda and Rappaport 1968:483).

Although Steward anticipated later "processual" archaeologists in his emphasis on cultural dynamics, his primary concerns were particularistic rather than generalizing. It was his goal to devise a scheme that could explain the occurrence of different types of cultures in similar environments, and of cultures with similar characteristics in widely differing environmental situations, "rather than . . . derive[ing] general principles applicable to any cultural-environmental situation" (Steward 1959:87). The cultural type was defined by the nature of the ecological adaptation reflected in the "core" characteristics, which Steward identified as those expressed in the technology and economy, plus the highest level of sociocultural integration achieved by the group, whether family band, village,

CHIEFDOM, or STATE. His method allowed both synchronic and diachronic analysis of short- and long-term evolutionary processes (Orlove 1977, 1980:238).

Steward saw the progression of societies through various levels of economic and social integration, from lesser to greater degrees of complexity, as an expression of the process of cultural EVOLUTION, a concept that is central to this theoretical scheme. He saw such evolution as being multilinear, with each culture following its own trajectory rather than repeating a fixed unilinear sequence of stages (Steward 1955, 1977).

Steward described the three basic procedures of cultural ecological research method as (1) analysis of the relationship between technology and the environment; (2) the study of behavior patterns implicated in exploiting a particular regional environment; and (3) determining the extent to which nonsubsistence aspects of the culture are affected by subsistence practices (Steward 1959:90–91). The principal objective of culture ecological research was "to determine whether similar adjustments occur in similar environments" (p. 92), and to account for cultural dissimilarities between populations occupying similar environments in terms of differences in their adaptive strategies.

While this defined the basic methodological goals, specific techniques for their realization developed only gradually, in the course of a number of important field studies utilizing cultural ecology as a paradigmatic framework for research. Among these were those of Stuart Struever, who employed cultural ecology in his studies of Woodland settlement and subsistence in the lower Illinois Valley (Struever 1968). In the 1970s Knud Fladmark applied cultural ecological principles in the construction of his paleoenvironmental model of Northwest Coast prehistory (Fladmark 1975). Cultural ecology has continued to provide a framework for archaeological investigations seeking to explain prehistoric cultures as ecologically adaptive systems (Bettinger 1978; Ferring 1986; Erlandson 1988). The continuing emphasis on subsistence and settlement pattern research in American archaeology is a direct result of Steward's cultural ecological orientation and method, which focused American archaeological research on those features of the cultural "core" most directly affected by environmental factors. The pioneering work of Steward's student Gordon R. Willey in settlement ARCHAEOLOGY (Willey 1953) was a result of his association with Steward, whose ideas and influence are apparent in Willey's work, as well as in many other ecologically oriented archaeological field studies since the 1960s.

The influence of the concepts of cultural ecology on contemporary archaeology in the Americas can scarcely be overestimated. The importance of environmental and ecological factors has assumed a paramount position in the thinking of most Americanist archaeologists in recent years, often to the exclusion of any humanistic factors as determinants of cultural patterns (Meighan 1982). While this mind-set has generated a plethora of studies and research designs producing quantifiable results, objective comparisons, and testable hypotheses, it has also substantially contributed to the current polarization of archaeology into two groups, the ecological-materialist "processualists" and the structuralist-oriented "postprocessualists" (see ARCHAEOLOGY). As Philip Kohl has pointed out (Kohl 1981:101), most beginning archaeological textbooks now in use in North America present a materialist viewpoint derived principally from the concepts first proposed by Steward, which have figured most prominently in shaping the theoretical orientation and research habits of several generations of American archaeologists. The benefits of this approach have been numerous, despite its limitations, and Steward's influence is likely to continue as a significant factor in shaping the archaeological goals of the future.

REFERENCES

Behrens, Clifford A. 1986. The cultural ecology of dietary change accompanying changing activity patterns among the Shipibo. Human Ecology 14(4):367–396.

Bettinger, R. L. 1978. Alternative adaptive strategies in the prehistoric Great Basin. Journal of Anthropological Research 34:27–46.

Erlandson, Jon McVey. 1988. Cultural ecology on the southern California coast at 5000 BP: a comparative analysis of CA-SBA-75. Coyote Press, Salinas, Calif.

Ferring, C. Reid. 1986. Late Holocene cultural ecology in the southern Plains: perspectives from Delaware Canyon, Oklahoma. Plains Anthropologist 31 (114, pt. 2):55–82.

Fladmark, Knut. 1975. A palaeoecological model for Northwest Coast prehistory. National Museum of Canada, Ottawa.

Kohl, Philip L. 1981. Materialist approaches in prehistory. Annual Review of Anthropology 10:89–118.

Larkin, Robert P., and Gary L. Peters. 1983. Cultural ecology. In A dictionary of concepts in human geography. Greenwood Press, Westport, Conn., pp. 49–52.

Meighan, Clement W. 1982. Environment and explanation in archaeology. In Culture and ecology: eclectic perspectives, John G. Kennedy and Robert B. Edgerton, eds. American Anthropological Association, Washington, D.C., pp. 84–94.

Murphy, R. F. 1977. Introduction: the anthropological theories of Julian H. Steward. In Evolution and ecology: essays on social transformations by J. H. Steward, Jane C. Steward and Robert F. Murphy, eds. University of Illinois Press, Urbana, pp. 1–39.

Orlove, B. S. 1977. Cultural ecology: a critical essay and a bibliography. Institute of Ecology Publication 13. University of California, Davis.

———. 1980. Ecological anthropology. Annual Review of Anthropology 9:235–273.

Steward, Julian H. 1955. The theory of culture change: the methodology of multilinear evolution. University of Illinois Press, Urbana.

———. 1959. The concept and method of cultural ecology, reprinted from The theory of culture change, in Readings in anthropology. Vol. 2: Cultural anthropology, Morton H. Fried, ed. Crowell, New York, pp. 81–95.

———. 1968. Cultural ecology. In International encyclopedia of the social sciences, D. I. Sills, ed. Macmillan, New York, vol. 4, pp. 337–344.

———. 1977. Evolution and ecology: essays on social transformation by Julian H. Steward, Jane C. Steward and Robert F. Murphy, eds. University of Illinois Press, Urbana.

Struever, Stuart. 1968. Woodland subsistence-settlement systems in the lower Illinois Valley. In New perspectives in archaeology, S. R. Binford and L. R. Binford, eds. Aldine, Chicago, pp. 285–312.

Vayda, A. P., and Roy Rappaport. 1968. Ecology, cultural and non-cultural. In Intro-
    duction to cultural anthropology, J. A. Clifton, ed. Houghton Mifflin, Boston,
    pp. 476–498.
Willey, Gordon R. 1953. Prehistoric settlement patterns in the Viru Valley, Peru. Bureau
    of American Ethnology/Bulletin 155. Smithsonian Institution, Washington, D. C.

SOURCES OF ADDITIONAL INFORMATION

Comprehensive discussions of Steward's cultural ecological method and theory, and
its development out of his Great Basin fieldwork, include Robert F. Murphy's "Introduction: the anthropological theories of Julian H Steward," in *Evolution and Ecology:
Essays on Social Transformation by Julian H. Steward*, Jane C. Steward and R. F.
Murphy, eds. (Urbana, University of Illinois Press, 1977), pp. 1–39. Another review of
the concept is in Robert A. Manners's obituary of Steward in *American Anthropologist*
75(1973):886–903, which includes a complete bibliography of Steward's publications.
A. P. Vayda and Roy Rappaport (1968; see References for citation) discuss Steward's
contribution within the historical context of the development of an ecological approach
in anthropology: "Ecology, cultural and non-cultural," in *Introduction to Cultural Anthropology*, James A. Clifton, ed. (Boston, Houghton Mifflin, 1968), pp. 476–497;
pp. 483–489 are specifically devoted to cultural ecology. Additional information may be
found in three review articles in *Annual Review of Anthropology*: Orlove 1980; Kohl
1981 (both cited above—see References); and R. M. Keesing, "Theories of culture,"
Annual Review of Anthropology 3(1974):373–397.

Most introductory texts on archaeology include some discussion of the basic concept
and method. See, e.g., David Hurst Thomas, *Archaeology* (New York, Holt, Rinehart
and Winston, 1979), pp. 121–126; Brian Fagan, *In the Beginning*, 6th ed. (Glenview,
Ill., Scott, Foresman, 1988), pp. 68–70; Robert Sharer and Wendy Ashmore, *Fundamentals of Archaeology* (Menlo Park, Calif., Benjamin Cummings, 1979), pp. 61–66.

For Steward's initial published statements on the merits of the cultural ecological
approach, see Steward, "Ecological aspects of southwestern society," *Anthropos*
32(1937):87–104; and *Basin-Plateau Aboriginal Sociopolitical Groups* (Washington,
D.C., Bureau of American Ethnology Bulletin 120, 1938). His most formalized expositions are in his article on cultural ecology for the *International Encyclopedia of the
Social Sciences* (see citation in References); in *The Theory of Culture Change* (pp. 30–
42; see References); and in "The concept and method of cultural ecology" (reprinted
1959; see References).

An informative discussion of the impact of cultural ecology on cultural anthropology
studies is Robert Winthrop, "Cultural ecology," in *A Dictionary of Concepts in Cultural
Anthropology* (Westport, Conn., Greenwood Press, 1991), pp. 47–50, which includes
bibliographic references.

For reports of current cultural ecological studies, see current and future issues of
American Anthropologist, *American Antiquity*, *Current Anthropology*, *Human Ecology*,
and *Annual Review of Anthropology*.

CULTURAL MATERIALISM. 1. As employed in archaeology, the general
concept that all aspects of human CULTURE are explicable in terms of the economic or productive system, which is considered to be the primary determinant
of a human society's social structure and of its ideological system, or superstructure. 2. Specifically, the method of cultural analysis and its rationale de-

veloped by Marvin Harris (1979), based upon the principle of economic determinism attributed to Karl Marx.

While materialist views of human culture and evolution can be traced back to the Enlightenment (Harris 1968; Kohl 1981), the method and theory of the approach called cultural materialism are firmly grounded in the theory of economic determinism first formulated by Karl Marx in the nineteenth century. In the first half of the twentieth century, Marxian principles were invoked to explain the development of past human societies by Vere Gordon Childe (1951), whose work subsequently influenced the growth of archaeology and its subdisciplines. A materialist orientation is a natural one to the archaeologist, given the nature of his or her primary data; and archaeologists have therefore tended to assume significant correlations between the material products of past human societies and the manner in which these societies functioned (Kohl 1981:90).

The most salient feature of the cultural materialist school of analysis is its emphasis on the primary causal role of economic and material factors in determining the growth and structure of society in all its aspects, from the system of production through the division of labor, patterns of family life, relations between the sexes, the class structure, and even the ideology or belief system. According to the cultural materialist viewpoint, all these social phenomena may be explained in terms of the economic system, or mode of production.

Marvin Harris, the principal exponent of the cultural materialist approach, has identified five "etic behavioral categories" common to all societies (Harris 1979). Two of these, the mode of production and the mode of reproduction, comprise the social *infrastructure*; domestic economy and political economy make up the *structure*; and the fifth category, the *superstructure*, is the realm of ideology, religion and its rituals, art, sports and entertainments—in short, all those areas of human activity not directly implicated in production, reproduction, or economy. Only the infrastructure is conceived as having determinative power, and therefore it is the nature of the modes of production and reproduction, which are most closely linked to the environment and to exploitation of its resources, that determines the characteristics of the social structure and superstructure. This position has much in common with Julian Steward's conception of economic and subsistence factors as comprising the "core" features of any given culture, which, together with environmental factors, may be used to explain cultural differences between human groups (Steward 1955; see also CULTURAL ECOLOGY). The basic principles of cultural materialism fit within the currently prevailing ecological materialist paradigm, which has provided the basic theoretical frame of reference for North American archaeology since the time of Steward's work in the 1930s, through the "NEW" ARCHAEOLOGY of the 1960s and 1970s, and up to the present.

Harris's cultural materialism, while providing an analytical scheme useful to archaeologists, does not deal directly with the role played by material culture in human societies, or how ARTIFACTS may provide information about specific ways in which the five behavioral categories may have operated in past societies known only through their material remains. Although some archaeologists consider this to be cultural materialism's most serious flaw, of equal importance is its inability to account adequately for characteristics of the superstructure in terms of modes of production and reproduction alone, a flaw that may be attributable to the failure to develop sufficient middle-range connecting arguments (see MIDDLE-RANGE RESEARCH).

Another problem in the application of Harris's behavioral categories to the analysis of real-world data is the difficulty of operationalizing them. Since these categories are so broadly conceived, and since all behavioral phenomena have both material and mental components, it may be virtually impossible to classify all human activities according to Harris's scheme (Adams 1981:603).

Attempts to operationalize Harris's categories and identify the causal relationships between the various elements of human experience have demonstrated the basically systemic nature of his analytical scheme, which has been described as

> . . . primarily unidirectional with feedback loops, superstructure and structure being conceived as acting back on infrastructure. The assumption underlying this notion is that infrastructure changes are consistently prior in time and more powerful in their deterministic effects. . . . (Cohen 1981:609)

An additional criticism is that despite Harris's attempt to make explicit all the assumptions on which his arguments are based, and his claim to having achieved this, unstated assumptions do in fact underlie a number of them (Schiffer 1983:192).

An overall weakness of the cultural materialist position, like that of the ecological materialist paradigm as a whole, is that it is supremely reductionistic in attempting to account for all cultural phenomena in economic and SUBSISTENCE terms, while ignoring the causal potential of emic superstructural categories, such as ideology, for determining specific qualities and characteristics of cultures past or present (see Johnson 1982a, 1982b). Despite the difficulty of objectifying and measuring the influences of human thought and belief on the growth and change of cultures, this continues to be a subject worthy of investigation by archaeologists, albeit a frequently neglected one.

Despite these myriad criticisms, archaeologists continue to find cultural materialism a useful interpretative framework, and some regard it as providing "the most powerful and productive set of premises extant in the discipline for the explanation of cultural similarity and difference, stability and change" (Price 1982:709). Barbara Price, in her 1982 position paper, devoted considerable energy to supporting the cultural materialist viewpoint as a superior alternative to the major competing paradigm, that of the cognitive structuralists (e.g., Leone 1982; Hodder 1982, 1986).

The influence of cultural materialist thought has been widespread in archaeological studies in the last third of the twentieth century, particularly in NEW WORLD ARCHAEOLOGY (e.g., Sanders and Price 1968; MacNeish 1972, 1978; Price 1977; Sanders 1977; Ross 1978). Although its precepts have not always been specifically invoked by the authors of archaeological studies, the influence of Harris's work continues to be discernible in most contemporary ecological-materialist research.

REFERENCES

Adams, Richard N. 1981. Natural selection, energetics, and "cultural materialism."
    Current Anthropology 22(6):603–624.
Childe, Vere Gordon. 1951. Social evolution. Watts, London.
Cohen, Ronald. 1981. [Comment on Adams, Natural selection, energetics, and "cultural
    materialism"]. Current Anthropology 22(6):609–610.
Harris, Marvin. 1968. The rise of anthropological theory. Crowell, New York.
———. 1979. Cultural materialism: the struggle for a science of culture. Random House,
    New York.
Hodder, Ian. 1986. Reading the past: current approaches to interpretation in archaeology.
    Cambridge University Press.
———, ed. 1982. Symbolic and structural archaeology. Cambridge University Press.
Johnson, Allen. 1982a. Reductionism in cultural ecology: the Amazon case. Current
    Anthropology 23:413–428.
———. 1982b. Nonreductionistic cultural ecology. In Culture and ecology: eclectic
    perspectives, John G. Kennedy and Robert B. Egerton, eds. AAA Special Pub-
    lication 15. Washington, D.C.
Kohl, Philip L. 1981. Materialist approaches in prehistory. Annual Review of Anthro-
    pology 10:89–118.
Leone, Mark P. 1982. Some opinions about recovering mind. American Antiquity
    47(4):742–760.
MacNeish, R. S. 1978. The science of archaeology? Duxbury Press, Belmont, Mass.
———, ed. 1972. The prehistory of the Tehuacán Valley. Vol. 5: Excavations and
    reconnaissance. University of Texas Press, Austin.
Price, Barbara J. 1977. Shifts in production and organization: a cluster-interaction model.
    Current Anthropology 18(2):209–234.
———. 1982. Culture materialism: a theoretical review. American Antiquity 47(4):709–
    741.
Ross, E. B. 1978. Food taboos, diet, and hunting strategy: the adaptation to animals in
    Amazon cultural ecology. Current Anthropology 19:1–36.
Sanders, William T. 1977. Resource utilization and political evolution in the Tehuacán
    Valley. In The explanation of prehistoric change, J. N. Hill, ed. University of
    New Mexico Press, Albuquerque, pp. 231–258.
Sanders, William T., and Barbara J. Price. 1968. Mesoamerica: the evolution of a
    civilization. Random House, New York.
Schiffer, Michael B. 1983. Cultural materialism: the struggle for a science of culture
    [review]. American Antiquity 48(1):190–194.
Steward, Julian H. 1955. The theory of culture change. University of Illinois Press,
    Urbana.

SOURCES OF ADDITIONAL INFORMATION

One of the most complete discussions of cultural materialism is in the essay by Philip
Kohl, "Materialist approaches in prehistory," *Annual Review of Anthropology*
10(1981):89–118, in which the author places Harris's scheme within the context of its
historical and philosophical antecedents and summarizes the literature of materialist
thought in both anthropology and archaeology. The intellectual foundations of Harris's
theoretical work are discussed by Guy Oakes in "The epistemological foundations of

cultural materialism," *Dialectical Anthropology* 6(1981):1–21. Brief introductory summaries may be found in Robert J. Wenke, "Explaining the evolution of cultural complexity: a review," *Advances in Archaeological Method and Theory* 4(1981):79–127 (pp. 87–92 cover cultural materialist explanation); and in such introductory archaeological texts as David Hurst Thomas, *Archaeology* (New York, Holt, Rinehart and Winston, 1979), pp. 118–120; Robert Sharer and Wendy Ashmore, *Fundamentals of Archaeology* (Menlo Park, Calif., Benjamin Cummings, 1979), p. 510, which emphasizes the influence of V. Gordon Childe on the development of the cultural materialist orientation; and Brian M. Fagan, *In the Beginning: An Introduction to Archaeology*, 6th ed. (Glenview, Ill., Scott, Foresman, 1988), p. 24.

One of the best critiques of the cultural materialist position is that by Drew Westen, "Cultural materialism: food for thought or bum steer?" *Current Anthropology* 22(6)(1984):603–624, who has pointed out a variety of difficulties with both the model and its applications. P. J. Magnarella has evaluated the Harris model from a probabilistic viewpoint in "Cultural materialism and the problem of probabilities," *American Anthropologist* 84(1982):138–145; Allen Johnson has addressed the problem of the reductionistic nature of all such explanatory schemes (Johnson 1982a, 1982b; see References for citation). Further evaluation may be found in reviews of Harris's *Cultural Materialism* (1979) by Michael Schiffer (see References); T. Beidelman in *American Journal of Sociology* 87(1980):1245–1247; and Anthony F. C. Wallace in *American Anthropologist* 82(1980):423–426.

For a succinct summary of a cultural materialist interpretation of the ritualistic *kula* exchange practiced in New Guinea, illustrating the productive potential of a materialist approach to such phenomena, see David Hurst Thomas, "The kula exchange in cultural materialist perspective," in his *Archaeology* (New York, Holt, Rinehart and Winston, 1979), pp. 122–123.

The Kohl review article cited above (Kohl 1981) is probably the best overall guide to the literature of cultural materialism up to the date of its publication, although it is now out-of-date. The Price paper in *American Antiquity* (see References) includes an extensive bibliography, though it, too, is now outdated. Westen (1984; see above) cites some slightly later publications, as well as some relevant Marxist literature.

To locate more recent literature referring to the work of Harris and cultural materialism, the reader should check recent issues of the journals *Dialectical Anthropology* and *American Anthropologist*. Searching the *Social Sciences Citation Index* for citations to Harris's *Cultural Materialism* is also recommended.

CULTURAL RESOURCE MANAGEMENT (CRM). The application of management skills, such as planning, organizing, directing, controlling, and evaluating, to the achievement of legally defined goals for preserving cultural remains of the past, including archaeological SITES. In the United States, legally mandated preservation efforts include both historic sites and buildings, and prehistoric archaeological remains, including shipwrecks.

Although archaeological excavation inevitably destroys sites, this destruction is offset by careful recordkeeping, analysis and interpretation of finds, CURATION of materials, and publication of findings in reports. If these conditions are not met, excavation is equivalent in its effect to the destructive activities of looters and treasure hunters, who in digging up and stealing ARTIFACTS destroy the unique information every find has to offer the archaeologist.

Modern development has now been recognized as being as destructive as looting in its effects on cultural materials (Fowler 1982, 1986). Concern over the increasing impact of urbanization, industrial expansion, and other development on archaeological resources has led to the enactment, over the past several decades, of laws designed to protect and preserve archaeological sites, both in the United States and in other nations aware of their prehistoric heritage. In addition to being strongly conservation-oriented, laws now in effect in the United States authorize the application of management principles and techniques to preserving cultural remains, both prehistoric and historic, for future generations, under the rubric of cultural resource managment, or CRM (McGimsey and Davis 1977; Knudson 1986).

Prior to the development of legislation, efforts to protect archaeological resources were sporadic. Private efforts in the past resulted in the preservation of the Great Serpent Mound in Ohio, and some other sites. Worldwide organizations, such as UNESCO, have carried out some heroic preservation efforts, notably the relocation of ancient Egyptian temples threatened by the Aswan Dam project on the Nile. A similar planned dam project on the Usumacinta River, which forms part of the border between Mexico and northwestern Guatemala, would inundate several entire standing remains of ancient Maya cities and has not fared so well. Postponed for nearly two decades by the intervention of archaeologists, environmentalists, and other concerned groups, this project is now proceeding, without any plan to preserve the impacted cultural remains.

The earliest CRM legislation passed in the United States was the Antiquities Act of 1906, which protected only sites on land owned or controlled by the federal government. Many sites were subsequently excavated and reported through efforts by the federal government during the large river basin and dam construction projects carried out under federal programs in the 1930s. With the beginning of freeway construction and extensive real estate development following World War II, SITE destruction reached wholesale proportions. The Reservoir Salvage Act of 1960 produced some large-scale rescue archaeology similar to efforts authorized by the federal government in the 1930s.

The Historic Preservation Act of 1966 was one of the first really effective laws aimed at preserving sites rather than merely recording them prior to their destruction. Under its terms, the federal government was required to set up a nationwide system of identifying and protecting "historic places," and the National Register of Historic Places was established. The law's provisions apply equally to prehistoric archaeological sites. A further provision was the protection of sites from the effects of development projects. The National Environmental Policy Act of 1969 went even further, outlining a broad policy of government planning for land use and resource management. With the passage of the Archaeological Resources Protection Act of 1979, removing archaeological materials from federal lands without a permit became a felony offense, with appropriate penalties; but unfortunately it gives no protection to sites on private lands, which continue to be plundered.

Enforcement of these laws has been extremely difficult, and penalties imposed on the few who have been prosecuted have been largely ineffective as a deterrent to the continuing destruction of sites. Professional organizations, such as the Society for American Archaeology and the Society of Professional Archaeologists, continue their lobbying and public education efforts for more effective laws and broader awareness of the problem. The activities of some private groups, such as the Archaeological Conservancy, which has purchased and preserved archaeological sites threatened with destruction, have also had an impact on the preservation effort.

The process of compliance with existing CRM laws has become a complicated and bureaucratic one. It consists of three steps: a review and assessment of cultural resources about to be impacted, with recommendations for their treatment; reporting of already identified sites in the target area, and recommending research needed to evaluate their significance (Tainter and Lucas 1983); and developing a management plan to implement the protection and preservation of endangered cultural remains. In practice, this can become a lengthy bureaucratic process, laden with red tape (Butler 1987).

CRM laws are often implemented by contractual arrangements between government agencies or private businesses and archaeologists; hence the phrase "contract archaeology," referring to the actual work of implementing CRM legislation. Many archaeologists now operate as independent contractors, carrying out the compliance process on a fee basis for companies or government agencies that must comply with local and federal preservation laws before undertaking activities impacting cultural resources.

The goals of academic and contract archaeology are sometimes incompatible, which has led to a certain polarization of interests between academic and contract archaeologists. While problem-focused research designs addressing questions of importance to archaeological researchers can conceivably be implemented by contracted archaeology projects, in practice this is seldom done (Berry 1984; Frison 1984). Limits on time and funding often result in purely descriptive investigations by contract archaeologists, and minimal reports of very limited distribution that are often inaccessible to most archaeologists as well as to the public. Compliance with the law is frequently minimal. The fact that contract projects now employ many more archaeologists than do academic institutions, and opportunities for academic employment are shrinking, has exacerbated this division.

Professional ethics with respect to contracted CRM projects is another problem area. Ethical questions related to the treatment of early human remains excavated from prehistoric burials are only one of many such problems contract archaeologists must face (Johnson 1977; McGimsey and Davis 1977; North Carolina, General Statutes, ch. 70, 1984). Ethics, professional training, and the compliance process are all matters requiring considerable attention and improvement.

Some of these issues are currently being addressed by professional organizations of archaeologists, with such laudable results as the professional code of ethics developed by the Society of Professional Archaeologists. Another important area that has scarcely been addressed, and one that will require ongoing efforts in the future, is the preservation of archaeological resources on private lands (Ruffini 1986).

REFERENCES

Berry, Michael S. 1984. Sampling and predictive modeling on federal lands in the West. American Antiquity 49(4):842–853.

Butler, William B. 1987. Significance and other frustrations in the CRM process. American Antiquity 52(4):820–829.

Fowler, Don D. 1982. Cultural resources management. Advances in Archaeological Method and Theory 5:1–50.

————. 1986. Conserving American archaeological resources. In American archaeology past and future. Smithsonian Institution/Society for American Archaeology, Washington, D.C., pp. 135–162.

Frison, George C. 1984. The Carter/Kerr-McGee Paleoindian sites: cultural resource management in archaeological research. American Antiquity 42(2):288–314.

Johnson, E., comp. 1977. Archaeology and native Americans. In The management of archaeological resources: The Airlie House report, C. R. McGimsey III and H. A. Davis, eds. Special publication of the Society for American Archaeology, Washington, D.C., pp. 90–96.

Knudson, Ruthann. 1986. Contemporary cultural resource management. In American archaeology past and future. Smithsonian Institution/Society for American Archaeology, Washington, D.C., pp. 395–413.

McGimsey, Charles R. III, and Hester A. Davis, eds. 1977. The management of archaeological resources: the Airlie House report. Special publication of the Society for American Archaeology, Washington, D.C.

North Carolina. Laws, etc. 1991. General Statutes of North Carolina, Chapter 70, Indian antiquities, archaeological resources and unmarked human skeletal remains protection. Charlottesville, Va., Michieco, pp. 81–90.

Ruffini, Franco. 1986. Public programs for protecting archaeological resources on private property. Columbus, Ohio. (Processed)

Tainter, Joseph A., and G. John Lucas. 1983. Epistemology of the significance concept. American Antiquity 48(4):707–719.

SOURCES OF ADDITIONAL INFORMATION

The most complete general statements of the goals and present state of cultural resource management are in Fowler 1982 and 1986 (see References for citations). The 1982 review article includes a very lengthy listing of bibliographic references and laws, still very useful although out-of-date. Also very informative is Leslie Wildesen's related article, "The study of impacts on archaeological sites," *Advances in Archaeological Method and Theory* 5(1982):51–96, which discusses the effects of fire and vandalism, as well as of natural processes such as erosion, on archaeological SITES, and includes an extensive bibliography. A third useful source of background information is the paper by Knudson (1986; see References). For one archaeologist's view of the field of CRM, see Leslie E.

Wildesen, "Cultural resource management: a personal view," *Practicing Anthropology* 2(2)(1980):10, 22–23. Questions of archaeological ethics relative to cultural resource management, preservation, the reburial issue, treatment of looted materials, and other matters are considered in the collection of papers edited by E. L. Green, *Ethics and Values in Archaeology* (New York, Free Press, 1984). The journals *American Antiquity*, *Archaeology*, and *Journal of Field Archaeology*, as well as *Annual Review of Anthropology* and annual volumes of *Archaeological Method and Theory*, should be consulted for latest publications.

CULTURE. 1. The sum of human knowledge and adaptive skills that have enabled the human species to survive and expand into all world environments. 2. The set of particular adaptive skills and strategies acquired by a human population, and transmitted through learning from one generation to the next within that group. 3. In archaeology, the totality of material remains, consisting of ARTIFACTS, ecofacts, surviving architecture, and observable contextual patterns documenting the lifeway of a past human population.

> . . . the American archaeologist . . . lacks a specific terminology that is standard with his fellow students, by means of which he can clearly express his maturing concepts. He stretches old meanings to apply to his needs, and finds himself justly criticised . . . for his extraordinarily indefinite, inaccurate uses of the term "culture," which, for want of a more specific term, is made to serve a multitude of specific purposes for which it never was intended. (McKern 1939:303)

The definition of culture is a problem that has long engaged the interest and energies of anthropologists and archaeologists. Many volumes have been devoted to the subject, and the literature is far too vast to be reviewed here (see, e.g., Kroeber and Kluckhohn 1952). Within archaeology, however, culture has taken on more limited and specific meanings, and the term is most frequently used to refer to the total configuration of artifactual remains, produced by humans in the past, that have survived in the ARCHAEOLOGICAL RECORD in the form of tools and other manufactured objects; or, more specifically, to the total material inventory of remains produced by members of a particular social group in the past. The present discussion will be confined to this more restricted concept of an *archaeological culture*. This usage of the term and its conceptual connotation have been discussed by C. F. Meinander:

> In archaeology, when we use the term "culture," it has a special significance. V. Gordon Childe (1929) was the first to define an "archaeological culture," but the concept was in use in the whole of Europe two or three decades before he came on the scene. I myself prefer to use David Clarke's definition of 1968: "An archaeological culture is a polythetic set of specific and comprehensive artifact types which consistently recur together in assemblages within a limited geographic area." (Meinander 1981:101–102)

An archaeological culture is in fact sometimes conceived in very limited terms, as consisting entirely of an ASSEMBLAGE of stone tools of restricted distribution, and representing a particular set of behavioral activities occurring in a particular time and place (Renfrew and Bahn 1991:485). This concept of culture was characteristic of archaeology in the earlier decades of the twentieth century.

Since the advent of the "new," processual archaeology in the 1960s, more inclusive definitions than this have become standard. The concept of culture has sometimes been extended to embrace all material vestiges of a past lifeway, including food remains and other ecofacts, pottery and/or basketry, art objects, architectural remains, hearths and other household features, and the patterns of relationship that may be discerned in the distributions of these remains within SITES.

Culture is now more frequently viewed by archaeologists as the total non-genetically transmitted adaptive pattern acquired and perpetuated through time by a human group, which will include not only the economic and technological adaptive systems reflected in its material remains, but also the social and ideological systems developed as part of its overall ADAPTATION. Ideological systems of the past are, of course, not directly accessible to the archaeologist, but many of their precepts and practices may be inferred, at least in part, from material evidence (Meltzer 1981).

Some postprocessual archaeologists have claimed that material culture shapes and embodies human behavior, including mental processes, and encodes past behavior in its attributes, which can be "read" like a text (Hodder 1986; Tilley 1990). The American archaeologist James Deetz has also regarded material culture as playing a dynamic role in society, not only *reflecting* human behavior but also *affecting* that behavior, much as Ian Hodder considers artifacts as "dynamic material symbols" playing an active role in shaping cultural behavior (Deetz 1974, 1977a, 1977b; Hodder 1989).

The possible ways in which artifacts may affect human motivation and behavior have most frequently been investigated by historical archaeologists, who have the advantage of written or oral accounts to document the importance of material objects in the lives of those who used them (Deetz 1977a, 1977b; Ferguson 1977; Fitting 1977; Hodder 1986, 1989; Meltzer 1981; Hugill and Dickson 1988). Material culture is also necessarily a strong focus of ethnoarchaeological investigations designed to reconstruct past behavior from the treatment accorded artifacts by the members of modern human groups (Ascher 1968, 1975; Hayden and Cannon 1984; see also ETHNOARCHAEOLOGY). A famous archaeological project in modern material culture studies (Ascher 1975; Rathje 1979; Meltzer 1981; Schlereth 1982, 1985; Miller 1987), designed to investigate various aspects of discard patterns of contemporary American households, including differences between socioeconomic groups in urban settings, has revealed some unexpected data concerning the formation of the ARCHAEOLOGICAL RECORD of our own time, as well as producing information useful for the teaching of archaeology (Rathje 1974); the latter is one of the major goals of modern material culture studies.

Other aims of this type of research include testing the validity of archaeological assumptions and principles, recording the archaeological record of today, and linking this record with that of the past (Rathje 1979; Lemmonier 1986).

REFERENCES

Ascher, Robert. 1968. Time's arrow and the archaeology of a contemporary community. In Settlement archaeology, K. C. Chang, ed. National Press Books, Palo Alto, Calif., pp. 43–52.

————. 1975. Tin-can archaeology. Historical Archaeology 8:7–16.

Childe, V. Gordon. 1929. The Danube in prehistory. Clarendon Press, Oxford.

Clarke, David L. 1968. Analytical archaeology. Methuen, London.

Deetz, James. 1974. A cognitive historical model for American material culture, 1620–1835. In Reconstructing complex societies, Charlotte B. Moore, ed. Supplement to Bulletin of the Schools of American Research No. 20.

————. 1977a. Material culture and archaeology—what's the difference? In Historical archaeology and the importance of material things, Leland Ferguson, ed. Special Publication Series No. 2. Society for Historical Archaeology, Tucson, pp. 9–12.

————. 1977b. In small things forgotten: the archaeology of early American life. Anchor Press/Doubleday, Garden City, N.Y.

Ferguson, Leland, ed. 1977. Historical archaeology and the importance of material things. Special Publication Series No. 2. Society for Historical Archaeology, Tucson.

Fitting, James E. 1977. The structure of historical archaeology and the importance of material things. In Historical archaeology and the importance of material things, Leland Ferguson, ed. Special Publication Series No. 2. Society for Historical Archaeology, Tucson, pp. 62–68.

Hayden, Brian, and Aubrey Cannon. 1984. The structure of material systems: ethnoarchaeology in the Maya highlands. SAA Papers No. 3. Society for American Archaeology, Washington, D.C.

Hodder, Ian. 1986. Reading the past: current approaches to interpretation in archaeology. Cambridge University Press.

————, ed. 1989. The meanings of things. Vol. 6: One world archaeology. Unwin Hyman, London.

Hugill, Peter J., and D. Bruce Dickson, eds. 1988. The transfer and transformation of ideas and material culture. Texas A&M Press, College Station.

Kroeber, A. L., and Clyde Kluckhohn. 1952. Culture: a critical review of concepts and definitions. Papers of the Peabody Museum of American Archaeology and Ethnology 47, no. 1. Harvard University, Cambridge, Mass.

Lemmonier, P. 1986. The study of material culture today: toward an anthropology of technical systems. Journal of Anthropological Archaeology 5(2):147–186.

McKern, W. C. 1939. The Midwestern Taxonomic Method as an aid to archaeological culture study. American Antiquity 4:301–313.

Meinander, C. G. 1981. The concept of culture in European archaeological literature. In Towards a history of archaeology, Glyn Daniel, ed. Thames and Hudson, London, pp. 100–111.

Meltzer, David J. 1981. Ideology and material culture. In Modern material culture: the archaeology of us, Richard A. Gould and Michael B. Schiffer, eds. Academic Press, New York, pp. 113–125.

Miller, Daniel. 1987. Material culture and mass consumption: social archaeology. Basil Blackwell, New York.

Rathje, William L. 1974. The garbage project: a new way of looking at the problems of archaeology. Archaeology 27(4):236–241.

———. 1979. Modern material culture studies. Advances in Archaeological Method and Theory 2:1–37.

Renfrew, Colin, and Paul Bahn. 1991. Archaeology: theories, methods and practice. Thames and Hudson, New York.

Schlereth, Thomas J., ed. 1982. Material culture studies in America. American Association for State and Local History. Nashville, Tenn.

———. 1985. Material culture: a research guide. University Press of Kansas, Lawrence.

Tilley, Christopher, ed. 1990. Reading material culture: structuralism, hermeneutics and post-structuralism. Basil Blackwell, Oxford and Cambridge, Mass.

SOURCES OF ADDITIONAL INFORMATION

An inclusive sample of the many ways in which anthropologists have defined the concept of culture may be found in Alfred Kroeber and Clyde Kluckhohn, *Culture: A Critical Review of Concepts and Definitions*, Papers of the Peabody Museum of American Archaeology and Ethnology, 47, no. 1 (Cambridge, Mass., Harvard University, 1952). For reviews of the concept of culture from the viewpoints of cultural anthropology and physical anthropology, respectively, see the two articles titled "Culture" in Robert Winthrop, *A Dictionary of Concepts in Cultural Anthropology* (Westport, Conn., Greenwood Press, 1991), pp. 50–61; and Joan Stevenson, *A Dictionary of Concepts in Physical Anthropology* (Westport, Conn., Greenwood Press, 1991), pp. 68–80, both of which include extensive bibliographical information.

Important publications in the area of archaeological material culture studies include A. M. Byers, "Structure, meaning, action and things, the duality of material cultural mediation," *Journal for the Theory of Social Behavior* 21(1)(1991):1–29; D. D. Davis, "Hereditary emblems: material culture in the context of social change," *Journal of Anthropological Archaeology* 4(3)(1985):149–176; and P. Lemmonier, "The study of material culture today: toward an anthropology of technical systems," *Journal of Anthropological Archaeology* 5(2)(1986):147–186, all of which include substantial lists of references to other recent literature. To update the information in these publications, the reader should consult latest issues of *American Antiquity*, *Journal of Anthropological Archaeology*, *Historical Archaeology*, and the pertinent annual reviews.

CULTURE AREA. 1. A concept used in archaeology that originated in ethnology and has been defined as "a geographic region within which the cultures show considerable similarity to each other and lack of similarity to cultures in adjacent areas" (Jennings 1968:4). 2. The basis of a taxonomic system for classifying cultures according to the distribution of cultural traits through geographic space.

The culture area concept was a consequence of the reaction against the developmentalist evolutionary thinking that dominated anthropology and archaeology in the nineteenth century. It represents the shift from diachronic to synchronic approaches to cultural phenomena that occurred around the end of the nineteenth century, a turning away from the study of cultural change through time to a greater emphasis on the description of cultures as they exist in the present.

Although the culture area concept as it is currently conceived and applied by anthropologists and archaeologists is usually attributed to Alfred Kroeber (Kroeber 1939), its roots go further back in time. As Kroeber himself noted (1939:4), the concept originated with the practice of classifying museum collections according to areas of geographic origin rather than according to developmental, evolutionary schemes such as the THREE-AGE SYSTEM.

In the late nineteenth century, the clustering of cultural features or traits within definable geographic areas, or ethnographic provinces, had been noted by the geographer Friedrich Ratzel and other members of the German-Austrian group of culture historians known as the Kulturkreislehre (Ratzel 1878–1880, 1896–1898). In 1895, a culture area classification for North America was worked out by Otis Mason (Winick 1958:38); and in a work published in 1915, William Henry Holmes used the museum method of classifying materials ''by ethnic areas, or areas of culture characterization'' (Holmes 1915:43) to divide the Americas into a 24-area scheme. Kroeber, in his later work dividing North America into his own cultural areas, cited some additional historical antecedents.

> By 1916, [the American linguist] Sapir in his Time Perspective discussed culture areas as something in general use; in 1917, Wissler codified those of native America—on the basis, largely, of current usage. There have been no serious modifications or criticisms of his scheme. (Kroeber 1939:4)

Kroeber further noted that the culture areal classifications developed by Holmes and by Clark Wissler (Wissler 1915) were essentially the same, differing only in some areas of eastern North America (Kroeber 1939:107). Kroeber's own scheme included some 19 culture areas of Mexico and Central America (1939:109–130), now usually included within the cultural ''superarea'' called Mesoamerica (Kirchhoff 1943, repr. 1952:19), which has also been termed an INTERACTION SPHERE (Freidel 1979). Kirchhoff, as well as Kroeber, took linguistic affiliations, in addition to material culture, SUBSISTENCE, and ceremonial practices, into consideration in characterizing these ethnogeographic units.

Although Kroeber's culture area classification for North and Central America comprises nearly 100 subdivisions (Kroeber 1939:Table 18), the ten largest units are those still used as ethnic cultural areas by American anthropologists and archaeologists for purposes of teaching and classification. These are usually called the Arctic, Subarctic, Northeast, Southeast, Plains, Southwest, California, Great Basin, Plateau, and Northwest Coast culture areas (Boxberger 1990).

Gordon Willey and Philip Phillips, in their landmark work developing basic archaeological units of analysis (Willey and Phillips 1958), defined an ''area'' as a spatial analytic unit corresponding to a geographic entity, but

> . . . very considerably larger than a region; it corresponds roughly to the *culture area*
> of the ethnographer. Archaeological areas, like regions have come into existence by
> common consent. . . . They tend to coincide with major physiographic divisions.
> (Willey and Phillips 1958:20; emphasis added)

As a unit of archaeological analysis, the culture area has retained both its
geographic and its cultural trait characteristics as part of its definition. Although
Willey and Phillips suggested a smaller unit, the *subarea*, as a logical subdivision
of the archaeological culture area, this has rarely been used by archaeologists,
who have tended to prefer the "region" as the next smaller analytic unit of
study.

One disadvantage of the culture area classifications that have been devised is
their dependence upon lists of "traits" for their definition. The cultural traits
used in defining culture areas have usually been the same ones used in the
construction of the first large anthropological data bank, the Human Relations
Area Files (HRAF), a project that originated with the Yale Cross-Cultural Survey
in 1937 and developed over several decades (Murdock 1957, 1962–1967; Murdock and White 1969; Moore 1970), as a tool for comparative cross-cultural
research. The comparative approach in ethnology, seeking common traits in
cultures of various types, enjoyed a vogue in American anthropology of the
1950s (Tax et al. 1952). Unfortunately, the cultural "traits," both material and
nonmaterial, that served as the basis for defining culture areas and for organizing
data in the HRAF, represent phenomena that frequently are not functionally
equivalent nor comparable in different cultural settings, but may have very
different meanings and derivations, as well as functions, in different societies.
The focus on cultural traits represents a now-outmoded approach to cultural data
that has been largely superseded by the study of cultures as adaptive systems.
Although the use of trait lists has been abandoned in both archaeology and
anthropology in favor of more holistic and dynamic approaches, some of the
products of earlier compilations of trait lists, including the HRAF and the culture
area concept, remain useful for organizing cultural data for some types of
analysis.

REFERENCES

Boxberger, Daniel L., ed. 1990. Native North Americans, an ethnohistorical approach.
    Kendall Hunt, Dubuque, Iowa.
Freidel, David A. 1979. Culture areas and interaction spheres: contrasting approaches to
    the emergence of civilization in the Maya lowlands. American Antiquity 44(1):36–
    54.
Holmes, William Henry. 1915. Areas of American culture characterization tentatively
    outlined as an aid in the study of the antiquities. In Anthropology in North America,
    by Franz Boas et al. G. E. Stechert, New York, pp. 42–75.
Jennings, Jesse D. 1968. Prehistory of North America. McGraw-Hill, New York.
Kirchhoff, Paul. 1943. Mesoamerica. Acta Americana 1:92–107. Mexico, D.F.
———. 1952. Mesoamerica. Reprinted in English translation by Norman McQuown, in
    Sol Tax et al., Heritage of conquest. Free Press, Glencoe, Ill., pp. 17–30. "Meso-

America" was printed as the opening chapter of Heritage of Conquest; The Eth-
nology of Middle America, by Sol Tax "and members of the Viking Fund Seminar
on Middle American Ethnology," which included (besides Kirchhoff and Tax):
Robert Redfield, Julio de la Fuente, Calixta Guiteras Holmes, Charles Wisdom,
Fernand Cámara, Benjamin D. Paul, Lois Paul, John Gillin, Ralph Beals, and
Gertrude B. Kurath.

Kroeber, Alfred L. 1939. Cultural and natural areas of native North America. University
of California Press, Berkeley.

Moore, Frank W. 1970. The Human Relations Area Files. In A handbook of method in
cultural anthropology, Raoul Naroll and Ronald Cohen, eds. Columbia University
Press, New York, pp. 640–675.

Murdock, George Peter. 1957. World ethnographic sample. American Anthropologist
59:664–687.

———. 1962–1967. Ethnographic atlas. In sequential issues of Ethnology.

Murdock, George Peter, and Douglas White. 1969. Standard cross-cultural sample. Ethnology 8:329–369.

Ratzel, Friedrich. 1878–1880. Die vereinigten Staaten von Nord-Amerika. 2 vols. R.
Oldenbourg, Munich.

———. 1896–1898. The history of mankind. A. J. Butler, translator. 3 vols. Macmillan,
New York. (Originally published 1885–1888)

Tax, Sol, et al. 1952. The sixteenth century and the twentieth: a comparison of culture
types and of culture areas. In Heritage of conquest, the ethnology of Middle
America. Free Press, Glencoe, Ill., pp. 262–281.

Willey, Gordon R., and Philip Phillips. 1958. Method and theory in American archaeology. University of Chicago Press.

Winick, Charles. 1958. Dictionary of anthropology. Littlefield, Adams, Ames, Iowa.

Wissler, Clark. 1915. Material cultures of the North American Indian. In Anthropology
in North America, by Franz Boas et al. G.E Stechert, New York, pp. 76–134.

SOURCES OF ADDITIONAL INFORMATION

Additional historical background on the culture area concept may be found in George
I. Quimby, "Cultural and natural areas before Kroeber," *American Antiquity*
19(1954):137–331. For information on culture areas of South America, see D. Stout,
"Culture types and culture areas in South America," *Papers of the Michigan Academy
of Science, Arts and Letters* 23(1938):73–86; and George P. Murdock, "The South
American culture areas," *Southwestern Journal of Anthropology* 7(1951):415–436. A
summary of the concept, including its role in diffusion studies and a critique, is in Robert
Winthrop, "Culture area," in *A Dictionary of Concepts in Cultural Anthropology* (Westport, Conn., Greenwood Press, 1991), pp. 61–63, which also includes a substantial
bibliography. Some applications of the culture area concept include M. Sivignon, "Frontier between two cultural areas, the case of Thessaly," *Annals of the New York Academy
of Sciences* 268(1976):43–58; G. Weiss, "The aboriginal culture areas of South America," *Anthropos* 75(3–4)(1980):405–415; C. Bernand and J. P. Digard, "From Tehran
to Tehuantepec: ethnology in the cultural area debate," *Homme* 26(1–2) (1986):63–80
(in French); and T. Buckley, "Kroeber theory of culture areas and the ethnology of
northwestern California," *Anthropological Quarterly* 62(1)(1989):15–26, as well as two
books: T. Jordan, *The European Culture Area, a Systematic Geography*, 2nd ed. (New
York, Harper & Row, 1988); and J. Cuisenier, *Europe as a Cultural Area* (The Hague,

Mouton, 1979). For later publications and information, see issues of *American Anthropologist*, *American Antiquity*, and *Ethnology*.

CULTURE HISTORY. A methodological approach to archaeological research centered on the problem of developing general chronologic schemes for relatively dating archaeological remains in terms of developmental cultural sequences.

Culture historians describe and classify archaeological materials in stylistic terms, and variation in STYLE is used as the basis of both typological and chronological classification. Historical chronologies are constructed from observation and study of stylistic changes in the material record, which are taken as indicative of temporal change as well in the overall pattern of the prehistoric culture under investigation.

Culture history in archaeology first appears in the work of members of the Kulturkreislehre school in Austria and Germany in the latter part of the nineteenth century (see CULTURE AREA), and was continued in Europe by the work of V. Gordon Childe in the early part of the twentieth century. However, in current usage the term refers specifically to the method developed by North American archaeologists in the early 1930s, utilizing the direct historical approach for constructing chronologies of prehistoric cultures known only through their material remains. It was the first attempt by American archaeologists to put archaeology on a scientific basis, and to remove it from the speculative and conjectural methods of earlier natural historians (Dunnell 1986:29).

Culture history is more concerned with statics, "with the space-time plotting of archaeological culture entities and . . . the relationships of these . . . one to another" (Willey 1985:351), than with the dynamic, or processual, aspect of cultural change. Its approach to archaeological data is essentially a descriptive and comparative one.

European culture historians developed a general historical sequence for the Old World beginning in the nineteenth century, in which several kinds of cultural chronology (Paleolithic/Mesolithic/Neolithic; Stone Age/Bronze Age/Iron Age; savagery/barbarism/civilization) were postulated for Europe and the Near East (Childe 1942; Trigger 1989; see also OLD WORLD ARCHAEOLOGY; PREHISTORY; THREE-AGE SYSTEM). A different chronological scheme was devised for the western hemisphere, beginning with the Paleo-Indian period, when nomadic hunting of Pleistocene megafauna was supposedly the principal method of SUBSISTENCE. This was followed by the Archaic period, a time when the inhabitants of the New World learned new methods of resource exploitation and ADAPTATION appropriate to the changed environment created by the recession of the continental ice sheets. The Formative period began with the appearance of pottery; this and subsequent cultural periods varied by individual geographic region. Such variants included Classic and Postclassic periods in some areas, characterized by the rise of ranked societies with permanent architecture and complex SOCIAL ORGANIZATION (see Willey and Phillips 1958; see also NEW WORLD ARCHAEOLOGY).

These cultural periods, based on relative chronologies derived from the study of stylistic variation in ARTIFACTS over time, established a basic framework for describing and classifying prehistoric SITES and material remains.

In American archaeology, the construction of culture history was achieved through the use of principles of the *direct historical approach*, beginning with the historically known Indian cultures of the New World and extrapolating backward by ANALOGY, from the characteristics of these directly observed aboriginal societies that had existed at the time of European contact to the prehistoric Indian cultures of the past (Steward 1942). The first culture historical synthesis of North American archaeology based on this principle was Alfred V. Kidder's *An Introduction to the Study of Southwestern Archaeology* (1924), published one year before V. Gordon Childe's culture-historical synthesis for Europe appeared (Childe 1925; Trigger 1989:188).

The second characteristic of the culture historic method was the use of "pattern or configurational descriptions" (Dunnell 1986:31). These were based on two underlying assumptions: (1) an inductive approach to research, in which generalizations are developed from many specific observations; and (2) a normative view of CULTURE which assumes that what a culture regards as normal behavior is determined by abstract rules, and further assumes that stylistic change in surviving ARTIFACTS reflects change in these behavioral rules (Fagan 1988:502). Both these assumptions are traceable to the work of Franz Boas, Nels C. Nelson, and others in the early twentieth century (Fagan 1988; Willey and Sabloff 1980).

To organize their data, culture historians required taxonomic units. Gordon Willey and Philip Phillips, in their *Method and Theory in American Archaeology* (1958), provided a classificatory scheme of chronological and spatial units comprising components and phases, regions and culture areas, stages, periods, horizons, and traditions, which was adopted as the standard for Americanist archaeology. Willey and Phillips's basic unit was the archaeological culture, a pattern or configuration of stylistic traits occurring together in space and time that could be seen to display temporal variation; and "variability . . . was a record of change. Variability allowed culture historians to tell time . . . " (Dunnell 1986:31).

The culture historical method as applied in archaeology consists of five basic steps, beginning with identification of a research area; this is followed by field reconnaissance and surface SURVEY of the area, then surface collection, to obtain artifact samples for developing a preliminary chronological sequence. The next step is selective excavation, to test the validity of the preliminary chronological sequence (by stratigraphic verification, if possible). The final step is analysis and classification of the excavation data, which will ultimately be used to refine the preliminary chronology into a generalizing synthesis. A basic goal of culture history was the development of culture historical area syntheses for regions, and finally for cultural areas. This five-step procedure constitutes the basic method of field archaeology followed by a majority of archaeologists in

America up to the beginning of problem-oriented field studies fostered by the "NEW" ARCHAEOLOGY of the 1960s and 1970s, and is still pursued by many traditionalists.

Gordon Willey (1985) has outlined some continuing problems in American archaeology that have preoccupied culture historians for several decades. Among these are the relationships of ancient Asian lithic industries to the earliest stone tool industries in the Americas; the origin and spread of ceramic technology in the New World; the historic relationships of the Hopewell culture to later Mississippian culture in North America, and of the pre-Columbian Mesoamerican cultures to those of North America. The resolution of such multifaceted problems as these will doubtless require their investigation using a variety of methodological and theoretical approaches, rather than simply the methods of culture history, as well as their redefinition in more specific terms at a variety of scales. That such problems continue to resist solution by the method of culture history is not surprising, for while "chronological and spatial ordering of archaeological data [is] a sound way of describing the past . . . [this] is of minimal use for explaining variability in the archaeological record or cultural process" (Fagan 1988:501). As Brian Fagan has noted, it is a useful approach for providing a framework for description, comparison, and chronological ordering of artifacts, but has little explanatory potential. Although culture history provides archaeological data and a methodology for obtaining and organizing them, it cannot tell us what they mean in dynamic, behavioral terms. Given these limitations, the culture historic approach constitutes an important methodological landmark in the historical development of archaeology as a scientific discipline.

REFERENCES

Childe, Vere Gordon. 1925. The dawn of European civilization. Routledge and Kegan Paul, London.

————. 1942. What happened in history. Pelican Books, Baltimore.

Dunnell, Robert C. 1986. Five decades of American archaeology. In American archaeology past and future, D. J. Meltzer, D. D. Fowler, and J. A. Sabloff, eds. Society for American Archaeology/Smithsonian Institution Press, Washington, D.C., pp. 23–49.

Fagan, Brian M. 1988. In the beginning: an introduction to archaeology, 6th ed. Scott, Foresman, Glenview, Ill.

Kidder, Alfred V. 1924. An introduction to the study of southwestern archaeology. Papers of the southwestern expedition, Phillips Academy No. 1. New Haven.

Steward, Julian H. 1942. The direct historical approach to archaeology. American Antiquity 7:337–343.

Trigger, Bruce G. 1989. A history of archaeological thought. Cambridge University Press.

Willey, Gordon R. 1985. Some continuing problems in New World culture history. American Antiquity 50(2):351–363.

Willey, Gordon R., and Philip Phillips. 1958. Method and theory in American archaeology. University of Chicago Press.

Willey, Gordon R., and Jeremy A. Sabloff. 1980. A history of American archaeology. 2nd ed. Thames and Hudson, London.

SOURCES OF ADDITIONAL INFORMATION

For further background on the development of culture historical studies, see Bruce Trigger, "Culture-historical archaeology," chapter 5 in his *A History of Archaeological Thought* (Cambridge, Cambridge University Press, 1989), pp. 148–206. V. Gordon Childe, in addition to his broad historical synthesis for Europe published in 1925 (see References), produced many detailed regional culture historical syntheses for various parts of Europe, including *The Prehistory of Scotland* (London, Kegan Paul, 1935); *Prehistoric Communities of the British Isles* (London, Chambers, 1940); "Archaeology in the U.S.S.R.," *Science* 145(1940):110–111; "Prehistory in the U.S.S.R. I. Palaeolithic and Mesolithic, A: Caucasus and Crimea," *Man* 42(1942):98–100; "Prehistory in the U.S.S.R. II. The Copper Age in south Russia," *Man* 42(1942):130–136; and "Archaeology in the U.S.S.R. The forest zone," *Man* 43(1943):4–9. Area syntheses for the New World include Alfred V. Kidder, *An Introduction to the Study of Southwestern Archaeology* (New Haven, Papers of the Southwestern Expedition, Phillips Academy No. 1, 1924); and Irvin B. Rouse, *Prehistory in Haiti: A Study in Method* (New Haven, Yale University Publications in Anthropology No. 21, 1939).

CURATION. In archaeology, the practice of retaining and maintaining tools or other ARTIFACTS over long periods of time, rather than discarding and replacing them when they become broken or worn.

Traditionally, curation in archaeology referred to the activities of museum personnel in storing, preserving, exhibiting, and interpreting material items of the past in museum collections (Marquardt et al. 1982). In recent years, the term has acquired a new principal meaning within the discipline, referring to past behavior with respect to the use and preservation of artifacts by those who made and used them (Hayden 1976; Bettinger 1979; Binford 1979).

With respect to implements, curation may involve resharpening or other restorative activities designed to ensure that the item remains functional, and may involve caching in locations where tools can be retrieved and reused at a later time. Items of a decorative or ritual nature, such as jewelry or ceremonial paraphernalia whose uses were primarily symbolic, were sometimes carefully stored and cared for by several generations, used only on special occasions, and treated in the same manner as modern heirlooms.

In contrast with tools made to be used once or only a few times and then thrown away, often at the site of their manufacture, curated tools were cared for, preserved, and repeatedly used over an extended period of time (Hayden 1976; Bettinger 1979). This assumed behavior provides the basis for distinguishing curated tools from those specifically created for a single, short-term task or episode; the latter are frequently referred to as improvised or expedient tools.

Lewis Binford was one of the first archaeologists to use the concept of curation in this sense consistently, to refer to behavior surrounding the manufacture and use of prehistoric tools (Binford 1979, 1980). In his ethnoarchaeological studies of the Nunamiut Eskimo, Binford noted that they removed tools after use at one SITE and kept them for future use at other sites (Binford 1973, 1976, 1978). He found that this group invested considerable time and labor in maintaining such tools to increase their use lives, resulting in very infrequent discard of butchering or woodcutting tools at the locations where they were used. This behavior would result in an inverse relationship between a tool's importance and frequency of use, and its appearance in the ARCHAEOLOGICAL RECORD (Binford 1976:263). Binford therefore distinguished curated from noncurated technologies in terms of contrasting tool frequencies occurring in the archaeological record. According to this view, only among noncurators are tool frequencies in archaeological deposits indicative of the relative importance of the activities for which they were used. In noncurated technologies, intersite variability in tool frequencies will be high, and will vary directly with seasonal SUBSISTENCE activities (see SEASONALITY). However, in curated technologies, relative frequencies of tool types in archaeological samples from several sites will vary independently of the frequency of activities in which they were used, and intersite variability will be relatively low, and independent of seasonal activity (Binford 1976:264–265).

Binford suggests these principles can be used to distinguish curation behavior from noncuration in past populations, using discard patterns inferable from the frequencies of various tool types in archaeological sites. It is worth noting that his conclusions, based on his Nunamiut data, were derived from observations on the uses of modern metal tools by contemporary people. Discard and curation patterns for the lithic tools used in the prehistoric past may have differed significantly from those Binford observed in the 1970s, when the cost of metal tools, as well as other factors, may have affected the frequency of curation behavior. For this reason, his conclusions from the Nunamiut data should be applied with caution to the interpretation of past lithic assemblages.

Curation may have been part of an overall logistic strategy that emphasized planning and preparation for unforeseen events. Such a strategy could also have included caching behavior and multipurpose procurement expeditions, for example, collecting raw materials for tools or other artifacts while on a hunting trip, such as Binford observed among the Nunamiut. However, Binford and others have tended to assume that expedient tools, improvised for a specific, immediate task and then abandoned after use, will predominate in most assemblages. Curated tools, on the other hand, will be retained for use in many repeated, and perhaps less frequently performed, tasks, and will therefore be discarded far less often. Hafted tools, requiring additional time and energy for fashioning handles and mounting, would be likely to be curated items because of the greater investment of effort they represent (Cahan, Keeley, and Van Noten 1979:662).

Archaeologically, curation is sometimes detectable from the survival in ASSEMBLAGES of artifacts that are stylistically much older than the majority of items. Frequently these are nonutilitarian items of ceremonial value. Carved jade ornaments dating to the Classic period of Maya civilization recovered from the "sacred well" at Chichén Itzá in the Yucatán, a site whose principal occupation was at a later time in Maya history (Terminal Classic/Postclassic), provide one example of this behavior. Such objects may not only have been preserved over a long period of time before becoming offerings, but also were very likely manufactured in locations remote from the site of their deposit, transported over a long distance, and subsequently treasured as heirlooms until being "sacrificed." Similar practices occur in numerous cultures in many parts of the world.

Curation has been invoked as one possible explanation for the observed variability between roughly contemporaneous Middle Paleolithic assemblages. However, more recent studies have produced other explanations for this phenomenon (Binford 1983; Rolland and Dibble 1990; see also ASSEMBLAGE; PALEOANTHROPOLOGY).

REFERENCES

Bettinger, R. L. 1979. Curation, statistics and settlement studies: a reply to Munday and Lincoln. American Antiquity 44(2):352–359.

Binford, Lewis R. 1973. Interassemblage variability—the Mousterian and the "functional" argument. In The explanation of culture change: models in prehistory, Colin Renfrew, ed. University of Pittsburgh Press.

———. 1976. Forty-seven trips: a case study in the character of archaeological formation processes. Reprinted in Working at archaeology, by L. R. Binford. Academic Press, New York, 1983, pp. 243–268.

———. 1978. Nunamiut ethnoarchaeology. Academic Press, New York.

———. 1979. Organization and formation processes: looking at curated technologies. Journal of Anthropological Research 35(3):255–273. Reprinted in Working at archaeology, pp. 269–286.

———. 1980. Willow smoke and dogs' tails: hunter-gatherer settlement systems and archaeological site formation. American Antiquity 45(2):4–20.

———. 1983. In pursuit of the past: decoding the archaeological record. Thames and Hudson, London.

Cahan, D., L. H. Keeley, and F. L. Van Noten. 1979. Stone tools, toolkits, and human behavior in prehistory. Current Anthropology 20(4):661–683.

Hayden, Brian. 1976. Curation: old and new. In Primitive art and technology, J. S. Raymond, B. Loveseth, C. Arnold, and G. Reardon, eds. Archaeological Association, University of Calgary, pp. 47–59.

Marquardt, William H., Anta Montet-White, and Sandra C. Scholtz. 1982. Resolving the crisis in archaeological collections curation. American Antiquity 47(2):409–418.

Rolland, Nicolas, and Harold L. Dibble. 1990. A new synthesis of Middle Paleolithic variability. American Antiquity 55(3):480–499.

SOURCES OF ADDITIONAL INFORMATION

Extended discussions of the principle of curation and its effects on artifact assemblages are relatively few. The reader is referred to Hayden 1976, and the publications by Binford (all cited above in References) for further information. Discussions of the application of the concept are somewhat more numerous. These include R. M. Gramly, "Raw materials source areas and curated tool assemblages," American Antiquity 45(4) (1980):823–833; Douglas B. Bamforth, "Technological efficiency and tool curation," American Antiquity 51(1) (1986):38–50; R. H. Towner and M. Warburton, "Projectile point rejuvenation, a technological analysis,'' *Journal of Field Archaeology* 17(3) (1990):311–321; and M. Kornfeld, K. Akoshima, and G. C. Frison, ''Stone tool caching on the North American plains: implications of the McKean site tool kit,'' *Journal of Field Archaeology* 17(3) (1990):301–309. For additional material, the reader is advised to examine future issues of *American Antiquity, Journal of Field Archaeology,* and *Journal of Anthropological Archaeology,* as well as forthcoming volumes of *Archaeological Method and Theory.*

D

DECIPHERMENT. The decoding of ancient scripts from early documents or inscriptions. Related terms: *epigraphy*, the study of an ancient writing system from inscriptions, for purposes of decipherment; *paleography*, the study and decipherment of ancient written documents.

The existence of a written script is always a great advantage to the archaeologist investigating an ancient CULTURE. In such cases, decipherment and archaeology complement each other in a symbiotic relationship, with archaeologist and epigrapher participating in a mutual feedback process in which archaeological evidence serves to clarify and flesh out the information in the texts being deciphered, while the content of the texts themselves adds to and clarifies understanding of the archaeological data, and sometimes serves as a check on the archaeologist's interpretations. Dialogue between the epigrapher and the archaeologist is essential for both; documents must be checked against archaeological evidence, and archaeological data must be checked against textual data, whenever this is available.

Since the beginning of archaeology as a professional discipline in the nineteenth century (see OLD WORLD ARCHAEOLOGY; PREHISTORY), Old World archaeologists, especially those engaged in studies of the early classical civilizations, have frequently themselves been epigraphers, who study the texts they discover in the course of excavating SITES. In the twentieth century, however, the field of epigraphy has attracted many scholars, both amateurs and professionals, outside the field of archaeology.

The first dramatic event of decipherment of an archaeological script occurred in the early 1820s, when Jean-François Champollion, a young French linguist and Egyptologist, succeeded in decoding the Egyptian hieroglyphic script from the multilingual texts inscribed on the Rosetta stone (Champollion 1965 [1822];

Pope 1975:68–84). The twentieth century has seen two more such major decipherments that have captured the interest of the public. The first of these occurred in 1952, when Michael Ventris, a British architect and avocational epigrapher, assisted by John Chadwick, decoded the script of the ancient Minoan civilization discovered by Sir Arthur Evans, called Linear B, by correctly identifying the language of texts inscribed on tablets Evans had excavated at Knossos as an archaic form of Greek (Chadwick 1970; Ventris and Chadwick 1953). The second was the decipherment of the Maya script of Mesoamerica, an achievement many scholars had long considered to be impossible, which occurred soon afterward, in the late 1950s (Knorozov 1958, 1967; Proskouriakoff 1960, 1963, 1964).

As the term itself suggests, decipherment is a form of cryptography, conducted through a deductive process of controlled experiment and hypothesis testing, resembling in some respects the work of a detective. Perhaps this is why, especially since the 1960s, the procedure has attracted the efforts of many amateur epigraphers, whose work has contributed significantly to the process of Maya decipherment, an accomplishment that has recently attracted a good deal of public attention.

During the course of efforts to decode and understand an unknown writing system, there is sometimes an accumulation of convergent evidence derived from different methodological approaches that produces a sudden breakthrough, or series of breakthroughs, and the code is "broken." John Chadwick, in his discussion of the decipherment of Linear B, likens this to "the initiation of a chain-reaction in atomic physics; once the critical threshold is passed, the reaction propagates itself" (Chadwick 1970:67). This phenomenon was very apparent in the Maya decipherment, where the convergence of knowledge gained through several lines of inquiry was a critical element in initiating the "chain reaction" (Berlin 1958; Knorozov 1958; Proskouriakoff 1960).

While the decipherment of Linear B was a dramatic and well-publicized event, the complexity of the problem solved by Ventris and Chadwick was considerably less than that of the decoding of the Maya script. The British scholars had the advantage of working with a script in an Indo-European language, with linguistic patterns similar to those of English and other modern European languages, a script with relationships to other previously decoded writing systems. The decipherers of Maya writing labored under a number of handicaps by comparison, which rendered their problem far more difficult, and its solution much less a foregone conclusion. The language of the script—or at least its modern variants— was a known fact. But Mayan is, of course, a non-Western language with a structure very different from the Indo-European languages, and there existed no other deciphered scripts to which it bore any genetic relationship. Since there are no equivalent scripts native to the New World, there could be no Rosetta stone to provide a "key" to this unknown script. This was the situation between 1958 and 1960, when the cumulative results of several different lines of research combined to produce a series of breakthroughs that led to the decoding of Mayan glyphic writing.

Maya decipherment capped a trio of important discoveries. First came the discovery by the Soviet linguist Yurii Knorozov that, in addition to the glyphs, Maya writing contained a number of phonetic signs, which he was able to identify from clarifying Bishop Diego de Landa's misunderstanding of the signs he had recorded in his famous sixteenth-century ethnography as "the Maya alphabet" (Tozzer 1941). Knorozov formulated a rule, which he called the *principle of synharmony*, for the combination of written phonetic syllables to form Maya words (Knorozov 1958, 1967). A second major discovery was made by the German scholar Heinrich Berlin, who identified the existence of "emblem glyphs," compound signs representing the names of ruling families at major Maya political centers, which may also have been used as the original names of these cities themselves (Berlin 1958). The third, and perhaps most significant, was the brilliant discovery by Tatiana Proskouriakoff, a Russo-American artist employed by the Carnegie Institution of Washington to make reconstruction drawings of Maya ruins, that glyphic inscriptions from the Maya sites of Piedras Negras, Guatemala, and Yaxchilan, Mexico, represented historical records of the ancient rulers of these two cities. The publication of her papers (Proskouriakoff 1960, 1963, 1964) was to revolutionize Maya research, preparing the way for reading of the hitherto unknown history of Maya civilization as it had been written nearly 2,000 years before (Chippindale, Hammond, and Sabloff 1988; Houston 1988). In the ensuing decades, archaeologists and epigraphers have been able to reconstruct dynasties, genealogies, ceremonies, alliances, wars, and political rivalries undreamed of by previous generations of Maya scholars (Schele and Miller 1986; Schele and Freidel 1990), and recent archaeological discoveries have further augmented epigraphers' interpretations of Maya texts (e.g., Culbert 1991).

The decipherments of Linear B and the Maya script clearly illustrate the different functions and purposes for which writing was designed and used by different societies in the past. The Mycenaean Greeks used Linear B and its antecedent script primarily for recording commercial transactions, which appears to have been the main purpose of a number of ancient Old World scripts. The Classic Maya, on the other hand, recorded the genealogies and military exploits of their kings, as did the Egyptians of the pharaonic period. Other uses for writing include recording prophecies and auguries; constructing tables of astronomical data for predicting eclipses and other celestial events; preparing almanacs; and recording herbal and medical recipes. The Mayas used writing for all these purposes, although the public inscriptions were confined to royal history and ceremony, with other kinds of information recorded in books. Ritual texts were frequently painted on ceramic vessels or incorporated into wall frescoes. Recording legal codes and writing letters are other important uses for writing that were utilized in some of the ancient Old World civilizations; the Mayas appear not to have used writing for these purposes.

Scholars have long noted that pictographic writing is often the first kind of written script to appear among peoples who have developed writing as an independent invention rather than by borrowing the technique from some already literate foreign people. In such cases, a type of proto-writing in the form of pictorial narratives often precedes the appearance of a fully developed pictographic script (Benson 1971; Smith 1973, 1983; Arnett 1983; Justeson 1986). Such scripts may evolve into logographic or hieroglyphic systems, and may eventually combine or replace these with a phonetic syllabary or alphabetic script (Boltz 1986:431; Isserlin 1982). Another important forerunner of writing is the use of tallying methods, ranging from the simple notched sticks employed by many preliterate peoples since Paleolithic times (Marshack 1972, 1979; Chase and Dibble 1987), to the complex tokens or counters of the Sumerians (Schmandt-Besserat 1981, 1982, 1986) and the *quipu* of the Peruvian Inca, a type of recordkeeping device that often precedes written numeration.

Epigraphers use a variety of methods to identify the nature of a script, that is, to determine whether the individual signs represent syllables, letters, or whole words, as well as to determine the language it was used to represent, since this basic information is essential for any subsequent decipherment effort. Comparison with other known scripts from the same geographic region is usually fruitful, when these are present. While the goals of the epigrapher will vary according to the particular script and the problems it presents, the principal aim will usually be to "break the code," that is, to identify the uses and functions of a sufficient number of the symbols employed in the script to predict contexts where each will occur, and to determine their grammatical nature (whether noun, verbal construction, preposition, etc.). This basic knowledge will usually enable a skilled epigrapher to interpret a variety of texts in which the known signs occur. An adequate corpus of texts is an indispensable requisite for decipherment, for purposes of comparison and verification, and lack of sufficient texts may present an insurmountable barrier to decipherment.

In the course of decipherment, signs of unknown meaning can sometimes be inferred from their context when adjacent symbols have been deciphered. It should be noted that decipherment is not equivalent to translation. The goal of translation is to render as nearly as possible the exact meaning of a text in another language, a process that becomes possible only after a script has been decoded and its structure thoroughly studied. Decipherment permits the general interpretation of the overall meaning and import of texts even though the meanings of some signs remain unknown.

Decipherment, along with the use of ethnohistoric documents and experimental archaeology, has become one of the most important methods used by archaeologists for testing hypotheses and existing interpretations regarding past civilizations. Decipherment of any extant hieroglyphic texts became a routine part of archaeological projects in the Maya area during the 1980s, and these have contributed considerably to the reconstruction of political history in the Maya region (Culbert 1991). Efforts continue to decode the writing system of the prehistoric Zapotec of the Mexican highlands, which, if successful, will undoubtedly contribute greatly to archaeologists' present knowledge of the history of this important early Mexican civilization (Marcus 1980; Whittaker 1980, 1982, 1983). To date, attempts at decipherment have been hindered by the lack of a sufficient number of texts.

The one Old World script that remains undeciphered is that of the Indus civilization, which exists only in the form of inscribed seals (Chippindale, Hammond, and Sabloff 1988), and is therefore unlikely to be deciphered unless additional and more extensive texts are found.

REFERENCES

Arnett, William S. 1983. The predynastic origins of Egyptian hieroglyphs: evidence for the development of rudimentary forms of hieroglyphs in Upper Egypt in the fourth millennium B.C. University Press of America, Washington, D.C.

Benson, Elizabeth P., ed. 1971. Mesoamerican writing systems, a conference at Dumbarton Oaks, October 30th and 31st, 1971. Dumbarton Oaks Research Library, Washington, D.C.

Berlin, Heinrich. 1958. El glifo "emblema" en las inscripciones mayas. Journal de la Société des Americanistes (Paris) n.s. 47:111–119.

Boltz, William G. 1986. Early Chinese writing. World Archaeology 17(3):420–436.

Chadwick, John. 1970. The decipherment of Linear B. 2nd ed. Cambridge University Press.

Champollion, J. F. 1965. Lettre à M. Dacier à l'alphabet des hiéroglyphes phonétiques [1822], trans. from the French by V. M. Conrad. In The world of archaeology, C. W. Ceram, ed. Thames and Hudson, London, pp. 162–170.

Chase, Philip G., and Harold L. Dibble. 1987. Middle Paleolithic symbolism: a review of current evidence and interpretations. Journal of Anthropological Archaeology 6:263–296.

Chippindale, C., N. Hammond, and J. A. Sabloff. 1988. The archaeology of Maya decipherment. Antiquity 62(234):119–122.

Culbert, T. Patrick, ed. 1991. Classic Maya political history: hieroglyphic and archaeological evidence. Cambridge University Press.

Houston, Stephen D. 1988. The phonetic decipherment of Mayan glyphs. Antiquity 62(234):126–135.

Isserlin, B.S.J. 1982. The earliest alphabetic writing. In Cambridge ancient history. Cambridge University Press, Cambridge and New York, vol. 3, pp. 794–818.

Justeson, John S. 1986. The origin of writing systems: Preclassic Mesoamerica. World Archaeology 17(3):437–458.

Knorozov, Yurii V. 1958. The problem of the study of the Maya hieroglyphic writing. American Antiquity 23:284–291.

———. 1967. The writing of the Maya Indians. Translation by Sophie Coe of chapters 1, 6, 7, and 9 of Pis'mennost'indeitseu maiia (Moscow, 1963). Tatiana Proskouriakoff, collaborating editor. Peabody Museum of Archaeology and Ethnology, Russian Translation Series No. 4. Cambridge, Mass.

Marcus, Joyce. 1980. Zapotec writing. Scientific American 242:50–64.

Marshack, Alexander. 1972. Upper Paleolithic notation and symbol. Science 178:817–828.

―――. 1979. Upper Paleolithic symbol systems of the Russian plain. . . . Current Anthropology 20(2):271–311.

Pope, Maurice. 1975. The story of archaeological decipherment: from Egyptian hieroglyphs to Linear B. Scribner's, New York.

Proskouriakoff, Tatiana. 1960. Historical implications of a pattern of dates at Piedras
Negras, Guatemala. American Antiquity 25:454–475.

―――. 1963. Historical data in the inscriptions of Yaxchilan. Estudios de Cultura Maya
3:149–167.

―――. 1964. Historical data in the inscriptions of Yaxchilan (part II). Estudios de
Cultura Maya 4:177–202.

Schele, Linda, and David Freidel. 1990. A forest of kings: the untold story of the ancient
Maya. William Morrow, New York.

Schele, Linda, and Mary Ellen Miller. 1986. The blood of kings: Dynasty and ritual in
Maya art. George Braziller/Kimbell Art Museum, New York.

Schmandt-Besserat, Denise. 1981. From tokens to tablets: a re-evaluation of the so-called
"numerical tablets." Visible Language 15:321–344.

―――. 1982. The emergence of recording. American Anthropologist 84:871–878.

―――. 1986. An ancient token system: the precursor to numerals and writing. Archaeology 39(6):32–39.

Smith, Mary Elizabeth. 1973. Picture writing from ancient southern Mexico: Mixtec place
signs and maps. University of Oklahoma Press, Norman.

―――. 1983. The Mixtec writing system. In The cloud people: divergent evolution of
the Zapotec and Mixtec civilizations, Kent V. Flannery and Joyce Marcus, eds.
Academic Press, New York, pp. 238–245.

Tozzer, Alfred M. 1941. Landa's Relacion de las cosas de Yucatan: a translation [of a
work originally published in 1566], edited with notes by Alfred M. Tozzer. Papers
of the Peabody Museum of Archaeology and Ethnology 18. Harvard University,
Cambridge, Mass.

Ventris, Michael G. F., and John Chadwick. 1953. Evidence for Greek dialect in the
Mycenaean archives. Journal of Hellenic Studies 73:84–103.

Whittaker, Gordon. 1980. The hieroglyphics of Monte Alban. Ph.D. dissertation, Yale
University.

―――. 1982. The tablets of Mound J at Monte Alban. International colloquium: the
Indians of Mexico in pre-Columbian and modern times, Martin Jansen and Th.
J. J. Leyenaar, eds. Rutgers, Leiden, pp. 50–86.

―――. 1983. The structure of the Zapotec calendar. In Calendars of Meso-america and
Peru, A. Aveni and G. Brotherston, eds. British Archaeological Reports, Oxford,
pp. 99–133.

SOURCES OF ADDITIONAL INFORMATION

For an overview of the decipherment of a number of Old World scripts, including
Egyptian hieroglyphics, Persian and Babylonian cuneiform, the Cretan script, and Linear
B, see *The Story of Archaeological Decipherment, from Egyptian Hieroglyphs to Linear
B*, by Maurice Pope (New York, Scribner's 1975). A historical compilation of deci-
pherments is *Reading the Past: Ancient Writing from Cuneiform to the Alphabet*, intro-
duction by J. T. Hooker (Berkeley, University of California Press/British Museum, 1990).
An account of the decipherment of Linear B and its relationship to other scripts is in
John Chadwick, *Linear B and Related Scripts* (London, British Museum Publications,

1987). For information on Asian writing systems, see D. Hawkins, "The origin and dissemination of writing in western Asia," in *The Origins of Civilisation*, P. R. S. Moorey, ed. (Oxford, Clarendon Press, 1979), pp. 128–165. Material on alphabetic writing may be found in Charles Keith Maisels, "The interactive evolution of alphabetic script," Appendix E in his *The Emergence of Civilization* (London and New York, Routledge, 1990), pp. 320–323; and A. R. Millard, "The infancy of the alphabet," *World Archaeology* 17(1986):390–398. A brief but informative account by Linda Schele of the decipherment of the Maya script of Mesoamerica may be found on pages 323–328 of *The Blood of Kings: Dynasty and Ritual in Maya Art*, by Linda Schele and Mary Ellen Miller (New York, George Braziller/Kimbell Art Museum, 1986). Information on the development of writing systems in Mesoamerica is included in the article by John S. Justeson in *World Archaeology* 17(3) (see References, above). The February 1986 issue of *World Archaeology* (vol. 17, no. 3) was devoted entirely to the topic of early writing systems. Articles cover the ancient scripts of Egypt, Uruk, Iran, Mesopotamia, Crete, Anatolia, India, China, and Mesoamerica.

The bibliography of this subject is difficult to access. The best bibliographies are in Justeson 1986 and the other specialized articles in vol. 17, no. 3 of *World Archaeology*. The substantial bibliography in the book by Pope (see References) is comprehensive for the Old World scripts he discusses, but now needs supplementing with those in the more recently published materials. In general, the most recent publications dealing with decipherment will be found in journals devoted to the disciplines associated with the archaeology, culture, and language of the area, such as *Latin American Antiquity* and *Mesoamerica* for the Mayan and Zapotec scripts, and journals in the field of classical archaeology and Oriental studies for the Old World scripts.

DIFFUSION. The process by which cultural traits and practices, such as institutions, art styles, ceremonial practices, and the manufacture and use of particular types of ARTIFACTS, spread across geographic space from one human population to another.

Diffusion, along with MIGRATION, EVOLUTION, and independent innovation, has long been considered by culture historians as one of the processes leading to sociocultural changes observable in the ARCHAEOLOGICAL RECORD. The principle of diffusion was used as an explanatory mechanism by the American anthropologist Clark Wissler, who adopted it from the archaeologist Nels C. Nelson, in the early part of the twentieth century (Nelson 1914, 1916; Wissler 1917, 1923). It was also an important concept in the Austrian Kulturkreislehre school of that time, which influenced the development of the CULTURE AREA concept in the United States, as well as the growth of British diffusionism (Graebner 1911; Kluckhohn 1936).

The mechanism of diffusion may be indirect contact between distant cultural groups through an intermediary, as in trade; the movement of an invading people into an already occupied territory; wars of conquest; migration; or other activities resulting in intercultural contact and the adoption of practices or elements of the donor group by the recipient group.

The diffusion concept has been utilized by several disciplines, notably geography (Blaut 1987), as well as by anthropologists. One of the earliest archaeological discussions of diffusion was in reference to European PREHISTORY, in a work by James Fergusson published in 1872, in which he traced the spread of the prehistoric practice of building megalithic tombs from the ancient civilization of India to North Africa and Europe (Renfrew 1979:31). Fergusson's position was quintessentially diffusionist. He assumed a single invention for a cultural trait—in this case, megalithic tombs—and its subsequent dispersion through contacts and communication with other geographic regions. Diffusionists have traditionally assumed that original human invention is a rare event, and therefore every significant innovative breakthrough in human history has occurred only once, and has subsequently been copied by others, either by direct exposure or via communication through an intermediary.

The idea of diffusion is rooted in the idea of CULTURE as an entity that can be conceived independently of society. This notion of culture is usually attributed to Edward B. Tylor, in his work *Primitive Culture* (Tylor 1871; Kroeber and Kluckhohn 1952:11). Although Tylor did not specifically discuss the geographic diffusion of culture, it has been suggested that this idea is implicit in his work (Adams 1978:2).

Archaeologists and anthropologists have usually distinguished between the direct diffusion or borrowing of cultural traits or trait complexes, and *stimulus diffusion* (Kroeber 1940). The latter phrase refers to the adoption of an idea or concept underlying a cultural practice or technical process, rather than its specific material expression in the donor culture, which may subsequently be expressed in the recipient culture in a different form. For example, the idea of domesticating animals and exercising control over them through practices such as herding, confinement in fenced areas, and selective breeding may be borrowed by contact with a cultural group in which cattle have been domesticated. If cattle are not present among the recipient group, the domestication of some other indigenous species may be undertaken as a result of this exposure. In this instance, it is the *concept* of animal domestication that is borrowed rather than the *practice* of cattle herding.

Some archaeologists also distinguish between primary and secondary diffusion. Primary diffusion is the introduction of an innovation along with a complex of other characteristics of the culture in which it was developed, as may occur with invasion or conquest of one cultural group by another. Secondary diffusion refers to the spread of an innovation beyond cultural boundaries when only the innovation is adopted and incorporated into the recipient culture, often in altered form (Trigger 1968).

Bruce Trigger has pointed out that diffusion refers to the spread of traits from individual to individual, and ultimately from group to group, rather than to their geographical movement along with their human carriers (Trigger 1968:27–28). Diffusion is therefore primarily a social, communicative process, rooted in contacts or encounters between essentially alien groups that may be rare and of fleeting duration. It represents a more subtle concept than that of migrationist explanations, in which cultural traits are thought to be simply transported through space as part of the cultural baggage of migrant human populations, and transplanted to new territories along with their human hosts.

In the early twentieth century, diffusion began to be invoked as a general explanatory principle to account for the existence of similar practices, beliefs, and material traits in societies occupying widely separated geographic areas of the world. Its popularity was a reaction to prevailing evolutionist views, which had been an entrenched part of the development of anthropology as a discipline in the latter part of the nineteenth century. The use of diffusion as an explanation for cultural change accompanied the widespread shift from a historical/diachronic approach to the phenomena of culture, to a synchronic one, emphasizing the distribution of cultures across geographic space rather than their local historical development.

Diffusion has frequently been invoked as an explanatory alternative to migration. Migration, however, never acquired the status of an abstract principle of explanation, as did diffusion. The heated arguments between early-twentieth-century advocates of these two processes as alternative explanations were waged primarily by anthropologists rather than archaeologists. Most archaeologists working in the first half of the twentieth century harbored diffusionist ideas, however, including V. Gordon Childe, who assumed that the cultural achievements of the classical civilizations had been introduced into Europe by diffusionist processes.

The most extreme example of diffusionist thinking was the position adopted and popularized by the Australian neurophysiologist Grafton Elliot Smith in the 1920s. He contended that all world civilizations resulted from exposure to the influence of ancient Egyptian civilization, an idea that seems to have originated with the Scandinavian Oscar Montelius, who first argued for the universal Egyptian influence in a work published at Stockholm in 1903. Smith was convinced of the absolute truth of this proposition, and set out to convince the public of its veracity in a series of popular publications, from newspaper articles to books (e.g., Smith 1927). Unfortunately, he succeeded so well that a sizable portion of the public remains convinced that the native civilizations of the New World were in fact the creation of wandering Egyptians who migrated to foreign soil, bringing pyramids and hieroglyphic writing with them.

Although contemporary archaeological diffusionists do not hold such extreme views as this, most remain convinced that many, if not all, cultural innovations were created only once, and spread to other localities from a single central source. Those who hold this position usually attempt to account for the existence of common "traits," such as stylistic or formal attributes shared by pottery produced in prehistoric South America and ceramics made in Asia at approximately the same time, by transoceanic contacts in prehistoric times. Although such views were once a part of mainstream archaeological thought, they have become increasingly unpopular since the 1940s or 1950s (Kehoe 1978). Dave Davis has pointed out that those who employ diffusionist arguments for such transoceanic contacts are inappropriately using diffusion as a single explanatory principle, rather than as only one of many causal processes resulting in cultural similarities as well as differences (Davis 1983:57).

Since 1970, several archaeological conferences have been devoted to the subject of diffusion (Riley 1971; Duke et al. 1978; Hugill and Dickson 1988). These have generated some lively discussion, as well as some serious efforts at modeling diffusion as one social process contributing to change in the archae-ological record (Hayden 1978). Today diffusion is rarely used as an explanation, partly because of the current unpopularity of monocausal explanations in ar-chaeology, where recent research has supported ideas that both cultural simi-larities and diversity are the result of the interaction of many complex variables, not all of which have yet been identified. In addition, there is little agreement concerning the exact nature and mechanisms of diffusion itself (Dunnell 1990:186), which has become an outmoded concept. Mainstream archaeology now tends to view each culture as a dynamic system with its own unique tra-jectory, each following its own pattern of invention, innovation, and borrowing from a finite range of technologies, art forms, and STYLES. Each culture will select from this range of possible variants those options that are useful or pleasing in terms of its own values and technoenvironmental constraints; but the dynamic processes and variables implicated in these decisions remain to be fully elucidated.

REFERENCES

Adams, W. Y. 1978. On migration and diffusion as rival paradigms. In Diffusion and Migration. Proceedings of the tenth annual archaeological conference of the Ar-chaeological Association of the University of Calgary, P. G. Duke, J. Ebert, G. Langemann, and A. P. Buchner, eds. Archaeological Association of the University of Calgary, pp. 1–5.

Blaut, J. M. 1987. Diffusionism: a uniformitarian critique. Annals of the Association of American Geographers 77(1):30–47. (Extensive bibliography)

Davis, Dave D. 1983. Investigating the diffusion of stylistic innovations. Advances in Archaeological Method and Theory 6:53–89.

Duke, P. G., J. Ebert, G. Langemann, and A. P. Buchner, eds. 1978. Diffusion and migration: their roles in cultural development. Proceedings of the tenth annual archaeological conference of the Archaeological Association of the University of Calgary.

Dunnell, Robert C. 1990. Review of The transfer and transformation of ideas and material culture, Peter J. Hugill and D. Bruce Dickson, eds. American Antiquity 55(1):185–186.

Fergusson, James. 1872. Rude stone monuments in all countries: their age and uses. J. Murray, London.

Graebner, F. 1911. Methode der Ethnologie. Winter, Heidelberg.

Hayden, Brian. 1978. A general diffusion model. In Diffusion and migration: their roles in cultural development. Proceedings of the tenth annual archaeological conference of the Archaeological Association of the University of Calgary, P. G. Duke, J. Ebert, G. Langemann, and A. P. Buchner, eds. Archaeological Association of the University of Calgary, pp. 106–124.

Hugill, Peter J., and D. Bruce Dickson, eds. 1988. The transfer and transformation of ideas and material culture. Texas A&M University Press, College Station.

Kehoe, Alice B. 1978. The dominance of diffusion and its decline in American anthropology. In Diffusion and migration: their roles in cultural development. Proceedings of the tenth annual conference of the Archaeological Association of the University of Calgary, P. G. Duke, J. Ebert, G. Langemann, and A. P. Buchner, eds. Archaeological Association, University of Calgary.

Kluckhohn, Clyde. 1936. Some reflections on the method and theory of the Kulturkreislehre. American Anthropologist 38(2):157–196.

Kroeber, Alfred L. 1940. Stimulus diffusion. American Anthropologist 42:1–20.

Kroeber, Alfred L., and Clyde Kluckhohn. 1952. Culture: a critical review of concepts and definitions. Papers of the Peabody Museum of American Archaeology and Ethnology, 47, no. 1. Harvard University, Cambridge, Mass.

Montelius, Oscar. 1903. Die typologische Methode: Die alteren Kulturperioden im Orient und in Europa, vol. 1. Selbstverlag, Stockholm.

Nelson, Nels C. 1914. Pueblo ruins of the Galisteo Basin. Anthropological Papers of the American Museum of Natural History 15, pt. 1. New York.

———. 1916. Chronology of the Tano ruins, New Mexico. American Anthropologist 18(2):159–180.

Renfrew, Colin. 1979. Before civilization: the radiocarbon revolution and prehistoric Europe. Cambridge University Press. (See Chapter 2)

Riley, Carroll L., J. Charles Kelley, Campbell W. Pennington, and Robert L. Rands, eds. 1971. Man across the sea: problems of pre-Columbian contacts. University of Texas Press, Austin.

Smith, Grafton Elliot. 1927. Culture: the diffusion controversy. W. W. Norton, New York.

Trigger, Bruce G. 1968. Beyond history: the methods of prehistory. Holt, Rinehart and Winston, New York.

Tylor, Edward B. 1871. Primitive culture: researches into the development of mythology, religion, language, art and custom. 2 vols. J. Murray, London.

Wissler, Clark. 1917. The American Indian. Oxford University Press, New York.

———. 1923. Man and culture. Crowell, New York.

SOURCES OF ADDITIONAL INFORMATION

Additional background and criticism on diffusion are in the review articles by Dave Davis (1983; see References for citation); and Edward M. Schortman and Patricia A. Urban, "Modeling interregional interaction in prehistory," *Advances in Archaeological Method and Theory* 11(1987):37–95 (pp. 40–48 are devoted to discussion of diffusion). An additional informational article is "Diffusion," in Robert Winthrop's *A Dictionary of Concepts in Cultural Anthropology* (Westport, Conn., Greenwood Press, 1991), pp. 82–85, which includes a bibliography of primary sources. For a sampling of the diffusion vs. migration debate, see the papers in *Diffusion and Migration: Proceedings of the Tenth Annual conference of the Archaeological Association of the University of*

Calgary, P. G. Duke, J. Ebert, G. Langemann, and A. P. Buchner, eds. (Calgary, Alberta, University of Calgary, 1978); of special interest is W. Y. Adams's paper "On migration and diffusion as rival paradigms" (pp. 1–5). Another volume of papers, from a symposium on pre-Columbian transoceanic contacts, is *Man Across the Sea*, edited by Carroll L. Riley et al. (see References for citation), which includes a theoretical treatment of diffusion versus independent invention by Stephen C. Jett, "Diffusion versus independent development: the bases of controversy," pp. 5–53.

An informal (and witty) rationale for diffusionism is Harold Gladwin's "Independent invention versus Diffusion," *American Antiquity* 2(1937):156–160. For a brief discussion of diffusionism versus processual explanation in archaeology, see "How to construct a 'traditional' explanation" and "The Processual Alternative" in chapter 12 of Renfrew and Bahn 1991 (see References; pp. 407–415). The brief chapter bibliography on p. 434 is the most current list of references available. The most extensive recent (1987) bibliography is in the critique by J. M. Blaut in *Annals of the Association of American Geographers* (see References). For more current publications, consult latest issues of the two pertinent annual reviews, *Annual Review of Anthropology* and *Archaeological Method and Theory*, and the journals *American Anthropologist* and *American Antiquity*.

E

ETHNOARCHAEOLOGY. 1. A subdiscipline of ARCHAEOLOGY, emphasizing the study of behavior among living populations that will affect the formation of future archaeological deposits, as a basis for making comparisons with the prehistoric ARCHAEOLOGICAL RECORD. 2. A set of methods for collecting and applying ethnographic data to make inferences about the past, including the use of ethnographic accounts and ethnohistorical records, the analytical use of ANALOGY, and various experimental approaches.

Ethnoarchaeology as a subdiscipline encompasses all theoretical and methodological approaches to combining and comparing ethnographic and archaeological data, with particular emphasis on the use of analogy to extrapolate from observed discard behavior among modern peoples, to similar processes in the past that produced the existing ARCHAEOLOGICAL RECORD. By observing behavioral patterns of living populations in the manufacture, use, and discard of ARTIFACTS, archaeologists can gain information for interpreting prehistoric archaeological deposits, and for testing working assumptions concerning past human behavior with respect to material CULTURE against contemporary examples. The ethnoarchaeologist observes living cultures from an archaeological point of view, and interprets archaeological remains of past cultures from an ethnographic perspective. Methods of data acquisition range from the archival to the experimental, and include consultation of early written accounts by travelers and explorers, and the use of museum collections as a basis for analogy and model building, in addition to field studies of contemporary peoples.

An important secondary aim of ethnoarchaeology is to utilize ethnographic data from contemporary populations to formulate predictive models of past behavior that can be tested using archaeological data. Underlying such models, and the principle of analogy on which they are based, are two basic assumptions, namely, the principle of UNIFORMITARIANISM, which assumes that processes observable in the present are basically the same as those operating in the past; and the supposition that humans tend to discard their material possessions in predictable, patterned ways, and therefore observations of discard behavior in living populations can provide valid clues to comparable behavior in the past.

Although the term *ethnoarchaeologist* appears in the literature as early as 1900 (Fewkes 1900), ethnoarchaeology as a distinct set of methods constituting a subdiscipline of archaeology began to develop only in the fifth and sixth decades of the twentieth century. Ethnographic data had long been used to interpret archaeological data, but conscious efforts to construct systematic models applying such data to archaeological research are a relatively recent phenomenon. Largely stimulated by the "direct historic approach" (Steward 1942; see also NEW WORLD ARCHAEOLOGY), and the uses of analogy by European prehistorians of the 1950s (Clark 1951, 1952; Childe 1956), American archaeologists began to accept the importance of ethnographic observation as a basis for constructing archaeological models. In 1961, Robert Ascher traced the historical background of the new subdiscipline and identified some of its more important theoretical and methodological issues, including those bearing on its relationship to another interpretative subdiscipline of archaeology, TAPHONOMY, the study of formative processes affecting the archaeological record (Ascher 1961). In the course of the 1960s a number of explicitly ethnoarchaeological projects were undertaken, many of them emphasizing the ecology of contemporary hunting and gathering societies (e.g., Gould 1968; Lee 1968; Woodburn 1968). Although these aroused considerable debate over the validity of using ethnographic analogy as an interpretative tool, such controversy contributed to the ensuing theoretical and methodological developments that became instrumental in defining the new subdiscipline.

During the 1970s interest in ethnoarchaeology increased, along with attention to problems inherent in applying information from experimental studies to the prehistoric past. By 1971 an entire issue of the journal *World Archaeology* (vol. 3, no. 2) was devoted to the uses of analogical reasoning in archaeology. In 1974 a UCLA monograph comprising a dozen papers, many reporting field studies, was published (Donnan and Clewlow 1974). Discussions of theoretical issues began to proliferate (Clark 1968; Orme 1973), and in 1977 an important review of ethnoarchaeology appeared (Stiles 1977) that remains one of the most thorough expositions of the subject. The late 1970s produced a number of field project reports, including Lewis Binford's study of the Nunamiut Eskimo (Binford 1978), Ian Hodder's work on western Kenya (Hodder 1977), and the results of J. E. Yellen's investigation of the !Kung bushmen (Yellen 1974, 1977a, 1977b). The 1970s also saw the initiation of a widely discussed long-term study of contemporary American trash disposal practices, the "Projet de Garbage," directed by William Rathje of the University of Arizona (Rathje 1974; Thomas 1979:416–422).

Interest in ethnoarchaeological studies continued to grow in the 1980s and 1990s. Debates over the uses and validity of ethnographic analogies and INFERENCE have continued (Gould and Watson 1982; Wylie 1982, 1985; Gould 1990; see also ANALOGY, INFERENCE). Since the early 1980s, the British archaeologist Ian Hodder of Cambridge has brought a structuralist orientation to ethnoarchaeology, in studies of material culture distribution patterns to investigate such problems as the identification of prehistoric ethnic units. His work emphasizes the dynamic functions of artifacts as material cultural symbols that he thinks may play an active role in the processes of cultural change (Hodder 1982a, 1982b).

A major problem in ethnoarchaeology, as in archaeology as a whole, has been that of obtaining adequate archaeological samples. Since the SAMPLING universe is unknown, preservation of a sufficient sample of typical artifacts, features, organic remains, and activity patterns in the archaeological record to represent past behavior must be assumed (Lee 1968; Gould 1974; Hayden 1978; see also SAMPLING). While information can be readily obtained from contemporary groups as a basis for comparison, remains surviving in archaeological deposits may constitute a biased sample of past behavior, due to differential preservation of remains as well as the effects of natural and cultural processes that affect the archaeological record (see TAPHONOMY).

Ethnoarchaeological models of prehistoric behavior may also require data that have not been consistently recorded by ethnographers. Variability in artifact forms, the reasons for observed spatial relationships among structures, and the specific areas within a SITE associated with such specialized activities as tool manufacture, cooking, and ritual, are categories of information not always recorded in ethnographies. Such data must often be gained through field observation and carefully designed experimental studies (Stiles 1977:92). Such studies may focus on the uses of specific kinds of artifacts in typical contexts, or experimental reproduction of artifacts themselves. Examples range from experiments in lithic tool use designed to reproduce wear patterns observed on tools from archaeological deposits, to attempts to reproduce Paleolithic cave paintings using only the pigments that would have been available to inhabitants of a late Pleistocene environment.

Ethnoarchaeological field studies may center on a particular activity, such as potterymaking (Longacre 1968, 1970, 1981, 1985; Stanislawski 1969a; Feinman 1985), refuse disposal (Rathje 1974; Hayden and Cannon 1984), or the procurement of raw materials; or they may be more broadly based, attempting to encompass the full range of SUBSISTENCE activities. In either case, physical traces left by important activities are carefully observed, and taphonomic processes affecting their preservation are identified insofar as possible (Schiffer 1976; Stiles 1977:93). An important area of investigation is that of food remains, including preserved animal and vegetable materials that can yield information on ecological ADAPTATION and subsistence strategies pursued by prehistoric groups. The effects of butchering practices and scavengers on such remains are also of interest, and have been the subject of several studies (e.g., Binford and Bertram 1977; Bonnichsen and Sorg 1989).

Investigators concentrating on relationships between artifacts and behavior have monitored processes of tool manufacture, use, and discard, noting the ways in which present populations perceive these implements from their own cultural perspective (Stanislawski 1969b, 1977; Hayden 1974, 1978; Hayden and Cannon 1984). Some studies of this nature have emphasized artifact patterning or stylistic factors as reflections of kinship organization or residence rules (e.g., Longacre 1968, 1970).

A further methodological approach is the examination of SITES abandoned within historic times, and comparing results with information obtained from living informants. A variant of this approach was Nicholas David's study of an occupied SITE that was treated as if it had been abandoned (David 1971). Studies of this kind may reveal complexities often obscured in the archaeological record.

Application of ethnoarchaeological methods in field studies has become a standard approach in the archaeology of the 1980s and 1990s. Theoretical work, however, has lagged behind the development of field methods and data collection, and hopes that ethnoarchaeology would result in the construction of middle-range theory to forge connective links between the static material record of the past and its present interpretation in dynamic, processual terms have not been realized. The development of such theory remains an area requiring the efforts of future ethnoarchaeologists.

REFERENCES

Ascher, Robert. 1961. Analogy in archaeological interpretation. Southwestern Journal of Anthropology 17:317–325.

Binford, Lewis R. 1978. Nunamiut ethnoarchaeology. Academic Press, New York.

Binford, Lewis R., and Jack B. Bertram. 1977. Bone frequencies—and attritional processes. In For theory building in archaeology, L. R. Binford, ed. Academic Press, New York, pp. 77–156.

Bonnichsen, R., and M. H. Sorg, eds. 1989. Bone modification: proceedings of the first international conference . . . Carson City, Nevada, August 1984. University of Maine, Center for Studies of Early Man, Orono.

Childe, V. Gordon. 1956. Piecing together the past. Routledge and Kegan Paul, London.

Clark, J. D. 1968. Studies of hunter-gatherers as an aid to the interpretation of prehistoric societies. In Man the hunter, R. B. Lee and Irven DeVore, eds. Aldine, Chicago.

Clark, J. G. D. 1951. Folk culture and the study of European prehistory. In Aspects of archaeology, W. F. Grimes, ed. Edwards, London.

———. 1952. Archaeologies, theories, and interpretations: Old World. In Anthropology today, A. L. Kroeber, ed. University of Chicago Press.

David, Nicholas. 1971. The Fulani compound and the archaeologist. World Archaeology 3:111–131.

Donnan, C. B., and C. W. Clewlow, Jr., eds. 1974. Ethnoarchaeology. Institute of Archaeology, Archaeological Survey Monograph 4. University of California, Los Angeles.

Feinman, Gary M. 1985. Changes in the organization of ceramic production in prehispanic

Oaxaca, Mexico. In Decoding prehistoric ceramics, Ben A. Nelson, ed. Southern Illinois University Press, Carbondale and Edwardsville, pp. 195–223.

Fewkes, J. W. 1900. Tusayan migration traditions. Bureau of American Ethnology, 19th Annual Report, pt. 2. Washington, D.C.

Gould, Richard A. 1968. Living archaeology: the Ngatatjara of Western Australia. Southwestern Journal of Anthropology 24:101–122.

———. 1974. Some current problems in ethnoarchaeology. In Ethnoarchaeology, C. B. Donnan and C. W. Clewlow, Jr., eds. Institute of Archaeology Monograph 4. University of California, Los Angeles.

———. 1990. Recovering the past. University of New Mexico Press, Albuquerque.

Gould, Richard, and Patty Jo Watson. 1982. The meaning and use of analogy in ethnoarchaeological reasoning. Journal of Anthropological Archaeology 1:355–381.

Hayden, Brian. 1974. Stone tool functions in the Western Desert. In Stone tools as cultural markers: change, evolution and complexity, R. V. S. Wright, ed. Australian Institute of Aboriginal Studies, Canberra, pp. 178–188.

———. 1978. Snarks in archaeology: or, inter-assemblage variability in lithics (a view from the Antipodes). In Lithics and subsistence: the analysis of stone tool use in prehistoric economies, Dave L. Davis, ed. Publications in Anthropology 20. Vanderbilt University, Nashville, Tenn., pp. 179–198.

Hayden, Brian, and Aubrey Cannon. 1984. The structure of material systems: ethnoarchaeology in the Maya highlands. SAA Papers No. 3. Society for American Archaeology, Washington, D.C.

Hodder, Ian. 1977. The distribution of material culture items in the Baringo District, western Kenya. Man 12:239–269.

———. 1982a. The present past: an introduction to anthropology for archaeologists. B. T. Batsford, London.

———. 1982b. Symbols in action: ethnoarchaeological studies of material culture. Cambridge University Press.

Lee, R. B. 1968. What hunters do for a living, or, how to make out on scarce resources. In Man the hunter, R. B. Lee and Irven DeVore, eds. Aldine, Chicago.

Longacre, William A. 1968. Some aspects of prehistoric society in east central Arizona. In New perspectives in archaeology, S. R. Binford and L. R. Binford, eds. Aldine, Chicago, pp. 89–102.

———. 1970. Archaeology as anthropology: a case study. Anthropological Papers of the University of Arizona No. 17. University of Arizona Press, Tucson.

———. 1981. Kalinga pottery: an ethnoarchaeological study. In Pattern of the past: studies in honor of David Clarke, Ian Hodder, Glynn Isaac, and Norman Hammond, eds. Cambridge University Press, pp. 49–66.

———. 1985. Pottery use-life among the Kalinga, northern Luzon, the Philippines. In Decoding prehistoric ceramics, Ben A. Nelson, ed. Southern Illinois University Press, Carbondale and Edwardsville, pp. 335–346.

Orme, Bryony. 1973. Archaeology and ethnography. In The explanation of culture change, C. Renfrew, ed. Duckworth, London, pp. 481–492.

Rathje, William L. 1974. The garbage project: a new way of looking at the problems of archaeology. Archaeology 27:236–241.

Schiffer, Michael B. 1976. Behavioral archaeology. Academic Press, New York.

Stanislawski, Michael B. 1969a. The ethnoarchaeology of Hopi pottery making. Plateau 42:27–33.

————. 1969b. What good is a broken pot? An experiment in Hopi-Tewa ethnoarchaeology. Southwestern Lore 35(1):11–18.

————. 1977. Ethnoarchaeology of Hopi and Hopi-Tewa pottery-making: styles of learning. In Experimental archaeology, D. Ingersoll, J. E. Yellen, and W. Macdonald,
eds. Columbia University Press, New York, pp. 378–408.

Steward, Julian H. 1942. The direct-historical approach to archaeology. American Antiquity 7:337–343.

Stiles, Daniel. 1977. Ethnoarchaeology: a discussion of methods and applications. Man
11:87–103.

Thomas, David Hurst. 1979. Archaeology. Holt, Rinehart and Winston, New York.

Woodburn, J. C. 1968. An introduction to Hadza ecology. In Man the hunter, R. B. Lee
and Irven DeVore, eds. Aldine, Chicago.

Wylie, Allison. 1982. An analogy by any other name is just as analogical: A commentary
on the Gould-Watson dialogue. Journal of Anthropological Archaeology 1:382–
401.

————. 1985. The reaction against analogy. Advances in Archaeological Method and
Theory 8:63–111.

Yellen, John E. 1974. The !Kung settlement pattern, an archaeological perspective.
Master's thesis, Harvard University, Cambridge, Mass.

————. 1977a. Archaeological approaches to the present: models for reconstructing the
past. Academic Press, New York.

————. 1977b. Cultural patterning in faunal remains: evidence from the !Kung bushmen.
In Experimental archaeology, D. W. Ingersoll, ed. Columbia University Press,
New York.

SOURCES OF ADDITIONAL INFORMATION

There are several detailed discussions of ethnoarchaeology providing both historical
background and basic methodological information. The paper by Daniel Stiles (1977; see
References), although now out-of-date with respect to recent developments, includes a
still-useful description of methods and applications, as well as a summary of literature
through the mid-1970s. An introduction to some theoretical issues in ethnoarchaeology
may be found in chapter 2 of Ian Hodder's *The Present Past* (1982; see References);
chapter 1 of the same work presents a discussion of the uses of ANALOGY. A useful
introduction by Carol Kramer to *Ethnoarchaeology, Implications of Ethnography for
Archaeology*, C. Kramer, ed. (New York, Columbia University Press, 1979) outlines
some basic theoretical assumptions, ethnoarchaeological objectives, data collection methods, and problems for future research.

A collection of papers in the area of modern material culture studies, titled *Modern
Material Culture: The Archaeology of Us*, Richard A. Gould and Michael B. Schiffer,
eds. (New York, Academic Press, 1981), includes discussions of method and theory as
well as examples of archaeological studies of present-day American cultural practices
relevant to ethnoarchaeology, among them graffiti, coin collecting, and recycling behavior. A second collection, from a 1978 symposium, is *Ethnography by Archaeologists:
1978 Proceedings of the American Ethnological Society*, Elisabeth Tooker, ed. (Washington, D.C., American Ethnological Society, 1982), which contains an important paper
by Jane K. Sallade and David P. Braun, based on fieldwork in Cyprus. Among notable

examples of the numerous studies of the ethnoarchaeology of potterymaking are Richard A. Krause, *The Clay Sleeps: an Ethnoarchaeological Study of Three African Potters* (University, University of Alabama Press, 1985); and Dean E. Arnold, *Ceramic Theory and Cultural Process* (Cambridge, Cambridge University Press, 1985). An ethnoarchaeological treatment of spatial analysis at the household level is Susan Kent's *Analyzing Activity Areas, an Ethnoarchaeological Study of the Use of Space* (Albuquerque, University of New Mexico Press, 1984).

In addition to the issue of *World Archaeology* devoted to analogy (vol. 3, no. 2, 1971), a more recent issue of the same journal (vol. 17, no. 2, 1985), devoted to ethnoarchaeology, contains 12 papers reporting studies in Africa, India, the Middle East, Thailand, Egypt, Europe, and Peru. For most recent publications, see bibliographic information in Richard Gould's book on ethnoarchaeology for a general audience (Gould 1990; see References), and current issues of *American Antiquity, Journal of Anthropological Archaeology*, and pertinent annual reviews.

EVOLUTION. 1. In biology, the theory that organisms will display "differential persistence of variability" (Dunnell 1980:38) through time, due to the operation of natural selection on the organism's genetic material. The result of this process is biological and behavioral change favoring the survival and persistence of those traits that are adaptive, that is, that promote or enhance the survival and reproduction of the individual organism (see also ADAPTATION). This is the essence of the theory of evolution proposed by Charles Darwin in the nineteenth century. 2. The philosophical idea that human CULTURES, like living organisms, become progressively more complex through time, through the effects of the selection process operating on human culture in a manner similar to the operation of natural selection on biological organisms. Both the biological and the cultural concepts of evolution are important in archaeology.

The basic idea of evolution has been traced as far back as Lucretius's *De rerum natura*. Composed in the first century BC, this was one of the earliest materialist expositions of the origin of life and the development of living creatures adapted to changing environmental conditions (Lucretius 1946). This idea did not receive further formal treatment in Western thought, however, until the eighteenth century, when it was developed by Jean Baptiste Lamarck, whose evolutionary model included the concept of inheritance of characteristics acquired by individuals during their lifetimes (Lamarck 1809). Other predecessors of Darwin who anticipated the main principles of evolutionary theory include the French paleontologist Georges Cuvier, and Darwin's own grandfather, Erasmus Darwin, who conceived most of his grandson's theory, with the exception of the principle of natural selection as the mechanism of evolutionary change (Glass 1959; Lowenberg 1959; Ospovat 1981).

While the concept of evolution as descent with modification resulting in cumulative change had long been present in Western thought, with Darwin it became a scientific principle (Darwin 1859). Previous schemes had been of a teleological nature, incorporating the idea that all development of living forms was directed toward the goal of improvement, or progress toward perfection, as part of an ordered universal plan ordained by the Creator. This developmentalist model was supported by observations of the paleontological record by nineteenth-century geologists such as Sir Charles Lyell (1830–1832, 1863). Beginning in the sixteenth century, contacts with human societies throughout the world that appeared to be in earlier stages of development than western European civilization lent support to a developmentalist view of humanity and human cultures, as well as of other living organisms (Grayson 1983).

By the late nineteenth century, the progressive stages of human social development had been formalized into the tripartite scheme of savagery, barbarism, and civilization employed by Lewis Henry Morgan in his work *Ancient Society* (Morgan 1877), each stage representing a different rung on the evolutionary ladder. Generalization from extant aboriginal societies to an overall model for the human past became an obvious step, one that provided the basis for interpreting the stone implements of early man encountered by the earliest European collectors and natural scientists, as well as the ancient structures dotting the European landscape. Recognition of the assumed similarity between living "savages" or "barbarians" and the lifeways of the past is clear in the anthropological literature of the late nineteenth century, including the works of Morgan, Sir John Lubbock (1865), and Edward Tylor (1871). This idea would later become the underlying basis for the use of ethnographic ANALOGY in interpreting archaeological data, and for the concept of sociocultural evolution of society as an entity distinct from human biology (Kroeber 1917; Steward 1956; Marks, Staski, and Schiffer, 1983; Turke 1984; Johnson and Earle 1987; Marks and Staski 1988; Klein 1989).

It can be argued that the principle of evolution or developmentalism is an implicit assumption underlying most of archaeological interpretation. The construction of cultural chronologies and ARTIFACT typologies usually follows a distinctive pattern characterized by progression from conditions of lesser to greater complexity, skill, and sophistication with increasing time. This is not, of course, a bias restricted to the field of archaeology, but may be seen as an essential part of the western European intellectual tradition from which the discipline arose, since the idea of progress has been an inherent part of that tradition since its earliest origins in the works of the classical philosophers.

In the early twentieth century, the use of evolutionary models for interpreting the ARCHAEOLOGICAL RECORD declined. This was in part a result of changing concepts of human culture, which was regarded by American anthropologists such as Alfred Kroeber and his students as a separate, "superorganic" entity evolving independently of human biological evolution, and subject to different selective processes (Kroeber 1917). The question of whether culture is a part of the biological adaptation of the human species, or a separate entity subject to "cultural selection" operating on individual cultural traits, is still being debated by archaeologists (Dunnell 1980, 1989; Rindos 1989; Durham 1990).

Since the 1960s, evolutionary arguments have again become important to archaeological explanation, beginning with the work of Julian Steward (1956) and Leslie White. Evolution was an essential part of the ANTHROPOLOGICAL ARCHAEOLOGY advocated by White's student Lewis Binford and other "new" processual archaeologists in the 1960s. Robert Dunnell has argued, however, that evolution as a scientific principle "has yet to be systematically applied in either sociocultural anthropology or archaeology," noting that the idea of cultural evolution derives from a completely different tradition than Darwinian evolution, being grounded in the social philosophy of Herbert Spencer and nineteenth-century anthropologists, and "is unrelated to Darwinian principles" (Dunnell 1980:37). Dunnell asserts that the biological theory developed by Darwin does indeed provide an appropriate explanatory approach for archaeology, if suitably adapted for the explanation of cultural phenomena of the past.

During the 1980s, several attempts were made to develop general evolutionary models for archaeological interpretation. One of the more successful of these was devised by R. D. Leonard and G. T. Jones (1987), who incorporated some of Robert Dunnell's suggestions (Dunnell 1980) into their proposed evolutionary paradigm. This model is "based on a selectionist perspective of change" and utilizes the biological evolutionary framework, which Dunnell regards as scientific, as distinct from the cultural evolutionary view, which is seen as lacking in explanatory power. In Leonard and Jones's model, artifacts are regarded as "part of the human phenotype," and their "fitness" is measured in terms of their "replicative success," much as human biological fitness is assessed in terms of reproductive success; mechanisms of selection can then be identified, and change explained in processual terms. Leonard and Jones set out to devise an inclusive explanatory scheme with general applicability, in which humans and their culture may be seen as subject to the same evolutionary and selective processes. This model has the advantage of greater simplicity and clarity than some of its cultural evolutionist counterparts.

Some recent attempts have also been made to develop evolutionary models of cultural change within the cultural evolutionary paradigm, in which culture is placed outside the realm of human biology and becomes subject to a set of rules different from those governing biological evolution. Several of these models have been reviewed by Durham (1990), including his own "coevolution model"; all of them regard cultural change as variation through time in the relative frequencies of "variant bundles" of cultural characteristics. These "variant bundles" are the units of selection; their change over time is effected through the operation of a number of different kinds of selective mechanisms, and a series of such mechanisms may be required to explain how change occurs, particularly when it occurs in different parts of the culture at different rates.

Robert Dunnell and others have noted that while Darwinian theory holds explanatory potential for archaeology, it cannot simply be transplanted in its biological form to account for cultural phenomena (Dunnell 1989; Pollitzer 1987). It must first be generalized in order to include cultural products as well as human genetic material. To date, Leonard and Jones appear to have made the best effort in this direction.

REFERENCES

Campbell, Bernard G. 1966. Human evolution: an introduction to man's adaptation. Aldine, Chicago.

Darwin, Charles. 1859. On the origin of species by means of natural selection . . . . J. Murray, London.

Dunnell, Robert C. 1980. Evolutionary theory and archaeology. Advances in Archaeological Method and Theory 3:35–99.

————. 1989. Aspects of the application of evolutionary theory in archaeology. In Archaeological thought in America, C. C. Lamberg-Karlovsky, ed. Cambridge University Press, pp. 35–49.

Durham, William H. 1990. Advances in evolutionary culture theory. Annual Review of Anthropology 19:187–210.

Glass, Bentley, ed. 1959. Foreunners of Darwin, 1745–1859. Johns Hopkins University Press, Baltimore.

Grayson, Donald K. 1983. The establishment of human antiquity. Academic Press, New York.

Johnson, A. W., and T. K. Earle. 1987. The evolution of human societies from foraging group to agrarian state. Stanford University Press, Stanford, Calif.

Klein, Richard G. 1989. The human career: human biological and cultural origins. University of Chicago Press.

Kroeber, Alfred L. 1917. The superorganic. Reprinted in The nature of culture, by Alfred L. Kroeber. University of Chicago Press, 1952, pp. 22–51.

Lamarck, Jean-Baptiste. 1809. Philosophie zoologique ou exposition des considérations relatives à l'histoire naturelle des animaux. Dentu, Paris.

Leonard, R. D., and G. T. Jones. 1987. Elements of an inclusive evolutionary model for archaeology. Journal of Anthropological Archaeology 6(3):199–219.

Lowenberg, Bert James. 1959. Darwin, Wallace, and the theory of natural selection. Arlington Books, Cambridge, Mass.

Lubbock, John. 1865. Prehistoric times, as illustrated by ancient remains and the manners and customs of modern savages. Williams and Norgate, London.

Lucretius. 1946. On the nature of things, by Lucretius: a new translation by Charles E. Bennett. Walter J. Black, Roslyn, N.Y.

Lyell, Charles. 1830–1832. The principles of geology. An attempt to explain the former changes of the earth's surface by reference to causes now in operation. 2 vols. J. Murray, London.

————. 1863. The geological evidences of the antiquity of man with remarks on the origin of species by variation. J. Murray, London.

Marks, J., and E. Staski. 1988. Individuals and the evolution of biological and cultural systems. Human Evolution 3:147–161.

Marks, J., E. Staski, and M. B. Schiffer. 1983. Cultural evolution—a return to the basics. Nature 302(5903):15–16.

Morgan, Lewis Henry. 1877. Ancient society. Charles H. Kerr, Chicago.

Ospovat, D. 1981. The development of Darwin's theory. Cambridge University Press, New York.

Pfeiffer, John E. 1978. The emergence of man. 3rd ed. Harper & Row, New York.

Pollitzer, William S. 1987. Two views of natural selection and evolution. Reviews in Anthropology 14(3):187–194.

Rindos, D. 1989. Undirected variation and the Darwinian explanation of cultural change. In Archaeological Method and Theory 1:1–45. University of Arizona Press, Tucson.

Sober, E., ed. 1986. Conceptual issues in evolutionary biology: an anthology. MIT Press, Cambridge, Mass.

Steward, J. H. 1956. Cultural evolution. Scientific American 194(5):69–80.

Turke, Paul W. 1984. On what's not wrong with a Darwinian theory of culture. American Anthropologist 86(3):663–668. (See bibliography)

Tylor, Edward. 1871. Primitive culture. 2 vols. J. Murray, London.

SOURCES OF ADDITIONAL INFORMATION

There are many introductory texts for students on the subject of human evolution, including Campbell 1966 and Pfeiffer 1978 (3rd ed.), though none of these is up to date. The more recent collection of papers edited by Sober (Sober 1986) includes discussions of many important issues in evolutionary theory. Some interesting philosophical treatments of human evolution are Mary Maxwell, *Human Evolution: A Philosophical Anthropology* (London and Sydney, Croom Helm, 1984); and Elliott Sober, *The Nature of Selection: Evolutionary Theory in Philosophical Focus* (Cambridge, Mass., MIT Press, 1984).

For extended discussion of the intellectual background of evolutionary theory, including the various influences on Darwin and others who developed similar theories in the nineteenth century, see Joan Stevenson, "Evolution," pp. 128–139, and "Natural Selection," pp. 279–281, in her *A Dictionary of Concepts in Physical Anthropology* (Westport, Conn., Greenwood Press, 1991); both articles include extensive bibliographic essays and lists of references. For philosophical background, as well as discussion of the role of evolutionism in anthropology and in the development of sociobiology in the 1980s, see Robert Winthrop, "Evolution," in his *A Dictionary of Concepts in Cultural Anthropology* (Westport, Conn., Greenwood Press, 1991), pp. 107–114.

A sampling of the controversy generated by evolutionary theory may be found in Peter J. Bowler, *Theories of Human Evolution: A Century of Debate, 1844–1944* (Baltimore, Johns Hopkins University Press, 1986). Discussions of the relationship between human biological and sociocultural evolution are in the papers in Napoleon A. Chagnon and W. Irons, eds., *Evolutionary Biology and Human Social Behavior* (North Scituate, Mass., Duxbury Press, 1979); and in the review by William Durham in *Annual Review of Anthropology* (1990; see References for complete citation). The Durham review also includes the most extensive up-to-date bibliography of literature on evolutionary theory now available.

For later material, future issues of *American Antiquity, American Anthropologist, Human Evolution, American Journal of Physical Anthropology*, and *Journal of Anthropological Archaeology* should be consulted, as well as annual volumes of *Annual Review of Anthropology* and *Archaeological Method and Theory*.

EXCHANGE. Any pattern of human interaction involving the giving and receiving of material goods. Such interaction may occur between members of a local community; adjacent communities within the same locality; or over long distances, involving members of different cultural systems who inhabit different geographic regions.

Exchange includes both transactions carried out primarily for economic reasons, such as trade; and ceremonial exchanges of so-called *primitive valuables* (Earle 1982a; Smith 1983), objects whose value is primarily symbolic and culturally determined rather than intrinsic, and whose exchange is of a social and ritual, rather than an economic, nature. What is exchanged in these various kinds of transactions may be gifts, symbolic objects, or commodities. Each of these has a different social role and meaning, and creates a different class of social relationships.

Trade has been defined by archaeologist Colin Renfrew, who has devoted much of his career to its study, as "reciprocal traffic, exchange, or movement of materials or goods through peaceful human agency" (Renfrew 1969:152), a definition accommodating all forms of human exchange. The archaeological study of exchange systems, and the role they may have played in the development of complex societies in the past, has been a subject of much investigation (Polanyi et al. 1957; Polanyi 1968; Renfrew 1969, 1975; Kohl 1975; Sabloff and Lamberg-Karlovsky 1975; Earle and Ericson 1977; Irwin-Williams 1977; Morris 1978; Fry 1980; Earle 1982b; Ericson and Earle 1982; Renfrew and Shennan 1982; Drennan 1984; Hirth 1984; Renfrew and Cherry 1986; Brumfiel and Earle 1987; Kirch 1988, 1991).

Earlier generations of archaeologists were likely to regard observed similarities in the material remains of widely separated prehistoric groups as evidence of MIGRATION or DIFFUSION, rather than of prehistoric trade. Archaeological research since the 1960s has demonstrated that numerous long-distance trading networks existed in many parts of the world in prehistoric times, linking distant populations through commercial and social contacts that were no doubt mutually beneficial to those who participated in them. The importance of the noneconomic, social functions of exchange was first noted by the French sociologist Marcel Mauss, whose *Essai sur le don*, published in 1925, emphasized this aspect of prehistoric interaction (Mauss 1967). Mauss interpreted what at first appeared to ethnologists to be economic transactions in some societies as constituting a form of social reciprocity, in which economic motives were often secondary, or even entirely absent.

The *kula* exchange, first observed by Bronislaw Malinowski during his pioneering research among the Massim of Melanesia in the early years of the twentieth century, and subsequently studied by many others, was of this type. More ceremonial activity than commercial transaction, the *kula* emphasized the relationship between those involved, which was of much greater value than what was being exchanged (Malinowski 1915, 1920, 1921, 1922; Tueting 1935; Uberoi 1962; Thomas 1979; Leach and Leach 1983; Macintyre 1983; Munn 1986; Kirch 1991). This system of interisland ceremonial exchange, which encompassed several archipelagoes of the South Pacific region, involved a complex pattern of exchanges of "primitive valuables," in the form of shell jewelry and other items circulating through a broad INTERACTION SPHERE. This system served to reinforce social bonds and maintain face-to-face contacts between members of different local communities, through the exchange of items endowed with symbolic value whose meaning was understood by all parties. Similar systems have been ethnographically identified in Papua and New Guinea. Subsequent archaeological research in Melanesia has revealed that commercial transactions and a trade in SUBSISTENCE commodities also existed in this region, beginning in the second millennium BC, a time when the *kula* may not yet have come into existence (Dalton 1984; Kirch 1991). Commerce is separate from ceremonial exchange in this region, and this may have been true in the prehistoric past as well, although archaeological evidence has not been found to support this assumption.

Studies of the *kula* and similar systems led to the development of the *substantivist* approach in economics, advocated by Karl Polanyi. This is an anthropologically oriented view in which economic behavior and process are to be interpreted within their cultural CONTEXT rather than from the point of view of formal Western economic theory. Substantivists include Polanyi, George Dalton, and Marshall Sahlins, who have used this orientation in their own research (Polanyi 1968, 1975; Dalton 1965, 1975, 1982, 1983; Sahlins 1972). *Formalist* economics, on the other hand, regards all trading transactions in terms of allocating scarce resources to alternative ends, and value is viewed as a function of supply-and-demand relationships in an impersonal setting. In formalist economics, all such activity is presumed to be motivated by the desire to maximize gain, a motive the formalists attribute rather vaguely to "human nature" and regard as a universal law. Charles Erasmus has applied the formalist approach cross-culturally in his work (Erasmus 1961). This position may reveal more about the social values of those who subscribe to it than about the nature of exchange activities in non-Western societies, where transfers of symbolic goods, such as the cowrie shell ornaments of the *kula*, may be carried out principally to maintain and reinforce social relationships, and may serve no function that could be called economic in formalist terms.

Polanyi distinguished three "modes" of exchange that have been observed in many different societies, a TYPOLOGY that has been widely adopted in archaeology. The first of these is *reciprocity*, the exchange of gifts between individuals who are usually social equals. The giving of the gift, and its acceptance, usually create a relationship of obligation, in which it is understood that the receiver is expected to make a similar gift to the donor in the future. This ritualized exchange is similar to economic *barter*, in which commodities or raw materials of equal value are traded between individuals, in a direct economic transaction conducted without the use of a currency.

The second type of exchange identified by Polanyi is *redistribution*. This type occurs in societies that have some formal centralized organization, such as a CHIEFDOM (Peebles and Kus 1977). It is a form of internal exchange, in which necessary commodities, which may include crops and foodstuffs as well as utilitarian or ritual goods manufactured by specialists, are collected from the population of a chiefdom or kingdom as tribute, and pooled in a central storage or collection facility. An administrative official, who is charged with this function by a chief, king, or other leader, will subsequently redistribute the collected goods, usually with the assistance of helpers, to the population, allocating the appropriate items in designated amounts to each individual household or other unit. In a ranked society, greater amounts of all desirable commodities are allocated to the ruler, his family, and other members of the elite class. Archaeological evidence for redistribution may include the presence of central storage facilities and other administrative structures.

Polanyi's third category is *market exchange*, in which economic transactions are carried out in a centrally located marketplace where bargaining occurs and prices are set by negotiation. Markets may be local, serving a single community or group of closely located communities, or international. The latter is exemplified in ports, where professional traders from many places bring their goods and carry out negotiations for selling and buying with other traders (Polanyi et al. 1957). Market exchange is greatly facilitated by the use of a currency, a standard medium of exchange that has been assigned an arbitrary value, or set of values, which can be given or received in exchanges in amounts equivalent to the value of the goods transferred. Currency may be money or almost any kind of small, portable object, such as minted coins or natural items, such as the cacao bean currency used in prehistoric Mesoamerica. Its form is less important than its agreed-upon value, its convenience, and its portability. Currencies often survive in the ARCHAEOLOGICAL RECORD, providing valuable data for the archaeologist. Prehistoric marketplaces may sometimes be identifiable archaeologically.

Archaeological evidence for trade consists of two basic kinds of data, namely, the presence of nonperishable raw materials unavailable in the local area and the presence of finished articles, such as pottery or tools, of nonlocal manufacture. Floral and faunal remains from species restricted to foreign ecozones are also indicative of trade, although these are rarely preserved (Morris 1978). Material evidence of trade is usually confined to inorganic raw materials and finished craft items. If prehistoric trade included foodstuffs, little evidence of this is likely to survive.

Although exotic items of obvious foreign manufacture or material may be relatively easy to identify in the archaeological record, tracing these to their sources can be a major problem whose difficulty varies with the nature of the material. Great progress has been made since the 1970s in the sourcing of some materials. This is especially true of obsidian, a valuable raw material for tools that was traded extensively in prehistoric Europe, the Americas, and the Pacific islands. Obsidian can often be traced to its localized supply sources from analysis of its chemical composition, which is distinctive for each source, using techniques such as X-ray fluorescence, neutron activation analysis, and optical spectrography (Vehik 1986; see ARCHAEOMETRY). Source locations for other raw materials, including jade and some of the clays used in potterymaking, can sometimes be determined by using similar methods (see also LITHICS; CERAMIC ANALYSIS). Patrick Kirch discussed some of these problems and methods in a review article.

> The recognition of exchange in prehistory depends . . . upon the ability to identify, and determine the source or provenience of, materials exotic to particular sites. . . . Identification of an object as of foreign origin is often the easiest task; determining its source can be exceedingly difficult. . . . In the current state of the art, it may only be possible to *characterize* a set of imported materials according to geochemical groups, without being able to attribute those groups to *source* localities. (Kirch 1991:142)

Commercial trade over long distances occurred in many prehistoric societies, particularly in those in which a CHIEFDOM or STATE level of sociopolitical organization had developed. The existence of complex societies with large populations is likely to create demands for more specialized goods in larger quantities than may be locally available. The development of trading networks and accompanying relationships of mutual economic dependence between widely separated peoples appears to have been an important factor in the growth of complex societies everywhere in the world (see CULTURAL COMPLEXITY). Such commercial relationships also served to facilitate other types of relationships between trading partners, including marriages and other social bonds, as well as political alliances formed for defensive purposes. A result was the creation of large networks of interaction involving peoples of varied culture, often spanning broad geographic areas and even linking different geographic regions. Such networks have been archaeologically documented in prehistoric Mesoamerica (Drennan 1984; Hirth 1984); North America (Cottrell 1985; Braun 1986); South America (Morris 1978); prehistoric Europe (Renfrew and Shennan 1982); Asia (Kohl 1978, 1979); and most other parts of the world (Earle and Ericson 1977; see also INTERACTION SPHERE).

Identifying the existence of specialized production can be of value to the archaeologist in the study of trade. The presence of high levels of sophistication and standardization in a certain class of ARTIFACT, such as pottery, is a good indicator of this (see SPECIALIZATION). Locations of specialist production centers may be pinpointed through such techniques as analysis of network patterns obtained from settlement studies. Network analysis can also be useful in identifying patterns of exchange in which middlemen were involved (Kirch 1991:144–145).

A key problem in the study of prehistoric trade is that of recovering or defining unequivocal archaeological evidence to distinguish trade items from goods acquired by such other means as direct collection of tribute from distant locations, or seizure of goods in raids or wars of conquest. Usually the only evidence is the presence of exotic items, often in burial contexts. For this reason, archaeologists have made considerable use of models based on archaeological data, supplemented by ethnographic information when available, to infer some of the processes and mechanisms of prehistoric trade that may be reflected in the ARCHAEOLOGICAL RECORD (Renfrew 1975; Sabloff and Lamberg-Karlovsky 1975; Fry 1980; Schortman and Urban 1987). Trade routes and mechanisms of exchange may be inferred from models based on observed spatial distributions simulating possible alternative processes whose operation would account for the observed patterns (Hodder and Orton 1976). Colin Renfrew has developed a down-the-line model for obsidian trade in the Near East, showing that each town at a successively further distance from a trading center passed on only a certain proportion of the goods it received from this center, resulting in an exponential decline in volume of goods moved with increasing distance from the trade center (Renfrew 1975). Renfrew has suggested that different parts of falloff curves produced by such models may reveal different exchange mechanisms in operation. He has also used CENTRAL PLACE THEORY for modeling long-distance trade. Other models have utilized network theory (Hodder and Orton 1976; Irwin-Williams 1977; Plog 1977), general SYSTEM THEORY (Wright and Zeder 1977), world system theory (Pailes and Whitecotton 1979), and a variety of other approaches (Fry 1980).

Other types of information on prehistoric societies may be obtained from the study of trade and exchange. Social change in regions where prehistoric trade networks were in operation may be reflected in changing configurations in distribution of trade goods through time, as well as by changes in the ARTIFACTS traded. Since the exchange of goods is accompanied by exchanges of important social information—ideas, symbols, values, religious and political concepts, and art STYLES, for example—information on prehistoric trade may yield material for the study of past cognitive systems as well as material systems. The role of trade as a factor in the development of complex societies has also become an important area of investigation since the 1970s (Zagarell 1986; Brumfiel and Earle 1987; Kipp and Schortman 1989).

One of the ultimate goals of studying prehistoric trade is to gain information for explaining the origins and development of exchange systems in human societies. Timothy Earle has noted that archaeology still lacks a body of theory to explain exchange and the ways in which it is related to other social processes, and believes that useful models for the archaeological study of this problem may be generated from substantivist and formalist economic theory (Earle 1982b). Attempts have been made to explain the phenomenon of exchange as adaptive behavior (Leach and Leach 1983), as a concomitant of colonization (Kirch 1988), and as an integral part of the mode of production (Thomas 1979), but to date no truly causal explanatory theory of exchange has been developed. Pending the possible development of such a theory, archaeologists continue to use all available methods to learn as much as possible concerning the mechanisms of exchange systems in the past, and to derive whatever can be inferred about the human motivations that prompted them from the study of their traces in the archaeological record.

REFERENCES

Braun, D. P. 1986. Midwestern Hopewellian exchange and supralocal interaction. In Peer polity interaction and sociopolitical change, C. Renfrew and J. F. Cherry, eds. Cambridge University Press, pp. 117–126.

Brumfiel, Elizabeth M., and Timothy K. Earle, eds. 1987. Specialization, exchange and complex societies. Cambridge University Press.

Cottrell, Marie G. 1985. Tomato Springs: the identification of a jasper trade and production center in southern California. American Antiquity 50:833–849.

Dalton, George. 1965. Primitive money. American Anthropologist 67:44–65.

———. 1975. Karl Polanyi's analysis of long-distance trade and his wider paradigm. In Ancient civilization and trade, J. A. Sabloff and C. C. Lamberg-Karlovsky, eds. University of New Mexico Press, Albuquerque, pp. 63–132.

———. 1982. Barter. Journal of Economic Issues 16:181–190.

———. 1984. The kula, past and present. [Review of The kula: new perspectives on Massim exchange, Jerry W. Leach and Edmund Leach, eds., Cambridge University Press, 1983; and The kula: a bibliography, by Martha Macintyre, Cambridge University Press, 1983]. American Anthropologist 86(4):943–953.

———, ed. 1983. Research in economic anthropology. JAI Press, Greenwich, Conn.

Drennan, Robert D. 1984. Long-distance movement of goods in the Mesoamerican Formative and Classic. American Antiquity 49(1):27–43.

Earle, Timothy K. 1982a. The ecology and politics of primitive valuables. In Culture and ecology: eclectic perspectives, J. Kennery and E. Edgerton, eds. American Anthropological Association Special Publication 15. Washington, D.C., pp. 65–83.

———. 1982b. Prehistoric economics and the archaeology of exchange. In Contexts for prehistoric exchange, J. E. Ericson and Timothy K. Earle, eds. Academic Press, New York, pp. 1–12.

Earle, T. K., and J. E. Ericson, eds. 1977. Exchange systems in prehistory. Academic Press, New York.

Erasmus, C. 1961. Man takes control. University of Minnesota Press, Minneapolis.

Ericson, J. E., and T. K. Earle, eds. 1982. Contexts for prehistoric exchanges. Academic Press, New York.

Fry, Robert E., ed. 1980. Models and methods in regional exchange. SAA Papers No. 1. Society for American Archaeology, Washington, D.C.

Hirth, Kenneth. 1984. Trade and exchange in early Mesoamerica. University of New Mexico Press, Albuquerque.

Hodder, Ian, and Clive Orton. 1976. Spatial analysis in archaeology. Cambridge University Press.

Irwin-Williams, Cynthia. 1977. A network model for the analysis of prehistoric trade. In Exchange systems in prehistory, Timothy Earle and J. E. Ericson, eds. Academic Press, New York, pp. 141–151.

Kipp, R. S., and E. M. Schortman. 1989. The political impact of trade in chiefdoms. American Anthropologist 91(2):370–385.

Kirch, Patrick V. 1988. Long distance exchange and island colonization: the Lapita case. Norwegian Archaeological Review 21:103–117.

———. 1991. Prehistoric exchange in western Melanesia. Annual Review of Anthropology 20:141–165.

Kohl, Philip L. 1975. The archaeology of trade. Dialectical Anthropology 1(1):43–50.
———. 1978. The balance of trade in southwestern Asia in the mid-third-millennium B.C. Current Anthropology 19:463–492.
———. 1979. The "world economy" in west Asia in the third millennium B.C. In South Asian Archaeology 1977, M. Taddei, ed. Istituto Universitario Orientale, Naples, pp. 55–85.
Leach, Jerry W., and Edmund Leach. 1983. The kula: new perspectives on Massim exchange. Cambridge University Press.
Macintyre, Martha. 1983. The kula: a bibliography. Cambridge University Press.
Malinowski, Bronislaw. 1915. The natives of Mailu: preliminary results of the Robert Mond research work in British New Guinea. Transactions of the Royal Society of South Australia 39:494–706.
———. 1920. Kula: the circulating exchanges of valuables in the archipelagoes of eastern New Guinea. Man 20:97–105.
———. 1921. The primitive economics of the Trobriand Islanders. Economic Journal 31:1–16.
———. 1922. Argonauts of the western Pacific. Routledge and Kegan Paul, London.
Mauss, Marcel. 1967. The gift. W. W. Norton, New York. (Originally published 1925)
Morris, Craig. 1978. The archaeological study of Andean exchange systems. In Social archaeology: beyond subsistence and dating, Charles Redman et al., eds. Academic Press, New York, pp. 315–327.
Munn, N. 1986. The fame of Gawa: a symbolic study of value transformation in a Massim society. Cambridge University Press.
Pailes, R., and J. Whitecotton. 1979. The greater southwest and the Mesoamerican "world system": an exploratory model of frontier relationships. In The frontier, vol. 2, W. Savage, Jr., and S. Thompson, eds. University of Oklahoma Press, Norman, pp. 105–121.
Peebles, Christopher S., and Susan M. Kus. 1977. Some archaeological correlates of ranked societies. American Antiquity 42(3):421–448.
Plog, Fred. 1977. Modeling economic exchange. In Exchange systems in prehistory, Timothy Earle and J. E. Ericson, eds. Academic Press, New York, pp. 127–140.
Polanyi, Karl. 1968. On the comparative treatment of economic institutions in antiquity: with illustrations from Athens, Mycenae, and Alalakh. In Primitive, archaic and modern economies: essays of Karl Polanyi, G. Dalton, ed. Doubleday, Garden City, N.Y., pp. 306–334.
———. 1975. Traders and trade. In Ancient civilization and trade, J. A. Sabloff and C. C. Lamberg-Karlovsky, eds. University of New Mexico Press, Albuquerque, pp. 133–154.
Polanyi, Karl, M. Arensberg, and H. Pearson, eds. 1957. Trade and market in the early empires. Free Press, Glencoe, Ill.
Renfrew, Colin. 1969. Trade and culture process in European prehistory. Current Anthropology 10:151–160.
———. 1975. Trade as action at a distance. In Ancient civilization and trade, J. Sabloff and C. C. Lamberg-Karlovsky, eds. University of New Mexico Press, Albuquerque, pp. 3–59.
Renfrew, Colin, and J. F. Cherry, eds. 1986. Peer polity interaction and sociopolitical change. Cambridge University Press.

Renfrew, Colin, and S. J. Shennan, eds. 1982. Ranking, resource and exchange: aspects of the archaeology of early European society. Cambridge University Press.

Sabloff, Jeremy, and C. C. Lamberg-Karlovsky, eds. 1975. Ancient civilization and trade. University of New Mexico Press, Albuquerque.

Sahlins, Marshall. 1972. Stone Age economics. Aldine, Chicago.

Schortman, Edward M., and Patricia A. Urban. 1987. Modeling interregional interaction in prehistory. Advances in Archaeological Method and Theory 11:37–95.

Smith, Timothy J. 1983. Wampum as primitive valuables. In Research in economic anthropology, George Dalton, ed. JAI Press, Greenwich, Conn., pp. 225–245.

Thomas, David H. 1979. The kula exchange in cultural materialist perspective. In his Archaeology. Holt, Rinehart & Winston, New York, pp. 122–123.

Tueting, L. T. 1935. Native trade in southeast New Guinea. B. P. Bishop Museum Occasional Paper 11, No. 15. Honolulu, pp. 3–43.

Uberoi, J. P. S. 1962. Politics of the kula ring: an analysis of the findings of Bronislaw Malinowski. Manchester University Press.

Vehik, S. C. 1986. The effects of trade on resource procurement behavior, a late prehistoric example from the southern Plains. Plains Anthropologist 31(114):141–154.

Wright, Henry, and Melinda Zeder. 1977. The simulation of a linear exchange system under equilibrium conditions. In Exchange systems in prehistory, Timothy K. Earle and Jonathan E. Ericson, eds. Academic Press, New York, pp. 233–254.

Zagarell, A. 1986. Trade, women, class, and society in ancient western Asia. Current Anthropology 27(5):415–430.

SOURCES OF ADDITIONAL INFORMATION

An extended discussion of the archaeological study of trade and exchange is in Chapter 9, "What contact did they have?" of Colin Renfrew and Paul Bahn's text, *Archaeology: Theories, Method and Practice* (New York, Thames and Hudson, 1991), pp. 307–338. The interrelated mechanisms of trade, specialization, and the growth of complexity are discussed in the papers in the volume edited by Brumfiel and Earle (see References for citation).

For access to recent archaeological literature on trade and exchange systems, several review articles exist, each including more than 100 references. These are P. S. Wells, "Cross-cultural interaction and change in recent Old-World research," *American Antiquity* 54(2) (1989):66–83; M. B. Schiffer and J. M. Skibo, "Theory and experiment in the study of technological change," *Current Anthropology* 28(5):595–622; Zagarell 1986; Schortman and Urban 1987; Kipp and Schortman 1989; Kirch 1991 (see References for citations). Issues of *American Antiquity, Current Anthropology, American Anthropologist, Journal of Anthropological Archaeology*, and future volumes of all pertinent annual reviews of research should be consulted for later information.

F

FIELD ARCHAEOLOGY. The on-site investigation of areas of past human activity and the recovery of material remains indicative of that activity, using such field techniques as surveying, controlled excavation, surface collection, stratigraphic interpretation, and careful recording of CONTEXTual information.

Field archaeology encompasses all the on-site activities carried out by "dirt" archaeologists in the course of their investigations, from the identification of SITE locations through final data analysis and reporting. A diversity of techniques go into fieldwork: SURVEY and mapping; excavating, cataloging, and preserving ARTIFACTS and features; collecting samples of soil, carbon, and biological remains for chemical analysis; documentation of excavations by stratigraphic soil profiles; on-site photography of site features; aerial photography and remote sensing of buried features; and a variety of other activities. In addition, background research and preparation for a field project, which include planning and staffing, obtaining funds and permits, surveying relevant literature on the sites to be investigated, and interviewing residents of the study area or other informants for additional background material, may be considered components of a field archaeology project. The critically important postexcavation activities that include detailed laboratory and interpretative studies, and the preparation of written reports of their results for publication, are also a part of field archaeology, and are often the most time-consuming portion of a field project (Alexander 1970; Fladmark 1978; Sharer and Ashmore 1979; Joukowsky 1980; Haag 1986; Fagan 1988; Renfrew and Bahn 1991).

In modern field archaeology, the formulation of a research design is a critical prerequisite to undertaking any major field project, since this will determine both the goals of the field research and the methods to be employed in attaining them. The goals of the project, as well as available staff and funding, will determine the selection of field techniques and SAMPLING strategies.

The first systematic, well-recorded archaeological field research, judged by modern standards, was that carried out by Thomas Jefferson in 1784, when he trenched a prehistoric burial mound on his property in Virginia and noted the presence of stratification, carefully recording his procedures and results (Jefferson 1787). This was, however, an isolated incident of modern field method that was not to be emulated until toward the end of the nineteenth century.

In 1860, Giuseppe Fiorelli undertook the next systematic excavation effort of record, at the buried Roman city of Pompeii. Under Fiorelli's direction, buildings were consolidated, wall paintings were preserved rather than removed, and plaster of Paris casts were made of the impressions of bodies buried by the eruption of Vesuvius in A.D. 79, when the city was destroyed (Daniel 1976:165; Trigger 1989:196).

The next major achievement in field archaeology was Heinrich Schliemann's discovery of the site of ancient Troy, which he located at Hissarlik in Turkey from information in Homer's *Iliad*, which Schliemann correctly interpreted as being at least in part a factual record of past events. Although Schliemann's field technique left much to be desired, he was able to interpret stratigraphic evidence from some of his excavations at Troy, and later in Greece (Renfrew and Bahn 1991:28).

Among those who contributed most to the development of current archaeological field methods were two English archaeologists, General Augustus Lane-Fox Pitt-Rivers and Sir William Flinders Petrie. Pitt-Rivers drew upon his military experience in surveying and mapping in his archaeological work. Like Thomas Jefferson, he excavated sites on his own estates, during which he carefully recorded the exact position of every item recovered. His site plans embody the strictest of archaeological standards, and his recordkeeping was meticulously accurate. Flinders Petrie was, like Pitt-Rivers, a careful excavator and recorder, collecting and describing every item recovered and fully publishing the results of his excavations in Egypt and Palestine between the 1880s and early 1940s. Petrie also developed his own chronological technique of SERIATION, called "sequence dating," which he used to build a chronology for data obtained from 2,200 graves in Upper Egypt (see SERIATION).

Contemporary field methods are the product of many such innovators. The multidisciplinary approach to field research, now routinely employed in North American archaeology, was pioneered by Alfred Kidder, who was also first to develop a regional strategy that included seriation and stratigraphic excavation to establish chronological sequences. In the 1950s, multidisciplinary research made possible the archaeological documentation of the beginnings of agriculture in both hemispheres, beginning with Robert Braidwood's work at Jarmo in Iraq (Braidwood and Braidwood 1950, 1953, 1960; Braidwood 1972, 1974), and continuing in the New World with the Tehuacán Valley project in Mexico, under the direction of Richard MacNeish (MacNeish and Byers 1967; MacNeish 1974, 1981; see also FOOD PRODUCTION).

Gradually evolving field techniques led to greater control of excavations.

Following natural stratification was often superseded by the use of arbitrary excavation levels, or the two were used in combination for maximum vertical control, with even lithic detritus and minor finds from each level preserved in "level bags." Artifacts and features were routinely cataloged and recorded in the course of their excavation, and all significant finds, as well as samples taken, were recorded on soil profiles. Field diaries, mapping, and in situ photography all contributed to more complete records. Today, much of the detailed record-keeping required for a field project can be done by using portable computers in the field, which greatly reduces the amount of paperwork a major dig required in the past.

Since the 1960s, many new field methods have been developed, as well as some specialized kinds of fieldwork. The growth of underwater archaeology, fostered by the efforts of George Bass (Bass 1970, 1980) and others, has resulted in the recovery of information from both historic and prehistoric shipwrecks by diver-archaeologists, as well as the collection of artifacts from inundated sites. Other wet sites, such as swamps and bogs, present another set of field conditions. Since organic materials are extraordinarily well preserved in a wet, anaerobic environment, investigations of wet sites have yielded such previously unavailable materials as Olmec woodcarvings, preserved bodies of humans who lived as long as 10,000 years ago, and whole households and their contents. Excavating wet sites required the development of special techniques, such as hose-screening, to remove preserved materials from their wet matrix.

The "NEW" ARCHAEOLOGY of the 1960s and 1970s had its own unique effects on field methods. The scientific approach prescribed by the "new" archaeologists led to the design of projects with very explicit goals, formulated in advance of survey or excavation. It popularized probabilistic sampling strategies and the standard use of sophisticated statistical techniques of processing field data (see QUANTIFICATION). Another result of this revolution in archaeological research was the increased use of experimental methods and ethnographic data in the course of archaeological field research (see ETHNOARCHAEOLOGY).

Current field research involves a complex sequence of procedures, beginning with formulation of the research design and ending with publication of the final report. For a major project, this sequence will normally include a literature survey, interviews with local residents, obtaining permits and permissions, staffing, and preparation of field facilities before the actual process of data acquisition is begun. The first phase of data acquisition itself will usually involve reconnaissance, preliminary surface survey and collection, and mapping, perhaps including aerial reconnaissance and photography, followed by surveying and grid layout for any sites selected for intensive systematic surface collection or test excavation. Actual digging is usually done with shovels to strip off deposits, keeping careful track of stratigraphic layers as well as arbitrary levels, if used. A separate field record is kept for each excavation unit, in which all finds are described and their context and associations carefully recorded. Excavated soil is routinely sieved through a fine wire-mesh screen, to recover any small items that may otherwise miss the excavator's notice. All artifacts are cataloged in the field, and features such as hearths and other fixtures (e.g., altars, benches) are cleared, recorded, photographed, and usually left in place. Stratigraphic profiles are made of each excavation unit, on which locations of important finds are recorded. Such profiles, in combination with artifact seriation and analysis, will provide the basic data for later constructing a relative chronology for the site, to be checked against any chronometric dates obtained from carbon samples or the use of other absolute dating methods (see CHRONOMETRIC DATING; RELATIVE DATING).

As field research progresses, the original research strategy may change, as a result of discoveries that necessitate modifications of the original plans. All steps and procedures require careful recording, and all records must be organized in a filing system, either manual or computerized, that will allow rapid retrieval of data for cross-checking and review as fieldwork progresses. Once the on-site field research is completed, all records will be used throughout the often lengthy laboratory phase of data analysis and interpretation, which may require the efforts of a number of experts representing a variety of academic disciplines, as well as the use of statistical procedures for computer analysis. Only when this portion of the study has been completed will the writing of reports for publication be possible.

Today European and North American large-scale field research projects often follow a procedure resembling that outlined above. In some other areas, however, significant differences in field methods will be found. For example, in Latin American countries, field archaeology often consists largely of cosmetic restoration efforts, directed at consolidating or restoring ruined structures to make archaeological sites more attractive to tourists, with only incidental recovery of ceramics and major artifacts and features, rather than research-oriented excavation or survey. Adoption of modern field methods has been slow and inconsistent in Latin America, and techniques such as flotation, permitting recovery of microfaunal and microbotanical remains, are rarely employed. Excavated deposits are frequently not sieved or screened to recover small artifacts and ecofacts, except in the course of projects directed by foreign archaeologists. Existing techniques frequently result in the loss of substantial amounts of information.

Because of the destructive nature of excavation, as well as its costliness, intensive surface survey has replaced excavation as the principal technique of field investigation in recent years, especially in North America. Such surveys can be carried out at a fraction of the cost of an excavation project, and new methods of locating archaeological remains through remote sensing and predictive modeling are being widely adopted (Kohler and Parker 1986; Scollar et al. 1990). This trend is likely to become more pronounced in the future, if present funding levels and pressures for preserving sites continue to exist.

New techniques of field archaeology and data analysis continue to be developed, as well as refinements of older methods. Chemical analyses of deposits can now be used to document site use even when ARTIFACTS are not present (Barba and Ortiz 1992); the use of remote sensing devices and electronic survey instruments greatly increases the ease and speed of surveys (Batey 1987). Nondestructive methods of evaluating the excavation potential of sites from patterns and characteristics of surface finds are being developed (Powell and Klasert 1984). Field methods based in the physical and engineering sciences that are now in use have greatly contributed to the efficiency of fieldwork, and perhaps even to the comparability of field data, facilitating future reanalysis of information when even more sophisticated methods are likely to be available.

REFERENCES

Alexander, John. 1970. The directing of archaeological excavations. J. Baker, London.
Barba, Luis, and Agustín Ortiz. 1992. Análisis químico de pisos de ocupación: un caso etnográfico en Tlaxcala, México. Latin American Antiquity 3(1):63–82.
Bass, George. 1970. Archaeology under water. Thames and Hudson and Penguin Books.
———. 1980. Marine archaeology: a misunderstood science. In Ocean Yearbook 2, Elisabeth Mann Borgese and Norton Ginsburg, eds. University of Chicago Press, pp. 137–152.
Batey, Richard A. 1987. Subsurface interface radar at Sepphones, Israel, 1985. Journal of Field Archaeology 14(1):1–8.
Braidwood, Robert J. 1972. Prehistoric investigations in southwestern Asia. Proceedings of the American Philosophical Society 116:310–320.
———. 1974. The Iraq Jarmo project. In Archaeological researches in retrospect, Gordon R. Willey, ed. Winthrop, Cambridge, Mass., pp. 59–83.
Braidwood, Robert J., and L. S. Braidwood. 1950. Jarmo: A village of early farmers in Iraq. Antiquity 24:189–195.
———. 1953. The earliest village communities of southwestern Asia. Journal of World History 1:278–310.
———. 1960. Prehistoric excavations in Iraqi Kurdistan. University of Chicago Press.
Daniel, Glyn. 1976. A hundred and fifty years of archaeology. Harvard University Press, Cambridge, Mass.
Fagan, Brian. 1988. In the beginning: an introduction to archaeology. 6th ed. Scott, Foresman, Glenview, Ill.
Fladmark, Knud R. 1978. A guide to basic archaeological field procedures. Department of Archaeology Publication No. 4. Simon Fraser University, Burnaby, B.C. (Canadian methods)
Haag, William G. 1986. Field methods in archaeology. In American archaeology, past and future, David J. Meltzer, Don D. Fowler, and Jeremy A. Sabloff, eds. Society for American Archaeology/Smithsonian Institution, Washington, D.C., pp. 63–76.
Jefferson, Thomas. 1787. Notes on the state of Virginia. John Stockdale, London. (Reprinted by University of North Carolina Press, Chapel Hill, 1954)
Joukowsky, Martha. 1980. A complete manual of field archaeology. Prentice-Hall, Englewood Cliffs, N.J. (American methods)
Kohler, Timothy A., and Sandra C. Parker. 1986. Predictive models for archaeological resource location. Advances in Archaeological Method and Theory 9:397–452.
MacNeish, Richard S. 1974. Reflections on my search for the beginnings of agriculture

in Mexico. In Archaeological researches in retrospect, Gordon R. Willey, ed. Winthrop, Cambridge, Mass., pp. 207–234.

————. 1981. Tehuacán's accomplishments. In Handbook of Middle American Indians Supplement 1: Archaeology, Victoria Bricker and Jeremy A. Sabloff, eds. University of Texas Press, Austin, pp. 31–47.

MacNeish, Richard S., and D. S. Byers. 1967. The prehistory of the Tehuacán Valley: environment and subsistence. University of Texas Press, Austin.

Powell, Shirley, and Anthony L. Klasert. 1984. A method for predicting the presence of buried structures on unexcavated artifact scatters. In Papers on the archaeology of Black Mesa, Arizona, vol. 2, Stephen Plog and Shirley Powell, eds. Southern Illinois University Press, Carbondale and Edwardsville, pp. 39–46.

Renfrew, Colin, and Paul Bahn. 1991. Archaeology: theories, method and practice. Thames and Hudson, New York.

Scollar, Irwin, A. Tabbagh, A. Hesse, and I. Herzog. 1990. Archaeological prospecting and remote sensing. Cambridge University Press.

Sharer, Robert, and Wendy Ashmore. 1979. Fundamentals of archaeology. Benjamin Cummings, Menlo Park, Calif.

Trigger, Bruce G. 1989. A history of archaeological thought. Cambridge University Press.

SOURCES OF ADDITIONAL INFORMATION

For basic information on field methods, see chapter 3 of Renfrew and Bahn (1991; cited in References above) and the field manuals by Joukowsky and Fladmark (see References). These and other field manuals, such as T. N. Hester, H. J. Shafer, and R. F. Heizer, *Field Methods in Archaeology*, 7th ed. (Palo Alto, Calif., Mayfield, 1987), outline standard method and practice in North America; other nations have developed field manuals reflecting their own current practice.

For an excellent and detailed step-by-step description of a modern archaeological field project, see "A case study in research design: the Quirigua project," in Sharer and Ashmore 1979, pp. 120–143 (see References). For a historical overview of the development of field archaeology in North America, see Haag 1986 (see References). The included bibliography will lead the reader to other relevant material.

For the latest applications of field methods, see current issues of *Journal of Field Archaeology* and *American Antiquity*.

FOOD PRODUCTION. The stage of economic development in which full dependence upon the cultivation of crops becomes the principal mode of SUBSISTENCE, often in combination with animal husbandry.

Food production refers to the mode of subsistence attained when agricultural products provide all, or nearly all, of the food consumed by a population, and is characterized by the appearance of various methods of agricultural intensification as populations enlarge. Such techniques as irrigation, crop rotation, hillside terracing, and intensive wetland cultivation are frequently developed to improve land productivity. Food-producing populations are sedentary, occupying permanent, large communities located in close proximity to the zones of cultivation and pasturage that provide their principal food source.

Speculation about the origins of agriculture has existed at least since the time of Lucretius. Such speculation increased among the philosophers of the seventeenth and eighteenth centuries, a time when interest in the past and the development of social institutions had been stimulated by discoveries of exotic peoples and a growing awareness of the antiquity of the human race.

Archaeologists and social scientists have long appreciated the critical importance of the transition to food production, an occurrence that transformed human societies from small groups of food collectors and villagers into large, complex populations of city dwellers. It has usually been assumed that food production was necessary to the development of permanent settlements and urban life, although a different view has been suggested (Bender 1975:22), and there is some archaeological evidence that a sedentary lifeway may have preceded the transition to agriculture in some areas (Henry 1985).

In the early years of the twentieth century, many archaeologists believed that food production had been discovered only once in human history, in a relatively small area of the Near East, and subsequently had been diffused throughout the world from this single primary center. It was suggested that as a consequence of this momentous discovery, a plethora of other cultural and technical changes also occurred, resulting in a "broad spectrum revolution" in the Neolithic period that led to rapid population increases, technological advances, and eventually the appearance of complex urban state societies (Childe 1929, 1936, 1940, 1957; Renfrew 1979). However, as a result of research during the past several decades, archaeological evidence has accumulated that suggests food production was discovered independently a number of times, at widely separated locations, over a long period of time (Braidwood 1952, 1958; Braidwood and Howe 1961; Butzer 1971a, 1971b; Flannery 1973, 1986; Hassan 1975, 1976; Harris 1977; MacNeish 1977, 1982; Ford 1981a, 1981b; Young et al. 1983; Buikstra, Konigsberg, and Bullington 1986; Russell 1988; Edwards 1989; Pearsall and Piperno 1990).

Archaeological models seeking to account for the major economic change from food collecting to food production can be divided into those that view this transition as a response to resource stress, such as would have occurred with a sudden population increase or major environmental change, and those regarding it as a logical stage in a continuous evolutionary development. Theories with a resource stress component began in archaeology with Sven Nilsson in the 1830s, although the idea of population pressure as a stimulus to the development of agriculture appears in European thought as early as the seventeenth century (Trigger 1989:7–8). The publication of Esther Boserup's *The Conditions of Agricultural Growth* (Boserup 1965) stimulated an explosion of theoretical models in archaeology seeking to account for the transition to food production, or for the beginning of agricultural intensification, by a sudden increase in population at some critical point in prehistory (Binford 1968; Harris 1972, 1977; Bronson 1977; Cohen 1977; Smith and Young 1983). An early environmental stress model developed by V. Gordon Childe (1936) was invalidated by ecological research that produced no paleoenvironmental evidence of the increasing desiccation he had postulated as a causal factor leading to agriculture. Population pressure models, in which population increase was considered to be the primary causal mechanism leading to food production, were rejected during the 1980s as too simplistic. Most archaeologists now believe the transition to production, like other major adaptive changes in human history, was the result of the complex interaction of many causal factors, and agricultural production may have been triggered by a varied range of conditions at different times in different geographic regions.

Archaeologists who have regarded the transition to food production as basically a logical consequence of the evolutionary process have included Robert Braidwood, Richard MacNeish, Kent Flannery, and David Rindos (Braidwood 1952, 1958; Braidwood and Howe 1961; MacNeish 1977, 1982, 1991; Rindos 1984). Flannery's systemic view prompted attempts to reconstruct the cultural processes leading to this economic shift in particular cases, resulting in his systemic models for the transition based on his work in Mexico and the Near East, in which he saw cultivation as a logical extension of the seasonally scheduled intensive collecting activities of complex hunter-gatherers (Flannery 1969, 1973, 1986).

Perhaps the most ambitious evolutionary model for the development of agriculture is that developed by David Rindos (Rindos 1984), whose food production model is actually incidental to his larger objective of constructing an overall research strategy for anthropology and archaeology based entirely on the principles of Darwinian evolution. Rindos set out to discover why farming should enhance human fitness by contributing to the survival and reproduction of the human individual. Noting the many natural coevolutionary symbiotic relationships that exist in nature between various species of plants and animals, Rindos used these to account for the origin of food production in human societies as an extension of a natural process. The model assumes that human populations will tend to increase with time; specialized production of particular domesticates and intensification techniques are seen as the consequences of population growth following the initial period of food production.

It is now recognized that the nature of the relationship between human population increases and the beginnings of food production is still not clearly discernible from the ARCHAEOLOGICAL RECORD. Although the continuous growth of populations in the Neolithic period is not in dispute, the material record is unclear as to whether the most rapid periods of growth preceded or followed the transition to agriculture, and the demographic situation may have varied from one geographic locality to another. The results of agricultural intensification are more evident, since this appears always to have been accompanied by a rapid increase in population growth rates. Archaeologists in the 1990s realize, however, that there is no simple causal link between demography and food production, and the subtle and complex manner in which these two variables may be related requires further exploration.

Diffusionist theories for the appearance of food production were still present in archaeology as recently as the 1970s. The theory that cultivation was introduced to the New World from a single center of invention in the Old World by means of transoceanic voyagers in prehistoric times, favored by the so-called diffusionist school of the early twentieth century, has now been largely discredited, despite attempts to produce evidence in its support (Sauer 1962; Barrau 1963; Carter 1977). Although numerous plant species have been suggested as candidates for early transport from the Old World, only four are likely to have been present on both sides of the Pacific before Columbus—namely cotton, sweet potato, coconut, and bottle gourd—and the botanical evidence for their early presence in both locations is highly equivocal (Pickersgill and Bunting 1969). It is probably significant that none of these constitutes a staple crop in either Asia or the Americas (but see below; and Hayden 1990).

An original scenario for the beginnings of cultivation is presented in a paper by Brian Hayden (Hayden 1990). Noting that the first crops to be cultivated by peoples in many parts of the world have not been the grains that eventually became dietary staples but cultigens from which prestige items might be made, such as the bottle gourd, or plants from which intoxicants, delicacies, or ornaments were manufactured, Hayden hypothesizes that the first crop cultivation was stimulated by the presence of "accumulators," competitive persons present in resource-rich communities where feasting and ceremonial activities were an important part of the CULTURE. Such persons sought to acquire these prestige-enhancing materials in quantity, in order to outclass their rivals, and in some instances gave them as gifts during feasting activities as a further means of enhancing their position. The latter phenomenon has been observed ethnographically in CHIEFDOM societies of the Northwest Coast, a resource-rich area where tobacco, another status-enhancing product, was one of the very few cultivated plants. This model presents a view of agriculture as a response to the beginnings of social differences, a result of social rather than economic or demographic processes.

Animal domestication was once thought to represent an earlier stage of development in the EVOLUTION of food production. Theorists of the nineteenth and early twentieth centuries believed that agriculture and sedentary settlement followed a period of "pastoralism," during which animals were herded by nomadic human populations who followed the seasonal foraging movements of their herds and lived in temporary or semipermanent camps near their animals' grazing areas. Only later, when crop cultivation began to replace the harvesting of wild grains and other plants, did food production completely replace a nomadic lifestyle and require settlement in permanent communities.

While a pattern of pastoralism has been established for some groups in the post-Pleistocene period, from both archaeological evidence and historical records, this is now known to have been a phenomenon of limited distribution. In some parts of the world, nothing resembling a "pastoral" phase has been observed. In at least some instances, this was simply due to the absence of mammals appropriate for domestication, such as bovids or ovines, as was true in the Americas after the end of the Pleistocene, until their reintroduction by the Spaniards at the time of the Conquest. The best archaeological evidence of pastoral ADAPTATIONS preceding the beginning of agriculture has been found in parts of Europe, India, and the Near East (Allchin 1972; Higgs and Jarman 1972). Some have suggested that here the cultivation of grains may have been prompted by a need to produce food not for humans but for domestic animals, when pasturelands began to be depleted from overgrazing (Hecker 1982; Henry 1985).

Current archaeological thinking about pastoralism has been profoundly affected by the large number of ethnoarchaeological hunter-gatherer studies of the 1980s, and by the influence of optimal foraging theory (Keegan 1986; see HUNTER-GATHERER ARCHAEOLOGY). As a result of these influences, the view of an evolutionary progression from hunter-gatherer to herding or cultivation is no longer commonly conceived as a series of transitions from one type of society to another. These changes are now more likely to be viewed as the adoption of alternative subsistence strategies that, either singly or in combination, were more appropriate to particular sets of environmental or social conditions at particular times (see, e.g., Layton, Foley, and Williams 1991).

It should be noted that many of the "theories" discussed above that attempt to account for the beginnings of food production and a settled lifeway which eventually resulted in urban civilization are not truly theories, in the strict sense of general explanations. Many of them apply only to specific cases, and are better described as scenarios, since they do not account in operational terms for the development of food production in the general case, although some attempts have been made to do this (e.g., Green 1980; Rindos 1984; Redding 1988). However, the contributions to our understanding of the origins of food production made by such investigators as Braidwood, MacNeish, Flannery, and others demonstrate that it is possible to do productive research and discover new insights into prehistoric subsistence change, including the transition to food production, without the advantage of a general theory. Such a theory would, however, make field research into the origins of agriculture more efficient, by generating hypotheses of general applicability that could be tested with field data.

REFERENCES

Allchin, B. 1972. Hunters or pastoral nomads? Late Stone Age settlements in western and central India. In Man, settlement and urbanism, Peter J. Ucko, Ruth Tringham, and G. W. Dimbleby, eds. Duckworth, London, pp. 115–119.

Barrau, J., ed. 1963. Plants and the migrations of Pacific peoples. Bishop Museum Press, Honolulu.

Bender, Barbara. 1975. Farming in prehistory: from hunter-gatherer to food producer. St. Martin's Press, New York.

Binford, Lewis R. 1968. Post-Pleistocene adaptations. In New perspectives in archaeology, S. R. Binford and L. R. Binford, eds. Aldine, Chicago, pp. 313–341.

Boserup, Esther. 1965. The conditions of agricultural growth: the economics of agrarian change under population pressure. Aldine, Chicago.

Braidwood, Robert. 1952. The Near East and the foundations of civilization. Oregon State System of Higher Education, Eugene.

————. 1958. Near Eastern prehistory. Science 127(3312):1419–1430.

Braidwood, Robert, and B. Howe. 1961. Prehistoric investigations in Iraqi Kurdistan. Studies in Ancient Oriental Civilization 31. Oriental Institute, University of Chicago.

Bronson, Bennet. 1977. The earliest farming: demography as cause and consequence. In The origins of agriculture, Charles Reed, ed. Mouton, The Hague.

Buikstra, Jane, Lyle Konigsberg, and Jill Bullington. 1986. Fertility and the development of agriculture in the prehistoric Midwest. American Antiquity 51:528–546.

Butzer, Karl W. 1971a. Agricultural origins in the Near East as a geographical problem. In Prehistoric agriculture, S. Struever, ed. The Natural History Press, Garden City, N.Y., pp. 209–235.

————. 1971b. The significance of agricultural dispersal into Europe and northern Africa. In Prehistoric agriculture, S. Struever, ed. The Natural History Press, Garden City, N.Y., pp. 313–334.

Carter, George F. 1977. A hypothesis suggesting a single origin of agriculture. In The origins of agriculture, Charles A. Reed, ed. Mouton, The Hague, pp. 89–133.

Chang, Claudia, and Harold A. Koster. 1986. Beyond bones: toward an archaeology of pastoralism. Advances in Archaeological Method and Theory 9:97–148.

Childe, Vere Gordon. 1929. The Danube in prehistory. Oxford University Press.

————. 1936. Man makes himself. Watts, London.

————. 1940. Prehistoric communities of the British Isles. W. and R. Chambers, London.

————. 1957. The dawn of European civilization. 6th ed. Routledge, London.

Cohen, Mark N. 1977. The food crisis in prehistory. Yale University Press, New Haven.

Edwards, Phillip C. 1989. Revising the broad spectrum revolution and its role in the origins of southwest Asian food production. Antiquity 63(239):225–246.

Flannery, Kent V. 1969. Origins and ecological effects of early domestication in Iran and the Near East. In The domestication and exploitation of plants and animals, P. J. Ucko and G. W. Dimbleby, eds. Duckworth, London, pp. 73–100.

————. 1973. The origins of agriculture. Annual Review of Anthropology 2:271–310.

————. 1986. Guila Naquitz: Archaic foraging and early agriculture in Oaxaca, Mexico. Academic Press, Orlando, Fla.

Ford, Richard I. 1981a. Gardening and farming before AD 1000: Patterns of prehistoric cultivation north of Mexico. Journal of Ethnobiology 1:6–27.

————. 1981b. New ideas about the origin of agriculture based on 50 years of museum-curated plant remains. In The research potential of anthropological museum collections, Anne-Marie E. Cantwell, James B. Griffin, and Nan A. Rothschild, eds. Annals of the New York Academy of Sciences, no. 276:345–356.

Green, Stanton W. 1980. Toward a general model of agricultural systems. Advances in Archaeological Method and Theory 3:311–355.

Harris, David R. 1972. The origins of agriculture in the tropics. American Scientist 60:180–193.

————. 1977. Alternative pathways toward agriculture. In The origins of agriculture, Charles Reed, ed. Mouton, The Hague, pp. 179–243.

Hassan, Fekri A. 1975. Diet, nutrition and agricultural origins in the Near East. In Origine de l'élévage et de la domestication, E. Higgs, ed. Union International des Sciences Préhistoriques et Protohistoriques, Paris, pp. 227–247.

————. 1976. The dynamics of agricultural origins in Palestine: a theoretical model. In The origins of agriculture, Charles Reed, ed. Mouton, The Hague.

Hayden, Brian. 1990. Nimrods, piscators, pluckers and planters: the emergence of food production. Journal of Anthropological Archaeology 9(1):31–69.

Hecker, Howard M. 1982. Domestication revisited: its implications for faunal analysis. Journal of Field Archaeology 9:217–236.

Henry, Donald O. 1985. Preagricultural sedentism: The Natufian example. In Prehistoric hunter-gatherers: the emergence of cultural complexity, T. Douglas Price and James A. Brown, eds. Academic Press, Orlando, Fla., pp. 365–384.

Higgs, E. S., and M. R. Jarman. 1972. The origins of plant and animal husbandry. In Papers in economic prehistory, E. S. Higgs, ed. Cambridge University Press, pp. 3–13.

Keegan, W. F. 1986. The optimal foraging analysis of horticultural production. American Anthropologist 88(1):92–107.

Layton, Robert, Robert Foley, and Elizabeth Williams. 1991. The transition between hunting and gathering and the specialized husbandry of resources: a socio-ecological approach. Current Anthropology 32(3):255–275.

MacNeish, Richard S. 1977. The beginnings of agriculture in central Peru. In The origins of agriculture, Charles Reed, ed. Mouton, The Hague.

———. 1981. Tehuacán's accomplishments. In Handbook of Middle American Indians. Supplement 1: Archaeology, Victoria Bricker and Jeremy Sabloff, eds. University of Texas Press, Austin, pp. 31–47.

———. 1991. The origins of agriculture and settled life. University of Oklahoma Press, Norman.

Pearsall, Deborah M., and Dolores R. Piperno. 1990. Antiquity of maize cultivation in Ecuador. Summary and reevaluation of the evidence. American Antiquity 55(2):324–337.

Pickersgill, Barbara, and A. H. Bunting. 1969. Cultivated plants and the Kon-Tiki theory. Nature 222:225–227.

Redding, R. W. 1988. A general explanation of subsistence change—from hunting and gathering to food production. Journal of Anthropological Archaeology 7(1):56–97.

Renfrew, Colin. 1979. Before civilization: the radiocarbon revolution and prehistoric Europe. Cambridge University Press.

Rindos, David. 1984. The origins of agriculture: an evolutionary perspective. Academic Press, New York.

Russell, Kenneth. 1988. After Eden: the behavioral ecology of early food production in the Near East and North Africa. BAR International Series 391. Oxford.

Sauer, Carl O. 1962. Agricultural origins and dispersals: the domestication of animals and foodstuffs. 2nd ed. MIT Press, Cambridge, Mass.

Smith, Philip E. L., and T. Cuyler Young, Jr. 1983. The force of numbers: population pressure in the central western Zagros 12,000-4500 B.C. In The hilly flanks and beyond, T. Cuyler Young, Jr., et al., eds. Oriental Institute, University of Chicago, pp. 141–162.

Trigger, Bruce G. 1989. A history of archaeological thought. Cambridge University Press.

Young, T. Cuyler, Jr., P. E. L. Smith, and P. Mortensen, eds. 1983. The hilly flanks and beyond: essays on the prehistory of southwestern Asia, presented to Robert J. Braidwood November 15, 1982. Studies in Ancient Oriental Civilization No. 36. Oriental Institute, University of Chicago.

SOURCES OF ADDITIONAL INFORMATION

The literature of explanations for the origins of food production is extensive, and it is possible to mention here only some of the more recent important additions to it.

A general summary and critique of explanatory models proposed up to the present is included in Richard W. Redding, "A general explanation of subsistence change: from hunting and gathering to food production," *Journal of Anthropological Archaeology* 7(1988):56–97, along with the author's own multistage continuum model and an extensive bibliography of the literature. Layton, Foley, and Williams (1991; see References for citation) also present a new, environmental change model for the transition, and include a substantial bibliography; another contribution is M. Rosenberg, "The mother of invention: evolutionary theory, territoriality, and the origins of agriculture," *American Anthropologist* 92(2) (1990):399–415. Phillip C. Edwards's critique of Kent Flannery's "broad spectrum" model (1989; see References) is also a source of numerous references to the literature. Critiques of existing models are quite plentiful; another is offered by Richard A. Gould in "Now let's invent agriculture, a critical review of concepts of complexity among hunter-gatherers," in *Prehistoric Hunter-Gatherers: The Emergence of Cultural Complexity,* T. D. Price and J. A. Brown, eds. (Orlando, Fla., Academic Press, 1985). Critiques of the population-pressure models are especially abundant; see Lawrence Keeley's "Hunter-gatherer economic complexity and 'population pressure': a cross-cultural analysis," *Journal of Anthropological Archaeology* 7(1988):373–411. Richard MacNeish has produced a general book, *The Origins of Agriculture and Settled Life* (Norman, University of Oklahoma Press, 1991).

Some considerations of the often-neglected archaeological evidence of pastoralism in the domestication process include P. T. Robertshaw and D. P. Collett, "The identification of pastoral peoples in the archaeological record: an example from East Africa," *World Archaeology* 15(1)(1983):67–78; and a review article devoted to the subject by Claudia Chang and Harold A. Koster, "Beyond bones: toward an archaeology of pastoralism," *Advances in Archaeological Method and Theory* 9(1986):97–148, which includes a 15-page bibliography.

For access to current and future publications, see forthcoming issues of *American Anthropologist, Antiquity, American Antiquity, Journal of Anthropological Archaeology, Annual Review of Anthropology, Annual Review of Ecology and Systematics,* and *Archaeological Method and Theory.*

G

GEOARCHAEOLOGY. 1. Archaeological research using the methods, techniques, and concepts of the earth sciences in the study of past environments, human paleoecology, and other geology-related problems in archaeology, integrating paleoenvironmental data with paleobiological data to reconstruct human ecosystems of the past. 2. An interdisciplinary subfield of archaeology explicitly focused on the depositional environment of ARTIFACTS. Also sometimes called archaeogeology. See also STRATIGRAPHY; UNIFORMITARIANISM.

Geoarchaeology deals with the time period in geological history since humans have inhabited the earth (Gladfelter 1981:344). Some of the earliest archaeological excavations to document the human past were undertaken by geologists of the nineteenth century, and natural scientists have worked with archaeologists since at least the time of Charles Lyell. The adoption of the concepts of UNIFORMITARIANISM and STRATIGRAPHY in geology were instrumental in leading to the acceptance of the idea of human antiquity, which provided the basic framework for archaeological study of human and cultural EVOLUTION (Hassan 1979; Grayson 1983). The geologist Sir Charles Lyell was concerned with the geological aspects of archaeology (Lyell 1863a, 1863b), and the link between the two disciplines remained a strong one that has become formalized only since the 1970s with the development of geoarchaeology.

In the early twentieth century, between the 1920s and 1940s, a number of geologists and geographers participated in interdisciplinary archaeological research efforts, and contributed both methods and concepts to the development of prehistoric archaeology (Butzer 1982:35–36). Collaborative empirical studies of this type increased in number during the two ensuing decades. In 1960, Karl Butzer demonstrated the usefulness of a geoenvironmental approach in archaeological SURVEY and SETTLEMENT PATTERN research (Butzer 1960), and in 1964 he developed a geological classification of archaeological sites for use in regional environmental archaeological studies (Butzer 1964, ch. 15; 1982:36). Butzer was the first to use the term GEOARCHAEOLOGY (Butzer 1973), but the concept was simultaneously developed by two other independent sources, appearing in the title of the published proceedings of a 1973 symposium (Davidson and Shackley 1976) and the names of symposia at the Geological Society of America meeting (Rapp et al. 1974).

Geoarchaeology is concerned with man-land relationships and interaction in the past, and especially with how these contributed to the formation of archaeological sites (Gladfelter 1977). A part of this is its focus upon the matrix material, the dirt surrounding the cultural remains recovered by the "dirt" archaeologist, and the environmental information it may reveal concerning the SITE and its history (Hassan 1978; Stein 1985, 1987; Stein and Rapp 1985).

The first formal definition of the field of geoarchaeology and its scope was by Colin Renfrew, in his introduction to the published proceedings of the symposium "Sediments in Archaeology," edited by D. A. Davidson and M. L. Shackley (Renfrew 1976). Renfrew noted the long-standing traditional relationship between the fields of geology and ARCHAEOLOGY and their more recent combination in the new subdiscipline, which investigates the geological aspects and circumstances of archaeological sites as deposits, as well as their subsequent history. The latter is also a primary concern of taphonomists, while the geoarchaeologist's chief concern is with the geological CONTEXT in which archaeological remains are found.

In America geoarchaeologists are often earth scientists with an archaeological interest, while in Britain they are more often professional archaeologists with a strong interest in one or more of the earth sciences, such as Quaternary geology, STRATIGRAPHY, petrography, or sedimentology (Shackley 1975). Bruce Gladfelter noted that a survey in the late 1970s (Burgess 1978) showed most geoarchaeological research in the United States at that time was being done by persons trained in geology and holding positions in museums, institutes, government agencies, or the private sector, rather than by those in academic positions, and that a large majority of them had no formal graduate training in archaeology. Many appear to have been engaged in contract archaeology projects (Gladfelter 1981:346).

At least five major areas of specialized interest had emerged in geoarchaeology by the early 1980s. These included survey techniques using geochemical and other remote sensing procedures for locating sites and features; documenting formative processes and the larger environmental context of sites; study of post-depositional disturbance processes; the use of absolute and RELATIVE DATING methods to develop temporal sequences for stratified deposits; and paleoenvironmental reconstruction (Gladfelter 1981:347). By this time, geoarchaeology had acquired a sufficient disciplinary identity to produce some doctoral dissertations (e.g., Fladmark 1975; Stein 1980). It had acquired no central theoretic orientation, although some geoarchaeologists have made use of models based on system theory (e.g., Fedele 1976). As Gladfelter has noted, geoarchaeology is an emergent field, one still seeking a distinctive identity as a subdiscipline of archaeology (Gladfelter 1981:358).

REFERENCES

Burgess, R. D. 1978. Some results of a geo-archaeological survey. Society for Archaeological Sciences Newsletter 1:1–2.

Butzer, Karl W. 1960. Archaeology and geology in ancient Egypt. Science 1132:1617–1624.

———. 1964. Environment and archaeology: an introduction to Pleistocene geography. Aldine, Chicago.

———. 1973. Spring sediments from the Acheulian site of Amanzi....Quaternaria 17:209–319.

———. 1982. Archaeology as human ecology. Cambridge University Press.

Davidson, D. A., and M. L. Shackley, eds. 1976. Geo-archaeology: earth science and the past. Duckworth, London.

Fedele, F. G. 1976. Sediments as palaeoland segments: the excavation side of study. In Geo-archaeology, D. A. Davidson and M. L. Shackley, eds. Duckworth, London, pp. 23–48.

Fladmark, Knud. 1975. A paleoecological model for Northwest Coast prehistory. Archaeological Survey of Canada Paper No. 43, National Museum of Man, Mercury Series. Ottawa.

Gladfelter, Bruce G. 1977. Geoarchaeology: the geomorphologist and archaeology. American Antiquity 42:519–538.

———. 1981. Development and directions in geoarchaeology. Advances in Archaeological Method and Theory 4:343–364.

Grayson, Donald K. 1983. The establishment of human antiquity. Academic Press, New York.

Hassan, Fekri A. 1978. Sediments in archaeology: methods and implications for palaeoenvironmental and cultural analysis. Journal of Field Archaeology 5:297–213.

———. 1979. Geoarchaeology: the geologist and archaeology. American Antiquity 44:267–270.

Lyell, Charles. 1863a. The antiquity of man. Athenaeum 41:523–525.

———. 1863b. The geological evidences of the antiquity of man with remarks on theories of the origin of species by variation. J. Murray, London.

Rapp, G., R. Bullard, and C. Albritton. 1974. Geoarchaeology? The Geologist 9:1.

Renfrew, Colin. 1976. Archaeology and the earth sciences. In Geo-archaeology, D. A. Davidson and M. L. Shackley, eds. Duckworth, London, pp. 1–5.

Shackley, M. L. 1975. Archaeological sediments: a survey of analytical methods. Wiley, New York.

———. 1981. Environmental archaeology. George Allen and Unwin, Boston.

Stein, Julie K. 1980. Geoarchaeology of the Green River shell mounds, Kentucky. Ph.D. dissertation, University of Minnesota. University Microfilms, Ann Arbor.

———. 1985. Interpreting sediments in cultural settings. In Archaeological sediments in context, J. K. Stein and W. R. Farrand, eds. Center for the Study of Early Man, University of Maine, Orono, pp. 5–19.

————. 1987. Deposits for archaeologists. Advances in Archaeological Method and Theory 11:337–395.

Stein, Julie K., and G. Rapp, Jr. 1985. Archaeological sediments: a largely untapped reservoir of information. In Contributions to Aegean archaeology, N. C. Wilkie and W. D. E. Coulson, eds. Center for Ancient Studies Publications in Ancient Studies 1. University of Minnesota, Minneapolis, pp. 143–159.

SOURCES OF ADDITIONAL INFORMATION

For further background material, see the review by Gladfelter in *Advances in Archaeological Method and Theory* 4 (1981; see References). This is the most comprehensive overview of the field, describing background, practice, and methods, and includes an illustrative geoarchaeological case study and extensive bibliography. Renfrew (1976; see References) gives only a brief overview.

Stein (1987) focuses on archaeological sediments in her review (see References); Dena F. Dincauze, in a review titled "Strategies for paleoenvironmental reconstruction in archaeology," *Advances in Archaeological Method and Theory* 11(1987):255–336, focuses on the paleoecological aspect. Karl Butzer has produced a very brief statement on method, "Toward an integrated, contextual approach in archaeology," *Journal of Archaeological Science* 5(1978):191–193, plus several applications, such as "Rise and fall of Axum, Ethiopia: a geoarchaeological interpretation," *American Antiquity* 46(1981):471–495; and "A 'marginality' model to explain major spatial and temporal gaps in the Old and New World Pleistocene settlement record," *Geoarchaeology* 3(1988):193–203. Fedele (1976; see References) attempts a theoretical approach, using models from David Clarke.

Some interesting applications are described in D. L. Drew, "Early man and where to look for him: geomorphic contexts," *Plains Anthropologist* 24(1979):269–281; and W. R. Farrand, "Sediment analysis of a prehistoric rock shelter: the Abri Pataud," *Quaternary Research* 5(1975):1–26.

Entree to the still rather sparse and scattered literature begins with the bibliographies in all the above-mentioned reviews. The Gladfelter review article (1981) also includes a substantial bibliography, but this is now out-of-date and needs to be supplemented with more recent material, such as the references listed in Stein 1987 and Dincauze 1987. Also check future issues of *Archaeological Method and Theory*, and the journals *Geoarchaeology*, *Quaternary Research*, *Journal of Archaeological Science*, *Journal of Field Archaeology*, and *American Antiquity* for current material.

H

HOUSEHOLD ARCHAEOLOGY. A subdivision of SETTLEMENT PATTERN archaeology specializing in the study of spatial patterning at the household level. Household archaeology may be considered as one aspect of settlement analysis, or as a specialized form of SPATIAL ANALYSIS.

The archaeology of the household as a social and spatial unit, although a relatively recent focus of research, has roots extending to the 1930s. Consideration of the ordinary family dwelling as an important unit worthy of archaeological study appeared in the work of the American archaeologist Robert Wauchope in that decade, as a result of his field studies in Mesoamerica (Wauchope 1934, 1938).

Household archaeology may also trace its historical antecedents to cultural anthropological studies of family and kinship structures and postmarital residence rules. Principles derived from these studies were first applied to the study of specifically archaeological problems by James Deetz (1965), William Longacre (1968), and James Hill (1968), who, together with William Haviland (1963) and K. C. Chang (1968), anticipated the flurry of development in the 1970s, when archaeological studies of residential remains as analytic units reflecting past activities carried out in the household began to emerge as a specialized area of study (Clarke 1972; Winter 1974; Calnek 1976; Flannery 1976; Reyna 1976; Brown 1977; Healan 1977; Stenholm 1979).

While the anthropologist George Murdock's earlier attempt to define residence rules for the generation of household units (Murdock 1949) did not prove particularly fruitful for archaeology, ethnographic and ethnohistorical studies have provided valuable resources for constructing analogies between past and recent household structures and composition, providing material for model building by archaeologists engaged in household studies of past communities (David 1971;

Hayden and Cannon 1982, 1984; Flannery 1983b). Ethnoarchaeological methodology has now become a standard approach in household studies, providing investigators with numerous insights into the past based on observations made in recent or contemporary communities (Kramer 1982; Smyth 1990; Widmer and Sheehey 1990; see also ETHNOARCHAEOLOGY).

For purposes of current investigations, the household, which has been defined as "an activity group and not necessarily a corporate social unit bound together by kinship or other social ties" (Wilk and Ashmore 1988:3), is taken as the basic unit of study, providing a microcosm of the society as a whole that may serve as an indicator of evolutionary change in SOCIAL ORGANIZATION at various scales or levels in the past.

During the 1980s, interest developed in investigating *activity areas*, the physical locations where specific activities such as butchering, cooking, weaving, or potterymaking were performed in the past (Kent 1983). The analysis of activity areas has contributed much to household archaeology, which tends to focus on those activities whose remains are identifiable within the household unit. A need for more precise terminology to denote the unit concepts of household archaeology than has traditionally been employed has been addressed by Wilk and Ashmore (1988:5–6), who offer a series of precise definitions of such terms as *household*, *coresidential group*, *dwelling*, and *house*, making it possible to employ such terms as analytic unit concepts when used according to their more restricted definitions (Wilk and Ashmore 1988:6).

While household studies have flourished in the western hemisphere (Glassie 1975; Calnek 1976; Brown 1977; Bawden 1982; Flannery 1983a, 1983b; Leventhal 1983; Rathje 1983; Tourtellot 1983; Webster and Abrams 1983; Wilk 1983, 1988; Stanish 1989; Storey and Widmer 1989), similar studies have also been carried out worldwide (e.g., Hammel 1980; Horne 1982; Herlihy 1984). Many of these have been more isolated efforts than household studies in the Americas, where a number of archaeological symposia have provided synthesis and exchange of data (e.g., Wilk and Ashmore 1988; MacEachern, Archer, and Garvin 1989).

The current goals of household archaeology include clarifying relationships between dwelling size and form, and residential group size; clarifying the nature of the coresidential group as a social unit; tracing social EVOLUTION from household remains; identification of economic and other activities performed at the household level, and how these vary within and between residential groups in the same society; and inferring the factors determining architectural form and variation in household remains within a community (Wilk and Ashmore 1988:19). Overall, household studies seek to delineate both household dynamics and the interaction of these basic social units with other social and economic entities in the local community, and with the society as a whole.

REFERENCES

Bawden, G. 1982. Community organization reflected by the household: a study of pre-Columbian social dynamics. Journal of Field Archaeology 9:165–181.

Brown, S. E. 1977. Household composition and variation in a rural Dominican village. Journal of Comparative Family Studies 3:257–267.

Calnek, E. E. 1976. The internal structure of Tenochtitlán. In The Valley of Mexico: Studies in prehispanic ecology and society, E. R. Wolf, ed. University of New Mexico Press, Albuquerque, pp. 287–302.

Chang, K. C. 1985. Study of the Neolithic social grouping: examples from the New World. American Anthropologist 60:198–334.

———, ed. 1968. Settlement archaeology. National Press Books, Palo Alto, Calif.

Clarke, David L. 1972. A provisional model of an Iron Age society and its settlement system. In Models in archaeology, David L. Clarke, ed. Methuen, London, pp. 801–869.

David, Nicholas. 1971. The Fulani compound and the archaeologist. World Archaeology 3:111–131.

Deetz, James. 1965. The dynamics of stylistic change in Arikara ceramics. Illinois Studies in Anthropology No. 4. University of Illinois Press, Urbana.

———. 1982. Households: a structural key to archaeological explanation. American Behavioral Scientist 25(6):717–724.

Flannery, Kent V. 1983a. The Tierras Largas phase and the analytical units of the early Oaxacan village. In The cloud people: divergent evolution of the Zapotec and Mixtec civilizations, Kent V. Flannery and Joyce Marcus, eds. Academic Press, New York, pp. 43–45.

———. 1983b. The legacy of the early urban period: an ethnohistoric approach to Monte Alban's temples, residences and royal tombs. In The cloud people . . . , Kent V. Flannery and Joyce Marcus, eds. Academic Press, New York, pp. 132–136.

———, ed. 1976. The early Mesoamerican village. Academic Press, New York.

Glassie, H. 1975. Folk housing in middle Virginia: a structural analysis of historic artifacts. University of Tennessee Press, Knoxville.

Hammel, E. A. 1980. Household structure in fourteenth-century Macedonia. Journal of Family History 5:242–273.

Haviland, William A. 1963. Excavation of small structures in the northeast quadrant of Tikal, Guatemala. Ph.D. dissertation, Department of Anthropology, University of Pennsylvania, Philadelphia.

Hayden, Brian D., and Aubrey Cannon. 1982. The corporate group as an archaeological unit. Journal of Anthropological Archaeology 1:132–158.

———. 1984. The structure of material systems: ethnoarchaeology in the Maya highlands. SAA Papers No. 3. Society for American Archaeology, Washington, D.C.

Healan, D. M. 1977. Architectural implications of daily life in ancient Tollan, Hidalgo, Mexico. World Archaeology 2:117–163.

Herlihy, D. 1984. Households in the early Middle Ages: symmetry and sainthood. In Households: comparative and historical studies of the domestic group, R. M. Netting, R. R. Wilk, and E. J. Arnould, eds. University of California Press, Berkeley, pp. 383–406.

Hill, James N. 1968. Broken K Pueblo: patterns of form and function. In New perspectives in archaeology, S. R. Binford and L. R. Binford, eds. Aldine, Chicago, pp. 103–142.

Horne, L. 1982. The household in space: dispersed holdings in an Iranian village. In Archaeology of the household, R. R. Wilk and W. L. Rathje, eds. American Behavioral Scientist 25:677–685.

Kent, Susan. 1983. Analyzing activity areas. University of New Mexico Press, Albuquerque.

Kramer, Carole. 1982. Ethnographic households and archaeological interpretation: a case of Iranian Kurdistan. In Archaeology of the household, R. R. Wilk and W. L. Rathje, eds. American Behavioral Scientist 25:663–675.

Leventhal, R. M. 1983. Household groups and Classic Maya religion. In Prehistoric settlement patterns: essays in honor of Gordon R. Willey, Evon Z. Vogt and R. M. Leventhal, eds. University of New Mexico Press, Albuquerque, pp. 55–76.

Longacre, William. 1968. Some aspects of prehistoric society in east central Arizona. In New perspectives in archaeology, S. R. Binford and L. R. Binford, eds. Aldine, Chicago, pp. 89–102.

MacEachern, Scott, David J. W. Archer, and Richard D. Garvin, eds. 1989. Households and communities: proceedings of the 21st annual Chacmool conference. Archaeological Association of the University of Calgary.

Murdock, George P. 1949. Social structure. Macmillan, New York.

Netting, Robert McC. 1982. Some home truths on household size and wealth. American Behavioral Scientist 25(6):641–662.

Rathje, William L. 1983. To the salt of the earth: some comments on household archaeology among the Maya. In Prehistoric settlement patterns, essays in honor of Gordon R. Willey, E. Z. Vogt and R. M. Leventhal, eds. University of New Mexico Press, Albuquerque, pp. 23–34.

Rathje, William L., and Randall H. McGuire. 1982. Rich men . . . poor men. American Behavioral Scientist 25(6):705–715.

Reid, J. Jefferson, and Stephanie M. Whittlesey. 1982. Households at Grasshopper Pueblo. American Behavioral Scientist 25(6):687–704.

Reyna, S. 1976. The extending strategy: regulation of household dependency ratio. Journal of Anthropological Research 32:182–199.

Smyth, Michael P. 1990. Reconstructing the past by reference to the present: the social implications of household activity organization at Sayil, Yucatán, Mexico. Paper presented at the 55th annual meeting of the Society for American Archaeology, Las Vegas, Nev.

Stanish, Charles. 1989. Household archeology: testing models of zonal complementarity in the south central Andes. American Anthropologist 92(2):7–24.

Stenholm, N. A. 1979. Identification of house structures in Mayan archaeology: a case study at Kaminaljuyu. In Settlement pattern excavations at Kaminaljuyu, Guatemala, J. W. Michels, ed. Pennsylvania State University Press, University Park, pp. 31–182.

Storey, Rebecca, and Randolph J. Widmer. 1989. Household and community structure of a Teotihuacán apartment compound: S3W1:33 of the Tlajinga barrio. Paper presented at the 21st annual Chacmool conference, University of Calgary.

Tourtellot, Gair. 1983. An assessment of Classic Maya household composition. In Prehistoric settlement patterns: essays in honor of Gordon R. Willey, E. Z. Vogt and R. M. Leventhal, eds. University of New Mexico Press, Albuquerque.

Wauchope, Robert. 1934. House mounds of Uaxactun, Guatemala. Carnegie Institution of Washington Publication 436, Contribution 7. Washington, D.C.

———. 1938. Modern Maya houses: a study of their archaeological significance. Carnegie Institution of Washington Publication 502. Washington, D.C.

Webster, David L., and E. M. Abrams. 1983. An elite compound at Copan, Honduras. Journal of Field Archaeology 10:285–296.

Widmer, Randolph J., and James J. Sheehey. 1990. Archaeological implications of architectural changes in the development cycle of a modern pottery workshop in

Teotihuacán. Paper presented at 55th annual meeting of the Society for American Archaeology, Las Vegas, Nev.

Wilk, Richard R. 1983. Little house in the jungle: the causes of variation in house size among modern Maya. Journal of Anthropological Archaeology 2:99–116.

———. 1988. Maya household organization: evidence and analogies. In Household and community in the Mesoamerican past, R. R. Wilk and Wendy Ashmore, eds. University of New Mexico Press, Albuquerque, pp. 135–151.

Wilk, Richard R., and Wendy Ashmore. 1988. Household and community in the Mesoamerican past. In Household and community in the Mesoamerican Past, R. R. Wilk and W. Ashmore, eds. University of New Mexico Press, Albuquerque, pp. 1–27.

———, eds. 1988. Household and community in the Mesoamerican past. University of New Mexico Press, Albuquerque.

Wilk, Richard R., and William L. Rathje. 1982. Household archaeology. American Behavioral Scientist 25(6):617–639.

Winter, Marcus. 1974. Residential patterns at Monte Alban, Oaxaca, Mexico. Science 185:981–987.

SOURCES OF ADDITIONAL INFORMATION

In 1982, an entire issue of *American Behavioral Scientist* (vol. 25, no. 6, July/August) was devoted to "Archaeology of the household: building a prehistory of domestic life," Richard R. Wilk and William L. Rathje, eds. Ten articles by Wilk and Rathje, Robert McC. Netting, Carol Kramer, Lee Horne, J. Jefferson Reid and Stephanie M. Whittlesey, Rathje and Randall McGuire, and James Deetz were included (see References for complete citations).

Some nonarchaeological household studies that have potential usefulness for providing data for ethnoarchaeological investigations in the areas covered include Nancie L. Solien Gonzalez, *Black Carib Household Structure, a Study of Migration and Modernization* (Seattle, University of Washington Press, 1969), based on the author's dissertation research in Belize during the 1950s; a collection of anthropological studies edited by Jack Goody, *The Developmental Cycle in Domestic Groups* (Cambridge, Cambridge University Press, 1985), which includes a paper by Derrick J. Stenning, "Household viability among the pastoral Fulani," a description of the group that served for one of the earliest (and most original) ethnoarchaeological studies, Nicholas David's "The Fulani compound and the archaeologist" (see ETHNOARCHAEOLOGY for complete reference); and Peter Laslett and Richard Wall, eds., *Household and Family in Past Time: Comparative Studies in the Size and Structure of the Domestic Group over the Last Three Centuries in England, France, Serbia, Japan and Colonial North America* . . . (Cambridge, Cambridge University Press, 1972).

A paper by Michael E. Smith, "Household possessions and wealth in agrarian states: implications for archaeology," Journal of Anthropological Archaeology 6 (1987):297–335, discusses problems of measuring household wealth from domestic artifactual remains. It includes the most extensive recent bibliography available for household studies.

For more recent material, current issues of *American Anthropologist, Journal of Field Archaeology, American Antiquity, Journal of Anthropological Research*, and *Journal of Anthropological Archaeology* should be consulted, as well as latest volumes of *Annual Review of Anthropology* and *Archaeological Method and Theory*.

HUNTER-GATHERER ARCHAEOLOGY. The specialized archaeological study of prehistoric groups pursuing a seasonally mobile foraging economic strategy, in which SUBSISTENCE is based on hunting wild game, fishing, and collecting wild plant foods. Such groups are usually small bands following a seasonal migratory cycle, moving frequently to take advantage of food resources when they are available in maximum amounts, and periodically joining with other such groups in larger temporary units during periods of harvest. See also SEASONALITY; SUBSISTENCE.

> Cultural Man has been on earth for some 2,000,000 years; for over 99 percent of this period he has lived as a hunter-gatherer. (Lee and DeVore 1968:3)

The beginnings of hunter-gatherer studies can be traced to the work of Julian Steward in the 1930s (Steward 1936, 1938). Steward's CULTURAL ECOLOGY, which offered both a theoretical and a methodological framework without precedent, was enthusiastically embraced by many ecologically oriented archaeologists. His approach permitted the use of environmental factors in explanation, mediated by technology and other features of CULTURE. Since hunter-gatherers are more closely dependent on environment than groups with other economic ADAPTATIONS, Steward first applied his principles of cultural ecology to hunting-gathering groups, whose entire culture often represents "core" features from the culture ecological viewpoint (Bettinger 1980:189–190).

Hunter-gatherer studies since the 1930s have resulted in "a basically descriptive general hunter-gatherer model that attempts to synthesize the salient characteristics of this lifeway" (Bettinger 1980:192). The principal features of this model are outlined by Richard Lee and Irven DeVore (1968:7), in their introduction to *Man the Hunter*, the first major collection of specialized hunter-gatherer research, as well as by Bettinger (1980). They include reliance on wild foods; the expenditure of only a fraction of the available time on resource procurement activities; low populations (30–70 percent of CARRYING CAPACITY; Birdsell 1958; Hayden 1972); and a small, egalitarian, mobile band (20–25 persons) with bilateral kinship affiliations and only informal leadership as the primary social unit (Birdsell 1968; Flannery 1968; Lee and Devore 1968; Sahlins 1968; Bettinger 1980).

This model was based to a large extent on data derived from archaeological studies. Archaeological hunter-gatherer research has stimulated ethnographic studies of contemporary hunter-gatherers in recent years, many of them conducted by archaeologists using the methods of ETHNOARCHAEOLOGY (Binford 1978; Hayden 1981). Hunter-gatherer archaeology has also contributed to the development of the concepts of CATCHMENT ANALYSIS and the idea of the subsistence-settlement system (Struever 1968; Jochim 1976; Binford 1980).

During the 1960s, archaeological studies of hunter-gatherers were used in modeling cultural processes leading toward sedentary, complex society (e.g., Flannery 1968). Since that time, archaeologists have begun to distinguish between "simple" or "egalitarian" hunter-gatherers (i.e., those described in the above model) and "complex hunter-gatherers," whose SOCIAL ORGANIZATION and economic activities appear to be leading in the direction of greater SEDENTARINESS, larger social units, and ultimately to a food-producing economy (Bender 1978; Kelly 1983, 1985; Flannery 1986; Johnson and Earle 1987). Such groups frequently display a more complex social structure, in which permanent social inequalities appear to be evolving, usually as a result of developing differences in access to critical resources by individuals or social units (see Price and Brown 1985).

Hunter-gatherer research conducted during the 1980s made extensive use of optimal foraging models derived from animal biology, and a substantial body of literature using this approach has been produced (see, e.g., the papers in Winterhalder and Smith 1981; Hawkes, Hill, and O'Connell 1982; Martin 1983; Smith 1983; Simms 1984; Hawkes and O'Connell 1981; Sih and Milton 1985; Belovsky 1987; Gould 1991). Although this approach affords a useful way of modeling subsistence, it has been criticized for being reductionistic, as well as for some of its assumptions, which may be invalid for human foragers, thereby undermining the utility of optimal foraging models for testing archaeological data (Thomas 1986:253).

Hunter-gatherer studies have continued to be an important area of archaeological research into the present, despite criticisms emphasizing the lack of a body of middle-range theory addressing the material consequences of procurement, production, utilization, and discard activities (Thomas 1986:247), a criticism often leveled at ARCHAEOLOGY as a whole.

Investigations have continued to emphasize evidence for the initial cultural changes that eventually transformed prehistoric hunter-gatherers into sedentary food producers with hierarchical societies (e.g., Matson 1985; Price and Brown 1985; Keeley 1988; Redding 1988; Hayden 1990; Layton, Foley, and Williams 1991). Ethnoarchaeological investigation of modern hunter-gatherers continues to be an important method of acquiring data for constructing models of past hunter-gatherer strategies and behaviors, to be tested against the ARCHAEOLOGICAL RECORD.

REFERENCES

Belovsky, Gary. 1987. Hunter-gatherer foraging: a linear programming approach. Journal of Anthropological Archaeology 6:29–76.
Bender, Barbara. 1978. Gatherer-hunter to farmer: a social perspective. World Archaeology 10:204–222.
Bettinger, Robert L. 1980. Explanatory/predictive models of hunter-gatherer adaptation. Advances in Archaeological Method and Theory 3:189–255.
Binford, Lewis R. 1978. Nunamiut archaeology. Academic Press, New York.
———. 1980. Willow smoke and dogs' tails: hunter-gatherer settlement systems and archaeological site formation. American Antiquity 45:4–20.
Birdsell, Joseph. 1958. On population structure in generalized hunting and collection populations. Evolution 12:189–205.
———. 1968. Some predictions for the Pleistocene based on equilibrium systems among

recent hunter-gatherers. In Man the hunter, R. B. Lee and I. DeVore, eds. Aldine, Chicago, pp. 229–240.

Flannery, Kent V. 1968. Archaeological systems theory and early Mesoamerica. In Anthropological archaeology in the Americas, B. Meggers, ed. Anthropological Society of Washington, Washington, D.C., pp. 67–87.

———. 1986. Guila Naquitz: Archaic foraging and early agriculture in Oaxaca, Mexico. Academic Press, Orlando, Fla.

Gould, Richard A. 1991. Arid-land foraging as seen from Australia—adaptive models and behavioral realities. Oceania 62(1):12–33.

Hawkes, Kristen, Kim Hill, and James O'Connell. 1982. Why hunters gather: optimal foraging and the Ache of eastern Paraguay. American Ethnologist 9:379–398.

Hawkes, Kristen, and James F. O'Connell. 1981. Affluent hunters? Some comments in light of the Alyawara case. American Anthropologist 83(3):622–626.

Hayden, Brian. 1972. Population control among hunter/gatherers. World Archaeology 4(2):205–221.

———. 1981. Subsistence and ecological adaptations of modern hunter/gatherers. In Omnivorous primates: gathering and hunting in human evolution, Robert S. Harding, ed. Columbia University Press, New York, pp. 344–422.

———. 1990. Nimrods, piscators, pluckers, and planters: the emergence of food production. Journal of Anthropological Archaeology 9:31–69.

Jochim, Michael. 1976. Hunter-gatherer subsistence and settlement: a predictive model. Academic Press, New York.

Johnson, Allen W., and Timothy Earle. 1987. The evolution of human societies, from foraging group to agrarian state. Stanford University Press, Stanford, Calif.

Keeley, Lawrence. 1988. Hunter-gatherer economic complexity and "population pressure": a cross-cultural analysis. Journal of Anthropological Archaeology 7:373–411.

Kelly, Robert L. 1983. Hunter-gatherer mobility strategies. Journal of Anthropological Research 39(3):277–306.

———. 1985. Hunter-gatherer mobility and sedentism: a Great Basin pilot study. Ph.D. dissertation, Department of Anthropology, University of Michigan, Ann Arbor.

Layton, R., R. Foley, and E. Williams. 1991. The transition between hunting and gathering and the specialized husbandry of resources—a socioecological approach. Current Anthropology 32(3):255–274.

Lee, Richard B., and Irven DeVore. 1968. Problems in the study of hunters and gatherers. In Man the hunter, R. B. Lee and I. DeVore, eds. Aldine, Chicago, pp. 3–12.

———, eds. 1968. Man the hunter. Aldine, Chicago.

Martin, John. 1983. Optimal foraging theory: a review of some models and their applications. [Review of Hunter-gatherer foraging strategies: ethnographic and archaeological analyses, Bruce Winterhalder and Eric Alden Smith, eds. University of Chicago Press, 1981]. American Anthropologist 85(3):612–629.

Matson, R. G. 1985. The relationship between sedentism and status inequalities among hunters and gatherers. In Status, structure and stratification, Marc Thompson, M. T. Garcia, and F. Ense, eds. Archaeological Association of the University of Calgary, pp. 245–252.

Price, T. Douglas, and James A. Brown, eds. 1985. Prehistoric hunter-gatherers: the emergence of cultural complexity. Academic Press, Orlando, Fla.

Redding, Richard. 1988. A general explanation of subsistence change: from hunting and gathering to food production. Journal of Anthropological Archaeology 7:56–97.

Sahlins, Marshall. 1968. Notes on the original affluent society. In Man the hunter, R. B. Lee and Irven DeVore, eds. Aldine, Chicago, pp. 85–89.

Sih, Andrew, and Katharine A. Milton. 1985. Optimal diet theory: should the !Kung eat mongongos? American Anthropologist 87(2):395–401.

Simms, Steven R. 1984. Aboriginal Great Basin foraging strategies: an evolutionary analysis. Ph.D. dissertation, Department of Anthropology, University of Utah, Salt Lake City.

Smith, Eric Alden. 1983. Anthropological applications of optimal foraging theory: a critical review. Current Anthropology 24(5):625–651.

Steward, Julian. 1936. The economic and social basis of primitive bands. In Essays in honor of A. L. Kroeber, R. H. Lowie, ed. University of California Press, Berkeley, pp. 331–350.

———. 1938. Basin-plateau aboriginal socio-political groups. Bureau of American Ethnology Bulletin 120. Washington, D.C.

Struever, Stuart. 1968. Woodland subsistence-settlement systems in the lower Illinois Valley. In New perspectives in archaeology, S. Binford and L. Binford, eds. Aldine, Chicago, pp. 285–312.

Thomas, David Hurst. 1986. Contemporary hunter-gatherer archaeology in America. In American archaeology, past and future, D. J. Meltzer, D. D. Fowler, and J. A. Sabloff, eds. SAA/Smithsonian, Washington, D.C., pp. 237–276.

Winterhalder, B., and E. Smith, eds. 1981. Hunter-gatherer foraging strategies. University of Chicago Press.

SOURCES OF ADDITIONAL INFORMATION

For original publications and statements about hunter-gatherers see Lee and DeVore 1968; for subsequent work see the review articles by Bettinger (1980) and Smith (1983) (see References, above), and the review by Stephen M. Perlman, "An optimum diet model, coastal variability, and hunter-gatherer behavior," *Advances in Archaeological Method and Theory* 3(1980):257–310, all of which include large bibliographies. Additional background information may be found in John Yellen and H. Harpending, "Hunter-gatherer populations and archaeological inference," *World Archaeology* 4(1972):244–253; and Carmel Schrire, ed., *Past and Present in Hunter-Gatherer Studies* (New York, Academic Press, 1984). A study of hunter-gatherer archaeological assemblage formation is J. C. Chatters, "Hunter-gatherer adaptation and assemblage structure," *Journal of Anthropological Archaeology* 6(4)(1987):336–375. David H. Thomas's critique (Thomas 1986; see References) is also useful, especially his extensive discussion of the applications and potential of optimal foraging theory in hunter-gatherer studies, as well as his comments on the interpretation of archaeological evidence.

In 1972, the journal *World Archaeology* devoted an issue to papers on nomadic pastoralists and hunter-gatherers (vol. 4, no. 2, October 1972), which includes important research on prehistoric transhumant adaptations in Europe, the Middle East, Asia, and Mexico, as well as treatments of population control among hunter-gatherers (Hayden 1972; see References), the use of inference in hunter-gatherer studies, and the origins of pastoral adaptations.

A discussion of the relationship between hunter-gatherers of today and the societies of the Paleolithic is Alain Testart's "Some major problems in the social anthropology of hunter-gatherers,'' *Current Anthropology* 29(1)(1988):1–31. Two publications using unusual approaches are Kristen Hawkes, James F. O'Connell, Kim Hill, and E. L. Charnov, "How much is enough? hunters and limited needs," *Ethology and Sociobiology* 6(1)(1835):3–15; and R. G. Reynolds, "A production system model of hunter-gatherer resource scheduling adaptations," *European Journal of Operations Research* 30(3)(1987):223–239.

The most recent comprehensive synthesis of hunter-gatherer studies is Fred R. Myers, "Critical trends in the study of hunter-gatherers," *Annual Review of Anthropology* 17 (1988):261–282, which includes a bibliography of 185 references to the literature up to 1988.

For most recent information, see current issues of *American Antiquity*, *American Anthropologist*, *Current Anthropology*, and volumes of *Archaeological Method and Theory* and *Annual Review of Anthropology*.

I

INFERENCE. 1. The psychological process of reconstructing unobservable past phenomena through logical reasoning from observable, empirical evidence. 2. A statement about the ARCHAEOLOGICAL RECORD arrived at through inferential reasoning.

Inferential arguments may be either deductive, when the conclusions follow necessarily from the premises, or inductive, when the conclusions are probabilistic rather than necessary (see M. H. Salmon 1976; Sullivan 1978). In archaeology, both types of inference have been employed in attempts to interpret the archaeological record of past material remains in terms of the dynamic causal processes of the past that led to its creation. Archaeologists also make use of statistical inferences, based on probability theory, in hypothesis testing and in estimating ranges of particular variables.

> Any statement that confers meaning in historical terms to observation made on the archaeological record is an inference. The justifications for such an inference must be robust arguments that link the properties (static matter) to the properties inferred (dynamic conditions). (Binford 1983:51)

Archaeological interpretation has always relied upon inferential arguments for explaining past phenomena that could have led to the deposition of material remains in the manner in which archaeologists recover them from the ground. Evidence of concern about archaeological inferences and their validity began to appear in the literature during the late 1950s and early 1960s, when some archaeologists were beginning to question the epistemological foundations of their interpretative methods (Smith 1955; Thompson 1956; MacWhite 1956; Spaulding 1960; Binford 1962). Interest peaked in the following decade, with the advent of the "NEW" ARCHAEOLOGY and its concern with epistemology and methods of scientific research and explanation (Binford 1962, 1964, 1965; Chang 1967;

Deetz 1968; Fritz 1972; Justeson 1973; W. Salmon 1973; Plog 1976; M. H. Salmon 1976, 1982; B. D. Smith 1977; P. J. Watson, LeBlanc, and Redman 1971; R. A. Watson 1976). This concern was accompanied by an increased use of statistical methods in analyzing archaeological data (Spaulding 1971, 1973), of probabilistic SAMPLING in archaeological research design, and of probabilistic models as a basis for archaeological inference (M. H. Salmon 1976, 1982; Sullivan 1978; Gibbon 1984, 1989; Kelley and Hanen 1988; P. J. Watson, LeBlanc, and Redman 1984).

The earliest debates on archaeological inference emphasized the deductive method, since these efforts were aimed at discovering scientific laws or lawlike generalizations that would constitute a theoretical basis and justification for explaining archaeological data as the inevitable products of past social phenomena or behavioral processes. Inductive arguments, and the possibilities these afford for prediction and innovative discovery, both essential for moving from observed data to new knowledge, were less favored by the "new" archaeologists of the 1960s in their search for laws (Kelley and Hanen 1988:266).

During the 1970s Bruce D. Smith (1977) proposed an inductive method of inference that he believed to be more appropriate to archaeological problems, which he referred to as the "hypothetico-analog method," based on probabilistic outcomes and employing the kind of reasoning proposed by Wesley Salmon (1967, 1973) and Merrilee Salmon (1976, 1982). John Justeson, in an earlier paper (1973), had outlined an approach to archaeological inference based on the principles and concepts of information theory, in which past cultural systems are treated as communication systems.

Archaeologists have often ranked inferences according to how far they appear to go beyond the empirical data used to support them. The limitations of archaeological inference have been discussed and debated since at least the late 1940s (Taylor 1948; M. A. Smith 1955; Binford 1968; Justeson 1973; Sullivan 1978:186–187), and have been attributed to the nature of archaeological data themselves, to methodological naiveté, and to inadequate concept development. Alan Sullivan has suggested that the chief problem inherent in these criticisms is the questionable assumptions about how past activities come to be represented by material remains.

> All activities are remote, since they occurred in the past. The problem lies in the inadequacies of our theories (and not just our methodologies . . .) to model how information about these different kinds of past activities is transmitted to the present in the form of material remains. (Sullivan 1978:186–187)

Sullivan goes on to propose a model for resolving this problem by outlining how information about the past is transmitted into the present via the material preserved in the archaeological record. This model, like that previously proposed by Justeson, is based in information theory, and on David Clarke's concept of "traces," those changes in the physical properties of archaeological objects or their relationships to one another that occur over time, and that constitute the basic units of information transmission about the past (see Sullivan 1978:192–210, for a complete discussion of his model and its underlying concepts).

Lewis Binford has noted that current inferential strategies restrict archaeologists to making limited assumptions from surviving data, and such assumptions should be kept as factual as possible, "far . . . from the 'technicolor' reconstructions common in our textbooks" (Binford 1984:165), which current methods cannot support or justify. Binford also warns against the hazard of committing the fallacy of affirming the consequent, as does Linda Patrik in her review on the nature of the archaeological record:

> If archaeology relied on the Hempelian model of inference alone, it would not be justified in deductively inferring the past causes of the [archaeological] record, because you cannot deduce a cause from an effect . . . this would be the fallacy of affirming the consequent. . . . (Patrik 1985:44–45)

In the 1980s and 1990s, archaeology has entered a period of "normal science" in which theoretical and methodological issues have been debated less often, and methods such as inference are more likely to be applied to specific problems in field research without more than a passing reference to their limitations, and little or no discussion of their epistemological foundations. The self-examination so characteristic of archaeology in the 1960s and 1970s is now on the wane, and appears unlikely to be revived until some new methodological or philosophical breakthrough stimulates another period of intensive inquiry and, perhaps, a revolutionary new approach to archaeological data and their interpretation. In the meantime, archaeologists will continue to rely upon the use of inferential techniques to explain their data, as they did for many years in the past, before this practice was called into question by the "new" archaeologists.

REFERENCES

Binford, Lewis R. 1962. Archaeology as anthropology. American Antiquity 28:217–225.
———. 1964. A consideration of archaeological research design. American Antiquity 29:425–451.
———. 1965. Archaeological systematics and the study of culture process. American Antiquity 31:203–210.
———. 1968. Archaeological perspectives. In New perspectives in archaeology, S. R. Binford and L. R. Binford, eds. Aldine, Chicago, pp. 5–32.
———. 1982. Meaning, inference and the material record. In Ranking, resources and exchange, C. Renfrew and S. Shannon, eds. Cambridge University Press. Reprinted in Working at archaeology, by Lewis R. Binford, Academic Press, New York, 1983, pp. 57–62.
———. 1983. Working at archaeology. Academic Press, New York.
———. 1984. Bones of contention: a reply to Glynn Isaac. American Antiquity 49(1):164–167.
Chang, K. C. 1967. Rethinking archaeology. Random House, New York.
Deetz, James F. 1968. The inference of residence and descent rules from archaeology

data. In New perspectives in archeology, S. R. Binford and L. R. Binford, eds. Aldine, Chicago, pp. 41–48.

Fritz, J. M. 1972. Archaeological systems for indirect observation of the past. In Contemporary archaeology, Mark P. Leone, ed. Southern Illinois University Press, Carbondale, pp. 135–157.

Gibbon, Guy. 1984. Anthropological archaeology. Columbia University Press, New York.

———. 1989. Explanation in archaeology. Blackwell, Oxford.

Justeson, John S. 1973. Limitations of archaeological inference: an information-theoretic approach with applications in methodology. American Antiquity 38:131–149.

Kelley, Jane H., and Marsha P. Hanen. 1988. Archaeology and the methodology of science. University of New Mexico Press, Albuquerque.

MacWhite, Eaoin. 1956. On the interpretation of archaeological evidence in historical and sociological terms. American Anthropologist 58:3–25.

Patrik, Linda E. 1985. Is there an archaeological record? Advances in Archaeological Method and Theory 8:27–62.

Plog, Stephen. 1976. The inference of prehistoric social organization from ceramic design variability. Michigan Discussions in Anthropology 1:1–47.

Salmon, Merrilee H. 1976. "Deductive" versus "inductive" archaeology. American Antiquity 41:376–381.

———. 1982. Philosophy and archaeology. Academic Press, New York.

Salmon, Wesley C. 1967. The foundations of scientific inference. University of Pittsburgh Press.

———. 1973. Logic. 2nd ed. Prentice-Hall, Englewood Cliffs, N.J.

Smith, Bruce D. 1977. Archaeological inference and inductive confirmation. American Anthropologist 79:598–617.

Smith, M. A. 1955. The limitations of inference in archaeology. Archaeological Newsletter 6:3–7.

Spaulding, Albert C. 1960. Statistical description and comparison of artifact assemblages. In The application of quantitative methods in archaeology, R. F. Heizer and S. F. Cook, eds. Viking Fund Publications in Anthropology No. 28. Chicago, pp. 60–83.

———. 1971. Some elements of quantitative archaeology. In mathematics in the archaeological and historical sciences, F. R. Hods on, D. G. Kendall and P. Tauta, eds. University Press of Edinburgh, pp. 3–16.

———. 1973. The concept of artifact type in archeology. Plateau 45:149–164.

Sullivan, Alan P. 1978. Inference and evidence in archaeology: a discussion of the conceptual problems. Advances in Archaeological Method and Theory 1:183–222.

Taylor, Walter W. 1948. A study of archeology. American Anthropological Association Memoirs No. 69, Washington, D.C.

Thompson, R. H. 1956. The subjective element in archaeological inference. Southwestern Journal of Anthropology 12:327–332.

Watson, Patty Jo, Stephen A. LeBlanc, and Charles L. Redman. 1971. Explanation in archaeology, an explicitly scientific approach. Columbia University Press, New York.

———. 1984. Archaeological explanation. Columbia University Press, New York.

Watson, R. A. 1976. Inference in archaeology. American Antiquity 41:58–66.

SOURCES OF ADDITIONAL INFORMATION

For some early, pre-"new" archaeology critical discussions of the use of inference and analogy in archaeological interpretation, see Gordon R. Willey, "Inference and analogy in archeology," in *An Appraisal of Anthropology Today*, Sol Tax, Loren C. Eiseley, Irvin Rouse, and C. F. Voeglin, eds. (Chicago, University of Chicago Press, 1953), pp. 251–254; and R. H. Thompson, "The subjective element in archaeological inference," *Southwestern Journal of Anthropology* 12(1956):327–332. Some treatments of inference as a method of scientific reasoning are J. R. Platt, "Strong inference," *Science* 146(1964):347–353; and H. Jeffreys, *Scientific Inference*, 3rd ed. (London and New York, Cambridge University Press, 1973). The major statement on the application of inference in archaeology is the review by Sullivan (1978; see References), which includes a comprehensive bibliography, now quite out-of-date. To update this valuable resource, another important discussion of the uses of archaeological inference in contemporary European structuralist archaeology is now available in Patty Jo Watson and Michael Fotiadis, "The razor's edge, symbolic-structuralist archaeology and the expansion of archaeological inference," *American Anthropologist* 92(3)(1990):613–629.

The journals *American Antiquity*, *Journal of Anthropological Archaeology*, and *American Anthropologist* should be monitored for future publications on inference, as should the appropriate annual reviews.

INTERACTION SPHERE. 1. An information and exchange network linking several different local CULTURES, where continuous patterned interaction occurs in the form of stylized or ritualized social contacts centered on trade, religious observances, diplomatic encounters, or other types of social transaction. 2. The initial phase in development of a regional economy, when region-wide institutions begin to emerge as a result of continuing interaction among local communities within the region. 3. A series of transactional systems crosscutting several local cultural traditions within the same geographic area, which are limited to certain cultural subsystems, such as mortuary practices, and have little or no permanent effect on SUBSISTENCE strategies or basic adaptive patterns.

Archaeologically, an interaction sphere is defined by the presence in the ARCHAEOLOGICAL RECORD of a set of shared material items providing evidence of ongoing contact between two or more local cultures and suggesting something of its nature, such as the ceremonial objects associated with a religious cult.

The interaction sphere as a specific theoretical concept was introduced into archaeology by Joseph R. Caldwell, Curator of Anthropology of the Illinois State Museum during the 1940s and 1950s. In his only published discussion of this concept, Caldwell described the prehistoric Hopewell cultural complex of North America (ca. 200 B.C.–A.D. 400) as the prototype (Caldwell 1964). Noting that interaction spheres tend to develop around some central organizing principle, Caldwell cited the complex of religious belief and mortuary practices shared by Hopewellian groups, archaeologically documented by distinctive artifacts found in graves over a wide geographical area. He proposed that several different kinds of interaction spheres may be discernible according to their shared organizing principle, each displaying its own set of diagnostic criteria. Other possible candidates he suggested were the Battle Ax culture of prehistoric Europe, the Olmec tradition of Mesoamerica, and the Chavin complex of South America. However, Caldwell confined his analysis to the Hopewell phenomenon, and this cultural tradition has become the prototypical example of the interaction sphere in subsequent archaeological discussions of the concept (Struever 1964; Struever and Vickery 1973; Struever and Houart 1975; Seeman 1979).

Several other interaction spheres have been identified and discussed in the archaeological literature. Lewis Binford proposed the existence of a Mississippian interaction sphere in the southeastern United States (Binford 1965; see also Fowler 1971). Others include Mesoamerica (Rathje 1973, 1977; Freidel 1979), the intermediate area between Mesoamerica and the central Andes (Myers 1978), the Chacoan interaction sphere in southwestern North America (Altschul 1978), and the Caribbean area (Keegan 1990; SAA 1990).

The interaction sphere concept was rooted in several earlier archaeological concepts, among them William Sanders's idea of the symbiotic region (Sanders 1956; Blanton 1976), and Braidwood and Willey's "regional tradition" as a development in the growth of CULTURAL COMPLEXITY (Braidwood and Willey 1962). Caldwell's theoretical innovation served to draw together within a broader conceptual framework a number of preexisting ideas regarding the role of regional communication and trade networks in promoting complexity (see also EXCHANGE).

It is no doubt more than coincidence that the interaction sphere concept, with its emphasis on the dynamic processes of interaction, was introduced into archaeology at a time when the focus was shifting from description of ARTIFACTS and SITES to attempts to explain these remains as the material consequences of prehistoric dynamic behavioral processes (Caldwell 1966). This focus on process was, of course, an important aspect of the "NEW" ARCHAEOLOGY of the 1960s by the time Caldwell's 1964 paper appeared.

Some subsequent system-oriented studies have used the interaction sphere as an analytic concept. David Freidel applied it as a theoretical framework to explain the evolution of civilization in the Maya Lowlands (Freidel 1979). Struever and Houart, in a systemic analysis of a group of Hopewell sites, made an attempt to construct a TYPOLOGY of interaction spheres along lines originally proposed by Caldwell (Struever and Houart 1975). Mark Seeman later analyzed their data, utilizing the principles of CENTRAL PLACE THEORY, with results strikingly different from Struever and Houart's (Seeman 1979).

There are some important differences between an interaction sphere and the somewhat similar concept of CULTURE AREA. In the culture area, a genetic relationship is assumed to exist between groups displaying cultural similarities who occupy the same geographic region. Cultural innovation is, in the culture area approach, viewed as a localized adaptive response to differing social and environmental conditions (Freidel 1979:36). In the interaction sphere model, the simple society adapted to its local environment is transformed in the course of becoming adapted to a new set of culturally created, regionwide conditions as a result of its participation in a regionwide information and exchange network. Cultural innovation in these circumstances becomes a function of CULTURE rather than an environmentally triggered adaptive process (Freidel 1979:53). It is perhaps significant that Caldwell himself occasionally used the phrase "interaction area" in preference to "culture area," to designate a region in which certain cultural patterns were widely distributed, infiltrating local cultures, because of its dynamic behavioral implications (Caldwell 1966:337).

Interaction spheres may exist at different scales, involving only the small communities within a limited area, communities of various sizes within a larger geographic region, or long-distance interregional transactions (Adams 1982). The transactions themselves may involve both tangibles and intangibles (SAA 1990:50), and may be of a strictly commercial nature, such as trade in utilitarian goods; or they may be primarily social, in the form of interregional marriage exchanges, kinship rituals or ceremonial reciprocity, or political alliances (Keegan 1990).

A useful typology of interaction spheres based on their organizing principles still remains to be developed. Comparisons of the proportion of secular commodities of exotic origin, relative to ritual goods, in archaeological deposits would be a logical first step toward developing such principles. Although the ARCHAEOLOGICAL RECORD may not provide all the needed information, it can frequently be supplemented by the informed use of ANALOGY to reconstruct prehistoric patterns of interaction.

The interaction sphere concept continues to be utilized by archaeologists, in particular by those engaged in regional studies or interregional analysis. In 1990, a symposium titled "Interaction Spheres in the Caribbean" was held at the annual meeting of the Society for American Archaeology; in it seven papers devoted to the subject were presented (SAA 1990); and it appears that the concept will continue to provide a useful analytic framework for archaeological studies at the regional and supraregional levels in coming years.

REFERENCES

Adams, William Hampton. 1982. Ethnography and archaeology of an American farming community: Silcott, Washington. In Ethnography by archaeologists, Elisabeth Tooker, ed. American Ethnological Society, Washington, D.C., pp. 43–62.

Altschul, Jeffrey H. 1978. The development of the Chacoan interaction sphere. Journal of Anthropological Research 34:109–146.

Binford, Lewis R. 1965. Archaeological systematics and the study of culture process. American Antiquity 31:203–210.

Blanton, Richard E. 1976. The role of symbiosis in adaptation and sociocultural change in the Valley of Mexico. In The Valley of Mexico: studies in pre-hispanic ecology and society, Eric R. Wolf, ed. University of New Mexico Press, Albuquerque, pp. 181–202.

Braidwood, Robert J., and Gordon R. Willey, eds. 1962. Courses toward urban life. Viking Fund Publications in Anthropology No. 32. Chicago.

Caldwell, Joseph R. 1964. Interaction spheres in prehistory. Illinois State Museum Scientific Papers 12, no. 6. Springfield, 133–156.

———. 1966. The new American archaeology. In New roads to yesterday: essays in archaeology, Joseph R. Caldwell, ed. Basic Books, New York. (Articles from Science)

Freidel, David A. 1979. Culture areas and interaction spheres: contrasting approaches to the emergence of civilization in the Maya lowlands. American Antiquity 44:36–54.

Fowler, Melvin L. 1971. Agriculture and village settlement in the North American East: the central Mississippi Valley area, a case history. In Prehistoric agriculture, Stuart Struever, ed. Natural History Press, Garden City, N.Y., pp. 391–403.

Keegan, William F. 1990. Interaction and the development of social complexity in the Northern Caribbean. Paper presented at symposium "Interaction Spheres in the Caribbean," 55th annual meeting of the Society for American Archaeology, Las Vegas, Nev.

Myers, Thomas P. 1978. Formative period interaction spheres in the Intermediate Area: archaeology of Central America and adjacent South America. In Advances in Andean archaeology, David L. Browman, ed. Mouton, The Hague.

Rathje, William L. 1973. Classic Maya development and denouement: a research design. In The Classic Maya collapse, T. Patrick Culbert, ed. University of New Mexico Press, Albuquerque, pp. 405–454.

———. 1977. The Tikal connection. In The origins of Maya civilization, R. E. W. Adams, ed. University of New Mexico Press, Albuquerque, pp. 374–382.

Sanders, William T. 1956. The central Mexican symbiotic region: a study in prehistoric settlement patterns. In Prehistoric settlement patterns in the New World, Gordon R. Willey, ed. Viking Fund Publications in Anthropology No. 23. Chicago, pp. 115–127.

Seeman, Mark F. 1979. The Hopewell interaction sphere: the evidence for interregional trade and structural complexity. Indiana Historical Society, Prehistory Research Series 5, no. 2. Indianapolis.

Society for American Archaeology. 1990. Program and abstracts of the 55th annual meeting. Washington, D.C.

Struever, Stuart. 1964. The Hopewell interaction sphere in Riverine-western Great Lakes cultural history. In Hopewellian studies, Joseph Caldwell and Robert Hall, eds. Illinois State Museum Scientific Papers No. 12. Springfield, pp. 85–106.

Struever, Stuart, and Gail L. Houart. 1975. An analysis of the Hopewell interaction sphere. In Social exchange and interaction, E. Wilmsen, ed. University of Michigan Museum of Anthropology Anthropological Papers No. 46. Ann Arbor.

Struever, Stuart, and Kent D. Vickery. 1973. The beginnings of cultivation in the Midwest-Riverine area of the United States. American Anthropologist 75:1197–1220.

SOURCES OF ADDITIONAL INFORMATION

There is relatively little literature on the nature and theoretical aspects of the interaction sphere concept. The best statements of it as an analytical principle remain those of Caldwell himself (Caldwell 1964, 1966; see References). Other discussions are in the review by D. W. Dragoo, "Some aspects of eastern North American prehistory: a review, 1975," *American Antiquity* 41(1976):3–27; and the paper by Freidel, who takes a more theoretical approach (Freidel 1979; see References). Most standard texts on archaeology do not include it in their coverage of archaeological concepts. Lewis Binford (1965; see References) devoted some brief discussion to the interaction sphere, its nature, and its usefulness as a unit of analysis, noting that although "I have seen the term used by other archaeologists . . . I have not been able to find it in the literature." William H. Adams briefly described a historic, small-scale interaction sphere in his ethnoarchaeological work on a modern farming community (Adams 1982; see References). A more recent treatment is in Edward M. Schortman and Patricia A. Urban, "Modeling interregional interaction in prehistory," *Advances in Archaeological Method and Theory* 11(1987):37–95, in which the authors discuss diffusion, trade, and other interactive processes, and provide an extensive bibliography.

For examples of the use of the interaction sphere concept in archaeological analysis, see items listed in References above. Future issues of *American Anthropologist* and *American Antiquity* should be checked for more recent literature.

L

LITHICS. 1. The technology of stoneworking. 2. The archaeological study of prehistoric stone tool technology, using a variety of experimental, analytical, and synthetic methods.

Lithics is the branch of prehistoric technology that has received more attention from archaeologists than any other. This is a consequence of the fact that stone is unique in being a material invariably preserved in archaeological deposits. Stone tools are therefore always available for study, even in sites where all other cultural remains have succumbed to the ravages of time. Because of their durability, lithic implements have traditionally served archaeologists as a principal basis for constructing preceramic CULTURE chronologies (Bordes 1968; Borden 1975).

Archaeologists are now becoming aware of the way in which this circumstance has biased interpretations of past cultures and their technology, and of how small a portion of that technology may be represented by surviving lithic remains. The countless books written on Paleolithic and Neolithic stone tool technology by archaeologists in the twentieth century, purporting to describe the development of technology in prehistoric times, describe only a fraction of the technical knowledge present in any prehistoric community. Nevertheless, many archaeologists continue to classify early archaeological cultures on the basis of stone tools alone, not only as a result of archaeological tradition and habit but also because this often is the only kind of material evidence available to document the technology of a prehistoric people.

The "Old" and "New" Stone Ages

The Paleolithic, or "Old" Stone Age, refers to the long period of stone tool technology when chipping and flaking were the basic techniques of stoneworking employed. The Neolithic, or "New" Stone Age, began at a later time when grinding and polishing were added to the lithic techniques available to stoneworkers (Bordaz 1970).

The first indications of stone tool manufacture and use by early hominids in Africa appeared at least 2 million years ago (Isaac 1983; see also PALEOAN- THROPOLOGY). Temporal changes in lithic technology occurred very slowly. In part, this was a result of the technological limitations imposed by the nature of the raw material itself. As a material for toolmaking, stone has quite limited possibilities, all of which were fully exploited by early toolmakers.

Archaeologists who have investigated tools found in association with ancient hominid remains have attempted to distinguish between rocks that show inten- tional modification for cultural purposes, and those that have been modified by animal activity or the action of natural weathering processes. While the artifactual nature of some presumed lithic ASSEMBLAGES remains controversial (e.g., that from the Calico Hills sites in the California desert; see Leakey, Simpson, and Clemento 1968; Simpson 1978; Duvall and Venner 1979), distinguishing the results of human stoneworking from the effects of natural processes is usually far easier for an experienced archaeologist than is the case with bone objects. Purposeful flaking of stone to produce a sharp cutting edge is distinctively different from the effects of natural fracture processes. Where uncertainty exists, further evidence, such as associations of the supposed tools with human remains, hearths, broken animal bones, or other material in the same deposit will some- times support the artifactual nature of the purported tools; and microscopic examination for residues of marks of use can frequently identify unworked lithic flakes that, although not intentionally sharpened, were utilized as implements in performing various tasks.

Certain kinds of stone were favored by early stone toolmakers because of their fracture properties. Among these were flint, chert, and obsidian—all very hard, homogeneous rocks that break systematically and predictably in a conic, or *conchoidal*, fracture pattern. This characteristic fracture pattern was utilized in planning tool shapes, and in determining the manner in which flakes were de- tached from a stone "core" to be fashioned into tools (Clark 1958; Crabtree 1966; Cotterell and Kamminga 1987).

Most early stone tools were made using the hammerstone technique. This consists of hitting one stone with another, to detach several large flakes from a pebble and produce a jagged cutting edge. Later, flakes were detached from both sides of the core to produce the first Oldowan "hand axes" made by the early African hominids, forerunners of the well-made Acheulean hand axes produced by *Homo erectus*. The sophisticated advances in stone tool technology made by the Neanderthals included the prepared core technique called Levallois, resulting in the removal of a flake of planned form by striking the prepared core.

A further refinement was the preparation of cores for the removal of long, thin blades, which were then trimmed to form knives and other specialized tools. This *blade technology*, which appeared during the Upper Paleolithic in Europe, was used worldwide. Blades could be trimmed with a piece of antler or wood or even by using the teeth.

Another important technique dating to Upper Paleolithic times was *pressure flaking*, in which flakes were removed from a core by "squeezing" them off, using controlled pressure. This was the most frequently used stoneworking technique in later prehistoric times, especially in the New World.

A third technique employed worldwide was microblade technology, used to produce very small tools of many kinds, called microliths. Some of these may have been mounted in wooden scythe handles and used for harvesting wild or cultivated grains.

Toward the close of the Paleolithic period, approximately 15,000 years ago, the new stoneworking techniques that would become typical markers of the Neolithic began to emerge, most likely in response to major changes in SUB-SISTENCE and life patterns that occurred as part of new worldwide human AD-APTATIONS to the changed post-Pleistocene environment. The principal change at this time was the adoption of abrasive techniques, such as grinding and polishing, allowing production of more efficient tools with smooth surfaces. This technology is the diagnostic marker of the Neolithic period in the Old World, and appears in the Archaic period in the New World archaeological chronology (see NEW WORLD ARCHAEOLOGY). Ground stone tools included the manos and metates required for processing seeds, when grains, which require grinding and cooking for greater digestibility and palatability, began to constitute a larger portion of human diets.

Lithic Analysis

Lithic analysis is basically of two types, namely, functional analysis and attribute analysis.

Functional analysis, in which ARTIFACT types are defined according to their dimensions, shapes, and presumed uses or functions for which they were designed, developed in the nineteenth century. An example of a functional tool type is the hand ax, whose name reflects its presumed use. This approach to stone artifact analysis is the one still favored by many Old World archaeologists (Symens 1986).

New World archaeologists have favored the alternative approach to lithic studies called *attribute analysis*, in which certain artifact features, or attributes, are used to infer both tool use and the processes of tool manufacture. An essential part of attribute analysis is the study of debitage, the detritus of waste flakes produced in the toolmaking process (Fladmark 1982). Types are often identified by applying statistical techniques.

Several other analytic approaches to lithic studies are of importance in lithic analysis and interpretation. *Lithic experimentation* consists of experimentally manufacturing stone tools (flint knapping), replicating the techniques employed in prehistoric times, a method pioneered in the United States by Don Crabtree (Crabtree 1966, 1972, 1975; Knudson 1982). Such techniques have been reconstructed with the aid of ethnographic material from a few twentieth-century populations still practicing flint knapping (Flenniken 1984:194–198).

Use-wear analysis involves both macro- and microscopic examination of wear patterns on the working edges of ancient tools, and comparing these with the patterns produced using experimentally manufactured tools. Such comparisons can often reveal whether a tool was used for butchering, woodworking, processing hides, cutting vegetable fibers, or other activities (Aldendorfer, Kimball, and Sievert 1989; Donahue 1988; Hayden 1979; Keeley 1980; Lewenstein 1987; Owen and Unrath 1986; Phillips 1988; Vaughn 1985; Yerkes 1983; Young and Banforth 1990).

Petrological analysis, the determination of the mineral composition of stone tools by microscopic examination of thin sections, allows identification of quarry locations from which the raw material was obtained (Shotton 1970; Hester and Heizer 1973; Wilson 1988). Such sourcing has been useful in reconstructing prehistoric trade in raw materials.

Refitting (also called retrofitting) requires collecting all the waste flakes from a toolmaking SITE and attempting to fit them together into the original nodules from which they were manufactured. This time-consuming process makes it possible to reconstruct the toolmaking process, and may even allow the archaeologist to determine the handedness or cerebral dominance of the prehistoric toolmaker, since this will be apparent from the sequence and location of chipping and flake removal (Cahen, Keeley, and Van Noten 1979).

These techniques, and other methods, such as stylistic analysis (Jelinek 1976; Wiessner 1983; see STYLE), now available for studying prehistoric technology have enabled archaeologists to acquire an increased understanding of technical habits of the past, and from this to determine how the implements manufactured by early toolmakers reflect the overall adaptive pattern of life in a particular set of environmental and cultural circumstances (Wilmsen 1970). New analytic techniques for studying stone tools continue to be developed, and knowledge of early lithic technology continues to expand, permitting both broader and deeper understandings of technological achievement in prehistoric societies, and of how early technologies served human lifeways.

REFERENCES

Aldendorfer, Mark S., Larry R. Kimball, and April Sievert. 1989. Microwear analysis in the Maya lowlands: the use of functional data in a complex-society setting. Journal of Field Archaeology 16(1):47–77.

Bordaz, J. 1970. Tools of the Old and New Stone Age. The Natural History Press, Garden City, N.Y.

Borden, C. E. 1975. Origins and development of early Northwest Coast culture to about 3,000 B.C. National Museum of Man, Mercury Series, Archaeological Survey of Canada, Paper No. 45. Ottawa.

Bordes, François. 1968. The Old Stone Age. McGraw Hill/World University Library, New York and Toronto.

Cahen, D., L. H. Keeley, and F. L. Van Noten. 1979. Stone tools, toolkits, and human behavior in prehistory. Current Anthropology 20:661–683.

Clark, J. Desmond. 1958. The natural fracturing of pebbles from the Batoka Gorge, Northern Rhodesia. Proceedings of the Prehistoric Society 24:64–77.

Cotterell, Brian, and Johan Kamminga. 1987. The formation of flakes. American Antiquity 52(4):675–708.

Crabtree, Don E. 1966. An introduction to flintworking. Part 1: An introduction to the technology of stone tools. Occasional Papers of the Idaho State University 28. Pocatello.

————. 1972. A stoneworker's approach to analyzing and replicating the Lindenmeier Folsom. Tebiwa 9:3–39.

————. 1975. The potential of lithic technology. In Primitive art and technology, J. S. Raymond et al., eds. Archaeological Association, University of Calgary, p. 106.

Donahue, R. E. 1988. Microwear analysis and site function of Pagleisi Cave, level 4A. World Archaeology 19(3):357–375.

Duvall, J. G., and W. T. Venner. 1979. A statistical analysis of lithics from the Calico site (SBCM 1500A), California. Journal of Field Archaeology 6:455–462.

Fladmark, Knut R. 1982. Microdebitage analysis: initial considerations. Journal of Archaeological Science 9:205–220.

Flenniken, J. Jeffrey. 1984. The past, present, and future of flintknapping: an anthropological perspective. Annual Review of Anthropology 13:187–203.

Hayden, Brian, ed. 1979. Lithic use-wear analysis. Academic Press, New York.

Hester, Thomas, and Robert F. Heizer. 1973. Bibliography of archaeology I: Lithic technology and petrography. Addison-Wesley Modules in Anthropology No. 29.

Isaac, Glyn. 1983. Aspects of the evolution of human behavior: an archaeological perspective. Canadian Journal of Anthropology 3:233–243.

Jelinek, A. 1976. Form, function and style in lithic analysis. In Cultural change and continuity: essays in honor of James Bennett Griffin, C. E. Cleland, ed. Academic Press, New York, pp. 19–33.

Keeley, Lawrence H. 1980. Experimental determination of stone tool uses: a microwear analysis. University of Chicago Press, Chicago.

Knudson, Ruthann. 1982. Obituary: Don E. Crabtree, 1912–1980 [with bibliography of his publications]. American Antiquity 47(2):336–343.

Leakey, L. S. B., Ruth D. Simpson, and Thomas Clemento. 1968. Archaeological excavations in the Calico Mountains, California: preliminary report. Science 160:1022–1023.

Lewenstein, Suzanne M. 1987. Stone tool use at Cerros: the ethnoarchaeological and use-wear evidence. University of Texas Press, Austin.

Owen, Linda R., and Guenther Unrath, eds. 1986. Technical aspects of microwear studies on stone tools. Early Man News, vols. 9, 11, pts. 1, 2. Commission for the Paleoecology of Early Man of INQUA . . . Institut für Urgeschichte, Tübingen.

Phillips, Patricia. 1988. Traceology (microwear) studies in the USSR. World Archaeology 19(3):349–356.

Shotton, F. W. 1970. Petrological examination. In Science in archaeology, a survey of progress and research, Don Brothwell and Eric Higgs, eds. Praeger, New York, pp. 571–577. (Revised and enlarged edition).

Simpson, R. D. 1978. The Calico Mountains archaeological site. In Early man in America from a circum-Pacific perspective, A. L. Bryan, ed. Occasional Papers No. 1. Department of Anthropology, University of Alberta, Edmonton, pp. 219–220.

Symens, Nicole. 1986. A functional analysis of selected stone artifacts from the Magdalenian site at Verberie, France. Journal of Field Archaeology 13(2):213–222.

Vaughn, Patrick C. 1985. Use-wear analysis of flaked tools. University of Arizona Press, Tucson.

Wiessner, Polly. 1983. Style and social information in Kalahari San projectile points. American Antiquity 48(2):253–276.

Wilmsen, Edwin N. 1970. Lithic analysis and cultural inference: a paleo-Indian case study. Anthropological Papers of the University of Arizona No. 16. University of Arizona Press, Tucson.

Wilson, Lucy. 1988. Petrography of the Lower Palaeolithic tool assemblages of the Cauve de l'Arago (France). World Archaeology 19(2):376–387.

Yerkes, Richard W. 1983. Microwear, microdrills, and Mississippian crafts specialization. American Antiquity 48(3):499–518.

Young, Donald, and Douglas M. Banforth. 1990. On the macroscopic identification of used flakes. American Antiquity 55(2):403–409.

SOURCES OF ADDITIONAL INFORMATION

All standard introductory archaeological texts include discussions of lithic technology and analysis. Some examples are in chapter 13, "Technology and artifacts," in Brian Fagan's *In the Beginning: An Introduction to archaeology*, 6th ed. (Glenview, Ill., Scott, Foresman, 1988), in which pp. 312–326 are devoted to stone tools; and Robert Sharer and Wendy Ashmore, *Fundamentals of Archaeology* (Menlo Park, Calif., Benjamin Cummings, 1979), pp. 295–304.

The review of flint knapping as an anthropological concept by Flenniken in the *Annual Review of Anthropology* (see References) takes a historical approach, and includes a useful bibliography.

In his paper "Prolegomena to a grammatical theory of lithic artifacts," *World Archaeology* 19(3) (February 1988):218–296, Fekri A. Hassan has criticized the present state of lithic studies, which he attributes to a failure of quantitative TYPOLOGY, and proposes a cognitive approach to lithic analysis incorporating the principles of European postprocessualism. Two issues of the journal *World Archaeology* have been devoted to lithic studies. Papers in Vol. 17(1) (June 1985), collectively titled "Studying stones," cover aspects of technology, microwear studies, petrography, Paleolithic assemblage variability, and the uses of structural stone. Papers included in vol. 19(3) (February 1988), "New directions in Palaeolithic archaeology," are more theoretical and interpretative; this issue includes the paper by Hassan cited above, as well as others on chronology and site functions.

The 1979 paper by Cahen, Keeley, and Van Noten in *Current Anthropology* (cited in References) addresses some of the most critical issues in lithic analysis and interpretation, including distinguishing curated from "expedient" tools (see CURATION), interpreting ASSEMBLAGE variability, and whether current lithic typologies actually reflect tool functions; some implicit assumptions underlying arguments on these points are also examined, and some nonstatistical methods for investigating these problems are discussed.

For access to the literature of lithic analysis, see the bibliographies in the works discussed above. These will need to be supplemented with more recent material by examining current issues of *American Antiquity*, the *Journal of Field Archaeology*, *Journal of Archaeological Science*, and *Lithic Technology*. Unfortunately, the annual review *Advances in Archaeological Method and Theory*, during its decade of publication, never included a review article on lithics. Forthcoming issues of its successor, *Archaeological Method and Theory*, should be monitored for the inclusion of a much-needed review.

M
_____

MIDDLE-RANGE RESEARCH. 1. A type of theoretical research into the formation processes of archaeological deposits. 2. A kind of empirical archaeological investigation in which behavior and events affecting SITE formation are directly observed in the present, and results are compared with data recovered through the excavation of prehistoric deposits.

Middle-range studies have as their goal "the isolation of diagnostic 'signatures' whose recognition in the ARCHAEOLOGICAL RECORD can inform us of the processes that led to the formation of that record" (Grayson 1986:77). The ultimate aim of middle-range research is the construction of middle-range theory, or "bridging theory," to explain the dynamic behavioral processes of the past that have left their material traces in the archaeological record. The archaeological subdisciplines of TAPHONOMY and ETHNOARCHAEOLOGY are examples of middle-range research.

Middle-range research in archaeology originated with the borrowing of the concept of middle-range theory from sociology, where it was introduced by Robert Merton in the 1940s. It was originally conceived as an intermediate level of theoretical abstraction, connecting higher-order theory with lower-order empirical studies (Merton 1948, 1949, 1967, 1968; Raab and Goodyear 1984).

In archaeology, middle-range research efforts have been directed toward developing a materialist epistemology for deriving explanation of past cultural behavior from the study of its material remnants. It first became a focus of archaeological interest in the 1960s. Since that time taphonomic, ethnoarchaeological, and experimental lithic studies have addressed the nature of relationships between past events and the material record, employing methods and techniques that include the use of analogical reasoning, constructing models of past behavior based on technological reconstruction, and observation of tool use and discard behavior among contemporary groups (Rathje 1974; Rathje and McCarthy 1977; Hayden and Cannon 1984; Rathje and Ritenbaugh 1984). Although these studies and procedures have resulted in scenarios of past behavior based on informed conjecture rather than speculation, they have not produced the lawlike generalizing statements about the action of cultural processes that Lewis Binford originally believed could be derived from this kind of research (Binford 1981, 1983, 1984).

Middle-range research encompasses not only past behavior affecting depositional processes but also the effects of natural phenomena (see TAPHONOMY). Methods of investigating cultural phenomena such as animal butchery, tool CURATION, recycling, trash disposal, grave robbing, and secondary burial are often based on field observation by ethnoarchaeologists and the use of written ethnographies and ethnohistoric materials when available, and rely heavily on the use of ANALOGY.

Although middle-range studies have been considered an area of theoretical importance in archaeology, in fact such research has been more productive of innovations in method than of new theoretical insights or generalizations. While little theory has resulted, archaeologists have learned from these efforts the importance of testing the accuracy of their interpretations against ethnoarchaeological field data whenever possible. This has had an important corrective effect on the interpretation of prehistoric data, and for this reason middle-range studies are likely to continue in the future, whether or not they result in a body of middle-range theory.

REFERENCES

Binford, Lewis R. 1981. Bones: ancient men and modern myths. Academic Press, New York.
————. 1983. In pursuit of the past. Thames and Hudson, New York
————. 1984. Faunal remains from Klasies River mouth. Academic Press, New York.
Grayson, Donald K. 1986. Eoliths, archaeological ambiguity, and the generation of "middle range" research. In American archaeology past and future, David J. Meltzer, Don D. Fowler, and Jeremy A. Sabloff, eds. Society for American Archaeology and Smithsonian Institution Press, Washington, D.C., pp. 77–133.
Hayden, Brian, and Aubrey Cannon. 1984. The structure of material systems: ethnoarchaeology in the Maya highlands. Society for American Archaeology, SAA Papers No. 3. Washington, D.C.
Merton, Robert. 1948. Discussion of Parsons. American Sociological Review 13:164–168.
————. 1949. Social theory and social structure. Free Press, New York.
————. 1967. On theoretical sociology. Free Press, New York.
————. 1968. Social theory and social structure. 3rd ed. Free Press, New York.
Raab, L. Mark, and Albert C. Goodyear. 1984. Middle-range theory in archaeology: a critical review of origins and applications. American Antiquity 49(2):255–268.
Rathje, William. 1974. The garbage project: a new way of looking at the problems of archaeology. Archaeology 27(4):236–241.

Rathje, William, and W. McCarthy. 1977. Regularity and variability in contemporary garbage. In Research strategies in historical archaeology, Stanley A. South, ed. Academic Press, New York.

Rathje, William, and Cheryl K. Ritenbaugh, eds. 1984. Household refuse analysis: theory, method and application in social science. Sage, Beverly Hills, Calif.

SOURCES OF ADDITIONAL INFORMATION

An extended discussion of middle-range research from a historical perspective may be found in Grayson (1986; see References), which includes an extensive bibliography. David Hurst Thomas, in a paper in the same volume as Grayson's, titled "Contemporary hunter-gatherer archaeology in America," *American Archaeology Past and Future*, D. J. Meltzer, D. D. Fowler, and J. A. Sabloff, eds. (Washington, D. C., Society for American Archaeology/Smithsonian Institution Press, 1986), pp. 237–276, covers some of the same major intellectual problems of middle-range studies discussed by Grayson, and reaches some contrasting conclusions. The most thorough coverage of middle-range research is in Raab and Goodyear (1984; see References), which traces its historical background and development, and discusses its basically nontheoretical nature.

An introductory discussion useful for the student or for acquiring general background may be found in Brian Fagan, *In the Beginning*, 6th ed. (Glenview, Ill., Scott, Foresman, 1988), pp. 402–428.

Some recent discussions of middle-range research representing very different theoretical orientations and methodologies are Robert L. Bettinger, "Archaeological approaches to hunter-gatherers," *Annual Review of Anthropology* 16 (1987):121–142 (see especially "The myth of middle-range theory," pp. 127–131); and Peter Kosso, "Method in archaeology: middle-range theory as hermeneutics," *American Antiquity* 56(4) (1991):621–627, which approaches the subject from a postprocessualist viewpoint.

For current research and recently published material, see latest volumes of *Archaeological Method and Theory* and *Annual Review of Anthropology*, and issues of *American Antiquity*, *American Anthropologist*, and *Journal of Anthropological Archaeology*.

MIGRATION. 1. The relatively rapid, purposeful movement of a human group into a new locality, with permanent relocation and settlement of the entire population in the new location. 2. Seasonal movements of nomadic human hunter-gatherers to take advantage of seasonally available resources; also called *transhumance* (see SEASONALITY). 3. A series of random population movements over a long period of time into a previously unoccupied area, resulting in the initial peopling of new geographic territories.

Migration theory has been present in anthropology and ARCHAEOLOGY ever since students of human culture began to examine the myths and traditional histories of non-Western peoples in the nineteenth century, most of which include at least one episode of migration (Adams, Van Gerven, and Levy 1978:483). Although once considered a sufficient explanation for variability in the AR-CHAEOLOGICAL RECORD indicative of cultural change, migration as a causal, explanatory process has fallen out of favor with archaeologists since the early years of the twentieth century, a fate it has largely shared with its one-time rival, DIFFUSION.

Migration was never formulated as a principle of historical explanation in the field of archaeology, although it has often been used as an ad hoc explanation for observed ethnic and linguistic change (Adams 1978:2). In the present climate of materialist, processual interpretations of archaeological evidence, such explanations are no longer in vogue, and are rarely invoked except in those cases where no reasonable alternative is possible. Such cases include the initial peopling and settlement of previously virgin territories, such as the American and Australian continents during the Pleistocene. The classic example of this type of migration is the peopling of the American continents by Old World populations, a process that may have occurred in waves over a period of several millennia.

Migrations of entire populations were very likely rare occurrences in prehistoric times, although some instances, such as the migratory voyages of the early Polynesians to distant islands in the Pacific, have been documented (Fagan 1987:147; Keegan and Diamond 1987). The more likely pattern proposed for the peopling of the Americas was a long series of movements of small groups over relatively short distances, by land or by water, extending over many millennia (Davies 1979; Fladmark 1979). The possibility of transoceanic migrations' significantly contributing to the settlement of the American continents has been repeatedly raised, particularly by diffusionists. Although this was once a hotly debated topic in Americanist archaeology, interest in such hypotheses has now declined, since similarities in individual cultural "traits" are no longer considered evidence for contact, and interpretations now seek overall patterns and processes to account for phenomena of the material record (Cherry 1981; Brochado 1985; Green and Perlman 1985).

Interest in the migrations to America has shifted to the demographic and cultural consequences of European contact (Crosby 1972), although the search for the sources of particular cultigens or cultural practices, as well as for the original homelands of various migratory populations, has continued to be a subject of speculative interest since the nineteenth century (Brinton 1871; Childe 1950; Emory 1959; Riley et al. 1971; Green 1981; Shutler 1983; Dillehay 1984; Finney 1985). Most archaeologists would now agree that while transoceanic contacts certainly occurred between the Norse Vikings and American Indians of the northern Atlantic coast (McGhee 1984), and very possibly between Polynesian or Asian voyagers and the Indians of western South America (Heyerdahl 1963), these intermittent and fleeting encounters most likely had no significant permanent impact on cultural development in the New World, which appears to have undergone an independent evolution (Davies 1979:241–243).

Archaeologists now tend to be more cautious in assigning directional "influences" when prehistoric migrations are hypothesized, since inferences regarding directionality are often very difficult to support using archaeological evidence. In the majority of cases where migration is a possible explanatory alternative, it is now usually offered in conjunction with a number of other behavioral processes to account for the observed evidence of change. This is in accordance with the current predisposition to avoid "monocausal" explanations for past cultural behavior. Such behavior is now likely to be viewed in systemic terms, as part of a complex web of subsystems interlinked in feedback relationships that sometimes lead to evolutionary change, and that are subject to multiple inputs from a variety of external sources.

Irving Rouse, an archaeologist who has long been interested in the archaeological study of human migration (Rouse 1958, 1976), has made a case for the continued viability of migration as an explanatory concept in archaeology (Rouse 1986) while observing the decline of its use for this purpose. Rouse distinguishes between the seasonal migrations of local groups (which he excludes from his discussion) and the large-scale movements of entire population groups, which are the object of his primary interest. The latter include not only the original peopling of new territories, such as Australia and the continents of the New World, but also "repeopling" by intrusive groups moving into already occupied lands, with the intrusive population supplanting the resident population. This process has frequently been called *invasion* (Clark 1966; West 1989), a somewhat misleading term that implies the use of military force, which may or may not occur as part of a population replacement.

Rouse, as well as some other investigators, has combined material from the archaeological record with linguistic and physical anthropological data to establish chronological frameworks for past population movements. Combining data derived independently by different approaches and methodologies provides a basis for checking conclusions developed from archaeological data against those of other investigators working from different data, to support or refute models utilizing migration as an explanatory process (see also Dyen 1956; Chew 1978; Heathcote 1978; Ehret and Posnansky 1982; Suarez 1985; Greenberg, Turner, and Zegura 1986; Rouse 1986). There is some evidence that migration as a possible explanation for phenomena observed from the ARCHAEOLOGICAL RECORD may be undergoing reconsideration (Anthony 1990).

REFERENCES

Adams, William Y. 1978. On migration and diffusion as rival paradigms. In Diffusion and Migration: Their roles in cultural development. Proceedings of the 10th annual archaeological conference, University of Calgary, P. G. Duke, J. Ebert, G. Langemann, and A. P. Buchner, eds., pp. 1–5.

Adams, William Y., Dennis P. Van Gerven, and Richard S. Levy. 1978. The retreat from migrationism. Annual Review of Anthropology 7:483–532.

Anthony, D. W. 1990. Migration in archaeology—the baby and the bathwater. American Anthropologist 92(4):895–914.

Brinton, Daniel Garrison. 1871. The Arawack language of Guiana in its linguistic and ethnological relations. Transactions of the American Philosophical Society n.s. 14 (art. 4):427–444.

Brochado, José Joaquim Justiniano Proenza. 1985. An ecological model of the spread of pottery and agriculture in eastern South America. Ph.D. dissertation, University of Illinois, Urbana.

Cherry, John. 1981. Pattern and process in the earliest colonization of the Mediterranean islands. In Proceedings of the Prehistoric Society (Cambridge) 47:41–68.

Chew, J. J. 1978. The prehistory of the Japanese languages in the light of evidence from the structures of Japanese and Korean. Asian Perspectives 19(1):190–200.

Childe, V. Gordon. 1950. Prehistoric migrations in Europe. Harvard University Press, Cambridge, Mass.

Clark, J. G. D. (Grahame). 1966. The invasion hypothesis in British archaeology. Antiquity 40(159):172–189.

Crosby, Alfred W., Jr. 1972. The Columbian exchange: biological and cultural consequences of 1492. Contributions in American Studies No. 2. Greenwood Press, Westport, Conn.

Davies, Nigel. 1979. Voyagers to the New World. Morrow, New York.

Dillehay, Tom D. 1984. A late Ice-Age settlement in southern Chile. Scientific American 251(4):106–117.

Dyen, Isidore. 1956. Language distribution and migration theory. Language 32(4):611–626.

Ehret, Christopher, and Merrick Posnansky, eds. 1982. The archaeological and linguistic reconstruction of African history. University of California Press, Berkeley and Los Angeles.

Emory, Kenneth P. 1959. Origin of the Hawaiians. Journal of the Polynesian Society 68(1):29–35.

Fagan, Brian M. 1987. The great journey: the peopling of ancient America. Thames and Hudson, New York.

Finney, Ben R. 1985. Anomalous westerlies, El Niño, and the colonization of Polynesia. American Anthropologist 87(1):9–26.

Fladmark, Knud. 1979. Routes: alternate migration corridors for early man in North America. American Antiquity 44(1):55–69.

Green, Roger C. 1981. Location of the Polynesian homeland: a continuing problem. In Studies in Pacific languages and cultures in honor of Bruce Biggs, J. Jollyman and A. Pawley, eds. Linguistic Society of New Zealand, Auckland, pp. 133–158.

Green, Stanton W., and Stephen W. Perlman. 1985. The archaeology of frontiers and boundaries. Academic Press, New York.

Greenberg, Joseph H., Christy G. Turner II, and Stephen L. Zegura. 1986. The Settlement of the Americas: a comparison of the linguistic, dental, and genetic evidence. Current Anthropology 27(5):477–497.

Heathcote, Gary M. 1978. Problems in interpreting migrations through osteometry. In Diffusion and Migration . . . , proceedings of the 10th annual archaeological conference, University of Calgary, P. G. Duke, J. Ebert, G. Langemann, and A.P. Buchner, eds., pp. 45–54.

Heyerdahl, Thor. 1963. Feasible ocean routes to and from the Americas in pre-Columbian times. American Antiquity 28(4):482–488.

Keegan, W. F., and J. Diamond. 1987. Colonization of islands by humans: a biogeographical perspective. In Advances in Archaeological Method and Theory 10:49–92.

McGhee, Robert. 1984. Contact between native North Americans and the medieval Norse: a review of the evidence. American Antiquity 49(1):4–26.

Riley, Carroll L., J. Charles Kelley, C. W. Pennington, and Robert L. Rands, eds. 1971.

Man across the sea: problems of pre-Columbian contacts. University of Texas Press, Austin.

Rouse, Irving. 1958. The inference of migrations from anthropological evidence. In Migrations in New World culture history, R. H. Thompson, ed. University of Arizona Social Science Bulletin No. 27, pp. 63–68.

———. 1976. Peopling of the Americas. Quaternary Research 6(4):597–612.

———. 1986. Migrations in prehistory: inferring population movements from cultural remains. Yale University Press, New Haven.

Shutler, Richard, Jr. 1983. The Australian parallel to the peopling of the New World. In Early man in the New World, Richard Shutler, ed. Sage, Beverly Hills, Calif., pp. 43–45.

Suarez, B. K., J. Crouse, and D. O'Rourke. 1985. Genetic variation in North Amerindian populations: the geography of gene frequencies. American Journal of Physical Anthropology 67:217–232.

West, Frederick H. 1989. The Americas: migrationism and New World origins [review of Greenberg, Turner and Zegura 1986]. In The interpretation of prehistory: essays from the pages of the Quarterly Review of Archaeology. Review of Archaeology 10(1):158–166. (Originally published in Quarterly Review of Archaeology 8[4], 1987)

SOURCES OF ADDITIONAL INFORMATION

For further background on the historical uses of migrationist explanations, and migration's former status as an alternative to DIFFUSION, see Adams (1978) and Adams, Van Gerven, and Levy (1978) on the decline of migrationist explanation (see References for citations). The latter includes a substantial bibliography.

A discussion of human migration as a biological phenomenon is in Joan Stevenson, "Migration," in her A Dictionary of Concepts in Physical Anthropology (Westport, Conn., Greenwood Press, 1991), pp. 259–264, which includes extensive bibliographic information. For an ethnological perspective, see Robert Winthrop, "Migration," in his A Dictionary of Concepts in Cultural Anthropology (Westport, Conn., Greenwood Press, 1991), pp. 187–189.

A book of papers on the initial peopling of the Americas is Out of Asia, Robert Kirk and Emoke Szathmary, eds. (Canberra, The Journal of Pacific History, 1985). The papers represent a variety of disciplinary approaches to the evidence for migration, including genetic studies, mitochondrial DNA variation, craniometry, and linguistic and cultural evidence.

Discussions of migration that may be indicative of a revival of archaeological interest are in Rouse (1986) and Anthony (1990; see References). The latter includes a bibliography of 114 references providing access to other literature. Future issues of American Antiquity and American Anthropologist, and appropriate annual review, should be checked for later publications.

MORTUARY ANALYSIS. The investigation of ancient human burials for information on past sociocultural systems. See also BIOCULTURAL STUDIES.

The analysis of skeletal remains, including their orientation and disposition, the grave goods or burial offerings interred with them, and the burial structures in which these are placed can provide many kinds of data on cultures of the past. Data on health and disease, diet and nutrition, paleodemographics, and cultural practices such as head deformation and dental decoration, as well as evidence of SOCIAL ORGANIZATION, trade relationships, and religious beliefs may be recovered or inferred from burials.

The study of burial customs has long been an important part of archaeology and anthropology (Yarrow 1891; Bushnell 1920; Macleod 1925; Kroeber 1927; Childe 1942, 1944, 1945). Purposeful interment of the dead has often been considered a diagnostic behavior of modern humans (*Homo sapiens sapiens*), setting them apart from earlier forms of *Homo sapiens* such as Neanderthal man, whose ostensible mortuary activities have been challenged and debated (Gargett 1989; Kooijmans 1989).

Ancient burial practices as indicators of religion and belief in an afterlife were the primary subject of interest to anthropologists and archaeologists of the nineteenth century. Such belief was at that time considered to be a component of the "psychic unity" shared by all humans, a view promoted by the German anthropologist Adolf Bastian (Bartel 1982:33) and widely adopted by other anthropologists of the time.

One of the first archaeologists to investigate burials in a systematic way was Sir John Lubbock, who devised a developmental TYPOLOGY of religious belief, beginning with atheism and progressing to monotheism. Lubbock described the burials he studied in terms of his "stages" of religious belief, assigning certain types and amounts of grave goods to each. He was among the first to recognize variable treatment of the dead according to age, sex, and social rank (Lubbock 1882). He later published the first statistical analysis of a series of mortuary data, based on his studies of 297 British tumulus burials, which included frequency data on grave types, body orientation, grave goods, burial method, and the relative wealth and labor investment represented (Lubbock 1900). Systematic investigations of burials for social and biological data using statistical techniques did not become common, however, until the 1970s and 1980s (Saxe 1970; Brown 1971; Gruber 1971; Hatch and Willey 1974; Hatch 1975, 1976, 1987; Tainter 1975, 1977; Rothschild 1979; Goldstein 1980, 1981; Blakely and Beck 1981; Chapman, Kinnes, and Randsborg 1981; Humphreys and King 1981; Orton and Hodson 1982; Parker-Pearson 1982; Milner 1984; Hatch and Geidel 1985; Mainfort 1985; Pearson et al. 1989).

The principles of mortuary analysis followed in contemporary archaeology were set forth by Arthur Saxe in his doctoral dissertation (Saxe 1970), using concepts derived from anthropological role theory (Tainter 1978:106). According to this approach, the roles an adult plays in society make up his or her social persona, and this multifaceted persona will be reflected in the treatment accorded an individual at death. In egalitarian societies infants will have few social identities, compared with adults. Therefore, if archaeologists find elaborate burials of infants, indicating a social persona more typical of an adult, they may assume that a principle of social ranking by birth is present, ascribing an inherited high status to the children of high-ranking persons (Tainter 1978).

Repeated archaeological examples attest that mortuary practices do in fact reflect the organization of society itself (Binford 1971), which has been confirmed ethnographically. It is therefore assumed that the mortuary treatment of the dead will vary according to the age, sex, and social status of the deceased. In hierarchical societies, the number of social classes or ranks present may be discernible from burials, if different mortuary treatment is given to the remains of persons belonging to different social levels or ranks (Peebles and Kus 1977). The orientation of the grave or body, the physical construction of grave or tomb, the body position, and the amount of postmortem manipulation are usually of social significance as well (Gruber 1971; Rothschild 1979).

Biological data derived from examination of skeletal remains may also provide important social information. Studies of skeletal remains can document episodes of famine, social differences in access to the most nutritious foods, disease and growth patterns and perhaps their relationship to social position or rank, the age at which children were weaned, life expectancies at various ages, birth and death rates, and a host of other factors (see also BIOCULTURAL STUDIES; PALEODEMOGRAPHY).

Patterns of interregional interaction and trade may be apparent from the presence of exotic goods in burials. Obsidian tools, and ornaments of gold, silver, jade, shell, or other materials not locally available, may have been imported from very distant locations, and can be traced to their sources to reconstruct prehistoric trade routes. Items such as these also reflect a society's level of technology and artistic skill, and may indicate the presence of full-time economic SPECIALIZATION in the society, as well as its patterns of wealth and consumption of nonutilitarian "elite" goods. Concentrations and distributions of such items as these in burials can be of great value to archaeologists in tracing the development of social ranking in formerly egalitarian societies, since "elite" items serve as markers of social change and growing complexity (Mainfort 1985; see also EXCHANGE).

Special mortuary treatment accorded certain classes or categories of individuals, such as women (see O'Shea and Zvelebil 1984; Sempowski 1986), or children, who in some societies are not given formal burial unless they have achieved a certain age, can be important indicators of the social significance of age and sex differences within an archaeological culture. Changes in burial practices are also revealing, since these usually reflect change in other aspects of society as well, including ideological and economic changes. The application of multivariate statistical techniques to the analysis of mortuary data continues to produce new insights into prehistoric society and behavior, contributing to a growing body of understandings of vanished lifeways.

REFERENCES

Bartel, Brad. 1982. A historical review of ethnological and archaeological analyses of mortuary practice. Journal of Anthropological Archaeology 1:32–58.
Binford, Lewis R. 1971. Mortuary practices: their study and their potential. In Approaches to the social dimensions of mortuary practices, James A. Brown, ed. SAA Memoirs No. 25. Washington D.C., pp. 6–29.

Blakely, Robert, and Lane A. Beck. 1981. Trace elements, nutritional status, and social stratification at Etowah, Georgia. Annals of the New York Academy of Sciences 376:417–431.

Brown, James A., ed. 1971. Approaches to the social dimensions of mortuary practices. SAA Memoirs No. 25. Washington, D.C.

Bushnell, D. I. 1920. Native cemeteries and forms of burial east of the Mississippi. Bureau of American Ethnology 71. Washington, D.C.

Chapman, Robert, I. Kinnes, and K. Randsborg, eds. 1981. The archaeology of death. Cambridge University Press.

Childe, Vere Gordon. 1942. The chambered cairns of Rousay. Antiquaries Journal 22:138–142.

———. 1944. Progress and archaeology. Watts, London.

———. 1945. Directional changes in funerary practices during 50,000 years. Man 4:13–19.

Gargett, Robert H. 1989. Grave shortcomings: the evidence for Neanderthal burial. Current Anthropology 30(2):157–190.

Goldstein, Lynne. 1980. Mississippian mortuary practices: a case study of two cemeteries in the lower Illinois Valley. Northwestern University Archaeological Program, Scientific Papers No. 4. Evanston, Ill.

———. 1981. One-dimensional archaeology and multi-dimensional people: spatial organization and mortuary analysis. In The Archaeology of death, R. Chapman, I. Kinnes, and K. Randsborg, eds. Cambridge University Press, pp. 53–69.

Gruber, J. W. 1971. Patterning in death in a late prehistoric village in Pennsylvania. American Antiquity 36:64–76.

Hatch, James W. 1975. Social dimensions of Dallas burials. Southeastern Archaeological Conference Bulletin 18:132–138.

———. 1976. Status in death: principles of ranking in Dallas Culture mortuary remains. Ph.D. dissertation, Pennsylvania State University, University Park.

———. 1987. Mortuary indicators of organizational variability among late prehistoric chiefdoms in the southeastern U.S. interior. In Chiefdoms in the Americas, Robert D. Drennan and Carlos A. Uribe, eds. University Press of America, Landon, Md., pp. 9–18.

Hatch, James W., and Richard A. Geidel. 1985. Status-specific dietary variation in two New World cultures. Journal of Human Evolution 14:469–476.

Hatch, James W., and Patrick Willey. 1974. Stature and status in Dallas society. Tennessee Archaeologist 30:107–131.

Humphreys, S. C., and Helen King, eds. 1981. Mortality and immortality: the anthropology and archaeology of death. Academic Press, London.

Kooijmans, L. P. Louwe. 1989. On the evidence for Neandertal burial. Current Anthropology 30(3):322–330.

Kroeber, Alfred L. 1927. Disposal of the dead. American Anthropologist 29:308–315.

Lubbock, John. 1882. The origin of civilization and the primitive condition of man. Longman, Green, London.

———. 1900. Prehistoric times. Williams and Norgate, London.

Mainfort, Robert C., Jr. 1985. Wealth, space, and status in a historic Indian cemetery. American Antiquity 50(3):555–579.

Macleod, W. C. 1925. Certain mortuary aspects of Northwest Coast culture. American Anthropologist 27:122–148.

Milner, George R. 1984. Social and temporal implications of variation among American Bottom Mississippian cemeteries. American Antiquity 49(3):468–488.

Orton, C. R., and F. R. Hodson. 1982. Rank and class: interpreting the evidence from prehistoric cemeteries. In Mortality and immortality: the anthropology and archaeology of death, S. C. Humphreys and Helen King, eds. Academic Press, London, pp. 103–115.

O'Shea, John, and Marek Zvelebil. 1984. Oleneostrovski mogilnik: Reconstructing the social and economic organization of prehistoric foragers in northern Russia. Journal of Anthropological Archaeology 3:1–40.

Parker-Pearson, Michael. 1982. Mortuary practices, society, and ideology: an ethnoarchaeological study. In Symbolic and structural archaeology, Ian Hodder, ed. Cambridge University Press, pp. 99–113.

Pearson, Richard, Jong-Wook Lee, Wonyoung Koh, and Anne Underhill. 1989. Social ranking in the kingdom of Old Silla, Korea: analysis of burials. Journal of Anthropological Archaeology 8:1–50.

Peebles, C. S., and S. Kus. 1977. Some archaeological correlates of ranked societies. American Antiquity 42:421–448.

Rothschild, Nan. 1979. Mortuary behavior and social organization at Indian Knoll and Dickson Mound. American Antiquity 44:658–675.

———. 1983. Review: The archaeology of death. American Antiquity 48(4):866–867.

Saxe, A. A. 1970. Social dimensions of mortuary practices. Ph.D. dissertation, University of Michigan.

Sempowski, Martha L. 1986. Differential mortuary treatment of Seneca women: some social inferences. Archaeology of Eastern North America 14:35–44.

Tainter, Joseph A. 1975. Social inferences and mortuary practices: an experiment in numerical classification. World Archaeology 7:1–15.

———. 1977. Woodland social change in west-central Illinois. Mid-Continental Journal of Archaeology 2(1):67–98.

———. 1978. Mortuary practices and the study of prehistoric social systems. Advances in Archaeological Method and Theory 1:105–141.

Yarrow, H. C. 1891. A further contribution to the study of mortuary customs of the North American Indians. 1st Annual Report of the Bureau of American Ethnology. Washington, D.C., pp. 89–206.

SOURCES OF ADDITIONAL INFORMATION

Joseph Tainter's 1978 review article (in the first volume of *Advances in Archaeological Method and Theory*; see References) presents an unbiased overview of concepts, issues, typologies, data selection, and quantitative methods in mortuary analysis, and cites important studies prior to 1978. The book by John O'Shea, *Mortuary Variability: An Archaeological Investigation* (New York, Academic Press, 1984), is a slightly more recent comprehensive treatment, focused on mortuary variability and problems of theory and method in mortuary studies; it also includes a wealth of field data from North America. Both these publications have extensive bibliographies that now require updating.

Bartel's 1982 review article (see References) gives additional historical treatment of the subject from the nineteenth century to the present, including a useful summary of European anthropological thought regarding mortuary practices; but his argument for a structuralist theoretical position in interpreting burial data is not likely to be acceptable to North American materialist archaeologists.

For information on analytical criteria and statistical techniques used in mortuary analysis, see Tainter 1978 and 1981; Braun 1981; and Rothschild 1979 (all in References). A review by Aubrey Cannon, "The historical dimension in mortuary expressions of status and sentiment," *Current Anthropology* 30(4)(1989):437–458, includes a list of more recent bibliographic references.

For other recent literature, check current issues of *World Archaeology*, *American Anthropologist*, *American Antiquity*, *Journal of Anthropological Archaeology*, and the pertinent annual reviews.

N

"NEW" ARCHAEOLOGY. The theoretical and methodological approach to archaeological research supported by Lewis Binford in the United States, and David L. Clarke in England, during the 1960s and 1970s; it advocates the use of scientific method, statistical procedures, and interpretative principles derived from cultural anthropology to develop general explanatory principles for phenomena observed from the ARCHAEOLOGICAL RECORD. Also called *processual archaeology*. See also ANTHROPOLOGICAL ARCHAEOLOGY.

The "new" archaeology has been widely regarded as a response to the long-standing lack of a unified body of interpretative theory in archaeology that had been noted by various critics beginning in the 1940s (e.g., Taylor 1948). It was also, however, a response to archaeological methodology of the time, which ended with description and the construction of cultural chronologies. The "new" archeologists, such as Binford, proposed more ambitious interpretative goals, and sought a body of theoretical principles that could be used to reconstruct the behavior of the past that had left its traces in the material remains of the archaeological record.

Prior to Julian Steward's development of CULTURAL ECOLOGY, American archaeology had remained largely atheoretic, and the emphasis had been placed on developing ARTIFACT typologies and chronological sequences. Much of this activity appears to have been motivated by the desire to discover the functions and social meanings of artifacts in their past CULTURE settings. However, it soon became clear that such interpretation required a theoretical framework, which was entirely lacking in archaeology at the midpoint of the twentieth century; the "new" archaeologists set out to fill this hiatus (Binford 1962, 1964, 1965, 1968; Clarke 1968, 1972; Fritz and Plog 1970; Watson, LeBlanc, and Redman 1971; Schiffer 1976; Salmon 1976, 1982; Salmon and Salmon 1979).

The "new" archaeologists advocated a problem-oriented program of archaeological research that included the formulation of falsifiable hypotheses that could be tested through evaluation and analysis of specific kinds of empirical data collected in the course of carefully designed field studies. Field investigations were to become only one part of an overall research design that would direct and shape the field investigation from beginning to end and define its goals in very explicit terms. According to Binford, the "new" archaeology's chief proponent, archaeological research was to become henceforth an explicitly scientific endeavor, beginning with the conscious statement of the researcher's underlying assumptions and evaluation of their validity, and proceeding to the construction of hypotheses, which would then be tested in the field. Results were to be quantifiable, and would be utilized to develop and modify a body of archaeological theory that would serve to generate further productive hypotheses.

Binford's goal was no less than the establishment of a science of archaeology. It was his hope that through the application of his proposed scientific research method, archaeological laws or lawlike statements might be discovered that would guide and shape all future interpretations of archaeological data. He proposed that by developing "middle-range" or "bridging" theory to identify and account for certain invariant taphonomic processes affecting archaeological deposits, archaeology would develop a body of general theory that would direct the discipline's future course, in a manner comparable with that in which the highly successful and generative Darwinian theory of EVOLUTION has come to direct research in biology since the mid-nineteenth century.

Although these ambitious theoretical goals have not been realized, Binford's influence upon archaeological research has been enormous. The fact that few American archaeologists now begin a field study without consciously formulating a research design, no matter how modest in its goals, is largely a result of the ideas he propounded in the 1960s and 1970s.

Because of the emphasis placed upon "process", that is, the dynamic behavioral aspect of past cultures, and in particular upon those processes contributing to the formation of the archaeological record, the "new" archaeology has also been called "processual archaeology." The opposing views of the structuralist-oriented European school that arose at the end of the 1970s as a reaction against the materialist bias of the "new" archaeology have thus been called "postprocessualism" (Hodder 1985; Tilley 1990).

An important part of the "new" archaeology has been its reliance on statistical methods utilizing the rapidly developing computer technology of the 1960s and 1970s which made it possible to analyze enormous amounts of field research data with great speed. Another prominent feature was the application of general SYSTEM THEORY and system analytic methods to the study and reconstruction of prehistoric cultures (Clarke 1968, 1972; Flannery 1972; Salmon 1976, 1982).

The "new" archaeology was a response to the interaction of a number of trends that emerged during the two decades preceding its appearance. Archaeology had, during its relatively brief history, been a notably pragmatic discipline, and its results had traditionally been reported in largely descriptive terms. Attempts at interpretation were often intuitive rather than systematic, and frequently were based on implicit analogies drawn from ethnographic data. As Binford pointed out, most such interpretation was based on unstated assumptions of which the analyst was often not consciously aware. As a result, excavational and analytic goals were poorly defined, and empirical data were difficult to interpret in the absence of a theoretical framework. A traditional response to this deficit had been the construction of elaborate typological and chronological schemes, in the hope that these would somehow enable the archaeologist to explain the data. Only with the recognition of the nature and multilevel character of scientific explanation, a result of the work of Karl Popper (Popper 1961, 1962), later popularized by Thomas Kuhn (Kuhn 1970), did the true character of archaeology's dilemma become clear, although the need for reform had been enunciated as early as the 1940s (Taylor 1948), and some preliminary attempts at theory building had been made in the same decade (Steward 1942).

In the wake of recent disaffection with the "new" archaeology among European archaeologists, it is important to emphasize the significance of this development in the history of the discipline, which has resulted in some far-reaching changes. Far from being a mere tidying up of field research methods, the "new" archaeology succeeded in defining some specific goals for the discipline that have been widely adopted. The most important and innovative of these was the goal of recovering the dynamic, processual aspects of the past, which focused on the study and definition of prehistoric cultural behavior.

The reforms offered by the British archaeologist David Clarke, at about the same time as Binford's proposals, were in many ways similar (Clarke 1968). An important difference was Clarke's insistence upon the "conceptual autonomy" of archaeology, which he believed should exist as a discipline in its own right, independent of both history and anthropology. He proposed that material culture constituted an independent system that should be studied and explained in its own terms. This approach has enjoyed some limited application in the United States (Rathje 1979), but has been more actively pursued in England, in particular by Ian Hodder (Hodder 1982, 1986). Clarke and his successors favored the use of formal mathematical models in their applications of SYSTEM THEORY to archaeological problems, rather than the more informal systemic models generally used by American practitioners (e.g., Flannery 1972).

The future direction of theoretical archaeology in America is uncertain at present. Some U.S. archaeologists, disillusioned by the failure of the scientific approach to produce the hoped-for theoretical results, have returned to doing primarily descriptive ecological studies, or have fallen back upon culture historical methods (Flannery 1982). British archaeologists of the "Cambridge School" associated with Hodder are gaining more influence on both sides of the Atlantic (Hodder 1985; Tilley 1990; Kosso 1991), but whether their "postprocessual" archaeology, based on a combination of historical, cognitive-structuralist, and linguistic methods, will gain widespread acceptance in North America is not yet clear. Some American archaeologists are pursuing the development of general theory based on Darwinian evolutionary principles (see, e.g., Leonard and Jones 1987), which may finally provide the long-awaited solution to the continuing atheoretical situation of American archaeology.

Despite the problems inherent in operationalizing many of its recommendations and reforms, and the realization that "general laws" in archaeology are likely to remain elusive, the explicitly scientific, problem-oriented approach and the use of quantitative methods of analysis, as well as probabilistic SAMPLING, have now become part of mainstream archaeological research, and are likely to remain so until more productive approaches to explanation are developed (Dunnell 1982; Gibbon 1984; Watson, LeBlanc, and Redman 1984; Kelley and Hanen 1988; Wylie 1988).

REFERENCES

Binford, Lewis R. 1962. Archaeology as anthropology. American Antiquity 28:217–225.
———. 1964. A consideration of archaeological research design. American Antiquity 29:425–441.
———. 1965. Archaeological systematics and the study of culture process. American Antiquity 31:203–210.
———. 1968. Archaeological perspectives. In New perspectives in archaeology, S. R. Binford and L. R. Binford, eds. Aldine, Chicago, pp. 5–32.
Clarke, David L. 1968. Analytical archaeology. Methuen, London.
———, ed. 1972. Models in archaeology. Methuen, London.
Dunnell, Robert C. 1982. Science, social science and common sense: the agonizing dilemma of modern archaeology. Journal of Anthropological Research 38:1–25.
Flannery, Kent V. 1972. The cultural evolution of civilizations. Annual Review of Ecology and Systematics 3:399–426.
———. 1982. The golden Marshalltown: a parable for the archaeology of the 1980s. American Anthropologist 84:265–278.
Fritz, John, and Fred T. Plog. 1970. The nature of archaeological explanation. American Antiquity 35:405–412.
Gibbon, Guy. 1984. Anthropological archaeology. Columbia University Press, New York.
Hodder, Ian. 1982. Symbols in action. Cambridge University Press, Cambridge.
———. 1985. Postprocessualist archaeology. Advances in Archaeological Method and Theory 8:1–26.
———. 1986. Reading the past: current approaches to interpretation in archaeology. Cambridge University Press, Cambridge.
Kelley, Jane H., and Marsha P. Hanen. 1988. Archaeology and the methodology of science. University of New Mexico Press, Albuquerque.
Kosso, Peter. 1991. Method in archaeology: middle-range theory as hermeneutics. American Antiquity 56(4):621–627.
Kuhn, Thomas J. 1970. The structure of scientific revolutions. 2nd ed. University of Chicago Press.
Leonard, R. D., and G. T. Jones. 1987. Elements of an inclusive model for archaeology. Journal of Anthropological Archaeology 6(3):199–219.

Popper, Karl. 1961. The logic of scientific discovery. Science Editions, New York.
————. 1962. Conjectures and refutations: the growth of scientific knowledge. Basic
    Books, New York; Routledge and Kegan Paul, London.
Rathje, William L. 1979. Modern material culture studies. Advances in Archaeological
    Method and Theory 2:1–37. Academic Press, New York.
Salmon, Merrilee H. 1976. "Deductive" versus "inductive" archaeology. American
    Antiquity 44:376–380.
————. 1982. Philosophy and archaeology. Academic Press, New York.
Salmon, Merrilee H., and Wesley C. Salmon. 1979. Alternative models of scientific
    explanation. American Anthropologist 81:61–74.
Schiffer, Michael. 1976. Behavioral archaeology. Academic Press, New York.
Steward, Julian H. 1942. The direct historical approach to archaeology. American An-
    tiquity 7:337–344.
Taylor, Walter W. 1948. A study of archaeology. American Anthropological Association
    Memoirs No. 69. Washington, D.C.
Tilley, Christopher, ed. 1990. Reading material culture: structuralism, hermeneutics, and
    post-structuralism. Basil Blackwell, Oxford and Cambridge, Mass.
Watson, Patty Jo, Stephen A. LeBlanc, and Charles L. Redman. 1971. Explanation in
    archaeology: an explicitly scientific approach. Columbia University Press, New
    York.
————. 1984 Archaeological explanation. Columbia University Press, New York.
Wylie, Alison. 1988. The new archaeology: tensions in theory and practice. Academic
    Press, New York.

SOURCES OF ADDITIONAL INFORMATION

Among the many retrospective discussions and evaluations of the "new" archaeology
that are now appearing in print, the book-length studies by Gibbon (1984), Kelley and
Hanen (1988), and Wylie (1988; all cited above in References) are the most thought-
provoking. The original statements of goals and methods in Watson, LeBlanc, and Redman
(1971, 1984; see References) are still worth reading. An excellent critique and evaluation
is R. A. Watson, "What the new archaeology has accomplished," *Current Anthropology*
32(3)(1991):275–291, which includes an up-to-date bibliography.

The clearest expositions of the competing postprocessualist paradigm are in Hodder
1986 (see References) and in a review article by Ian Hodder, "Postprocessualist archaeology," *Advances in Archaeological Method and Theory* 8(1985):1–26. An intriguing
treatment of postprocessualism by one of the leading exponents of the "new" archaeology,
Patty Jo Watson, is the paper by Watson and M. Fotiadis, "The razor's edge: symbolic-
structuralist archaeology and the expansion of archaeological inference," *American Anthropologist* 92(3)(1990):613–629.

For forthcoming literature on the new archaeology and the development of the postprocessualist reaction to it, see future annual volumes of *Annual Review of Anthropology*
and *Archaeological Method and Theory*, and current issues of *Journal of Anthropological
Archaeology, American Antiquity,* and *American Anthropologist.*

NEW WORLD ARCHAEOLOGY. The study of CULTURES present in North,
South, and Central America prior to the time of European contact, through the
recovery and investigation of their material remains.

Also called *American (or Americanist) studies*, New World archaeology is not exclusively confined to the prehistoric period before written records; it also includes the archaeological investigation of material remains dating to the time of initial contact with European civilization in the early sixteenth century, and study of European records of the conquest period, as well as of native documents produced by the literate civilizations of Mexico during the millennium prior to European contact.

The history of New World, or Americanist, archaeology may be said to begin with the earliest speculations concerning the origins of the native Americans, soon after Columbus's voyages of discovery (Acosta 1604; Beals 1957), which has remained a central question in the development of New World archaeology. Speculation on American Indian origins have traced them to the ancient tribes of Israel, to the legendary "lost continents" of Atlantis and Mu (Wauchope 1962), and other sources. Rational explanations date back to the late sixteenth century, when Father José de Acosta suggested the ancestors of the native Americans had migrated from one or more locations in Europe or Asia, traveling across land bridges that might have connected the continents in the past. This strikingly modern idea is now supported by knowledge of geological history and the events of the Pleistocene epoch, and is widely accepted (Carter 1978; Fladmark 1979, 1983; Willey and Sabloff 1980; Shutler 1983; Bryan 1986).

Early speculation about the Indians was also an outgrowth of the humanistic-antiquarian tradition inherited from the Old World, whose influence continued to be a significant one in American archaeology throughout the nineteenth century, contributing to the growth and persistence of the "Mound Builder" concept. The latter notion attributed the large mounds and effigy earthworks in the central and eastern United States to the prehistoric presence of an unknown foreign civilized race, the "Mound Builders," who presumably were of Old World origin (Silverberg 1968). It was then believed that the "primitive" American Indians could not have built structures of this scale and complexity, a racist notion very much in keeping with late-nineteenth-century Indian policies of the U.S. government.

The earliest field investigations in America, like those in the Old World, were often motivated by the antiquarian desire to acquire objects for collections, and only secondarily to uncover evidence to support speculations about the American past. An exception to this was the work of Thomas Jefferson. The third president of the United States was sufficiently interested in the native population and its past to conduct the first controlled stratigraphic excavations on the North American continent, which were also among the first anywhere in the world. Jefferson's work on an Indian mound located on his Virginia plantation, duly reported in his publication *Notes on the State of Virginia* (1787), was an early model of fieldwork that remained unparalleled for more than a hundred years.

The work of Jefferson was the first instance of the empirical approach that would become a continuing characteristic of American archaeologists, in contrast with their European counterparts. While archaeology in the Old World, and in

Europe in particular, has always been closely aligned with history and the humanistic disciplines, American archaeology was to become closely associated with the developing field of anthropology from its outset, and has remained more empirically and scientifically oriented up to the present (see also OLD WORLD ARCHAEOLOGY; PREHISTORY).

The classificatory-descriptive period in American archaeology (ca. 1840–1914; Willey and Sabloff 1980) began in the 1840s with the work of Ephraim Squier and Edwin H. Davis, who undertook surveys of the North American Indian mounds to record what was left of them before they were destroyed by development—a concern still very much alive among American archaeologists. Squier and Davis accepted the idea of a "Mound Builder race," which was finally refuted by excavations led by Cyrus Thomas for the U.S. Bureau of American Ethnology (Squier and Davis 1848; Thomas 1894). Thomas was among the first to use the so-called "direct historical approach" in American archaeology, a technique based on the use of ANALOGY to extrapolate backward in time from the material culture of contemporary native peoples to make inferences about the lifeway of their ancestors, who manufactured similar artifacts and occupied the same geographic area. This method has continued to be an important part of American archaeology up to the present (Kidder 1936; Steward 1942).

In Middle America, the classificatory-descriptive period began with the explorations of John L. Stephens and Frederick Catherwood in the region of the ancient Maya civilization, which provided scholars and the public with the first accurate descriptions and illustrations of many major ruins, and stimulated archaeological investigation of the area by Alfred Maudslay, Teobert Maler, and many others (Maudslay 1889–1902; Maler 1901, 1903; Stephens 1963, 1969).

In both Central and South America, archaeology was aided from the beginning by the existence of early written accounts by Spanish explorers and clerics, including the detailed descriptions of the Maya civilizations by Diego de Landa (1941), and of the Aztecs by Bernardino de Sahagún (1950–1970) and Bernal Diaz del Castillo (1908–1916), as well as a number of general histories (e.g., Oviedo Y Valdez 1950; Vazquez de Espinosa 1968). Knowledge of the prehispanic cultures of these areas, as well as of their flora, fauna, and geography, was further supplemented by information obtained from responses to a questionnaire distributed by the Spanish Crown in the late 1570s to Catholic bishops and local officials of Central and South America; its surviving remnant has been published as *Relaciones Geográficas* (1898; see also Mignon 1987). While this body of material has no exact counterpart in North America, some early descriptions and drawings of the North American natives and their towns, as well as of the flora and fauna of the southeastern United States, dating to the sixteenth century, have survived (Smith 1624; Lorant 1965).

Other developments of the classificatory-descriptive period in the Americas included the beginning of stratigraphic excavations, pioneered by Max Uhle in California and Peru, Nels Nelson in the southwestern United States, and Manuel

Gamio in Mexico (Uhle 1903, 1907; Gamio 1913; Nelson 1916; Bernal 1980; see also STRATIGRAPHY).

During the classificatory-historical period (1914–1960, per Willey and Sabloff 1980), the American past, previously thought to be a period of unknown length and unchanging, uniform culture, began to be charted from the results of stratigraphic excavation, and cultural chronologies based on these excavations and the new technique of artifact SERIATION began to be developed (see also RELATIVE DATING). The work of Alfred Kidder at Pecos Pueblo in the American Southwest was especially important to this development (Kidder 1924, 1931, 1936); a comparable chronological sequence for the southeastern United States was the contribution of James A. Ford (Ford 1938, 1962). Chronology was to become "the central theme . . . in American archaeology" during this period (Willey and Sabloff 1980:83), and remained the dominant concern up to the advent of "new" processual archaeology in the 1960s.

Allied to the concern with developing chronologies was a secondary preoccupation with classification of archaeological data. Artifact typologies, reflecting temporal changes in the STYLES and attributes of material objects, became the bases for developing cultural sequences that, it was hoped, would permit the construction of culture historical syntheses for each major culture area. In actuality, classification and chronology became almost ends in themselves during this time, and the goal of broad syntheses proved to be elusive. This period produced the first major attempt to develop a standardized system of archaeological systematics, in the work of Gordon Willey and Philip Phillips, which was based on an earlier classification outlined by W. C. McKern (McKern 1939; Willey and Phillips 1958).

Willey and Phillips devised a cultural chronology for the New World, a basic sequence that, with some local modifications, has been widely adopted and is still in use. In this chronological scheme, New World PREHISTORY began with the Paleo-Indian period (sometimes called the Lithic), encompassing all cultural developments up to the end of the Pleistocene epoch approximately 12,000 years ago, a period when populations are believed to have supported themselves by hunting large game animals that inhabited the Americas during the Pleistocene. The Paleo-Indian period was followed by the Archaic period, a time roughly comparable to the European Neolithic and marked by changes in lithic technology; New World populations underwent a broad-spectrum readaptation to the altered climatic and ecological conditions created by the recession of the continental ice sheets, resulting in rises in sea level and the extinction of the biggame fauna. The appearance of pottery, cultivated crops, and permanent village settlements marked the beginning of the Formative period.

Although the times when these various periods began varied from one geographic region to another, the sequence was assumed to be basically similar everywhere up to this point, although each region experienced its own unique local cultural trajectory. Different terms designate these local developments,

beginning with the Formative period. In the eastern United States, the developed
Formative is designated the Woodland cultural period, which was succeeded by
the Mississippian. In the American Southwest, the Formative was followed by
cultural developments designated Anasazi, Hohokam, and Mogollon, whose
manifestations vary from one locality to another. In Mesoamerica, the Formative
(here sometimes called the Preclassic) was followed by a Classic period of
florescent civilization, and a succeeding Postclassic period, a time of population
dislocation, warfare, and sweeping cultural change. This basic sequence, with
local variants, has been applied to all of Mesoamerica. Similar sequences with
locally variant terminology exist for South America and the Arctic area (Willey
and Phillips 1958; Fiedel 1987).

In the latter part of the classificatory-historical era in New World archaeology,
some landmark regional field projects were undertaken. The earliest of these,
and perhaps the most influential on later research, was the Tehuacán Valley
project, begun in the 1950s under the direction of Richard MacNeish. This was
an early example of the kind of problem-oriented research on a broad scale that
was to become characteristic of the ensuing "explanatory period." In the Tehuacán Valley of Puebla, Mexico, MacNeish set out to discover and document
the beginnings of maize agriculture in Mesoamerica, in a multidisciplinary field
effort that would continue for many years and yield a wealth of ecological, as
well as archaeological, data (Byers and MacNeish 1967–1976). This was also
a period when the self-examination and change that were to occur in archaeology
during the 1960s were anticipated in the writings of such critics as Walter Taylor,
who pointed out the need for revision in archaeology's goals and field methods
(Taylor 1948).

The early 1960s ushered in the "explanatory period" in New World archaeology (Willey and Sabloff 1980), with the appearance of the so-called "NEW"
ARCHAEOLOGY with its innovative research designs and methods, and an increased emphasis on cultural processes of the past, which has continued into the
present (Binford 1962, 1964; see also "NEW" ARCHAEOLOGY; ARCHAEOLOGY;
ANTHROPOLOGICAL ARCHAEOLOGY).

Currently, the methodological aims of the "NEW" ARCHAEOLOGY have become
incorporated into the mainstream of research, although no body of archaeological
theory has developed, as had been hoped. American archaeology is now in a
stage of "normal science" (Kuhn 1962), and new attempts at theory-building
will most likely await the next period of revolutionary change and upheaval.

Several major long-standing research problems continue to preoccupy New
World archaeologists in the last decade of the twentieth century. A primary area
of concern and continuing controversy is determination of the time when humans
first entered the western hemisphere. This question is a multifaceted one. The
number of migratory episodes that occurred, the routes followed, and the behavioral processes and motivations that resulted in the initial population of the
Americas are some of its different aspects, all problems that continue to engage
the attention of many New World archaeologists, as well as physical anthro-

pologists and linguists (Fladmark 1979; Greenberg, Turner, and Zegura 1986; see also MIGRATION). Another is the chief mode of SUBSISTENCE pursued by the earliest Americans (Martin and Wright 1967; Dincauze 1984). Still another problem is that early archaeological sites which can be reliably dated have frequently produced chronometric dates that most researchers believe are too late to represent an initial migratory episode, which most conservative estimators would now place at approximately 20,000 years ago (Meltzer 1989). Chronometric dates obtained using various methods from the physical sciences have been a further subject of controversy, and virtually all of these suggesting settlement prior to approximately 12,000–13,000 years ago have been rejected and revised to more recent estimates (Adovasio et al. 1980; Guidon and Delibrias 1986; see also CHRONOMETRIC DATING). Some related questions concern the possible existence of an ''ice-free corridor'' during periods of glacial advance that would have made migration by land a possibility, and the problematic nature of ARTIFACTS from several controversial early sites (Dillehay 1986; Guidon 1986, 1991; Guidon and Delibrias 1986; Dillehay and Collins 1988).

The question of pre-Columbian transoceanic contacts between Old World populations and native American groups has long been a topic of considerable archaeological controversy (see DIFFUSION). Once a matter of burning concern to diffusionists, this has become a subject of diminished archaeological attention in recent years, since the decline in popularity of DIFFUSION as an explanatory process. Most would now agree that such contacts very likely occurred many times in the past, but were probably isolated incidents involving small numbers of individuals, and had only minimal impact on the native cultures of the New World.

Another problem area of continuing importance in New World archaeology is estimating the sizes and characteristics of precontact populations. Since a large proportion—perhaps as much as 95 percent—of the indigenous New World population died of European diseases in the contact period, little is known of original population sizes and characteristics. Some studies have documented population declines in North America before actual contact with Europeans occurred, a possible result of the indirect spread of pathogens from the areas of initial contact, such as the West Indies and Yucatán, via human vectors, a consequence of trading relationships between South America, Mesoamerica, North America, and the Caribbean in pre-Columbian times (Dobyns 1983; Ramenofsky 1987; Campbell 1989).

Another unexplained phenomenon documented in the ARCHAEOLOGICAL RECORD of North America, as in that of other parts of the world, is the extraordinary disappearance of the large animals present during the Pleistocene. Species such as the woolly mammoth, mastodon, giant bison, saber-toothed tiger, and giant sloth, to mention only a few, disappeared entirely worldwide in a relatively short time. This unprecedented episode of mass extinction has been attributed to overhunting by human populations (Martin and Wright 1967; Martin 1973, 1982), although there is little evidence that humans were present in sufficient numbers anywhere in the world during the Pleistocene to have an impact of this scale. The primary competing hypothesis attributes these extinctions to the radical environmental and climatic changes that occurred when the ice sheets receded. However, the causal agents and processes involved in these extinctions have not yet been satisfactorily explained.

These are only a few examples of some areas requiring future attention in New World archaeology; a variety of other problems also remain uninvestigated or underinvestigated. Future research will doubtless generate still further questions, and there is little likelihood that archaeologists will ever exhaust the opportunities for further productive work in the Americas.

REFERENCES

Acosta, José de. 1604. The naturall and morall historie of the East and West Indies, E.G., trans. V. Sims for E. Blount and W. Aspley, London.

Adovasio, J. M., J. D. Gunn, J. Donahue, R. Stuckenrath, J. E. Guilday, and K. Volman. 1980. Yes, Virginia, it really is that old: a reply to Haynes and Mead. American Antiquity 45:588–595.

Beals, Ralph L. 1957. Father Acosta on the first peopling of the New World. American Antiquity 23:182–183.

Bernal, Ignacio. 1980. A history of Mexican archaeology. Thames and Hudson, London.

Binford, Lewis R. 1962. Archaeology as anthropology. American Antiquity 28(2):217–225.

———. 1964. A consideration of archaeological research design. American Antiquity 29:425–441.

Bryan, A. L., ed. 1986. New evidence for the Pleistocene peopling of the Americas. Center for the Study of Early Man, University of Maine, Orono.

Byers, D. S., and Richard S. MacNeish, eds. 1967–1976. The prehistory of the Tehuacán Valley. 5 vols. University of Texas Press, Austin.

Campbell, Sarah K. 1989. Post-Columbian culture history in the northern Columbia Plateau. Ph.D. dissertation, Department of Anthropology, University of Washington, Seattle.

Carter, George F. 1978. The American Paleolithic. In Early man in America from a circum-Pacific perspective, A. L. Bryan, ed. Archaeological Researches International, Edmonton, Alberta, pp. 10–19.

Diaz del Castillo, Bernal. 1908–1916. The true history of the conquest of New Spain ... from the only exact copy made of the original manuscript, Alfred Percival Maudslay, trans. 5 vols. Hakluyt Society, 2nd series. London, pp. 23–25, 30, 40.

Dillehay, Tom D. 1986. The cultural relationships of Monte Verde: a late Pleistocene settlement site in the subantarctic forest of south-central Chile. In New evidence for the Pleistocene peopling of the Americas, A. L. Bryan, ed. Center for the Study of Early Man, University of Maine, Orono, pp. 319–338.

Dillehay, T. D., and M. B. Collins. 1988. Early cultural evidence from Monte Verde in Chile. Nature 332:150–152.

Dincauze, Dena. 1984. An archaeo-logical evaluation of the case for pre-Clovis occupations. Advances in World Archaeology 3:275–323.

Dobyns, H. 1983. Their number become thinned. University of Tennessee Press, Knoxville.

Fiedel, Stuart J. 1987. Prehistory of the Americas. Cambridge University Press.

Fladmark, Knud R. 1979. Routes: alternate migration corridors for early man in North America. American Antiquity 44:55–69.

———. 1983. Times and places: environmental correlates of mid-to-late Wisconsinan human population expansion in North America. In Early man in the New World, Richard Shutler, Jr., ed. Sage, Beverly Hills, Calif., pp. 13–41.

Ford, James A. 1938. A chronological method applicable to the Southeast. American Antiquity 3(3):260–264.

———. 1962. A quantitative method for deriving cultural chronology. Pan American Union Technical Manual No. 1. Washington, D.C.

Gamio, Manuel. 1913. Arqueología de Atzcapotzalco, D.F., Mexico. Proceedings, Eighteenth International Congress of Americanists, London, pp. 180–187.

Greenberg, Joseph H., Christy G. Turner II, and Stephen L. Zegura. 1986. The settlement of the Americas: a comparison of the linguistic, dental and genetic evidence. Current Anthropology 27(5):477–497.

Guidon, Niede. 1986. Las unidades culturales de São Raimundo Nonato, sudeste del estado de Piauí, Brazil. In New evidence for the Pleistocene peopling of the Americas, A. L. Bryan, ed. Center for the Study of Early Man, University of Maine, Orono, pp. 157–172.

Guidon, N., and B. Arnaud. 1991. The chronology of the New World: two faces of one reality. World Archaeology 23(2):167–178.

Guidon, Niede, and G. Delibrias. 1986. Carbon-14 dates point to man in the Americas 32,000 years ago. Nature 321:769–771.

Jefferson, Thomas. 1787. Notes on the state of Virginia. John Stockdale, London. (Reprinted by University of North Carolina Press, Chapel Hill, 1954)

Kidder, Alfred V. 1924. An introduction to the study of southwestern archaeology, with a preliminary account of the excavations at Pecos. Papers of the Southwestern Expedition, Phillips Academy No. 1. Yale University Press, New Haven.

———. 1931. The pottery of Pecos, vol. 1. Papers of the Southwestern Expedition, Phillips Academy. Yale University Press, New Haven.

———. 1936. Speculations on New World prehistory. In Essays in anthropology. University of California Press, Berkeley, pp. 143–152.

Kuhn, Thomas S. 1962. The structure of scientific revolutions. University of Chicago Press.

Landa, Diego de. 1941. Landa's Relación de las cosas de Yucatán; a translation [of a work originally published in 1566], edited with notes by Alfred M. Tozzer. Papers of the Peabody Museum of Archaeology and Ethnology 18. Harvard University, Cambridge, Mass.

Lorant, Stefan, ed. 1965. The New World: the first pictures of America made by John White and Jacques LeMoyne and engraved by Theodore DeBry, with contemporary narratives of the French settlements in Florida 1562–1565 and the English colonies in Virginia 1585–1590. Rev. ed. Duell, Sloan and Pearce, New York.

Maler, Teobert. 1901–1903. Researches in the central portion of the Usumatsintla Valley. Memoirs of the Peabody Museum 2, nos. 1, 2. Cambridge, Mass.

Martin, Paul S. 1973. The discovery of America. Science 179:969–974.

———. 1982 The pattern and meaning of holarctic mammoth extinction. In Paleoecology of Beringia, David M. Hopkins, John V. Matthews, Jr., Charles E. Schweger, and Steven B. Young, eds. Academic Press, New York, pp. 399–408.

Martin, Paul S., and H. E. Wright, eds. 1967. Pleistocene extinctions. Yale University Press, New Haven.

Maudslay, Alfred P. 1889–1902. Archaeology. Biologia Centrali Americana. 4 vols. Porter and Dulau, London.

McKern, W. C. 1939. The Midwestern Taxonomic Method as an aid to archaeological study. American Antiquity 4:301–313.

Meltzer, David J. 1989. Why don't we know when the first people came to North America? American Antiquity 54(3):471–490.

Mignon, Molly R. 1987. The questionnaire of Felipe II: an English translation. Appendix to Maya animal protein procurement and utilization: an assessment of the ethnohistoric evidence. Ph.D. dissertation, Department of Archaeology, Simon Fraser University, Burnaby, B.C., Canada, pp. 301–309.

Nelson, Nels. 1916. Chronology of the Tano ruins, New Mexico. American Anthropologist 18(2):159–180.

Oviedo y Valdez, Gonzalo Fernández de. 1950. Natural history of the West Indies, translated and edited by Sterling A. Stoudemire. University of North Carolina Studies in the Romance Languages and Literature No. 32. Chapel Hill.

Ramenofsky, Ann. 1987. Vectors of death: the archaeology of European contact. University of New Mexico Press, Albuquerque.

Relaciones Geográficas. 1898. Colección de documentos inéditos relativos al descubrimiento, conquista y organización de las antiguas posesiones españolas de ultramar, segunda serie. . . . Madrid. (Originally published 1578–1584)

Sahagún, Bernardino de. 1950–1970. Florentine codex: General history of the things of New Spain. English translation by Charles E. Dibble and Arthur J. O. Anderson. 12 vols. The School of American Research/University of Utah, Provo.

Shutler, Richard Jr., ed. 1983. Early man in the New World. Sage, Beverly Hills, Calif.

Silverberg, Robert. 1968. Mound Builders of ancient America: the archaeology of a myth. New York Graphic Society, Greenwich, Conn.

Smith, John. 1624. The generall historie of Virginia, New-England and the Summer Isles, with the names of the adventurers, planters and governours from their first beginning, Ano 1584, to this present 1624. . . . Also the maps and descriptions of all those countryes, their commodities, people, government, customes, and religion yet knowne. . . . Michael Sparkes, London.

Squier, Ephraim G., and E. H. Davis. 1848. Ancient monuments of the Mississippi Valley. Smithsonian Contributions to Knowledge 1. Washington, D.C.

Stephens, John Lloyd. 1963. Incidents of travel in Yucatan, with illustrations by Frederick Catherwood. 2 vols. Dover, New York. (Originally published in 1843).

———. 1969. Incidents of travel in Central America, Chiapas, and Yucatan. 2 vols. Dover Books, New York. (Reprint of a work originally published in 1841)

Steward, Julian H. 1942. The direct historical approach to archaeology. American Antiquity 7:337–344.

Taylor, Walter W. 1964. A study of archaeology. Southern Illinois University Press, Carbondale. (Originally printed as No. 69 of the Memoirs of the American Anthropological Association in 1948)

Thomas, Cyrus. 1894. Report of the mound explorations of the Bureau of Ethnology.

Smithsonian Institution, Bureau of Ethnology, Twelfth Annual Report. Washington, D.C.

Uhle, Max. 1903. Pachacamac. University of Pennsylvania Press, Philadelphia.

———. 1907. The Emeryville shellmound. University of California Publications in American Archaeology and Ethnology 7, no. 1. Berkeley.

Vazquez de Espinosa, Antonio. 1968. Description of the Indies (c. 1620) . . . translated by Charles Upson Clark. Smithsonian Institution Press, Washington, D.C.

Wauchope, Robert. 1962. Lost tribes and sunken continents: myth and method in the study of American Indians. The University of Chicago Press.

Willey, Gordon R., and Philip Phillips. 1958. Method and theory in American archaeology. University of Chicago Press.

Willey, Gordon R., and Jeremy A. Sabloff. 1980. A history of American archaeology. 2nd ed. W. H. Freeman, San Francisco.

SOURCES OF ADDITIONAL INFORMATION

For a general historical overview of New World prehistory and archaeology, see Stuart J. Fiedel, *Prehistory of the Americas* (Cambridge, Cambridge University Press, 1987). An introductory summary of what is known of the prehistoric period in North America, plus a brief description of the development of American archaeology, may be found in "North American prehistory," by Molly R. Mignon, in *Native North Americans, an Ethnohistoric Approach*, Daniel L. Boxberger, ed. (Dubuque, Iowa, Kendall/Hunt, 1990), pp. 1–21. For a comprehensive, detailed account of the development of archaeology in the Americas, particularly in North America, see Gordon R. Willey and Jeremy A. Sabloff, *A History of American Archaeology* (2nd ed., 1980; see References for complete citation. A 3rd ed. is in preparation). Brian M. Fagan, *Ancient North America: The Archaeology of a Continent* (New York, Thames and Hudson, 1991), is an up-to-date popular treatment of the same subject.

Discussions of individual topics in American archaeology and some major contributions to theory and method during the period between 1935 and 1985 are included in the fiftieth anniversary issue of *American Antiquity* (vol. 50, no. 2, April 1985), and in the SAA anniversary volume, *American Archaeology Past and Future*, edited by David J. Meltzer, Don D. Fowler, and Jeremy A. Sabloff (see References for complete citation). The papers in *Archaeological Thought in America*, edited by C. C. Lamberg-Karlovsky (Cambridge, Cambridge University Press, 1989), present some excellent discussions of a variety of specific topics in the intellectual and methodological history of American archaeology.

Information on the archaeology of some of the Latin American countries is in Ignacio Bernal, *A History of Mexican Archaeology* (London, Thames and Hudson, 1980); and Richard W. Keatinge, ed., *Peruvian Prehistory* (Cambridge, Cambridge University Press, 1988); and the papers by Guidon (1986, 1991), Guidon and Delibrias (1986), Dillehay (1986) and Dillehay and Collins (1988; see References for all citations).

A review article with extensive bibliography on the "early man" problem is W. N. Irving's "Context and chronology of early man in the Americas," *Annual Review of Anthropology* 14(1985):529–555. R. E. Taylor and Clement W. Meighan, in their book *Chronologies in New World Archaeology* (New York, Academic Press, 1978), include "hemispheric projections" correlating New World regional chronologies on the endpapers. (See also RELATIVE DATING.)

The bibliographies in the background sources listed above provide access to much of the literature published through the late 1980s. To update these with more recent material, the forthcoming 3rd ed. of Gordon R. Willey and Jeremy A. Sabloff, *A History of American Archaeology*, should be consulted when it becomes available, as well as future issues of such research journals as *American Antiquity*, *Latin American Antiquity*, and *Ancient Mesoamerica*. Forthcoming annual volumes of *Archaeological Method and Theory* and *Annual Review of Anthropology* should be consulted for future review articles on New World archaeology and prehistory.

O

OLD WORLD ARCHAEOLOGY. The body of data acquired from speculation, field research, theoretical efforts, and chronological studies concerning the prehistoric peoples and lifeways of Africa, Asia, Europe, and the Near and Middle East; or the research efforts that have resulted in this body of data.

Old World archaeology encompasses biblical archaeology and the archaeology of the classical civilizations of Egypt, India, the Near East, and the early civilizations of the Mediterranean area, as well as the prehistoric period of Europe and Asia (Cook 1931; Bietak 1979; Davis et al. 1980; Roe 1981; Dyson 1982; Ammerman and Cavalli-Sforza 1984; Kohl 1984; Schild 1984; Adler 1985; Gamble 1986; Geddes 1986; Bernal 1987; Castleder 1987; Shennan 1987; Simek 1987; Stoneman 1987; Gibson and Geselowitz 1988; Dyson 1989; Higham 1989; Keeley and Cahan 1989; Maricenko and Vinogradov 1989; Soffer 1989). Traditionally, Old World studies have not included paleoanthropological research recently conducted in African countries to document the EVOLUTION of the human species and its hominid predecessors, although European prehistoric archaeology, particularly as it relates to current thinking about the transition to *Homo sapiens sapiens*, is an important part of Old World archaeology (Jelinek 1982a; Binford 1985; Mellars 1989; Dibble and Mellars 1990; Rolland and Dibble 1990; see also ARCHAEOLOGY; PALEOANTHROPOLOGY; PREHISTORY).

The origins of Old World archaeology coincide with the birth of the discipline itself in early-nineteenth-century Europe (see ANTIQUARIANISM). The humanistic and historical orientation of the antiquarian collectors of Europe who were the first archaeologists has persisted in European archaeology up to the present time. This is especially evident in the work of classical archaeologists, whose interest in the ancient civilizations of the Near East and Mediterranean regions was long heavily weighted toward the interpretation of inscriptions and works of art produced by these cultures (Cook 1931; Woolley 1950; Lloyd 1981; Bernal 1987; Stoneman 1987). This bias also exists to a certain extent among many specialists in biblical archaeological studies (Kenyon 1979; Van Seters 1983; Adler 1985) and in what was formerly called Egyptology, although studies of ancient Egyptian civilization have traditionally encompassed a wide range of archaeological interests and specialties (Petrie 1959; Butzer 1976; Bietak 1979; Reid 1985; Wenke 1986, 1989; Kemp 1989).

The standard chronology for Old World archaeology originated in Europe in the late nineteenth century, rooted in the early excavations of Jacques Boucher de Perthes at Abbeville and the THREE-AGE SYSTEM developed several decades earlier by Christian Thomsen and Jens Worsaae in Denmark (Thomsen 1836; Boucher de Perthes 1860, 1861). The Paleolithic and Neolithic periods were initially named and defined by Sir John Lubbock in his first book, *Pre-historic Times, as Illustrated by Ancient Remains and the Manners and Customs of Modern Savages* (1865). Lubbock proposed the term "Paleolithic" for the time "when man shared the possession of Europe with the Mammoth, the Cave Bear, the Woolly-haired Rhinoceros, and other extinct animals," and "Neolithic" for the age of polished stone implements (Lubbock 1865, quoted in Daniel 1967:109). The Neolithic was subsequently divided into four subdivisions by the Swedish archaeologist Oscar Montelius, who also worked out a series of subdivisions for the Bronze Age (Montelius 1888). A. C. Carlyle, who conducted field excavations in the Vindhya Hills of India between 1868 and 1888, was the first to suggest the idea of a Mesolithic period, characterized by ASSEMBLAGES of geometric microliths (Binford 1968:314). These have been interpreted as having been made for mounting in scythes, with many small sharp-edged flake tools assembled into complex tools for cutting grains. The Mesolithic has been viewed as a transitional period when vegetable foods were becoming a larger and more significant component of diets, and the harvesting of wild grains and initial cultivation of some plant species acquired greater economic importance (Bar-Yosef 1980; Cauvin and Sanlaville 1981; Jelinek 1982b; Price 1983).

In the succeeding Neolithic period, populations would turn increasingly to cultivation as the principal SUBSISTENCE activity, and the previous nomadic residence pattern of hunter-gatherers would be replaced by settlement in permanent communities. These developments were thought to have originated in the Near East, and later spread into western Europe by way of the Mediterranean area, a route of DIFFUSION subsequently followed by later innovations such as metallurgy and the technology of the Bronze and Iron ages. This was the model proposed by V. Gordon Childe (Childe 1925, 1929, 1934) and supported (at least in its initial assumptions concerning agriculture) by significant field projects documenting the origins of agriculture in the Middle East (Braidwood and Cambel 1980; Braidwood 1982; Braidwood and Braidwood 1983). However, as a result of the recalibration of an original series of radiocarbon dates for the appearance of important technological innovations in western Europe and the Near East,

Childe's model was refuted, resulting in sweeping revisions in interpretation of the early history of these two regions and the directionality of influence (Renfrew 1979).

The earliest archaeological investigations in Europe were, quite naturally, concerned with local cultural and skeletal evidence of early occupation by Paleolithic peoples. Interest in Paleolithic studies was later extended to Africa and Asia, as a result of important early discoveries of fossil hominid remains in China and southern Africa. In the latter case, this resulted in studies of human origins and early hominid ADAPTATIONS becoming the major focus of African archaeology (see also PALEOANTHROPOLOGY).

A cultural chronology for the Paleolithic, based on the "type SITE" concept and dividing the period into Lower (Abbevillian, Acheulean), Middle (Mousterian), and Upper (Perigordian-Aurignacian-Solutrean-Magdalenian), was initially devised by Old World archaeologists for western Europe, and correlated with the four principal glacial periods into which geologists had divided the European Pleistocene. This basic cultural/chronological scheme has been extended and adapted to other areas of the Old World, including Africa, where the earliest cultural remains of the Lower Paleolithic are termed Oldowan. Oldowan cultures, named for the type site of Olduvai Gorge, consist of a complex of early unifacially worked chopping tools that precedes the appearance of the Acheulean in a number of localities. The Acheulean (from the site of St. Acheul in France) is characterized by the appearance of a distinctive form of bifacially chipped hand ax, representing a more developed technology than the Oldowan. Cultural remains of the Middle Paleolithic are designated Mousterian, and are frequently associated with the physical remains of *Homo sapiens neanderthalensis*. This complex has been the subject of controversy between the late distinguished French archaeologist François Bordes and Lewis Binford, with Bordes maintaining that variation between Mousterian stone tool assemblages from different sites reflects ethnic differences in their manufacturers, while Binford attributes this variation to differences in site function (Binford and Binford 1966, 1969; Bordes and de Sonneville-Bordes 1970; Bordes 1978; Binford 1983).

The end of the Mousterian cultural period is often associated with the disappearance of Neanderthal man and the first appearance of modern *H. sapiens sapiens*, which some archaeologists now believe occurred at the Middle-to-Upper Neolithic transition (Jelinek 1982a, 1988; Binford 1985; Mellars 1989; Dibble and Mellars 1990; Rolland and Dibble 1990). The relatively sudden appearance of revolutionary innovations in the material record at this time, which included cave art, more sophisticated tools and hunting methods, religious practices, and definite evidence of human burial, is attributed to the appearance of modern humans, and the culture of the Neanderthals has accordingly been downgraded. It has even been suggested that Neanderthal man possessed neither articulate speech, nor religion, nor other manifestations of symbolic thought, and should therefore no longer be classified as belonging to the species *sapiens*, although the evidence on which these allegations have been based is far from clear-cut. This position acquired considerable popularity among Old World archaeologists during the 1980s.

The chronological/cultural sequence developed for the European Paleolithic became the prototype for Paleolithic chronologies outside of western Europe as well, including parts of Africa, Asia, and eastern Europe, although not all of the cultural "phases" of the European Paleolithic were found to occur elsewhere. The European sequence cannot be applied to the New World, where a separate evolution of the Paleolithic seems to have occurred.

Archaeological work in the Middle Eastern area of the Old World (Central Asia), a region formerly included within the territories of the Soviet Union, began in the very early years of the twentieth century with the excavations of the American archaeologist Raphael Pumpelly. Soviet archaeology in this area did not begin until the post-World War II period (Kohl 1985). Investigations of some spectacular Bronze Age sites with deep stratified deposits, such as Altyn Depe in Turkmenistan, have been an important focus of Soviet studies here (Kohl 1981; Masson 1981), although Paleolithic studies have not been neglected. Several major English-language area syntheses for this region were published during the 1970s and 1980s (Masson and Sarianidi 1972; Gupta 1979; Ranov and Davis 1979; Davis, Ranov, and Dodonov 1980; Kohl 1981, 1984, 1985; Dergachev 1989). Paleolithic research in the Soviet Union concentrated in the Siberian area, where remains of Pleistocene fauna such as the woolly mammoth have been preserved in areas of permafrost (Ranov and Davis 1979; Davis, Ranov, and Dodonov 1980; Okladnikov and Pospelova 1982; Davis 1983). With the dissolution of the Soviet Union, the future of archaeological research in these regions has become uncertain.

East Asian archaeology (continental China, Japan) developed entirely independently of the western hemisphere. Archaeology in China is much older than European archaeology, and although the exact time of its origin cannot be pinpointed, there is evidence of excavation of prehistoric remains as early as the Warring States period (ca. 450–221 B.C.) in Chinese history. As in Europe, the earliest archaeological activities in China were associated with ANTIQUARI-ANISM, which may be nearly as old as Chinese civilization itself. The Chinese equivalent of the three-age system of cultural periods when implements were made first of stone, then bronze, and finally iron, anticipated that developed by Thomsen for Europe by over a thousand years. Despite these early archaeological developments, however, the concept of a Paleolithic culture during the Pleistocene does not appear in China until the twentieth century; and the ideas and techniques of modern archaeology were not adopted until the 1930s (Chang 1986). In spite of its long tradition, Chinese archaeology remains unknown territory to most Western archaeologists, aside from the discoveries of "Peking man" at Chou-k'ou-tien in 1920, and subsequent finds of other *Homo erectus* specimens in the 1960s. Only a few Western scholars have worked in this area, and the resulting Western-language literature is small (e.g., Boule et al. 1928;

Black et al. 1933; Teilhard de Chardin 1941; Andersson 1943; Movius 1944, 1949, 1955; Maringer 1950; Rudolph 1963; Aigner 1981). With the publication of the English-language works of K. C. Chang, the history of Chinese archaeology has become easily accessible to Western archaeologists (Chang 1977, 1984, 1986).

In Japan, archaeological research has revealed the existence of Paleolithic sites with cultural remains that have been assigned ages in excess of seventy thousand years before the present, although these dates are controversial (Ikawa-Smith 1978; Ikawa-Smith (ed.) 1978; Serizawa 1978). Middle and Upper Paleolithic occupation of the Japanese islands has not been documented (Reynolds 1985).

The African continent, which has produced the earliest known remains of prehuman hominids, appears to have been the location where the human species originally evolved, stimulating interest in Paleolithic and protohuman studies. African archaeology began with Raymond Dart's discovery of the Taung (South Africa) skull in 1924. This juvenile cranium was the first fossil remnant of an australopithecine hominid. Subsequent discoveries of australopithecine remains were made in the Transvaal, prior to the discovery of an East African form at Olduvai Gorge (Tanzania) in the late 1950s. More recent specimens have been found in Kenya north and east of Lake Turkana, and in southern and central Ethiopia. All date to the period prior to 1 million years ago, and the earliest examples may be of Pliocene date (Wolpoff 1980:131–133). The Paleolithic period has been the principal focus of African archaeology, aside from the development of Egyptian civilization in North Africa (McIntosh and McIntosh 1983; Lubell, Sheppard, and Jackes 1984; Parkington 1984). (For further discussion of the African Paleolithic, see PALEOANTHROPOLOGY).

The Paleolithic period is still an area of intensive study and current controversy in Old World studies (Schild 1984; Straus and Clark 1986; Simek 1987; Gowlett 1988; Soffer 1989). Some differing approaches were noted by François Bordes in his foreword to *The Old Stone Age*:

> There are a variety of schools in the field of prehistory. In France, the emphasis is . . . on stratigraphy and typology; in the English-speaking countries, on the relationship between man and his environment; in the USSR, on palaeosociology. . . . There are historical reasons for this. . . . In France, the first study of prehistory was the work of naturalists. The Americans, . . . with primitive peoples still living among them, were able to study their relationship with the environment. The Soviet interest in palaeosociology comes partly from their Marxist outlook. (Bordes 1968:7–8)

Although European archaeologists have traditionally been less explicitly interested in theoretical issues than Americans, a shift toward a more anthropologically oriented approach and an interest in prehistoric behavioral processes has been noted since the 1970s, and the influence of such British archaeologists as Ian Hodder and Colin Renfrew has led to a current interest in past symbolic behavior (Bogucki 1985; see also COGNITIVE ARCHAEOLOGY). This interest began with the work of André Leroi-Gourhan (1965), Alexander Marshack (1972), and

Margaret Conkey (1978, 1980, 1982) on European Palaeolithic art and symbolism, and is becoming an area of increasing interest both to structuralist-
oriented European archaeologists and to their materialist counterparts in North
America (see ARCHAEOLOGY; "NEW" ARCHAEOLOGY; NEW WORLD
ARCHAEOLOGY).

REFERENCES

Adler, Rudolph J. 1985. Biblical beginnings: archaeology and the roots of scripture.
    Prentice-Hall, Englewood Cliffs, N.J.
Aigner, Jean S. 1981. Archaeological remains in Pleistocene China. Deutsches Archaeo-
    logisches Institut, Kommission für Allgemeine und Vergleichende Archaeologie,
    Bonn.
Ammerman, A. J., and L. L. Cavalli-Sforza. 1984. The Neolithic transition and the
    genetics of populations in Europe. Princeton University Press, Princeton, N.J.
Andersson, J. G. 1943. Researches into the prehistory of the Chinese. Bulletin of the
    Museum of Far Eastern Antiquities, 15, Stockholm.
Bar-Yosef, O. 1980. Prehistory of the Levant. Annual Review of Anthropology 9:101–
    161.
Bernal, M. 1987. Black Athena: the Afroasiatic roots of classical civilization. Vol. 1:
    The fabrication of ancient Greece, 1785–1985. Free Association Books, London.
Bietak, M. 1979. The present state of Egyptian archaeology. Journal of Egyptian Ar-
    chaeology 65:156–160.
Binford, Lewis R. 1968. Post-Pleistocene adaptations. In New perspectives in archae-
    ology, S. R. Binford and L. R. Binford, eds. Aldine, Chicago, pp. 313–341.
———. 1983. The challenge of the Mousterian. In In pursuit of the past. Thames and
    Hudson, New York, pp. 79–94.
———. 1985. Human ancestors: changing views of their behavior. Journal of Anthro-
    pological Archaeology 4(4):292–327.
Binford, Lewis R., and Sally R. Binford. 1966. A preliminary analysis of functional
    variability in the Mousterian of Levallois facies. American Anthropologist 68:238–
    295.
———. 1969. Stone tools and human behavior. Scientific American 220:70–84.
Black, Davidson, P. Teilhard de Chardin, C. C. Young, and W. C. Pei. 1933. Fossil
    man in China. Geological Survey of China, Memoirs, ser. A. Peiping, p. 11.
Bogucki, Peter. 1985. Theoretical directions in European archaeology [Annual review
    of Old World archaeology 1]. American Antiquity 50(4):780–788.
Bordes, François. 1968. The Old Stone Age, J. E. Anderson, trans. McGraw-Hill, New
    York.
———. 1978. Typological variability in the Mousterian layers at Pech de l'Aze I, II,
    and IV. Journal of Anthropological Research 34:181–193.
Bordes, François, and Denise de Sonneville-Bordes. 1970. The significance of variability
    in Palaeolithic assemblages. World Archaeology 2(1):61–73.
Boucher de Perthes, J. 1860. De l'homme antédiluvien et de ses oeuvres. Jung-Treuttel,
    Paris.
———. 1861. Sur les silex taillés trouvés dans le diluvium de département de la Somme;
    remarques de M. Boucher de Perthes à l'occasion d'une communication récente

sur les pierres travaillées par les habitants primitifs des Gaules. Comptes Rendus Hebdomadaires de l'Académie des Sciences 52:300–302.

Boule, M., H. Breuil, E. Licent, and P. Teilhard de Chardin. 1928. Le paléolithique de la Chine. Archives de l'Institut de Paléontologie Humaine, Mémoire No. 4. Paris.

Braidwood, L. S., ed. 1982. Prehistoric village archaeology in south-eastern Turkey. British Archaeological Reports, International Series, No. 138. Oxford.

Braidwood, Robert J., and L. S. Braidwood, eds. 1983. Prehistoric archaeology along the Zagros flanks. Oriental Institute Publications no. 105. Chicago.

Braidwood, Robert J., and H. Cambel. 1980. Prehistoric research in southeastern Anatolia. Eddebiyat Facultesi Basimevi, Istanbul.

Butzer, Karl W. 1976. Early hydraulic civilization in Egypt. University of Chicago Press.

Castleder, Rodney. 1987. The Stonehenge people: an exploration of life in Neolithic Britain 4700–2000 BC. Routledge and Kegan Paul, London.

Cauvin, J., and P. Sanlaville. 1981. Prehistoire du Levant. Centre National de la Recherche Scientifique, Paris.

Chang, Kwang-chih. 1977. Chinese archaeology since 1949. Journal of Asian Studies 36:623–646.

———. 1984. China. In Annual review of Old World archaeology, part II: current research in Europe, the Near and Middle East, and China," Peter S. Wells, coordinator. American Antiquity 49(4):754–756.

———. 1986. The archaeology of Ancient China. Fourth edition. Yale University Press, New Haven.

Childe, Vere Gordon. 1925. The dawn of European civilization. K. Paul, Trench, Trubner, London.

———. 1929. The Danube in prehistory. Clarendon, Oxford.

———. 1934. New light on the most ancient East: the oriental prelude to European prehistory. Appleton-Century, New York.

Conkey, Margaret W. 1978. Style and information in cultural evolution: towards a predictive model for the Paleolithic. In Social archaeology: beyond subsistence and dating, Charles L. Redman et al., eds. Academic Press, New York, pp. 61–85.

———. 1980. Context, structure and efficacy in Paleolithic art and design. In Symbol as sense, M. L. Foster and S. H. Brandes, eds. Academic Press, New York, pp. 225–248.

———. 1982. Boundedness in art and society. In Symbolic and structural archaeology, Ian Hodder, ed. Cambridge University Press, pp. 115–128.

Cook, Arthur Bernard. 1931. The rise and progress of classical archaeology. Cambridge University Press.

Daniel, Glyn. 1967. The origins and growth of archaeology. Crowell, New York.

———. 1976. A hundred and fifty years of archaeology. Harvard University Press, Cambridge, Mass.

Davis, Richard S. 1983. Theoretical issues in contemporary Soviet Paleolithic archaeology. Annual Review of Anthropology 12:403–428. (98 references)

Davis, Richard S., V. A. Ranov, and A. E. Dodonov. 1980. Early man in Soviet Central Asia. Scientific American (December):130–137.

Dergachev, V. 1989. Neolithic and Bronze Age cultural communities of the steppe zone of the USSR. Antiquity 63(241):793–802.

Dibble, Harold, and P. Mellars, eds. 1990. New perspectives on human adaptation and behavior in the Middle Paleolithic. University of Pennsylvania Press, Philadelphia.

Dyson, Stephen L. 1982. Archaeological survey in the Mediterranean Basin: a review of recent research. [Annual review of Old World archaeology] American Antiquity 47(1):87–98.

———. 1989. The role of ideology and institutions in shaping classical archaeology in the nineteenth and twentieth centuries. In Tracing archaeology's past, Andrew L. Christenson, ed. Southern Illinois University Press, Carbondale and Edwardsville, pp. 127–135.

Gamble, Clive. 1986. The Paleolithic settlement of Europe. Cambridge University Press, New York.

Geddes, David S. 1986. Neolithic, Chalcolithic and Early Bronze in west Mediterranean Europe. [Annual review of Old World archaeology] American Antiquity 51(4):763–778.

Gibson, D. Blair, and Michael N. Geselowitz, eds. 1988. Tribe and polity in late prehistoric Europe: demography, production and exchange in the evolution of complex social systems. Plenum Press, New York.

Gowlett, J. A. J. 1988. Introduction to "New Directions in Paleolithic Archaeology" issue. World Archaeology 19(3):59–61.

Gupta, S. P. 1979. Archaeology of Soviet Central Asia and the Iranian borderlands. 2 vols. B. R. Publishing, Delhi.

Higham, Charles. 1989. The archaeology of mainland Southeast Asia from 10,000 B.C. to the fall of Angkor. Cambridge University Press.

Ikawa-Smith, Fumiko. 1978. History of early Palaeolithic research in Japan. In Early Palaeolithic in South and East Asia, F. Ikawa-Smith, ed. Mouton, The Hague.

———. 1982. Co-traditions in Japanese archaeology. World Archaeology 13:296–309.

———, ed. 1978. Early Palaeolithic in South and East Asia. Mouton, The Hague.

Jelinek, A. 1982a. The Middle Paleolithic in the southern Levant, with comments on the appearance of Homo sapiens. In The transition from the Lower to Middle Paleolithic and the origin of modern man, A. Ronen, ed. BAR International Series 151. British Archaeological Reports, Oxford, pp. 57–101.

———. 1982b. The Tabun cave and Paleolithic man in the Levant. Science 216:1369–1375.

———. 1988. Technology, typology, and culture in the Middle Paleolithic. In Upper Pleistocene prehistory of western Eurasia, H. L. Dibble and A. Montet-White, eds. The University Museum, University of Pennsylvania, Philadelphia, pp. 199–212.

Keeley, Lawrence H., and Daniel Cahan. 1989. Early Neolithic forts and villages in northeast Belgium: a preliminary report. Journal of Field Archaeology 16(2):157–176.

Kemp, Barry J. 1989. Ancient Egypt: anatomy of a civilization. Routledge, London.

Kenyon, Kathleen M. 1979. Archaeology of the Holy Land. 4th ed. Norton, New York.

Kohl, Philip L. 1984. Central Asia: Palaeolithic beginnings to the Iron Age (L'Asie centrale dès origines à l'Age du Fer). Editions Recherche sur les Civilisations, "synthèse" 14, Paris.

———. 1985. Recent research in Central Asia [Annual review of Old World archaeology] American Antiquity 50(4):789–795.

———, ed. 1981. The Bronze Age civilization of Central Asia: recent Soviet discoveries. M. E. Sharpe, Armonk, N.Y.

Leroi-Gourhan, André. 1965. Treasures of prehistoric art. Abrams, New York.

Lloyd, Seton H. 1981. Foundations in the dust: a story of Mesopotamian exploration. 2nd ed. Thames and Hudson, London.

Lubell, David, Peter Sheppard, and Mary Jackes. 1984. Continuity in the Epipaleolithic of northern Africa with emphasis on the Maghreb. Advances in World Archaeology 3:143–191.

Lubbock, John. 1865. Pre-historic times, as illustrated by ancient remains and the manners and customs of modern savages. Williams and Norgate, London.

Maricenko, K., and Yuri Vinogradov. 1989. The Scythian period in the northern Black Sea region (750–250 B.C.). Antiquity 63(241):803–813.

Maringer, John. 1950. Contribution to the prehistory of Mongolia. Statens Etnografiska Museum, Stockholm.

Marshack, Alexander. 1972. The roots of civilization. McGraw-Hill, New York.

Masson, V. M. 1981. Altyn-depe. Trudi Iu. T.A.K.E. 18.

Masson, V. M., and V. I. Sarianidi. 1972. Central Asia: Turkmenia before the Achaemenids. Thames and Hudson, London.

McIntosh, S. K., and R. J. McIntosh. 1983. Current directions in West African prehistory. Annual Review of Anthropology 12:215–258.

Mellars, P. 1989. Major issues in the emergence of modern humans. Current Anthropology 30:349–385.

Montelius, Oscar. 1888. The civilization of Sweden in heathen times. London.

Movius, Hallam L., Jr. 1944. Early man and Pleistocene stratigraphy in southern and eastern Asia. Papers of the Peabody Museum 19. Harvard University, Cambridge, Mass.

———. 1949. The Lower Palaeolithic cultures of southern and eastern Asia. Transactions of the American Philosophical Society, n.s. 38, pt. 4, pp. 329–420.

———. 1955. Palaeolithic archaeology in southern and eastern Asia, exclusive of India. Cahiers d'Histoire Mondiale 2:257–282, 520–553.

Okladnikov, A. P., and G. A. Pospelova. 1982. Ulalinka, the oldest palaeolithic site in Siberia. Current Anthropology 23:710–712.

Parkington, John. 1984. Changing views of the Later Stone Age of South Africa. Advances in World Archaeology 3:89–142.

Petrie, W. M. Flinders. 1959. The making of Egypt. Sheldon, London.

Price, T. Douglas. 1983. The European Mesolithic [Annual review of Old World archaeology] American Antiquity 48(4):761–778.

Ranov, V. A., and R. S. Davis. 1979. Toward a new outline of the Soviet Central Asian Palaeolithic. Current Anthropology 20(2):249–270.

Reid, D. 1985. Indigenous Egyptology: the decolonization of a profession. Journal of the American Oriental Society 105:233–246.

Renfrew, Colin. 1979. Before civilization: the radiocarbon revolution and prehistoric Europe. Cambridge University Press.

Reynolds, T. E. G. 1985. The Early Paleolithic of Japan. Antiquity 59:93–96.

Roe, Derek A. 1981. The Lower and Middle Paleolithic periods in Britain. Routledge and Kegan Paul, London.

Rolland, Nicolas, and Harold L. Dibble. 1990. A new synthesis of Middle Paleolithic variability. American Antiquity 55(3):480–499.

Rudolph, Richard C. 1963. Preliminary notes on Sung archaeology. Journal of the American Oriental Society 22:169–177.

Schild, Romuald. 1984. Terminal Paleolithic of the north European plain: a review of lost chances, potential, and hopes. Advances in World Archaeology 3:193–274.

Serizawa, C. 1978. The Stone Age of Japan. Asian Perspectives 19:1–14.

Shennan, S. J. 1987. Trends in the study of later European prehistory. Annual Review of Anthropology 16:365–382.

Simek, Jan F. 1987. Spatial order and behavioural change in the French Paleolithic. Antiquity 61(1):25–40.

Soffer, Olga. 1989. Storage, sedentism and the Eurasian Palaeolithic record. Antiquity 63(241):719–732.

Stoneman, R. 1987. Land of the lost gods: the search for classical Greece. University of Oklahoma Press, Norman.

Straus, Lawrence G., and Geoffrey A. Clark, eds. 1986. La Riera cave: Stone Age hunter-gatherer adaptations in northern Spain. Department of Anthropology, Anthropological Research Papers No. 36. Arizona State University, Tempe.

Teilhard de Chardin, P. 1941. Early man in China. Institut de Géo-Biologie, Peking.

Thomsen, C. J. 1836. Ledetraad til nordisk oldkyndighed. S. L. Møller, Copenhagen.

Van Seters, J. 1983. In search of history: historiography in the ancient world and the origins of biblical history. Yale University Press, New Haven.

Wenke, Robert J. 1986. Old Kingdom community organization in the western Egyptian Delta. Norwegian Archaeological Review 19(1):15–33.

———. 1989. Patterns in prehistory. 3rd ed. Oxford University Press, New York.

Wolpoff, Milford H. 1980. Paleo-anthropology. Knopf, New York.

Woolley, C. Leonard. 1950. Digging up the past. Penguin Books, Harmondsworth, U.K.

SOURCES OF ADDITIONAL INFORMATION

The literature of Old World archaeology is vast, and an adequate description of it would require several volumes. In addition to its overwhelming size, much of this literature has been published in languages and locations that make it inaccessible to American scholars. For these reasons, the emphasis here will be on broadly synthetic works in English whose bibliographic references will direct researchers to more specific and specialized studies in areas of particular interest.

There are now several works on the history of archaeology that provide information on the development of Old World archaeology. Of these, both Bruce Trigger, *A History of Archaeological Thought* (Cambridge, Cambridge University Press, 1989), and Glyn Daniel, *A Hundred and Fifty Years of Archaeology* (Cambridge, Mass., Harvard University Press, 1976), are oriented toward the intellectual history of archaeology. Donald Grayson, in *The Establishment of Human Antiquity* (New York, Academic Press, 1983), provides a detailed historical overview of the processes resulting in the eventual acceptance of the idea of human antiquity. For those lacking ready access to primary sources, Glyn Daniel has reprinted extensive passages from the influential works of John Frere, Boucher de Perthes, Sir John Lubbock, Oscar Montelius, and Thomas Jefferson, plus many others, in his *The Origins and Growth of Archaeology* (1967; see References for complete citation).

The archaeological history of China has been made accessible to Western scholars in the works of Kwang-shih Chang, whose *The Archaeology of Ancient China* (New Haven, Yale University Press, 1986) has now appeared in four editions, of which the last two (1977 and 1986) are supplementary to each other, the third edition containing material that has been omitted from the fourth, which includes new data supplementing that in its predecessor, making it necessary to consult both editions for complete coverage.

Journals published in Western languages in this field to update Chang's work include *Journal of the American Oriental Society*, *Journal of Asian Studies*, and *Bulletin of the Museum of Far Eastern Antiquities, Stockholm*. A good background overview of the Chinese Paleolithic is chapter 1 in Chang 1986 (see References).

The best ongoing coverage of recent research and publication in Old World archaeology has been the periodic reviews in the journal *American Antiquity*. Originally an annual feature, the "Review of Old World archaeology" became biennial in the late 1980s. No review has appeared since 1989, suggesting that this feature has been dropped, which is serious loss, since there is no comparable ongoing coverage elsewhere.

The February 1988 issue of *World Archaeology* (vol. 19, no. 3) is devoted to Old World research on the Paleolithic. The articles cover a variety of problems concerning the Paleolithic in Europe, Africa, and India, including subsistence (Sturdy and Webley), lithic technology and analysis (F. Hassan; Patricia Phillips; Lucy Wilson), Paleolithic art as an information system (Mithen), chronology (McBreaty), regional adaptive systems (Straus et al.), and paleoenvironmental studies (Biagi and Cremaschi). The brief introduction to the issue by J. A. J. Gowlett presents some interesting historical background on current research problems and methods.

For the most recent information and publication, current issues of the journals *Antiquity*; *American Antiquity*; *Classical Journal*; *Archaeology*; *Journal of Egyptian Archaeology*; *American Journal of Archaeology*; and *Journal of Anthropological Archaeology* should be monitored, as well as the appropriate annual reviews.

P

PALEOANTHROPOLOGY. The study of hominids and protohumans from their fossilized skeletal remains and surviving material record, using the methods of a variety of disciplines, with the goal of acquiring information about the EVOLUTION and lifeways of the early ancestors of modern *H. sapiens sapiens*. (See also BIOCULTURAL STUDIES; EVOLUTION.)

> Paleoanthropology is a multidisciplinary science, which its practitioners aim to evolve into an interdiscipinary one. It encompasses not only the study of "fossil man," now rephrased human paleontology, but also aspects of the earth sciences, prehistoric archaeology, behavioral science, palynology, vertebrate and invertebrate paleontology, taphonomy, comparative and functional morphology, biomechanics, systematics, evolutionary theory, and molecular biology. (Tuttle 1988:391)

As Russell Tuttle notes, paleoanthropology is a multifaceted realm of research, combining methods and concepts borrowed from a diversity of disciplines. Like BIOCULTURAL STUDIES, paleoanthropology depends upon archaeological field methods for recovering most of its primary data, and draws its theoretical concepts and methodology from physical anthropology and the biological sciences, as well as from archaeology.

Paleoanthropology's roots lie in the work of Louis and Mary Leakey at Olduvai Gorge, beginning in the 1950s (L. S. B. Leakey 1951, 1961; M. D. Leakey 1970, 1971, 1975). The Leakeys utilized the varied expertise of scientists from several disciplines in their search for the origins of humanity. This multidisciplinary approach has been continued in the work of their son Richard in Kenya (Leakey and Leakey 1978), and was adopted by F. Clark Howell in his field research in Ethiopia and Spain. Since the 1970s, theirs has become the standard approach to field studies concentrated on acquiring evidence of early man and human origins (R. Leakey 1977; Tuttle 1988).

Since humans appear to have originated and evolved on the African continent, much of the archaeological effort in paleoanthropological research has been concentrated in this region. This work has resulted in the discovery of a number of significant hominid fossils and cultural traces, from the *Homo habilis* finds at Olduvai to the widely publicized *Australopithecus afarensis* specimen called "Lucy" in Ethiopia, and the traces of early hominid locomotion in the famous footprints at Laetoli, Tanzania (M. Leakey et al. 1976; Leakey and Hay 1979; Johanson and Edey 1981; Johanson, Taieb, and Coppens 1982; Stern and Susman 1983; Blumenschine and Masao 1991). Resulting data have raised a number of important questions about the differences between the australopithecines and members of the genus *Homo*, which have not yet been resolved (Butzer and Isaac 1975; Johanson and White 1979; Coppens 1980; Falk 1987).

In recent years, paleoanthropological research has concentrated on several key problems. Some of these lie in the realm of human biology and molecular anthropology, while others involve the role of CULTURE, as well as biological factors, in human EVOLUTION and ADAPTATION, and are more directly related to archaeological research.

Among the questions of concern to biologically oriented paleoanthropologists is When did the first hominids appear? In the late 1960s, Vincent Sarich and A. C. Wilson devised the idea of a "molecular clock," and used serum albumins from living apes and humans in serological studies to estimate the time when the hominid and pongid lines diverged from their common ancestral lineage (Sarich and Wilson 1967; Sarich 1968, 1971). The utility of the molecular clock concept is diminished, however, by the fact that it is based on a number of unverifiable assumptions, most importantly that the rate of molecular evolution has remained constant throughout time, which has not been supported by recent research (Li and Tanimura 1987).

A more recent group of studies headed by Rebecca Cann has approached this question on the basis of genetics. Cann and her associates have reconstructed human phylogeny using mitochondrial DNA, which is passed only through females to their offspring. The resulting "Eve hypothesis," which traces all living human populations to a common ancestral female who lived in Africa in the remote past, has generated considerable controversy, as well as attracting media attention (Wilson, Cann, et al. 1985; 1988; Cann, Stoneking, and Wilson 1987; Lewin 1987; Wilson, Stoneking, Cann, et al., 1987; Stoneking and Cann 1989; Brown 1990; Foley 1991).

Paleoanthropological problems more directly related to archaeological research objectives include work prompted by new hypotheses concerning the nature of the earliest human SUBSISTENCE and adaptation. Until about 1980, it was assumed that early human groups supported themselves primarily by hunting game, following a life pattern similar to that of twentieth-century–hunter-gatherers (Isaac 1976, 1978). More recently, faunal remains originally thought by zooarchaeologists to be the remnants of species hunted by early humans have been restudied using taphonomic methods, including such techniques as examination of bones under the scanning electron microscope, and comparing bone ASSEMBLAGES of species presumably hunted by humans with collections of bones from the dens of hyenas and other predators. These resulted in reinterpretations suggesting that early man habitually scavenged the carcasses of species killed by other animal predators, and may have lacked the technology for efficient hunting until a much later time (Shipman and Phillips-Conroy 1977; Brain 1981; Isaac 1981, 1983, 1984; Shipman 1983, 1986; Binford 1984, 1985; Stahl 1984). Such findings have contributed to a different model of early hominid adaptation and lifeway, in which food-getting and survival would have been much more opportunistic than among modern hunter-gatherers, whose subsistence behavior necessarily incorporates a considerable amount of foresight and planning, as well as amassing large amounts of environmental information (Bunn and Kroll 1986; Blumenschine 1987; Turner 1988; see also HUNTER-GATHERER ARCHAEOLOGY).

An important area of intensive current investigation and debate involving both paleoanthropologists and archaeologists focuses on a second major transition in human evolution, at least equally important as the transition from australopithecine to *Homo*. This is the far more recent appearance of fully "modern" humans, *Homo sapiens sapiens*, and their replacement of such archaic forms as the Neanderthals, which has been termed the "human revolution" (Mellars and Stringer 1989). Much of this research is centered on questions relating to the biological and behavioral origins of modern humans, whose evolution is now thought by many investigators to have been a far more rapid and recent phenomenon than former gradualistic views had indicated (Mellars 1990:vii). Many now place the time of the appearance of *H. sapiens sapiens* at the Middle-to-Upper Paleolithic transition, or roughly 50,000 years ago.

While some of the archaeological research related to this matter has concentrated on cultural and chronological evidence (e.g., Clarke 1988; Reynolds 1990; Chamberlain 1991; Timei and Yinyun 1991), an abundant portion of it has attempted to infer the cognitive abilities of archaic humans, including their linguistic capabilities and capacity for other forms of symbolic behavior, and to compare these with those of modern humans (Chase and Dibble 1987; Davidson and Noble 1989; Mellars 1989; Mellars and Stringer 1989; Foster 1990; Klein 1990; Lindly and Clark 1990; Marshack 1990; Otte 1990). An important question addressed by most of this research is the relationship of Neanderthals to ourselves, that is, what role this species played in the evolutionary process (Stringer 1982; White 1982). In the 1940s, it was assumed that the Neanderthals were ancestral to modern humans, and at least some researchers would still agree that this group did contribute to our genetic heritage (Wolfpoff 1989). Overall, however, there has been a downgrading of the inferred intelligence and cognitive abilities of Neanderthal man vis-à-vis those of modern humans, and an increased emphasis on the cognitive and intellectual contrast between that species and ourselves. Many investigators now believe Neanderthals lacked articulate speech, religion, art, and other forms of symbolic expression—in short, most of what we would call culture, and would place the appearance of human culture at the beginning of the Upper Paleolithic, making this a very recent occurrence in terms of evolutionary time (Wynn 1979, 1985, 1986; Trinkaus 1986, 1989; Binford 1989; Whallon 1989; Graves 1991).

The related subject of the EVOLUTION and first appearance of human language has stimulated considerable interest and debate with respect to the "Neanderthal problem" and the transition to modern humans (Isaac 1976; Pfeiffer 1982; Parker 1985; White 1985; Davidson and Noble 1989; Bateman et al. 1990; Marshack 1990). While most of the debate has centered on the Middle-to-Upper Paleolithic transition in Europe, it has been extended to other areas as well, such as the Far East, where evidence suggests a similar transformation, although the fossil record of this area indicates a different evolutionary background for *Homo sapiens sapiens* than that of Europe or Africa (Orguera 1984; Binford and Ho 1985; Binford and Stone 1986; Pope 1988; Mellars and Stringer 1989; Stringer 1989).

Much of this research is still in too early a stage to be realistically evaluated, but some of its conclusions are very controversial. Making valid inferences concerning the presence or absence of distinctly human cognitive and physiological characteristics in archaic humans of the late Middle Paleolithic from existing material evidence requires more sophisticated models than those employed in the past, if such inferences are to be supported with currently available data. Meanwhile, the debate over the origins of our species promises to continue unabated.

REFERENCES

Bateman, Richard, Ives Goddard, Richard O'Grady, V. A. Funk, Rich Mooi, W. John Kress, and Peter Cannell. 1990. Speaking of forked tongues: the feasibility of reconciling human phylogeny and the history of language. Current Anthropology 31(1):1–24.

Binford, Lewis R. 1984. Faunal remains from Klasies River mouth. Academic Press, New York.

———. 1985. Human ancestors: changing views of their behavior. Journal of Anthropological Archaeology 4(4):292–327.

———. 1989. Isolating the transition to cultural adaptations: an organizational approach. In The emergence of modern humans: biocultural adaptations in the later Pleistocene, Erik Trinkaus, ed. Cambridge University Press, pp. 18–41.

Binford, Lewis R., and C. K. Ho. 1985. Taphonomy at a distance: Zhoukoudian, "the cave home of Beijing man"? Current Anthropology 26(4):413–443.

Binford, Lewis R., and Nancy M. Stone. 1986. Zhoukoudian: a closer look. Current Anthropology 27(5):453–475.

Blumenschine, Robert J. 1987. Characteristics of an early hominid scavenging niche. Current Anthropology 28(4):383–407.

Blumenschine, Robert J., and F. T. Masao. 1991. Living sites at Olduvai Gorge, Tanzania—preliminary landscape archaeology results in the basal Bed II lake margin zone. Journal of Human Evolution 21(6):451–462.

Brain, C. K. 1981. The hunters or the hunted? An introduction to African cave taphonomy. University of Chicago Press.

Brown, Michael H. 1990. The search for Eve. Harper & Row, New York.

Bunn, Henry T., and Ellen M. Kroll. 1986. Systematic butchery by Plio/Pleistocene hominids at Olduvai Gorge, Tanzania. Current Anthropology 27(5):431–452.

Butzer, Karl W., and Glyn L. Isaac, eds. 1975. After the australopithecines. Mouton, The Hague.

Cann, Rebecca L. 1988. DNA and human origins. Annual Review of Anthropology 17:127–143.

Cann, Rebecca L., M. Stoneking, and A. C. Wilson. 1987. Mitochondrial DNA and human evolution. Nature 325:31–36.

Chamberlain, A. T. 1991. A chronological framework for human origins. World Archaeology 23(2):137–146.

Chase, Philip G., and Harold L. Dibble. 1987. Middle Paleolithic symbolism: a review of current evidence and interpretations. Journal of Anthropological Archaeology 6:263–296.

Clarke, R. L. 1988. Habiline handaxes and paranthropine pedigree at Sterkfontein. World Archaeology 20(1):1–12.

Coppens, Y. 1980. The differences between *Australopithecus* and *Homo:* preliminary conclusions from the Omo research expeditions's studies. In Current argument on early man, L.-K. Konigsson, ed. Pergamon, Oxford, pp. 207–225.

Davidson, Iain, and William Noble. 1989. The archaeology of perception: traces of depiction and language. Current Anthropology 30(2):125–155.

Falk, Dean. 1987. Hominid paleoneurology. Annual Review of Anthropology 16:13–30.

Foley, Robert. 1991. Recent palaeoanthropology as an epic [review of *The search for Eve*, by Michael H. Brown]. Current Anthropology 32(2):207–208.

Foster, Mary LeCron. 1990. Symbolic origins and transitions in the Paleolithic. In The emergence of modern humans: an archaeological perspective, Paul Mellars, ed. Edinburgh University Press, pp. 517–539.

Graves, Paul. 1991. New models and metaphors for the Neanderthal debate. Current Anthropology 32(5):513–541.

Isaac, Glyn. 1976. Stages of cultural elaboration in the Pleistocene: possible archaeological indicators of the development of language capabilities. Annals of the New York Academy of Sciences 280:275–288.

———. 1978. Food-sharing and human evolution: archaeological evidence from the Plio-Pleistocene of East Africa. Journal of Anthropological Research 34:311–325.

———. 1981. Archaeological tests of alternative models of early hominid behaviour: excavation and experiments. Philosophical Transactions of the Royal Society of London B292:177–188.

———. 1983. Bones in contention: Competing explanations for the juxtaposition of early Pleistocene artifacts and faunal remains. In Animals and archaeology: hunters and their prey, J. Clutton-Brock and C. Grigson, eds. British Archaeological Reports, Oxford, pp. 3–19.

———. 1984. The archaeology of human origins: studies of the Lower Pleistocene in East Africa 1971–1981. In Advances in World Archaeology 3:1–87.

Johanson, Donald C., and Maitland Edey. 1981. Lucy: the beginnings of humankind. Simon and Schuster, New York.

Johanson, Donald C., M. Taieb, and Y. Coppens. 1982. Pliocene hominids from the Hadar Formation, Ethiopia (1973–1977). . . . American Journal of Physical Anthropology 57:373–402.

Johanson, Donald C., and T. D. White. 1979. A systematic assessment of early African hominids. Science 203:321–330.

Klein, Sheldon. 1990. Human cognitive changes at the Middle to Upper Palaeolithic transition: the evidence of Boker Tachtit. In The emergence of modern humans: an archaeological perspective, Paul Mellars, ed. Edinburgh University Press, pp. 499–516.

Leakey, Lewis S. B. 1951. Olduvai Gorge: a report on the evolution of the hand-axe culture in Beds I–IV. Cambridge University Press.

————. 1961. Very early East African Hominidae and their ecological setting. In African ecology and human evolution, F. C. Howell and Bourliere, eds. Aldine, Chicago, pp. 448–457.

Leakey, Mary D. 1970. Early artefacts from the Koobi Fora area. Nature 226:228–230.

————. 1971. Olduvai Gorge: excavations in Beds I & II, 1960–1963. Cambridge University Press.

————. 1975. Cultural patterns in the Olduvai sequence. In After the australopithecines, K. W. Butzer and G. Ll. Isaac, eds. Mouton, The Hague, pp. 477–493.

Leakey, Mary D., and R. L. Hay. 1979. Pliocene footprints in the Laetoli beds at Laetoli, north Tansania. Nature 278:317–323.

Leakey, Mary D., R. L. Hay, G. H. Curtis, R. E. Drake, M. K. Jackes, and T. D. White. 1976. Fossil hominids from the Laetoli beds. Nature 262:460–466.

Leakey, M. G., and R. E. Leakey. 1978. Koobi Fora research project, vol. 1. The fossil hominids and an introduction to their context, 1968–1984. Clarendon Press, Oxford.

Leakey, Richard E. F. 1977. Origins. Dutton, New York.

Lewin, R. 1987. The unmasking of mitochondrial Eve. Science 238:24–36.

Li, Wen-hsiung, and Masako Tanimura. 1987. The molecular clock runs more slowly in man than in apes and monkeys. Nature 326:93–96.

Lindly, J. M., and G. A. Clark. 1990. Symbolism and modern human origins. Current Anthropology 31(3):233–261.

Marshack, Alexander. 1990. Early hominid symbol and evolution of the human capacity. In The emergence of modern humans: an archaeological perspective, Paul Mellars, ed. Edinburgh University Press, pp. 457–498.

Mellars, Paul. 1989. Major issues in the emergence of modern humans. Current Anthropology 39:349–385.

————, ed. 1990. The emergence of modern humans: an archaeological perspective. Edinburgh University Press.

Mellars, P., and C. B. Stringer, eds. 1989. The human revolution. University of Edinburgh Press.

Orguera, L. 1984. Specialization and the Middle/Upper Paleolithic transition. Current Anthropology 25:73–98.

Otte, Marcel. 1990. From the Middle to the Upper Paleolithic: the nature of the transition. In The emergence of modern humans: an archaeological perspective, Paul Mellars, ed. Edinburgh University Press, pp. 438–456.

Parker, Sue Taylor. 1985. A socio-technological model for the evolution of language. Current Anthropology 26(5):617–639.

Pfeiffer, J. E. 1982. The creative explosion. Harper & Row, New York.

Pope, Geoffrey G. 1988. Recent advances in Far Eastern paleoanthropology. Annual Review of Anthropology 17:43–77.

Reynolds, T. E. G. 1990. The Middle-Upper Palaeolithic transition in southwestern France: interpreting the lithic evidence. In The emergence of modern humans: an archaeological perspective, Paul Mellars, ed. Edinburgh University Press, pp. 262–275.

———. 1991. Revolution or resolution? the archaeology of modern human origins. World Archaeology 23(2):155–166.

Rightmire, G. Philip. 1988. *Homo erectus* and later Middle Pleistocene humans. Annual Review of Anthropology 17:239–259.

Sarich, Vincent M. 1968. The origin of the hominids: an immunological approach. In Perspectives on human evolution 1, S. L. Washburn and P. C. Jay, eds. Holt, Rinehart and Winston, New York, pp. 94–121.

———. 1971. A molecular approach to the question of human origins. In Background for man, P. Dolhinow and V. Sarich, eds. Little, Brown, Boston, pp. 60–81.

Sarich, Vincent M., and A. C. Wilson. 1967. Rates of albumin evolution in primates. Proceedings of the National Academy of Sciences 58:142–148.

Shipman, Pat. 1983. Early hominid lifestyle: hunting and gathering or foraging and scavenging? In Animals and archaeology: 1. Hunters and their prey, Juliet Clutton-Brock and C. Grigson, eds. BAR International Series, Oxford, pp. 31–49.

———. 1986. Scavenging or hunting in early hominids: theoretical framework and tests. American Anthropologist 88(1):27–43.

Shipman, Pat, and J. Phillips-Conroy. 1977. Hominid tool-making versus carnivore scavenging. American Journal of Physical Anthropology 46:77–86.

Stahl, A. B. 1984. Hominid dietary selection before fire. Current Anthropology 25:151–168.

Stern, J. T., and R. L. Susman. 1983. The locomotor anatomy of *Australopithecus afarensis*. American Journal of Physical Anthropology 60:279–317.

Stoneking, Mark, and Rebecca L. Cann. 1989. African origins of human mitochondrial DNA. In The human revolution: behavioural and biological perspectives on the origins of modern humans, Paul Mellars and Chris Stringer, eds. University of Edinburgh Press, pp. 17–30.

Stringer, C. B. 1982. Towards a solution to the Neanderthal problem. Journal of Human Evolution 11:431–438.

———. 1989. The origins of early modern humans: a comparison of the European and non-European evidence. In The human revolution, P. Mellars and C. B. Stringer, eds. University of Edinburgh Press, pp. 232–244.

Timei, Chen, and Zhang Yinyun. 1991. Palaeolithic chronology and the possible coexistence of *Homo erectus* and *Homo sapiens* in China. World Archaeology 23(2):147–154.

Trinkaus, Erik. 1986. The Neanderthals and modern human origins. Annual Review of Anthropology 15:193–218.

———, ed. 1989. The emergence of modern humans: biocultural adaptations in the later Pleistocene. Cambridge University Press.

Turner, Alan. 1988. Relative scavenging opportunities for East and South African Plio-Pleistocene hominids. Journal of Archaeological Science 15:327–341.

Tuttle, Russell H. 1988. What's new in African paleoanthropology. Annual Review of Anthropology 17:391–426.

Whallon, Robert. 1989. Elements of cultural change in the later Palaeolithic. In The human revolution: behavioural and biological perspectives on the origins of modern humans, vol. 1, P. Mellars and C. B. Stringer, eds. Edinburgh University Press, pp. 433–454.

White, Randall. 1982. Rethinking the Middle/Upper Paleolithic transition. Current Anthropology 23:169–192.

———. 1985. Thoughts on social relationships and language in hominid evolution. Journal of Social and Personal Relationships 2:95–115.

Wilson, A.C., Rebecca L. Cann, et al. 1985. Mitochondrial DNA and two perspectives on evolutionary genetics. Biological Journal of the Linnean Society 26:375–400.

Wilson, A. C., M. Stoneking, R. L. Cann, et al. 1987. Mitochondrial clans and the age of our common mother. In Human genetics, proceedings of the seventh international congress, F. Vogel and K. Sperling, eds. Springer-Verlag, Berlin, pp. 158–164.

Wolfpoff, Milford H. 1989. The place of the Neanderthals in human evolution. In The emergence of modern humans: biocultural adaptations in the later Pleistocene, Erik Trinkaus, ed. Cambridge University Press, pp. 97–141.

Wynn, Thomas. 1979. The intelligence of later Acheulean hominids. Man 14:371–391.

———. 1985. Piaget, stone tools, and the evolution of human intelligence. World Archaeology 17(1):32–43.

———. 1986. Archaeological evidence for the evolution of modern human intelligence. In The Pleistocene prespective: precirculated papers of the World Archaeological Congress, Southampton, 1986, M. Day, R. Foley, and Wu Rukang, eds. Allen and Unwin, London.

SOURCES OF ADDITIONAL INFORMATION

For a general introduction to paleoanthropology, see Milford H. Wolfpoff, *Paleoanthropology* (New York, Alfred A. Knopf, 1980); and the review by Nicholas Toth and Kathy D. Schick, "The first million years: the archaeology of protohuman culture," *Advances in Archaeological Method and Theory* 9 (1986):1–96. A review article on the evolution of the human brain and its capabilities is Dean Falk's "Hominid paleoneurology," *Annual Review of Anthropology* 16(1987):13–30. A review by Henry T. Bunn, "A taphonomic perspective on the archaeology of human origins," *Annual Review of Anthropology* 20 (1991):433–467, discusses effects of taphonomic factors on the archaeological record of early man.

There is a large body of literature and review articles in this field. Tuttle, in his 1988 review (see References), attempting to cover only the literature on African paleoanthropology, cited nearly 600 references to publications of the 1960s, 1970s, and 1980s. The twenty-page bibliography in Toth and Schick (see above) gives a good overview of publication to 1986. More specialized reviews include Randall R. Skelton, Henry M. McHenry, and Gerrell M. Drawhorn, "Phylogenetic analysis of early hominids," *Current Anthropology* 27(1) (1986):21–43; G. Philip Rightmire, "*Homo erectus* and later Middle Pleistocene humans," *Annual Review of Anthropology* 17 (1988):239–259; Robert J. Blumenschine's review of early hominid scavenging (1987; see References); and the review of paleoanthropology in the Far Eastern countries by Geoffrey G. Pope (1988; see References).

The recent explosion of interest in the Middle-to-Upper Paleolithic transition and the emergence of modern humans has generated a superabundance of publications. Reviews covering some of this literature include Erik Trinkaus, "The Neanderthals and modern human origins," *Annual Review of Anthropology* 15(1986):193–218; Paul Mellars, "Major issues in the emergence of modern humans," *Current Anthropology* 39(1989):349–385; and L. Orguera, "Specialization and the Middle-Upper Paleolithic transition," *Current Anthropology* 25(1984):73–98. Others devoted to particular aspects of the transition, such as language and symbolic development, include Falk (1987), Graves (1991), and Davidson and Noble (1989; see References for complete citations).

Collections of papers are even more numerous. Some of the more important of these are Trinkaus 1989; Mellars and Stringer 1989; Mellars 1990 (all cited in References); and J. F. Hoffecker and C. A. Wolf, eds., *The Early Upper Paleolithic: Evidence from Europe and the Near East* (Oxford, British Archaeological Report, BAR International Series 437, 1988).

For further coverage of this ongoing avalanche of publication, consult latest volumes of *Annual Review of Anthropology* and current issues of *American Journal of Physical Anthropology*, *Journal of Human Evolution*, *American Anthropologist*, *World Archaeology*, *American Antiquity*, and *Journal of Anthropological Archaeology*.

PALEODEMOGRAPHY. 1. An interdisciplinary subdivision of archaeology, devoted to the study of the characteristics of prehistoric human populations from information in the ARCHAEOLOGICAL RECORD. Also called *demographic archaeology*. 2. The study of human skeletal remains from archaeological burials as a basis for making demographic inferences about past population characteristics. See also BIOCULTURAL STUDIES; CARRYING CAPACITY.

Paleodemographers seek to determine such population parameters as group composition, population sizes and densities, age composition, rates of population growth, sex ratios, and birth and mortality rates of past populations, as well as changes that occurred in these through time, using ARTIFACTS, settlement data, food remains, and environmental data supplemented by ethnographic or historical records that may be available. Such data are used in constructing explanatory models and formulating hypotheses concerning past cultural processes, and their relation to population dynamics. Investigations are often made by physical anthropologists working with archaeologists.

Paleodemographic research is a fairly recent area of specialized study, having arisen only since the 1930s. The first studies now regarded as paleodemographic date to the 1930s and 1940s (Vallois 1937; Weidenreich 1939; Angel 1947). While these early investigations were focused on problems of limited scope, paleodemographers since then have developed broader goals. Today paleodemographers may seek to establish the possible range of human social structure, or to elucidate such concepts as CARRYING CAPACITY (Howell 1986:219, 229–230) from their analyses of human remains, in addition to the more descriptive goal of establishing population parameters for now-extinct human groups.

Like other specialized subdisciplines of archaeology, paleodemography has both empirical and theoretical dimensions and objectives. The former are represented in field studies of particular populations (Haviland 1969, 1972; Tolstoy and Fish 1975; Storey 1985; Schlanger 1988; Corruccini, Brandon, and Handler 1989); the latter, by various attempts to define concepts and establish a theoretical framework for comparing past populations (Hayden 1975; Zubrow 1975; Howell 1976, 1986:229).

Since the 1960s, paleodemographic research has been important in archaeological studies of the beginnings of FOOD PRODUCTION, accumulating data to address important issues regarding the possibly causal role of population dynamics in this major cultural transition (Boserup 1965; Harner 1970; Bronson 1975; Cowgill 1975; Handwerker 1983; Cohen and Armelagos 1984). Related to this issue is the matter of human fertility and reproduction in the past, and the possible use of population control measures in prehistoric times (Hayden 1972; Cashdan 1985; Holland 1989).

A central problem in the study of prehistoric populations is that of estimating group sizes in the past. Two principal approaches to this problem utilized by archaeologists have been (1) to use settlement data, and in particular occupied living floor area, to estimate sizes of local groups at particular times; and (2) to assess the carrying capacity of the inhabited environment, that is, the maximum number of humans the habitat could have supported.

Estimates made from occupied floor area are likely to yield more realistic results, in general, since these are most often made using ethnographic or historical data on populations descended from the prehistoric group of interest, in addition to the archaeological settlement data. The demographer Raoul Naroll (Naroll 1962) derived an equation for determining population size from occupied living space that has been refined and heavily utilized in subsequent archaeological research. According to this formula, the population of a community is roughly equivalent to one tenth of the total area in square meters of all occupied floor space in an archaeological unit, such as a household, a village, a valley, or other region. While this is a useful rule of thumb, it is overgeneralized, and must be modified to take local and individual variation into account. Other such formulas have been devised, for instance, by S. F. Cook and Robert F. Heizer, whose formula allowed 25 square feet (2.325 square meters) for each of the first six people occupying a dwelling space, and 100 square feet (9.3 square meters) for each additional person. Other modifications have been based upon ethnographic data available for local populations in various parts of the world, allowing more refined estimates to be made of local group sizes in prehistoric times.

Population estimates for hunter-gatherer groups who lack permanent settlements have been made from formulas based on ethnographic data collected from contemporary hunting and gathering peoples, whose current local group size varies from approximately 15 to 50 persons, and averages between 20 and 30, ranges probably very similar to those of food-collecting populations in the prehistoric past. Artifact numbers and distribution densities, as well as human skeletal, faunal, and botanical remains, have also been used in making estimates of prehistoric populations (Howells 1960; Hassan 1981).

Population size estimates for large areas made on the basis of archaeological evidence alone remain educated guesses, even if derived from the best available data and mathematical techniques. Studies from the same base data can produce widely differing results, depending upon the investigator's initial assumptions and the techniques of analysis employed; and because of the unavoidable imprecision of both data and results, paleodemographers will normally attempt to establish only a reasonable range of estimated population rather than to arrive at precise figures. Estimates of world population in Paleolithic times range, for example, from as few as 5 million persons to more than 20 million (Renfrew and Bahn 1991:400).

Other aspects of prehistoric populations that have been subject to paleodemographic study include population densities in the past. Although densities may be easily estimated from house counts in combination with the use of formulas such as Naroll's, such procedures are compromised by the difficulty of establishing contemporaneity of occupation of the dwelling units in any given sample, and allowances must be made for error in making such judgments.

Physical anthropologists have made a considerable contribution to the field of paleodemography through their studies of human skeletal remains from archaeological burials. Fertility and mortality rates in the past, as well as life expectancies and data on health and disease, can be estimated from burial populations of sufficient size to provide a statistically adequate sample (see, e.g., Storey 1985; Corruccini, Brandon, and Handler 1989; see also BIOCULTURAL STUDIES).

In recent years, paleodemographic studies have been criticized on various grounds. Fekri Hassan has pointed out that empirical data on the demography of prehistoric peoples are scant and of variable quality. This situation is improving as fieldworkers become more skilled in the systematic collection of reliable data for demographic analysis from archaeological projects now in progress (Webster and Freter 1990). Others have contended that paleodemographic methods are so biased and imprecise that resulting data are virtually worthless (Bocquet-Appel and Masset 1982). The key arguments presented by J.-P. Bocquet-Appel and C. Masset have been answered by two experienced paleodemographers (Jane Buikstra and Lyle W. Konigsberg), and found to be "extreme," although they concede that there is considerable need to refine techniques for accurately estimating age from skeletal remains of older adults, and for standardizing techniques used for making such age estimates to ensure comparability of resulting data produced by different investigators.

An emerging area of paleodemographic studies is that concerned with the investigation of disease patterns and distribution in the past, and their effects on prehistoric population sizes and structure (Dobyns 1983; Ramenofsky 1987). An especially fertile area for such investigation is the entire inhabited area of the New World at the time of European contact, in the late fifteenth and early sixteenth centuries. New World populations had previously been free of infectious epidemic diseases, and consequently had no resistance to them. The result was death on an unprecedented scale. Although the exact dimensions of the resulting demographic disaster cannot yet be accurately assessed (Dobyns 1983), archaeologists have begun to find evidence that in many areas, the introduction of European disease organisms actually preceded the arrival of Europeans themselves, sometimes by several decades (Ramenofsky 1987; Campbell 1989). Diseases such as smallpox, spread by human intermediaries such as traders and visitors moving from Central to North and South America, raged through Native American groups, depopulating large areas prior to the first Spanish arrivals. Paleoepidemiologic studies documenting these events, while still in an early stage of development, have produced some intriguing results that will no doubt become far more refined through future work.

REFERENCES

Angel, J. Lawrence. 1947. The length of life in ancient Greece. Journal of Gerontology 2:18–24.

Bocquet-Appel, Jean-Pierre, and Claude Masset. 1982. Farewell to paleodemography. Journal of Human Evolution 11:321–333.

Boserup, Esther. 1965. The conditions of agricultural growth. Aldine, Chicago.

Bronson, Bennet. 1975. The earliest farming: demography as a cause and consequence. In Population, ecology and social evolution, S. Polger, ed. Mouton, The Hague, pp. 53–78.

Brothwell, D. R. 1971. Palaeodemography. In Biological aspects of demography, W. Brass, ed. Taylor and Francis, London, pp. 111–130.

Buikstra, Jane E., and L. W. Konigsberg. 1985. Paleodemography: critiques and controversies. American Anthropologist 87:316–333.

Campbell, Sarah K. 1989. Post-Columbian culture history in the northern Columbia Plateau. . . . Doctoral dissertation, Department of Anthropology, University of Washington, Seattle.

Cashdan, Elizabeth A. 1985. Natural fertility, birth spacing, and the "first demographic transition." American Anthropologist 87(3):650–653.

Cohen, Mark N., and George J. Armelagos. 1984. Paleopathology at the origin of agriculture. Academic Press, Orlando, Fla.

Corruccini, Robert S., Elizabeth M. Brandon, and Jerome S. Handler. 1989. Inferring fertility from relative mortality in historically controlled cemetery remains from Barbados. American Antiquity 54(3):609–614.

Cowgill, George L. 1975. On causes and consequences of ancient and modern population changes. American Anthropologist 77:505–525.

Dobyns, Henry F. 1983. Their number become thinned: native American population dynamics. . . . University of Tennessee Press/Newberry Library Center for the History of the American Indian, Knoxville.

Handwerker, W. Penn. 1983. The first demographic transition: an analysis of subsistence choices and reproductive consequences. American Anthropologist 85:5–27.

Harner, M. J. 1970. Population pressure and social evolution of agriculturalists. Southwestern Journal of Anthropology 26:67–86.

Hassan, Fekri A. 1981. Demographic archaeology. Academic Press, New York.

Haviland, William A. 1969. A new population estimate for Tikal, Guatemala. American Antiquity 34:429–432.

———. 1972. Family size, prehistoric population estimates and the ancient Maya. American Antiquity 37(1):135–139.

Hayden, Brian. 1972. Population control among hunter-gatherers. World Archaeology 4:205–221.

———. 1975. The carrying capacity dilemma: an alternative approach. American Antiquity 40:11–21.

Holland, Thomas D. 1989. Fertility in the prehistoric Midwest: a critique of unifactorial models. American Antiquity 54(3):614–625.

Howell, Nancy. 1976. Toward a uniformitarian theory of human paleodemography. In The demographic evolution of human populations, R. H. Ward and K. M. Weiss, eds. Academic Press, New York, pp. 25–40.

———. 1986. Demographic anthropology. Annual Review of Anthropology 15:219–246.

Howells, W. W. 1960. Estimating population numbers through archaeological and skeletal remains. In The application of quantitative methods in archaeology, R. F. Heizer and S. F. Cook, eds. Viking Fund Publication in Anthropology No. 28. Quadrangle Books, Chicago, pp. 158–180.

Konigsberg, Lyle W., Jane E. Buikstra, and Jill Dillington. 1989. Paleodemographic correlates of fertility: a reply to Corruccini, Brandon and Handler and to Holland. American Antiquity 54(3):626–636.

Naroll, Raoul. 1962. Floor area and settlement population. American Antiquity 27:587–589.

Ramenofsky, Ann F. 1987. Vectors of death: the archaeology of European contact. University of New Mexico Press, Albuquerque.

Renfrew, Colin, and Paul Bahn. 1991. Archaeology: theories, methods and practice. Thames and Hudson, New York.

Schlanger, Sarah H. 1988. Patterns of population movement and long-term population growth in southwestern Colorado. American Antiquity 53(4):773–793.

Storey, Rebecca. 1985. An estimate of mortality in a pre-Columbian urban population. American Anthropologist 87(3):519–535.

Tolstoy, Paul, and Suzanne K. Fish. 1975. Surface and subsurface evidence for community size at Coapexco, Mexico. Journal of Field Archaeology 2:97–101.

Vallois, H. V. 1937. La durée de la vie chez l'homme fossile. Anthropologie 47:499–532.

Webster, David, and Ann Corrine Freter. 1990. The demography of Late Classic Copan. In Precolumbian population history in the Maya lowlands, T. Patrick Culbert and Don S. Rice, eds. University of New Mexico Press, Albuquerque, pp. 37–61.

Weidenreich, F. 1939. The duration of life of fossil man in China and the pathological lesions found in his skeleton. Chinese Medical Journal 55:34–44.

Zubrow, E. B. W. 1975. Prehistoric carrying capacity: a model. Benjamin Cummings, Menlo Park, Calif.

SOURCES OF ADDITIONAL INFORMATION

Review articles summarizing the literature are not numerous in the field of paleodemography, especially in recent years. In the late 1970s, two such articles appeared in annual review volumes, both by Fekri Hassan: "Demography and archaeology," *Annual Review of Anthropology* 8(1979):137–160; and "Demographic archaeology," *Advances in Archaeological Method and Theory* 1(1978):49–103. The only more recent review has been Nancy Howell's "Demographic anthropology," *Annual Review of Anthropology* 15(1986):219–246, which is oriented more toward studies of present populations.

For background information on paleodemography, there are informative discussions in Hassan 1981 (see References) and L. L. Allen et al., "Demography and human origins," *American Anthropologist* 84(1982):888–896. Kenneth M. Weiss (1973; see References for citation) demonstrates the use of mathematical methods of demographic theory to develop life tables for human populations both past and present, using data from both living and skeletal populations, and showing how models can be constructed to predict mortality from a fertility model and used to investigate human demographic change over long spans of time.

For more recent literature, consult articles and book reviews in current issues of *American Anthropologist* and *American Antiquity*, and future volumes of the major annual reviews.

PREHISTORY. 1. The time in the human career before the invention of writing and the keeping of written records. 2. The study of preliterate cultures of the past, which is a principal focus of modern archaeological studies. See also ANTIQUARIANISM; ARCHAEOLOGY; OLD WORLD ARCHAEOLOGY; PALEO-ANTHROPOLOGY.

Although the terms *prehistory* and *archaeology* are sometimes used interchangeably, *prehistory* is more correctly confined to denoting the concept of a preliterate, prehistoric period in the human career that can be investigated using the methods of a variety of disciplines, including those of history and archaeology.

The term *prehistory* was first employed in 1833 by Paul Tournal, a French amateur geologist who excavated bone deposits in a number of caves and published his findings in the 1820s and 1830s (Tournal 1833; Bernal 1980:9). The first subsequent use of the concept of prehistory and prehistoric time dates to 1851, when Daniel Wilson used it in the title of his book *The Archaeology and Prehistoric Annals of Scotland*, published in that year (Daniel and Renfrew 1988). It later appears in Sir Edward Tylor's monumental work of anthropology, *Primitive Culture* (1871). The concept of prehistory was also present among archaeologists in other parts of Europe during the mid-nineteenth century, although understandings of the term and the concept may have been quite variable and individualistic.

In the seventeenth century, Bishop James Ussher and Dr. John Lightfoot attempted to fix the date of the creation of the world and humankind. Their source was Martin Luther's calculations based on genealogical information in the biblical book of Genesis, corrected by the astronomer Johannes Kepler from solar eclipse cycles (Ussher 1658; Toulmin and Goodfield 1965:76; Clark 1970). Collectively, the date of October 23, 4004 B.C. was arrived at as the time of the biblical creation, and the biblical flood was reckoned to have occured in 2501 B.C. These dates were widely accepted until well into the nineteenth century, making the idea of prehistory, as a time before written records were known, quite unnecessary, since in this scheme there was no time when humans did not have a knowledge of writing. It was not until the evidence of a much greater antiquity of the world itself, and of the human species as well, began to be discovered and correctly interpreted, that scholars began to realize humans had inhabited the earth for an immense period of time before learning to record the events of their lives in written scripts (Lyell 1863; Grayson 1983).

By the year 1858, when both Alfred Wallace's and Charles Darwin's evolutionary theories were presented to the Linnaean Society, the idea of human antiquity, while by no means universally accepted, was an established issue in the intellectual life of the time. The chief obstacle to acceptance of the concept of prehistory was the notion of the fixity and permanence of all biological species, each of which was believed to occupy a unique position in a great chain of being laid down by God at the moment of creation, which was presumed to be eternal, perfect, and unchanging. Since the disappearance of a single link would destroy the whole, the extinction of any species, as well as the creation of new ones, was impossible. In this paradigm (as we would now call it) there was no place for EVOLUTION, nor especially for the idea that the human species had developed from some different prehuman animal form in the distant past (Grayson 1983:44; Daniel and Renfrew 1988:23).

Although Linnaeus had included man in his biological taxonomy with the other primates (Linnaeus 1735), the acceptance of the idea of a common descent for humans and the other primates met with considerable resistance until the twentieth century, and is still rejected by some fundamentalist religious groups in the United States. The final acceptance of human antiquity, and a long period of human experience before written history, would depend upon the recognition of stone tools found in association with the skeletal remains of the predecessors of modern humans.

Folk interpretations of early stone tools found in Europe prior to the beginning of the Renaissance attributed them to various fanciful origins, ranging from weapons made by elves or other spirits to the residues of thunderbolts. The first European scholar to interpret early human tools correctly was probably Michele Mercati, who, at the end of the sixteenth century, suggested these objects were "the weapons of a primitive folk ignorant of metallurgy" (Daniel and Renfrew 1988:30), an opinion echoed 50 years later by William Dugdale in his *History of Warwickshire* (1656), and still later by Robert Plot, first keeper of the Ashmolean Museum, in a history published in 1681. The first formal account of the discovery of such tools in association with the bones of extinct animals was made by John Frere. Frere's report of his finds at Hoxne in Suffolk, made to the Society of Antiquaries in 1797 (Frere 1800), aroused little attention or discussion at the time. It was not until the findings of Jacques Boucher de Perthes in the Somme River gravels near Abbeville, France, attracted public attention in the 1830s and 1840s, that the controversy over human prehistory became widespread (Boucher de Perthes 1859, 1860).

Recognition of stone ARTIFACTS for what they were was achieved somewhat earlier in Scandinavia than elsewhere in Europe. In Denmark, collections of early Stone tools led to the development of Christian Thomsen's THREE-AGE SYS-

TEM. Thomsen published his museum catalog incorporating the three-age approach within only 35 years of the publication of Frere's discoveries, and before the publication of Boucher de Perthes's theory of human antiquity in his *De la création* (Frere 1800; Thomsen 1836; Boucher de Perthes 1838–1841, 1859, 1860). The existence of a ''stone age'' in remote antiquity, preceding the invention of metallurgy, was quickly adopted by Scandivanian archaeologists, and Thomsen's Stone, Bronze, and Iron ages eventually became the principal basis for organizing museum collections throughout Europe, including that of the British Museum, although this acceptance was not complete until after 1850 (see OLD WORLD ARCHAEOLOGY; THREE-AGE SYSTEM).

Ultimately, the adoption of the idea of prehistory depended not only upon the archaeological discoveries of Frere, Boucher de Perthes, and others but equally upon the effects of the two key theoretical achievements of the nineteenth century, namely UNIFORMITARIANISM and EVOLUTION, which together formed the cornerstone for the disciplines of archaeology, geology, and biology. Prehistory has continued to be a central concept in both archaeology and anthropology, representing the interpretation of evidence for the vast, unrecorded expanse of the preliterate human past, whose history has been partially reconstructed through the painstaking efforts of several generations of prehistoric archaeologists whose work has only begun.

REFERENCES

Bernal, Ignacio. 1980. A history of Mexican archaeology. Thames and Hudson, London.
Boucher de Perthes, J. 1838–1841. De la création. Essai sur l'origine et la progression des êtres. 5 vols. Treuttel et Wurtz, Paris.
———. 1859. Sur les silex taillés des bancs diluviens de la Somme. Comptes Rendus Hebdomadaires de l'Académie des Sciences 49:581.
———. 1860. De l'homme antédiluvien et de ses oeuvres. Jung-Treuttel, Paris.
Clark, Grahame. 1970. Aspects of prehistory. University of California Press, Berkeley and Los Angeles.
Daniel, Glyn, and Colin Renfrew. 1988. The idea of prehistory. Edinburgh University Press.
Dugdale, William. 1656. The antiquities of Warwickshire, illustrated. . . . T. Warren, London.
Frere, John. 1800. Account of flint weapons discovered at Hoxne in Suffolk. Archaeologia 13:204–205.
Grayson, Donald K. 1983. The establishment of human antiquity. Academic Press, New York.
Linnaeaus, Carolus. 1735. Systema naturae. T. Haak, Leyden.
Lubbock, J. 1900. Prehistoric times. 6th ed. Williams and Norgate, London.
Lyell, C. 1863. The geological evidence of the antiquity of man. Murray, London.
Plot, Robert. 1681. The natural history of Staffordshire. Oxford.
Thomsen, Christian Juergen. 1836. Ledetraad til nordisk oldkyndighed. National Museum, Copenhagen.
Toulmin, Stephen, and June Goodfield. 1965. The discovery of time. Harper & Row, New York.

Tournal, Paul. 1833. Considérations générales sur le phénomène des cavernes à ossemens. Annales de Chimie et de Physique 52:161–181.

Tylor, Edward B. 1871. Primitive culture. J. Murray, London.

Ussher, James. 1658. Annals of the world. Deduced from the origin of time, and continued to the beginning of the Emperour Vespasian's reign. . . . E. Tyler for J. Crook and G. Bedell, London.

SOURCES OF ADDITIONAL INFORMATION

Donald Grayson's *The Establishment of Human Antiquity* (New York, Academic Press, 1983) provides a comprehensive overview of the development of prehistory as a concept in Western intellectual history, as well as a lengthy bibliography that includes many primary sources. Another useful introduction to the subject is *The Idea of Prehistory*, by Glyn Daniel and Colin Renfrew (Edinburgh, Edinburgh University Press, 1988). Their bibliographic essay is, however, slanted more toward British publications and popular rather than scholarly sources than is Grayson's list. A very readable introduction to prehistory is Grahame Clark's *Aspects of Prehistory* (Berkeley and Los Angeles, University of California Press, 1970), which includes a final chapter ("The Dawn of Self Awareness," pp. 105–146) in which Clark considers the cognitive aspects of prehistory.

A summary review of European prehistoric studies is S. J. Shennan, "Trends in the study of later European prehistory," *Annual Review of Anthropology* 16(1987):365–382, which has a bibliography of over 100 references. Other important historical works on the development of the idea of prehistory, and those who contributed to it, include A. Laming-Emperaire, *Origines de l'archéologie préhistorique en France* (Paris, Picard, 1964); B. D. Lynch and T. F. Lynch, "The beginnings of a scientific approach to prehistoric archaeology in 17th and 18th century Britain," *Southwestern Journal of Anthropology* 24(1968):33–65; K. Sklenar, *Archaeology in Central Europe: The First 500 Years* (Leicester, U.K., Leicester University Press, 1983); B. M. Marsden, *Pioneers of Prehistory: Leaders and Landmarks in English Archaeology (1500–1900)* (Ormskirk, U.K., Hesketh, 1984); P. Levine, *The Amateur and the Professional: Antiquarians, Historians and Archaeologists in Victorian England, 1838–1886* (Cambridge, Cambridge University Press, 1986); Glyn Daniel, *The Origins and Growth of Archaeology* (Crowell, New York, 1967), and *A Hundred and Fifty Years of Archaeology* (Cambridge, Mass., Harvard University Press, 1975); Glyn Daniel and Colin Renfrew, *The Idea of Prehistory* (1988; see References); and Bruce G. Trigger, *Beyond History: The Methods of Prehistory* (New York, Holt, Rinehart and Winston, 1968) and *A History of Archaeological Thought* (Cambridge, Cambridge University Press, 1989).

For more recent publications, current issues of *Ethnohistory* and other historical journals should be consulted, as well as *Antiquity, American Antiquity, American Anthropologist*; and latest volumes of *Annual Review of Anthropology* should be checked for a more up-to-date review article.

PSEUDOARCHAEOLOGY. Any of a number of current pseudoscientific systems of interpreting the human past, based upon scientifically insupportable, and often irrational, sets of assumptions concerning ARCHAEOLOGY and PREHISTORY. Also called *cult archaeology* (Cole 1980), *folk archaeology* (Michlovic 1990, 1991), and *alternative archaeology* (Hodder 1986).

Some recent examples of pseudoarchaeological interpretations of the human past that have enjoyed considerable popularity and notoriety include the proposition that civilization was originally introduced to the earth by "ancient astronauts" from outer space (Von Daniken 1970); the claim that great civilizations once flourished on the "lost continents" of Atlantis and Mu, which are now purportedly buried beneath the oceans; and that archaeological sites can be located by psychics using extrasensory perception. These are all imaginative scenarios based on unscientific examinations of various kinds of archaeological evidence, some of which have been presented in publications as valid alternatives to the standard interpretations of archaeologists.

As Robert Sharer and Wendy Ashmore noted in their discussion of the phenomenon (Sharer and Ashmore 1979), pseudoarchaeology has been with us for a long time. Irrational and simplistic explanations for complex phenomena and the unknown are probably as old as humanity itself.

The myths, cosmologies, and cosmogonies of all peoples contain references to the intervention of deities and other supernatural beings to account for the origins of the earth, the universe, and humankind. These early attempts at explanation are, however, different in kind from the simplistic, unscientific solutions to various problems in interpreting the human past offered by pseudoarchaeologists as legitimate explanations. The early mythmakers were concerned with explaining the phenomena of the natural world in ways that made sense to them in terms of their own cultural values. Modern pseudoarchaeologists, on the other hand, are usually aware of existing scientific explanations for the material remains and events of past civilizations, but find these unsatisfying on an emotional level. The alternative scenarios they devise tend to reduce the issues to absolute, either/or terms, and emphasize the elimination of uncertainty. The resulting simplistic explanation, however irrational, is less conducive to anxiety than the contemplation of the unknowable and the inexplicable, and of the unanswerable questions this generates; and many archaeological explanations are only partial, incomplete ones, offered tentatively pending the recovery of fuller data, which the public finds unsatisfying. Proponents of pseudoarchaeological explanations are usually hostile to scientific archaeologists and their opinions, although they often seek their professional support to gain authoritative validation for their own positions (Cole 1980).

Many pseudoarchaeological systems have been based in religious doctrine or alternative belief systems, and have sometimes been used to argue in support of such systems. A number of these, including theosophy and Mormonism, were popular in the nineteenth century, and their explanations for surviving phenomena of the past became a part of their creeds. The MIGRATION from the Near East to America in pre-Christian times of Hebrew peoples, who subsequently constructed the mounds and earthworks of North America, is a part of the doctrine of the Mormon Church, as is the attribution of the great cities of pre-Columbian Mesoamerica to a later wave of migrants from the Old World (Silverberg 1968; Book of Mormon 1980). The idea of a foreign race of "mound builders" who inhabited North America in ancient times and constructed the numerous surviving mounds and earthworks of the southern and eastern states was widely accepted in the nineteenth century, and was taken over and incorporated into the teachings of the Mormon Church. Adherents of the Theosophical Society accepted the doctrine of their leaders that high civilizations had existed many thousands of years ago on the "lost continents" of Atlantis and Mu, colonists from which settled the New World and were responsible for the later civilizations of Central America (Wauchope 1962). Both these explanatory systems, along with some others, grew out of philosophical concern over the origins of the native peoples of the New World, which arose immediately after Columbus's voyages and has continued into the twentieth century (see also MIGRATION; NEW WORLD ARCHAE-OLOGY). The late American archaeologist Robert Wauchope has written a lively and very readable account of the "folk" explanations that have been devised for this and other perplexing phenomena (Wauchope 1962).

In addition to the problem of Amerindian origins, pseudoarchaeology in the twentieth century has introduced additional themes and types of explanatory argument that have enjoyed some popularity with the public. Among these are the ideas of Erich von Daniken, who has used visits to earth by ancient astronauts to account for events and passages in the Old Testament, as well as for the development of early civilizations, including that of the Maya (Von Daniken 1970). Barry Fell and others have presented arguments and "evidence" for very early human occupation of the American continents, as well as for the existence of extremely ancient inscriptions in unknown scripts in North America (Fell 1976, 1978; Christensen 1970). Such pseudoexplanatory schemes as these have been found to have widespread influence on the thinking of college students (Bainbridge 1978; Feder 1984), presenting a challenge to all scientific archaeologists to make their discoveries known to the public in more meaningful and understandable terms.

A commonly recurring theme in pseudoarchaeology is hyperdiffusionism, the idea that all major human advances, such as civilization, occurred only once and were subsequently spread to other parts of the world by prehistoric contact. Similarities in art styles, customs, or other cultural traits in widely separated populations are taken to constitute "proof" of such contact. Adherents of this approach have sometimes attributed the origins of New World civilizations to colonists from ancient Egypt, from the lost continents of Atlantis and Mu (Churchward 1926, 1931, 1933; Donnelly 1882), or, among those who agree with von Daniken, to contact with astronauts from other planets. This practice of explaining all cultural commonalities in diffusionist terms, which assumes a single invention for every innovation from pyramids to farming, ignores human inventiveness as well as the common psychological nature of all people that leads them to devise similar solutions to similar problems. In this respect, it is an approach resembling that of many anthropologists and archaeologists of earlier generations, when monocausal explanations of many kinds, including diffusionist ones, were in vogue. Contemporary archaeologists who have investigated the remnants of past cultures are now acutely aware that no human situation is, or ever has been, so simple as this. Tracing the growth and decline of a past culture more often resembles attempting to unravel a complicated fabric whose threads lead off in myriad directions toward origins that remain elusive, posing continuing challenges to even the most knowledgeable.

The extremist fringe of pseudoarchaeology is what has been termed "psychic archaeology" (Goodman 1976; Cole 1980; Feder 1980; McKusick 1982, 1984), which combines the use of dowsing as a technique for locating archaeological sites, the interpretation of artifacts by ESP, and the acceptance of a number of features of other "cult" archaeologies, including influences from Atlantis and Mu, spiritualism, and degenerationism. This branch, as John Cole points out, appears to be "a subcategory of the larger, popular paranormal cult movement . . . which is more reliant upon anecdote, haphazard experiment, and populist exhortation on occult themes than the other[s] . . . " (Cole 1980:15).

Robert Sharer and Wendy Ashmore, in their introductory textbook of archaeology (Sharer and Ashmore 1979), define pseudoarchaeology as the "use of real or imagined archaeological evidence to justify nonscientific accounts about the past" (p. 567), and describe this phenomenon as it presently exists in these terms:

> The term *pseudo-archaeology* refers to a body of popularized accounts that use real or imaginary evidence to justify nonscientific and often overly dramatic reconstructions of prehistory . . . a specific case of the larger phenomenon of pseudo-science which plagues many branches of scientific study. Pseudo-scientists take dramatic stances on unconventional theories, attacking established scientific positions with highly selective data and accusing their proponents of narrow-mindedness and intellectual prejudice. In fact, the pseudo-scientists themselves are usually the ones who are guilty of such unscholarly sins. (Sharer and Ashmore 1979:540)

Nigel Davies, who has devoted an entire book to discussion of this subject (Davies 1979), has noted that pseudoexplanations present "doctored" scientific explanations, oversimplified for the public, that are usually stated in sensational terms to arouse curiosity: "Since the days of the first shamans, Man has been mesmerized by the cult of the mysterious, which made renewed strides in the nineteenth century and remains a growth industry today" (Davies 1979: 241–242).

The truth of this statement is attested by the appeal of supermarket tabloids headlining purportedly true accounts of contacts with extraterrestrials, communication with the dead, and other events beyond the realm of normal human experience, which are also currently popular themes in commercial films. It is perhaps the appeal of the exotic, of the thrillingly extraordinary, that underlies the popularity of pseudoarchaeological explanations and the willingness of the public to believe them. Such scenarios apparently fulfill a psychological need to believe in the reality of experience beyond the mundane, a need also served by the tabloids and the movies. As long as this need exists, there will doubtless be those who, whether sincere believers in the stories they concoct or charlatans who consciously set out to deceive the public, will continue to invent imaginative, if unscientific, ways to explain easily the complex and often seemingly inexplicable events of the past, as well as many eager believers willing to accept their explanations.

REFERENCES

Bainbridge, W. S. 1978. Chariots of the gullible. Skeptical Inquirer 3(2):33–48.
The Book of Mormon. 1980. The Book of Mormon, an account written by the hand of Mormon . . . taken from the plates of Nephi. The Church of Jesus Christ of Latter-day Saints, Salt Lake City.
Christensen, R. T. 1970. Did the Phoenicians cross the Atlantic? Society for Early Historic Archaeology, Newsletter and Proceedings No. 118 (January 12):1–9.
Churchward, James. 1926. The lost continent of Mu. Washburn, New York.
———. 1931. The children of Mu. Washburn, New York.
———. 1933. The sacred symbols of Mu. Washburn, New York.
Cole, John R. 1980. Cult archaeology and unscientific methods and theory. Advances in Archaeological Method and Theory 3:4–37.
Cole, John R., Kenneth L. Feder, Francis B. Harrold, Raymond A. Eve, and Alice B. Kehoe. 1990. On ''Folk archaeology in anthropological perspective.'' Current Anthropology 31(4):390–395. (Commentary)
Davies, Nigel. 1979. Voyagers to the New World. William Morrow, New York.
Donnelly, Ignatius T. T. 1882. Atlantis: The antediluvian world. Harper, New York.
Feder, Kenneth L. 1980. Psychic archaeology: the anatomy of irrationalist prehistoric studies. The Skeptical Inquirer 4(4):32–43.
———. 1984. Irrationality and popular archaeology. American Antiquity 49(3):525–541.
Fell, Barry. 1976. America, B.C. Quadrangle, New York.
———. 1978. Vermont's ancient sites and the larger picture of trans-Atlantic visitations to America, B.C. In Ancient Vermont, W. Cook, ed. Castleton State College, Castleton, Vt., pp. 70–84.
Goodman, J. 1976. Psychic archaeology: time machine to the past. Putnam's, New York.
———. 1982. American genesis: the American Indian and origins of modern man. Berkeley Books, New York.
Hodder, Ian. 1986. Reading the past. Cambridge University Press.
McKusick, Marshall. 1982. Psychic archaeology: theory, method and mythology. Journal of Field Archaeology 9(1):99–118. (A review article)
———. 1984. Psychic archaeology from Atlantis to Oz. Archaeology 37(5):48–52.
Michlovic, Michael G. 1990. Folk archaeology in anthropological perspective. Current Anthropology 31(1):103–107.
———. 1991. On archaeology and folk archaeology: a reply. Current Anthropology 32(3):321–322.
Sharer, Robert, and Wendy Ashmore. 1979. Pseudo-archaeology. In Fundamentals of archaeology. Benjamin Cummings, Menlo Park, Calif., pp. 540–545.
Silverberg, Robert. 1968. Mound builders of ancient America: the archaeology of a myth. New York Graphic Society, Greenwich, Conn.
Von Daniken, E. 1970. Chariots of the gods? Putnams, New York, and Souvenir Press, London, 1969.
Wauchope, Robert. 1962. Lost tribes and sunken continents. University of Chicago Press.

SOURCES OF ADDITIONAL INFORMATION

The most comprehensive and best-informed discussions of the cult phenomenon are the 1980 review article by John Cole in *Advances in Archaeological Method and Theory* (see References); Robert Wauchope's 1962 book, *Lost Tribes and Sunken Continents* (Chicago, University of Chicago Press); the more recent volume by Nigel Davies (Davies 1979; see References for citation); the collection of papers in Francis B. Harrold and Raymond A. Eve, eds., *Cult Archaeology and Creationism: Understanding Psuedoscientific Beliefs About the Past* (Ames, University of Iowa Press, 1987); and the discussions by J. R. Cole, K. L. Feder, F. B. Harrold and R. A. Eve, and Alice B. Kehoe, "On folk archaeology in anthropological perspective," *Current Anthropology* 31(4) (1990):390–393; and Stephen Williams, "Fantastic messages from the past," *Archaeology* 41(5) (1988):62, 64, 70.

Cole's treatment is perhaps the most comprehensive and penetrating, and includes a still-useful, lengthy bibliography. The Wauchope volume was the first published discussion of the cult phenomenon by an archaeologist, and remains a landmark work on the subject. Davies's book, *Voyages to the New World* (New York, William Morrow, 1979), covers most of the major themes of prehistoric contacts and diffusion from Old World to New, including theories of the "lost continents" of Atlantis and Mu (which he traces to their historical roots), the migrationist doctrines of the Mormon Church, and the voyages of ancient mariners, to mention only a few. He also discusses some of the mystical and occultist movements that grew out of and fostered the preservation of some of these ideas, especially during the late nineteenth and early twentieth centuries, placing more recent cultists' ideas in a broader historical perspective. The book contains an extensive bibliography, now out-of-date but still useful.

The book by Harrold and Eve (1987; see above) includes ten articles treating the subject from a variety of viewpoints, including the handling of pseudoarchaeological beliefs among college students in the classroom (see also Feder 1984). More recent discussions include the 1990 article by Michlovic in *Current Anthropology* (see References), the commentary by Cole et al. in the same publication (1990), and the author's reply (Michlovic 1991: see References), which include substantial bibliographies.

The article by Feder in *American Antiquity* (Feder 1984; see References) should be required reading for all archaeologists who teach beginning college classes in archaeology. His discussion of factors leading to the influences of cultist thinking that he observes in his own students is especially convincing.

The subject of pseudoarchaeology has been quite frequently discussed in archaeological journals since the 1980s, and current issues of journals such as *American Antiquity* and *Archaeology* should be consulted for the most recent material, pending another review comparable to Cole's (Cole 1980).

_Q_

QUANTIFICATION. The use of formal or mathematical methods, especially statistical concepts and procedures, in the analysis and interpretation of archaeological data.

Quantitative treatment of archaeological data affords an objective means of measuring patterning and determining whether observed patterns are or are not significant, and sometimes allows archaeologists to support or refute hypotheses with quantified empirical data. Quantitative methods are also used for modeling archaeological research problems, and for testing research models using metric data acquired from field research.

The chief purpose of quantifying archaeological data is the need to generalize from the large number of individual observations the archaeologist acquires from collections of ARTIFACTS, ecofacts, and spatial and contextual data concerning them. Quantification also establishes a convenient comparative framework for data collected by several investigators from different sources. Descriptive statistics provide a rigorous method for summarizing data in ways that quickly reveal any significant patterns that may emerge from the analysis.

Quantification of the simple descriptive kind has long been a part of archaeological analysis, going back virtually to the beginning of "scientific" archaeology in the 1930s and 1940s (Clark and Stafford 1982:100). The earliest such efforts were aimed at deriving and clarifying cultural chronologies, at classifying or describing ASSEMBLAGES in terms of artifact type frequencies, or at deriving artifact types themselves, based on combinations and frequencies of various metric or descriptive traits (Driver and Kroeber 1932). Quantification in archaeology remained in this state into the 1950s, when the earliest research using statistical INFERENCE began to appear.

Prior to the 1960s, the rather limited uses made of statistical methods by archaeologists were usually restricted to descriptive techniques for summarizing or reducing quantitative information in ways that would highlight patterns and relationships which could be readily discerned on cursory examination of data tables or other kinds of summary data displays.

The use of statistics in problem-oriented research began in the early 1960s, as one aspect of the "NEW" ARCHAEOLOGY and its objective of recovering data that would reveal the behavioral processes of the past; but it was not until the 1970s that explicit SAMPLING strategies, based on probability theory, became a frequent feature of archaeological research designs (Clark 1982; Clark and Stafford 1982). Such sampling designs have now become routine, and since about 1970 the use of statistical and probabilistic methods has become a standard part of archaeological data collection and analysis. The availability of sophisticated computer equipment, and of software packages enabling archaeologists to apply a variety of previously inaccessible techniques, including those of multivariate analysis, to their data has led to the explosion of statistically oriented archaeological literature (Doran and Hodson 1975). Unfortunately this literature includes numerous examples "where the power and sophistication of the mathematics far outstrip both the relevance and reliability of the data . . . " (Cowgill 1986:370). Data reliability continues to be a problem in archaeology, where small sample sizes and inconsistent methods and standards for data collection can lead to major distortions, contributing to such problems as incomparability of results and underestimation of ASSEMBLAGE diversity.

In archaeology, quantitative methods have been applied to such problems as ARTIFACT classification; the construction of cultural chronologies from stratigraphic data; SPATIAL ANALYSIS of settlement data and mapping of artifact distributions on sites; hypothesis testing, using whatever quantitative data may be available; studies of prehistoric ecology and SUBSISTENCE, including faunal and paleobotanical studies; modeling various kinds of research problems; and recently the measurement of archaeological diversity (Heizer and Cook 1960; Ford 1962; Hodson, Kendall, and Tautu 1971; Spaulding 1971; Clarke 1972; Keighley 1973; Orton 1973, 1980; Cowgill 1974, 1982, 1986, 1989; Grayson 1979; Renfrew 1979; Whallon and Brown 1982; Hietala 1984; Leonard and Jones 1989; see also ARCHAEOMETRY).

The use of quantitative data for constructing simulation models has had a mixed success at best (Sabloff 1981), due to the virtual impossibility of identifying and quantifying all possibly relevant variables that may affect results when modeling the complex cultural situations with which archaeologists deal.

Quantitative and statistical literacy are now absolutely necessary parts of an archaeologist's skills. It is quite possible that in the future, statistical methods will replace the time-honored intuitive and inferential methods on which archaeological interpretation has been traditionally based, and will become the standard procedure for collecting and reporting archaeological data in all situations.

REFERENCES

Clark, G., and C. R. Stafford. 1982. Quantification in American archaeology: a historical perspective. World Archaeology 14:98–119.

Clark, G. A. 1982. Quantifying archaeological research. Advances in Archaeological Method and Theory 5:217–273.

Clarke, David L., ed. 1972. Models in archaeology. Methuen, London.

Cowgill, George L. 1974. Quantitative studies of urbanization at Teotihuacán. In Mesoamerican archaeology: new approaches, Norman Hammond, ed. Duckworth, London, pp. 363–396.

————. 1982. Clusters of objects and associations between variables: two approaches to archaeological classification. In Essays in archaeological typology, R. Whallon and J. Brown, eds. Center for American Archaeology Press, Evanston, Ill., pp. 30–55.

————.1986. Archaeological applications of mathematical and formal methods. In American archaeology past and future, David J. Meltzer, Don D. Fowler, and Jeremy A. Sabloff, eds. Society for American Archaeology/Smithsonian Institution Press, Washington, D.C., pp. 369–393.

————. 1989. Formal approaches in archaeology. In Archeological thought in America, C. C. Lamberg-Karlovksy, ed. Cambridge University Press, pp. 74–88.

Doran, J. E., and F. R. Hodson. 1975. Mathematics and computers in archaeology. Harvard University Press, Cambridge, Mass.

Driver, H. E., and A. L. Kroeber. 1932. Quantitative expression of cultural relationships. University of California Publications in American Archaeology and Ethnology 31:211–256.

Ford, J. A. 1962. A quantitative method for deriving cultural chronology. Pan American Union Technical Manual 1. Washington, D.C.

Grayson, Donald K. 1979. On the quantification of vertebrate archaeofaunas. Advances in Archaeological Method and Theory 2:199–237.

Heizer, R. F., and S. F. Cook. 1960. Quantitative methods in archaeology. Viking Fund Publications in Anthropology 28. University of Chicago Press.

Hietala, Harold J., ed. 1984. Intrasite spatial analysis in archaeology. Cambridge University Press.

Hodson, F. R., D. G. Kendall, and P. Tautu, eds. 1971. Mathematics in the archaeological and historical sciences. Edinburgh University Press.

Keighley, J. 1973. Some problems in the quantitative interpretation of ceramic data. In The explanation of culture change: models in prehistory, Colin Renfrew, ed. Duckworth, London, pp. 131–136.

Leonard, Robert D., and George T. Jones, eds. 1989. Quantifying diversity in archaeology. Cambridge University Press.

Orton, Clive R. 1973. The tactical uses of models in archaeology—the SHERD project. In The explanation of culture change: models in prehistory, Colin Renfrew, ed. Duckworth, London, pp. 137–139.

————. 1980. Mathematics in archaeology. Collins, London.

Renfrew, Colin. 1979 Transformations: mathematical approaches to culture change. Academic Press, New York.

Sabloff, Jeremy A., ed. 1981. Simulations in archaeology. University of New Mexico Press, Albuquerque.

Spaulding, A. C. 1971. Some elements of quantitative archaeology. In Mathematics in the archaeological and historical sciences, F. R. Hodson, D. G. Kendall, and P. Tautu, eds. Edinburgh University Press, pp. 3–16.

Whallon, Robert, and James A. Brown, eds. 1982. Essays on archaeological typology. Center for American Archaeology Press, Evanston, Ill.

SOURCES OF ADDITIONAL INFORMATION

Background sources on the use of quantitative methods in archaeology are fairly numerous. The review by Clark in *Advances in Archaeological Method and Theory* (Clark 1982; see References) discusses the historical development of formal methods in archaeology as well as their uses, and reviews the literature listed in the 11-page bibliography. The two general discussions by Cowgill (1986, 1989; see References) are equally useful; Doran and Hodson (1975; see References) is still an informative source for computer applications. The specialized reviews by Grayson on problems of faunal data analysis (1979; see References), and R. Barry Lewis, "The analysis of contingency tables in archaeology," *Advances in Archaeological Method and Theory* 9(1986):276–310, are essential for those utilizing the methods they cover.

Book-length treatments of subjects in quantification include Mark S. Aldenderfer, ed., *Quantitative Research in Archaeology: Progress and Prospects* (Newbury Park, Calif., Sage, 1987); and Stephen Shennan, *Quantifying Archaeology* (Academic Press, New York, 1988). An article evaluating the results of applying formal methods to archaeological data is Jim Doran, "Formal methods and archaeological theory, a perspective," *World Archaeology* 18(1)(1986):20–32.

The June 1982 issue of *World Archaeology* (vol. 14, no. 1) was devoted to quantitative methods; its nine papers cover a broad range, including applications in ceramic analysis, zooarchaeology, taphonomy, lithics, cluster analysis, and spatial analysis, as well as the historical treatment by Clark and Stafford (see References).

For latest literature on quantitative methods, current issues of *American Antiquity, American Anthropologist, Journal of Archaeological Science,* and *Archaeometry* should be consulted, as well as *Annual Review of Anthropology* and *Archaeological Method and Theory* for possible future reviews.

R

RELATIVE DATING. Estimation of the ages of ARTIFACTS relative to one another by establishing a chronological sequence of events in the past, and relating specific finds to this known sequence. Unlike CHRONOMETRIC DATING, relative dating cannot produce absolute dates in actual calendar years, but can determine which items from the material record are older or younger than others, and aid in the construction of useful chronological schemes based upon stratigraphic relationships, stylistic and technological change, and other factors.

A central problem in archaeology since its beginning has been that of establishing a time frame for the prehistoric past (Petrie 1899; Spier 1917; Brainerd 1951; Robinson 1951; Ford 1962; Rowe 1962a, 1962b; Renfrew and Sterud 1969; Schiffer 1975; Taylor and Meighan 1978; Graslund 1987; Bird and Frankel 1991; Chamberlain 1991). In the nineteenth century, the discovery of the vast amount of time that humans have lived on the earth raised questions about the sequence of events in this greatly expanded human past, in addition to raising philosophical questions. For archaeologists, a major problem became that of developing a means of classifying this huge expanse of time, a way of ordering past cultural developments in a manner that would make it possible to acquire a coherent perspective for interpreting the past and its material remains. Relative methods of dating were the initial response to this need for a temporal perspective, and until the development of chronometric dating techniques in the physical sciences in the twentieth century, these were the only methods available. Many of them remain useful today, and are sometimes used in conjunction with chronometric methods now available (Michels 1972; Read 1979).

Relative dating methods are of three basic types. The first is a group based on principles derived from geology. Among these are methods utilizing the principles of STRATIGRAPHY and superposition, according to which older materials will underlie later ones in stratified deposits (Rowe 1961). Also included in this category are geochronological methods derived from geologic dating of the Pleistocene epoch. One of these is dating from deep-sea cores, which reflect the known periodic worldwide climatic changes that accompanied alternating periods of glacial advance and the warmer interglacials. Another geological technique is the dating of archaeological deposits associated with ash layers from volcanic eruptions of known date. Cultural materials underlying and overlying such levels can be relatively dated as older or younger than the eruption date (Aitken 1988, 1990).

Methods based on biological data include the study of faunal remains of past food species, and relating these to known spatial and temporal distributions of such species in the past; and *palynology*, in which pollen diagrams obtained from sequences at specific archaeological sites are related to vegetational time charts developed for various parts of the world covering the past 10,000 years. Another biologically based technique is that of ordering fossilized skeletal remains of early humans and hominids in a developmental sequence, according to the principles of evolutionary theory.

The third category of relative dating methods is based on human cultural characteristics, including technological development. The THREE-AGE SYSTEM devised by Christian J. Thomsen in the 1830s was the first example of this type of relative chronology, in which human cultural development was classified into three "ages" according to the principal material used for making artifacts (Thomsen 1836; Rodden 1981). The earliest of these was the Stone Age, in which all implements were made from lithic materials; this was followed by "ages" of bronze and iron. This scheme was later revised to reflect significant temporal changes in stoneworking technology, by dividing the Stone Age into the Paleolithic period, when only chipped and flaked tools were produced, and the Neolithic period, when grinding and polishing technologies were added to stoneworking techniques. A third period, the Mesolithic, characterized by many small tools called microliths, was a later addition.

Two other relative dating methods using cultural principles were of great importance to archaeologists prior to the development of chronometric techniques, and have remained useful into the present. The first of these is SERIATION, a method pioneered by Sir Flinders Petrie in the 1890s, in which artifacts are arranged into a temporal or other linear sequence according to observed, regularly recurring patterns of stylistic variation. This technique has been of great value in establishing ceramic sequences for entire archaeological regions, and continues to be a principal dating technique for archaeological materials of many kinds (Petrie 1899; Smith 1955; Kendall 1963; Dunnell 1970; Gelfand 1971; Cowgill 1972; Marquardt 1978; Braun 1985; see also SERIATION). The second method is *cross-dating*, in which artifacts of known date and provenance occur in foreign contexts, usually as trade goods, allowing the archaeologist to date the foreign cultural context in which they are found. For example, a Roman amphora manufactured in the first century B.C. may be recovered from an archaeological deposit in a fishing hamlet on the Baltic, permitting the excavator to date any materials associated with it in the same stratigraphic level to the time period of its manufacture.

This group of basic relative dating methods permitted archaeologists to develop chronological sequences for most archaeologically studied areas of the world during the first half of the twentieth century. Today they continue to be used, often in combination with chronometric methods such as radiocarbon dating or inscriptional records, for constructing and refining regional cultural sequences. Together, they have enabled archaeologists to establish a chronological orientation to the prehistoric past that has permitted coherent interpretations of the material remains of early human groups to be developed, and allowed inferences to be made about the dynamic processes of human interaction in the past that resulted in the creation of the ARCHAEOLOGICAL RECORD (Kitchen 1991).

REFERENCES

Aitken, Martin J. 1988. The Thera eruption, continuing discussion of the dating I. Resume dating. Archaeometry 30(1):165–182.

———. 1990. Science-based dating in archeology. Longman, London.

Barros, Philip L. F. de 1982. The effects of variable site occupation span on the results of frequency seriation. American Antiquity 47(2):291–315.

Bird, C. F. M., and David Frankel. 1991. Problems in constructing a prehistoric regional sequence: Holocene south-east Australia. World Archaeology 23(2):179–192.

Brainerd, George W. 1951. The place of chronological ordering in archaeological analysis. American Antiquity 14(4):301–313.

Braun, D. P. 1985. Absolute seriation: a time-series approach. In For concordance in archaeological analysis: bridging data structure, quantitative technique, and theory, C. Carr, ed. Westport, Kansas City, Mo., pp. 509–539.

Chamberlain, A. T. 1991. A chronological framework for human origins. World Archaeology 23(2):137–146.

Cowgill, G. L. 1972. Models, methods and techniques for seriation. In Models in archaeology, David L. Clarke, ed. Methuen, London, pp. 381–424.

Dunnell, Robert C. 1970. Seriation method and its evaluation. American Antiquity 35:305–319.

Ford, James A. 1962. A quantitative method for deriving cultural chronology. Pan American Union, Technical Manual No. 1. Washington, D.C. Reprinted as Museum Brief No. 9, Museum of Anthropology, University of Missouri-Columbia, 1972.

Gelfand, Alan E. 1971. Seriation methods of archaeological materials. American Antiquity 36:263–274.

Graslund, Bo. 1987. The birth of prehistoric chronology: dating methods and dating systems in nineteenth-century Scandinavian archaeology. Cambridge University Press.

Kendall, David G. 1963. A statistical approach to Flinders Petrie's sequence-dating. Bulletin of the International Statistical Institute 40:657–680.

Kitchen, K. A. 1991. The chronology of ancient Egypt. World Archaeology 23(2):201–208.

Marquardt, William H. 1978. Advances in archaeological seriation. Advances in Archaeological Method and Theory 1:257–314.

Michels, Joseph W. 1972. Dating methods. Annual Review of Anthropology 1:113–126.

Petrie, W. M. Flinders. 1899. Sequences in prehistoric remains. Journal of the Royal Anthropological Institute n.s. 29:295–301.

Read, Dwight W. 1979. The effective use of radiocarbon dates in the seriation of archaeological sites. In Radiocarbon dating, R. Berger and H. E. Suess, eds. University of California Press, Los Angeles, pp. 89–94.

Renfrew, Colin, and Gene Sterud. 1969. Close-proximity analysis: a rapid method for the ordering of archaeological materials. American Antiquity 34(3):265–277.

Robinson, W. S. 1951. A method for chronologically ordering archaeological deposits. American Antiquity 14(4):293–301.

Rodden, J. 1981. The development of the three age system: archaeology's first paradigm. In Towards a history of archaeology, Glyn Daniel, ed. Thames and Hudson, London, pp. 51–68.

Rowe, John H. 1961. Stratigraphy and seriation. American Antiquity 26(3):324–330.

———. 1962a. Stages and periods in archaeological interpretation. Southwestern Journal of Anthropology 18:40–54.

———. 1962b. Worsaae's Law and the use of grave lots for archaeological dating. American Antiquity 28(2):129–137.

Schiffer, Michael B. 1975. Arrangement vs. seriation of sites: a new approach for relative temporal relationships. In The Cache River archaeological project . . . , M. B. Schiffer and J. H. House, eds. Arkansas Archaeological Survey Research Series 8. Fayetteville, pp. 257–263.

Smith, Robert E. 1955. Ceramic sequence at Uaxactun, Guatemala, vols. 1 and 2. Middle American Research Institute Publication no. 20. Tulane University, New Orleans.

Spier, Leslie. 1917. An outline for a chronology of Zuni ruins. American Museum of Natural History Anthropological Papers 18, no. 3. New York.

Taylor, R. E., and D. W. Meighan, eds. 1978. Chronologies in New World archaeology. Academic Press, New York.

Thomsen, C. J. 1836. Ledetraad til nordisk oldkyndighed. Stockholm.

Timei Chen and Zhang Yinyun. 1991. Palaeolithic chronology and the possible coexistence of Homo erectus and Homo sapiens in China. World Archaeology 23(2):147–154.

SOURCES OF ADDITIONAL INFORMATION

For historical background material on seriation, see L. Johnson, Jr., "Introduction to imaginary models for archaeological scaling and clustering," in Models in Archaeology, David L. Clarke, ed. (London, Methuen, 1972), pp. 309–379, historical material on pp. 315–318; Kendall 1963; and Rowe 1961 (see References for citations). For an overall discussion of seriation techniques, their theoretical foundations, and the role of seriation in archaeological research, see the review article by William H. Marquardt, "Advances in archaeological seriation," in Advances in Archaeological Method and Theory 1(1978):257–314; also see SERIATION.

Other reviews of dating methods are Jeffrey S. Dean, "Independent dating in archaeological analysis," Advances in Archaeological Method and Theory 1(1978):223–255; and Barbara A. Purdy and David E. Clark, "Weathering of inorganic materials: dating and other applications," Advances in Archaeological Method and Theory 10(1987):211–253.

World Archaeology 23, no. 2 (October 1991) is devoted to chronologies in archaeology;

the introductory paper by J. A. J. Gowlett, "Introduction: uncertain time" (pp. 135–136), discusses the current role of relative dating. Other papers discuss chronologies for human origins, Paleolithic chronology in China, problems in New World, Australian, and Egyptian chronologies, and the development of greater precision in relative sequences.

For other current literature, consult forthcoming issues of *American Antiquity*, *Journal of Field Archaeology*, *World Archaeology*, and *Archaeometry*, as well as appropriate annual reviews.

S

SAMPLING. The procedure for selecting archaeological units for detailed investigation by excavation, surface collection, or other methods. Sampling strategies used by most contemporary archaeologists are based on probability theory, although nonprobabilistic sampling methods, which have traditionally been employed by archaeologists for more than a century, are still used to some extent.

Since funding is very rarely available for investigating archaeological sites or site groups in their entirety, archaeologists must employ sampling techniques to select a limited number of spatial areas, or sampling units, that are likely to yield data representative of the site or area as a whole. The selection of units for excavation or intensive surface collection is now most frequently a probabilistic sampling procedure, at least in a project's initial stages. Sampling strategy will depend on many factors, including project goals and the size of the unit that will be investigated; but the overall aim of any sampling strategy is to maximize the degree to which the sample is representative of the site's contents as a whole (Read 1986).

The basic assumption of sampling theory is that the characteristics of a *population*—that is, the totality of all units, such as archaeological SITES, people, ARTIFACTS, excavation units, or whatever is being investigated—can be estimated, within a certain defined range of error, by determining the characteristics of a carefully chosen sample of its members. This sample is normally selected by applying the laws of probability.

Sampling by probability theory has been widely used by archaeologists only since the 1960s (Nance 1983). Prior to that time, sampling was generally of the "grab" or judgmental types (see below), based on convenience, visibility of remains, or the archaeologist's preferences or opinions concerning the potentially most productive places to dig. Probabilistic sampling began to be adopted as a standard archaeological research technique as part of the statistically based methodology developed by "new" archaeologists of the 1960s and 1970s (Binford 1975; Chenhall 1975; Redman 1975; Flannery 1976a, 1976b, 1976c; Plog 1976).

According to probability theory, the best representation of a population's statistically defined characteristics, or parameters, can be obtained by taking a *random sample*, one in which each unit of the sampled population has an equal chance of being selected for investigation. Random sampling has become quite popular in recent decades, particularly among North American archaeologists, as a method for obtaining reliable data from limited excavation.

Random samples are developed by using a table of random numbers to select from the universe of units in an archaeological site or SURVEY area those that will become part of the sample to be collected or excavated. When a study area is surveyed, a grid-square or other systematic method of dividing the area into equal, numbered units will be laid out. Each unit is assigned a unique number, and the random number table is used to select those to be investigated. Using this method results in a *simple random sample*, that is, one in which each unit has an equal probability of being included in the sample.

In many, if not most, research situations, the simple random sampling method will require some refinement in order to ensure collecting representative data. This will be true if, for example, the site's boundaries have not been clearly defined or cannot be located with certainty, or if random sampling results in oversampling of some areas of the site and excludes other areas (Renfrew and Bahn 1991). In such instances, a *stratified random sampling* method may be applied, in which the area of study is divided into different zones, based on current land use (e.g., forest vs. cultivated land) or physical features such as differences in elevation, soil, or vegetation zones, with each zone allotted a number of sampling units proportional to its area in relation to the whole. If 90 percent of the study area is covered by forest, 90 percent of the sampling units must be in the forested zone, and so on.

A second solution to this problem is *systematic sampling*. Using this method, a sample consisting of equally spaced units will be selected, for instance, every third grid square. This method has its hazards, the main one being that one risks missing (or including) every example in a regular pattern of distribution, resulting in a very biased sample. Combining stratification with systematic random sampling is a solution to this problem. A stratified systematic random sample also makes it possible to extend the grid-square system in any direction, making it unnecessary to define site boundaries, and is therefore very useful in situations where boundary definition is difficult or impossible. Stratified systematic random sampling has proven to be a highly efficient strategy in many archaeological situations.

In addition to these probabilistic methods, archaeologists may still use nonprobabilistic sampling when it is warranted by circumstances. Nonprobabilistic methods may be regarded as complementing probabilistic methods to some degree, since the latter are often used in the earlier stages of a field project, and the former in the later stages, when considerable information about the site has already been acquired.

Among the most common of nonprobabilistic methods is what is usually called judgmental sampling, a procedure in which the archaeologist decides, on the basis of what he or she knows about the area of investigation, to pursue additional excavations in nonrandomly selected parts of the site. This may be done to increase the number of rare artifacts recovered, or to fully expose an entire known structure, burial, or other feature. Such excavation may also be pursued when probabilistic sampling has revealed information on what kinds of localities within the SITE are most likely to yield significant concentrations of artifacts or features, which will then be nonrandomly selected for further work (Shott 1987).

Another nonprobabilistic method of sampling sometimes employed by archaeologists engaged in reconnaissance surveys is what is called "grab" sampling. As the name implies, this is an uncontrolled, opportunistic method, which is most often used when limitations of time or accessibility of remains make it the only practical one. For example, a survey team may decide to record only those sites with structures that can be seen with binoculars, through heavy vegetation cover while traveling through an isolated area on a dirt track traversable only by a four-wheel-drive vehicle. Such a strategy might be used if time, weather conditions, or other constraints do not permit exploration on foot. Results, of course, will be highly biased, in ways that cannot be statistically measured or described.

An important part of sampling is selecting an appropriate sampling fraction, or determining what size of sample will be necessary in order to obtain representative results. The requisite percentage of the target area that will constitute an adequate sample is determined by using an appropriate statistical formula for the sampling method selected (Asch 1975:175–178).

The type of physical units constituting the sample will normally be part of the research design, and will depend upon such factors as the amount of prior knowledge about the site or area of investigation, and whether project goals emphasize producing a complete inventory of common artifacts, or are focused on architectural features, spatial analysis, establishing chronological relationships, or other objectives, since collecting each of these types of data may require a different sampling method. Basically, the physical units used in sampling will be either quadrats, that is, grid squares, or transects. The latter are linear paths, or traverses, that comprise a large, lengthy segment of the landscape. Transects are frequently used as sampling units in regional surveys, or for investigating settlement in areas covered by dense vegetation, such as tropical rain forest. Transect sampling has frequently been used in such tropical environments as Mesoamerica. A notable example of this type of sampling research was the study of settlement density in the intersite area between the prehistoric Maya cities of Tikal and Yaxha in the Department of El Petén, Guatemala, by Anabel Ford, in which the investigator surveyed 40 percent of a 500-meter-wide transect through the rain forest extending the entire 28-kilometer distance separating these two major ruined cities (Ford 1981, 1986).

Quadrat or test-pit sampling is a standard method that can be used in a variety of situations. Test pits, excavated grid squares selected for excavation by the sampling design, are especially useful for investigating deep, stratified sites with many occupation levels, since stratigraphy will usually be visible on the walls of the test pit, facilitating the construction of a relative chronology. Test-pit sampling is also a useful technique in regional surveys when visibility of surface remains is poor, although it may not reveal the presence of small, low-density sites (Nance and Ball 1986).

The *scale* at which the investigation is focused (e.g., household, community, region) will also be important in choosing sampling designs. Sampling methods selected will often differ from season to season in an ongoing project, with nonprobabilistic strategies, especially judgmental sampling, perhaps replacing random methods to varying degrees as more information is acquired about the area under study (Redman 1987).

Sampling strategies, like research designs, must be frequently reevaluated in order to obtain the data required to meet project goals, which are also likely to undergo change during the course of a major field investigation. Charles Redman, in his critique of archaeological sampling methods and research design, suggests that evaluation should be done during, or at the conclusion of, each stage of a project (Redman 1987).

While each probabilistic sampling method presents problems of reliability and bias, these can usually be mitigated by modifying the sampling design. Probabilistic methods have the considerable advantage of allowing statistical analysis of resulting data, and will doubtless continue to constitute a standard approach used in archaeological research design for many years to come.

REFERENCES

Asch, David L. 1975. On sample size problems and the uses of nonprobabilistic sampling. In Sampling in archaeology, James W. Mueller, ed. University of Arizona Press, Tucson, pp. 170–191.

Binford, Lewis R. 1975. Sampling, judgment and the archaeological record. In Sampling in archaeology, J. W. Mueller, ed. University of Arizona Press, Tucson, pp. 251–257.

Chenhall, Robert G. 1975. A rationale for archaeological sampling. In Sampling in archaeology, J. W. Mueller, ed. University of Arizona Press, Tucson, pp. 3–15.

Flannery, K. V. 1976a. Sampling by intensive surface collection. In The early Mesoamerican village, Kent V. Flannery, ed. Academic Press, New York, pp. 51–61.

———. 1976b. Excavating deep communities by transect samples. In The early Mesoamerican village, Kent V. Flannery, ed. Academic Press, New York, pp. 68–72.

———. 1976c. The trouble with regional sampling. In The early Mesoamerican village, K. V. Flannery, ed. Academic Press, New York, pp. 159–160.

Ford, Anabel. 1981. Conditions for the evolution of complex societies: the development of the central lowland Maya. Ph.D. dissertation, Department of Anthropology, University of California, Santa Barbara.

————. 1986. Population growth and social complexity, an examination of settlement and environment in the central Maya lowlands. Anthropological Research papers No. 35. Arizona State University, Tempe.

Nance, Jack D. 1983. Regional sampling in archaeological survey: the statistical perspective. Advances in Archaeological Method and Theory 6:289–356.

Nance, Jack D., and Bruce F. Ball. 1986. No surprises? The reliability and validity of test pit sampling. American Antiquity 51(3):457–483.

Plog, Stephen. 1976. Relative efficiencies of sampling techniques for archaeological surveys. In The early Mesoamerican village, K. V. Flannery, ed. Academic Press, New York, pp. 136–158.

Read, Dwight. 1986. Sampling procedures for regional surveys: a problem of representativeness and effectiveness. Journal of Field Archaeology 13(4):477–491.

Redman, Charles L. 1975. Productive sampling strategies for archaeological sites. In Sampling in archaeology, James W. Mueller, ed. University of Arizona Press, Tucson, pp. 147–154.

————. 1987. Surface collection, sampling and research design: a retrospective. American Antiquity 52(2):249–265.

Renfrew, Colin, and Paul Bahn. 1991. Archaeology: theories, methods and practice. Thames and Hudson, New York.

Shott, Michael J. 1987. Feature discovery and the sampling requirements of archaeological evaluations. Journal of Field Archaeology 14(3):359–371.

SOURCES OF ADDITIONAL INFORMATION

For a brief, useful elementary summary (with illustrations) of archaeological sampling strategies, see pp. 66–67 in Renfrew and Bahn (1991); for a more detailed discussion, see Plog 1976 (citations in References). Another source of basic information is S. Ragir, "A review of techniques for archaeological sampling," in *Field Methods in Archaeology*, R. Hester, R. G. Heizer, and J. A. Graham, eds. (Palo Alto, Calif., Mayfield, 1967), pp. 181-198. For an in-depth discussion of individual sampling methods, their appropriate uses, and relative merits, see the papers in James W. Mueller, ed., *Sampling in Archaeology* (Tucson, University of Arizona Press, 1975).

A review of twenty years' experience with the use of various sampling strategies, and an evaluation of those that have proved most useful in particular kinds of situations, as well as suggestions and valuable commentary on the frequent need for combining a variety of strategies in a single project, is Redman 1987 (see References), which also includes a review of the literature through the mid-1980s. This is a very practical treatment of how sampling does (and does not) work in real-world situations. Redman also emphasizes the importance of changing sampling methods as the site becomes better known, that is, in later seasons, judgmental sampling becomes more important and random sampling less so; and surface collection may not always be a warranted first step.

For criticism of sampling practices in archaeology, see the critical review by Bonnie Laird Hole, "Sampling in archaeology: a critique," *Annual Review of Anthropology* 9(1980):217–234. For discussion of statistical problems in sampling, see the paper by Jack Nance (1983; see References). For discussions of reliability, see George Cowgill, "Some sampling and reliability problems in archaeology," in *Archéologie et calculateurs: Problèmes semiologiques et mathématiques*, M. J. Gardin and M. Gardin, eds. (Paris, Centre National de la Recherche Scientifique, 1970), pp. 161–175; and B. A. Nicholson, "A comparative evaluation of four sampling techniques and of the reliability of microdebitage as a cultural indicator in regional surveys," *Plains Anthropologist* 28(1983):278–281.

For access to recent literature, see the bibliographies in Nance and Ball 1986; Redman 1987; and Shott 1987 (see References). To update this material, see current issues of *American Antiquity*, *Journal of Archaeological Science*, and the most recent annual volumes of *Archaeological Method and Theory* and *Annual Review of Anthropology*.

SEASONALITY. 1. The scheduled collection of food resources by human groups at specific times of the year when the resources of a particular microenvironment are most abundant, often while in temporary camps established near the resource location to facilitate its exploitation. 2. The settlement system of human populations characterized by periodic seasonal changes of residence in order to be close to important food resources at the time when they are most abundant. Also called *transhumance*. 3. The focus of archaeological investigations of indicators in the ARCHAEOLOGICAL RECORD of seasonal exploitation by past human populations of one or more specific food resources, using the methods of BIOARCHAEOLOGY to determine the season of their most intensive exploitation.

Gregory Monks, in a review of seasonality, has noted that archaeological seasonality studies are an area of investigation that has not been well defined in terms of its scope, goals, and methods (Monks 1981). The concept of human seasonality, the seasonally scheduled movements of populations for purposes of exploiting resources at times when they are most abundant, emerged from ecologically oriented archaeological studies of SUBSISTENCE and SETTLEMENT PATTERNS in the late 1950s and 1960s. In particular, the investigations by Richard MacNeish (MacNeish 1964, 1967, 1972, 1981; MacNeish, Patterson, and Neely 1972) and Kent Flannery (1968) of early maize cultivation in the Tehuacán Valley of Puebla, Mexico, resulted in a model for the development of an agricultural economy in Mesoamerica from an earlier pattern of seasonally scheduled resource collection. According to this model, the transition from hunting and gathering to FOOD PRODUCTION was accomplished through an intermediate period when food resources were systematically exploited by increasingly larger aggregations of people, according to a seasonally scheduled pattern. In this model, "population pressure and environmental factors are not sufficient conditions for plant domestication, but cultural factors, such as scheduling and diffusion, are" (MacNeish 1981:42). In other words, localized seasonal scheduling of harvest activities, and the spread of this behavioral pattern to a wider area, became the primary cultural processes that ultimately led to the development of an agricultural economy in this region.

According to the seasonality model developed by Kent Flannery (Flannery 1968), small family bands of hunter-gatherers exploiting the same resource area first began to come together at some seasons, forming temporarily larger social units, or macrobands, during the harvest season. Their seasonal encampments formed identifiable archaeological SITES, in which the remnants of their food-gathering activities have been preserved in varying degrees. This seasonal scheduling of specialized resource procurement had the long-range effects of contracting the size of the home range and promoting an increasingly sedentary lifeway.

The annual seasonal round of these hunter-gatherers gradually became contracted, with groups occupying fewer resource camps for longer periods at a time. Eventually, the habit of making several moves during the year was reduced to a pattern of perhaps two seasonal moves between two principal resource zones located in different microenvironments, each having its own distinctive set of food resources. In Flannery's model, these temporary residential sites were most likely to be located where two or more resource zones intersected or overlapped, allowing more efficient exploitation. For example, an area where nuts could be harvested by one segment of the population while deer were being hunted during their fat season by another segment would have permitted a more efficient use of available human energy than concentration on a single resource, as well as contributing to dietary diversity.

By the time this stage was reached, a human population residing for half the year in a location where a few crops were being cultivated could, during the other portion of the year, relocate to a camp near a forested area to harvest wild nuts and hunt the animals that were abundant in the forest environment. Foods procured during this time of intensive activity could then be preserved and transported back to the home site or hamlet for storage, to supplement the products of small-scale cultivation during the balance of the year. Over time, such a pattern may easily have altered into one in which only the younger men left the community for a time to hunt deer, perhaps taking with them some of the youths to collect nuts, while the women, children, and older males remained in what was becoming their permanent home community to tend the crops. In this manner, an increasing pattern of SEDENTARINESS became established. Flannery analyzed this change in system theoretic terms, and attempted to account for each change in terms of positive feedback processes (Flannery 1968).

The periodic experience of living in larger population units, with a resulting increase in the breadth and intensity of social contacts outside the local group, prepared seasonal populations for the time when, with full agricultural production, they would live in larger, permanent communities. These temporary macroband aggregations would also have provided opportunities for mate selection outside the local group, and for the sharing of important common rituals and ceremonies, an activity that itself may have become an important part of the regularly scheduled cycle. In Mesoamerica, where the archaeological evidence for this model was acquired, seasonal scheduling of rituals could have been a very significant factor in development of the regionwide ceremonial calendar shared by all native Mesoamerican peoples, which is still observed in many localities. In the more mundane realm, the necessity of developing methods for preserving foods, and facilities for storing them, contributed to both technological innovation and the growth of organizational complexity, processes that further contributed to the development of a more complex pattern of life (Flannery 1972).

Gregory Monks defines seasonality as "the time of year at or during which a particular event is most likely to occur" (Monks 1981:178), and adopts the concept of the "economic season" proposed by M. A. Jochim (1976:45) as a unit of analysis in seasonality studies. The economic season is derived from the recurring annual sequence of predictable subsistence-related events, and does not necessarily correspond to a four-season scheme. Estimating seasons at which particular cultural and subsistence activities took place in the past permits archaeologists to reconstruct subsistence patterns, and the ways in which these influenced, and were influenced by, other subsystems of the CULTURE, such as religion and its associated rituals.

Human seasonality is part of the subsistence and settlement system of a community, and characteristically leaves its traces in the archaeological SETTLEMENT PATTERN, as well as in the material culture and bioarchaeological remains of transhumant populations. Seasonal movements of human groups are distinguishable from MIGRATION in their periodic, temporary nature. Although seasonal changes of residence may involve the relocation of an entire human community, this is a short-term phenomenon, repetitive and structured, in contrast with the permanent relocation in a new regional habitat characteristic of migrating populations.

Ethnographic studies have provided considerable data on periodic population movements dictated by seasonal resource availability (Suttles 1951, 1960; Barnett 1955; Oberg 1973; Jochim 1976; Stuart 1977; Blomberg 1983; Henderson 1983; Powell 1984; Rocek 1988). Such studies are an invaluable adjunct to the now-abundant archaeological evidence of seasonality that has been recovered from many parts of the world (Borden 1960; Coutts and Higham 1971; Bahn 1977; Smith 1978; Wills and Windes 1989). Paul Bahn has investigated sites of European reindeer herders of the late Pleistocene which suggest that seasonal movements of human populations in the past reflect the annual migratory patterns of preferred prey species, especially when these have become semidomesticated or subject to loose herding (Bahn 1977). Shellfish middens have long provided archaeologists with information on seasonal collecting activities of both hunter-gatherers and horticultural peoples (Ham and Irvine 1975; Claasen 1986). Settlement archaeologists now recognize the significance of temporary extraction camps for groups moving toward a sedentary life pattern, in broadening the resource catchment area of their increasingly permanent communities (Jochim 1976; Mortensen 1983), and are able to recognize how changing SUBSISTENCE strategies and seasonal patterns at the close of the Pleistocene epoch are reflected in the archaeological record (Binford 1968, 1980).

Seasonal settlement patterns observed archaeologically range from short-term camps, minor sites used for a few days by small groups and located near special resources, to long-term "macroband" camps. The former are located in caves or open-air sites with a few isolated hearths, sometimes contain some small animal remains or evidence of large animal butchering, and have low diversity and density of lithic artifacts (Butzer 1982:231). "Macroband" camps are typically larger, more complex open-air or cave sites occupied for several weeks or months, near water and seasonal food resources, with abundant specialized ARTIFACTS and ecofacts, and frequently have series of relatively shallow deposits reflecting repeated reoccupation, sometimes with remnants of larger structures, and substantial trash-midden accumulations (Butzer 1982:231).

Study of bioarchaeological evidence for the seasonal capture of faunal species is the principal method of archaeological seasonality studies (Monks 1981; see also BIOARCHAEOLOGY; ZOOARCHAEOLOGY). Such investigations are predicated on the assumption that migratory faunal species will be hunted at only one season of the year in any location, and are therefore indicative of seasonal site occupation by humans. Since paleontological data show that seasonal animal MIGRATION patterns have not changed in the past 12,000–15,000 years (Bokonyi 1972:121), seasonal hunting in the past can be inferred from archaeological remains of prey species found where migrating species now spend certain seasons of the year. Wild mammals also bear their young at certain seasons, so ages of animals at death (determinable from osteological markers and stages of tooth eruption) are another indicator of seasonality (Higgs and White 1963; House and Farrow 1968; Weide 1969; Bourque, Morris, and Spiess 1978; Clark 1974; Ham and Irvine 1975). Others include seasonal shedding of antlers by cervids, growth patterns in shells of marine shellfish, and other distinctive skeletal markers (see also ZOOARCHAEOLOGY). Remains of plant species edible only at certain seasons are another useful indicator of seasonality (MacNeish, Patterson, and Neely 1972).

Careful analysis of ecofacts from sites can be used to test hypotheses about seasonal versus year-round site occupation. A good illustration of the use of this technique at a Mississippian SITE in Missouri is reported by Bruce Smith (1978). This study is also an example of the use of multiple working hypotheses in seasonality studies, favored by Monks (1981) as a productive research strategy in this important and growing area of specialized archaeological research.

REFERENCES

Bahn, P. G. 1977. Seasonal migration in southwest France during the late glacial period. Journal of Archaeological Science 4:245–257.
Barnett, H. G. 1955. The Coast Salish of British Columbia. University of Oregon Press, Eugene.
Binford, Lewis R. 1968. Post-Pleistocene adaptation. In New perspectives in archaeology, S. R. Binford and L. R. Binford, eds. Aldine, Chicago, pp. 313–341.
———. 1980. Willow smoke and dogs' tails. American Antiquity 45(1):4–20.
Blomberg, Belinda. 1983. Mobility and sedentism: The Navajo of Black Mesa, Arizona. Center for Archaeological Investigations Research Paper No. 32. Southern Illinois University, Carbondale.
Bokonyi, S. 1972. Zoological evidence for seasonal or permanent occupation of prehistoric settlements. In Man, settlement and urbanism, P. J. Ucko, R. Tringham, and G. W. Dimbleby, eds. Duckworth, London, pp. 121–126.

Borden, Charles E. 1960. DjRi3, an early site in the Fraser Canyon, British Columbia. National Museum of Canada Bulletin No. 162. Ottawa, pp. 101–118.

Bourque, B., J. K. Morris, and A. Spiess. 1978. Determining the season of death of mammal teeth from archaeological sites: a new sectioning technique. Science 199:530–531.

Butzer, Karl W. 1982. Spatial integration II: socioecological models for settlement analysis. In Archaeology as human ecology, Cambridge University Press, pp. 230–257.

Claasen, Cheryl. 1986. Shellfishing seasons in the prehistoric southeastern United States. American Antiquity 51(1):21–37.

Clark, G. R. II. 1974. Growth lines in invertebrate skeletons. Annual Review of Earth and Planetary Sciences 2:77–99.

Coutts, P. J. F., and C. Higham. 1971. The seasonal factor in prehistoric New Zealand. World Archaeology 2:266–277.

Flannery, Kent V. 1968. Archaeological systems theory and early Mesoamerica. In Anthropological archaeology in the Americas, Betty J. Meggers, ed. Anthropological Society of Washington, Washington, D. C., pp. 67–87.

————. 1972. The cultural evolution of civilizations. Annual Review of Ecology and Systematics 3:399–426.

Ham, L. C., and M. Irvine. 1975. Techniques for determining seasonality of shell middens from marine mollusk remains. Syesis 8:363–373.

Henderson, E. 1983. Social organization and seasonal migrations among the Navajo. The Kiva 48:279–307.

Higgs, E. S., and J. P. White. 1963. Autumn killing. Antiquity 37:282–289.

House, M. R., and G. E. Farrow. 1968. Daily growth banding in the shell of the cockle, *Cardium edule*. Nature (London) 219:1384–1386.

Jochim, M. A. 1976. Hunter-gatherer subsistence and settlement: a predictive model. Academic Press, New York.

MacNeish, Richard S. 1964. The origins of New World civilization. Scientific American November 1964; reprinted in Avenues to antiquity: readings from Scientific American, pp. 169–177.

————. 1967. An interdisciplinary approach to an archaeological problem. In Prehistory of the Tehuacán Valley. Vol. 1: Environment and subsistence, D. S. Byers, ed. University of Texas Press, Austin, pp. 14–24.

————. 1972. The evolution of community patterns in the Tehuacán Valley of Mexico and speculations about the cultural processes. In Man, settlement and urbanism, P. J. Ucko, R. Tringham, and G. W. Dimbleby, eds. Duckworth, London, pp. 67–93.

————. 1981. Tehuacán's accomplishments. In Handbook of Middle American Indians. Supplement 1: Archaeology, Victoria Bricker and Jeremy Sabloff, eds. University of Texas Press, Austin, pp. 31–47.

MacNeish, Richard S., F. A. Patterson, and J. A. Neely. 1972. The archaeological reconnaissance. In Prehistory of the Tehuacán Valley. Vol. 5: Excavations and reconnaissance, R. S. MacNeish, ed. University of Texas Press, Austin, pp. 341–360.

Monks, Gregory G. 1981. Seasonality studies. Advances in Archaeological Method and Theory 4:177–240.

Mortensen, Peder. 1983. Patterns of interaction between seasonal settlements and early villages in Mesopotamia. In The hilly flanks and beyond: essays on the prehistory of southwestern Asia, presented to Robert J. Braidwood; T. Cuyler Young, Jr., Philip E. L. Smith, and Peder Mortensen, eds. Studies in Ancient Oriental Civilization No. 36. The Oriental Institute of the University of Chicago, pp. 207–229.

Oberg, Kalervo. 1973. The social economy of the Tlingit Indians. J. J. Douglas, Vancouver, B.C.

Powell, Shirley. 1984. The effects of seasonality on site space utilization: a lesson from Navajo sites. In Papers on the archaeology of Black Mesa, Arizona, vol. 2, S. Plog and S. Powell, eds. Southern Illinois University Press, Carbondale, pp. 117–126.

Rocek, Thomas R. 1988. The behavioral and material correlates of site seasonality: lessons from Navajo ethnoarchaeology. American Antiquity 53(3):523–536.

Smith, Bruce D. 1978. Prehistoric patterns of human behavior: a case study in the Mississippi Valley. Academic Press, New York.

Stuart, D. E. 1977. Seasonal phases in Ona subsistence, territorial distribution and organization: implications for the archaeological record. In For theory building in archaeology, L. R. Binford, ed. Academic Press, New York, pp. 251–283.

Suttles, Wayne P. 1951. The economic life of the Coast Salish of Haro and Rosario Straits. Ph.D. dissertation, Department of Anthropology, University of Washington, Seattle.

———. 1960. Affinal ties, subsistence, and prestige among the Coast Salish. American Anthropologist 62:296–305.

Weide, M. M. 1969. Seasonality of Pismo clam collecting at ORA-82. Archaeological Survey Annual Report 2. University of California at Los Angeles, pp. 131–141.

Wills, W. H., and Thomas C. Windes. 1989. Evidence for population aggregation and dispersal during the Basketmaker III period at Chaco Canyon, New Mexico. American Antiquity 54(2):347–369.

SOURCES OF ADDITIONAL INFORMATION

The review article by Monks in *Advances in Archaeological Method and Theory* 4(1981):177–240, which remains the only summary of seasonality research available to date, concentrates on the role and uses of bioarchaeological analysis in seasonality studies. While it provides a good overview of these aspects, there is relatively little emphasis on human scheduling or settlement patterns. The best exposition on these points is still Kent Flannery's 1968 paper, "Archaeological systems theory and early Mesoamerica" (see References).

For a review of much of the literature on the transition from seasonality to sedentariness in Mesoamerica up to about 1980, see Barbara Stark's topical synthesis, "The rise of sedentary life," in *Handbook of Middle American Indians, Supplement 1: Archaeology*, Victoria Bricker and Jeremy Sabloff, eds. (Austin, University of Texas Press, 1981), pp. 345–372.

More recent treatments of the subject of seasonality to update these now out-of-date basic sources may appear in the current literature from time to time, and can be located by searching in the current *Annual Review of Anthropology*, *Annual Review of Ecology and Systematics*, *Archaeological Method and Theory*, and *Current Anthropology*.

SEDENTARINESS. Long-term or permanent residence of a human population in a single location, as distinguished from a pattern of seasonal or transhumant movement between two or more locations throughout the year. In a sedentary community, all, or at least the greater portion, of the residents will normally remain in the same residential locality all year. Sedentariness is often called *sedentism* in the archaeological literature. (See also SEASONALITY.)

The concept of sedentariness has not been clearly defined in the archaeological literature, and the term or its alternative, *sedentism*, is used to refer to several different patterns of settlement and community life (Rafferty 1985). Some archaeologists would apply the term only to those groups whose members live in permanent, year-round communities and have no alternative place of residence, such as a seasonal camp for specialized resource procurement (Higgs and Vita-Finzi 1972). Others would regard groups with some members following a pattern of restricted, seasonally scheduled change of residence as displaying a sedentary pattern (Rice 1975). Those favoring this kind of definition tend to interpret sedentariness as a continuous variable, a matter of degree rather than an absolute, making it possible to refer to settlement types such as "semipermanent sedentary" communities (Beardsley et al. 1956).

In general, archaeologists tend to apply the term *sedentary* to a fairly broad range of settlement practices, including those in which the local population, or a part of it, spends part or even most of the year at several different locations, as well as those in which the entire community remains throughout the year at a single, permanent location. Some would include groups such as the Coast Salish of the Northwest Coast of North America, who follow an annual seasonal round of moves but habitually return to a permanent winter village, among sedentary peoples. In short, there is considerable flexibility in the interpretation of the concept, and many archaeologists appear to conceive of sedentariness as a continuous phenomenon.

Sedentarization, the trend from a seasonal to a more permanent SETTLEMENT PATTERN, is commonly viewed as an adaptive cultural process, although this is not often made explicit in the literature. At least one anthropologist has specifically recognized the processual nature of sedentarization, and even stated that it is not necessarily irreversible, noting that while nomads often become sedentary, the reverse has also been observed ethnographically (Salzman 1980). In both cases, the change, according to Salzman, is one of degree, a point on a continuum, and does not imply a revolution in lifeway.

Those who view sedentariness as a significant and permanent change rather than a matter of degree have sometimes regarded it as a "stage" in cultural EVOLUTION, with consequences that go far beyond an alteration in settlement pattern (Sahlins and Service 1960; Braidwood 1975; Harris 1978; Eder 1984). Proponents of this position may view the phenomenon of permanent settlement as part of the so-called "broad spectrum revolution" marking the Old World Neolithic, which occurred when the SUBSISTENCE base underwent a transition from hunting and gathering to FOOD PRODUCTION, involving a reorganization of the society's energy capture systems in a manner promoting greater efficiency. This change may have been effected by exploiting new, and more localized, resources, by developing new methods of resource procurement, or both, such that resource productivity was either maintained or enhanced, without the need for continuing to expend human energy in periodic group moves to alternative resource locations. However, the energy conserved by remaining in one location may be offset to some extent by the necessity for building permanent storage facilities and participating in trading networks with distant peoples to obtain resources not locally available (Rafferty 1985). In any case, the absolutist view of sedentariness implies a *qualitative* change in the total life pattern of a human population, with permanent consequences.

Sedentariness as an archaeological concept developed with the earliest archaeological investigations of evidence for the appearance of agriculture in the Near East during the 1940s, when excavations of early villages in Iraq, Iran, the Levant, and other localities by interdisciplinary teams of workers were carried out under the initial leadership of Robert Braidwood of the University of Chicago. Prior to revisions in earlier thinking that began to appear in the 1960s as a consequence of these and other investigations of past economy and human ecology (e.g., Flannery 1968, 1969; MacNeish 1973), agriculture had long been regarded as a necessary precondition for sedentary settlement (Braidwood 1952, 1975). Since the time these earliest projects investigating the transition to FOOD PRODUCTION were undertaken, archaeological evidence of permanently occupied sedentary communities with nonagricultural economies has accumulated from many parts of the world, weakening the basis of arguments for agriculture as a requirement for sedentariness.

The case of the native populations of the Northwest Coast of North America had long been known, and considered aberrant, although the patterns of settlement observed ethnographically among these peoples could not qualify them as sedentary by any definition requiring that some part of the population remain in the permanent village all year (Suttles 1951; Barnett 1955). These groups provide an example illustrative of a pattern of sedentariness cum mobility, in which a population with a permanent residence (in this case, permanent winter villages with substantial architecture) makes trips throughout the year to other areas to procure seasonal resources, always returning to their main settlement, where important ceremonial activities are centered. Since resource trips involved *all* members of the community, resulting in temporarily vacating the main settlement, the Coast Salish pattern would have to be considered a minimal example of sedentariness, one that would, by some definitions of the concept, not qualify as a sedentary pattern at all (see, e.g., Rice 1975:97).

Another instance of sedentariness without agriculture is that of the Cotton Preceramic peoples of coastal Peru (Moseley 1975; Moseley and Feldman 1988). It is perhaps significant that these early sedentary Andeans, like the Coast Salish of the Pacific Northwest and other relatively sedentary maritime-adapted coastal groups (Renouf 1988), had an economy based on shellfish collecting and the procurement of other marine resources, an economic pattern sometimes considered a "subset" of hunting-gathering economies displaying some of the characteristics of sedentary peoples (Yesner 1980).

Other examples of early sedentary nonagriculturists, however, have been found in relatively arid inland environments (Lee 1972; Bar Yosef 1983; Wills and Winde 1989), with economic patterns based on specialized selective hunting or incipient animal husbandry, and intensive collecting. The requirement of evidence for crop cultivation as a criterion of sedentariness still persists, however, adding to the imprecision of the concept, which is sometimes viewed as an aspect of economy rather than as primarily a phenomenon of settlement. It is perhaps more useful to consider sedentariness as a broader concept, with settlement in permanent communities occurring as one consequence of the technological and organizational changes associated with certain kinds of changes in economic strategy (Rafferty 1985:124).

Archaeological evidence of sedentariness is of several kinds. Settlement patterns are marked by the appearance of larger units, accompanied by evidence of longer SITE occupation in the form of more substantial architecture, including specialized ceremonial and administrative structures, and deeper accumulations of midden deposits. There is sometimes evidence of community planning, with structures nonrandomly aligned according to some fixed pattern or consistent directional orientation. A greater variety of ARTIFACT types, including specialized tools, is typical, reflecting an increased range of community activities and some degree of SPECIALIZATION. Storage vessels and facilities occupy a more prominent place in the material inventory, sometimes including both pottery and basketry, as well as underground chambers or pits, storerooms, and granaries. Special-purpose SITES or activity areas, such as quarries and workshops, may be present, and a marked temporal increase in the overall variety, number, size, and distribution of sites is commonly found. Taken together, the settlement evidence is usually indicative of larger local population aggregates.

Population growth has been considered to be one of the long-term correlates of sedentariness, especially in combination with agriculture, although it has not generally been possible to distinguish cause from effect in this area through archaeological evidence alone (Binford 1968; Roth 1981; see also FOOD PRODUCTION; PALEODEMOGRAPHY). Other developments that have been considered consequences of sedentariness include more complex forms of sociopolitical organization, crop agriculture using various intensification techniques (irrigation, terracing), and a overall tendency toward increasing CULTURAL COMPLEXITY, sometimes culminating in urban civilization.

REFERENCES

Barnett, H. G. 1955. The Coast Salish of British Columbia. University of Oregon Press, Eugene.

Bar Yosef, Ofer. 1983. The Natufian in the southern Levant. In The hilly flanks and beyond: essays on the prehistory of southwestern Asia presented to Robert J.

Braidwood; T. Cuyler Young, Jr., Philip E. L. Smith, and Peder Mortensen, eds. Studies in Ancient Oriental Civilization No. 36. The Oriental Institute of the University of Chicago, pp. 11–32.

Beardsley, R. K., Preston Holder, A. D. Krieger, B. J. Meggers, John B. Rinaldo, and Paul Kutsche. 1956. Functional and evolutionary implications of community patterning. In Seminars in archaeology: 1955, R. Wauchope, ed. SAA Memoir No. 22. Society for American Archaeology, Washington, D.C., pp. 130–157.

Binford, Lewis R. 1968. Post-Pleistocene adaptation. In New perspectives in archaeology, S. R. Binford and L. R. Binford, eds. Aldine, Chicago, pp. 313–341.

Braidwood, Robert J. 1952. The Near East and the foundations of civilization. Oregon State System of Higher Education, Eugene.

———. 1975. Prehistoric men. 8th ed. Scott, Foresman, Glenview, Ill.

Eder, James F. 1984. The impact of subsistence change on mobility and settlement pattern in a tropical forest foraging economy: some implications for archaeology. American Anthropologist 86(4):837–853.

Flannery, Kent V. 1968. Archaeological systems theory and early Mesoamerica. In Anthropological archaeology in the Americas, B. J. Meggers, ed. Anthropological Society of Washington, Washington, D.C., pp. 67–87.

———. 1969. Origins and ecological effects of early domestication in Iran and the Near East. In The domestication and exploitation of plants and animals, J. Ucko and G. W. Dimbleby, eds. Aldine, Chicago, pp. 73–100.

Harris, David R. 1978. Settling down: an evolutionary model.... In The evolution of social systems, J. Friedman and M. J. Rowlands, eds. University of Pittsburgh Press, pp. 401–417.

Higgs, E. S., and C. Vita-Finzi. 1972. Prehistoric economies: a territorial approach. In Papers in economic prehistory, E. S. Higgs, ed. Cambridge University Press, pp. 27–36.

Lee, Richard B. 1972. Population growth and the beginning of sedentary life among the !Kung bushmen. In Population growth: anthropological implications, Brian Sponner, ed. MIT Press, Cambridge, Mass., pp. 329–342.

MacNeish, Richard S. 1973. The evolution of community patterns in the Tehuacán Valley of Mexico and speculations about the cultural processes. In Ecology and agricultural settlements, R. Tringham, ed. Warner Modular Publications, Andover, Mass.

Moseley, Michael E. 1975. The maritime foundations of Andean civilization. Benjamin Cummings, Menlo Park, Calif.

Moseley, Michael E., and Robert A. Feldman. 1988. Fishing, farming, and the foundations of Andean civilization. In The archaeology of prehistoric coastlines, G. Bailey and J. Parkington, eds. Cambridge University Press, pp. 125–134.

Rafferty, Janet E. 1985. The archaeological record on sedentariness: recognition, development and implications. Advances in Archaeological Method and Theory 8:113–156.

Renouf, M. A. P. 1988. Sedentary coastal hunter-fishers: an example from the Younger Stone Age of northern Norway. In The archaeology of prehistoric coastlines, Geoff Bailey and John Parkington, eds. Cambridge University Press, pp. 102–115.

Rice, Glenn. 1975. A systematic explanation of change in Mogollon settlement patterns.

Ph.D. dissertation, Department of Anthropology, University of Washington, Seattle.

Roth, Eric A. 1981. Sedentism and changing fertility patterns in a northern Athapascan isolate. Journal of Human Evolution 10:413–425.

Sahlins, Marshall D., and Elman R. Service, eds. 1960. Evolution and culture. University of Michigan Press, Ann Arbor.

Salzman, P. C., ed. 1980. When nomads settle. Praeger, New York.

Suttles, Wayne P. 1951. The economic life of the Coast Salish of Haro and Rosario Straits. Ph.D. dissertation, Department of Anthropology, University of Washington, Seattle.

Wills, W. H., and Thomas C. Winde. 1989. Evidence for population aggregation and dispersal during the Basketmaker III period in Chaco Canyon, New Mexico. American Antiquity 54(2):347–369.

Yesner, David R. 1980. Maritime hunter-gatherers: ecology and prehistory. Current Anthropology 21:727–750.

SOURCES OF ADDITIONAL INFORMATION

The only comprehensive review article on sedentariness as a distinctive archaeological concept is that by Janet Rafferty (Rafferty 1985; see References), which will undoubtedly serve as the principal background and intermediary source on the subject for some time. A comparable review of the considerable literature on the transition to permanent settlement in Mesoamerica appears in Barbara L. Stark's "The rise of sedentary life," in *Handbook of Middle American Indians, Supplement 1: Archaeology*, Victoria Bricker and Jeremy A. Sabloff, eds. (Austin, University of Texas Press, 1981), pp. 345–372.

Several more limited discussions of various aspects of sedentariness appear in the literature. Among the most significant of these are Barbara Bender's consideration of possible explanations for the development of sedentariness, which she maintains must include social as well as economic and ecological factors; see Barbara Bender, "Gatherer to farmer: a social perspective," *World Archaeology* 10(2) (1978):204–222. Others include Olga Soffer's discussion of the role of storage in the development of sedentary life in Eurasia, "Storage, sedentism and the Eurasian Palaeolithic record," *Antiquity* 63(1989):719–732; and James Eder's fairly lengthy and thoughtful discussion of the concepts of sedentariness and seasonal mobility, and their relation to archaeological theory (Eder 1984; see References). All three articles include substantial bibliographies.

The only volume dealing solely with the phenomenon of sedentariness is the collection of anthropological papers edited by Salzman (see References), none of which deal with sedentariness in an archaeological population. The festschrift presented to Robert Braidwood, *The Hilly Flanks and Beyond: Essays on the Prehistory of Southwestern Asia* (see Bar Yosef 1983, in References, for complete citation), contains a number of papers touching on the process of sedentarization as an adjunct to the transition to FOOD PRO-DUCTION in this region. An interesting ethnoarchaeological study of the shift to sedentary settlement in a modern Navajo population is reported by Belinda Blomberg in *Mobility and Sedentism: The Navaho of Black Mesa, Arizona* (Carbondale, Center for Archaeological Investigations Research Paper No. 32, Southern Illinois University, 1983).

A unique method for detecting the transition to a year-round sedentary settlement pattern has been described by Brian Hesse in "Rodent remains and sedentism in the Neolithic: evidence from Tepe Ganj Dareh, eastern Iran," *Journal of Mammalogy* 60(4) (1979):856–877. Hesse suggests that the frequency of *Mus musculus* remains in archaeological sites can be used to document the shift from seasonal to permanent occupation of sites, and supports this with evidence from the Neolithic site of Tepe Ganj Dareh, where the frequency of remains of this domestic house mouse increased dramatically with the beginning of mud-brick architecture and goat husbandry.

Some discussions of sedentariness as an adaptive pattern and its consequences are in D. P. Braun, "Coevolution of sedentism, pottery technology and horticulture in the central Midwest, 200 BC–AD 600," in *Emergent Horticultural Economies of the Eastern Woodlands*, W. F. Keegan, ed. (Carbondale, Southern Illinois University Center for Archaeological Investigations, Occasional Papers No. 7, 1987), pp. 153–181; and Susan Kent, ed., *Farmers as Hunters: The Implications of Sedentism* (Cambridge, Cambridge University Press, 1989). A major literature review is M. J. O'Brien, "Sedentism, population growth, and resource selection in the Woodland Midwest: a review," *Current Anthropology* 28(1987):177–197.

SERIATION. 1. The arrangement or ordering of data units or phenomena in a sequence or series according to some consistent principle, such that the position of any item relative to any other reflects their degree of similarity or stylistic relatedness, or their temporal, chronological relationship to one another. 2. In archaeology, a RELATIVE DATING technique in which the contents of an ASSEMBLAGE are arranged in such a way that the frequencies of various kinds of ARTIFACTS form battleship-shaped curves through time (Deetz 1967). 3. Any sequential, unidimensional system of ordering or sorting archaeological units, whether artifacts, stylistic categories, ecofacts, soil samples, or other items, according to some principle other than STRATIGRAPHY or superposition. (See also RELATIVE DATING; TYPOLOGY.)

Seriation, in its simplest definition, is the arrangement of phenomena or data into linear series according to some consistent principle of ordering. In archaeology, seriation is most often concerned with chronology or time-ordering of data, although this may be accomplished using nontemporal criteria, such as stylistic factors. Unlike STRATIGRAPHY, which is derived from the geological principle of superposition, seriation has been said to have its theoretical framework entirely in cultural history (Rouse 1967; Dunnell 1970; Willey and Sabloff 1980:93).

While the concept of seriation is usually attributed to Sir Flinders Petrie, in actuality it first appears in the work of the early-nineteenth-century Danish scholar Christian Juergen Thomsen, since it is implicit in Thomsen's THREE-AGE SYSTEM (Klindt-Jensen 1975:49–57; Trigger 1989:418). Petrie was, however, the first to develop a seriational *method*, which he called "sequence dating." In the 1890s he used this method to organize ceramics recovered from a series of Egyptian tombs, which also provided a relative dating sequence for these materials (Petrie 1899).

Seriation is used to arrange comparable units along a continuum in such a way that the position of each unit reflects its degree of similarity to other units. This may be accomplished by scaling, that is, assigning a numerical value to each unit, or by ranking. If the criteria used to order the units are reliable chronological indicators, the resulting sequence can be used as a relative dating method (Marquardt 1978:258).

Seriations of ceramic remains from archaeological SITES have frequently been used to build relative chronologies for entire regions or cultures. A classic example is the ceramic sequence developed by Robert E. Smith for the Maya site of Uaxactun in Guatemala, which now serves as the basic sequence for the Maya area. Pottery assemblages from other sites throughout the Maya region have subsequently been correlated with this sequence, and thereby relatively dated (Smith 1955). Similar seriations were developed earlier in the twentieth century by Alfred Kroeber (1916) and Leslie Spier (1917) for Zuni pottery in the American Southwest.

A number of innovations have contributed to the usefulness of seriation since the 1960s (Rowe 1961, 1962; Kendall 1963; Renfrew and Sterud 1969; Gelfand 1971; Cowgill 1972; Schiffer 1975; Meighan 1977; Read 1979; Barros 1982; Braun 1985). The graphical technique developed by James A. Ford (Ford 1962) was designed to reflect changing patterns in the relative frequencies of different pottery types from the same unit. Since the mid-1960s seriation has greatly benefited from the use of computers (Hole and Shaw 1967; Graham, Galloway, and Scollar 1976).

REFERENCES

Barros, Philip L. F. de. 1982. The effects of variable site occupation span on the results of frequency seriation. American Antiquity 47(2):291–315.

Braun, D. P. 1985. Absolute seriation: a time-series approach. In For concordance in archaeological analysis: bridging data structure, quantitative technique, and theory, C. Carr, ed. Westport, Kansas City, Mo., pp. 509–539.

Cowgill, G. L. 1972. Models, methods and techniques for seriation. In Models in archaeology, D. L. Clarke, ed. Methuen, London, pp. 381–424.

Deetz, James. 1967. Invitation to archaeology. Doubleday, New York.

Dunnell, Robert C. 1970. Seriation method and its evaluation. American Antiquity 35:305–319.

Ford, J. A. 1962. A quantitative method for deriving cultural chronology. Panamerican Union Technical Manual 1. Washington, D.C.

Gelfand, Alan E. 1971. Seriation methods of archaeological materials. American Antiquity 36:263–274.

Graham, I., P. Galloway, and I. Scollar. 1976. Model studies in computer seriation. Journal of Archaeological Science 3(1):1–30.

Hole, F., and M. Shaw. 1967. Computer analysis of chronological seriation. Monograph in Archaeology 53, No. 4. Rice University Studies, Houston, Tex.

Kendall, David G. 1963. A statistical approach to Flinders Petrie's sequence-dating. Bulletin of the International Statistical Institute 40:657–680.

Klindt-Jensen, O. 1975. A history of Scandinavian archaeology. Thames and Hudson, London.

Kroeber, Alfred L. 1916. Zuni potsherds. Anthropological Papers 18, No.:1–17. American Museum of Natural History, New York.

Marquardt, William H. 1978. Advances in archaeological seriation. Advances in Archaeological Method and Theory 1:257–313.

Meighan, Clement W. 1977. Recognition of short time periods through seriation. American Antiquity 42(4):628–629.

Petrie, W. M. Flinders. 1899. Sequences in prehistoric remains. Journal of the Royal Anthropological Institute n.s. 29:295–301.

Read, Dwight W. 1979. The effective use of radiocarbon dates in the seriation of archaeological sites. In Radiocarbon dating, R. Berger and H. E. Suess, eds. University of California Press, Los Angeles, pp. 89–94.

Renfrew, Colin, and Gene Sterud. 1969. Close-proximity analysis: a rapid method for the ordering of archaeological materials. American Antiquity 34(3):265–277.

Rouse, I. 1967. Seriation in archaeology. In American historical anthropology: essays in honor of Leslie Spier, C. L. Riley and W. W. Taylor, eds. Southern Illinois University Press, Carbondale, pp. 153–195.

Rowe, J. H. 1961. Stratigraphy and seriation. American Antiquity 26(3):324–330.

———. 1962. Worsaae's Law and the use of grave lots for archaeological dating. American Antiquity 28:129–137.

Schiffer, Michael B. 1975. Arrangement vs. seriation of sites: a new approach for relative temporal relationships. In The Cache River archaeological project: M. B. Schiffer and J. H. House, eds. Arkansas Archaeological Survey Research Series 8. Fayetteville, pp. 257–263.

Smith, Robert E. 1955. Ceramic sequence at Uaxactun, Guatemala, vols. 1 and 2. Middle American Research Institute Publication No. 20. Tulane University, New Orleans.

Spier, Leslie. 1917. An outline for a chronology of Zuni ruins. American Museum of Natural History Anthropological Papers 18, No. 3. New York.

Trigger, Bruce G. 1989. A history of archaeological thought. Cambridge University Press.

Willey, Gordon R., and Jeremy A. Sabloff. 1980. A history of American archaeology. 2nd ed. W. H. Freeman, San Francisco.

SOURCES OF ADDITIONAL INFORMATION

For historical background material on seriation, consult Kendall (1963); Rouse (1967:154–155); and Rowe (1962). For an overall discussion of seriation techniques currently in use, their theoretical foundations, and the role of seriation in contemporary archaeological research, see the review article by Marquardt (1978). Good earlier discussions are in Rouse (1967), Dunnell (1970), and Cowgill (1972). (See References for all works cited.)

For access to the literature, see the extensive bibliography in Marquardt 1978, which now requires updating. For this purpose, consult indexes to research journals such as *American Antiquity*, as well as current issues of this and *Journal of Archaeological Science* and *Archaeometry*, and latest issues of *Archaeological Method and Theory* for a more up-to-date review. See also references and additional sources listed in CHRONOMETRIC DATING and RELATIVE DATING.

SETTLEMENT PATTERN. 1. The spatial distribution of human habitation and activity over the geographic landscape, reflected in archaeological remains and their location relative to one another. 2. A statement describing observable regularities or relationships among structures within a prehistoric community, usually in terms of what these reveal about the relationships of environmental features to sociocultural factors, such as residence rules, and their influence on the location, size, and density of settlements. 3. An abstract model of a particular type of settlement configuration, defined from the characteristic distribution of structures on the landscape in a pattern that can be described as nucleated, linear, or dispersed. (See also SPATIAL ANALYSIS.)

Settlement pattern is a concept used in archaeology in several different senses, of which the three defined above are the most common. Settlement analysis itself was originally conceived by geographers as encompassing the three basic ideas of direction, distance, and connectivity embodied in the spatial organization of human communities (Vita-Finzi and Higgs 1970).

Archaeologists have usually applied one of two basic approaches to the study and modeling of settlement patterns. The first of these, the ecological determinants approach, assumes that habitation sites are located rationally, with locational decisions determined by proximity to water and other critical resources; this is also the basic assumption underlying CATCHMENT ANALYSIS. The second analytic approach is that of locational analysis, based on other concepts borrowed from geography, including CENTRAL PLACE THEORY.

Settlement pattern studies developed during the 1930s, following somewhat different courses in England and the United States. British settlement archaeology, linking environmental factors to the distribution of archaeological remains, was stimulated by Cyril Fox's work in the 1920s, studies of relationships between vegetation patterns and settlement that later affected American settlement archaeology (Fox 1943; Sharer and Ashmore 1979:421).

While the earliest roots of North American settlement archaeology may be traced to the investigations of Lewis Henry Morgan of North American Indians in the 1880s (Morgan 1881), the beginnings of American settlement pattern research are usually attributed to Julian Steward. Steward's ecological approach and Great Basin research led him to the recognition of residential patterns that appeared to reflect both environmental and cultural factors (Steward 1937). Steward provided the inspiration for the first formal settlement pattern study, conducted by his student Gordon R. Willey, in the Viru Valley of Peru, in which Willey developed a methodological framework for settlement research using the SITE, rather than the ARTIFACT, as the basic unit of analysis (Willey 1953). Willey has continued to play a key role in the development of American settlement pattern research (Willey 1956; Willey and Bullard 1965; Willey et al. 1965; Vogt and Leventhal 1983). Walter Taylor's critique of American archaeology, which emphasized the neglect of archaeological research focused at the household level, also served as an important stimulus to the growth of settlement archaeology in the United States (Taylor 1948). In the decade following Willey's initial study, a number of settlement research studies were undertaken, and some of them were reported in a volume of papers devoted to settlement pattern research published in 1968 (Chang 1968).

Settlement studies can be focused at a variety of scales, ranging from specialized activity areas within a single room of a dwelling to the distribution of sites throughout an entire geographic region. These different scales are reflected in the hierarchy of levels and units of analysis used in settlement studies. The smallest such level or unit is the activity area, the locus within a single structure or on a single occupation surface of a particular kind of activity, such as tool-making, woodcarving, cooking, or food processing. The next level of analysis above the activity area is the household (see HOUSEHOLD ARCHAEOLOGY). A household unit will vary according to family size and structure, the number of individuals present, whether all of them lived under one roof or in several closely spaced separate structures, and so on.

Succeedingly larger units of settlement analysis are variable, depending upon the nature of the community and its degree of complexity. In larger communities, a level between the household and the community as a whole, such as the neighborhood, may be recognized. This kind of unit is characteristic of urban communities, and is very often related to the presence of specialized economic activities such as manufacturing or skilled crafts.

The next major level in the hierarchy of settlement units is usually that of the SITE. The site is an extremely variable unit, and may consist of anything from a location used for two hours to butcher a deer carcass to a city of many thousands. Usually, however, a site is conceived of as a community, a place occupied by a distinct group of people on a more or less permanent basis, or at least for a particular season of each year. A community is composed of a cluster of house-hold units comprising a larger unit that may have been a temporary camp, a cave dwelling, a pithouse village, a farming hamlet, a town, or a city. SITES can also be special-purpose, nonresidential locations, such as kill sites where hunters butchered their prey; military forts or outposts; trading stations; places where specialized manufacturing activities (e.g., potterymaking, obsidian carving) were carried on; or sources of important natural resources where raw materials were mined or quarried, in addition to residential communities of all types.

The largest level or unit at which settlement is usually studied archaeologically is the region. This can be defined geographically as well as culturally, and frequently refers to a spatially distinct area occupied by people participating in the same CULTURE during a particular period of time; it often coincides with a geographically definable area with physical boundaries, such as a valley, a basin, or a river drainage. A number of important settlement studies at the regional scale have been carried out in Mesoamerica, including that conducted in the Valley of Oaxaca by Kent Flannery and his students (Flannery 1976) and the classic study of the Basin of Mexico by William Sanders and his associates (Sanders, Parsons, and Santley 1979). Settlement studies at the regional scale are often only one part of a larger overall research design or objective, involving an interdisciplinary effort utilizing the knowledge and skills of specialists in a multiplicity of scientific and technical fields. Richard MacNeish's ecologically oriented research project in the Tehuacán Valley, which included work on set-tlement patterns, but whose overall aim was defining the origins of maize agriculture in Mesoamerica, is a case in point (Byers 1967; MacNeish, Peterson, Flannery 1970; MacNeish et al. 1975).

Other settlement units that have become subjects of archaeological investigation include intersite areas (Ford 1981) and site catchment areas (see CATCHMENT ANALYSIS).

In addition to levels or units of settlement, human communities may display particular characteristic spatial forms or shapes affording another analytic approach using settlement configuration as a criterion for classification. The basic shape of a community on the landscape, easily observable from the air, may be described as *linear*, when spread in the stringlike pattern often displayed by communities built along riverbanks; *nucleated*, when most of the structures are aggregated around a central core area; or *dispersed*, in which structures are located at intervals with intervening spaces, rather than distributed in a continuous pattern. Remote sensing technology has become an important tool in identifying settlement configurations, which are frequently much more apparent from the air than on the ground (see ARCHAEOMETRY).

Settlement pattern studies, often conducted in combination with ecological research or investigations of prehistoric SUBSISTENCE, have become a highly specialized aspect of the overall study of spatial patterning, or SPATIAL ANALYSIS, in archaeology, which has produced its own body of research literature (Hodder and Orton 1976; Clarke 1977; Hodder 1978).

REFERENCES

Byers, Douglas S., ed. 1967. The prehistory of the Tehuacán Valley. Vol. 1: Environment and subsistence. University of Texas Press, Austin.

Clarke, David L., ed. 1977. Spatial archaeology. Academic Press, London.

Chang, K. C., ed. 1968. Settlement archaeology. National Press Books, Palo Alto, Calif.

Flannery, Kent V., ed. 1976. The early Mesoamerican village. Academic Press, New York.

Ford, Anabel. 1981. Conditions for the evolution of complex societies: the development of the central lowland Maya. Ph.D. dissertation, Department of Anthropology, University of California, Santa Barbara.

Fox, Cyril. 1943. A Beaker barrow enlarged in the Middle Bronze Age. The Archaeological Journal 99:1–32.

Hodder, Ian, ed. 1978. The spatial organisation of culture. Duckworth, London.

Hodder, Ian, and Clive Orton. 1976. Some models for settlement patterns. In Spatial analysis in archaeology. Cambridge University Press, pp. 53–97.

MacNeish, Richard S. 1956. Prehistoric settlement patterns on the northeastern periphery of Mesoamerica. In Prehistoric settlement patterns in the New World, Gordon R. Willey, ed. Viking Fund Publications in Anthropology No. 23. Wenner-Gren Foundation for Anthropological Research, New York.

———. 1972. The evolution of community patterns in the Tehuacán Valley of Mexico and speculations about the cultural processes. In Man, settlement and urbanism, P. J. Ucko, R. Tringham, and G. W. Dimbleby, eds. Duckworth, London, pp. 67–93.

MacNeish, Richard, Fredrick A. Peterson, and Kent V. Flannery. 1970. The prehistory of the Tehuacán Valley. Vol. 3: Ceramics, Richard S. MacNeish, gen. ed. University of Texas Press, Austin.

MacNeish, Richard S., Melvin L. Fowler, Angel Garcia Cook, Frederick A. Peterson, Antoinette Nelken-Turner, and James A. Neely. 1975. The prehistory of the Tehuacán Valley. Vol. 5: Excavations and reconnaissance, Richard S. MacNeish, gen. ed. University of Texas Press, Austin.

Morgan, Lewis Henry. 1881. Houses and house-life of the American aborigines. U.S. Government Printing Office, Washington, D.C.

Sanders, William, Jeffrey Parsons, and William Santley. 1979. The Basin of Mexico: ecological process in the evolution of a civilization. Academic Press, New York.

Sharer, Robert, and Wendy Ashmore. 1979. Fundamentals of archaeology. Benjamin Cummings, Menlo Park, Calif.

Steward, Julian. 1937. Ecological aspects of southwestern society. Anthropos 32:87–104.

Taylor, Walter W. 1948. A study of archaeology. American Anthropological Association Memoir No. 69. Washington, D.C.

Vita-Finzi, C., and E. S. Higgs. 1970. Prehistoric economy in the Mt. Carmel area of Palestine: site catchment analysis. Proceedings of the Prehistoric Society 36:1–37.

Vogt, Evon Z., and Richard M. Leventhal, eds. 1983. Prehistoric settlement patterns: essays in honor of Gordon R. Willey. University of New Mexico Press, Albuquerque; Peabody Museum of Archaeology and Ethnology, Harvard University, Cambridge, Mass.

Willey, Gordon R. 1953. Prehistoric settlement patterns in the Viru Valley, Peru. Bureau of American Ethnology Bulletin 155. Washington, D.C.

———, ed. 1956. Prehistoric settlement patterns in the New World. Viking Fund Publications in Anthropology No. 23. Wenner-Gren Foundation for Anthropological Research, New York.

Willey, Gordon R., and William R. Bullard, Jr. 1965. Prehistoric settlement patterns in the Maya lowlands. In Handbook of Middle American Indians, vol. 2, Robert Wauchope, gen. ed. University of Texas Press, Austin, pp. 360–377.

Willey, Gordon R., William R. Bullard, Jr., J. B. Glass, and J. C. Gifford. 1965. Prehistoric Maya settlement in the Belize Valley. Peabody Museum of Archaeology and Ethnology Paper No. 54. Harvard University, Cambridge, Mass.

SOURCES OF ADDITIONAL INFORMATION

Summaries of the development, techniques, and achievements of settlement pattern analysis may be found in many introductory texts, including Sharer and Ashmore 1979 (pp. 421–434; see References); Brian Fagan, *In the Beginning*, 6th ed. (Scott, Foresman, Glenview, Ill., 1988), pp. 429–469; and Colin Renfrew and Paul Bahn, *Archaeology: Theories, Methods and Practice* (Thames and Hudson, New York, 1991), pp. 158–162. Descriptions of settlement studies of many different cultures at varied scales of analysis, as well as discussions of methods and theoretical aspects of settlement pattern research, may be found in the festschrift dedicated to Gordon R. Willey (Vogt and Leventhal 1983; see References).

A discussion of the use of settlement models in archaeology, emphasizing those derived from geography (including central place models), by Susan Evans and Peter Gould, "Settlement Models in Archaeology," appeared in *Journal of Anthropological Archae-*

ology 1(1982):275–304, and included a substantial bibliography. A review devoted exclusively to the archaeological study of settlement by Jeffrey R. Parsons is "Archaeological settlement patterns," *Annual Review of Anthropology* 2(1972):127–150, but its bibliography is now out-of-date. The synthesis by Roland Fletcher, "Settlement archaeology: world-wide comparisons," *World Archaeology* 18(1)(1986):59–83, has an extensive bibliography covering some of the literature published in the intervening period.

More recent studies of interest include L. J. Gorenflo and N. Gale, "Mapping regional settlement in information space," *Journal of Anthropological Archaeology* 9(3)(1990):240–274; and A. P. Sullivan, "Investigating the archaeological consequences of short-duration occupations," *American Antiquity* 57(2)(1992):99–115. *World Archaeology* (vol. 19, no. 1, June 1987), devoted to the topic of urbanization, included two papers in the field of settlement archaeology: Timothy Taylor's "Aspects of settlement diversity and its classification in southeast Europe" (pp. 1–22) and Maurizio Gualtieri's "Fortification and settlement organization: an example from pre-Roman Italy" (pp. 30–46).

For later material, current issues of *Antiquity, American Antiquity, Journal of Field Archaeology, World Archaeology,* and *Journal of Anthropological Archaeology* should be consulted, and the pertinent annual reviews should be monitored.

SITE. The fundamental spatial unit of archaeological investigation, consisting of a concentration on the landscape of material evidence of past human activity (Deetz 1967:11).

The collection of material evidence indicating the presence of an archaeologic site may consist of scatters of ARTIFACTS on the ground surface; dwelling remains or structures; storage pits, garbage dumps, or middens; human burials; animal kill sites or butchery sites, marked by concentrations of bones and tools; hearths, campsites, workshops, or a combination of these within a single area. Sites may also consist of submerged features and remains, such as shipwrecks, deposits of artifacts in ancient wells or ponds, and bogs or wetlands in which bodies and other organic materials are preserved.

The problem of defining the site is a basic one in archaeology. Traditionally, a site has been equated with a prehistoric community, the most common level at which archaeological research was focused before the second half of the twentieth century. Since the "NEW" ARCHAEOLOGY of the 1960s, archaeological research has concentrated on a broader range of units, representing different scales and types of analysis; and the site itself as the basic unit of investigation has had to be redefined to reflect this increased variety. The manner in which this is done will depend upon many variable factors, such as the nature of the CULTURE being investigated, if this is known at the time research is begun; the scale (region, local community, household, activity area) at which the project is focused; the physical location and characteristics of surface material remains; and the intensity of the field research, that is, if the site is to be sampled, how much of the surveyed area will be exposed.

Defining a site in terms of its physical limits or boundaries can be extremely difficult, since these can be determined with certainty only if the site is excavated in its entirety. Because of limited time and funds, as well as the destructive nature of excavation, this is almost never done. SAMPLING designs for site investigation must therefore be based on assumptions concerning site characteristics, which are usually extrapolated from a preliminary surface SURVEY rather than from certain knowledge.

Sites can be classified into types based on their content, location, size, ARTIFACT distributions, the inferred group size or composition of the occupants, or function. Examples of functional site classes are dwelling, storage, tool manufacture, ceremonial, and burial or mortuary sites. A site may comprise a single surface artifact scatter, an isolated house, monument, or ceremonial structure, or an enormous city, as well as units of all sizes and types intervening between these extremes. Human group sizes represented by a site may range from the nuclear family to large urban or regional populations of hundreds of thousands or even millions of persons, and may include seasonal macrobands, small, isolated groups of hunters occupying seasonal camps, or groups of specialized craftspeople who carried out their manufacturing activities at special locations.

Of all possible ways of classifying and characterizing sites, the most common and useful have usually been those based on scale or on function. Site classifications based on scale allow archaeologists to develop site hierarchies. These may comprise a broad range of site sizes and types, from the isolated family household and its activity areas to the large, multisite geographic region occupied by a people sharing a single culture. Such hierarchies provide a very useful analytic framework for SETTLEMENT PATTERN research, as well as for identifying patterns of intercommunity and interregional interaction and trade. Classifying sites by function, on the other hand, facilitates the location and study of particular activities of social and economic importance, such as potterymaking, flint knapping, or food processing, in the community of study, providing information on resource utilization, ecology, and SUBSISTENCE patterns.

The development of aerial photography for site discovery produced a scheme for classifying sites into abstract types based on their appearance from the air. O. G. S. Crawford, a British geographer who pioneered aerial photography as a method of locating archaeological sites in the 1920s, developed such a classification, in which sites were designated as "shadow sites," visible from shadows cast by surface irregularities such as pithouse depressions at sunrise or sunset; "soil sites," where remains are visible from the air through variations in soil color, or frost, snow, or moisture marking; and "crop sites," revealed by the variable growth of crops over subsurface structures, which creates patterns following the outlines of such structures (Scollar et al. 1990:33–77). More recently, instruments for locating sites with subsurface remains from the ground, based on magnetism (Aitken 1969; Scollar et al. 1990:375–590), soil resistivity to electric currents (Clark 1969; Scollar et al. 1990:307–374), and soil surface temperature variations (Scollar et al 1990:591–635), have been developed, as well as methods for predicting subsurface remains from characteristics of surface artifact scatters (Powell and Klasert 1984).

Defining the site conceptually was not often explicitly addressed by archaeologists prior to the 1960s, and the meaning of the term was accepted as part of the body of implicit, unstated assumptions and concepts shared by archaeologists until the "new" archaeology underlined the necessity of defining and examining all such assumed understandings.

The first formal treatment of the site as a conceptual and analytical unit was that by Gordon Willey and Philip Phillips, in their comprehensive attempt to develop a standardized systematics for American archaeological research (Willey and Phillips 1958). In this endeavor, they drew upon the terminology and concepts developed in the 1930s by W. C. McKern as part of his so-called "Midwestern Taxonomic Method" (McKern 1939). McKern, however, although he distinguished between varieties of sites, did not include the site as an analytic unit or concept in his taxonomic scheme, which was composed of abstract, interpretative units rather than empirical categories.

Willey and Phillips defined sites as "archaeological materials . . . occur[ring] in discrete clusters . . . in space," and included as part of their definition and description the "discovery of their boundaries" (Willey and Phillips 1958:16). The authors went on to define and characterize the site as the basic (and smallest) spatial archaeological unit.

> A *site* is the smallest unit of space dealt with by the archaeologist and the most difficult to define. Its physical limits, which may vary from a few square yards to as many square miles, are often impossible to fix. About the only requirement ordinarily demanded of the site is that it be fairly continuously covered by remains of former occupation, and the general idea is that these pertain to a single unit of settlement, which may be anything from a small camp to a large city. Upon excavation, of course, it rarely turns out to be that simple. The site is the basic unit for stratigraphic studies; it is an almost certain assumption that cultural changes here can only be the result of the passage of time. It is in effect the *minimum operational unit of geographical space* [emphasis added]. (Willey and Phillips 1958:18)

As is immediately evident, this definition does not adequately cover every type of spatial entity that would be considered a "site" in current archaeological research; but it represents a thoughtful and useful early attempt at a comprehensive definition of a very basic analytical concept.

Prior to Willey and Phillips's pioneering effort, the importance of sites as the primary units of archaeological study and analysis had been recognized by Graham Clark, as well as by Walter Taylor as part of the "conjunctive approach" he proposed in the course of his critical work, *A Study of Archaeology* (Taylor 1948), many of whose suggestions were to be incorporated into the methods of the "new" archaeologists of the 1960s and 1970s. Taylor favored a strongly materialist approach to archaeological data, in which data should be reported in such a manner as to enable future reanalysis by other investigators. The site was the basic unit to be used for developing a chronological sequence and syntheses of material remains, which would then be used to discover the pattern of life followed at the site in the past. Only when the site had been fully studied, analyzed, and described could its contents be compared with those of other sites. Intersite comparisons would then form the basis of understanding broader life patterns within a larger territory. Taylor's emphasis on reconstructing lifeways from material remains representing single sites echoed the approach advocated by Graham Clark in the late 1930s (Trigger 1989:277–278).

With the advent of the "NEW" ARCHAEOLOGY, the focus on single sites was to shift to an emphasis on the role played by individual sites in regional site systems and networks (Dunnell and Dancey 1983:267), a reorientation to the ARCHAEOLOGICAL RECORD from a local to a regional scale that has been attributed to the influence of Lewis Binford's work (Nance 1983:289). While it is true that many of the large-scale archaeological surveys of the 1970s and beyond were regionally rather than individual site-oriented (see, e.g., Sanders, Parsons, and Santley 1979; Keller and Rupp 1983), many were focused at the level of the site, and new methods and strategies of ecological and economic investigation, such as CATCHMENT ANALYSIS—which is usually termed *site catchment analysis*—have been concentrated on the site as the primary unit of study. Indeed, as David H. Thomas has pointed out, Binford himself considered the site and the region to be equally valid units of investigation and analysis.

> Binford also based his 1964 discussion on the site concept when he argued that there are only two basic sampling universes in excavation or fieldwork: the region and the site. "Populations of sites must be investigated within a universe defined in spatial terms, the region. Populations of cultural items and features must be investigated within a universe defined by . . . the site." (Binford 1964:433; quoted in Thomas 1975:61)

Thomas goes on to point out that although the site concept is accepted as archaeology's minimal spatial unit, it is not necessarily its minimal *operational* unit (Thomas 1975:62); and in non-site-oriented projects, both smaller units (e.g., artifacts, excavation units, activity areas, features) and larger ones, such as the geographic region, may become the primary units of interest.

At present, while interest in regional studies is still strong, the individual site continues to be a basic operational unit in archaeological research, even in projects emphasizing the investigation of smaller units, such as households, as well as larger ones. Surveys continue to discover and define sites, even when these are not the primary units of interest, and an increasing variety of site types continues to be identified. Despite so-called "siteless" surveys and the growth of studies concentrated on activity areas and HOUSEHOLD ARCHAEOLOGY since the 1970s, the traditional concept of the site remains an integral part of archaeological research and interpretation, and one that is not likely to disappear in the future.

REFERENCES

Aitken, Martin. 1969. Magnetic location. In Science in archaeology, rev. and enl. ed., Don Brothwell and Eric Higgs, eds. Praeger, New York, pp. 681–694.
Binford, Lewis R. 1964. A consideration of archaeological research design. American Antiquity 29:425–441.

Clark, Anthony. 1969. Resistivity surveying. In Science in archaeology, rev. and enl. ed., Don Brothwell and Eric Higgs, eds. Praeger, New York, pp. 695–707.

Deetz, James. 1967. Invitation to archaeology. Natural History Press, New York.

Dunnell, Robert C., and William S. Dancey. 1983. The siteless survey: a regional scale data collection strategy. Advances in Archaeological Method and Theory 6:267–297.

Keller, D. R., and D. W. Rupp, eds. 1983. Archaeological survey in the Mediterranean area. BAR International Series 155. Oxford.

McKern, William C. 1939. The Midwestern Taxonomic Method as an aid to archaeological study. American Antiquity 4:301–313.

McManamon, Francis P. 1984. Discovering sites unseen. Advances in Archaeological Method and Theory 7:223–292.

Nance, Jack D. 1983. Regional sampling in archaeological survey: the statistical perspective. Advances in Archaeological Method and Theory 6:289–356.

Powell, Shirley, and Anthony L. Klasert. 1984. A method for predicting the presence of buried structures on unexcavated artifact scatters. In Papers on the archaeology of Black Mesa, Arizona, vol. 2, Stephen Plog and Shirley Powell, eds. Southern Illinois University, Carbondale and Edwardsville, pp. 39–46.

Sanders, William T., Jeffrey R. Parsons, and Robert S. Santley. 1979. The Basin of Mexico: ecological processes in the evolution of a civilization. Academic Press, New York.

Scollar, Irwin, A. Tabbagh, A. Hesse, and I. Herzog. 1990. Archaeological prospecting and remote sensing. Cambridge University Press.

Taylor, Walter W. 1948. A study of archaeology. American Anthropological Association, Menasha, Wis.

Thomas, David Hurst. 1975. Nonsite sampling in archaeology: up the creek without a site? In Sampling in archaeology, J. W. Mueller, ed. University of Arizona Press, Tucson, pp. 61–81.

Trigger, Bruce G. 1989. A history of archaeological thought. Cambridge University Press.

Willey, Gordon R., and Philip Phillips. 1958. Method and theory in American archaeology. University of Chicago Press.

SOURCES OF ADDITIONAL INFORMATION

Definitions of the site concept may be found in Willey and Phillips 1958, and in Deetz 1967, p. 11 (see References for full citations). For a discussion of site types, see Ian Hodder and Clive Orton, *Spatial Analysis in Archaeology* (London and New York, Cambridge University Press, 1976), p. 18. Much of their information is taken from the list and discussion of site types in the Addison-Wesley module *Settlement Patterns in Archaeology*, by K. C. Chang (Reading, Mass., Addison-Wesley Module 24, 1972), pp. 1–26, which may be consulted for more detail.

For a brief but pithy discussion of the site as the basic unit of archaeology, including its temporal context as determined from stratigraphy, formation processes, preservation and disturbance processes, and especially its geological environment, see Colin Renfrew's introductory essay "Archaeology and the earth sciences," in *Geoarchaeology: Earth Science and the Past*, D. A. Davidson and M. L. Shackley, eds. (London, Duckworth, 1976), pp. 1–5.

Discussions of the site as a concept are now quite uncommon in the literature. For possible future publications, forthcoming issues of *Current Anthropology* and *American Antiquity* should be consulted, as well as annual volumes of *Archaeological Method and Theory*.

SOCIAL ORGANIZATION. The set of informal, unwritten rules by which a human society is ordered into a coherent scheme or structure.

The structures of human societies are usually based on some general organizational principle. This may be genetic relatedness among individuals, in societies organized along kinship lines; in more complex societies, the organizing principle may be social inequality, expressed in hierarchies of ranks, classes, or other groups of unequal status. In cultural evolutionary thought, social organization is conceived as developing progressively from simple, kin-based systems to more complex structures with increasing degrees of differentiation, whether based on differences in wealth, power, personality traits, or manipulative skills. In anthropology, social organization is often equated with the study of kinship systems.

Sociopolitical structures have traditionally been viewed by archaeologists from an evolutionary perspective, as proceeding from small and simple to larger and more complex. This view is expressed, either implicitly or explicitly, in the hierarchical typologies of social units developed to describe levels of social organization observed in human societies throughout the world at various times, beginning with the initial three-stage scheme of cultural EVOLUTION proposed by Lewis Henry Morgan in the middle of the nineteenth century (Morgan 1851), and continuing up to the present (Sahlins and Service 1960; Service 1962, 1975; Sanders and Webster 1978; Braun and Plog 1982; Johnson and Earle 1987).

Morgan's early classification of societies was a three-part scheme, in which all CULTURES could be categorized as representing a state of savagery, barbarism, or civilization. This classificatory scheme was based on the mode of SUBSISTENCE, with savagery encompassing all hunting-and-gathering societies, barbarism all nomadic herders or pastoralists, and civilization all complex, urban societies supported by agriculture. Morgan assumed that characteristic forms of social and political organization would be found associated with each mode of subsistence (Feinman and Neitzel 1984:40). Archaeological research, however, has demonstrated that little may be inferred about social organization from knowledge of subsistence practices alone; study of SETTLEMENT PATTERNS, SITE distributions, burial practices, and community size are also essential for determining social organization (Hole 1968).

A four-stage evolutionary typology of human social organization was developed in the early 1960s by Elman Service (Service 1962). Service characterized four types of social structure, each representing a developmental stage and progressing from simplest to most complex. This is the band-tribe-chiefdom-state sequence, which has been widely used in anthropology and archaeology since

Service's original exposition. A similar four-part classificatory scheme was proposed by Morton Fried at about the same time (Fried 1960, 1967).

The simplest, and therefore supposedly earliest, social unit in Service's classification is the *band*, conceived as a small, family-based group numbering perhaps 25 persons or less, which may grow to about twice that size before fissioning into two such groups. The band represents the highest (and only) level of social integration found in the smallest nomadic groups of simple hunter-gatherers; such groups typically lack formal leadership. Archaeological evidence of this level of social organization usually consists of temporary open campsites, sometimes in combination with a semipermanent winter base camp. Many cave occupations also appear to represent the band level of organization (see Damas 1969; Williams 1974; HUNTER-GATHERER ARCHAEOLOGY).

The next level above the band is termed a *tribe*. The tribe is not a well-defined entity, and the term and concept have been criticized and rejected by many social theorists, as well as archaeologists, on the ground that the tribal concept possesses no real analytic value (Willey and Phillips 1958:19–20). Some, such as Colin Renfrew, have employed alternative terms, such as *segmentary society* (Renfrew and Bahn 1991), to describe this level of social organization. The characteristics that define a tribe are not standardized, and no consensus exists regarding what they should be. Tribes may differ from bands only in the size of their membership. They are usually conceived as relatively large, egalitarian social groups that may number up to several thousand persons, without formalized status differences other than that of group leader, or chief. The chief's authority may be transitory, of limited scope, and lacking in enforcement powers, as well as in any mechanism for its perpetuation on a chief's death. Chiefs in tribal societies often attain their position through the exercise of their personal abilities or charisma. The concept of the tribe may also include territoriality, with members of a tribal population occupying some definable geographic unit or area, although they may move from one location to another within this area on a seasonal basis, and there may be no permanent, sedentary settlements. Archaeological evidence for this level of social organizational unit is difficult to establish, since the tribe concept itself remains problematical.

In both the band and the tribe, kinship is presumed to be the primary mechanism of social integration, and the society is organized along the lines of genetic relationships among its members. This may also be true in societies displaying the next level of organization, namely the CHIEFDOM, although complex chiefdoms may develop other criteria for defining and distinguishing the social roles of particular individuals.

In chiefdoms, an individual or a lineage group will attain power over the entire social unit, usually by acquiring wealth through control of the means of production or by trade with outside groups. The resulting economic power subsequently becomes the basis for political power, which is passed on to appropriate members of the ruling lineage on the death of a paramount chief. Lineage groups in chiefdom societies may be ranked in relation to one another, from lowest to highest, in a type of organization that has been called the "conical clan" (Kirchhoff 1955; Peebles and Kus 1977).

CHIEFDOMS and STATES have the additional feature of intervening levels of organizational authority between the family or household level and the highest level of government. In a state, the number of such intermediate levels will be greater than that in a chiefdom. A convenient rule of thumb that has been used to define a state from the ARCHAEOLOGICAL RECORD is that at least three levels of organization between the household level and the top level of governmental organization must be identifiable. States have other distinctive characteristics as well, which may include a governmentally sanctioned religion or ideological system justifying or rationalizing the existing form of sociopolitical organization in ideological terms, such as the concept of divine right of rulership.

Archaeological evidence for social and political organization may be subtle and difficult to verify. Clues to sociopolitical structures of the past are obtained by archaeologists from study and interpretation of ARTIFACT distributions, settlement pattern data, and stylistic variation in artifacts. Other kinds of evidence on how past societies were organized may be recovered from burials, where grave goods interred with the deceased will frequently reflect differences of status and rank when these are present, and from examination of public architecture designed for administrative, civic, or governmental purposes, together with any artifacts consistently found in such structures (Peebles and Kus 1977).

Archaeologists may concentrate on settlement data to identify various kinds of social units from the archaeological record, and attempt to distinguish how many different levels of integration appear to be present from the analysis of these data. This approach may be used in conjunction with the comparative study of burials and grave goods (Brown 1971; Chapman, Kinnis, and Randsborg 1981). However, such evidence can provide only a basis for making INFERENCES based on social structures observed ethnographically in more recent societies. Models derived from ethnoarchaeological studies of such contemporary societies can be tested using empirical evidence from archaeological excavation. Such tests rely heavily on the goodness of fit between the model and the data from the archaeological record, which may support or fail to support expectations based on the model. Instances in which a predictive model is not supported by the data will require other explanatory strategies, and may lead to the application of alternative methods of analysis.

Current archaeological practice places less emphasis on the detection of specific social organizational levels or types, such as those outlined by Service and Fried, and more on acquiring data that will support inferences regarding behavioral processes implicated in social organizational structures, and the changes these may have undergone at different points along the developmental trajectories of prehistoric societies. Such inferences are now likely to result from tests of models derived from ethnoarchaeological studies of contemporary groups, or from descriptions in the ethnohistoric literature that may suggest how such processes operated in the past. Although each society is unique, all those displaying a similar level of integration and organization will have common features that can be used for constructing useful models of past behavior to interpret the static data of the past recovered from the archaeological record.

REFERENCES

Braun, D. P., and S. Plog. 1982. Evolution of "tribal" social networks: theory and prehistoric North American evidence. American Antiquity 47(3):504–525.

Brown, James A., ed. 1971. Approaches to the social dimensions of mortuary practice. Memoirs of the Society for American Archaeology No. 25. Washington, D.C.

Chapman, Robert, I. Kinnis, and K. Randsborg, eds. 1981. The archaeology of death. Cambridge University Press.

Damas, D., ed. 1969. Contributions to anthropology: band societies. National Museum of Canada Bulletin 228. Ottawa.

Feinman, Gary, and Jill Neitzel. 1984. Too many types: an overview of sedentary prestate societies in the Americas. Advances in Archaeological Method and Theory 7:39–102.

Fried, Morton H. 1960. On the evolution of social stratification and the state. In Culture in history, S. Diamond, ed. Columbia University Press, New York, pp. 713–731.

————. 1967. The evolution of political society: an essay in political anthropology. Random House, New York.

Hole, Frank. 1968. Evidence of social organization from western Iran. In New perspectives in archaeology, Sally Binford and Lewis R. Binford, eds. Aldine, Chicago, pp. 245–266.

Johnson, Allen W., and Timothy Earle. 1987. The evolution of human societies, from foraging group to agrarian state. Stanford University Press, Stanford, Calif.

Kirchhoff, Paul. 1955. The principles of clanship in human society. Davidson Anthropological Journal 1:1–10.

Morgan, Lewis Henry. 1851. Ancient Society. Henry Holt, New York.

Peebles, Christopher, and Susan Kus. 1977. Some archaeological correlates of ranked societies. American Antiquity 42(3):421–448.

Renfrew, Colin, and Paul Bahn. 1991. Archaeology: theories, methods and practice. Thames and Hudson, New York.

Sahlins, Marshall D., and Elman R. Service. 1960. Evolution and culture. University of Michigan Press, Ann Arbor.

Sanders, William T., and David Webster. 1978. Unilinealism, multilinealism, and the evolution of complex societies. In Social archaeology: beyond subsistence and dating, Charles L. Redman et al., eds. Academic Press, New York, pp. 249–302.

Service, Elman R. 1962. Primitive social organization. Random House, New York.

————. 1975. Origins of the state and civilization. Norton, New York.

Willey, Gordon R., and Philip Phillips. 1958. Method and theory in American archaeology. University of Chicago Press.

Williams, B. J. 1974. A model of band society. Memoirs of the Society for American Archaeology No. 29. Washington, D.C.

SOURCES OF ADDITIONAL INFORMATION

For background information on the concept of social organization and the basic principles of social structure, an older discussion from an anthropological viewpoint, which is still useful, is James L. Gibbs, Jr., "Social organization," in Horizons of Anthropology, Sol Tax, ed. (Chicago, Aldine, 1964), pp. 160–170. A volume of studies of sociopolitical structures in the prehistoric American Southwest from archaeological evidence is Stead-man Upham, Kent G. Lightfoot, and Roberta A. Jewett, eds., *The Sociopolitical Structure of Prehistoric Southwestern Societies* (Boulder, Colo., Westview Press, 1989). The extensive bibliography in the 1984 review article by Feinman and Neitzel in *Advances in Archaeological Method and Theory* (see References) includes many references to publications related to sociopolitical organization and its underlying principles.

For an introductory exposition of the band/tribe/chiefdom/state typology, see the two volumes by Elman Service (1962, 1975; see References). Descriptions of the organization of band societies may be found in B. J. Williams, *A Model of Band Society* (Washington, D.C., Memoirs of the Society for American Archaeology No. 29, 1974); and in the volume of papers presented at the Conference on Band Organization, Ottawa, 1965, published as *Contributions to Anthropology: Band Societies*, David Damas, ed. (Ottawa, National Museum of Canada Bulletin No. 228, Anthropological Series No. 84, 1969). Additional material may be found in the references cited at the end of the article HUNTER-GATHERER ARCHAEOLOGY.

For discussions of tribal societies, see Morton Fried, *The Notion of Tribe* (Menlo Park, Calif., Benjamin Cummings, 1975); David Braun and Stephen Plog, "Evolution of 'tribal' social networks: theory and prehistoric North American evidence," *American Antiquity* 47(3)(1982):504–526, which includes an extensive bibliography; and Barbara Bender, "Emergent tribal formations in the American midcontinent," *American Antiquity* 50(1)(1985):52–62, in which the author treats tribal society and its identifying characteristics from a Marxist perspective.

For detailed discussion of the CHIEFDOM and STATE levels of social organization, see the articles on these concepts in this volume, together with recommended sources.

Most recent literature may be found in current journals, including *American Antiquity* and *Journal of Anthropological Archaeology*. Latest annual reviews should also be checked for review articles.

SPATIAL ANALYSIS. The investigation of patterned regularities that are directly observable, or statistically discoverable, in distributions of archaeological remains on a landscape or its subdivisions. Also called *locational analysis*.

The study of the spatial dimension of archaeology is concerned with the investigation of spatial relationships among ARTIFACTS, ecofacts, facilities, and features, and the detection of patterning in their distributions relative to one another and to larger units. This area of study is broadly directed toward acquiring an understanding of past human behavior in its locational CONTEXT at a variety of different scales, from individual activity areas to interaction at the macroregional level. It makes use of statistical methods, and of techniques derived from geography, in the study of human settlement location, especially to infer economic and ecological factors or principles that appear to affect the location of human communities. Studies focused on smaller-scale units include analyses of patterning in remains found in activity areas or households.

The domain of locational or spatial archaeology was outlined by the British archeologist David Clarke in the 1970s. He defined this area of study in broad terms:

> Spatial archaeology might be defined as—the retrieval of information from archaeological . . . [data] and the study of the spatial consequences of . . . activity patterns within and between features and structures and their articulation with sites, site systems and their environments . . . the study of the flow and integration of activities within and between structures, sites and resource spaces . . . archaeology deals . . . with human activities at every scale, the traces and artefacts left by them, the physical infrastructure which accommodated them, the environments that they impinged upon and the interaction between all these aspects. (Clarke 1977:9)

This wide-ranging, comprehensive definition encompasses the entire field of SETTLEMENT PATTERN research and all of its specialized subdivisions. Clarke also outlined the various levels, or scales, of spatial investigation and discussed some relevant theories and models common to spatial studies (Clarke 1977:10–32). He noted that geographical models and distribution maps have been favored methods of studying spatial patterning in Europe since the time of Cyril Fox (Fox 1922; Losch 1954; Haggett 1977).

In the United States, spatial archaeology has been more concerned with studies of SOCIAL ORGANIZATION and settlement patterns "rather than artefacts and distribution maps; the anthropological dimension became stronger and the geographical aspect diminished" (Clarke 1977:3). This is especially evident in the ethnoarchaeological work of Lewis Binford (Binford 1978, 1983), which emphasizes the importance of developing appropriate methods for detecting and interpreting the tremendous variability in past human utilization of space that is evident in the ARCHAEOLOGICAL RECORD. Binford believes patterning observable in SITES is understandable and explicable only from information obtained through actualistic studies, such as those he undertook among the Nunamiut Eskimo in the 1970s (Binford 1978), an opinion now shared by many others (see ETHNOARCHAEOLOGY).

Generally speaking, in America spatial analysis has been a part of SETTLEMENT PATTERN research, and has drawn much of its focus and methodology from ethnoarchaeological studies such as Binford's. Many recent spatial studies by North American archaeologists have been focused on small scales of analysis, such as the activity area or the household (see HOUSEHOLD ARCHAEOLOGY), rather than on larger units such as the region, although studies on this scale have also been carried out (e.g., Blanton et al. 1981). While current work represents aspects of spatial archaeology on a variety of scales, there seems to be little recognition of any overlying unity of goals or theoretical approach (Agorsah 1988).

Currently, spatial analysis makes use of a variety of methods and techniques, including ARTIFACT and SITE distribution mapping, SITE system analysis, and almost any kind of quantitative approach focused on spatial relationships among archaeological remains such as features, artifacts, and facilities, in which investigators seek to determine the significance of observed regularities and patterns in the distribution of such units, or of larger units such as whole sites or regions engaged in interactive trading networks (Hodder 1972, 1978; Hodder and Orton

1976). Patterns are interpreted as indicative of the relative effects of environmental, economic, and sociopolitical factors on the location and distribution of sites and on distributions of smaller units within sites. Statistical techniques are employed to determine how much of the observed patterning can be explained by each of a possible range of such factors (Whallon 1973, 1974, 1984; Earle 1976; Pinder, Shimada, and Gregory 1979). Investigators interested in identifying factors involved in the choice of site location frequently employ mathematical or theoretical models of this process, and devise ways to test these using empirical data (see, e.g., Green 1973; Crumley 1979). Trend surface analysis has also been employed to highlight important trends, for example, the distribution density within a defined, mapped area of a particular category of ARTIFACT, which is often useful for reconstructing patterns of EXCHANGE or trade of particular items (Renfrew and Bahn 1991:323).

REFERENCES

Agorsah, Emmanuel Kofi. 1988. Evaluating spatial behavior patterns of prehistoric societies. Journal of Anthropological Archaeology 7:231–247.
Binford, Lewis R. 1978. Nunamiut ethnoarchaeology. Academic Press, New York.
———. 1983. People in their lifespace. In In Pursuit of the past: decoding the archaeological record. Thames and Hudson, New York, pp. 144–192.
Blanton, Richard E., Stephen Kowalewski, Gary Feinman, and Jill Appel. 1981. Ancient Mesoamerica: a comparison of change in three regions. Cambridge University Press.
Clarke, David L., ed. 1977. Spatial archaeology. Academic Press, New York.
Crumley, Carole L. 1979. Three locational models: an epistemological assessment for anthropology and archaeology. Advances in Archaeological Method and Theory 2:141–173.
Earle, Timothy K. 1976. A nearest neighbor analysis of two Formative settlement systems. In The early Mesoamerican village, Kent V. Flannery, ed. Academic Press, New York, pp. 196–223.
Fox, Cyril. 1922. The archaeology of the Cambridge region. Cambridge University Press.
Green, Ernestene L. 1973. Location analysis of prehistoric Maya sites in northern British Honduras. American Antiquity 38(3):279–293.
Haggett, Peter, Andrew D. Cliff, and Allan Frey. 1977. Locational analysis in human geography. 2nd ed. Edward Arnold, London.
Hodder, Ian. 1972. Locational models and the study of Romano-British settlement. In Models in archaeology, David L. Clarke, ed. Methuen, London, pp. 887–909.
———. 1977. Some new directions in the spatial analysis of archaeological data at the regional scale (macro). In Spatial archaeology, David L. Clarke, ed. Academic Press, New York, pp. 223–352.
———, ed. 1978. The spatial organisation of culture. Duckworth, London.
Hodder, Ian, and Clive Orton. 1976. Spatial analysis in archaeology. Cambridge University Press, London and New York.
Losch, August. 1954. The economics of location. Translated from the second revised edition by William H. Woglom. . . . Yale University Press, New Haven.
Pinder, D., I. Shimada, and D. Gregory. 1979. The nearest neighbor statistic: archaeological application and developments. American Antiquity 44:430–445.

Renfrew, Colin, and Paul Bahn. 1991. Archaeology: theories, methods and practice. Thames and Hudson, New York.

Whallon, Robert, Jr. 1973. Spatial analysis of occupation floors. Vol. 1: Application of dimensional analysis of variance. American Antiquity 38:266–278.

———. 1974. Spatial analysis of occupation floors. Vol. 2: Nearest neighbor analysis. American Antiquity 39:16–34.

———. 1984. Unconstrained clustering for the analysis of spatial distributions in archaeology. In Intrasite spatial analysis in archaeology, H. J. Hietala, ed. Cambridge University Press, pp. 242–277.

SOURCES OF ADDITIONAL INFORMATION

For a basic, general explanation of spatial analysis and distribution studies, see Chapter 9 in *Archaeology: Theories, Methods and Practice,* by Colin Renfrew and Paul Bahn (New York, Thames and Hudson, 1991), especially pp. 320–327. The paper in Clarke 1977 by Ian Hodder (see References) outlines the area of study, and accounts for the apparent randomness of many archaeological distributions, but requires some statistical background.

Access to literature of intrasite spatial analysis through the early 1980s, together with a lengthy discussion of goals and analytic techniques for such analysis, is available in the review article by Christopher Carr, "The nature of organization of intrasite archaeological records and spatial analytic approaches to their investigation," *Advances in Archaeological Method and Theory* 7(1984):103–222. A collection of papers on the same subject was also published in the same year, titled *Intrasite Spatial Analysis in Archaeology*, Harold Hietala, ed. (Cambridge, Cambridge University Press, 1984).

A number of papers on spatial analysis deal with new methods and techniques. Among these are M. R. Attwell and M. Fletcher, "An analytical technique for investigating spatial relationships," *Journal of Archaeological Science* 14(1)(1987):1–11; A. Voorrips and J. M. O'Shea, "Conditional spatial patterning: beyond the nearest neighbor," *American Antiquity* 52(3)(1987):500–521; K. L. Kvamme, "One-sample tests in regional archaeological analysis, new possibilities through computer technology," *American Antiquity* 55(2)(1990):367–381; and S. M. Wilson and D. J. Melnick, "Modeling randomness in locational archaeology," *Journal of Archaeological Science* 47(4)(1990):403–412.

For the most recent publications on spatial analysis, current issues of the journals *American Antiquity, Journal of Archaeological Science*, and *Journal of Anthropological Archaeology* should be consulted, as well as *Current Anthropology* and *Archaeological Method and Theory* for more recent reviews.

SPECIALIZATION. The presence in a society of persons who engage in economic activities not directly related to SUBSISTENCE or the production of life's basic necessities, who devote all or a significant part of their time to other pursuits. Such persons may be priests or other ritual specialists; craftsmen or artisans skilled in various technological processes; scribes, artists, or musicians; administrators; or economic specialists, such as professional merchants or traders. Specialization is characteristically associated with culturally complex societies, such as CHIEFDOMS and STATES.

Anthropologists and archaeologists have usually interpreted the origins of specialization by using one of three types of models: a commercial development model, an adaptationist model, or a political model (Brumfiel and Earle 1987:1). Traditionally, a model similar to the one developed by Friedrich Engels in the 1880s (Engels 1972) has been adopted, which assumes that production of a food surplus is a necessary prerequisite for the presence of specialists in a society, and therefore specialization would not be found in preagricultural groups (Gamble 1982).

With the beginning of intensive studies of modern hunter-gatherers in the 1960s, however, it became clear that this assumption is not necessarily valid. Marshall Sahlins was among the first to question this assumption, maintaining that, on the basis of his own observations, hunter-gatherers had more leisure time for specialized activities than those living in agricultural societies (Sahlins 1958, 1972).

The political structure of centralized societies, such as chiefdoms and states, facilitates specialization; the latter, in turn, increases the efficiency of production. Part-time specialization can and does exist without production of a surplus. Most hunter-gatherer societies have at least part-time ritual specialists, such as shamans; these specialists do, however, engage in subsistence activities during part of their time, as do all members of a hunting-gathering society.

Archaeological evidence of specialization consists of several types of data. According to Peebles and Kus (1977), a principal indicator is the presence of monuments or monumental architecture, which requires planning; the mobilization of a large work force; and the organization and coordination of the latter's activities, which implies the presence of administrative specialists. Large-scale public works, such as irrigation systems and other methods of agricultural intensification, are further evidence of administrative specialization (Abrams 1987). Craft specialization will leave traces of the presence of organized production beyond the household level, on either an interhousehold or an intercommunity basis. If a society is producing specialized goods as a commercial activity, this will be detectable in the presence of uniformity or standardization of form in the products manufactured, as well as their production in large quantities, with production activities frequently confined to specialized locations.

Maurizio Tosi has developed some detailed criteria for recovering indicators of craft specialization in the ARCHAEOLOGICAL RECORD. Tosi identifies evidence for specialized production and labor allocation at several organizational levels, including the household, the intrasettlement specialized activity area (of which he distinguishes four types), and the extralocal center of specialized production. He lists six classes of archaeological indicators for specialized craft production: the presence of processing facilities, such as kilns; tools for manufacturing other tools, such as molds for metal casting; residues of manufacturing processes, such as lithic debitage, metal slag, and other detritus; semifinished products, including flint blocks or cores, and metal ingots; stocks of unworn, unused products awaiting distribution; and materials awaiting recycling or repair, such as worn knife blades in need of resharpening (Tosi 1984:23–27).

Detailed archaeological evidence for craft specialization among the early Inca collected by Craig Morris (Morris and Thompson 1985) shows that a group of women specialized in the production of clothing and beer in a segregated work area dedicated to these activities. Their archaeological traces were supplemented by ethnohistoric records to reconstruct the organization of a prehistoric craft.

> [At] Huanuco Pampa . . . [Andes] . . . a compound of 50 buildings [was] given over to the making of beer and clothing. Thousands of special ceramic jars and dozens of spindle whorls and weaving implements provided the archaeological clues; the ethnohistoric record linked these with beer and cloth production, more particularly with a special social class of Inca women know as *aklla*, who were kept segregated from the rest of the population . . . the compound [was] enclosed by a surround wall with a single entrance—and the density of occupational refuse suggested the presence of permanently segregated *aklla* craft specialists. (Renfrew and Bahn 1991:193)

Among the first occupations to become specialized were lithic toolmaking and potterymaking. Other early specialists most probably included shaman/priests with specialized knowledge of curing procedures and other rituals. Associated with the latter was usually a body of specialized knowledge of the medicinal properties of herbs, plants, and animal products. Although specialties such as ritual and curing may leave fewer traces in the archaeological record than manufacturing activities, some evidence may survive in the form of preserved ritual paraphernalia, or even of concentrations of preserved remains of medicinal herbs or plants, although this is quite rare.

Differentiating between full-time and part-time specialization from the archaeological record can be challenging. Peebles and Kus (1977) maintain this can be done by determining the level of sociopolitical organization present, since they assume a direct correlation between full-time specialization and a state level of organization, with part-time specialization confined to chiefdoms. In actuality, the situation is rarely that simple, and many kinds of data will usually be required to determine both the form of government and the presence of full- or part-time specialists (Peregrine 1991).

Commercial production may exist in chiefdoms as well as states, since products confined to the use of elites and ritual specialists are frequently an important focus of trade in such societies, and are manufactured in large quantities for this purpose. A well-known example is the production of thousands of widely traded copper and mica ornaments by societies of the prehistoric Hopewell culture of North America (Prufer 1964). In chiefdoms and states alike, specialization at the household level may exist alongside commercial production in dedicated manufacturing areas. Tosi's research into craft specialization in ancient Iraq has demonstrated this situation, where textile manufacture and leatherworking were carried out only in residential areas, while stone tools and gem carving were confined to specialized workshop areas (Tosi 1984).

More recent archaeological research into ancient craft specialization (Evans 1978; Chang 1980; Muller 1984; Morris and Thompson 1985; Tobert 1985; Arnold 1987; Brumfiel 1987; Earle 1987; Galvin 1987; Santley, Arnold, and Pool 1989) typically employs a variety of quantitative techniques, including multivariate statistical methods, to simplify and clarify the often highly complex information retrieved from the archaeological record, and to detect significant patterns that permit more detailed and sophisticated interpretations of these data than were possible in the past. Such methods may permit the construction of models for interpreting prehistoric economic systems (e.g., Gilman 1976, 1987) that can shed light on the cultural dynamics implicated in the development and operation of such systems, and the changes they underwent through time.

REFERENCES

Abrams, Elliot M. 1987. Economic specialization and construction personnel in Classic Period Copan, Honduras. American Antiquity 52(3):485–499.

Arnold, Jeanne. 1987. Craft specialization in the prehistoric Channel Islands. University of California Publications in Anthropology 18. Berkeley.

Brumfiel, Elizabeth M. 1987. Elite and utilitarian crafts in the Aztec state. In Specialization, exchange, and complex societies, Elizabeth M. Brumfiel and Timothy K. Earle, eds. Cambridge University Press, pp. 102–118.

Brumfiel, Elizabeth M., and Timothy K. Earle. 1987. Specialization, exchange, and complex societies: an introduction. In Specialization, exchange, and complex societies, E. M. Brumfiel and T. K. Earle, eds. Cambridge University Press, pp. 1–9.

———, eds. 1987. Specialization, exchange, and complex societies. Cambridge University Press.

Chang, Kwang-Chih. 1980. Shang civilization. Yale University Press, New Haven.

Earle, Timothy K. 1987. Specialization and the production of wealth: Hawaiian chiefdoms and the Inka empire. In Specialization, exchange, and complex societies, E. M. Brumfiel and T. K. Earle, eds. Cambridge University Press, pp. 64–75.

Engels, Friedrich. 1972. The origins of the family, private property and the state, E. Reed, ed., R. Vernon, trans. Pathfinder Press, New York. (Originally published in 1884)

Evans, Robert K. 1978. Early craft specialization: an example from the Balkan Chalcolithic. In Social archaeology: beyond subsistence and dating, Charles L. Redman et al., eds. Academic Press, New York, pp. 113–129.

Galvin, Kathleen F. 1987. Forms of finance and forms of production: the evolution of specialized livestock production in the ancient Near East. In Specialization, exchange, and complex societies, Elizabeth M. Brumfiel and Timothy K. Earle, eds. Cambridge University Press, pp. 119–129.

Gamble, Clive. 1982. Leadership and ''surplus'' production. In Ranking, resources and exchange, C. Renfrew and S. Shennan, eds. Cambridge University Press, pp. 100–105.

Gilman, Antonio. 1976. Bronze Age dynamics in southeast Spain. Dialectical Anthropology 1:307–319.

———. 1987. Unequal development in Copper Age Iberia. In Specialization, exchange, and complex societies, Elizabeth M. Brumfiel and Timothy K. Earle, eds. Cambridge University Press, pp. 22–29.

Morris, C., and D. Thompson. 1985. Huanuco Pampa: An Inca city and its hinterland. Thames and Hudson, London.

Muller, Jon. 1984. Mississippian specialization and salt. American Antiquity 49(3):489–507.

Peebles, Christopher S., and Susan M. Kus. 1977. Some archaeological correlates of ranked societies. American Antiquity 42(3):421–448.

Peregrine, Peter. 1991. Some political aspects of craft specialization. World Archaeology 23(1):1–11.

Prufer, Olaf H. 1964. The Hopewell complex of Ohio. Hopewellian Studies, Illinois State Museum Scientific Papers 12. Springfield.

Renfrew, Colin, and Paul Bahn. 1991. Archaeology: theories, methods and practice. Thames and Hudson, New York.

Sahlins, Marshall. 1958. Social stratification in Polynesia. University of Washington Press, Seattle.

———. 1972. Stone age economics. Aldine, Chicago.

Santley, Robert S., P. J. Arnold III, and C. A. Pool. 1989. The ceramics production system at Matacapan, Veracruz, Mexico. Journal of Field Archaeology 16(1):107–132.

Tobert, Natalie. 1985. Craft specialisation: a seasonal camp in Kebkebiya. World Archaeology 17(2):278–288.

Tosi, Maurizio. 1984. The notion of craft specialization and its representation in the archaeological record of early states in the Turanian Basin. In Marxist perspectives in archaeology, M. Spriggs, ed. Cambridge University Press, pp. 22–52.

SOURCES OF ADDITIONAL INFORMATION

A brief discussion of specialization in relation to trade and exchange is in the introductory first chapter by Elizabeth Brumfiel and Timothy Earle to their 1987 volume of papers (see References for citation). For discussions of the question of the necessity of a surplus as a prerequisite to specialization, see Gamble 1982 and Sahlins 1972 (see References for complete citations).

Volume 23, no. 1 (June 1991) of *World Archaeology* is devoted to craft production and specialization. The eight papers included range from Peregrine's discussion of the relationship between craft specialization, the production and consumption of elite goods, and political centralization (see References), to articles focusing on the specialized production of pottery, beads, lithic tools, and metal products at a variety of locations in both hemispheres.

Unfortunately there is no general review of the literature of specialization. A review of literature pertaining to a limited aspect and time period is L. Orguera, "Specialization and the Middle/Upper Paleolithic transition," *Current Anthropology* 25(1984):73–98.

Current issues of *American Antiquity*, *World Archaeology*, *Journal of Anthropological Archaeology*, and *American Anthropologist* should be checked for more recent publications; the *Annual Review of Anthropology* and *Archaeological Method and Theory* should also be monitored for future review articles.

STATE. A level of sociopolitical organization characterized by a strong, centralized bureaucratic government and a professional ruling class whose legitimacy is based on some claim or principle other than kinship, with established mechanisms for perpetuating the governmental structure independently of the individuals occupying its key positions.

The state is a form of human sociopolitical organization in which a population is united by allegiance to a single sovereign form of government. In archaeology, a state must be defined both in terms of its spatial dimensions and in terms of its characteristic organizational structure, insofar as this can be identified from the material record. (See also CHIEFDOM; SOCIAL ORGANIZATION.)

A classic definition of the state as it is understood within archaeology is that formulated by Robert Carneiro in 1970:

> A state is an autonomous political unit, encompassing many communities within its territory and having a centralized government with the power to draft men for war or work, levy and collect taxes, and decree and enforce laws. (Carneiro 1970:733)

This definition includes most of what have traditionally been regarded as the requisite characteristics of a state, namely autonomy, territoriality, and a strong, enforcing central government with many smaller social units under its administrative control. The last-mentioned attribute also implies a certain scale with respect to population and territorial size, relatively larger than that of other sociopolitical units.

The concept of statehood has been present in Western thought since the time of the ancient Greeks, when it was discussed by Plato and Aristotle with reference to the Greek polis, or city-state. The state in its present meaning, and as a normative concept, first appeared in the sixteenth century, when it was introduced into European thought by Niccolo Machiavelli at a time when the nation-states of Europe were developing (Watkins 1968).

Defining the state and delineating the social processes leading to its formation in early civilizations has long been a subject of interest to historians and anthropologists, as well as to philosophers and political scientists. Edward Tylor (1871), Lewis Henry Morgan (1877), and Sir Henry Maine (1861) all speculated on the development of prehistoric sociopolitical organization during the early days of anthropology, using the assumptions of the nineteenth-century evolutionists; and Herbert Spencer in the 1880s actually developed a political typology of preindustrial societies that has subsequently been used to define various levels and concepts of SOCIAL ORGANIZATION, including the state (Spencer 1967[1882]). Robert Lowie produced a book on the origins of the state in the 1920s (Lowie 1927).

Some theorists have assigned varying degrees of importance to the role of conflict or warfare in state formation, and the relative importance of enforcing powers as an integral component of state government (Haas 1981; Webster 1975).

Ronald Cohen and Elman Service (1978), Jonathan Haas (1982), and others have distinguished between theories of state formation emphasizing the role of conflict as a primary causal variable, of which Morton Fried (Fried 1960) and Robert Carneiro (Carneiro 1970, 1981) have developed notable examples, and theories placing greater importance on the processes of social integration, or "managerialism" (Maisels 1990:203), such as that of Elman Service. According to Service, the state was the logical culmination of the growth of bureaucratic structures and institutions that developed with increasing social complexity (Service 1975). Others have assigned causal importance to long-distance trading and exchange networks in the development of the state (Brumfiel and Earle 1987; Johnson and Earle 1987), while others have stressed economic factors implicated in the mode of production. The latter include various Marxian interpretations of sociopolitical development, such as those of Marvin Harris (Harris 1968, 1979) and Jonathan Friedman (Friedman 1975). More recently, Charles Spencer has distinguished between two major current positions regarding state formation, based in the two principal views of the evolutionary process held by contemporary neoevolutionists. The first of these he terms the *transformationalist/punctualtionalist* position, in which the state is regarded as being qualitatively different from previous governmental forms, attained through stepwise change, and achieved relatively rapidly by transformation. The second, the *gradualist* or *continualist* position, views statehood as an arbitrary organizational "type" imposed on a continuum of evolutionary development. Spencer himself favors the transformationalist position (Charles Spencer 1990).

In archaeology, problems of defining the state have been focused on acquiring adequate archaeological evidence to document its presence. Since archaeologists deal primarily with the material aspect of civilizations and other cultural entities, their concern with defining the state is usually centered on acquiring empirical evidence for the existence of prehistoric state societies, and with developing ways in which their presence may be detected from material remains surviving in the ARCHAEOLOGICAL RECORD. Since the 1960s, many processual archaeologists have addressed this problem (e.g., Wright and Johnson 1975; Peebles and Kus 1977; Price 1978; Charles Spencer 1979, 1982, 1990). One of the earliest systematic attempts to document state formation from examination of the archaeological record, in combination with ethnohistorical material, was that of Service (Service 1975). Haas later devised an empirical test of the relative validity of conflict vs. integration models of state formation using only material evidence, which forced him to conclude that available archaeological data are inadequate for confirming or refuting either model, although what evidence exists provides stronger support for conflict theory than for the integrationist position (Haas 1982).

Identifying the presence of a state level of sociopolitical organization, and distinguishing it from less complex forms such as the CHIEFDOM by attempting to define the number of hierarchical levels of organization that can be verified from the archaeological record, has become another key problem in twentieth-century archaeology, one that has generated considerable discussion and debate (Sanders and Webster 1978; Cohen and Service 1978; Haas 1979, 1982; Jones and Kautz 1981). A closely related question has been the controversy regarding the existence and archaeological detectability of primary, or "pristine," states and "secondary" states. The latter are viewed by those who make this distinction as brought into being by contact with a "pristine" state, and are often characterized as typically "nonurban" in settlement pattern (see Sanders and Price 1968; Price 1978; Charles Spencer 1982, 1990).

The need to develop reliable criteria for identifying states in terms of their material correlates that can be verified or falsified from archaeological evidence is apparent. One such set of criteria, suggested by Herbert Spencer's "doubly compound" societal type as elaborated by Robert Carneiro (Spencer 1967; Carneiro 1981:45–46, 68–69), would define the state archaeologically by detecting the presence of three levels of territorial and political organization, namely a local or village level; a larger districtwide level, with local villages administered under the direction of a larger political unit; and a state level, in which local and district-level structures are subordinate to "a single, overarching polity" (Carneiro 1981:69). This TYPOLOGY, of course, requires a set of empirically verifiable, material criteria for its detection in the archaeological record (see Peebles and Kus 1977).

Many archaeologists regard settlement data and other spatial patterning as the primary evidence for state detection; others stress the importance of public architecture as the primary distinguishing characteristic; and others emphasize artifacts of an administrative or elite nature, and their distribution patterns in the archaeological record of complex sites. The combination of all these categories of material evidence is necessary for addressing questions as complex as those regarding the processes of prehistoric state formation.

Another important preoccupation of archaeologists investigating complex cultures since the 1960s has been defining the social and cultural processes implicated in state formation. Robert Carneiro, in his classic paper on the state, defined social *circumscription* as the primary independent dynamic variable leading to the formation of states. Circumscription occurs when land, resources, and social opportunity all become severely restricted, usually as a consequence of population expansion and resulting ecological pressures (Carneiro 1970; Graber and Roscoe 1988; Schacht 1988).

Other sociocultural processes leading to the rise of state bureaucracies, under the conditions of social systemic stress that may require the state as a survival mechanism, were identified and discussed by Kent Flannery in another classic paper (Flannery 1972).

An example of developing and applying archaeological evidence for a state level of organization in southwestern Iran is the work of Henry Wright and Gregory Johnson (1975). The archaeological evidence cited in support includes the presence of large towns with extensive areas of elaborate architecture; inscribed tablets written in an undeciphered Proto-Elamite script, of which only the numbers can be read but that appear to be summaries of receipts and expenditures; the presence of "administrative artifacts," such as seals of both stamp and cylinder types, used to identify bills of lading for shipments by illiterate transporters; evidence of a four-level hierarchy of settlement (based on SITE sizes and numbers); and evidence of major changes in population size and density, as well as in densities of imported and exported materials and manufactured goods, throughout the period of state formation and statehood. The authors' position with respect to the dynamics of state formation appears to belong in the transformationist/punctuationist camp. They note, however, that although the southwestern Iran area has been intensely studied by archaeologists for nearly a century, archaeological data supporting primary state formation in this area are "remarkably incomplete" (Wright and Johnson 1975:283); and the problems of determining the relative influence and causal importance of different system variables in the state formation process remain unresolved.

A more recent treatment of the mechanisms leading to state formation may be found in Charles Spencer (1990). He regards the state as one of a very limited number of basic variable forms that human sociopolitical organization may take, and that may evolve from the complex chiefdom. Spencer agrees with Henry Wright (Wright 1977) that a state will successfully emerge from a chiefdom only via a transformational or punctuational process. He presents two archaeological examples of primary state formation, both from Mesoamerica (Monte Alban and Teotihuacán). Among the archaeological criteria for state formation that he cites are dramatic increases in the number and variety of administrative facilities (i.e., public buildings); evidence of larger populations, concentrated in nucleated, centralized communities that served as administrative decision-making centers; an inscriptional record; construction of massive defensive walls; and the appearance of warrior societies with animal "logos." Such evidence as that cited in these two studies is, of course, not entirely conclusive and could be interpreted in support of other developments than state formation. But until such time as unique archaeological markers for the presence (or absence) of statehood may be identified, evidence such as that cited by these authors, and by Haas (1982), remains the best available for making precise identifications of the forms of prehistoric sociopolitical organization from the material record of the past.

REFERENCES

Brumfiel, Elizabeth M., and Timothy K. Earle, eds. 1987. Specialization, exchange, and complex societies. Cambridge University Press.
Carneiro, Robert L. 1970. A theory of the origin of the state. Science 169:733–738.
———. 1981. The chiefdom, precursor of the state. In The transition to statehood in the New World, G. D. Jones and Robert Kautz, eds. Cambridge University Press, pp. 37–79.
———. 1987. The evolution of complexity in human societies and its mathematical expression. International Journal of Comparative Sociology 28 (3–4):111–128.
———. 1988. The circumscription theory, challenge and response. American Behavioral Scientist 31(4):497–511.

Cohen, Ronald, and Elman R. Service, eds. 1978. Origins of the state: the anthropology of political evolution. Institute for the Study of Human Issues, Philadelphia.

Flannery, Kent V. 1972. The cultural evolution of civilizations. Annual Review of Ecology and Systematics 3:399–426.

Fried, Morton. 1960. On the evolution of social stratification and the state. In Culture in history: essays in honor of Paul Radin, Stanley Diamond, ed. Columbia University Press, New York, pp. 713–731.

Friedman, J. 1975. Tribes, states, and transformations. In Marxist analyses and social anthropology, M. Bloch, ed. Wiley, New York, pp. 161–202.

Graber, R. B., and P. B. Roscoe. 1988. Circumscription and the evolution of society: introduction [editorial]. American Behavioral Scientist 31(4):405–415.

Haas, Jonathan. 1979. The evolution of the prehistoric state: toward an archaeological analysis of political organization. Ph.D. dissertation, Department of Anthropology, Columbia University.

———. 1981. Class conflict and the state in the New World. In The transition to statehood in the New World, G. D. Jones and R. R. Kautz, eds. Cambridge University Press, pp. 80–102.

———. 1982. The evolution of the prehistoric state. Columbia University Press, New York.

Harris, Marvin. 1968. The rise of anthropological theory. Crowell, New York.

———. 1979. Cultural materialism: the struggle for a science of culture. Random House, New York.

Johnson, A. W., and T. K. Earle. 1987. The evolution of human societies from foraging group to agrarian state. Stanford University Press, Stanford, Calif.

Jones, Grant D., and Robert R. Kautz, eds. 1981. The transition to statehood in the New World. Cambridge University Press.

Lowie, Robert. 1927. The origin of the state. Harcourt, Brace & World, New York.

Maine, Henry S. 1861. Ancient law. Reprinted Peter Smith, Gloucester, Mass., 1970.

Maisels, Charles Keith. 1990. The emergence of civilization, from hunting and gathering to agriculture, cities, and the state in the Near East. Routledge, London and New York.

Morgan, Lewis Henry. 1877. Ancient society. Reprint ed., Eleanor Leacock, ed. Peter Smith, Gloucester, Mass., 1963.

Patterson, Thomas, and Christine Gailey, eds. 1987. Power relations and state formation. Archaeology Section, American Anthropological Association, Washington, D.C.

Peebles, Christopher, and Susan Kus. 1977. Some archaeological correlates of ranked societies. American Antiquity 42(3):421–428.

Price, Barbara. 1978. Secondary state formation: an explanatory model. In The origins of the state, Ronald Cohen and Elman R. Service, eds. Institute for the Study of Human Issues, Philadelphia, pp. 161–186.

Roscoe, P. B. 1988. From big-men to the state, a processual approach to circumscription theory. American Behavioral Scientist 31(4):472–483.

Sanders, William T., and Barbara Price. 1968. Mesoamerica, the evolution of a civilization. Random House, New York.

Sanders, William T., and David Webster. 1978. Unilinealism, multilinealism, and the evolution of complex societies. In Social archaeology, Charles Redman et al., eds. Academic Press, New York, pp. 249–302.

Schacht, R. M. 1988. Circumscription theory. American Behavioral Scientist 31(4):438–448.

Service, Elman R. 1975. Origins of the state and civilization: the process of cultural evolution. W. W. Norton, New York.

Spencer, Charles S. 1979. Irrigation, administration, and society in Formative Tehuacán. In Prehistoric social, political, and economic development in the area of the Tehuacán Valley. University of Michigan Museum of Anthropology, Technical Reports 11. Ann Arbor.

———. 1982. The Cuicatlan Canada and Monte Alban: a study of primary state formation. Academic Press, New York.

———. 1990. On the tempo and mode of state formation: neoevolutionism reconsidered. Journal of Anthropological Archaeology 9(1):1–30.

Spencer, Herbert. 1967. The evolution of society: selections from Herbert Spencer's Principles of sociology [1882], Robert L. Carneiro, ed. University of Chicago Press.

Tylor, Edward B. 1871. Primitive culture. J. Murray, London.

Watkins, Frederick M. 1968. State II: the concept. International encyclopedia of the social sciences 15. Macmillan and Free Press, New York, pp. 150–157.

Webster, David. 1975. Warfare and the evolution of the state: a reconsideration. American Antiquity 40:464–470.

Wright, Henry T. 1977. Toward an explanation of the origin of the state. In The explanation of prehistoric change, James N. Hill, ed. University of New Mexico Press, Albuquerque.

Wright, Henry T., and Gregory A. Johnson. 1975. Population, exchange and early state formation in southwestern Iran. American Anthropologist 77(2):267–289.

SOURCES OF ADDITIONAL INFORMATION

The most thorough general treatment of the subject of state formation from an archaeological point of view is in Jonathan Haas's published doctoral dissertation (Haas 1982; see References), which includes the most comprehensive review and discussion of conflict and integrationist theories of state formation (see especially chapters 2 and 3). Briefer coverage of this theme may be found in Cohen and Service 1978 (in the introduction by Ronald Cohen), and in Maisels (1990, chapter 7; both cited in References).

For further discussion of conflict theories of state formation, see the classic paper by Carneiro (1970) and *American Behavioral Scientist* (vol. 31, no. 4, 1988), which is devoted to discussions of Carneiro's circumscription theory of state formation. Further material on conflict theories is in Haas 1981; Fried 1960; and Webster 1975 (all listed in References).

For historical material on the development of the concept of the state, see Watkins 1968, and the accompanying article in the *International Encyclopedia of the Social Sciences*, vol. 15, by Morton Fried, "State I: the institution" (New York, Macmillan and Free Press, 1968), pp. 143–150.

Discussions of the problems inherent in archaeologically testing for the presence of the state are in Service 1975 and Haas 1981, 1982 (see References).

The excellent bibliography in Haas 1982 is now out-of-date but still useful. The bibliography in Spencer 1990 updates this somewhat, although Spencer's coverage is far less comprehensive. Key sources should be checked in recent updates of the *Social Sciences Citation Index* for supplementary and more recent material. Current issues of

Journal of Anthropological Archaeology, *American Antiquity*, and *Current Anthropology* should also be checked for the most recent literature, as well as the appropriate annual review volumes.

STRATIGRAPHY. The layered pattern of archaeological deposits in deep archaeological sites, where strata containing cultural materials from different occupations of the SITE have been successively deposited one over another. The sequence of cultural strata will be visible on the walls of a trench cut through the deposits, allowing the archaeologist to construct a relative chronology of the SITE's occupation history. (See also RELATIVE DATING.)

Stratigraphy is based on the concept of deposition and depositional events (Stein 1987:337). Sequences of layered deposits are used by archaeologists for relatively dating cultural materials occurring in these deposits, as well as for reconstructing characteristics of the past environment from deposits of soils and botanical remains, and for analyzing the depositional and taphonomic processes that lead to the formation of archaeological SITES.

The term and basic concepts of stratigraphy are derived from geology. Stratification of rocks in superimposed layers was observed and described by the Scottish geologist James Hutton in his *Theory of the Earth* (Hutton 1795). The "law of superposition," the principle underlying stratigraphy, had been first enunciated by Nicolaus Steno in 1669, and was later applied by the British geologist William "Strata" Smith in the early nineteenth century (Steno 1669; Smith 1816; Daniel 1976:37–38; Renfrew and Bahn 1991:22). According to this principle, archaeological strata, like geological strata, lie one upon another like the layers of a cake, with earlier deposits underlying later ones. Smith was able to assign relative ages to geological strata by observing fossilized faunal remains in each stratum, noting that extinct species occurred only in the lowest levels, with modern species in upper levels. Smith was one of the first geologists to argue for an orderly deposition of fossils and geological layers in the past, in accordance with natural processes observable in the present. This principle of UNIFORMITARIANISM was later supported by Charles Lyell, although it was not readily accepted by those favoring a catastrophist interpretation of earth history (Lyell 1830–1833; Daniel 1976).

According to the law of superposition, the archaeologist assumes that any item found in the lowermost levels of a stratigraphic sequence, whether ARTIFACT, fossil, or unworked stone, was deposited earlier in time than materials occurring in the strata lying above it, assuming that the deposits are undisturbed. Artifacts, bones, and features occurring in association—that is, in the same depositional stratum or level—are assumed to be contemporaneous, or at least to belong to the same cultural period, in the absence of evidence of disturbance. This is the so-called "law of association," which, together with the law of superposition, forms the basic framework for the interpretation of archaeological data (see also CONTEXT).

Although the principles of stratigraphy were outlined by William Smith early in the nineteenth century, controlled techniques of stratigraphic excavation in archaeology were not developed until many decades later. Although the greater antiquity of deposits containing only stone tools, in contrast with those containing metal implements, was recognized by European investigators in the eighteenth century, it was not until the nineteenth century, when Scandinavian archaeologists such as Christian Thomsen and Jens Worsaae developed the THREE-AGE SYSTEM, that stratigraphic principles were used in excavation to support the chronological nature of these deposits (Grayson 1983:14; see also Klindt-Jensen 1975; Graslund 1981; Rodden 1981).

The method of stratigraphic excavation requires carefully removing each layer of deposits according to its natural shape and outline, proceeding from top to bottom, that is, the reverse order to that in which the layers were originally deposited (Harris 1989:159). One of the first excavators to employ this technique was Thomas Jefferson, who had an amateur interest in archaeology. Jefferson excavated prehistoric Indian mounds on his Virginia plantation, using stratigraphic methods and keeping careful records (Jefferson 1797). Although this is a notable early example of modern field method, it had no immediate successors, until the work of Giuseppe Fiorelli at Pompeii in the 1860s (Trigger 1989:196; Willey and Sabloff 1980:29). Stratigraphic excavation as a standard field technique was not adopted until the early years of the twentieth century, with the work of William Dall in Alaska (Dall 1877), Max Uhle in California and Peru (Uhle 1903, 1907, 1910, 1913), Manuel Gamio in Mexico (Gamio 1913, 1922), and Nels Nelson in the southwestern United States (Nelson 1909, 1910, 1914, 1916, 1920).

In addition to carefully removing the natural layers and their contents, and recording all finds by CONTEXT, stratigraphic excavation will also involve developing a stratigraphic profile for each trench or other excavation unit. Layers are normally easy to distinguish, due to variations in soil color and texture, and in the types and concentrations of inclusions in each layer. A sketch is made of this profile for each wall of the excavation unit on which stratification is visible, and each plan is clearly identified by the SURVEY coordinates of the excavation unit and the directional orientation of the individual wall being charted. Levels are described in terms of soil type and color, inclusions, and other characteristics, such as relative particle size, looseness or compaction or the matrix material, rodent disturbance or other intrusions. Locations of features, soil or carbon samples taken, artifact concentrations, or major artifact finds may also be included in the profile drawing. Since many archaeologists now use arbitrary levels of various thicknesses (e.g., 10 or 20 cm) for vertical excavation control, these should be superimposed on the drawing of the stratigraphic profile, to facilitate the exact location of any excavated item during the postexcavation period of data analysis (see also CONTEXT; FIELD ARCHAEOLOGY).

Today, stratigraphic excavation and interpretation are important features of modern archaeological field technique, routinely employed by most professional archaeologists, who use either natural strata, arbitrary excavation levels, or a combination of these to control their data. Although newer methods of CHRON-OMETRIC DATING have been developed for more precisely dating archaeological deposits and their cultural contents, the principle of stratigraphy remains basic to developing site chronologies, acting as a check on results obtained from radiocarbon dating and other techniques that may be used when organic materials are preserved. In areas where conditions do not favor organic preservation, stratigraphy remains the principal basis for developing relative chronologies.

REFERENCES

Dall, William H. 1877. On succession in the shell-heaps of the Aleutian Islands. In Contributions to North American Ethnology 1. U. S. Department of the Interior, Washington, D.C., pp. 41–91.

Daniel, Glyn. 1976. A hundred and fifty years of archaeology. Harvard University Press, Cambridge, Mass.

Daniels, S. G. H., and S. J. Freeth, eds. 1970. Stratigraphy, an interdisciplinary symposium. Institute of African Studies. University of Ibadan, Occasional Publication No. 19. Ibadan, Nigeria

Gamio, Manuel. 1913. Arqueología de Atzcapotzalco, D. F., México. Proceedings, Eighteenth International Congress of Americanists, London, pp. 180–187.

————. 1922. La población del Valle de Teotihuacán. 3 vols. Secretaría de Fomento, Mexico, D. F.

Graslund, Bo. 1981. The background to C. J. Thomsen's Three Age System. In Towards a history of archaeology, Glyn Daniel, ed. Thames and Hudson, London, pp. 45–50.

Grayson, Donald K. 1983. Sequence and stratigraphy: documenting change in earth history. In The establishment of human antiquity. Academic Press, New York, pp. 11–26.

Harris, Edward C. 1989. Principles of archaeological stratigraphy. 2nd ed. Academic Press, New York.

Hutton, James. 1795. Theory of the earth, with proofs and illustrations. 2 vols. Cadell and Davies. Edinburgh. (Originally publisned 1785)

Jefferson, Thomas. 1797. Notes on the state of Virginia. John Stockdale, London. Reprinted University of North Carolina Press, Chapel Hill, 1954.

Klindt-Jensen, Ole. 1975. A history of Scandinavian archaeology. Thames and Hudson, London.

Lyell, Charles. 1830–33. The principles of geology: an attempt to explain the former changes of the earth's surface by reference to causes now in operation. 2 vols. J. Murray, London.

Nelson, Nels C. 1909. Shellmounds of the San Francisco Bay region. University of California Publications in American Archaeology and Ethnology 7(4). Berkeley, pp. 319–348.

————. 1910. The Ellis Landing shellmound. University of California Publications in American Archaeology and Ethnology 7(5). Berkeley, pp. 357–426.

————. 1914. Pueblo ruins of the Galisteo Basin. Anthropological Papers of the American Museum of Natural History 15, pt. 1. New York.

————. 1916. Chronology of the Tano ruins, New Mexico. American Anthropologist 18(2):159–180.

————. 1920. Notes on Pueblo Bonito. In Pueblo Bonito, G. H. Pepper, ed. Anthropological Papers of the American Museum of Natural History 27. New York.

Renfrew, Colin, and Paul Bahn. 1991. Archaeology: methods, theories and practice. Thames and Hudson, New York.

Rodden, Judith. 1981. The development of the Three Age System: archaeology's first paradigm. In Towards a history of archaeology, Glyn Daniel, ed. Thames and Hudson, London, pp. 51–68.

Smith, William. 1816. Strata identified by organised fossils. W. Arding, London.

Stein, Julie. 1987. Deposits for archaeologists. Advances in Archaeological Method and Theory 11:337–395.

Steno, Nicolas. 1669. De solido intra solidum naturaliter contento dissertationis prodromus. Extypographia sub signo stellae, Florence.

Trigger, Bruce. 1989. A history of archaeological thought. Cambridge University Press.

Uhle, Max. 1903. Pachacamac. University of Pennsylvania Press, Philadelphia.

————. 1907. The Emeryville shellmound. University of California Publications in American Archaeology and Ethnology 7(1). Berkeley.

————. 1910. Über die fruhkulturen in der umgebung von Lima. In Sixteenth International Congress of Americanists, Vienna [Proceedings]. Vienna, A. Hartleben, pp. 22–45.

————. 1913. Die ruinen von Moche. Journal de la Société des Americanistes de Paris 10:95–117.

Willey, Gordon R., and Jeremy A. Sabloff. 1980. The stratigraphic revolution. In A history of American archaeology, 2nd ed. W. H. Freeman, San Francisco, pp. 84–93.

SOURCES OF ADDITIONAL INFORMATION

A historical summary of the concept of stratigraphy and detailed discussion, including differences between its geological and archaeological applications, may be found in the Stein 1987 review article, which also includes an extensive bibliography (see References). An excellent informative discussion of stratigraphic field methods, including some historical background material, may be found in J. H. Rowe, "Stratigraphy and seriation," *American Antiquity* 26(3)(1961):324–330. B. M. Conkin and J. E. Conkin, eds., *Stratigraphy, Foundations and Concepts* (New York, Van Nostrand Reinhold, 1984), which contains reprints from key works in the history of geological stratigraphy from the time of Steno onward, with editorial discussion and comments, is a valuable source for the history and development of stratigraphy.

Some of the earliest stratigraphic excavations in the New World were those by Manuel Gamio at sites in western Mexico, described and discussed in Ignacio Bernal, *A History of Mexican Archaeology* (London, Thames and Hudson, 1980), chapter 8: "Potsherds victorious," pp. 160–189.

Additional information may be found in Donald Grayson, *The Establishment of Human Antiquity* (New York, Academic Press, 1983), chapter 2: "Sequence and stratigraphy: documenting change in earth history," pp. 11–26. Instructional guides to procedures and stratigraphic interpretation may be found in S. G. H. Daniels and S. J. Freeth, eds., *Stratigraphy, an Interdisciplinary Symposium* (Institute of African Studies, University of Ibadan, Occasional Publication No. 19, 1970); and in H. Gasche and O. Tunca, "Guide to archaeostratigraphic classification and terminology: definitions and principles," *Journal of Field Archaeology* 10 (1983):325–335.

For access to recent literature, see the extensive bibliography in Stein 1987 (see References); to update this, consult current annual reviews and issues of *American Antiquity*, *Current Anthropology*, and *Journal of Field Archaeology*.

STYLE. 1. Formal variation in shape, pattern, or design of an ARTIFACT that carries cultural meaning, and may therefore serve as a form of symbolic communication among producers and users of the artifact, but is independent of the implement's functional purpose or use. 2. The sum of diagnostic features of any artifact that is used to identify its cultural affiliation by suggesting its time and place of origin. 3. "Formal variation in material culture that transmits information about personal and social identity" (Wiessner 1983:256).

The archaeological concept of style and stylistic variation as a basis for classifying artifacts according to their time and place of origin dates back at least to the second decade of the nineteenth century. The Danish scholar Christian Thomsen made use of factors of style, such as decorative design characteristics, as one of his criteria for classifying artifacts in museum collections, in an early attempt at devising a scheme of systematics for relatively dating archaeological materials (Trigger 1989:76). In the late nineteenth and early twentieth centuries, style would become one of several significant factors contributing to the development of typologies and chronologies for classifying artifacts of various kinds. However, it was only with the appearance of processual archaeology in the 1960s that stylistic variation in artifacts began to be used for making INFERENCES about various aspects of prehistoric SOCIAL ORGANIZATION. Research efforts by James Deetz (Deetz 1965), James N. Hill (1970), and William Longacre (1970), among others, established the validity of stylistic change as an index of temporal change in such social practices as postmarital residence. Although the assumptions on which some of these studies were based have been called into question by various critics, style has continued to be regarded as an important factor both in the analysis of archaeological remains and in the use of resulting data for making inferences concerning the behavioral dynamics of past societies. Similarities in stylistic factors, such as decorative designs, have been measured statistically, as a method for determining the degree and intensity of interaction between different communities that utilized similar designs or other decorative elements in their manufactured items (Plog 1978).

Since the 1960s, style and its definition have become increasingly important in archaeological analysis and interpretation, and resulting debates have produced a growing body of literature. Some key problems include the question of whether STYLE as expressed in artifacts reflects the ethnicity of their manufacturers, a key aspect of what has been called the "Mousterian problem" (Binford 1973; Sackett 1985), a continuing debate regarding the interpretation of the archaeological record of the European Middle Paleolithic. While stylistic factors have traditionally been treated separately from factors relating to the functions for which prehistoric implements were designed (Dunnell 1978), the materialist orientation of the "NEW" ARCHAEOLOGY that developed in the 1960s created philosophical problems in the archaeological definition and application of the concept of style, which tends to resist strictly materialist treatment, since it is "always grounded in some cultural context or frame of reference" (Conkey and Hastorf 1990:2).

The relationship between stylistic and functional attributes of artifacts has also been a subject of extensive discussion among archaeologists, some of whom have regarded these as complementary (see, e.g., Sackett 1982).

A number of attempts have been made to define and codify style into types, based upon its application to different artifact types and contexts. Although some have devised as many as five distinct categories of style (e.g., Plog 1983), dual or three-part schemes have usually been more successful (Sackett 1982; Hill 1985). Hill has distinguished what he refers to as two primary "theories" of style (Hill 1985). The first of these, which he calls the "social interaction theory," views style as nonfunctional and nonadaptive, and as conveying only "passive" data about contacts between prehistoric groups, a view he discerns in the work of James Deetz (1965), William Longacre (1970), Stephen Plog (1980), J. A. Voss (1977), and Robert Whallon (1968), as well as his own early work (Hill 1970, 1985). According to this view, the degree of stylistic similarity observable in material items manufactured by different groups is an index of the amount and intensity of social interaction between them. The second theory, which Hill calls the "information exchange theory," sees style as both functional and adaptive in fostering "group identity, integration and boundary mainte- nance" (Hill 1985:366). This second dynamic, social information-transmitting concept of style in archaeological materials has been favored by numerous ar- chaeologists in recent years, in particular by ceramic specialists. James Sackett, who has written extensively on the analysis of style in archaeology as well as on its theoretical aspects (Sackett 1977, 1982, 1985, 1986a, 1986b, 1990), refers to this as the "iconological" view of style, and notes that it underlies the entire area of analysis sometimes called "ceramic sociology."

Sackett also distinguishes two additional categories of style. The first of these he calls the "standard" archaeological view, which regards style and stylistic attributes as devices for placing artifacts both geographically and chronologically on a culture-historical continuum. The second is his own view of style, which assigns equal and complementary responsibility for all observable formal vari- ation in artifacts to functional and stylistic factors, which he calls "isochrestism" (see Sackett 1982).

Another source of debate concerns the validity of applying stylistic concepts to lithic artifact analysis. The "two theories" scheme described by Hill applies principally to the area of CERAMIC ANALYSIS, and has been employed extensively by ceramic specialists. Ideas about style in lithic analysis have frequently been confined to discussions of whether or not these reveal ethnic differences (Binford 1973, 1983, 1986, 1989; Conkey 1978; Sackett 1982). However, studies by Polly Wiessner of lithic artifacts and their uses among the Kalahari !Kung San

(Wiessner 1983, 1985) suggest a dynamic, informational stylistic aspect of such artifacts that may prove important in inferring past behavioral processes (see Conkey and Hastorf 1990:13).

A doctoral dissertation by Dorothy Hosler (Hosler 1986) discusses such stylistic factors as shape, color, texture, and even sound as important information-bearing attributes of material objects, and suggests that the particular forms these take in a given community are determined by both CONTEXT and past historical traditions of tool use and manufacture in that group (Conkey and Hastorf 1990:13).

In the traditional culture-historical approach to archaeology, the concept of style was useful primarily for establishing chronologies and tracing interaction and lines of influence between different human groups in the past. At present, it is most often viewed as one aspect of "coded information about variability in the functioning of past cultural systems" (Conkey and Hastorf 1990:15), that is, as a way of communicating information on past social systems through the use of certain decorative patterns and other nonfunctional attributes (Wobst 1977; Conkey 1978; Miksic 1989). This informational aspect has led to the formulation of new questions of an epistemological and theoretical nature, some of which have been dealt with in a collection of papers from a conference devoted entirely to discussion of the nature and applications of style in archaeology (Conkey and Hastorf, eds. 1990). These discussions address a variety of questions and problems that promise to become the subject of further debate by both processual and postprocessual archaeologists in the years to come.

REFERENCES

Binford, Lewis R. 1973. Interassemblage variability—the Mousterian and the "functional" argument. In The explanation of culture change, C. Renfrew, ed. Duckworth, London, pp. 227–254.
———. 1983. In pursuit of the past. Thames and Hudson, New York.
———. 1986. An Alyawara day: making men's knives and beyond. American Antiquity 51(3):547–562.
———. 1989. Styles of style. Journal of Anthropological Archaeology 8(1):51–67.
Conkey, Margaret W. 1978. Style and information in cultural evolution: Toward a predictive model for the Paleolithic. In Social archaeology: beyond subsistence and dating, Charles L. Redman et al., eds. Academic Press, New York, pp. 61–86.
Conkey, Margaret W., and Christine Hastorf. 1990. Chapter 1: introduction. In The uses of style in archaeology, M. W. Conkey and C. Hastorf, eds. Cambridge University Press.
———, eds. 1990. The uses of style in archaeology. Cambridge University Press.
Deetz, James. 1965. The dynamics of stylistic change in Arikara ceramics. University of Illinois Press, Urbana.
Dunnell, Robert C. 1978. Style and function: a fundamental dichotomy. American Antiquity 43(2):192–202.
Hill, James N. 1970. Broken K Pueblo: Prehistoric social organization in the American Southwest. University of Arizona, Anthropological Papers No. 18, Tucson.

———. 1985. Style: a conceptual evolutionary framework. In Decoding prehistoric ceramics, Ben A. Nelson, ed. Southern Illinois University Press, Carbondale and Edwardsville, pp. 362–385.

Hosler, Dorothy. 1986. The origins, technology and social construction of ancient west Mexican metallurgy. Unpublished Ph.D. dissertation, University of California, Santa Barbara.

Longacre, William A. 1970. Archaeology as anthropology: a case study. Anthropological Papers No. 17. University of Arizona, Tucson.

Miksic, J. N. 1989. Archaeological studies of style, information transfer and the transition from classical to Islamic periods in Indonesia. Journal of Southeast Asian Studies 20(1):1–10.

Plog, Stephen. 1978. Social interaction and stylistic similarity: a reanalysis. Advances in Archaeological Method and Theory 1:143–182.

———. 1980. Stylistic variation in prehistoric ceramics: design analysis in the American Southwest. Cambridge University Press, London.

———. 1983. Analysis of style in artifacts. Annual Review of Anthropology 12:125–142.

Sackett, James R. 1977. The meaning of style in archaeology: a general model. American Antiquity 42(3):369–380.

———. 1982. Approaches to style in lithic archaeology. Journal of Anthropological Archaeology, 1(1):59–112.

———. 1985. Style and ethnicity in the Kalahari: a reply to Wiessner. American Antiquity 50(1):154–159.

———. 1986a. Style, function, and assemblage variability: a reply to Binford. American Antiquity 51(3):628–634.

———. 1986b. Isochrestism and style. Journal of Anthropological Archaeology 5:266–277.

———. 1990. Style and ethnicity in archaeology: the case for isochrestism. In The uses of style in archaeology, M. W. Conkey and C. Hastorf, eds. Cambridge University Press, pp. 32–43.

Trigger, Bruce. 1989. A history of archaeological thought. Cambridge University Press.

Voss, J. A. 1977. The Barnes site: functional and stylistic variability in a small Paleo-Indian assemblage. Mid-Continental Journal of Archaeology 2:253–305.

Whallon, Robert. 1968. Evidence of late prehistoric social organization in New York state. In New perspectives in archaeology, Sally R. Binford and Lewis R. Binford, eds. Aldine, Chicago, pp. 223–244.

Wiessner, Polly. 1983. Style and social information in Kalahari San projectile points. American Antiquity 48(2):253–276.

———. 1985. Style or isochrestic variation? A reply to Sackett. American Antiquity 50(1):160–166.

Wobst, H. Martin. 1977. Stylistic behavior and information exchange. In Papers for the director: research essays in honor of James B. Griffin, Charles E. Cleland, ed. Academic Press, New York, pp. 317–342.

SOURCES OF ADDITIONAL INFORMATION

The best overview and discussion of major current issues in the treatment of style in archaeology is the lucid and articulate introductory paper by Margaret Conkey and Christine Hastorf in their collection of papers on this subject (Conkey and Hastorf 1990; and Conkey and Hastorf, eds., 1990; see References). Additional background information may be found in all of the papers by James Sackett (see References). A classic early discussion of style is "Style," by Meyer Schapiro, in *Anthropology Today*, Alfred L. Kroeber, ed. (Chicago, Aldine, 1953), pp. 287–312.

For an outline of the two theories of style underlying ceramic sociology, see Hill 1985 (in References); for discussions of the "social interaction" theory, see Wobst 1977 (in References), and Dorothy K. Washburn and R. G. Matson, "Use of multidimensional scaling to display sensitivity of symmetry analysis of patterned design to spatial and chronological change: examples from Anasazi prehistory," in *Decoding Prehistoric Ceramics*, Ben A. Nelson, ed. (Carbondale and Edwardsville, (Southern Illinois University Press, 1985), pp. 75–101. For detailed discussion of the iconological and isochrestic theories of style, as well as the "standard" concept of style, see Sackett 1982 and 1990 (see References).

A number of important papers have appeared on various aspects and interpretations of style in archaeology. Among these are two papers by Roy Larick on the social and ethnic meanings of stylistic factors in spears used by a group of pastoralists in Kenya: "Spears, style and time among Maa-speaking pastoralists," *Journal of Anthropological Archaeology* 4(3)(1985):206–220; and "Age grading and ethnicity in the style of Loikop (Samburu) spears," *World Archaeology* 18(2)(1986):269–283. A paper relating to the "Mousterian problem" using data from North Africa is P. Vanpeer, "Interassemblage variability and Levallois styles, the case of the northern African Middle Paleolithic," *Journal of Anthropological Archaeology* 10(2)(1991):107–151; another discussion published in the same journal dealing with style and symbolism in Paleolithic artifacts is P. G. Chase, "Symbols and Paleolithic artifacts: style, standardization and the imposition of arbitrary form," *Journal of Anthropological Archaeology* 10(3)(1991):193–214.

Access to the growing literature on this subject begins with the 1978 review article by Stephen Plog in *Advances in Archaeological Method and Theory* (see References), which includes a four-page bibliography. This should be updated with the substantial bibliographies in Binford 1989 (see References), and in the 1991 articles by Chase and Vanpeer in the *Journal of Anthropological Archaeology* (see above). In addition, issues of this journal and *American Antiquity* should be checked for more recent papers, and latest issues of *Current Anthropology* and annual volumes of *Archaeological Method and Theory* should be monitored for later review articles.

SUBSISTENCE. The primary or dominant strategy employed by a human population for getting a living from the environment, comprising all the principal economic (food-getting and energy-extracting) activities engaged in, such as scavenging, hunting, fishing, loose herding, and the harvesting and cultivation of plants.

The subsistence activities engaged in by human groups cover a very broad range. The processes of getting a living may include scavenging the carcasses of dead animals; hunting wild animals; herding, taming, or domestication and selective breeding of various animal species; fishing, shellfishing, and hunting marine mammals; harvesting and cultivating wild plants, horticulture, or small-scale garden cropping; full-scale FOOD PRODUCTION with intensive agriculture and specialized cropping; and the various combinations of these that occur in typical mixed economies. In evolutionary schemes, economies based on certain of these activities are often assigned to hierarchical "levels" of development, with scavenging representing a lower, and therefore earlier, level than hunting, and gathering of wild plant foods being regarded as antecedent to cultivation, horticulture, and sedentary agriculture. In contemporary archaeological research, the study of subsistence is usually viewed as encompassing everything in the ARCHAEOLOGICAL RECORD related to such activities, including ARTIFACTS, biological remains, settlement and locational data, and all other material remains implicated in past economic behavior.

Archaeological interest in the study of subsistence economies of the past can be traced back to at least the fourth decade of the nineteenth century. In the 1830s and 1840s, the Scandinavian zoologist and paleontologist Sven Nilsson, a student of the paleontologist Georges Cuvier and a contemporary of Christian Thomsen, who devised the earliest classificatory scheme for organizing museum artifact collections, became interested in the study of prehistoric subsistence. Nilsson compared stone and bone implements of prehistoric date with those obtained by ethnographers from modern hunter-gatherers. His studies included an appreciation of use-wear patterns on tools as indications of their uses in different kinds of subsistence activities, anticipating methods that would not become widespread in archaeology until more than a century later (Nilsson 1868:4; Trigger 1989:80). Nilsson agreed with some eighteenth-century philosophers that increasing population had led humans to the creation of food-producing economies, an idea much later adopted by twentieth-century archaeologists as the basis for a number of so-called "population pressure" models for the invention of agriculture (Boserup 1965). Nilsson's studies of the subsistence practices of early inhabitants of Scandinavia were published between 1836 and 1843, and were later translated into English (Nilsson 1868).

Systematic archaeological studies of subsistence were not undertaken until the 1940s, when they began to develop in both Europe and the United States. Grahame Clark was one of first to seek new techniques for using archaeological evidence of resource utilization and subsistence patterns in prehistoric times (Clark 1952, 1954, 1972, 1974; Trigger 1989). Clark's excavations at Star Carr in East Yorkshire between 1949 and 1951 were aimed in part at recovering organic food remains and other ecological data to document subsistence patterns and land use at this Mesolithic site (Clark 1974). His *Prehistoric Europe: The Economic Basis* (1952) was an attempt to reconstruct European subsistence from the end of the Pleistocene up to historic times, from data in the then-extant archaeological literature (Trigger 1989:268), using a functionally oriented approach.

In the United States, subsistence studies were stimulated by the pioneering work of Julian Steward (Steward 1936, 1937), which led him to develop his method and theory of CULTURAL ECOLOGY (Steward 1955). Steward's work in North America was complemented by Robert Braidwood's field studies of early farming in the Near East, which first documented the beginnings of settled life in several prehistoric agricultural villages in Iraq, using the expertise of a team of interdisciplinary researchers (Braidwood 1950, 1953, 1974). The development of radiocarbon dating techniques during the 1940s, when these research projects were in progress, permitted the first precise CHRONOMETRIC DATING of biological materials from archaeological CONTEXTS.

The New World counterpart of Braidwood's search for the major subsistence change from hunting and gathering to food production in Iraq was the Tehuacán Valley project in the Mexican Sierra de Tamaulipas, directed by archaeologist Richard MacNeish. MacNeish set out to document the beginnings of maize cultivation in Mesoamerica, using the same broad interdisciplinary investigative approach as had Braidwood in the Iraq Jarmo project (MacNeish 1964, 1972, 1974; Mangelsdorf, MacNeish, and Willey 1964; MacNeish and Byers 1967).

In the decades that have elapsed since these first major research efforts directed toward documenting the transition from hunting and gathering to agriculture in different parts of the world, a number of smaller-scale studies, employing similar methodologies and motivated by similar goals, have been carried out (see, e.g., Flannery 1965, 1969; Lee 1979; Zagarell 1989). At present, multidisciplinary field research has become the norm, and ecological studies of subsistence activities are now a standard part of almost all archaeological field investigations.

The archaeological study of subsistence practices has been fostered and stimulated in recent years by the ascendancy of the ecological approach that has prevailed in American archaeology since the time of Julian Steward, with its overarching emphasis on subsistence and human ecological ADAPTATION in the past. Indeed, in a broad sense the realm of subsistence studies comprises nearly all of contemporary archaeological research, which tends to be concentrated on the economic and ecologically adaptive aspects of past human behavior, and the investigation of other aspects of past societies is most frequently undertaken with a view to understanding their relationship to subsistence activities.

Archaeologists since the 1960s have used a variety of investigative approaches to the study of past subsistence strategies, and the ways in which these may have evolved toward food production. Among the factors that are usually examined are data on environmental conditions in the past, including vegetation patterns reflected in pollen profiles and botanical remains such as carbonized seeds, and animal species available to prehistoric hunters as revealed by bone deposits retrieved from archaeological contexts. Changes in SETTLEMENT PATTERNS, as well as patterns of prehistoric trade, warfare, tool manufacture, and even ideology, have all been investigated in relation to the matter of obtaining a living from the environment.

One approach that has become popular since the 1960s has been the archaeological study of hunter-gatherers and their strategies for getting a living from their environment (Lee and DeVore 1968; Bettinger 1980, 1987; Conkey 1980; Price and Brown 1985; Thomas 1986; Myers 1988; Yellen 1989). Animal butchering practices have been investigated among modern hunter-gatherers by ethnoarchaeologists seeking to construct middle-range arguments for interpreting faunal remains found in archaeological SITES (Binford and Bertram 1977; Binford

1978a, 1978b, 1980, 1981, 1983; Bettinger 1987). Others have applied optimal foraging theory derived from biology to the study of prehistoric subsistence (Keene 1979, 1981, 1982, 1983; Winterhalder 1981; Winterhalder and Smith 1981; Martin 1983; Kurland and Beckerman 1985), while still others have developed or applied economic models based on decision theory to address the problem (Yellen 1977; Earle 1980). Yet another approach is that of paleonutritionists, who have identified the relative amounts of meat, fish, and grains in prehistoric diets from trace element and carbon isotope studies of archaeological human bone as a basis for inferring dominant subsistence strategies of past human communities (Wing and Brown 1979; Chisholm, Nelson, and Schwarz 1983; Gilbert and Mielke 1985; Larsen 1987). In addition, paleodemographic studies of population patterns and growth rates in the past from archaeological evidence have sought to document a demographic necessity for the dramatic shift from hunting and gathering to food production (Boserup 1965). Studies of animal domestication also seek to document this process, using zooarchaeological data showing changes in animal body size and other characteristics that commonly occur as a result of the domestication process and the effects of selective breeding (see ZOOARCHAEOLOGY).

This research has generated a wealth of data that have been subjected to new techniques of data analysis, and has greatly expanded the perspective of archaeologists investigating subsistence questions of theoretical significance, including the reasons for the transition to food production, although to date they have not resulted in any single, widely accepted explanatory model for this phenomenon. The search for such models continues as part of efforts in the theoretical realm (Earle 1980; Rindos 1984; Redding 1988). Meanwhile, interdisciplinary subsistence research goes on, acquiring new techniques and generating further data that may someday lead to more complete answers to such questions.

REFERENCES

Bettinger, Robert L. 1980. Explanatory/predictive models of hunter-gatherer adaptation. Advances in Archaeological Method and Theory 3:189–256.

———. 1987. Archaeological approaches to hunter-gatherers. Annual Review of Anthropology 16:121–142.

Binford, Lewis R. 1978a. Dimensional analysis of behavior and site structure: learning from an Eskimo hunting stand. American Antiquity 43:330–361.

———. 1978b. Nunamiut ethnoarchaeology. Academic Press, New York.

———. 1980. Willow smoke and dogs' tails: hunter-gatherer settlement systems and archaeological site formation. American Antiquity 45:4–20.

———. 1981. Bones: ancient men and modern myths. Academic Press, New York.

———. 1983. In pursuit of the past: decoding the archaeological record. Thames and Hudson, New York.

Binford, Lewis R., and J. B. Bertram. 1977. Bone frequencies—and attritional processes. In For theory building in archaeology. . . . L. R. Binford, ed. Academic Press, New York, pp. 77–156.

Boserup, Esther. 1965. The conditions of agricultural growth. Aldine, Chicago.

Braidwood, Robert J. 1950. Jarmo: a village of early farmers in Iraq. Antiquity 24:189–195.

———. 1953. The earliest village communities of southwestern Asia. Journal of World History 1:278–310.

———. 1974. The Iraq Jarmo project. In Archaeological research in retrospect, Gordon R. Willey, ed. Winthrop, Cambridge, Mass., pp. 61–83.

Chisholm, Brian S., Erle D. Nelson, and Henry Schwarz. 1983. Marine and terrestrial protein in prehistoric diets on the British Columbia Coast. Current Anthropology 24:396–398.

Clark, Grahame. 1952. Prehistoric Europe: the economic basis. Methuen, London.

———. 1954. Excavations at Star Carr. Cambridge University Press.

———. 1972. Star Carr: a case study in bioarchaeology. McCaleb Module No. 10. Addison-Wesley Modular Publications, Reading, Mass.

———. 1974. Prehistoric Europe: the economic basis. In Archaeological researches in retrospect, Gordon R. Willey, ed. Winthrop, Cambridge, Mass., pp. 31–57.

Conkey, Margaret W. 1980. The identification of prehistoric hunter-gatherer aggregation sites: the case of Altamira. Current Anthropology 21(5):609–630.

Earle, Timothy K. 1980. A model of subsistence change. In Modeling change in prehistoric subsistence economies, T. K. Earle and A. L. Christensen, eds. Academic Press, New York, pp. 1–29.

Flannery, Kent V. 1965. The ecology of early food production in Mesopotamia. Science 147:1247–1256.

———. 1969. The origins and ecological effects of early domestication in Iran and the Near East. In The domestication and exploitation of plants and animals, P. J. Ucko and G. W. Dimbleby, eds. Duckworth, London, pp. 73–100.

Gilbert, Robert I., Jr., and James H. Mielke, eds. 1985. The analysis of prehistoric diets. Academic Press, New York.

Keene, A. 1979. Economic optimization models and the study of hunter-gatherer subsistence-settlement systems. In Transformations: mathematical approaches to culture change, C. Renfrew and K. Cooke, eds. Academic Press, New York, pp. 369–404.

———. 1981. Optimal foraging in a nonmarginal environment: a model of prehistoric subsistence strategies in Michigan. In Hunter-gatherer foraging strategies, Bruce Winterhalder and E. A. Smith, eds. University of Chicago Press, pp. 171–193.

———. 1982. Prehistoric foraging in a temperate forest: a linear programming model. Academic Press, New York.

———. 1983. Biology, behavior and borrowing: a critical examination of optimal foraging theory in archaeology. In Archaeological hammers and theories, J. A. Moore and A. S. Keene, eds. Academic Press, New York, pp. 137–155.

Kurland, Jeffrey A., and Stephen J. Beckerman. 1985. Optimal foraging and hominid evolution: labor and reciprocity. American Anthropologist 87(1):73–95.

Larsen, Clark Spencer. 1987. Bioarchaeological interpretations of subsistence economy and behavior from human skeletal remains. Advances in Archaeological Method and Theory 10:339–445.

Lee, Richard B. 1979. The !Kung San: men, women and work in a foraging society. Cambridge University Press.

Lee, Richard B., and Irvin DeVore. 1968. Man the hunter. Aldine, Chicago.

MacNeish, Richard S. 1964. Ancient Mesoamerican civilization. Science 193:3606.
———. 1967. A summary of the subsistence. In Prehistory of the Tehuacán Valley, vol. 1, D. Byers, ed., University of Texas Press, Austin, pp. 290–309.
———. 1972. The prehistory of the Tehuacán Valley: chronology and irrigation. University of Texas Press, Austin.
———. 1974. Reflections on my search for the beginnings of agriculture in Mexico. In Archaeological researches in retrospect, Gordon R. Willey, ed. Winthrop, Cambridge, Mass., pp. 207–234.
MacNeish, Richard S., and D. S. Byers. 1967. The prehistory of the Tehuacán Valley: environment and subsistence. University of Texas Press, Austin.
Mangelsdorf, Paul, Richard S. MacNeish, and Gordon R. Willey. 1964. Origins of agriculture in Middle America. In Handbook of Middle American Indians, vol. 1, Robert Wauchope and Robert C. West, eds. University of Texas Press, Austin, pp. 427–445.
Martin, J. F. 1983. Optimal foraging theory: a review of some models and their applications. American Anthropologist 85:612–629.
Myers, Fred R. 1988. Critical trends in the study of hunter-gatherers. Annual Review of Anthropology 17:261–282.
Nilsson, Sven. 1868. The primitive inhabitants of Scandinavia, 3rd ed., J. Lubbock, trans. Longmans, Green, London.
Price, T. Douglas, and James A. Brown, eds. 1985. Prehistoric hunter-gatherers: the emergence of cultural complexity. Academic Press, Orlando, Fla.
Redding, R. W. 1988. A general explanation of subsistence change—from hunting and gathering to food production. Journal of Anthropological Archaeology 7(1):56–97.
Rindos, David. 1984. The origins of agriculture: an evolutionary perspective. Academic Press, New York.
Steward, Julian H. 1936. The economic and social basis of primitive bands. In Essays in anthropology presented to A. L. Kroeber, R. Lowie, ed. University of California Press, Berkeley, pp. 331–345.
———. 1937. Ecological aspects of southwestern society. Anthropos 32:87–104.
———. 1955. Theory of culture change. University of Illinois Press, Urbana.
Thomas, David Hurst. 1986. Contemporary hunter-gatherer archaeology in America. In American archaeology, past and future, D. J. Meltzer, D. D. Fowler, and J. A. Sabloff, eds. Smithsonian Institution Press, Washington, D.C., pp. 237–276.
Trigger, Bruce G. 1989. A history of archaeological thought. Cambridge University Press.
Wing, Elizabeth S., and Antoinette B. Brown. 1979. Paleonutrition: method and theory in prehistoric foodways. Academic Press, New York.
Winterhalder, Bruce. 1981. Optimal foraging strategies and hunter-gatherer research in anthropology: theory and models. In Hunter-gatherer foraging strategies, B. Winterhalder and E. A. Smith, eds. University of Chicago Press, pp. 13–35.
Winterhalder, Bruce, and E. A. Smith, eds. 1981. Hunter-gatherer foraging strategies. University of Chicago Press.
Yellen, John E. 1977. Archaeological approaches to the present: models for reconstructing the past. Academic Press, New York.
———. 1989. The present and the future of hunter-gatherer studies. In Archaeological

thought in America, C. C. Lamberg-Karlovsky, ed. Cambridge University Press, pp. 103–116.

Zagarell, Allen. 1989. Pastoralism and the early state in greater Mesopotamia. In Archaeological thought in America, C. C. Lamberg-Karlovsky, ed. Cambridge University Press, pp. 180–301.

SOURCES OF ADDITIONAL INFORMATION

For general background information on the archaeological study of subsistence, there are introductory discussions in most standard textbooks. Some examples are "Reconstructing ancient subsistence systems," in Robert Sharer and Wendy Ashmore, *Fundamentals of Archaeology* (Menlo Park, Calif., Benjamin Cummings, 1979), pp. 414–419; chapter 14, "Subsistence and diet," in Brian Fagan, *In the Beginning*, 6th ed. (Glenview, Ill., Scott, Foresman, 1988), pp. 355–401; and chapter 7, "What did they eat? Subsistence and diet," in Colin Renfrew and Paul Bahn, *Archaeology: Methods, Theories and Practice* (New York, Thames and Hudson, 1991), pp. 233–270.

There has not been a review published on the specific subject of subsistence or subsistence change. The discussion by Earle (1980; see References) is still useful, but his bibliography is out-of-date. The two reviews by Bettinger (1980, 1987; see References) on hunter-gatherer adaptation can be used to supplement this in a limited way, and the 1987 review adds more recent material through the mid-1980s.

Two papers representing different current approaches to the transition to a food-producing economy are R. Layton, R. Foley, and E. Williams, "The transition between hunting and gathering and the specialized husbandry of resources, a socioecological approach," *Current Anthropology* 32(3)(1991):255–274, which includes 125 references to relevant literature; and M. Rosenberg, "The mother of invention: evolutionary theory, territoriality, and the origins of agriculture," *American Anthropologist* 92(2)(1990):399–415, which also includes a substantial bibliography. For the most current literature, issues of *American Antiquity* and *Journal of Anthropological Archaeology* should be consulted, and latest volumes of *Archaeological Method and Theory* and the *Annual Review of Anthropology* should be monitored for an up-to-date review.

SURVEY. 1. The systematic search for remains of human activity or habitation in the past, through careful examination of land surfaces for ARTIFACTs, outlines of structures or features, concentrations of frequently cultivated vegetational species gone wild, or other superficial evidence. Such surveys are carried out to locate SITES, or to assess the archaeological resources of a region, and may involve the use of remote sensing techniques and aerial photography (see ARCHAEOMETRY), as well as ground exploration. Also called *archaeological prospecting* (Scollar et al. 1990) and *reconnaissance*. 2. The procedure of mapping and laying out a controlled grid over a site, using appropriate instruments, to establish a set of permanent reference points that will serve as coordinates for describing the locations of all features and artifacts subsequently discovered within the grid.

Survey, like excavation, requires a carefully formulated research design, including a strategy for SAMPLING the area of study, which will usually be based on probability theory (Judge, Ebert, and Hitchcock 1975). A survey is generally conducted within a controlled grid or other organized scheme, established as part of the research design, to facilitate the accurate mapping of finds in their location of discovery. The layout of this grid is accomplished using surveying techniques developed by civil engineers, cartographers, and topographic surveyors, employing appropriate technical instruments, such as transits or theodolites. The British archaeologist Sir Mortimer Wheeler (1890–1976) was among the first to use the grid-square system in laying out a site plan (Renfrew and Bahn 1991:30). Like General Pitt-Rivers, he acquired his technical knowledge of survey techniques from his military experience, and later applied it in his archaeological work.

Although the concept of survey or reconnaissance to locate archaeological sites has been a part of FIELD ARCHAEOLOGY for many decades, the large-scale survey was stimulated by development of regional studies in archaeology during the 1960s and 1970s. Since that time a number of such regional surveys have been undertaken, and intensive surface survey has become a principal method of field study, often serving as an alternative to excavation (Sanders 1965; Cherry and Shennan 1978; Blanton et al. 1979; Sanders, Parsons, and Santley 1979; Keller and Rupp 1983).

Surveys are basically of three kinds: (1) those conducted to discover sites; (2) those conducted of known site areas, to select those areas of greatest potential for further intensive study; (3) those carried out to assess, salvage, or preserve the archaeological resources of an entire region, in which the region itself is the major focus rather than individual sites lying within it. The latter is the so-called "siteless" or "nonsite" survey, which is frequently conducted where archaeological resources are being threatened by development projects (Thomas 1975; Dunnell and Dancey 1983). Such surveys have become a basic technique employed in CULTURAL RESOURCE MANAGEMENT studies, since they provide a quick and relatively inexpensive method for assessing archaeological resources to be impacted by urban expansion, road construction, or other development projects (Doelle 1977). The goals of these three kinds of survey strategies are not necessarily incompatible. Surveys prompted and funded as conservation or resource assessment projects can produce results of considerable research value, when they are guided from the beginning by a research design that permits the acquisition of the appropriate data (Schiffer, Sullivan, and Klinger 1978).

Surveys vary greatly in their intensity, with those of least intensity the most common. A survey area is usually walked by a team of surveyors placed at preestablished distances from one another, each assigned to record the resources in his/her survey area, and the ground surface is systematically searched by each surveyor for archaeological remains (Ammerman and Feldman 1978; Ammerman 1981). Since the success of a survey depends on careful observation, the best method of search is usually on foot. Where this is impossible, survey can be done by boat, four-wheel-drive vehicle, horseback, or muleback, but this will require sacrificing considerable information that might have been retrieved by walking the survey area.

Investigations of entire regional landscapes by these methods is now a major part of archaeological field research, and may serve as background for later planned excavations of selected portions of the survey region, as well as functioning as a substitute for excavation in some cases. For site location and regional resource assessment, remote techniques, such as aerial reconnaissance, satellite photography, and side-looking airborne radar are sometimes employed, as well as magnetic and electrical resistivity techniques, although the cost of these methods restricts their use to the larger, best-financed projects.

Surface survey, with collection of surface remains, has become an increasingly popular low-cost, nondestructive substitute for excavation since the 1960s. Since funds for excavation are increasingly unavailable, and surveys can be used to acquire data at modest cost and without the inevitable site destruction that occurs with excavation, this trend can be expected to continue. New techniques for nondestructive investigation and assessment continue to be developed that, along with the use of predictive models, allow archaeological sites to be studied and preserved rather than permanently destroyed by excavation. Such techniques are also useful when limited excavation is planned, by permitting the location of subsurface structures from careful study of surface finds before excavation is begun, leading the archaeologist to pursue excavation only where it is most likely to be productive of new information (Chomko 1974; Powell and Klasert 1984; Kohler and Parker 1986; Scollar et al. 1990).

REFERENCES

Ammerman, A. J. 1981. Surveys and archaeological research. Annual Review of Anthropology 10:63–88.

Ammerman, Albert J., and M. W. Feldman. 1978. Replicated collection of site surfaces. American Antiquity 43:734–740.

Blanton, R. E., Jill Appel, Laura Finsten, Steve Kowalewski, Gary Feinman, and Eva Fisch. 1979. Regional evolution in the Valley of Oaxaca, Mexico. Journal of Field Archaeology 6:369–390.

Cherry, John F., and S. J. Shennan. 1978. Sampling cultural systems: some perspectives on the application of probabilistic regional survey in Britain. In Sampling in contemporary British archaeology, J. F. Cherry, C. S. Gamble, and S. J. Shennan, eds. BAR International Series 50. Oxford, pp. 17–48.

Chomko S. A. 1974. A survey technique for delimiting activity areas within a site, parts I and II. Missouri Archaeological Society Newsletter 278:1–5 and 279:1–7.

Doelle, W. H. 1977. A multiple survey strategy for cultural resource management studies. In Conservation archaeology: a guide for cultural resources management studies, M. B. Schiffer and G. J. Gumerman, eds. Academic Press, New York, pp. 201–209.

Dunnell, Robert C., and William S. Dancey. 1983. The siteless survey: a regional scale data collection strategy. Advances in Archaeological Method and Theory 6:267–287.

Judge, W. James, James I. Ebert, and Robert K. Hitchcock. 1975. Sampling in regional archaeological survey. In Sampling in archaeology, James W. Mueller, ed. University of Arizona Press, Tucson, pp. 82–123.

Keller, D. R., and D. W. Rupp, eds. 1983. Archaeological survey in the Mediterranean area. BAR International Series 155. Oxford.

Kohler, Timothy A., and Sandra C. Parker. 1986. Predictive models for archaeological resource location. Advances in Archaeological Method and Theory 9:397–452.

Powell, Shirley, and Anthony L. Klasert. 1984. A method for predicting the presence of buried sructures on unexcavated artifact scatters. In Papers on the archaeology of Black Mesa, Arizona, vol. 2, Stephen Plog and Shirley Powell, eds. Southern Illinois University Press, Carbondale and Edwardsville, pp. 39–46.

Renfrew, Colin, and Paul Bahn. 1991. Archaeology: methods, theories and practice. Thames and Hudson, New York, pp. 61–100.

Sanders, William T. 1965. The cultural ecology of the Teotihuacán Valley: a preliminary report of the results of the Teotihuacán Valley project. Department of Anthropology, Pennsylvania State University, University Park.

Sanders, William T., Jeffrey R. Parsons, and Robert S. Santley. 1979. The Basin of Mexico: ecological processes in the evolution of a civilization. Academic Press, New York.

Schiffer, Michael B., Alan P. Sullivan, and Timothy C. Klinger. 1978. The design of archaeological survey. World Archaeology 10(1):1–29.

Scollar, I., A. Tabbagh, A. Hesse, and I. Herzog. 1990. Archaeological prospecting and remote sensing. Cambridge University Press.

Thomas, David H. 1975. Nonsite sampling in archaeology: up the creek without a site? In Sampling in archaeology, J. W. Mueller, ed. University of Arizona Press, Tucson, pp. 61–81.

SOURCES OF ADDITIONAL INFORMATION

For a comprehensive, practical introduction to field survey methods and techniques, see chapter 1, "Site surveying," in *A Guide to Basic Archaeological Field Procedures*, by Knud R. Fladmark (Burnaby, B.C., Department of Archaeology, Simon Fraser University, Publication No. 4, 1978), pp. 3–21. Mapping methods are covered in chapter 2 of the same publication. An overview of current methods of survey, remote sensing, and field techniques may be found in chapter 3, "Where? Survey and excavation of sites and features," in Renfrew and Bahn 1991, pp. 61–100 (see References). Remote techniques now in use for locating sites are discussed in Scollar et al. 1990 (see References). Guidelines for archaeologists who must choose among a variety of survey and site-discovery techniques are provided by Francis McManamon in a review article that also summarizes a large body of literature through the early 1980s, "Discovering sites unseen," *Advances in Archaeological Method and Theory* 7(1984):223–292.

There is a great variety of review articles with extensive bibliographies on various aspects of survey, all published during the 1980s. The most useful of these are A. J. Ammerman, "Surveys and archaeological research," *Annual Review of Anthropology* 10(1981):63–88; Robert S. Dunnell and William S. Dancey, "The siteless survey: a regional scale data collection strategy," *Advances in Archaeological Method and Theory* 6(1983):267–287; Jack Nance, "Regional sampling in archaeological survey: the statistical perspective," *Advances in Archaeological Method and Theory* 6(1983):289–356; McManamon 1984 (see above); and Timothy A. Kohler and Sandra C. Parker, "Predictive models for archaeological resource location," *Advances in Archaeological Method and Theory* 9(1986):397–452. Two more specialized reviews are Michael Parrington, "Remote sensing," *Annual Review of Anthropology* 12(1983):105–124; and John W. Weymouth, "Geophysical methods of archaeological site surveying," *Advances in Archaeological Method and Theory* 9(1986):311–395. All of these now need to be updated.

For a lively first-person discussion of some of the problems of field survey in a tropical jungle environment, see Arlen F. Chase's article "Jungle surveying: mapping the archaeological site of Caracol, Belize," in *P.O.B., Point of Beginning* 13(3):10–12.

Pending publication of a more recent comprehensive literature review, the above-mentioned bibliographic publications should be supplemented by examining current issues of *American Antiquity*, *Journal of Field Archaeology*, and *Current Anthropology* for recent material.

SYSTEM THEORY. A theoretical and methodological approach used in archaeology since the 1960s, as an interpretative tool for analyzing and describing cultural dynamics in terms of the systemic processes and feedback relationships of general system theory.

Archaeological system theory is based on the general system theory developed by Ludwig von Bertalanffy (1962, 1968), W. Ross Ashby (1958), and others in the 1950s and 1960s. General system theory may be regarded as an intellectual hybrid, descended from biology on one side and engineering technology on the other. Its appearance, which coincided roughly with that of the "NEW" ARCHAEOLOGY, was timely, and it was quickly seized upon by many archaeologists as a less deterministic analytical alternative to the organic model for explaining sociocultural development in the past (Butzer 1980).

One of the chief advantages of the systems approach in archaeology is its focus on the dynamic dimension of CULTURE, in which static data are viewed primarily in terms of their past utility as part of a cultural process, or system. At the same time, the emphasis placed upon feedback mechanisms, viewed as "mutual causal processes" (Maruyama 1963; Flannery 1968), places the problem of causality within a synchronic rather than a developmental framework, permitting the explanation of cultural change in processual terms and even allowing such change to be viewed as of a random or probabilistic, rather than a conventionally causal, nature. System theory is therefore not truly explanatory, but is more realistically described as a method that can permit the dynamic behavioral processes leading to change in cultural systems to be mechanistically described; but it does not produce causal explanations as these are traditionally conceived.

The systems approach was adopted and given further impetus by the "new" archaeologists of the 1960s and 1970s. Lewis Binford, in a 1965 paper, emphasized the multivariate nature of culture, which lends itself readily to modeling in terms of various subsystems (Binford 1965). David Clarke also explicitly advocated the advantages of using the systems approach (Clarke 1968, 1972).

A number of efforts to account for archaeological evidence and patterning in terms of systemic processes and feedback relationships have been made since the early 1960s. The application of the systems approach developed along with the methodology of CULTURAL ECOLOGY, as a natural outgrowth of the study of changing temporal relationships between cultures and their environments, in which the mechanisms of ecosystemic change are an important part of the adaptive process and lend themselves to modeling in systemic terms.

Instead of the fixed cycle of growth, development, and decline dictated by the organic model of culture (see Butzer 1980), systemic models allow the interpretation of complex cultures as unique systems, each of which follows its own particular trajectory. A special attraction of the systems approach for "new" archaeologists was its emphasis on the dynamic, processual aspect of prehistoric cultures. At the same time, it fit in well with earlier work of the British functionalist anthropologists, in particular that of A. R. Radcliffe-Brown, whose concept of societies as social systems had been modeled on biological systems, using the organic model (Radcliffe-Brown 1935, 1952, 1957).

General system theory has been employed in several ways by archaeologists. Some, such as David Clarke, have regarded it as a potential theory of archaeology, while others have seen it as a body of concepts useful in describing social processes in terms of such mechanisms as deviation and feedback (Flannery 1968, 1972; Hole, Flannery, and Neely 1969; Webster 1977; Butzer 1980). It has also been used as a source of techniques for modeling the dynamics of past cultures, sometimes with the aid of simulation models (Doran 1970) as a source of testable hypotheses for predicting regularities in all systems of a particular class, such as SUBSISTENCE, and as a model for explanation (Clarke 1968; Watson, LeBlanc, and Redman 1971).

David Clarke's massive work *Analytical Archaeology* (1968) was the most thoroughgoing attempt to utilize a general system theoretic approach in constructing archaeological theory. In the course of his discussion, Clarke identified material culture as constituting not only a system for environmental regulation and control but also as an information system. The information-systemic nature of material culture is a concept reflected in the analytic methods of Ian Hodder and other "postprocessualists" of the 1980s and 1990s, which assign a dynamic role to ARTIFACTS as "material symbols" implicated in the processes of cultural change (Hodder 1982, 1986).

In general, archaeologists have been quite selective in their use of system theoretic methods, and have usually applied system theory principles on a small scale. Kent Flannery has used systemic concepts to address several continuing archaeological problems, including the origin of FOOD PRODUCTION (Flannery 1968) and the development of CULTURAL COMPLEXITY and the STATE (Flannery 1972). His 1968 paper analyzing the processes leading to the transition to food production in Mesoamerica in system theoretic terms, and his later theoretical paper seeking to identify the processes leading to the formation of complex STATE societies, which Flannery regards as hierarchical control systems (Flannery 1972), have become classics of archaeological systems analysis.

Early promoters of system theory anticipated its application in constructing computer simulation models of sociocultural systems of the past, using empirical data. Attempts to put this into practice have made abundantly clear the apparent impossibility of identifying all possible causal variables that affect such systems, aside from the practical problem of recovering sufficient archaeological evidence for modeling them adequately (see, e.g., Willey and Shimkin 1973).

System theory has been criticized as lacking theoretical status, as having little or no relevance to archaeological problems (Salmon 1978), as being simply another method of functional explanation under a new rubric, and as having limited explanatory value because of its failure to account for phenomena in conventional causal terms. It has also been called reductionistic, a justified criticism, since most of its applications to archaeological research problems have usually ended up accounting for higher-order phenomena, such as political and religious structures, in terms of lower-order systems, such as SUBSISTENCE and economic subsystems. But the key problem in its application to complex social systems lies in the requirement of identifying and modeling all significant subsystem variables. In the case of any sociocultural system, this is not possible; nor is there any way to verify whether this might actually have been accomplished in any particular case. These problems are a consequence of the multivariate nature of cultural systems, which has led archaeologists to focus on only certain limited categories of variables or subsystems in attempting to analyze sociocultural phenomena using system theoretic methods.

Despite these limitations on its applicability, the systems approach has proved to be a fruitful one for archaeology, as the work of Flannery and others has demonstrated. System theory continues to provide archaeologists with a useful method for modeling certain important subsystems of prehistoric cultures, especially those of SUBSISTENCE and settlement, provided the limitations of the method are acknowledged and taken into consideration.

REFERENCES

Ashby, W. Ross. 1958. General systems theory as a new discipline. General Systems 3:1–6.
Bertalanffy, Ludwig von. 1962. General system theory, a critical review. General Systems 7:1–20.
———. 1968. General system theory: foundations, development, applications. Rev. ed. George Braziller, New York.
Binford, Lewis R. 1965. Archaeological systematics and the study of culture process. American Antiquity 32:203–209.
Butzer, Karl W. 1980. Civilizations: organisms or systems? American Scientist 68:517–523.
Clarke, David L. 1968. Analytical archaeology. Methuen, London.
———, ed. 1972. Models in archaeology. Methuen, London.
Doran, James. 1970. Systems theory, computer simulations and archaeology. World Archaeology 1:289–298.
Flannery, Kent V. 1968. Archaeological systems theory and early Mesoamerica. In Anthropological archaeology in the Americas, Betty J. Meggers. Anthropological Society of Washington, Washington, D.C.

————. 1972. The cultural evolution of civilizations. Annual Review of Ecology and
    Systematics 3:399–426.

Hodder, Ian. 1982. Theoretical archaeology: a reactionary view. In Symbolic and struc-
    tural archaeology, Ian Hodder, ed., Cambridge University Press, pp. 1–16.

————. 1986. Reading the past: current approaches to interpretation in archaeology.
    Cambridge University Press.

Hole, Frank, Kent Flannery, and James A. Neely. 1969. Prehistory and human ecology
    of the Deh Luran Plain: an early village sequence from Khuzistan, Iran. Memoirs
    of the Museum of Anthropology No. 1. University of Michigan, Ann Arbor.

Maruyama, Mogorrah. 1963. The second cybernetics: deviation-amplifying mutual causal
    processes. American Scientist 51:164–179.

Radcliffe-Brown, A. R. 1935. On the concept of function in social science. American
    Anthropologist 37:394–402.

————. 1952. Structure and function in primitive society. Free Press, Glencoe, Ill.

————. 1957. A natural science of society. Free Press, Glencoe, Ill.

Salmon, Merrilee. 1978. What can systems theory do for archaeology? American An-
    tiquity 43:174–183.

Watson, Patty Jo, Stephen LeBlanc, and Charles Redman. 1971. Explanation in archae-
    ology: an explicitly scientific approach. Columbia University Press, New York.

Webster, David. 1977. Warfare and the evolution of Maya civilization. In The origins
    of Maya civilization, R. E. W. Adams, ed. University of New Mexico Press,
    Albuquerque, pp. 335–372.

Willey, Gordon R., and Dimitri B. Shimkin. 1973. The Maya collapse: a summary view.
    In The Classic Maya collapse, T. P. Culbert, ed. School of American Research
    Advanced Seminar Series. University of New Mexico Press, Albuquerque,
    pp. 457–503.

SOURCES OF ADDITIONAL INFORMATION

A still-useful general discussion of the principles of system theory and its potential for
archaeological research is the review article by Fred Plog, "Systems theory in archeological research," *Annual Review of Anthropology* 4(1975):207–224; although its bibliography is now hopelessly out-of-date with respect to recent literature, it contains
references to a number of basic background sources that, like this article, are still useful
as introductions to the subject, as well as some classic early studies, such as Flannery's.
The discussion in Salmon (1978; See References) is also still very informative. These
sources are recommended as background reading, since the discussions of system theory
and archaeological applications of the systems approach in many beginning archaeology
textbooks tend to be very brief and superficial.

Some applications of the systems approach include J. W. G. Lowe, "Qualitative
systems theory, its utility and limitations," *Journal of Anthropological Research* 41(1)
(1985):42–62; and R. G. Reynolds, "A production system model of hunter-gatherer
resource scheduling adaptations," *European Journal of Operational Research*
30(3)(1987):237–239.

There is at present no up-to-date, comprehensive review of the literature in this field.
On-line search of the *Social Sciences Citation Index* for works citing particular authors
of important archaeological systems studies is recommended for retrieving recent
literature.

T
_____

TAPHONOMY. A subdiscipline of archaeology devoted to the investigation of formative and disturbance processes affecting the ARCHAEOLOGICAL RECORD, especially those affecting the deposition of faunal remains. Such processes encompass all the events intervening between the time of initial deposition and the time of recovery of remains by the archaeologist or paleontologist. (See also ZOOARCHAEOLOGY.)

Taphonomy, a category of MIDDLE-RANGE RESEARCH originally developed within the field of paleontology, has now become an important branch of zooarchaeological studies. First defined by the Russian paleontologist I. A. Efremov as "the science of the laws of embedding or burial, the study of the transition . . . of organics from the biosphere into the lithosphere" (Efremov 1940; quoted in Lyman 1987b:117), taphonomy has also been defined as "the study of differences between a fossil ASSEMBLAGE and the community(ies) from which it derived . . ." (Hill 1978). Taphonomy literally means "the laws of burial" (Behrensmeyer and Hill 1980:xi; Olson 1980:5), and is concerned with all the processes that affect remains in archaeological CONTEXTs up to the time of their removal from the SITE of deposition by the archaeologist.

Although most archaeological taphonomic studies have been concerned with the investigation of faunal remains (Grayson 1978, 1981, 1982, 1983, 1984, 1985), and sometimes with the use of resulting data for reconstructing past ecology, archaeologists such as Michael Schiffer and others have included a somewhat broader range of materials within taphonomic studies. Some would place human cultural remains (Schiffer 1976, 1983, 1987) and plant remains (Miksicek 1987), as well as human osteological remains (Behrensmeyer 1975; Nelson and Sauer 1984), within its scope.

The principal objectives of taphonomic studies within the field of archaeology are (1) the identification and description of processes resulting in the formation of archaeological deposits; and (2) recovering environmental data to facilitate paleoecological reconstruction of past environments that affected prehistoric human ADAPTATION, as a part of the study of prehistoric SUBSISTENCE and economy.

The term and concept of taphonomy first appeared in the literature of paleontology in 1940, in a paper by I. A. Efremov titled "Taphonomy: A New Branch of Paleontology," published in the *Pan-American Geologist* (Efremov 1940). As Olson has observed (Olson 1980:6), taphonomy originally had essentially the same meaning as the term *biostratinomy*, namely those processes affecting the remains of an organism between death and final burial, now frequently called *perthotaxic factors* (Lyman 1987b). Taphonomy is now usually divided into biostratinomic and diagenetic studies, the latter focused on postburial processes that affect organic materials between final burial and recovery (Lawrence 1979a, 1979b; Lyman 1987b). However, Olson also notes that a universal set of "laws" accounting for taphonomic processes has yet to be established; and while it is possible to determine some common properties in assemblages from different sites, the circumstances creating each assemblage are unique, making generalization about taphonomic processes difficult (Olson 1980:9). Taphonomists must make uniformitarian assumptions in constructing their depositional histories, relying on the principle that formative and disturbance processes now affecting faunal and other archaeological deposits are essentially similar to those in the past, whose operation generated the existing archaeological record.

Laboratory methods utilized by taphonomists for studying faunal remains include the use of scanning electron microscopy (SEM), to examine bones for patterned marks indicative of butchering or other treatment by humans, and to distinguish these from marks attributable to natural processes. However, no completely reliable set of criteria for making such distinctions with certainty has yet been developed (Lyman 1987a; Bonnichsen and Sorg 1988).

An important emphasis of taphonomic studies is disturbance or *transformational* processes. These factors that affect deposits after initial deposition, in the interval between deposition and recovery, are termed *diagenetic* factors by taphonomists. The archaeologist Michael Schiffer has distinguished two types of disturbance process. Those which are the result of human cultural activity (e.g., plowing, grave robbing) he calls "C-transforms," while those attributable to natural processes, such as freezing and thawing (cryoturbation) or rodent activity, are termed "N-transforms" (Schiffer 1976).

Most of the processes taphonomists deal with are of natural or animal origin, and often have little connection to human behavior. The effects of human behavior are, of course, relevant to taphonomic studies; and many taphonomists are primarily concerned with being able to distinguish between the results of human activity and other factors affecting archaeological materials, particularly animal bones (Binford and Bertram 1977). Distinguishing the marks of human activity on bones from those resulting from natural or animal agents is in fact a key problem for taphonomists, since this distinction may be crucial for detecting a human presence at a particular site at a particular time in the past. Preoccupation with this question has generated a number of experimental studies (see, e.g., Gifford-Gonzalez et al. 1985; Stanford, Bonnichsen, and Morlan 1981), although results of these have not yet led to the development of general principles for distinguishing conclusively between the results of human and animal activity on archaeological bone.

Despite the imprecise nature of much of the data, sampling problems, and the difficulties inherent in connecting fossilized bones with animal communities of the past, taphonomic studies of archaeofaunal materials continue to provide archaeologists with useful data on hunting patterns, preferred food species, butchering and cooking habits, and material on other human SUBSISTENCE activities in the past, as well as indications of past environmental characteristics that influenced patterns of human ADAPTATION and animal utilization in a variety of past situations. For these reasons, this specialized area of investigation will doubtless continue to be an important part of future archaeological studies.

REFERENCES

Behrensmeyer, Anna K. 1975. Taphonomy and paleontology in the hominid fossil record. Yearbook of Physical Anthropology 19:30–50.

Behrensmeyer, Anna K., and Andrew P. Hill, eds. 1980. Fossils in the making: vertebrate taphonomy and paleoecology. University of Chicago Press.

Binford, Lewis R., and J. B. Bertram. 1977. Bone frequencies—and attritional processes. In For theory building in archaeology, Lewis R. Binford, ed., Academic Press, New York, pp. 77–153.

Bonnichsen, R., and M. Sorg, eds. 1988. Bone modification. Center for the Study of Early Man, Univerity of Maine, Orono.

Efremov, I. A. 1940. Taphonomy: a new branch of paleontology. Pan-American Geologist 74:81–93.

Gifford-Gonzalez, Diane P., et al. 1985. The third dimension in site structure: an experiment in trampling and vertical dispersal. American Antiquity 50(4):803–818.

Grayson, Donald K. 1978. Reconstructing mammalian communities: a discussion of Shotwell's method of paleoecological analysis. Paleobiology 4:77–81.

———. 1981. A critical view of the use of archaeological vertebrates in paleoenvironmental reconstruction. Journal of Ethnobiology 1:28–38.

———. 1982. Review of bones: ancient men and modern myths, by L. R. Binford. American Anthropologist 84:439–440.

———. 1983. The paleontology of Gatecliff shelter: small mammals. In The archaeology of Monitor Valley. Vol. 2: Gatecliff shelter, by D. H. Thomas. American Museum of Natural History Anthropological Papers 19(1):99–135.

———. 1984. Quantitative zooarchaeology. Academic Press, New York.

———. 1985. The paleontology of Hidden Cave: birds and mammals. In The archaeology of Hidden Cave, Nevada, D. H. Thomas, ed. American Museum of Natural History Anthropological Papers 61(1):125–161.

Hill, Andrew P. 1978. Taphonomical background to fossil man—problems in paleoecology. In Geological background to fossil man, V. W. Bishop, ed. Scottish Academic, Edinburgh, pp. 87–100.

Lawrence, D. R. 1979a. Biostratinomy. In Encyclopedia of paleontology, R. W. Fair-bridge and D. Jablonski, eds. Dowden, Hutchinson and Ross, Stroudsburg, Pa., pp. 99–103.

———. 1979b. Diagenesis of fossils—fossildiagenese. In Encyclopedia of Paleontology, pp. 245–247.

Lyman, R. Lee. 1987a. Archaeofaunas and butchery studies: a taphonomic perspective. Advances in Archaeological Method and Theory 10:249–337.

———. 1987b. Zooarchaeology and taphonomy: a general consideration. Journal of Ethnobiology 7(1):93–117.

Miksicek, Charles H. 1987. Formation processes of the archaeobotanical record. Advances in Archaeological Method and Theory 10:211–247.

Nelson, Dorothy A., and Norman J. Sauer. 1984. An evaluation of postdepositional changes in the trace element content of human bone. American Antiquity 49(1):141–147.

Olson, Everett C. 1980. Taphonomy: its history and role in community evolution. In Fossils in the making, Anna K. Behrensmeyer and Andrew P. Hill, eds. University of Chicago Press, pp. 5–19.

Schiffer, Michael B. 1976. Behavioral archaeology. Academic Press, New York.

———. 1983. Toward the identification of formation processes. American Antiquity 48(4):675–706.

———. 1987. Formation processes of the archaeological record. University of New Mexico Press, Albuquerque.

Stanford, Dennis, Robson Bonnichsen, and Richard E. Morlan. 1981. The Ginsberg experiment: modern and prehistoric evidence of bone flaking technology. Science 212:434–440.

SOURCES OF ADDITIONAL INFORMATION

For background material and an introduction to the field of taphonomic studies, the reader is referred to the introductory text by Patricia Shipman, *Life History of a Fossil: An Introduction to Vertebrate Taphonomy and Paleoecology* (Cambridge, Mass., Harvard University Press, 1981); to the collection of papers in the 1980 volume edited by Behrensmeyer and Hill, *Fossils in the Making* (see References); and the article by Anna K. Behrensmeyer, "Taphonomy and Paleontology in the Hominid Fossil Record," *Yearbook of Physical Anthropology* 19(1975):30–50.

With respect to reviews and bibliographic sources, as well as the volume of literature available, the field of taphonomy has an embarrassment of riches. Between 1979 and 1987, the annual *Advances in Archaeological Method and Theory* published no fewer than six review articles on various aspects of taphonomic studies and related subjects. The initial volume (1978) included "A survey of disturbance processes in archaeological site formation," by W. Raymond Wood and Donald Lee Johnson (pp. 315–381); vol. 2 (1979) included Donald Grayson's "On the quantification of vertebrate archaeofaunas" (pp. 199–237). In vol. 4 (1981), a major review by Diane Gifford appeared, titled "Taphonomy and paleoecology, a critical review of archaeology's sister disciplines" (pp. 365–438), which included over 12 pages of bibliographic references. Vol. 5 (1982) contained the first of R. Lee Lyman's reviews, "Archaeofaunas and subsistence studies" (pp. 331–393), which included a section on taphonomy and subsistence analysis, and concluded with a 16-page bibliography of literature, most of it published in the 1970s and early 1980s. Two reviews appeared in vol. 10 (1987): Charles H. Miksicek's "Formation processes of the archaeobotanical record'' (pp. 211–247), followed by Lyman's second review, ''Archaeofaunas and butchery studies: a taphonomic perspective'' (pp. 249–337); both were accompanied by extensive bibliographies.

The continuing volume of publication in taphonomic studies is astounding. In 1991, *Annual Review of Anthropology* published a review by Henry T. Bunn, ''A taphonomic perspective on the archaeology of human origins'' (20:433–467). Papers published in *Journal of Archaeological Science* and *Journal of Human Evolution* alone since 1987, covering the taphonomy of both faunal and botanical remains, are too numerous to list here. Several studies have appeared in issues of *Current Anthropology*. Book publications include George C. Frison and L. C. Todd, *The Colby Mammoth Site: Taphonomy and Archaeology of a Clovis Kill in Northern Wyoming* (Albuquerque, University of New Mexico Press, 1986); *Bone Modification*, Rob Bonnichsen and M. Sorg, eds., a volume of papers presented at the First International Conference on Bone Modification at Carson City, Nevada, in 1984 (Orono, Center for the Study of Early Man, University of Maine, 1988); and *Problem Solving in Taphonomy: Archaeological and Paleontological Studies from Europe, Africa and Oceania*, S. U. Solomon, Iain Davidson, and D. I. Watson, eds. (University of Queensland, TEMPUS, Archaeology and Material Culture Studies in Anthropology, vol. 2, 1990).

THREE-AGE SYSTEM. The classification of human PREHISTORY into a sequence of three technological ages, namely Stone Age, Bronze Age, and Iron Age, according to the principal raw material used for tool manufacture during a particular time frame in the past.

The initial tripartite classificatory/chronological scheme based on technological materials was formulated in the early nineteenth century by the Danish archaeologist Christian J. Thomsen (Thomsen 1836). Although originally developed as a system for organizing ARTIFACTS in the collection of the Danish National Museum, of which Thomsen served as curator, the three-age scheme eventually became the basis of a relative chronology for European archaeology as well as for arranging archaeological museum collections throughout Europe.

Thomsen was one of a number of Scandinavian archaeologists who investigated and interpreted the antiquities of their own nations for a substantial period before archaeology developed on the European continent. Thomsen's protégé, Jens Worsaae (1821–1885), who worked with Thomsen as a museum volunteer, was to become the first professional prehistoric archaeologist, as well as the first professor of archaeology at the University of Copenhagen. Thomsen, who remained a museum archaeologist all his life, postulated that his three ages reflected three successive developmental stages of the human past, and made some speculations concerning the nature of the society and CULTURE associated with each age. Worsaae, on the other hand, was an avid fieldworker, and his stratigraphic excavations confirmed and refined Thomsen's chronology, providing material evidence to test Thomsen's speculations (Trigger 1989:80–81).

According to Thomsen's speculative scenario, during the Stone Age all tools were made of stone, bone, or wood, and clothing was made chiefly of animal skins. In the succeeding Bronze Age, when weapons and implements were made first of copper, and later of bronze, copper technology developed, first by cold-hammering and later by casting. Knowledge of iron smelting came much later, and Thomsen suggested it most likely developed in the Mediterranean area and was introduced into northern Europe by "people from the shores of the Black Sea, about the time of Julius Caesar . . . '' (Daniel 1971:85).

In one of his several works on the history of archaeology, Glyn Daniel noted that the idea of a ''stone age'' did not originate with Thomsen.

> . . . the idea of an age of stone existed in the writings of Greek philosophers and historians, and the recognition of stone implements as such by antiquaries and geologists in the sixteenth, seventeenth, and eighteenth centuries . . . prepared the way for the recognition as a historical fact of a stone age in the human past . . . [but] it was the writings of Scandinavian historians and archaeologists, and their work in museums and in excavation, that established not only the idea of a stone age, but a sequence of three ages in the prehistoric past—Stone, Bronze, and Iron. The Three-Age system has very properly been described by Joseph Dechelette as ''the basis of prehistory,'' and by R. A. S. Macalister as ''the cornerstone of modern archaeology.'' (Daniel 1971:79)

The Stone Age was subsequently divided into stages by French archaeologists of the 1860s: into a Paleolithic, or Old Stone Age, when lithic technology was confined to percussion, chipping, and flaking; and a Neolithic, or New Stone Age, beginning with the first major innovations of stone grinding and polishing. A third division, the Mesolithic period of microlith technology, was a somewhat later addition (see LITHICS).

Charles Maisels has pointed out that the three-age system had much earlier origins than those cited by Daniel:

> Though the modern stone-bronze-iron succession, with its ethnographic parallels, derives ultimately from Mercati (1541–93), whose *Metallotheca* was suppressed until 1717, the first recorded ''Ages System'' is . . . that contained in Hesiod's *Works and Days* . . . of the eighth century BC, a mytho-moral system describing successive ''races (*genos*) of men.'' (Maisels 1990, app. F, p. 324)

The scheme of Hesiod (1973:62) was based on the idea that humankind had originally inhabited an ''Age of Gold,'' and then degenerated through an ''Age of Silver'' to subsequent ages of Bronze and Iron. But the sixteenth-century work of Mercati was a direct anticipation of the scheme devised by Thomsen in the first half of the nineteenth century. Some of the earlier versions of this Scandinavian scheme assumed there were ages of stone, copper, and iron (Daniel 1971:79), with bronze replacing copper in later versions.

Worsaae eventually succeeded Thomsen as director of the National Museum. At the age of 22 he published his *The Primeval Antiquities of Denmark* (1843), a work of remarkable sophistication in its advocacy of comparative archaeological studies, as well as in its attention to field techniques and the importance of archaeological CONTEXT, in which Worsaae made use of Thomsen's three-age chronologic sequence. Worsaae later split the Stone and Bronze ages into two principal divisions each, although these did not correspond to those now in use (Graslund 1987). The three-age system was adopted by the British Museum in the 1860s, and eventually was widely accepted as a standard classificatory method for organizing museum collections.

Another kind of three-stage chronologic scheme, based on economic factors and social organization, was an outgrowth of a scheme of sociocultural evolution developed by Sven Nilsson, professor of zoology at Lund, Sweden, in the 1830s. This rough chronology of human prehistory consisted of the three stages of savagery, barbarism (nomadic pastoralism), and civilization (supported by agriculture), which was adopted by Edward B. Tylor in his monumental work of cultural anthropology, *Primitive Culture* (1871). This savagery-barbarism-civilization scheme persisted well into the twentieth century before it was perceived to be a gross oversimplification of social EVOLUTION, which is no longer routinely regarded as the unilinear phenomenon suggested by early observations of the ARCHAEOLOGICAL RECORD of the Old World but as multilinear, and far more complex than previously supposed. Although this second three-stage cultural classificatory system had no direct relationship to the three-part sequence of technological "ages" devised and formalized by Thomsen, it served as a useful organizational principle in anthropology and archaeology, and afforded a method of associating particular kinds of SUBSISTENCE and social patterns with the three major stages of technological development that underlay Thomsen's scheme.

The three-age system of Thomsen has withstood the test of time rather well. It has fared far better than its social evolutionary counterpart, and with the addition of some revisions and refinements, still serves as a basic relative chronology for OLD WORLD ARCHAEOLOGY.

It should be noted that Thomsen's three-age sequence was based upon archaeological knowledge derived entirely from Old World field data, much of it acquired in the Near East and Mediterranean areas, which were the ones best known to archaeologists of Thomsen's and Worsaae's generations. Although a roughly similar developmental sequence has since been traced in the Americas, the terminology and time frame for the New World "Stone Age" is somewhat different; and there are no true equivalents for a Bronze Age or Iron Age in the western hemisphere (see NEW WORLD ARCHAEOLOGY). The striking variability between Old World and New World cultural history contributed significantly to the development of present multilinear evolutionary models as better approximations of the events of the past than simple unilinear schemes, such as those devised by Thomsen and Nilsson. The early work of the Scandinavian archaeologists should not be underestimated, however, for it marked the birth of professionalism in archaeology, with the creation of the first chronological framework for interpreting the material remains of the past and organizing them in a useful manner for study (see also ANTIQUARIANISM; ARCHAEOLOGY; PREHISTORY). In this respect, the three-age system was indeed archaeology's first "paradigm" (Rodden 1981).

REFERENCES

Daniel, Glyn. 1971. The three-age system. In The origins and growth of archaeology. Crowell, New York, pp. 79–98.

——. 1976. The spread of the three-age system. In A hundred and fifty years of archaeology. Harvard University Press, Cambridge, Mass., pp. 77–84.

Graslund, Bo. 1981. The background to C. J. Thomsen's three age system. In Towards a history of archaeology, Glyn Daniel, ed. Thames and Hudson, London, pp. 45–50.

——. 1987. The birth of prehistoric chronology. Cambridge University Press.

Hesiod. 1973. Theogony. D. Wender, trans. Penguin, Harmondsworth, U.K.

Lubbock, John. 1865. Pre-historic times, as illustrated by ancient remains, and the manners and customs of modern savages. Williams and Norgate, London.

Maisels, Charles Keith. 1990. The emergence of civilization, from hunting and gathering to agriculture, cities, and the state in the Near East. Routledge, London and New York.

Rodden, Judith. 1981. The development of the three age system: archaeology's first paradigm. In Towards a history of archaeology, Glyn Daniel, ed. Thames and Hudson, London, pp. 51–68.

Thomsen, Christian Juergen. 1836. Ledetraad til nordisk oldkyndighed. National Museum, Copenhagen. (Trans. into English, 1848)

Trigger, Bruce. 1989. A history of archaeological thought. Cambridge University Press.

Tylor, Edward B. 1871. Primitive culture: researches into the development of mythology, religion, language, art and custom. 2 vols. J. Murray, London.

Worsaae, Jens J. A. 1849. The primeval antiquities of Denmark, W. J. Thoms, trans. Parker, London. (Originally published in 1843)

SOURCES OF ADDITIONAL INFORMATION

The most detailed discussions of Thomsen's three-age system are in Daniel 1971, 1976; Graslund 1981; and Rodden 1981 (see References). There is some additional information in Gordon Willey and Jeremy Sabloff's *A History of American Archaeology* (San Francisco, W. H. Freeman, 1980), pp. 3–5; and in Bruce Trigger, *A History of Archaeological Thought* (Cambridge, Cambridge University Press, 1989). For additional material, consult the bibliographies in Maisels (1990) and Trigger (1989; see References).

TYPOLOGY. 1. The process of creating an ordered system for classifying archaeological data into *types* (mutually exclusive classes), which usually are empirically defined according to an established set of criteria, for purposes of facilitating description, comparison, and interpretation of ARTIFACTs in terms of standardized categories. 2. The classificatory system or scheme that is the end result of the typological process. Types are defined by the consistent clustering of shared attributes; the unit types within a typology are often arranged hierarchically, with larger units each comprising all smaller units assigned to the class.

The process of classifying the world and its contents into categories is a universally human one, and practical typologies form an important component of every human culture's sensemaking system. The units utilized in the construction of these systems may vary radically from one culture to another, however, as well as the kinds of criteria used to define them. The mental processes employed in their construction are often largely intuitive. Archaeological typologies share certain common characteristics with these "folk" classifications, including the use of intuition in their construction and the utilization of unit categories that are at least to some extent culture-dependent (Berlin 1973). Archaeological classification differs from folk classification in consciously employing logical reasoning as well as intuition in developing typologies, and may sometimes make use of categories that can be defined statistically (quantitatively) as well as descriptively (qualitatively).

The conscious use of logical processes such as deductive and inductive reasoning in classification goes back at least to the time of the Greek philosopher Porphyry (third century A.D.). The logical approach to classification has resulted in some very broadly useful and flexible systematics, of which the Linnaean classification of biological species is probably the best known (Linnaeus 1735) and which has long been used as a model of classification (Mayr 1942; Simpson 1945).

The first specifically archaeological system of classification was the THREE-AGE SYSTEM devised by Christian J. Thomsen in the 1830s, which, like later ones, was designed to classify portable artifacts. In Thomsen's scheme, artifacts were sorted according to their material of manufacture, and this attribute was used as a basis for organizing museum collections into broad culture-chronological categories. Chronology was to become a major concern in European archaeology, one that played a major role in shaping the discipline of archaeology, and the characteristics of artifacts that form the basis of typologies were accorded chronological importance. The importance of artifact classification in European archaeology in the latter part of the nineteenth century is apparent in the chronological work of Sir Flinders Petrie (Petrie 1899), and of the Swedish archaeologist Oscar Montelius, who developed a typological method based on Thomsen's work (Montelius 1903).

In American archaeology, classification and typology had a very different development. Here, artifact ASSEMBLAGES frequently had components that, in European terminology, were both Paleolithic and Neolithic, and the existence of a surviving aboriginal population provided a basis for inferring artifact functions by using ethnographic ANALOGY. The American ARCHAEOLOGICAL RECORD lacked the distinct temporal changes visible in that of the Old World, making the construction of chronologies a major goal of classificatory efforts, which in fact became a virtually exclusive goal of American archaeology in first half of the twentieth century (Robinson 1951; Rowe 1962).

The development of typologies in American archaeology began late in the nineteenth century, with the efforts of the Smithsonian archaeologists Charles Rau and Thomas Wilson, which were designed to classify lithic projectile points. Rau devised a four-part intuitive scheme based on differences of size and shape; Wilson's version of this system arranged it into a two-level hierarchy (Rau 1876; Wilson 1899). Ceramic typologies did not develop until much later, although in the late nineteenth century William Henry Holmes grouped pottery vessels into groups according to their attributes, and regarded temporal changes in forms as having chronological significance (Holmes 1886a, 1886b, 1903). The standard type/variety method of ceramic classification now in use was a by-product of the later typological synthesis that resulted in the classificatory system now widely in use in America (Wheat, Gifford, and Wasley 1958; Smith, Willey, and Gifford 1960; Sabloff and Smith 1969).

American archaeological classification has usually been a pragmatic process, dictated by the demands of the immediate situation or problem being investigated. This produced a multiplicity of types and typologies of limited usefulness for the general case, and often resulted in the use of categories and terminology that are not broadly comparable. A consequence of this has been a number of formal efforts to create standardized terms and analytic units that have uniform meaning in all circumstances, while preserving terminology that has acquired general usage (Steward and Setzler 1938; Steward 1954; Clay 1965; Hill and Evans 1972; Read 1974). As Robert Dunnell has pointed out, however, such classificatory efforts have not often distinguished between types as devices of measurement and types as empirical categories. This ambiguity has contributed to numerous debates on the objective "reality" of archaeological types, in which a major issue has been whether such types represent *emic* categories that would be recognizable and meaningful to those who created the artifacts, or are merely *etic* devices superimposed on the data by the archaeologist (Read 1982, 1989; Whallon 1982; Dunnell 1988).

At present, most American archaeologists utilize a synthetic system of classification based on the work of James Ford, Alex Krieger, and Irving Rouse, employing terms and intuitive concepts inherited from earlier classificatory efforts and adapted to form a typology that served the aims of American culture historians (Ford 1938, 1952, 1954, 1962; Rouse 1939, 1960, 1970; Krieger 1944, 1960). An early effort to achieve standardization and overcome the problem of multiple classifications with nonequivalent categories was the so-called Midwestern Taxonomic Method (McKern 1939), designed as a descriptive system without any intent to serve as a chronological scheme. This classificatory scheme contains many of the categories adapted, enlarged, and elaborated by Gordon Willey and Philip Phillips in their own, more fully developed effort at defining a standard classificatory system (Willey and Phillips 1958).

New efforts to devise typologies for archaeology were stimulated by the shift of focus from chronology to past behavior that occurred with the "NEW" ARCHAEOLOGY of the 1960s and 1970s (Binford 1965; Binford and Sabloff 1982). Among these were the use of statistical techniques to define ARTIFACT types (Spaulding 1953), and other mathematical approaches, including cluster analysis (Clarke 1968; Sneath and Sokal 1973; Doran and Hodson 1975; Christensen and Read 1977; Cowgill 1982; Kronenfeld 1985), which had some historical antecedents in the work of Alfred Kroeber and William McKern (Dunnell 1988:187). Quantitative methods have been central to many recent efforts to develop a rigorous archaeological systematics (see, e.g., papers in Whallon and Brown 1982). This is a goal long pursued by Robert Dunnell, who since the early 1970s has noted that a scientific systematics, while essential, has not developed in archaeology due to the lack of a body of general theory from which such a systematics could be deduced (Dunnell 1971, 1986). Until such time as a more rigorous classificatory system may be devised, the practical typological system now in use among American archaeologists, representing the synthetic compromise that arose from the work of such archaeologists as Rouse, Ford, and Krieger between the 1930s and 1960s, continues to be relied upon.

REFERENCES

Berlin, Brent. 1973. Folk systematics in relation to biological classification and nomenclature. Annual Review of Ecology and Systematics 4:259–271.

Binford, Lewis R. 1965. Archaeological systematics and the study of culture process. American Antiquity 31:203–210.

Binford, Lewis R., and Jeremy A. Sabloff. 1982. Paradigms, systematics, and archaeology. Journal of Anthropological Research 38:137–153.

Christensen, Anders L., and Dwight W. Read. 1977. Numerical taxonomy, R-mode factor analysis, and archaeological classification. American Antiquity 42(2):163–179.

Clarke, David L. 1968. Analytical archaeology. Methuen, London.

Clay, R. Berle. 1965. Typological classification, attribute analysis, and lithic variability. Journal of Field Archaeology 3(3):303–311.

Cowgill, George L. 1982. Clusters of objects and associations between variables: two approaches to archaeological classification. In Essays on archaeological typology, R. Whallon and J. A. Brown, eds. Center for American Archaeology Press, Evanston, Ill., pp. 30–55.

Doran, J. E., and F. R. Hodson. 1975. Mathematics and computers in archaeology. Harvard University Press, Cambridge, Mass.

Dunnell, Robert C. 1971. Systematics in prehistory. Free Press, New York.

———. 1978. Style and function: a fundamental dichotomy. American Antiquity 43:192–202.

———. 1986. Five decades of American archaeology. In American archaeology past and future . . . , D. J. Meltzer, D. D. Fowler, and J. A. Sabloff, eds. Society for American Archaeology/Smithsonian Institution Press, Washington, D.C., pp. 23–49.

———. 1988. Methodological issues in Americanist artifact classification. Advances in Archaeological Method and Theory 9:149–207.

Ford, James A. 1938. A chronological method applicable to the Southeast. American Antiquity 3:260–264.

———. 1952. Measurements of some prehistoric design developments in the southeastern states. American Museum of Natural History Anthropological Papers 43, no. 3. New York.

———. 1954. The type concept revisited. American Anthropologist 56:42–54.

———. 1962. A quantitative method for deriving cultural chronology. Pan American Union, Washington, D.C.

Hill, J. N., and R. K. Evans. 1972. A model for classification and typology. In Models in archaeology, David L. Clarke, ed. Methuen, London, pp. 231–273.

Holmes, William Henry. 1886a. Pottery of the ancient Pueblos. In Fourth Annual Report of the Bureau of Ethnology. Smithsonian Institution, Washington, D.C., pp. 257–360.

———. 1886b. Ancient pottery of the Mississippi Valley. In Fourth Annual Report of the Bureau of Ethnology. Smithsonian Institution, Washington, D.C., pp. 361–436.

———. 1903. Aboriginal pottery of the eastern United States. In Twentieth Annual Report (1898–1899) of the Bureau of American Ethnology. Smithsonian Institution, Washington, D.C.

Krieger, Alex D. 1944. The typological concept. American Antiquity 9(3):271–288.

———. 1960. Archaeological typology in theory and practice. In Man and culture: selected papers of the Fifth International Congress of Anthropological and Ethnological Sciences, Anthony F. C. Wallace, ed. University of Pennsylvania Press, Philadelphia, pp. 141–151.

Kronenfeld, David B. 1985. Numerical taxonomy: old techniques and new assumptions. Current Anthropology 26(1):21–41.

Linnaeus, Carolus. 1735. Systema naturae, sive regna tria naturae systematice proposita per classes, ordines, genera et species. T. Haak, Leyden.

Mayr, Ernst. 1942. Systematics and the origin of species. Columbia Biological Series 13, Columbia University, New York.

McKern, William C. 1939. The Midwestern Taxonomic Method as an aid to archaeological study. American Antiquity 4:301–313.

Montelius, Gustav Oscar. 1903. Die typologische methode: die alteren kulturperioden im Orient und in Europa, vol. 1. Selbstverlag, Stockholm.

Petrie, Sir W. M. Flinders. 1899. Sequences in prehistoric remains. Journal of the Royal Anthropological Institute of Great Britain and Ireland 29:295–301.

Rau, Charles. 1876. The archaeological collections of the United States National Museum in charge of the Smithsonian. Smithsonian Contributions to Knowledge 22, no. 4. Washington, D.C.

Read, Dwight W. 1974. Some comments on typologies in archaeology and an outline of a methodology. American Antiquity 39(2):216–242.

———. 1982. Toward a theory of archaeological classification. In Essays on archaeological typology, Robert Whallon and James A. Brown, eds. Center for American Archaeology Press, Evanston, Ill., pp. 56–92.

———. 1989. Intuitive typology and automatic classification—divergence or full circle. Journal of Anthropological Archaeology 8(2):158–188.

Robinson, W. S. 1951. A method for chronologically ordering archaeological deposits. American Antiquity 16:293–301.

Rouse, Irving. 1939. Prehistory in Haiti: a study in method. Yale University Publications in Anthropology 21. New Haven.

———. 1960. The classification of artifacts in archaeology. American Antiquity 25(3):313–323.

———. 1970. Classification for what? Comments on Analytical archaeology, by D. L. Clarke. Norwegian Archaeological Review 3:9–12.

Rowe, John H. 1962. Stages and periods in archaeological interpretation. Southwestern Journal of Anthropology 18(1):40–54.

Sabloff, Jeremy A., and Robert E. Smith. 1969. The importance of both analytic and taxonomic classification in the type-variety system. American Antiquity 34(3):278–285.

Simpson, George Gaylord. 1945. The principles of classification and a classification of mammals. Bulletin of the American Museum of Natural History 85. New York.

Smith, R. E., G. R. Willey, and J. C. Gifford. 1960. The type-variety concept as a basis for the analysis of Maya pottery. American Antiquity 25(3):330–340.

Sneath, P. H. A., and Robert R. Sokal. 1973. Numerical taxonomy. W. H. Freeman, San Francisco.

Spaulding, Albert C. 1953. Statistical techniques for the discovery of artifact types. American Antiquity 18:305–313.

Steward, Julian H. 1954. Types of types. American Anthropologist 56:54–57.

Steward, Julian H., and Frank M. Setzler. 1938. Function and configuration in archaeology. American Antiquity 4(1):4–10.

Whallon, Robert. 1982. Variables and dimensions: the critical step in quantitative typology. In Essays on archaeological typology, R. Whallon and J. A. Brown, eds. Center for American Archeology Press, Evanston, Ill., pp. 127–161.

Whallon, Robert, and James A. Brown, eds. 1982. Essays on archaeological typology. Center for American Archeology Press, Evanston, Ill.

Wheat, J. B., James Gifford, and W. Wasley. 1958. Ceramic variety, type cluster, and ceramic system in southwestern pottery analysis. American Antiquity 24:34–47.

Willey, Gordon R., and Philip Phillips. 1958. Method and theory in American archaeology. University of Chicago Press.

Wilson, Thomas. 1899. Arrowheads, spearheads and knives of prehistoric times. In Report of the U.S. National Museum for 1897, part 1. Washington, D.C., pp. 811–988.

SOURCES OF ADDITIONAL INFORMATION

A volume devoted to the problem of archaeological systematics, considered from both a pragmatic viewpoint and in its philosophical dimension, is William Y. Adams and Ernest W. Adams, *Archaeological Typology and Practical Reality: A Dialectical Approach to Artifact Classification and Sorting* (Cambridge, Cambridge University Press, 1991). For an overview of the development of typology in American archaeology, as well as a lucid discussion of some philosophical issues implicated in classification, see Robert Dunnell, ''Methodological issues in Americanist artifact classification,'' *Advances in Archaeological Method and Theory* 9(1986):149–207, which includes almost 14 pages of bibliographic references to additional literature. A more recent paper by Dwight Read, ''Intuitive typology and automatic classification—divergence or full circle,'' *Journal of Anthropological Archaeology* 8(2)(1989):158–188, includes additional references. For the most current discussions, see issues of *American Antiquity*, *Journal of Anthropological Archaeology*, *Current Anthropology*, and annual volumes of *Archaeological Method and Theory*.

U

UNIFORMITARIANISM. The doctrine that processes occurring in the physical world were essentially the same in the past as in the present, and present conditions are the result of the continuing operation of such processes.

In archaeology, uniformitarianism is conceived as the principle that all natural processes, whether of a biological, cultural, or geological nature, observable in the present are basically similar to those that operated in the remote past. This is the major theoretical premise underlying the use of analogic reasoning in the interpretation of archaeological remains, and therefore plays a key role in all such interpretation.

The historical roots of uniformitarianism lie in the eighteenth and nineteenth centuries, when it first appeared as a reaction against biblical catastrophism. Catastrophism was the notion that the earth as it exists today resulted from a series of cataclysmic events caused by divine intervention in the past. Among these was the great Flood, described in the Old Testament, the Gilgamesh Epic, and other early sources, an event that was central to the development of the idea of catastrophism, which took its alternative name of *diluvialism* from this scriptural event of the past. This was the prevailing view when, in the seventeenth century, Archbishop James Ussher announced that the date of the earth's creation was October 23, 4004 B.C., and the biblical Flood had occurred in 2501 B.C. (Hookyas 1963, 1970; Daniel 1975; Trigger 1989; see also PREHISTORY).

One of the first natural scientists to oppose this view was the physician and amateur geologist James Hutton. In his *Theory of the Earth* (1788), Hutton described the earth as a self-sustaining machine whose present and future operation were seen as essentially the same. This uniformitarian view was next expressed nearly three decades later by William "Strata" Smith (1769–1839), a geologist who rejected catastrophic theory, favoring instead the view that the earth's rocks and fossils were the products of continuous, natural geologic processes that led to the formation of layered deposits of these materials all over the world (Smith 1816, 1817).

Although the primary concept of uniformitarianism is often attributed to Hutton (Hutton 1788), who initially maintained that the earth had been formed by natural and gradual processes, its first explicit statement was by Sir Charles Lyell, in his *Principles of Geology* (Lyell 1830–1833), a work that greatly influenced Charles Darwin during the period when he was formulating his theory of EVOLUTION. The concept was later inherited by archaeology from the field of geology, where it still constitutes one of the main principles underlying the interpretation of fossils by paleontologists (Cunningham 1977).

George Gaylord Simpson (Simpson 1970) has noted that the uniformitarian view in reality encompasses two concepts, namely uniformitarianism and actualism, the latter referring to processes similar to those of the past still operating in the present, as distinct from those of the past. The concept of actualism has been adopted by some ethnoarchaeologists who have undertaken "actualistic" studies, using presently observed behavioral and natural processes as a basis for making analogic extrapolations to the archaeological past (Schiffer 1976; see also ETHNOARCHAEOLOGY). Both ETHNOARCHAEOLOGY and taphonomic studies rely on the soundness of the concepts of uniformitarianism and actualism as a part of their philosophical foundation, since both represent efforts to explain the past, and the existing ARCHAEOLOGICAL RECORD, in terms of processes that continue to be observable in the present.

Lewis Binford (1977:8) has suggested that some classes of data from the past may better support uniformitarian assumptions than others. In particular, he suggests that archaeological materials documenting past human ecologic ADAPTATION may provide the most reliable data available for constructing middle-range arguments that rely on uniformitarian assumptions. These data include the frequency of occurrence in archaeological SITES of various types of animal bones traceable to currently known species, and the manner in which humans of the past utilized and organized space as a setting for their activities (Binford 1977). In their settlement and SUBSISTENCE studies of past human populations, archaeologists since the 1960s have assumed that such data as these reflect conditions in the past that have not changed and can be readily and reliably documented from available material evidence.

Uniformitarianism continues to be a basic philosophical principle underlying all current archaeological interpretation, and is especially essential to the subdisciplines of ethnoarchaeology and TAPHONOMY, whose methodologies are entirely reliant on uniformitarian assumptions concerning the processes of the past that led to the formation of the present archaeological record.

REFERENCES

Binford, Lewis R. 1977. General introduction. In For theory building in archaeology, Lewis R. Binford, ed. Academic Press, New York, pp. 1–13. Reprinted in his Working at Archaeology. Academic Press, New York, 1983, pp. 31–39.

Cunningham, F. F. 1977. Lyell and uniformitarianism. Canadian Geographer 21(2):164–175.

Daniel, Glyn. 1975. One hundred and fifty years of archaeology. London, Duckworth.

Hookyas, R. 1963. Natural law and divine miracle: the principle of uniformity in geology, biology and theology. Brill, Leiden.

————. 1970. Catastrophism in geology, its scientific character in relation to actualism and uniformitarianism. North-Holland, Amsterdam.

Hutton, James. 1788. A theory of the earth. Transactions of the Royal Society of Edinburgh 1:209–304.

Lyell, Charles. 1830–1833. Principles of geology, being an attempt to explain the former changes of the earth's surface by reference to causes now in operation. 3 vols. J. Murray, London.

Schiffer, Michael. 1976. Behavioral archaeology. Academic Press, New York.

Simpson, George Gaylord. 1970. Uniformitarianism; an inquiry into principle, theory and method in geohistory and biohistory. In Essays in evolution and genetics in honor of Theodosius Dobzhansky. Appleton-Century-Crofts, New York, pp. 43–96.

Smith, William. 1816. Strata identified by organized fossils, containing prints on colored paper of the most characteristic specimens in each stratum. W. Arding, London.

————. 1817. Stratigraphical system of organized fossils, with reference to the specimens of the original geological collection in the British Museum. . . . E. Williams, London.

Trigger, Bruce. 1989. A history of archaeological thought. Cambridge University Press.

SOURCES OF ADDITIONAL INFORMATION

For a further discussion of the principle of uniformitarianism and its development, see the article "Uniformitarianism" in Joan Stevenson, *A Dictionary of Concepts in Physical Anthropology* (Westport, Conn., Greenwood Press, 1991), pp. 405–409, which includes references to other sources of information. Additional discussion may be found in Donald Grayson, *The Establishment of Human Antiquity* (New York, Academic Press, 1983).

For literature on concepts of time in relation to the development of uniformitarianism and other principles of modern scientific thought, see the review by G. N. Bailey, "Concepts of time in Quaternary prehistory," *Annual Review of Anthropology* 12 (1983):165–191.

Z

ZOOARCHAEOLOGY. The study of faunal remains from archaeological CON-
TEXTS, usually as a method of gaining information on prehistoric diet and SUB-
SISTENCE. Sometimes equated with its principal method, faunal analysis, or the
examination and interpretation of animal bones recovered from archaeological
SITES, zooarchaeology is a specialized subdivision of the broader archaeological
subdiscipline BIOARCHAEOLOGY, and is closely allied with the subdiscipline of
TAPHONOMY (Lyman 1987a, 1987b).

The systematic recovery and analysis of animal bones from archaeological
sites has become a standard field technique only since the 1970s. Formerly, such
remains were sometimes collected and preserved by archaeologists, but rarely
were studied in any detail, although a few notable exceptions have been reported
in the literature (see, e.g., Mercer 1975[1896]), and large collections resulting
from a conscious effort to obtain a representative sample were a great rarity until
the 1970s (but see Pollock and Ray 1957). Often, animal bones found in sites
were simply discarded, since their significance for archaeological research had
not yet been realized. Their systematic collection and analysis were a consequence of reforms in field methods and research goals that resulted from interdisciplinary field research of the 1950s and the "NEW" ARCHAEOLOGY of the
two ensuing decades. Since the 1960s, increased interest in gaining information
about prehistoric diet and subsistence has led to new field methods for recovering
as much information as possible. Animal bones, as well as teeth, antlers, and
shells, are now as routinely collected as ARTIFACTS, since data of this kind are
now recognized as very important for developing accurate reconstructions of
past lifeways and subsistence practices.

Zooarchaeology is part of the larger subdisciplinary field of bioarchaeology,
which is concerned with the study of any once-living material found in archae-

ological sites. The goals of bioarchaeological studies are similar to those of paleoecology, which is primarily concerned with reconstructing past environments and human ways of interacting with them; both fields share many methods and research techniques. In general, bioarchaeologists are involved in the study and analysis of biological ecofacts; and zooarchaeologists are primarily concerned with those ecofacts representing animal remains, as well as with artifacts made from durable animal parts.

While animal remains recovered from archaeological sites may include the whole zoological spectrum, vertebrate species are usually better represented archaeologically than invertebrates, not only because of their greater size but also because bone, being hard and durable, is more likely to survive in archaeological deposits than are softer tissues. Exceptions are those invertebrate species with shells, since shell preserves archaeologically in many environmental situations and may actually survive in greater quantity than animal bone in some contexts. Other body parts that frequently survive in the ARCHAEOLOGICAL REC-ORD include teeth, antlers, and tusks.

The archaeological preservation of bone and other animal parts is affected by all the transformational processes that are of concern to students of taphonomy. Just as animal remains are usually better preserved than plant remains, bones of large animal species are more often preserved than those of smaller species, increasing the likelihood that mammals will be overrepresented in most archaeological bone ASSEMBLAGES. The bones of domestic mammals can usually be distinguished from those of their wild relatives by differences in average physical size, and by the differing ranges of individual variation that exist between wild and domestic forms (Clutton-Brock 1989).

Small species, and in particular invertebrates such as insects and their larvae, are likely to be grossly underrepresented in archaeological deposits (Brothwell and Jones 1978), and their recovery usually requires special field methods and equipment (Clason and Prummel 1977). While large bones will often survive longer, small bones are usually covered sooner by soil deposits and are therefore less subject to weathering.

Bones deposited on the ground surface are always vulnerable to gnawing and trampling by animal predators, and are therefore more likely to be modified prior to burial than are small, quickly buried bones. The presence of predators, and the occurrence of mass or catastrophic animal kills resulting from natural disasters, group hunts such as buffalo drives, severe winters, drought, or disease, sometimes leave their evidence in large concentrations of preserved skeletal remains. At sites where large animal kills are preserved, such as the Olsen-Chubbuck site in Colorado (Olsen 1964), scavengers have not been able to dispose of all the carcasses, and many complete skeletons may survive in relatively intact form. Such finds are, however, quite rare.

Although animal kill sites are archaeologically rare, animal deaths due to predation by both humans and other animals are common at water sources, and many animal remains have been recovered from these high-risk locations. Posthumous water transport of bone, sometimes over considerable distance, often occurs if death takes place near a river or stream. Bone subjected to such processes presents the archaeologist with interpretative challenges similar to those posed by redeposited stone tools.

Most animal deaths occur in circumstances unfavorable to bone preservation. Typically, bones will be gnawed and scattered by predators or scavengers, or destroyed by weathering, water transport, or acid soil conditions, and therefore will not become part of the ARCHAEOLOGICAL RECORD.

Postmortem events further affect archaeological bone (see TAPHONOMY). The effects of such activities as butchering by humans, gnawing by animals, and transport by natural processes have been observed in experimental situations in recent years. "Actualistic" studies in African game parks where animal kills have occurred have shown that different species of animals attack and chew bones in different ways, resulting in different survival rates and distributions of archaeological bone. Some predators will eat the bones along with the flesh of their prey. Scavengers will clean the bones of carcasses killed by other animals. Dogs reduce bones according to a characteristic pattern, attacking areas of large muscle attachment first, then cracking open the outer bone to reach the marrow (Binford and Bertram 1977). This kind of information can often assist the archaeologist in reconstructing the events leading up to the deposition of a particular concentration of bone deposits.

A key problem in zooarchaeological studies is one also central to taphonomists, namely, that of distinguishing the effects of intentional human modification of bone from the effects of natural agencies, such as animal trampling. This is a major problem area in interpreting faunal remains. The bone ASSEMBLAGE found at Old Crow Flats in the Yukon Basin, where bone objects identified as artifacts may be better explained as the result of postdepositional events, is a case in point (Morlan 1984). Such assemblages as this are of importance for addressing questions relating to the time of initial human MIGRATIONS from Asia to the New World. A second well-known example of a problematical bone assemblage is that from the Namib Desert in southern Africa, collected by Raymond Dart, who named it the "osteodontokeratic culture," attributing bone modification to the intentional tool-manufacturing efforts of australopithecine hominids (Dart 1957). Restudy of this collection by C. K. Brain indicated that the condition of the bones was more likely produced by the activities of cave hyenas (Brain 1969).

Attempts to develop reliable criteria for distinguishing the effects of human from animal activity on bone continue to be made (see, e.g., Bonnichsen and Sorg 1988). Even bones found in association with undisputed artifacts require interpretation, since apparent "cut marks" attributable to human butchering can also result from animal gnawing.

The principal method of attacking this problem has been that of actualistic studies, involving direct observation of animal kills and subsequent consumption of the carcass, as well as observing human hunting and butchering behavior, and noting any significant differences between the effects of these two classes of activity on the bones of particular species (Binford and Bertram 1977; Stanford, Bonnichsen, and Morlan 1981). Studies of scavenging are also useful, especially since there is now evidence that early hominids may have been primarily scavengers rather than hunters (Binford 1984). Other objectives of actualistic research include determining the effects of SEASONALITY on animal behavior, and how these are reflected archaeologically in the types of prey pursued by humans at different times of the year.

Archaeofaunal specialists use a variety of quantitative methods in the analysis of their material (Grayson 1978a, 1978b, 1979, 1984), and employ several kinds of metric indexes to describe faunal assemblages. To assess the abundance of a species in the past, zooarchaeologists can make estimates from bone counts of the total animal "biomass," or meat resources available, in particular environments at particular times. Minimum numbers of individuals (MNI) of each represented species can be determined by sorting bones into skeletal elements that could represent a single animal, and repeating this procedure for all the bones in an assemblage. Bone assemblages also may be quantified by simply counting the total number of bones or bone fragments from each species, to obtain an index of the number of identified specimens present (NISP). Problems and methods of quantifying vertebrate faunal remains have frequently been discussed in the literature (White 1953; Bokonyi 1970; Wolff 1975; Grayson 1978a, 1979, 1984; Smith 1979; Fieller and Turner 1982; Lyman 1987c).

Despite the many problems involved in quantifying and interpreting faunal assemblages, zooarchaeologists continue to make a very valuable contribution to archaeological research by increasing knowledge and understanding of human patterns of animal use in the past.

REFERENCES

Binford, Lewis R. 1984. Faunal remains from Klasies River mouth. Academic Press, New York.

Binford, Lewis R., and J. B. Bertram. 1977. Bone frequencies—and attritional processes. In For theory building in archaeology, Lewis R. Binford, ed. Academic Press, New York, pp. 77–153.

Bokonyi, S. 1970. A new method for the determination of the number of individuals in animal bone material. American Journal of Archaeology 74:291–292.

Bonnichsen, Robson, and M. Sorg, eds. 1988. Bone modification. Center for the Study of Early Man, University of Maine, Orono.

Brain, C. K. 1969. The contribution of Namib Desert Hottentots to an understanding of australopithecine bone accumulations. Scientific Papers of the Namib Desert Research Station 39. Wolvis Bay, Africa, pp. 13–22.

Brothwell, Don, and R. Jones. 1978. The relevance of small mammal studies to archaeology. In Research problems in zooarchaeology, D. Brothwell, K. D. Thomas, and J. Clutton-Brock, eds. Institute of Archaeology, Occasional Publication No. 3. London, pp. 47–57.

Clason, A. T., and W. Prummel. 1977. Collecting, sieving and archaeozoological research. Journal of Archaeological Science 4:171–175.

Clutton-Brock, Juliet. 1989. A natural history of domesticated animals. University of Texas Press, Austin.

Dart, Raymond A. 1957. The Osteodontokeratic culture of *Austalopithecus prometheus*. Transvaal Museum Memoirs 10. Praetoria, South Africa.

Fieller, N. R. J., and A. Turner. 1982. Number estimation in vertebrate samples. Journal of Archaeological Science 9:49–62.

Grayson, Donald K. 1978a. Minimum numbers and sample size in vertebrate faunal analysis. American Antiquity 43(1):53–65.

———. 1978b. Reconstructing mammalian communities: a discussion of Shotwell's method of paleoecological analysis. Paleobiology 4:77–81.

———. 1979. On the quantification of vertebrate archaeofaunas. Advances in Archaeological Method and Theory 2:199–237.

———. 1984. Quantitative zooarchaeology. Academic Press, New York.

Lyman, R. Lee. 1987a. Archaeofaunas and butchery studies: a taphonomic perspective. Advances in Archaeological Method and Theory 10:249–337.

———. 1987b. Zooarchaeology and taphonomy: a general consideration. Journal of Ethnobiology 7(1):93–117.

———. 1987c. On the analysis of vertebrate mortality profiles: sample size, mortality type, and hunting pressure. American Antiquity 52(1):125–142.

Mercer, Henry C. 1975. The hill-caves of Yucatán: a search for man's antiquity in the caverns of Central America. University of Oklahoma Press, Norman. (Originally published in 1896)

Morlan, Richard E. 1984. Problems of interpreting modified bones from the Old Crow Basin, Yukon Territory. Paper presented at the First International Conference on Bone Modification, Carson City, Nev.

Olsen, Stanley J. 1964. Mammal remains from archaeological sites. Papers of the Peabody Museum of Archaeology and Ethnology 56 no. 1. Harvard University, Cambridge, Mass.

Pollock, H. E. D., and Clayton E. Ray. 1957. Notes on vertebrate animal remains from Mayapan. Carnegie Institution of Washington Current Reports 41. Washington, D.C.

Smith, Bruce D. 1979. Measuring the selective utilization of animal species by prehistoric human populations. American Antiquity 44:155–160.

Stanford, Dennis, Robson Bonnichsen, and Richard E. Morlan. 1981. The Ginsberg experiment: modern and prehistoric evidence of bone flaking technology. Science 212:434–440.

White, Theodore E. 1953. A method of calculating the dietary percentage of various food animals utilized by aboriginal peoples. American Antiquity 38(4):396–398.

Wolff, R. G. 1975. Sampling and sample size in ecological analyses of fossil mammals. Paleobiology 2:195–204.

SOURCES OF ADDITIONAL INFORMATION

For background material on zooarchaeology, see the introduction by Patricia Shipman, *Life History of a Fossil: An Introduction to Vertebrate Taphonomy and Paleoecology* (Cambridge, Mass., Harvard University Press, 1981); and the papers in Anna K. Behrensmeyer and Andrew P. Hill, eds., *Fossils in the Making: Vertebrate Taphonomy and*

Paleoecology (Chicago, University of Chicago Press, 1980). Treatments of specialized classes of materials are discussed in Richard W. Casteel, "Comparison of column and whole unit samples for recovering fish remains," *World Archaeology* 8(2)(1976):192–196; H. K. Kenward, "The value of insect remains as evidence of ecological conditions on archaeological sites," in *Research Problems in Zooarchaeology*, D. Brothwell, K. D. Thomas, and J. Clutton-Brock, eds. (London, Institute of Archaeology Occasional Paper No. 3, 1978), pp. 25–28; and S. A. Chomko and B. M. Gilbert, "Bone refuse and insect remains: their potential for temporal resolution of the archaeological record," *American Antiquity* 56(4)(1991):680–686. Information on field methods for recovering remains is in Clason and Prummel 1977 (see References).

For access to the large body of zooarchaeological literature, see the reviews by Donald Grayson (1979; see References) and by R. Lee Lyman, "Archaeofaunas and subsistence studies," *Advances in Archaeological Method and Theory* 5(1982):332–393, and Lyman's later review in the same publication (1987a; see References). To update the bibliographic information in these, check latest annual volumes of *Archaeological Method and Theory* and current issues of *Current Anthropology* for a more recent review; also consult current issues of the journals *American Antiquity*, *Journal of Archaeological Science*, *World Archaeology*, *Paleobiology*, and *Quaternary Research* for latest publications.

Name Index

Acosta, Jose de, 215
Adams, Robert McC., 64
Arnold, Dean, 67
Ascher, Robert, 183
Ashby, W. Ross, 331
Ashmore, Wendy, 174, 253, 255
Ashurbanipal, King of Assyria, 25
Aveni, Anthony, 16

Bahn, Paul, 274
Bass, George, 158
Bastian, Adolf, 205
Berlin, Heinrich, 127
Bettinger, Robert L., 178
Binford, Lewis R., 2, 9, 22, 27, 41, 96–
    97, 121–122, 138, 145, 183, 185, 188,
    199, 210, 211, 212, 227, 293, 300,
    331, 349
Boas, Franz, 119
Bocquet-Appel, Jean-Pierre, 246
Bordes, François, 41, 227, 229
Boserup, Esther, 55, 56, 162
Boucher de Perthes, J., 26, 226, 250,
    251
Braidwood, Robert, 44, 157, 163, 165,
    188, 279, 322–323
Brain, C. K., 353
Butzer, Karl, 169–170

Caesar Augustus, 25
Caldwell, Joseph R., 187–188, 189
Cann, Rebecca, 237
Carlyle, A. C., 226
Carneiro, Robert, 56, 72, 307, 308, 309
Catherwood, Frederick, 216
Chadwick, John, 126
Champollion, Jean-Francois, 125
Chang, K. C., 173, 229
Childe, V. Gordon, 104, 111, 118, 119,
    133, 162–163, 226, 227
Chisholm, Michael, 59
Christaller, Walter, 59, 61–63, 64
Clark, Grahame, 44, 292, 293, 322
Clarke, David, 2, 111, 184, 210, 212,
    299–300, 331, 332
Cohen, Mark, 96
Cohen, Ronald, 308
Cole, John, 255
Conkey, Margaret, 230
Cook, S. F., 245
Cowgill, George, 57, 259
Crabtree, Don, 194
Crawford, O.G.S., 291
Cuvier, Georges, 143, 322

Dall, William, 314
Dalton, George, 149

Daniel, Glyn, 340
Dart, Raymond, 229, 353
Darwin, Charles, 143, 250, 349
Darwin, Erasmus, 143
David, Nicholas, 140
Davies, Nigel, 255
Davis, Dave, 133–134
Davis, Edwin H., 216
Deetz, James, 67, 112, 173, 317, 318
DeVore, Irven, 178
Diaz del Castillo, Bernal, 216
Douglass, A. E., 76
Dugdale, William, 37, 250
Dunnell, Robert, 3, 145, 344, 345
Durham, William H., 2, 145

Earle, Timothy K., 73, 152
Efremov, I. A., 335, 336
Engels, Friedrich, 303
Erasmus, Charles, 149
Errington, D. L., 55
Esper, Johann, 37
Evans, Arthur, 76, 126

Fagan, Brian, 38, 120
Fell, Barry, 254
Fergusson, James, 132
Fiorelli, Giuseppe, 157, 314
Fladmark, Knud, 101
Flannery, Kent V., 59, 93, 163, 165,
    212, 272–274, 287, 309, 332
Ford, Anabel, 269–270
Ford, James A., 66, 217, 284, 344, 345
Fox, Cyril, 286, 300
Freidel, David, 188
Frere, John, 26, 38, 250, 251
Fried, Morton, 296, 308
Friedman, Jonathan, 308

Gamio, Manuel, 216–217, 314
Gargett, Robert, 94
Gifford, James C., 67
Gladfelter, Bruce, 170
Glock, Albert, 24
Gould, Richard A., 6, 7

Haas, Jonathan, 308, 310
Hammerstrom, F. N., 55

Harris, Marvin, 104–105, 308
Hassan, Fekri, 57, 246
Haviland, William, 173
Hawkes, Christopher, 34
Hawkins, Gerald, 16
Hayden, Brian, 94, 164
Heizer, Robert F., 245
Herodotus, 11
Hesiod, 340
Higgs, Eric, 58–59
Hill, James N., 173, 317, 318
Hodder, Ian, 22, 30–31, 112, 138, 139,
    212, 229
Holmes, William Henry, 115, 344
Hosler, Dorothy, 319
Houart, Gail L., 188
Howell, F. Clark, 236
Hutton, James, 313, 348, 349

Jefferson, Thomas, 157, 215, 314
Jochim, M. A., 274
Johnson, Gregory, 64, 309–310
Jones, George T., 145, 146, 213
Justeson, John, 184

Kepler, Johannes, 249
Kidder, Alfred V., 5, 119, 157, 217
Kirch, Patrick, 2, 151
Knorozov, Yurii, 127
Kohl, Philip, 102
Krieger, Alex, 344, 345
Kroeber, Alfred L., 100, 115, 144, 284,
    344
Kuhn, Thomas, 212, 218
Kus, Susan M., 303, 304

Lamarck, Jean-Baptiste, 143
Landa, Diego de, 127, 216
Lane-Fox Pitt-Rivers, Augustus, 26, 157,
    328
Leakey, Lewis, 236
Leakey, Mary, 236
Leakey, Richard, 236
Lee, Richard, 178
Leonard, R. D., 145, 146, 213
Leroi-Gourhan, Andre, 229
Levi-Strauss, Claude, 30
Libby, Willard, 76

Lightfoot, John, 249
Linnaeus, Carolus, 12, 250, 343
Lockyer, J. N., 16
Longacre, William, 67, 173, 317, 318
Lowie, Robert, 307
Lubbock, John, 144, 205, 223, 226
Lucretius, 143, 162
Luther, Martin, 249
Lyell, Charles, 144, 169, 313, 349

McGuire, Randall, 94
Machiavelli, Niccolo, 307
McKern, William, 217, 292, 344
MacNeish, Richard S., 157, 163, 165,
    218, 272, 287–288, 323
Maine, Henry, 307
Maisels, Charles, 340
Maler, Teobert, 216
Malinowski, Bronislaw, 148
Malthus, Thomas, 55
Marcus, Joyce, 64
Marshak, Alexander, 229
Marx, Karl, 104
Mason, Otis, 115
Masset, Claude, 246
Maudslay, Alfred P., 216
Mauss, Marcel, 148
Mercati, Michele, 250, 340
Merton, Robert, 198
Monks, Gregory, 272, 274, 275
Montelius, Oscar, 226, 343
Morgan, Lewis Henry, 144, 286, 295,
    307
Morris, Craig, 304
Murdock, G. P., 173

Nabonidus, 25
Naroll, Raoul, 245, 246
Nelson, Nels C., 119, 131, 216, 314
Nilsson, Sven, 162, 322, 341
Nyerup, Rasmus, 12

Obert, Kalervo, 72, 73
Olson, Everett C., 336

Patrik, Linda, 21, 185
Paynter, Robert, 94, 96
Peebles, Christopher S., 303, 304

Petri, William Flinders, 157, 263, 283,
    343
Phillips, Philip, 67, 115–116, 119, 207,
    217, 283, 292, 344
Plog, Fred, 94
Plog, Stephen, 318
Plot, Robert, 37, 250
Polanyi, Karl, 149–150
Popper, Karl, 212
Porphyry, 343
Price, Barbara, 93, 105
Proskouriakoff, Tatiana, 127
Pumpelly, Raphael, 228

Radcliffe-Brown, A. R., 332
Rappaport, Roy, 56
Rathje, William, 138
Ratzel, Friedrich, 115
Rau, Charles, 343
Redman, Charles, 270
Renfrew, Colin, 148, 152, 170
Rice, Prudence, 69
Rindos, David, 163
Rouse, Irving, 202, 344, 345

Sackett, James, 318
Sahagun, Bernardino de, 216
Sahlins, Marshall, 149, 303
Salmon, Merrilee, 184
Salmon, Wesley C., 184
Salzman, P. C., 278
Sanders, William, 93, 188, 287
Sarich, Vincent, 237
Saxe, Arthur, 205
Schiffer, Michael B., 335, 336
Schliemann, Heinrich, 157
Seeman, Mark, 188
Service, Elman R., 73, 295–296, 308
Sesostris III, King of Egypt, 25
Sharer, Robert, 253, 255
Simpson, George Gaylord, 349
Smith, Bruce D., 184, 275
Smith, Grafton Elliot, 133
Smith, Robert E., 67, 284
Smith, William "Strata," 313, 314, 348–
    349
Spencer, Charles, 308, 310
Spencer, Herbert, 2, 145, 307, 309

Spier, Leslie, 284
Squier, Ephraim, 216
Steno, Nicolaus, 313
Stephens, John Lloyd, 216
Steponaitis, Vincas, 73
Steward, Julian, 44, 59, 72–73, 100–101,
    102, 104, 145, 156, 178, 189, 210,
    286, 297, 322, 323
Struever, Stuart, 101, 188
Sullivan, Alan P., 89–90, 184–185

Taylor, Walter W., 27, 212, 218, 286,
    292–293
Thom, Alexander, 16
Thomas, Cyrus, 5, 216
Thomas, David Hurst, 293
Thomsen, Christian Juergen, 12, 226,
    228, 250–251, 263, 283, 314, 317,
    322, 339–340, 341, 343
Tosi, Maurizio, 303–304
Tournal, Paul, 249
Tylor, Edward B., 132, 144, 249, 307,
    341

Uhle, Max, 216, 314
Ussher, James, Archbishop, 25, 249, 348

Ventris, Michael, 126
Vita-Finzi, Claudio, 58–59

von Bertalanffy, Ludwig, 331
von Daniken, Erich, 254
Voss, J. A., 318

Wallace, Alfred, 250
Wasley, William W., 67
Watson, Patty Jo, 7, 214
Wauchope, Robert, 173, 254
Wenke, Robert, 93
Whallon, Robert, 318
Wheat, Joe Ben, 67
Wheeler, Mortimer, 328
White, Leslie, 2, 145
Wiessner, Polly, 318–319
Wilk, Richard R., 174
Willey, Gordon R., 67, 101, 115–116,
    119, 120, 188, 217, 286, 292, 344
Wilson, A. C., 237
Wilson, Daniel, 249
Wilson, Thomas, 343
Wing, Elizabeth, 49
Wissler, Clark, 115, 131
Worsaae, J.J.A., 12, 226, 314, 339,
    340–341
Wright, Henry, 309–310
Wylie, Alison, 7, 22

Yellen, J. E., 138

Subject Index

Page numbers of concept entries appear in *italics*.

Absolute dating. *See* Chronometric
Dating
Activity Area. *See* Household
Archaeology; Settlement Pattern; Site;
Spatial Analysis
Actualistic Studies. *See*
Ethnoarchaeology; Zooarchaeology
Adaptation, *1–5*. *See also* Evolution
Agriculture. *See* Food Production
Analogy, *5–8*. *See also*
Ethnoarchaeology; Inference
Animal Domestication. *See* Food
Production; Zooarchaeology
Anthropological Archaeology, *8–11*. *See
also* "New" Archaeology
Antiquarianism, *11–15*. *See also*
Archaeology; Prehistory
Archaeoastronomy, *15–21*
Archaeobotany. *See* Bioarchaeology
Archaeological Record, *21–24*
Archaeological Theory. *See* Archaeology;
"New" Archaeology; Middle-Range
Research
Archaeology, *24–33*. *See also*
Antiquarianism; Prehistory
Archaeometry, *34–37*. *See also*

Chronometric Dating; Relative Dating;
Seriation
Archaic Period. *See* New World
Archaeology
Art. *See* Cognitive Archaeology
Artifact, *37–40*. *See also* Assemblage;
Ceramic Analysis; Lithics
Assemblage, *40–43*
Association. *See* Context; Stratigraphy
Astroarchaeology. *See* Archaeoastronomy
Attribute. *See* Lithics; Typology

Band. *See* Hunter-Gatherer Archaeology;
Social Organization
Biblical Archaeology. *See* Old World
Archaeology
Bioarchaeology, *44–48*. *See also*
Biocultural Studies; Zooarchaeology
Biocultural Studies, *48–54*. *See also*
Bioarchaeology; Mortuary Analysis
Bronze Age. *See* Relative Dating; Three-
age System
Burial Practices. *See* Mortuary Analysis

Carbon 14 Dating. *See* Chronometric
Dating

Carrying Capacity, *55–58. See also* Paleodemography

Catastrophism. *See* Uniformitarianism

Catchment Analysis, *58–61*

Central Place Theory, *61–66. See also* Catchment Analysis; Spatial Analysis

Ceramic Analysis, *66–71*

Chiefdom, *72–75. See also* Cultural Complexity; Social Organization; State

Chronology. *See* Chronometric Dating; Culture History; Relative Dating; Three-Age System

Chronometric Dating, *76–81. See also* Relative Dating

Civilization. *See* Cultural Complexity; State

Classical Archaeology. *See* Old World Archaeology

Classification. *See* Typology

Cognitive Archaeology, *81–88*

Context, *88–90*

Contract Archaeology. *See* Cultural Resource Management

Craft Specialization. *See* Specialization

Cult Archaeology. *See* Pseudoarchaeology

Cultural Change. *See* Adaptation; Evolution

Cultural Chronology. *See* Culture History; Relative Dating; Three-Age System

Cultural Complexity, *91–99. See also* Chiefdom; State

Cultural Ecology, *99–103*

Cultural Evolution. *See* Evolution

Cultural Materialism, *103–107*

Cultural Resource Management, *107–111*

Culture, *111–114. See also* Culture History

Culture Area, *114–118*

Culture History, *118–121*

Culture Process. *See* Adaptation; Diffusion; Evolution; "New" Archaeology

Curation, *121–124*

Dating. *See* Archaeometry; Chronometric Dating; Relative Dating

Decipherment, *125–131*

Demographic Archaeology. *See* Paleodemography

Dendrochronology. *See* Chronometric Dating

Diagenesis. *See* Taphonomy

Diffusion, *131–136. See also* Migration

Direct Historical Approach. *See* Culture History; Ethnoarchaeology; New World Archaeology

Domestication. *See* Food Production

Ecofact. *See* Bioarchaeology

Ecological Archaeology. *See* Bioarchaeology; Cultural Ecology; Geoarchaeology

Economic Specialization. *See* Specialization

Egyptology. *See* Old World Archaeology

Epigraphy. *See* Decipherment

Ethnoarchaeology, *137–143*

Evolution, *143–147. See also* Adaptation

Excavation. *See* Field Archaeology

Exchange, *147–155. See also* Interaction Sphere

Experimental Archaeology. *See* Ethnoarchaeology

Explanation. *See* Archaeology; "New" Archaeology

Faunal Analysis. *See* Zooarchaeology

Feature. *See* Field Archaeology; Settlement Pattern

Field Archaeology, *156–161*

Flintknapping. *See* Lithics

Folk Archaeology. *See* Pseudoarchaeology

Food Production, *161–168. See also* Subsistence

Formative Processes. *See* Taphonomy

Geoarchaeology, *169–172*

Hieroglyphics. *See* Decipherment

Household Archaeology, *173–177. See also* Settlement Pattern; Site; Spatial Analysis

Human Relations Area Files (HRAF). *See* Culture Area
Hunter-Gatherer Archaeology, *178–182*

Ice Age. *See* Geoarchaeology; Old World Archaeology
Iconography. *See* Cognitive Archaeology; Decipherment
Ideology. *See* Cognitive Archaeology
Industrial Archaeology. *See* Cultural Resource Management
Inference, *183–187*. *See also* Analogy
Inscription. *See* Decipherment
Interaction Sphere, *187–191*. *See also* Exchange
Iron Age. *See* Three-Age System

Kulturkreislehre. *See* Culture Area; Culture History; Diffusion

Language. *See* Cognitive Archaeology; Paleoanthropology
Law of Association. *See* Context; Stratigraphy
Law of Superposition. *See* Context; Stratigraphy
Lithics, *192–197*
Locational Analysis. *See* Settlement Pattern; Spatial Analysis
Looting. *See* Antiquarianism

Mapping. *See* Field Archaeology; Survey
Marxist Archaeology. *See* Cultural Materialism
Material Culture. *See* Archaeological Record; Culture
Materialism. *See* Archaeology; Cultural Materialism
Medicine Wheel. *See* Archaeoastronomy
Megalith. *See* Archaeoastronomy
Mesolithic. *See* Old World Archaeology; Relative Dating
Method. *See* Archaeology; Field Archaeology
Middle-Range Research, *198–200*. *See also* Ethnoarchaeology; Taphonomy
Migration, *200–204*. *See also* Diffusion
Mortuary Analysis, *204–209*

Moundbuilders. *See* New World Archaeology; Pseudoarchaeology

Natural Selection. *See* Adaptation; Evolution
Neanderthal Man. *See* Cognitive Archaeology; Old World Archaeology; Paleoanthropology
Neolithic. *See* Lithics; Old World Archaeology; Relative Dating
"New" Archaeology, *210–214*. *See also* Anthropogical Archaeology
New World Archaeology, *214–224*

Old World Archaeology, *225–235*
Optimal Foraging. *See* Food Production; Hunter-Gatherer Archaeology; Subsistence

Paleoanthropology, *236–244*
Paleodemography, *244–249*
Paleoecology. *See* Bioarchaeology; Geoarchaeology
Paleoethnobotany. *See* Bioarchaeology
Paleography. *See* Decipherment
Paleoindian Period. *See* New World Archaeology
Paleolithic. *See* Lithics; Old World Archaeology; Relative Dating
Paleontology. *See* Old World Archaeology; Prehistory; Stratigraphy; Uniformitarianism
Paleonutrition. *See* Biocultural Studies
Paleopathology. *See* Biocultural Studies
Palynology. *See* Bioarchaeology; Relative Dating
Pastoralism. *See* Food Production; Subsistence; Three-Age System
Petroglyph. *See* Cognitive Archaeology; Decipherment
Pictograph. *See* Cognitive Archaeology; Decipherment
Pleistocene. *See* Geoarchaeology
Polity. *See* Chiefdom; Social Organization; State
Postprocessual Archaeology. *See* Archaeology; "New" Archaeology
Pothunting. *See* Antiquarianism

Pottery. *See* Ceramic Analysis
Prehistory, *249–252. See also*
    Archaeology
Primitive Valuable. *See* Exchange
Processual Archaeology. *See*
    Anthropological Archaeology; "New"
    Archaeology
Provenience. *See* Context
Pseudoarchaeology, *252–257*

Quantification, *258–261*
Quaternary Studies. *See* Geoarchaeology

Radiocarbon Dating. *See* Chronometric
    Dating
Random Sample. *See* Sampling
Reconnaissance. *See* Survey
Relative Dating, *262–266. See also*
    Chronometric Dating; Culture History;
    Stratigraphy; Three-Age System
Religion. *See* Cognitive Archaeology
Remote Sensing. *See* Archaeometry;
    Field Archaeology

Sampling, *267–272*
Seasonality, *272–277*
Sedentariness, *278–283*
Sedentism. *See* Sedentariness
Seriation, *283–285. See also* Relative
    Dating
Settlement Pattern, *285–290*
Site, *290–294. See* Taphonomy
Site Catchment Analysis. *See* Catchment
    Analysis
Social Organization, *295–299*
Spatial Analysis, *299–302. See also*
    Settlement Pattern
Specialization, *302–306*

State, *307–313. See also* Chiefdom;
    Cultural Complexity
Statistical Analysis. *See* "New"
    Archaeology; Quantification
Stone Age. *See* Lithics; Old World
    Archaeology; Three-Age System
Stratigraphy, *313–317*
Structuralism. *See* Archaeology
Style, *317–321*
Subsistence, *321–327. See also* Food
    Production; Hunter-Gatherer
    Archaeology; Seasonality
Superposition. *See* Context; Stratigraphy
Surface collection. *See* Field
    Archaeology; Survey
Survey, *327–331*
Symbolic Behavior. *See* Cognitive
    Archaeology
Systematics. *See* Typology
System Theory, *331–334*

Taphonomy, *335–339*
Taxonomy. *See* Typology
Three-Age System, *339–342*
Trade. *See* Exchange
Transformation. *See* Evolution
Transhumance. *See* Seasonality
Transoceanic contacts. *See* Diffusion;
    Migration
Tribe. *See* Cultural Complexity; Social
    Organiation
Typology, *342–347*

Uniformitarianism, *348–350*

Writing. *See* Cognitive Archaeology;
    Decipherment

Zooarchaeology, *351–356*

About the Author

MOLLY RAYMOND MIGNON is an academic librarian who has taught both library science and archaeology and has done archaeological fieldwork in North America. She is currently owner and President of Mayan Adventures, Inc., an archaeological tour group.